THE
BEDFORD
READER

By X. J. Kennedy and Dorothy M. Kennedy

Knock at a Star: A Child's Introduction to Poetry, 1982
The Bedford Reader, 1982; Second Edition, 1985

By X. J. Kennedy

Poetry

Cross Ties: Selected Poems, 1985
Hangover Mass, 1984
French Leave: Translations, 1984
Three Tenors, One Vehicle (with James Camp and Keith Waldrop), 1975
Emily Dickinson in Southern California, 1974
Celebrations After the Death of John Brennan, 1974
Breaking and Entering, 1971
Bulsh, 1970
Growing into Love, 1969
Nude Descending a Staircase, 1961

Fiction and verse for children

The Forgetful Wishing Well: Poems for Young People, 1985
The Owlstone Crown, 1983
Did Adam Name the Vinegarroon? 1982
The Phantom Ice Cream Man, 1979
One Winter Night in August, 1975

Anthologies

Tygers of Wrath: Poems of Hate, Anger, and Invective, 1981
Pegasus Descending: A Book of the Best Bad Verse (with James Camp and Keith Waldrop), 1971

Textbooks

Literature: An Introduction to Fiction, Poetry, and Drama, 1976; Third Edition, 1983
An Introduction to Fiction, 1976; Third Edition, 1983
An Introduction to Poetry, 1966; Fifth Edition, 1982
Messages: A Thematic Anthology of Poetry, 1973
Mark Twain's Frontier (with James Camp), 1963

THE
—BEDFORD—
READER
SECOND EDITION

EDITED BY

X. J. Kennedy & Dorothy M. Kennedy

A Bedford Book

ST. MARTIN'S PRESS • NEW YORK

Library of Congress Catalog Card Number: 84–51142
Manufactured in the United States of America
9 8 7 6 5
f e d c b a
For information, write St. Martin's Press, Inc.,
175 Fifth Avenue, New York, N.Y. 10010
Editorial Offices: Bedford Books of St. Martin's Press,
29 Commonwealth Avenue, Boston, MA 02116

ISBN: 0–312–07119–1

Text and cover design: Anna Post
Front cover photo: Dan Morrill
Back cover photo: Alan Oransky

ACKNOWLEDGMENTS

Maya Angelou, "Champion of the World." From *I Know Why the Caged Bird Sings*, by Maya Angelou. Copyright © 1969 by Maya Angelou. Reprinted by permission of Random House, Inc.

Russell Baker, "Universal Military Motion." Copyright © 1981 by The New York Times Company. Reprinted by permission.

William F. Buckley, Jr., "Why Don't We Complain?" Reprinted by permission of Wallace & Sheil Agency, Inc. Copyright © 1960, 1963 by William F. Buckley, Jr. First published in *Esquire*.

Kenneth Burke, "Classifying Proverbs." Excerpt from "Literature as Equipment for Living" in *The Philosophy of Literary Form* (Los Angeles: University of California Press, 1974). Reprinted by permission of the author.

Bruce Catton, "Grant and Lee: A Study in Contrasts." From *The American Story*, Earl Schenck Miers, editor. © 1956 by Broadcast Music, Inc. Reprinted by permission.

Malcolm Cowley, "Vices and Pleasures: The View from 80." An excerpt from *The View from 80* by Malcolm Cowley. Copyright © 1976, 1978, 1980 by Malcolm Cowley. Reprinted by permission of Viking Penguin Inc.

Joan Didion, "In Bed." From *The White Album* by Joan Didion. Copyright © 1979 by Joan Didion. Reprinted by permission of Simon & Schuster, Inc.

Annie Dillard, "Lenses." From *Teaching a Stone to Talk: Expeditions and Encounters* by Annie Dillard. Copyright © 1982 by Annie Dillard. Reprinted by permission of Harper & Row, Publishers, Inc.

(Continued on page 592)

PREFACE
FOR INSTRUCTORS

"A writer," declares Saul Bellow, "is a reader moved to emulation." On the belief that students can be stirred by reading to become more effective writers *The Bedford Reader* is built. Yet the book offers more than model essays. It tries to show how effective writing is written — not supposedly, but in the working practices of some of the best American writers of our day. Speaking for themselves, these writers address your students. They tell how they cope with writing problems. Some of these problems — what to write about, where to find examples, how to organize — are problems every student writer knows.

Here are forty-nine essays, a few classic and many contemporary, to lead students to carry out familiar purposes in writing: to narrate, to describe, to explain, to argue and persuade. As we suggest in the Introduction, these rhetorical modes and their subvarieties may be regarded not as machines to feed with verbiage, but as natural forms that can help fulfill purposes. Like waves in water, they may be seen to rise, take shape, and disintegrate in the flow of a writer's prose. That they can prompt student writers to discover much more to say, many instructors familiar with both rhetorical tradition and with the findings of recent composition theory are well aware. It is not as formulas but as methods of invention and fruition that this book presents these modes and invites students to make use of them.

In choosing essays, we have let in none that we did not enjoy reading and would not want to teach. Some essays (good old Thurber and Mitford!) will seem as familiar and trustworthy as Otis elevators; and the instructor can rely on them to lift a class discussion to a higher floor. Other essays, we believe, are likely candidates for classroom immortality, though they first saw print only a few months ago. Fortunately, we have been guided in our choices. Many students used the questionnaire at the back of the book to voice their feelings. More than 130 instructors who taught from the first edition liked and disliked certain essays and told us so.

WHAT'S NEW?

With rare exceptions, these instructors were satisfied customers. Why then is so much of this second edition changed — twenty-six new essays out of forty-nine? One good reason came from Bettie M. Sellers of Young Harris College: she professed to have no complaints about the book "except that the teacher tires of the same essays over and over, quarter after quarter." Another reason is that, after mulling the instructors' advice, we believed that by trying harder we might better serve their needs. While we have retained from the first edition twenty-three selections given high marks for teachability, we have striven to pack the book with still more grade A material. Not every change will be to all likings. May the day soon arrive when every instructor can request an individually computer-tailored table of contents.

The winds of change most strongly buffeted the Postscripts on Process. Although these statements remain, as in the first edition, first-hand accounts of how professional writers write (all of them written especially for *The Bedford Reader*), this time all ten are new. To be sure, we were determined to keep the book's unique focus on the writing process. But instead of again commissioning both essays and postscripts, we sought a wider choice. From hundreds of recently published essays, we chose the most teachable we could find (three of them among the best-liked selections in the first edition) by contemporary American writers of nonfiction whose work we keenly admire. (To find a first-rate analogy essay by a writer willing to do a postscript stymied us, but an obliging second-rate writer came along, full of passionate intensity. His is the book's one essay not previously published: "Writing with a DECmate II: Building Sand Castles.")

Then we asked all ten writers to tell us how they wrote their essays and, if they wished, how they ordinarily write. We could not have expected the range and depth and vivacity of their replies. We are profoundly grateful to Maxine Hong Kingston, Annie Dillard, Roger Rosenblatt, Jeff Greenfield, John Train, Paul Fussell, Marie Winn, Joseph Epstein, and Richard Rodriguez for taking your students into their confidence. We trust you will find their statements various, useful and provocative, fun to read, rich in surprise. If this edition of *The Bedford Reader* strikes you as at all special, and not just one more item to sell to the used textbook hawks, then that happy fact, we suspect, will be due to these fine writers and their graciousness.

You will notice, too, the enriched Introduction, with its new advice on reading an essay and a sample essay (by Lewis Thomas) followed by the editors' analysis. We hope that, if you care to assign this feature for outside reading, it will save you time both in and out of class.

Although our explanations of rhetorical modes drew little complaint, we have severely revised some of them anyway, seeking to offer students more practical help. Questions on essays have been rethought in the light of user experience; writing topics have been added, subtracted, or revised.

THE STRUCTURE OF THIS BOOK

At the start of each chapter, we set forth each mode of discourse: what it is and what it can do (*The Method*) and how to use it (*The Process*). Then follows a paragraph-length example of each method in action. After each of these examples, we tell how we wrote it. To lend these paragraph-examples interest and consistency, all focus on the same subject: television.

Because life has already prepared most students to write a first-person memoir, this book begins with narration. Description follows, on the theory that students can then be asked to write a sensory report of a person, place, or thing. Next come the methods of exposition: from example (basic and continually useful) to analogy (most difficult, useful just once in a while). Last in line stand two inclusive methods that call into play all the other methods that students have learned. Definition (Chapter 9), usually considered a method of exposition, often invites a writer to employ description, comparison, classification, or any other method. Argument (Chapter 10) also seizes on whatever methods it requires. Either or both of these last chapters may help in reviewing any of the preceding chapters. (Instructors who wish to concentrate on Argument and Persuasion will find this chapter enlarged by two more essays than the first edition had. They will find argument, too, in all four essays in *For Further Reading*.) If you don't see eye to eye with us, or you wish to take up the rhetorical modes in a different sequence, nothing will hinder you. If you care to ignore rhetorical modes and teach by subjects, themes, or genres, please see the list of *Essays Arranged by Subject* at the back of the book. For brief discussions of every selection in the book, see the *Instructor's Manual to Accompany* The Bedford Reader, Second Edition.

After each essay (except the four essays for further reading), we offer three groups of questions. *Questions on Meaning and Purpose* focus on content; *Questions on Writing Strategy* point not only to the method shown in a chapter, but to recognizing audience, organizing, using transitions, and whatever else a writer does in writing effectively. *Questions on Language* take in, besides matters of style and diction, any vocabulary words in an essay that may give students trouble. You will find an ample supply of questions — more, we trust, than will need to be asked. In any of the questions, terms in CAPITAL LETTERS refer the student to a glossary in the back of the book, *Useful Terms*.

Besides the *Suggestions for Writing* that follow each essay, additional writing topics will be found at the end of every chapter. If you don't assign a specific topic but let students discover their own, perhaps these suggestions will start them on the road to discovery.

ACKNOWLEDGMENTS

Besides the debts we acknowledge in our first edition (and the book still bears the clear imprints of Richard S. Beal and Sylvan Barnet), we have contracted more. Thomas Whissen of Wright State University supplied a long list of helpful comments and suggestions, including scores of fresh writing topics he has found successful. We have helped ourselves liberally to his ideas, leaving some of his excellent topics in his own words. Members of the Alternate English Staff of Middlesex County College in Edison, N.J., worked out a course outline using *The Bedford Reader* as the major tool. We learned from them all: Santi Buscemi, Emanuel di Pasquale, Naomi Given, Albert Nicolai, Ken Rader, and Julia Meyers.

Instructors who, at the publisher's invitation, wrote their detailed comments and rated the effectiveness of our essays were Cora Agatucci, Anne Agee, Dorothy Bankston, Arthur L. Barrett, R. Bartolameolli, Alan D. Boehm, Bruce Bawer, Margaret H. Brofman, Kenneth H. Byron, Victor L. Cahn, Thomas Carmelo Caramagno, Kathleen L. Carroll, Brenda Catto, Steven R. Centola, Margaret Cesa, William Cooper, Daniel Cornell, Lois M. Craig, Bruce A. Crissinger, M. L. Cruikshank, Linda Dyer Doran, Cynthia A. Eby, Charles Fanning, Randy Fertel, Janet M. Foltz, Marilyn Frank, Cynthia S. Frederick, J. L. Funston, H. B. Galloway, Ideale Gambera, M. Garbowsky, Jennifer M. Ginn, Marilyn Glaim, Jean Goodihe, Steve Harvey, Rick Hascal, Charles S. Haynes, Janet Hettenbach, Clyde M. Hoffman, Van Hook, Wayne P. Hubert, E. H. Hunter Davis, Rita A. Jensen, Howard Jones, B. M. H. Kelly, Theodore Knight, Rebecca Koontz, Daniel R. Kragon, Marlena F. Lange, Phyllis Kutt Leith, Karen Locke, Joan MacDonald, A. B. MacLeod, Rebecca Martin, William B. Martin, George McElroy, Nellie McCrory,

Vickie McQuay, Barbara G. Merkel, Gary L. Merritt, Arthur
A. Molitierno, Charles A. Morrow, John Mullen, Janet Norton,
Maria C. Palileo, Margaret B. Palmer, Christine Pavel, Fred R.
Pfister, Mary Pinard, Richard Podgorski, Harry Preble, Sol Ra-
bushka, Honora M. F. Rankine-Galloway, Ann F. Rauten-
strauch, Julie Reahard, Clarita M. Reed, Lois Rew, Mary Ann
Rishel, Beverly A. Rocho, Mardee M. Rose, Michael Russo,
Kent C. Ryden, Teresita Sellers, Gay P. Sibley, Bill Siverly,
Carol L. Snyder, William B. Stone, Barbara Stout, Marilyn
Swanson, Catherine Swatta, Susan Taylor, Maxine Turnage,
Patricia Urbos, Elizabeth Vanderventer, Dorothy Wall, Verna
Watterson, Katherine White, Resa Willis, Barbara M. Williams,
Susan L. Wing, Margarit C. Woodbridge, Janet E. Worthing-
ton, Gloria L. Young, and Spencer Zimmerman.

Erika Lindemann and members of the teaching staff in the
composition program at the University of North Carolina,
Chapel Hill, gave reactions in person. For other advice, corrections, and reactions, we thank David L. Ackiss, Tucker Arnold,
Laird H. Barber, Martha Bargo, Kathleen Brown, Sister Mary-
anna Childs, John P. Cooney, Elizabeth R. Hatcher, Janet Ruth
Heller, Patricia Johansson, M. W. Matheny, Robert McGovern,
Robert K. Miller, Julie Michitsch, Sara Mott, George W. Pol-
lock, Robert Sprich, Jean M. Szczypien, John W. Taylor, and
Wallace Taylor. They gave us more good counsel than we could
take.

Charles H. Christensen, publisher of Bedford Books, helped
us shape this new edition every step of the way, as did Joan Fein-
berg, associate publisher. Jane Aaron gave valuable advice;
Nancy Lyman fought the battle of permissions; and Sue Warne,
by her incisive comments on our editorial explanations of certain modes, prompted us to try, try again. We remain grateful to
former students at Ohio University, the University of Michigan,
the University of North Carolina (Greensboro), and Tufts University for friendly and enlightening skirmishes over their
themes.

X. J. Kennedy and Dorothy M. Kennedy

CONTENTS

2 DESCRIPTION: Writing with Your Senses   73

In sensuous detail, the writer describes both migraine headache in general and the visits of the uninvited "friend" that she herself endures.

A master wordsmith takes his young son on a pilgrimage to a scene from his own past, and arrives at a startling realization.

Wistfully, the author of *1984* sets out to describe his ideal English pub: a joyful spot for a game of darts (with nobody getting skewered), a hearty lunch, a pint of warm stout with family and friends.

As a child, staring at microscopic animals in her basement laboratory, the writer unknowingly may have prepared herself to behold — and capture in words — two magnificent swans.

In this friendly, fascinating account of the making of "Lenses," Dillard takes us into a rewriter's workshop. She reveals a few crucial improvements she made in her essay, and gives pointers you can follow when you describe.

3 EXAMPLE: Pointing to Instances   115

Suddenly, as you're walking home, an attacker grabs you by the hair. You stab at him blindly with a knife. You kill him. Can you go to jail? Giving examples of all-too-possible situations, a professor of law informs you of your rights.

Self-service gas is rapidly becoming the American way of motoring. What could be rottener? asks a writer who vividly recalls the bad old days of yore.

"He was one of the greatest scientists the world has ever known, yet if I had to convey the essence of Albert Einstein in a single word, I would choose *simplicity*." So begins an essay rich in examples, among them intimate stories that stick in memory.

Some old people die in mansions crammed with possessions, others produce great paintings despite arthritic hands. In a lively, wise, and example-studded essay, an insider tells what may be in store for you.

THE
BEDFORD
READER

INTRODUCTION

WHY READ? WHY WRITE?
WHY NOT PHONE?

In recent years, many prophets have forecast the doom of the written word. Soon, they have argued, books and magazines will become museum pieces. Newspapers will be found only in attics. The mails will be replaced by a computer terminal in every home.

Although the prophets have been making such forecasts for decades, their vision is far from realized. Books remain more easily portable than computer terminals and television sets — cheaper, too, and in need of less upkeep and energy. The newspaper reader continues to obtain far more information in much less time than the viewer of the six o'clock news. Most business is still conducted with the aid of paper. A letter or memoran-

dum leaves no doubt about what its writer is after. It is a permanent record of thought, and it lies on its recipient's desk, expecting something to be done about it.

The day may come when we will all throw away our pens
and typewriters, to compose on the glowing screens of word
processors and transmit paragraphs over cables; still, it is doubtful that the basic methods of writing will completely change.
Whether on paper or on screens, we will need to arrange our
thoughts in a clear order. We will still have to explain them to
others plainly and forcefully.

That is why, in almost any career or profession you may enter, you will be expected to read continually, and also to write.
This book assumes that reading and writing are a unity. Deepen
your mastery of one and you deepen your mastery of the other.
The experience of carefully reading an excellent writer, noticing
not only what the writer has to say but also the quality of its saying, rubs off (if you are patient and perceptive) on your own
writing. "We go to college," said poet Robert Frost, "to be given
one more chance to learn to read in case we haven't learned in
high school. Once we have learned to read, the rest can be
trusted to add itself unto us."

USING THE BEDFORD READER

In this book, we hope you will find at least a few essays you'll
enjoy and just possibly care to remember. *The Bedford Reader*
contains work by several of the finest nonfiction writers whose
keyboards stay busy nowadays, and by some of the finest whose
pens scratched earlier.

The essays range widely. They deal with more than just
writing and literature and such usual concerns of English
courses; they cut broadly across a college curriculum. You'll find
writings on science, law, history, medicine, biology, zoology, art,
business and finance, women's studies, mathematics, sociology,
education, child development, anthropology, natural resources,
computers, sports, politics and government. Some writers recall
their childhoods, their families, their own college days. Some
discuss matters perhaps controversial: drug use, the threat of nu-

clear war, censorship, funerals, sex roles, class distinctions, bilingual schooling, the death penalty. Some are intently serious; others, lightheartedly funny. In all, these essays reveal some of the kinds of nonfiction you will meet in your other college courses. Such reading is the diet of well-informed people with lively minds — who, of course, aren't found only on campuses.

These essays have been chosen for one main purpose: to show you how good writers write. Don't feel glum if at first you see an unbridgeable distance in quality between Mark Twain's writing and yours. Good grief! Of course there's a distance: Twain is an immortal with a unique style that he went on perfecting for over half a century. You don't have to *judge* your efforts by comparison. The idea is to gain whatever sense of language and whatever writing techniques you can — and if you're going to learn from other writers, why not go to the best of them? You want to know how to define an idea so that the definition is memorable? Read Twain. You want to know how to tell a story about your college experience and make it hilarious? Read James Thurber. Before long, by the sweat of your brow, you may even narrow that unbridgeable distance noticeably.

This book has another aim: to provoke fresh thoughts of your own to write about. Just mulling over the views these writers advance, going on with their hints, agreeing and disagreeing with them, may set your mind in motion. You may be led to search your own knowledge and experience (or do some looking up in a library) and so discover ideas, points to make, and examples you didn't expect to find.

As a glance over the table of contents will show, the essays in *The Bedford Reader* illustrate ten familiar methods of writing. These methods aren't classroom games; they're practical ways to generate ideas, to say what you have to say, and to give shape to it. To begin with, of course, you'll need something worth saying. The method isn't supposed to be an empty jug to pour full of any old dull words. Neither is it meant to be a straitjacket woven by fiendish English teachers to pin your writing arm to your side and keep you from expressing yourself naturally. Amazingly, these methods can be ways to discover what you know, what you need to know, and what you'll want to write

about. Give them a try. See if they don't help you find more to
say, more that you feel is worth saying. Good writers believe
their own words. That is why readers, too, believe them.

Suppose, for example, you set out to write about two popular singers — their sounds, their styles, their looks, what they
are like offstage — by the method of comparison and contrast.
With any luck, you may find the method prompting you to notice similarities and differences between the two singers that you
hadn't dreamed of noticing. At least, hundreds of teachers and
tens of thousands of students have found that, in fact, these rhetorical methods can help you to invent and discover. Such little
miracles of creating and finding take place with heartening regularity.

Reading the essays in *The Bedford Reader*, you'll find that
some writers will stick to one rhetorical method all the way
through. Narration is the single method in Maya Angelou's
"Champion of the World," since the writer tells a story from
first word to last. But in the flow of most expository prose, methods tend to rise, take shape, and disperse like waves in a tide. Often you'll find a writer using one method for a paragraph or
two, then switching to another. In "The Black and White Truth
about Basketball," Jeff Greenfield mainly compares and contrasts the styles of black and white players, but he begins with a
paragraph that follows another method: giving examples. Later,
he gives still more examples; he briefly describes Julius Erving
and John Havlicek in action; he defines the terms *rhythm*,
"*black*" *basketball*, and "*white*" *basketball*. Clearly, Greenfield
employs whatever methods suit his purpose: to explain the differences between two playing styles.

In truth, these rhetorical methods are like oxygen, iron, and
other elements that make up substances in nature: all around
us, but seldom found alone and isolated, in laboratory-pure
states. Analogy, the method of explaining the familiar in terms
of the unfamiliar, is obviously central to Dick Gregory's "If You
Had To Kill Your Own Hog," even though Gregory develops
his analogy in only three of his eight paragraphs. In this book,
don't expect an essay in a chapter called *Description* or *Process
Analysis* to describe or analyze a process in every single line. We
promise you only that the method will be central to the writer's

purpose in the essay — and that you'll find the method amply (and readably) illustrated.

Following every essay, you'll find questions to help you analyze it and learn from it. In some of these questions, certain terms appear in CAPITAL LETTERS. These are words helpful in discussing both the essays in this book and the essays you write. If you'd like to see such a term defined and illustrated, you can find it in the glossary at the back of the book: Useful Terms. This section offers more than just brief definitions. It is there to provide you further information and support.

We have tried to give this book still another dimension. We wanted to break out of the neatly swept classroom and go into a few workshops littered with crumpled sheets and forgotten coffee cups, where some of the better professional writing in North America these days actually takes place. Accordingly, we invited the writers of ten essays to tell us how they wrote, or how they write. After their essays (one at the end of each chapter), you will find a *Postscript on Process*. Read these after you've read each essay. Don't miss them; they're entertaining. The writers reveal various things: why they wrote, where they gathered inspiration, how they revised, what problems they met, what solutions they worked out. From what some of them say, you ought to take comfort and cheer. You aren't the only one who ever finds writing tough work.

READING AN ESSAY

Whatever career you enter, most of the reading you will do — for business, not for pleasure — will probably be hasty. You'll skim: glance at words here and there, find essential facts, catch the drift of an argument. To cross oceans of print, you won't have time to paddle: you'll need to hop a jet. By skimming, you'll be able to tear through a pile of junk mail, or quickly locate the useful parts of a long report. You'll keep up with the latest issue of a specialized journal aimed at members of your trade or profession: *Computer Times*, perhaps, or the *Journal of the American Medical Association*, or *Boarding Kennel Proprietor*.

But reading essays, in order to learn from them how to write better, calls for reading word by word. Your aim is to jimmy open good writers' writings and see what makes them go. You're looking for pointers to sharpen your skills and help you put your own clear, forceful paragraphs together. Unless with one sweeping, analytic look (like that of Sherlock Holmes sizing up a new client) you can take in everything in a rich and complicated essay, expect to spend an hour or two in its company. Does the essay assigned for today remain unread, and does class start in five minutes? "I'll just breeze through this little item," you might tell yourself. But no, give up. You're a goner.

Good writing, as every writer knows, demands toil; and so does analytic reading. Never try to gulp down a rich and potent essay without chewing; all it will give you is indigestion. When you're going to read an essay in depth, seek out some quiet place — a library, a study cubicle, your room (provided it doesn't also hold two roommates playing poker). Flick off radio, stereo, or television. What writer can outsing Michael Jackson or Luciano Pavarotti, or outshout a kung fu movie? The fewer the distractions, the easier your task will be.

How do you read an essay? Exactly how, that is, do you read it analytically, to learn how a good writer writes, and so write better yourself? Let's look at an actual essay. It won't be the easiest in this book, but it will be worth your time. In it you will meet a few difficulties, and find out how to get over them.

Before you even start to read this — or any — essay you'll find clues to its content and to its writer's biases. Notice:

The Title.   Often the title will tell you the writer's subject. That's what the title of this particular essay declares: It is "On Smell." Sometimes a title immediately states the THESIS of the essay, the main point it will make: "Let's Abolish Smoking," or perhaps "A Cigarette Is a Constitutional Right." It may make its point in a question: "Why Don't We Complain?" A title also may reveal TONE: the writer's attitude toward the material. If a work is called "A Serious Call to the Devout and Holy Life," the title gives you an idea of the writer's approach, all right; and so does that of a less formal essay, "Oops! How's That Again?" — whose writer, we might guess, views the subject (whatever it may be) with light humor. The reader, in turn, approaches each work in a different way — with serious intent, or prepared to laugh. Some titles spell out what a writer proposes to do ("Grant and Lee: A Study in Contrasts"), and may indicate, too, a particular readership ("For the Adventurous Few: How to Get Rich"). Some titles reveal more than others, no doubt, but a title sits atop its essay like a neon sign. Usually, it tells you what's inside. To pick a pungent title for an essay of your own is a skill worth cultivating.

Who Wrote It. Whatever you know about a writer — background, special training, previous works, outlook or ideology — often will help you guess in advance, before you read a word of the essay, the assumptions on which it is built. Is the writer a political conservative? Expect an argument against more federal aid to the underprivileged. Is the writer a liberal? Expect an argument in favor of more such aid, and fewer nuclear missiles. Is the writer a black activist? A feminist? An internationally renowned philosopher? A popular television comedian? By who writers are, you will know them; you may even know beforehand a little of what they will say. To help provide such knowledge, this book supplies biographical notes. Here, let us just note that the author of "On Smell" is Lewis Thomas, a distinguished physician and medical administrator, and one of the most highly regarded writers of our day.

Where the Essay Was First Published. Clearly, it matters to a writer's credibility whether an article called "Living Mermaids: An Amazing Discovery" first saw print in *Scientific American*, a magazine for scientists and for nonscientists who follow what's happening in science, or in a popular tabloid weekly, sold at supermarket checkout counters, that is full of eye-popping sensations. But no less important, finding out where an essay first appeared can tell you for whom the writer was writing. In this book we'll strongly urge you as a writer to think of your readers and try to look at what you write as if through their eyes. Knowing something about the original readers of the essays you study will help you to develop this ability. (After you have read the sample essay, we'll further consider how having a sense of your reader helps you write.)

When the Essay Was First Published.   Knowing in what year an essay was first printed may give you another key to understanding it. A 1984 essay on mermaids will contain statements of fact more recent and more reliable than an essay printed in 1700 — although the older essay might contain valuable information, too, and perhaps some delectable language, folklore, and poetry. In *The Bedford Reader*, we try to tell you, in a brief introductory note on every essay, when and where the essay was originally printed. If you're reading an essay elsewhere — say, in one of the writer's books — you can find this information on the dust jacket or the copyright page.

The essay you're about to read, Lewis Thomas's "On Smell," first appeared in the *New England Journal of Medicine*, a magazine for medical professionals. In 1983 Thomas included it in a book with a completely unclinical title: *Late Night Thoughts on Listening to Mahler's Ninth Symphony*. If you'd guess from these facts that Thomas is expert at making scientific matters clear and enjoyable to readers with no special training, you'd guess right. He loves to revel in what all of us know, and in what scientists don't know yet. Nothing delights him more than a mystery of nature still to be penetrated.

Because Thomas originally addressed his essay to doctors, nurses, paramedics, and medical administrators, you can expect him to spring a few technical words on you. If you meet any, take them in your stride. When, in reading a rich and complicated essay with a knotty vocabulary, you run into a word or an unfamiliar name you don't understand, see if you can figure it out from context. If a word stops you cold and you feel lost, circle it in pencil; you can always look it up later. (We will have more to say later about reading with a pencil. Some readers feel more confident with pencil in hand from the start.)

On first reading an essay, you don't want to bog down over every unfamiliar word, every troublesome particular. Size up the forest first; later on, you can squint at the acorns all you like. To begin with, glimpse the essay in its entirety. When you start to read "On Smell," as you are about to do, don't even think about dissecting it. Just follow what the writer has to say. You'll find what Lewis Thomas says well worth your while.

On Smell

· Lewis Thomas ·

The vacuum cleaner turned on in the apartment's back bed-   1
room emits a high-pitched lament indistinguishable from the
steam alarm on the teakettle in the kitchen, and the only way of
judging whether to run to the stove is to consult one's watch:
there is a time of day for the vacuum cleaner, another time for
the teakettle. The telephone in the guest bedroom sounds like
the back-door bell, so you wait for the second or third ring before moving. There is a random crunching sound in the vicinity
of the front door, resembling an assemblage of people excitedly
taking off galoshes, but when listened to carefully it is recognizable as a negligible sound, needing no response, made by the ancient elevator machinery in the wall alongside the door. So it
goes. We learn these things from day to day, no trick to it.
Sometimes the sounds around our lives become novel confusions, harder to sort out: the family was once given a talking
crow named Byron for Christmas, and this animal imitated
every nearby sound with such accuracy that the household was
kept constantly on the fly, answering doors and telephones, oil-
ing hinges, looking out the window for falling bodies, glancing
into empty bathrooms for the sources of flushing.

We are not so easily misled by vision. Most of the things be-   2
fore our eyes are plainly there, not mistakable for other things
except for the illusions created for pay by professional magicians
and, sometimes, the look of the lights of downtown New York
against a sky so black as to make it seem a near view of eternity.
Our eyes are not easy to fool.

Smelling is another matter. I should think we might fairly   3
gauge the future of biological science, centuries ahead, by esti-
mating the time it will take to reach a complete, comprehensive
understanding of odor. It may not seem a profound enough
problem to dominate all the life sciences, but it contains, piece
by piece, all the mysteries. Smoke: tobacco burning, coal smoke,
wood-fire smoke, leaf smoke. Most of all, leaf smoke. This is the
only odor I can *will* back to consciousness just by thinking

9

about it. I can sit in a chair, thinking, and call up clearly to mind the smell of burning autumn leaves, coded and stored away somewhere in a temporal lobe, firing off explosive signals into every part of my right hemisphere. But nothing else: if I try to recall the thick smell of Edinburgh in winter, or the accidental burning of a plastic comb, or a rose, or a glass of wine, I cannot do this; I can get a clear picture of any face I feel like remembering, and I can hear whatever Beethoven quartet I want to recall, but except for the leaf bonfire I cannot really remember a smell in its absence. To be sure, I know the odor of cinnamon or juniper and can name such things with accuracy when they turn up in front of my nose, but I cannot imagine them into existence.

The act of smelling something, anything, is remarkably like   4
the act of thinking itself. Immediately, at the very moment of perception, you can feel the mind going to work, sending the odor around from place to place, setting off complex repertoires throughout the brain, polling one center after another for signs of recognition, old memories, connections. This is as it should be, I suppose, since the cells that do the smelling are themselves proper brain cells, the only neurones whose axones carry information picked up at first hand in the outside world. Instead of dendrites they have cilia, equipped with receptors for all sorts of chemical stimuli, and they are in some respects as mysterious as lymphocytes. There are reasons to believe that each of these neurones has its own specific class of receptors; like lymphocytes, each cell knows in advance what it is looking for; there are responder and nonresponder cells for different classes of odorant. And they are also the only brain neurones that replicate themselves; the olfactory receptor cells of mice turn over about once every twenty-eight days. There may be room for a modified version of the clonal-selection theory to explain olfactory learning and adaptation. The olfactory receptors of mice can smell the difference between self and nonself, a discriminating gift coded by the same H-2 gene locus governing homograft rejection. One wonders whether lymphocytes in the mucosa may be carrying along this kind of genetic information to donate to new generations of olfactory receptor cells as they emerge from basal cells.

The most medically wonderful of all things about these   5 brain cells is that they do not become infected, not very often anyway, despite their exposure to all the microorganisms in the world of the nose. There must exist, in the mucus secretions bathing this surface of the brain, the most extraordinary antibiotics, including eclectic antiviral substances of some sort.

If you are looking about for things to even out the disparity 6 between the brains of ordinary animals and the great minds of ourselves, the superprimate humans, this apparatus is a good one to reflect on in humility. Compared to the common dog, or any rodent in the field, we are primitive, insensitive creatures, biological failures. Heaven knows how much of the world we are missing.

I suppose if we tried we could improve ourselves. There are, 7 after all, some among our species with special gifts for smelling — perfume makers, tea tasters, whiskey blenders — and it is said that these people can train themselves to higher and higher skills by practicing. Perhaps, instead of spending the resources of our huge cosmetic industry on chemicals for the disguising or outright destruction of odors we should be studying ways to enhance the smell of nature, facing up to the world.

In the meantime, we should be hanging on to some of the 8 few great smells left to us, and I would vote for the preservation of leaf bonfires, by law if necessary. This one is pure pleasure, fetched like music intact out of numberless modular columns of neurones filled chockablock with all the natural details of childhood, firing off memories in every corner of the brain. An autumn curbside bonfire has everything needed for education: danger, surprise (you know in advance that if you poke the right part of the base of leaves with the right kind of stick, a blinding flare of heat and fragrance will follow instantly, but it is still an astonishment when it happens), risk, and victory over odds (if you jump across at precisely the right moment the flare and sparks will miss your pants), and above all the aroma of comradeship (if you smell that odor in the distance you know that there are friends somewhere in the next block, jumping and exulting in their leaves, maybe catching fire).

It was a mistake to change this, smoke or no smoke, carbon 9 dioxide and the greenhouse effect or whatever; it was a loss to give up the burning of autumn leaves. Now, in our haste to protect the environment (which is us, when you get down to it), we rake them up and cram them into great black plastic bags, set out at the curb like wrapped corpses, carted away by the garbage truck to be buried somewhere or dumped in the sea or made into fuel or alcohol or whatever it is they do with autumn leaves these days. We should be giving them back to the children to burn.

When first looking into an essay as rich and complex as "On Smell," you are like a person who arrives at the doorway of a large and lively room, surveying a party going on inside. Taking a look around the room, you catch the overall picture: the locations of the food and the drinks, of people you know, of people you don't know but would certainly like to. You have just taken such an overview of Thomas's essay. Now, stepping through the doorway of the essay and going on in, you can head for whatever beckons most strongly.

Well, what will it be? If it is writing skills you want, then go for those elements that took skill or flair or thoughtful decision on the writer's part. Most likely, you'll need to reread the essay more than once, go over the difficult parts several times, with all the care of someone combing a snag from the mane of an admirable horse.

In giving an essay this going-over, many students — some of the best — find a pencil in hand as good as a currycomb. It concentrates the attention wonderfully. These students underline (and perhaps star) the main idea in an essay (if the book is theirs); they underline any idea that strikes them as essential. They score things with vertical lines; they bracket passages. They vent their feelings ("Bull!," "Says who?," "Hear! Hear!"). They jot notes in the margins. Such pencilwork, you'll find, helps you behold the very spine of an essay, as if in an X-ray view. You'll feel you have put your own two cents into it. While reading this way, you're being a writer. Your pencil tracks will jog your memory, too, when you review for a test, when you take part in class discussion, or when you want to write about what you've read. (In *The Bedford Reader*, by the way, paragraphs in essays are numbered, to help you refer to them.) Some sophisticates scorn pencils in favor of markers that roll pink or yellow ink over a word or a line, leaving it legible. (But you can't write notes in a margin with such markers.) Whether you read with close attention and a pencil, or with a marker, or with close attention alone, look for the following elements.

1. Meaning and Purpose. "No man but a blockhead," declared Samuel Johnson, "ever wrote except for money." Perhaps the industrious critic, journalist, and dictionary maker was remembering his own days as a literary drudge in London's Grub Street; but surely most people who write often do so for other reasons.

When you read an essay, you'll find it rewarding to ask, "What is this writer's PURPOSE?" By purpose, we mean the writer's apparent reason for writing: what he or she was trying to achieve. A purpose is as essential to a good, pointed essay as a destination is to a trip. It affects every choice or decision the writer makes. (On vacation, of course, carefree people sometimes climb into a car without a thought and go happily rambling around; but if a writer rambles like that in an essay, the reader may plead, "Let me out!") In making a simple statement of a writer's purpose, we might say that the writer writes *to narrate*, or *to describe*, or *to explain*, or *to persuade*. To state a purpose more fully, we might say not just that a writer writes to narrate, but "to tell a story to illustrate the point that when you are being cheated it's a good idea to complain," or "to tell a horror story to entertain us and make chills shoot down our spines." If the essay is an argument meant to convince, a fuller statement of its writer's purpose might be: "to win us over to the writer's opinion that San Antonio is the most livable city in the United States," or "to convince us to take action: write our representative and urge more federal spending for the rehabilitation of criminals."

"But," the skeptic might object, "how can I know a writer's purpose? I'm no mind reader, and even if I were, how could I tell what Jonathan Swift was trying to do? He's dead and buried." And yet writers living and dead reveal their purposes in what they write, just as visibly as a hiker leaves footprints.

What is Lewis Thomas's purpose in "On Smell"? If you care to be exact, it might help to speak of his *main* or *central purpose*, for his essay accomplishes more than one. To be sure, Thomas entertains us in his recollection of Byron the crow and in his description of the fun of jumping over bonfires as a child. But is entertainment his uppermost purpose? No, for his essay isn't pure fun to read. Thomas seems determined to convince us of something. Although the essay does some explaining — of smell — it mainly argues a point. Thomas unites his essay with one purpose above all others. It is to convince us that we should keenly appreciate our smellers and the natural world they register. How can you tell it is?

You can tell if you ask: What is the THESIS of this essay — the point made for a purpose? Some writers will come right out, early on, and sum up this central idea in a sentence or two. George Orwell, in his essay "Politics and the English Language," states the gist of his argument in his second paragraph:

> Modern English, especially written English, is full of bad habits which spread by imitation and which can be avoided if one is willing to take the necessary trouble. If one gets rid of these habits one can think more clearly, and to think clearly is a necessary first step towards political regeneration.

Orwell's thesis is obvious early on. Sometimes, however, a writer will state the main point only in a summing up at the end. Other writers won't come out and state their theses in any neat Orwellian capsule at all. Even so, the main point of a well-unified essay will make itself clear to you — so clear that you can sum it up in a sentence of your own.

In "On Smell," the last sentence in paragraph 7 seems crucial to the essay: "Perhaps, instead of spending the resources of our huge cosmetic industry on chemicals for the disguising or outright destruction of odors we should be studying ways to enhance the smell of nature, facing up to the world." And yet Thomas's essay contains no one thesis sentence you can underline. You might sum up its main idea like this: To smell great smells is a privilege that everyone ought to enjoy. (You could put this main idea many ways. Another: Not to smell a wonderful smell is not quite fully to live.) Practice in finding a thesis in an essay helps you to state one of your own.

There's another way to make a writer's controlling purpose stand out for you. The purpose will become evident if, pencil in hand, you work through every paragraph. Look for the main idea in each. If you find a sentence that sums up the main idea, underline it before it gets lost. You've discovered a TOPIC SENTENCE. Often, because each new paragraph tends to introduce a new idea, the topic sentence will come first, or early. You won't always find a topic sentence in every paragraph, though, for many a competent writer works by intuition, taking up one idea at a time, but not consciously writing by the topic sentence method. If no topic sentence stands out, you can scribble next to the paragraph a few words to sum up its main idea, whatever that seems to you.

This isn't just a meaningless exercise in meaning-spotting. Get in the habit of thinking, "An idea calls for a paragraph," and then when you write, the fine art of paragraphing may come more easily to you.

In Thomas's opening paragraph, a careful reader might find two main ideas: *Sounds need sorting out*; and a related idea, *Some sounds are hard to sort.* Next to the paragraph, in order to remember its ideas, the reader might scribble a note to this effect. Paragraph 2 proves simpler. The reader can underline its first sentence. (The other two sentences just rephrase the idea and amplify it.) In paragraph 3, again there are two main ideas: that it will take biologists a long time to understand smelling, and that leaf smoke is the only smell the writer can recall. Paragraphs 4, 5, 6, 7, 8, and the last paragraph, 9, are cinches. In each, the opening sentence announces the main idea.

Point by point, as you can see, Thomas fulfills his purpose: to convince us that smell, unique among our senses, is worth cherishing. The process of smelling is mysterious, he maintains in paragraph 3, beyond present-day understanding. It's a shame, he affirms in paragraph 6, that we don't train ourselves to detect smells as keenly as dogs can: "Heaven knows how much of the world we are missing." (His purpose is showing, right there.) In paragraph 7, he argues that we ought not get rid of smells by perfuming them away; we should cultivate them. To close, he argues for the preservation of his favorite smell of all: that of leaf bonfires. Children, he affirms, should not be deprived of it. Although Thomas gives us a medical account of the process by which we detect odors, his essay adds up to much more. Read as a whole, it seems a glad diatribe on behalf of smelling and smells: a psalm to the sensuous world that only a blockhead (as Samuel Johnson would say) or a blocked nose will miss.

When you write an essay, to have such a clear-cut purpose in mind gives you a powerful advantage. You're heading toward a goal. You control the progress of your essay from beginning to end. The more exactly you can define this purpose, the easier you'll find it to fulfill. It will help your writing flow along smoothly, hang together, and add up. You'll be wise to write it down before you even start writing — to be able to look at it, to keep in mind exactly where you're aiming to arrive.

2. *Writing Strategy.* One of the most valuable ways to notice a good writer's STRATEGY (an inclusive name for whatever practices make for good writing) is to ask: What AUDIENCE (or readership) does this writer write for? An audience influences writers' attitudes toward their material, expressed (or implied) views, choice of language, choice of examples, and more. Why bother to wonder whom the writer wrote for? To make yourself, as a writer, more clearly aware of your own readers. Writing a job application, you'll want to imagine what a prospective employer is looking for. Writing a paper for your instructor and other members of your class, you'll have to try to engage them and hold them and tell them what they'll need to know.

Whether or not you can clearly identify your audience and recognize their faces, you always have to write — at least, rewrite — with a sense that *somebody* out there is reading you. Otherwise, you may babble on pointlessly. Now and again you'll want to step back from your work, sit down in your reader's seat, and look at your own words with detachment and (if need be) resentment and boredom and bafflement. Then make any necessary repairs: add any information you left out; subtract any that your reader wouldn't need to be told; rewrite anything that to your reader might sound as simpleminded as a talking cow, or too murky to fathom.

We've already indicated Thomas's original audience: doctors and other people in the medical profession. But even if we hadn't told you, you could have identified this audience from the essay itself: from terms such as *neurones, dendrites, receptors, lymphocytes, H-2 gene locus,* and *homograft rejection.* That Thomas doesn't bother to define these terms indicates that he expects his trained readers to be familiar with them. That he printed his essay again, however, in a book for general sale, suggests that he wrote not exclusively for medical professionals, but for anyone — anyone who might care.

If, as a writer aware of his readers, Lewis Thomas holds our interest and engages our sympathies, it will pay us to ask: How does he succeed? You'll notice that Thomas keeps involving his audience by referring to common (or uncommon yet intriguing) experiences. At one time, most of us have faced at least one of the problems Thomas cites in his opening paragraph: trying to tell a doorbell from a ringing phone. That detail involves us. Then, although none of us has owned a talking crow named Byron, we take an interest in this mischief-working bird. The mention of him sounds promising. Willingly, we read a few lines about him and are rewarded to learn of his uncanny ability to sound like a toilet flush.

What else in Thomas's essay strikes us as fresh and memorable? For one thing, notice Thomas's use of concrete, specific details. They illuminate his discussion at every turn. Note, for instance, his examples of superior human whiffers (in paragraph 7): "perfume makers, tea tasters, whiskey blenders." Note (in 8) the description of the joy of burning leaves. These specifics lend his essay vividness. They stick in his reader's memory.

Here, then, is a valuable tip for your own writing: Illustrate each main idea, each general statement. Give examples galore — it's a rare student writer who uses too many. (If you are such a writer, you can always delete a few. Cutting a first draft is easy; adding more examples to it can be hard.)

Any devices that organize the essay and help it attain COHERENCE — help it follow smoothly and logically and sensibly, and stick together — are worth inspecting. TRANSI-

TIONS, or verbal connections, are such devices: "In the meantime . . .," paragraph 8 begins. (For a list of the different kinds of
transitions, with examples, see Useful Terms, page 583.) So are
reminders of what the writer has said already: "Smelling is another matter" (paragraph 3) — a reference back to matters discussed before.

   3. Language and Vocabulary. Thomas, you'll notice, is a
writer whose language is richly various. It isn't entirely hefty and
technical. Many arrays of common one-syllable words, many expressions from speech lend his prose style vigor and a certain
conversational ease and naturalness: "So it goes," "such things
. . . when they turn up in front of my nose," "Heaven knows,"
"I suppose," "we should be hanging on to some of the few great
smells left to us," "sparks will miss your pants." Besides, he is a
master of FIGURES OF SPEECH: bits of colorful language not
to be taken literally. (For a rundown of figures of speech, see
Useful Terms, page 576.) One such vivid bit is his memorable
SIMILE (or likening of one thing to another) of "great black
plastic bags, set out at the curb like wrapped corpses" (paragraph 9).
   But in paragraph 4, it is true, the language develops medical
complications. Technical terms gang up on us. Some become
clear from other words around them. To make sense of *responder
and nonresponder cells*, you need no medical degree. (Evidently,
they are cells that respond to odors and cells that don't.) When
we, your editors, first read this paragraph, we didn't know what
to make of the *clonal-selection theory*, or of the *H–2 gene locus*. We
still don't know, and we don't greatly care. If we wanted to
know more about brain functions, or needed to, we would have
looked up those technical words. Yet we felt we could follow
Thomas's thesis and take in his purpose and pick out his main
ideas, and that was good enough for us, however ignorant of the
clonal-selection theory we remained.
   We assure you that, while questions in this book point to
troublesome or unfamiliar words, only you can decide if they are
worth looking up. No one expects you to be a slave to your dictionary — just to become a frequent and judicious client of it.

As a writer, you can have no traits more valuable than a fondness for words, a curiosity about strange ones, and a yen to enlarge your working word supply. Get in the habit of looking up any words that stop understanding, that come from a kind of knowledge you care about, or that sound so great you want to store them in your memory.

In reading essays, why not ask yourself: What am I looking for? Information? Ideas to set in motion my own ideas for writing? Words I don't know, to extend my vocabulary? A demonstration of how an excellent writer writes?

It never hurts to wonder: What's in this essay for me? Thomas has much to give us. Besides explaining how wonderful our noses are — those forgettable, cold-catching bumps on our faces that need blowing — he indicates how we might more keenly relish life. In his rich, beautifully exampled argument, he seeks not merely to explain the process of smell (which, after all, no one fully understands). His audience isn't only doctors; it's everybody. His purpose is to wake us up to what our senses bring us, to make us more poignantly alive.

· 1 ·

NARRATION

Telling a Story

THE METHOD

"What happened?" you ask a friend who sports a luminous black eye. Unless he merely grunts, "A golf ball," he may answer you with a narrative — a story, true or fictional.

"OK," he sighs, "you know The Tenth Round? That nightclub down by the docks that smells of formaldehyde? Last night I heard they were giving away $500 to anybody who could stand up for three minutes against this karate expert, the Masked Samurai. And so . . ."

You lean forward. At least, you lean forward *if* you love a story. Most of us do, particularly if the story tells us of people in action or in conflict, and if it is told briskly, vividly, and with insight into the human heart. *Narration*, or storytelling, is therefore a powerful method by which to engage and hold the attention of listeners — readers as well. A little of its tremendous power flows to the public speaker who starts off with a joke, even a stale joke ("A funny thing happened to me on my way over here . . ."), and to the preacher who at the beginning of a sermon tells of some funny or touching incident he has observed. In its opening paragraph, an article in a popular magazine ("Vampires Live Today!") will give us a brief, arresting narrative: perhaps the case history of a car dealer who noticed, one moonlit night, his incisors strangely lengthening.

At least a hundred times a year, you probably resort to narration, not always for the purpose of telling an entertaining story, but usually to explain, to illustrate a point, to report information, to argue, or to persuade. That is, although a narrative can run from the beginning of an essay to the end, more often in your writing (as in your speaking) a narrative is only a part of what you have to say. It is there because it serves a larger purpose. In truth, because narration is such an effective way to put across your ideas, the ability to tell a compelling story — on paper, as well as in conversation — may be one of the most useful skills you can acquire.

The term *narrative* takes in abundant territory. A narrative may be short or long; factual or imagined; as artless as a tale told in a locker room, or as artful as a novel by Henry James. A narrative may instruct and inform, or simply divert and regale. It may set forth some point or message, or it may be as devoid of significance as a comic yarn or a horror tale whose sole aim is to curdle your blood. In *The Bedford Reader*, our concern is not with fiction (a branch of imaginative literature), but with narration as the telling of true stories. (If you care to study narration in fiction, read novels: *Pride and Prejudice, David Copperfield, War and Peace, Anna Karenina, Madame Bovary, Huckleberry Finn*, or other classics suggested by your instructor. Not only do such works exhibit masterly storytelling, but they are also a great way to spend rainy nights.)

A novel is a narrative, but a narrative doesn't have to be long. Sometimes an essay will include several brief stories. See, for instance, Arthur R. Miller's example-filled essay "Self-Defense" (page 121) and William F. Buckley's argument "Why

Don't We Complain?" (page 455). A type of story often used to illustrate a point is the *anecdote*, a short, entertaining account of a single incident. Sometimes told of famous persons, anecdotes add color and life to history, biography, autobiography, and every issue of *People* magazine. Besides being fun to read, an anecdote can be deeply revealing. W. Jackson Bate, in his biography of Samuel Johnson, traces the growth of the great eighteenth-century critic and scholar's ideas, and, with the aid of anecdotes, he shows that his subject was human and lovable. As Bate tells us, Dr. Johnson, a portly and imposing gentleman of fifty-five, had walked with some friends to the crest of a hill, where the great man,

> delighted by its steepness, said he wanted to "take a roll down." They tried to stop him. But he said he "had not had a roll for a long time," and taking out of his pockets his keys, a pencil, a purse, and other objects, lay down parallel at the edge of the hill, and rolled down its full length, "turning himself over and over till he came to the bottom."

However small the event it relates, this anecdote is memorable — for one reason, because of its attention to detail: the exact list of the contents of Johnson's pockets. In such a brief story, a superhuman figure comes down to human size. In one stroke, Bate reveals an essential part of Johnson: his boisterous, hearty, and boyish sense of fun.

An anecdote may be used to explain a point. Asked why he had appointed to a cabinet post Josephus Daniels, the harshest critic of his policies, President Woodrow Wilson replied with an anecdote of an old woman he knew. On spying a strange man urinating through her picket fence into her flower garden, she invited the offender into her yard because, as she explained to him, "I'd a whole lot rather have you inside pissing out than have you outside pissing in." By telling this story, a rude *analogy* (see Chapter 7 for more examples), Wilson made clear his situation in regard to his political enemy more succinctly and pointedly than if he had given a more abstract explanation. As a statesman, Woodrow Wilson may have had his flaws; but as a storyteller, he is surely among the less forgettable.

THE PROCESS

So far, we have considered a few uses of narration. Now let us see how you tell an effective story.

Every good story has a purpose. Perhaps the storyteller seeks to explain what it was like to be a black American in a certain time and place (as Maya Angelou does in "Champion of the World" in this chapter); perhaps the teller seeks merely to entertain us. Whatever the reason for its telling, an effective story holds the attention of readers or listeners; and to do so, the storyteller shapes that story to appeal to its audience. If, for instance, you plan to tell a few friends of an embarrassing moment you had on your way to campus — you tripped and spilled a load of books into the arms of a passing dean — you know how to proceed. Simply to provide a laugh is your purpose, and your listeners, who need no introduction to you or the dean, need be told only the bare events of the story. Perhaps you'll use some vivid words to convey the surprise on the dean's face when sixty pounds of literary lumber hit him. Perhaps you'll throw in a little surprise of your own. At first, you didn't take in the identity of this passerby on whom you'd dumped a load of literary lumber. Then you realized: It was the dean!

Such simple, direct storytelling is so common and habitual that we do it without planning in advance. The *narrator* (or teller) of such a personal experience is the speaker, the one who was there. (The first two selections in this chapter, by James Thurber and Maya Angelou, tell of such personal experiences, narrated by their writers in the first person, *I*.) Of course, a personal experience told in the first person can use some artful telling and some structuring. (In the course of this discussion, we'll offer advice on telling stories of different kinds.)

When a story isn't the narrator's own experience but a recital of someone else's, or of events that are public knowledge, then the narrator proceeds differently. Without expressing opinions, he or she steps back and reports, content to stay invisible. Instead of saying, "I did this, I did that," he narrates an event or events in the third person: "The dean did this, he did that." The storyteller may have been on the scene; if so, he will probably write as a spectator, from his own point of view. If he puts together what happened from the testimony of others, he tells the story from the *point of view* (or angle of seeing) of a *nonparticipant* (a witness who didn't take part). He sets forth events *objectively*: without bias, as accurately and dispassionately as possible.

For this reason, the narrator of a third-person story isn't a character in the eyes of his audience. Unlike the first-person writer of a personal experience, he isn't the main actor; he is the cameraman, whose job is to focus on what transpires. Most history books and news stories are third-person narratives. (In this chapter, the second two selections, by Calvin Trillin and Maxine Hong Kingston, illustrate third-person narration.) An *omniscient* narrator, one who is all-knowing, can see into the minds of the characters. Sometimes, as in a novel or any imagined story, a writer finds it effective to give us people's inmost thoughts. Whether omniscient narration works or not depends on the storyteller's purpose. Note how much Woodrow Wilson's anecdote would lose if the teller had gone into the thoughts of his characters: "The old woman was angry and embarrassed at seeing the stranger . . ." Clearly, Wilson's purpose was to make a point, not to explore psychology.

Whether you tell of your own experience or of someone else's, you need a whole story to tell. Before starting to write, do some searching and discovering. One trusty method to test your memory (or to make sure you have all the necessary elements of a story) is that of a news reporter. Ask yourself:

1. *What* happened?
2. *Who* took part?
3. *When?*
4. *Where?*
5. *Why* did this event (or these events) take place?
6. *How* did it happen?

That last *how* isn't merely another way of asking what happened. It means: In exactly what way or under what circumstances? If the event was a murder, how was it done — with an ax or with a bulldozer? Journalists call this handy list of questions "the five W's and the H."

Well-prepared storytellers, those who first search their memories (or do some research and legwork), have far more information on hand than they can use. The writing of a good story calls for careful choice. In choosing, remember your purpose and your audience. If you're writing that story of the dean and the books to give pleasure to readers who are your friends, delighted to hear about the discomfort of a pompous administrator, you will probably dwell lovingly on each detail of his consternation. You would tell the story differently if your audience were strangers who didn't know the dean from Adam. They would need more information on his background, reputation for stiffness, and appearance. If, suspected of having deliberately contrived the dean's humiliation, you were writing a report of the incident for the campus police, you'd want to give the plainest possible account of the story — without drama, without adornment, without background, and certainly without any humor whatsoever.

Your purpose and your audience, then, clearly determine which of the two main strategies of narration you're going to choose: to tell a story by *scene* or to tell it by *summary*. When you tell a story in a scene, or in scenes, you visualize each event as vividly and precisely as if you were there — as though it were a scene in a film, and your reader sat before the screen. This is the strategy of most fine novels and short stories — of much excellent nonfiction as well. Instead of just mentioning people, you portray them. You recall dialogue as best you can, or you invent some that could have been spoken. You include *description* (a mode of writing to be dealt with fully in our next chapter).

For a lively example of a well-drawn scene, see Maya Angelou's account of a tense crowd's behavior as, jammed into a small-town store, they listen to a fight broadcast (in "Champion of the World," beginning on page 40). Angelou prolongs one scene for almost her entire essay. Sometimes, though, a writer will draw a scene in only two or three sentences. This is the brevity we find in W. Jackson Bate's glimpse of the hill-rolling Johnson. Unlike Angelou, Bate evidently seeks not to weave a tapestry of detail, but to show, in telling of one brief event, a trait of his hero's character.

When, on the other hand, you tell a story by the method of summary, you relate events concisely. Instead of depicting people and their surroundings in great detail, you set down what happened, in relatively spare narrative form. Most of us employ this method in most stories we tell, for it takes less time and fewer words. A summary is to a scene, then, as a simple stick figure is to a portrait in oils. This is not to dismiss simple stick figures as inferior. A story told in summary may be as effective as a story told in scenes, in lavish detail. In his fable "But a Watch in the Night" (page 316), James Rettie, by the method of summary, covers in six pages the history of the earth for the past 757 million years. Within so brief a space, Rettie can't paint with verbal brush strokes the scene of the building of King Cheops's Great Pyramid. Indeed, the whole of Egyptian history rates a passing mention, while eleven words wrap up the discovery of America. Yet Rettie does what he sets out to do: He conveys to a general reader, not a scientist, the vastness of geologic time and the relatively brief history of human life on earth. The story, though told in bare summary, is spellbinding.

Again, your choice of a method depends on your answer to the questions you ask yourself: What is my purpose? What is my audience? How fully to flesh out a scene, how much detail to include — these choices depend on what you seek to do, and on how much your audience needs to know in order to follow you. Read the life of some famous person in an encyclopedia, and you will find the article telling its story in summary form. Its writer's purpose, evidently, is to recount the main events of a whole life in a short space. But glance through a book-length biography of the same celebrity, and you will probably find scenes in it. A biographer writes with a different purpose: to present a detailed portrait roundly and thoroughly, bringing the subject vividly to life.

To be sure, you can use both methods in telling a single story. Often, summary will serve a writer who passes briskly from one scene to the next, or hurries over events of lesser importance. Were you to write, let's say, the story of a man's fiendish passion for horse racing, you might decide to give short shrift to most other facts of his life. To emphasize what you consider essential, you might begin a scene with a terse summary: "Seven years went by, and after three marriages and two divorces, Lars found himself again back at Hialeah." (A detailed scene might follow.)

Good storytellers know what to emphasize. They do not fall into a boring drone: "And then I went down to the club and I had a few beers and I noticed this sign, Go 3 MINUTES WITH THE MASKED SAMURAI AND WIN $500, so I went and got knocked out and then I had pizza and went home." In this lazily strung-out summary, the narrator reduces all events to equal unimportance. A more adept storyteller might leave out the pizza and dwell in detail on the big fight.

Some storytellers assume that to tell a story in the present tense (instead of the past tense, traditionally favored) gives events a sense of immediacy. Presented as though everything were happening right now, the story of the Masked Samurai might begin: "I duck between the ropes and step into the ring. My heart is thudding fast." You can try the present tense, if you like, and see how immediate it seems to you. Be warned, however, that nowadays so many fiction writers write in this fashion that to use the past tense may make your work seem almost fresh and original.

In narration, the simplest method is to set down events in *chronological order*, the way they happened. To do so is to have your story already organized for you. A chronological order is therefore an excellent sequence to follow unless you can see some special advantage in violating it. Ask: What am I trying to do? If you are trying to capture your reader's attention right away, you might begin *in medias res* (Latin, "in the middle of things"), and open with a colorful, dramatic event, even though it took place late in the chronology. If trying for dramatic effect, you might save the most exciting or impressive event for last, even though it actually happened early. By this means, you can keep your readers in suspense for as long as possible. (You can return to earlier events by a *flashback*, an earlier scene recalled.) Let your purpose be your guide. In writing a news story, a reporter often begins with the conclusion, placing the main event in the *lead*, or opening paragraph. Dramatically, this may be the weakest method to tell the story; yet it is effective in this case because the reporter's purpose is not to entertain but rather to tell quickly what happened, for an audience impatient to learn the essentials. Calvin Trillin has recalled why, in telling a story, he deliberately chose not to follow a chronology:

> I wrote a story on the discovery of the Tunica treasure which I couldn't begin by saying, "Here is a man who works as a prison guard in Angola State Prison, and on his weekends he sometimes looks for buried treasure that is rumored to be around the Indian village." Because the real point of the story centered around the problems caused when an amateur wanders on to professional territory, I thought it would be much better to open with how momentous the discovery was, that it was the most important archeological discovery about Indian contact with the European settlers to date, and *then* to say that it was discovered by a prison guard. So I made a conscious choice *not* to start with Leonard Charrier working as a prison guard, not to go back to his boyhood in Bunkie, Louisiana, not to talk about how he'd always been interested in treasure hunting — hoping that the reader would assume I was about to say that the treasure was found by an archeologist from the Peabody Museum at Harvard.[1]

Trillin, by saving for late in his story the fact that a prison guard made the earthshaking discovery, effectively took his reader by surprise.

No matter what order you choose, either following chronology or departing from it, make sure your audience can follow it. The sequence of events has to be clear. This calls for transitions of time, whether they are brief phrases that point out exactly when each event happened ("Seven years later," "A moment earlier"), or whole sentences that announce an event and clearly locate it in time ("If you had known Leonard Charrier ten years earlier, you would have found him voraciously poring over every archeology text he could lay his hands on in the public library").

In a story Mark Twain liked to tell aloud, a woman's ghost returns to claim her artificial arm made of gold, which she wore

---

[1]"A Writer's Process: A Conversation with Calvin Trillin," by Alice Trillin, *Journal of Basic Writing* (Fall/Winter 1981), p. 11. Trillin's story, "The Tunica Treasure," appeared in *The New Yorker*, July 27, 1981.

in life and which her greedy husband had unscrewed from her corpse. Carefully, Twain would build up suspense as the ghost pursued the husband upstairs to his bedroom, stood by his bed, breathed her cold breath on him, and intoned: *"Who's got my golden arm?"* Twain used to end his story by suddenly yelling at a member of the audience, *"You've got it!"* — and enjoying the victim's shriek of surprise. That final punctuating shriek may be a technique that will work only in oral storytelling; yet, like Twain, most storytellers like to end with a bang if they can. The final impact, however, need not be so obvious. As Maya Angelou demonstrates in her story in this chapter, you can achieve impact just by leading to a point. In an effective written narrative, a writer usually hits the main events of a story especially hard, often saving the best punch (or the best karate chop) for the very end.

NARRATION IN A PARAGRAPH

Oozing menace from beyond the stars or from the deeps, televised horror powerfully stimulates a child's already frisky imagination. As parents know, a "Creature Double Feature" has an impact that lasts long after the click of the OFF button. Recently a neighbor reported the strange case of her eight-year-old. Discovered late at night in the game room watching *The Exorcist,* the girl was promptly sent to bed. An hour later, her parents could hear her chanting something in the darkness of her bedroom. On tiptoe, they stole to her door to listen. The creak of springs told them that their daughter was swaying rhythmically to and fro and the smell of acrid smoke warned them that something was burning. At once, they shoved open the door to find the room flickering with shadows cast by a lighted candle. Their daughter was sitting up in bed, rocking back and forth as she intoned over and over, "Fiend in human form . . . Fiend in human form . . ." This case may be unique; still, it seems likely that similar events take place each night all over the screen-watching world.

Comment. This paragraph puts an anecdote to work to support a thesis statement: the claim, in the second sentence, that for children the impact of TV horror goes on and on. The story relates a small, ordinary, but disquieting experience taken from the writer's conversation with friends. A bit of suspense is introduced, and the reader's curiosity is whetted, when the parents steal to the bedroom door to learn why the child isn't asleep. The crisis — the dramatic high moment in the story when our curiosity is about to be gratified — is a sensory detail: the smell of smoke. At the end of the paragraph, the writer stresses the importance of these events by suggesting that they are probably universal. In a way, he harks back to his central idea, reminding us of his reason for telling the story. Narration, as you can see, is a method for dramatizing your ideas.

· James Thurber ·

JAMES THURBER (1894–1961), a native of Columbus, Ohio, made himself immortal with his humorous stories of shy, bumbling men (such as "The Secret Life of Walter Mitty") and his cartoons of men, women, and dogs that look as though he had drawn them with his foot. (In fact, Thurber suffered from weak eyesight and had to draw his cartoons in crayon on sheets of paper two or three feet wide.) As Thurber aged and approached blindness, he drew less and less, and wrote more and more. His first book, written with his friend E. B. White, is a takeoff on self-help manuals, *Is Sex Necessary?* (1929). His later prose includes *My Life and Hard Times* (1933), from which "University Days" is taken; *The Thirteen Clocks*, a fable for children (1950); and *The Years with Ross* (1959), a memoir of his years on the staff of *The New Yorker*.

University Days

Ohio State University in World War I may seem remote from your own present situation, but see if you don't agree that this story of campus frustration is as fresh as the day it was first composed. Notice how, with beautiful brevity, Thurber draws a scene, introduces bits of revealing dialogue, and shifts briskly from one scene to another.

I passed all the other courses that I took at my university, but I could never pass botany. This was because all botany students had to spend several hours a week in a laboratory looking through a microscope at plant cells, and I could never see through a microscope. I never once saw a cell through a microscope. This used to enrage my instructor. He would wander around the laboratory pleased with the progress all the students were making in drawing the involved and, so I am told, interesting structure of flower cells, until he came to me. I would just be standing there. "I can't see anything," I would say. He would be-

32

gin patiently enough, explaining how anybody can see through a microscope, but he would always end up in a fury, claiming that I could *too* see through a microscope but just pretended that I couldn't. "It takes away from the beauty of flowers anyway," I used to tell him. "We are not concerned with beauty in this course," he would say. "We are concerned solely with what I may call the *mechanics* of flars." "Well," I'd say, "I can't see anything." "Try it just once again," he'd say, and I would put my eye to the microscope and see nothing at all, except now and again a nebulous milky substance — a phenomenon of maladjustment. You were supposed to see a vivid, restless clockwork of sharply defined plant cells. "I see what looks like a lot of milk," I would tell him. This, he claimed, was the result of my not having adjusted the microscope properly, so he would readjust it for me, or rather, for himself. And I would look again and see milk.

I finally took a deferred pass, as they called it, and waited a year and tried again. (You had to pass one of the biological sciences or you couldn't graduate.) The professor had come back from vacation brown as a berry, bright-eyed, and eager to explain cell-structure again to his classes. "Well," he said to me, cheerily, when we met in the first laboratory hour of the semester, "we're going to see cells this time, aren't we?" "Yes, sir," I said. Students to right of me and to left of me and in front of me were seeing cells; what's more, they were quietly drawing pictures of them in their notebooks. Of course, I didn't see anything. 2

"We'll try it," the professor said to me, grimly, "with every adjustment of the microscope known to man. As God is my witness, I'll arrange this glass so that you see cells through it or I'll give up teaching. In twenty-two years of botany, I — " He cut off abruptly for he was beginning to quiver all over, like Lionel Barrymore,[1] and he genuinely wished to hold onto his temper; his scenes with me had taken a great deal out of him. 3

So we tried it with every adjustment of the microscope 4

[1] A noted American stage, radio, and screen actor (1878–1954).—EDS.

known to man. With only one of them did I see anything but blackness or the familiar lacteal opacity, and that time I saw, to my pleasure and amazement, a variegated constellation of flecks, specks, and dots. These I hastily drew. The instructor, noting my activity, came back from an adjoining desk, a smile on his lips and his eyebrows high in hope. He looked at my cell drawing. "What's that?" he demanded, with a hint of a squeal in his voice. "That's what I saw," I said. "You didn't, you didn't, you *didn't!*" he screamed, losing control of his temper instantly, and he bent over and squinted into the microscope. His head snapped up. "That's your eye!" he shouted. "You've fixed the lens so that it reflects! You've drawn your eye!"

Another course that I didn't like, but somehow managed to   5
pass, was economics. I went to that class straight from the botany class, which didn't help me any in understanding either subject. I used to get them mixed up. But not as mixed up as another student in my economics class who came there direct from a physics laboratory. He was a tackle on the football team, named Bolenciecwcz. At that time Ohio State University had one of the best football teams in the country, and Bolenciecwcz was one of its outstanding stars. In order to be eligible to play it was necessary for him to keep up in his studies, a very difficult matter, for while he was not dumber than an ox he was not any smarter. Most of his professors were lenient and helped him along. None gave him more hints in answering questions or asked him simpler ones than the economics professor, a thin, timid man named Bassum. One day when we were on the subject of transportation and distribution, it came Bolenciecwcz's turn to answer a question. "Name one means of transportation," the professor said to him. No light came into the big tackle's eyes. "Just any means of transportation," said the professor. Bolenciecwcz sat staring at him. "That is," pursued the professor, "any medium, agency, or method of going from one place to another." Bolenciecwcz had the look of a man who is being led into a trap. "You may choose among steam, horse-drawn, or electrically propelled vehicles," said the instructor. "I might suggest the one which we commonly take in making long journeys across land." There was a profound silence in which everybody stirred uneasily, including Bolenciecwcz and Mr. Bassum. Mr.

Bassum abruptly broke this silence in an amazing manner. "Choo-choo-choo," he said, in a low voice, and turned instantly scarlet. He glanced appealingly around the room. All of us, of course, shared Mr. Bassum's desire that Bolenciecwcz should stay abreast of the class in economics, for the Illinois game, one of the hardest and most important of the season, was only a week off. "Toot, toot, too-tooooooot!" some student with a deep voice moaned, and we all looked encouragingly at Bolenciecwcz. Somebody else gave a fine imitation of a locomotive letting off steam. Mr. Bassum himself rounded off the little show. "Ding, dong, ding, dong," he said, hopefully. Bolenciecwcz was staring at the floor now, trying to think, his great brow furrowed, his huge hands rubbing together, his face red.

"How did you come to college this year, Mr. Bolenciecwcz?" asked the professor. "*Chuffa* chuffa, *chuffa* chuffa."   6

"M'father sent me," said the football player.   7

"What on?" asked Bassum.   8

"I git an 'lowance," said the tackle, in a low, husky voice, obviously embarrassed.   9

"No, no," said Bassum. "Name a means of transportation. What did you *ride* here on?"   10

"Train," said Bolenciecwcz.   11

"Quite right," said the professor. "Now, Mr. Nugent, will you tell us — "   12

If I went through anguish in botany and economics — for different reasons — gymnasium work was even worse. I don't even like to think about it. They wouldn't let you play games or join in the exercises with your glasses on and I couldn't see with mine off. I bumped into professors, horizontal bars, agricultural students, and swinging iron rings. Not being able to see, I could take it but I couldn't dish it out. Also, in order to pass gymnasium (and you had to pass it to graduate) you had to learn to swim if you didn't know how. I didn't like the swimming pool, I didn't like swimming, and I didn't like the swimming instructor, and after all these years I still don't. I never swam but I passed my gym work anyway, by having another student give my gymnasium number (978) and swim across the pool in my place. He was a quiet, amiable blond youth, number 473, and he would have seen through a microscope for me if we could have got   13

away with it, but we couldn't get away with it. Another thing I
didn't like about gymnasium work was that they made you strip
the day you registered. It is impossible for me to be happy when I
am stripped and being asked a lot of questions. Still, I did better
than a lanky agricultural student who was cross-examined just
before I was. They asked each student what college he was in —
that is, whether Arts, Engineering, Commerce, or Agriculture.
"What college are you in?" the instructor snapped at the youth
in front of me. "Ohio State University," he said promptly.

    It wasn't that agricultural student but it was another a   14
whole lot like him who decided to take up journalism, possibly
on the ground that when farming went to hell he could fall back
on newspaper work. He didn't realize, of course, that that would
be very much like falling back full-length on a kit of carpenter's
tools. Haskins didn't seem cut out for journalism, being too embarrassed to talk to anybody and unable to use a typewriter, but
the editor of the college paper assigned him to the cow barns,
the sheep house, the horse pavilion, and the animal husbandry
department generally. This was a genuinely big "beat," for it
took up five times as much ground and got ten times as great a
legislative appropriation as the College of Liberal Arts. The agricultural student knew animals, but nevertheless his stories were
dull and colorlessly written. He took all afternoon on each of
them, on account of having to hunt for each letter on the typewriter. Once in a while he had to ask somebody to help him
hunt. "C" and "L," in particular, were hard letters for him to
find. His editor finally got pretty much annoyed at the farmer-
journalist because his pieces were so uninteresting. "See here,
Haskins," he snapped at him one day, "why is it we never have
anything hot from you on the horse pavilion? Here we have two
hundred head of horses on this campus — more than any other
university in the Western Conference except Purdue — and yet
you never get any real lowdown on them. Now shoot over to
the horse barns and dig up something lively." Haskins shambled
out and came back in about an hour; he said he had something.
"Well, start it off snappily," said the editor. "Something people
will read." Haskins set to work and in a couple of hours brought
a sheet of typewritten paper to the desk; it was a two-hundred-

word story about some disease that had broken out among the horses. Its opening sentence was simple but arresting. It read: "Who has noticed the sores on the tops of the horses in the animal husbandry building?"

Ohio State was a land grant university and therefore two 15 years of military drill was compulsory. We drilled with old Springfield rifles and studied the tactics of the Civil War even though the World War was going on at the time. At 11 o'clock each morning thousands of freshmen and sophomores used to deploy over the campus, moodily creeping up on the old chemistry building. It was good training for the kind of warfare that was waged at Shiloh but it had no connection with what was going on in Europe. Some people used to think there was German money behind it, but they didn't dare say so or they would have been thrown in jail as German spies. It was a period of muddy thought and marked, I believe, the decline of higher education in the Middle West.

As a soldier I was never any good at all. Most of the cadets 16 were glumly indifferent soldiers, but I was no good at all. Once General Littlefield, who was commandant of the cadet corps, popped up in front of me during regimental drill and snapped, "You are the main trouble with this university!" I think he meant that my type was the main trouble with the university but he may have meant me individually. I was mediocre at drill, certainly — that is, until my senior year. By that time I had drilled longer than anybody else in the Western Conference, having failed at military at the end of each preceding year so that I had to do it all over again. I was the only senior still in uniform. The uniform which, when new, had made me look like an interurban railway conductor, now that it had become faded and too tight made me look like Bert Williams in his bellboy act.[2] This had a definitely bad effect on my morale. Even so, I had become by sheer practice little short of wonderful at squad maneuvers.

One day General Littlefield picked our company out of the 17

---

[2]A popular vaudeville and silent-screen comedian of the time, Williams in one routine played a hotel porter in a shrunken suit.—Eds.

whole regiment and tried to get it mixed up by putting it through one movement after another as fast as we could execute them: squads right, squads left, squads on right into line, squads right about, squads left front into line, etc. In about three minutes one hundred and nine men were marching in one direction and I was marching away from them at an angle of forty degrees, all alone. "Company, halt!" shouted General Littlefield. "That man is the only man who has it right!" I was made a corporal for my achievement.

The next day General Littlefield summoned me to his office. 18 He was swatting flies when I went in. I was silent and he was silent too, for a long time. I don't think he remembered me or why he had sent for me, but he didn't want to admit it. He swatted some more flies, keeping his eyes on them narrowly before he let go with the swatter. "Button up your coat!" he snapped. Looking back on it now I can see that he meant me although he was looking at a fly, but I just stood there. Another fly came to rest on a paper in front of the general and began rubbing its hind legs together. The general lifted the swatter cautiously. I moved restlessly and the fly flew away. "You startled him!" barked General Littlefield, looking at me severely. I said I was sorry. "That won't help the situation!" snapped the General, with cold military logic. I didn't see what I could do except offer to chase some more flies toward his desk, but I didn't say anything. He stared out the window at the faraway figures of co-eds crossing the campus toward the library. Finally, he told me I could go. So I went. He either didn't know which cadet I was or else he forgot what he wanted to see me about. It may have been that he wished to apologize for having called me the main trouble with the university; or maybe he had decided to compliment me on my brilliant drilling of the day before and then at the last minute decided not to. I don't know. I don't think about it much any more.

QUESTIONS ON MEANING AND PURPOSE

1. In what light does Thurber portray himself in "University Days"? Is his self-portrait sympathetic?
2. Are Bolenciecwcz and Haskins stereotypes? Discuss.
3. To what extent does Thurber sacrifice believability for humorous EFFECT? What is his main PURPOSE?

QUESTIONS ON WRITING STRATEGY

1. How do Thurber's INTRODUCTION, his TRANSITIONS, and his CONCLUSION heighten the humor of his essay?
2. Criticize the opening sentence of the story Haskins writes about horse disease (quoted in paragraph 14).
3. Thurber does not explain in "University Days" how he ever did fulfill his biological sciences requirement for graduation. Is this an important omission? Explain.
4. Do you find any support in Thurber's essay for the view that he is genuinely critical of certain absurdities in college education?

QUESTIONS ON LANGUAGE

1. Be sure to know what the following words mean: nebulous (paragraph 1); lacteal opacity, variegated (4).
2. Explain how Thurber's word choices heighten the IRONY in the following phrases: "like falling back full-length on a kit of carpenter's tools" (paragraph 14); "a genuinely big 'beat' " (14); "the decline of higher education in the Middle West" (15).
3. What is a land grant university (paragraph 15)?
4. Where in his essay does Thurber use colloquial DICTION? What is its EFFECT?

SUGGESTIONS FOR WRITING

1. How does Thurber's picture of campus life during the days of World War I compare with campus life today? What has changed? What has stayed the same? Develop your ideas in a brief essay.
2. Write an essay called "High-School Days" in which, with a light touch, you recount two or three anecdotes from your own experience, educational or otherwise.

· Maya Angelou ·

MAYA ANGELOU was born Marguerita Johnson in St. Louis in 1928. After an unpleasantly eventful youth by her account ("from a broken family, raped at eight, unwed mother at sixteen"), she went on to join a dance company, star in an off-Broadway play (*The Blacks*), write three books of poetry, produce a series on Africa for PBS-TV, act in the television-special series "Roots," serve as a coordinator for the Southern Christian Leadership Conference at the request of Martin Luther King, Jr., and accept three honorary doctorates. She is best known, however, for the four books of her searching, frank, and joyful autobiography — beginning with *I Know Why the Caged Bird Sings* (1970), which she adapted for television, through her most recent volume, *The Heart of a Woman* (1981).

Champion of the World

"Champion of the World" is the nineteenth chapter from *I Know Why the Caged Bird Sings*; the title is a phrase taken from it. Remembering her childhood, the writer tells how she and her older brother, Bailey, grew up in a town in Arkansas. The center of their lives was grandmother and Uncle Willie's store, a gathering place for the black community. On the night when this story takes place, Joe Louis, the "Brown Bomber" and the hero of his people, defends his heavyweight title against a white contender.

The last inch of space was filled, yet people continued to wedge themselves along the walls of the Store. Uncle Willie had turned the radio up to its last notch so that youngsters on the porch wouldn't miss a word. Women sat on kitchen chairs, dining-room chairs, stools and upturned wooden boxes. Small children and babies perched on every lap available and men leaned on the shelves or on each other. 1

The apprehensive mood was shot through with shafts of gaiety, as a black sky is streaked with lightning. 2

"I ain't worried 'bout this fight. Joe's gonna whip that 3 cracker like it's open season."

"He gone whip him till that white boy call him Momma." 4

At last the talking was finished and the string-along songs 5 about razor blades were over and the fight began.

"A quick jab to the head." In the Store the crowd grunted. 6 "A left to the head and a right and another left." One of the listeners cackled like a hen and was quieted.

"They're in a clinch, Louis is trying to fight his way out." 7

Some bitter comedian on the porch said, "That white man 8 don't mind hugging that niggah now, I betcha."

"The referee is moving in to break them up, but Louis fi- 9 nally pushed the contender away and it's an uppercut to the chin. The contender is hanging on, now he's backing away. Louis catches him with a short left to the jaw."

A tide of murmuring assent poured out the doors and into 10 the yard.

"Another left and another left. Louis is saving that mighty 11 right . . . " The mutter in the Store had grown into a baby roar and it was pierced by the clang of a bell and the announcer's "That's the bell for round three, ladies and gentlemen."

As I pushed my way into the Store I wondered if the an- 12 nouncer gave any thought to the fact that he was addressing as "ladies and gentlemen" all the Negroes around the world who sat sweating and praying, glued to their "master's voice."[1]

There were only a few calls for R. C. Colas, Dr. Peppers, 13 and Hires root beer. The real festivities would begin after the fight. Then even the old Christian ladies who taught their children and tried themselves to practice turning the other cheek would buy soft drinks, and if the Brown Bomber's victory was a particularly bloody one they would order peanut patties and Baby Ruths also.

Bailey and I laid the coins on top of the cash register. Uncle 14 Willie didn't allow us to ring up sales during a fight. It was too

---

[1]"His master's voice," accompanied by a picture of a little dog listening to a phonograph, was a familiar advertising slogan. (The picture still appears on RCA Victor records.)—Eds.

noisy and might shake up the atmosphere. When the gong rang
for the next round we pushed through the near-sacred quiet to
the herd of children outside.

"He's got Louis against the ropes and now it's a left to the   15
body and a right to the ribs. Another right to the body, it looks
like it was low . . . Yes, ladies and gentlemen, the referee is sig-
naling but the contender keeps raining the blows on Louis. It's
another to the body, and it looks like Louis is going down."

My race groaned. It was our people falling. It was another   16
lynching, yet another Black man hanging on a tree. One more
woman ambushed and raped. A Black boy whipped and
maimed. It was hounds on the trail of a man running through
slimy swamps. It was a white woman slapping her maid for being
forgetful.

The men in the Store stood away from the walls and at at-   17
tention. Women greedily clutched the babes on their laps while
on the porch the shufflings and smiles, flirtings and pinching of
a few minutes before were gone. This might be the end of the
world. If Joe lost we were back in slavery and beyond help. It
would all be true, the accusations that we were lower types of
human beings. Only a little higher than apes. True that we were
stupid and ugly and lazy and dirty and, unlucky and worst of all,
that God Himself hated us and ordained us to be hewers of
wood and drawers of water, forever and ever, world without
end.

We didn't breathe. We didn't hope. We waited.   18

"He's off the ropes, ladies and gentlemen. He's moving   19
towards the center of the ring." There was no time to be relieved. The worst might still happen.

"And now it looks like Joe is mad. He's caught Carnera with   20
a left hook to the head and a right to the head. It's a left jab to
the body and another left to the head. There's a left cross and a
right to the head. The contender's right eye is bleeding and he
can't seem to keep his block up. Louis is penetrating every
block. The referee is moving in, but Louis sends a left to the
body and it's an uppercut to the chin and the contender is dropping. He's on the canvas, ladies and gentlemen."

Babies slid to the floor as women stood up and men leaned   21
toward the radio.

"Here's the referee. He's young. One, two, three, four, five, 22
six, seven . . . Is the contender trying to get up again?"

All the men in the store shouted, "NO." 23

" — eight, nine, ten." There were a few sounds from the au- 24
dience, but they seemed to be holding themselves in against tremendous pressure.

"The fight is all over, ladies and gentlemen. Let's get the mi- 25
crophone over to the referee . . . Here he is. He's got the Brown
Bomber's hand, he's holding it up . . . Here he is . . ."

Then the voice, husky and familiar, came to wash over us — 26
"The winnah, and still heavyweight champeen of the world
. . . Joe Louis."

Champion of the world. A Black boy. Some Black mother's 27
son. He was the strongest man in the world. People drank Coca-
Colas like ambrosia and ate candy bars like Christmas. Some of
the men went behind the Store and poured white lightning in
their soft-drink bottles, and a few of the bigger boys followed
them. Those who were not chased away came back blowing
their breath in front of themselves like proud smokers.

It would take an hour or more before the people would leave 28
the Store and head for home. Those who lived too far had made
arrangements to stay in town. It wouldn't do for a Black man
and his family to be caught on a lonely country road on a night
when Joe Louis had proved that we were the strongest people in
the world.

QUESTIONS ON MEANING AND PURPOSE

1. What do you take to be the author's PURPOSE in telling this
   story?
2. What connection does Angelou make between the outcome of the
   fight and the pride of the black race? To what degree do you think
   the author's view is shared by the others in the store listening to
   the broadcast?
3. To what extent are the statements in paragraphs 16 and 17 to be
   taken literally? What function do they serve in Angelou's narrative?

4. Primo Carnera was probably *not* the Brown Bomber's opponent on the night Maya Angelou recalls. Louis fought Carnera only once, on June 25, 1935, and it was not a title match; Angelou would have been no more than seven years old at the time. Does the author's apparent error detract from her story?

QUESTIONS ON WRITING STRATEGY

1. What details in the opening paragraphs indicate that an event of crucial importance is about to take place?
2. How does Angelou build up SUSPENSE in her account of the fight? At what point were you able to predict the winner?
3. Comment on the IRONY in Angelou's final paragraph.
4. How many stories does "Champion of the World" contain? What are they?
5. What EFFECT does the author's use of direct quotation have on her narrative?

QUESTIONS ON LANGUAGE

1. Explain what the author means by "string-along songs about razor blades" (paragraph 5).
2. How does Angelou's use of NONSTANDARD ENGLISH contribute to her narrative?
3. Be sure you know the meanings of these words: apprehensive (paragraph 2); assent (10); ambushed, maimed (16); ordained (17); ambrosia, white lightning (27).

SUGGESTIONS FOR WRITING

1. In a brief essay, write about the progress and outcome of a recent sporting event and your reaction to the outcome. Include enough illustrative detail to bring the contest to life.
2. Write an essay based on some childhood experience of your own, still vivid in your memory.

· Calvin Trillin ·

CALVIN TRILLIN, distinguished commentator on American life, was born in 1935, grew up in Kansas City, Missouri, and earned his B.A. from Yale in 1957. From 1960 to 1963, he worked as a reporter and writer for *Time* magazine. Since then he has been a staff writer for *The New Yorker* and since 1978 a columnist for the *Nation.* Trillin has written nine lively books, whose subjects range from food (*Alice, Let's Eat,* 1978) to politics (*Uncivil Liberties,* 1982). *Killings* (1984) is his most recent book.

It's Just Too Late

This essay first appeared as one of a series called "U.S. Journal," which Trillin contributed to *The New Yorker* until 1982. The author has since included the narrative in *Killings,* a collection of factual chronicles of violent death in America. The book, says Trillin, "is meant to be more about how Americans live than about how some of them die. . . . A killing often seemed to present the best opportunity to write about people one at a time."

Knoxville, Tennessee
March 1979

Until she was sixteen, FaNee Cooper was what her parents sometimes called an ideal child. "You'd never have to correct her," FaNee's mother has said. In sixth grade, FaNee won a spelling contest. She played the piano and the flute. She seemed to believe what she heard every Sunday at the Beaver Dam Baptist Church about good and evil and the hereafter. FaNee was not an outgoing child. Even as a baby, she was uncomfortable when she was held and cuddled. She found it easy to tell her parents that she loved them but difficult to confide in them. Particularly compared to her sister, Kristy, a cheerful, open little girl two and a half years younger, she was reserved and introspective. The thoughts she kept to herself, though, were

1

45

apparently happy thoughts. Her eighth-grade essay on Christmas — written in a remarkably neat hand — talked of the joys
of helping put together toys for her little brother, Leo, Jr., and
the importance of her parents' reminder that Christmas is the
birthday of Jesus. Her parents were the sort of people who might
have been expected to have an ideal child. As a boy, Leo
Cooper had been called "one of the greatest high-school basketball players ever developed in Knox County." He went on to
play basketball at East Tennessee State, and he married the
homecoming queen, JoAnn Henson. After college, Cooper became a high-school basketball coach and teacher and, eventually, an administrator. By the time FaNee turned thirteen, in
1973, he was in his third year as the principal of Gresham Junior
High School, in Fountain City — a small Knox County town
that had been swallowed up by Knoxville when the suburbs began to move north. A tall man, with curly black hair going on
gray, Leo Cooper has an elaborate way of talking ("Unless I'm
very badly mistaken, he has never related to me totally the content of his conversation") and a manner that may come from
years of trying to leave errant junior-high-school students with
the impression that a responsible adult is magnanimous, even
humble, about invariably being in the right. His wife, a high-
school art teacher, paints and does batik, and created the name
FaNee because she liked the way it looked and sounded — it
sounds like "Fawn-*ee*" when the Coopers say it — but the impression she gives is not of artiness but of soft-spoken small-town
gentility. When she found, in the course of cleaning up FaNee's
room, that her ideal thirteen-year-old had been smoking cigarettes, she was, in her words, crushed. "FaNee was such a perfect
child before that," JoAnn Cooper said some time later. "She
was angry that we found out. She knew we knew that she had
done something we didn't approve of, and then the rebellion
started. I was hurt. I was very hurt. I guess it came through as
disappointment."

　　Several months later, FaNee's grandmother died. FaNee   2
had been devoted to her grandmother. She wrote a poem in her
memory — an almost joyous poem, filled with Christian faith in
the afterlife ("Please don't grieve over my happiness/Rejoice

with me in the presence of the Angels of Heaven"). She also took some keepsakes from her grandmother's house, and was apparently mortified when her parents found them and explained that they would have to be returned. By then, the Coopers were aware that FaNee was going to have a difficult time as a teenager. They thought she might be self-conscious about the double affliction of glasses and braces. They thought she might be uncomfortable in the role of the principal's daughter at Gresham. In ninth grade, she entered Halls High School, where JoAnn Cooper was teaching art. FaNee was a loner at first. Then she fell in with what could only be considered a bad crowd.

Halls, a few miles to the north of Fountain City, used to be known as Halls Crossroads. It is what Knoxville people call "over the ridge" — on the side of Black Oak Ridge that has always been thought of as rural. When FaNee entered Halls High, the Coopers were already in the process of building a house on several acres of land they had bought in Halls, in a sparsely settled area along Brown Gap Road. Like two or three other houses along the road, it was to be constructed basically of huge logs taken from old buildings — a house that Leo Cooper describes as being, like the name FaNee, "just a little bit different." Ten years ago, Halls Crossroads was literally a crossroads. Then some of the Knoxville expansion that had swollen Fountain City spilled over the ridge, planting subdivisions here and there on roads that still went for long stretches with nothing but an occasional house with a cow or two next to it. The increase in population did not create a town. Halls has no center. Its commercial area is a series of two or three shopping centers strung together on the Maynardville Highway, the four-lane that leads north into Union County — a place almost synonymous in east Tennessee with mountain poverty. Its restaurant is the Halls Freezo Drive-In. The gathering place for the group FaNee Cooper eventually found herself in was the Maynardville Highway Exxon station.

At Halls High School, the social poles were represented by the Jocks and the Freaks. FaNee found her friends among the Freaks. "I am truly enlightened upon irregular trains of thought

aimed at strange depots of mental wards," she wrote when she
was fifteen. "Yes! Crazed farms for the mental off — Oh! I
walked through the halls screams & loud laughter fill my ears —
Orderlys try to reason with me — but I am unreasonable! The
joys of being a FREAK in a circus of imagination." The little
crowd of eight or ten young people that FaNee joined has been
referred to by her mother as "the Union County group." A
couple of the girls were from backgrounds similar to FaNee's,
but all the boys had the characteristics, if not the precise addresses, that Knoxville people associate with the poor whites of
Union County. They were the sort of boys who didn't bother to
finish high school, or finished it in a special program for slow
learners, or got ejected from it for taking a swing at the principal.

      "I guess you can say they more or less dragged us down to   5
their level with the drugs," a girl who was in the group — a girl
who can be called Marcia — said recently. "And somehow we
settled for it. It seems like we had to get ourselves in the pit before we could look out." People in the group used marijuana and
Valium and LSD. They sneered at the Jocks and the "prim and
proper little ladies" who went with the Jocks. "We set ourselves
aside," Marcia now says. "We put ourselves above everyone.
How we did that I don't know." In a Knox County high school,
teenagers who want to get themselves in the pit need not main-
line heroin. The Jocks they mean to be compared to do not
merely show up regularly for classes and practice football and
wear clean clothes; they watch their language and preach temperance and go to prayer meetings on Wednesday nights and
talk about having a real good Christian witness. Around Knoxville, people who speak of well-behaved high-school kids often
seem to use words like "perfect," or even "angels." For FaNee's
group, the opposite was not difficult to figure out. "We were into
wicked things, strange things," Marcia says. "It was like we were
on some kind of devil trip." FaNee wrote about demons and vul-
tures and rats. "Slithering serpents eat my sanity and bite my
ass," she wrote in an essay called "The Lovely Road of Life," just
after she turned sixteen, "while tornadoes derail and ever so
swiftly destroy every car in my train of thought." She wrote a lot
about death.

FaNee's girl friends spoke of her as "super-intelligent." Her   6
English teacher found some of her writing profound — and disturbing. She was thought to be not just super-intelligent but
super-mysterious, and even, at times, super-weird — an intro-
verted girl who stared straight ahead with deep-brown, nearly
black eyes and seemed to have thoughts she couldn't share. Nobody really knew why she had chosen to run with the Freaks —
whether it was loneliness or rebellion or simple boredom. Marcia thought it might have had something to do with a feeling
that her parents had settled on Kristy as their perfect child. "I
guess she figured she couldn't be the best," Marcia said recently.
"So she decided she might as well be the worst."

Toward the spring of FaNee's junior year at Halls, her prob-   7
lems seemed to deepen. Despite her intelligence, her grades were
sliding. She was what her mother called "a mental dropout."
Leo Cooper had to visit Halls twice because of minor suspen-
sions. Once, FaNee had been caught smoking. Once, having
ducked out of a required assembly, she was spotted by a favorite
teacher, who turned her in. At home, she exchanged little more
than short, strained formalities with Kristy, who shared their
parents' opinion of FaNee's choice of friends. The Coopers had
finished their house — a large house, its size accentuated by the
huge old logs and a great stone fireplace and outsize "Paul Bun-
yan"–style furniture — but FaNee spent most of her time there
in her own room, sleeping or listening to rock music through
earphones. One night, there was a terrible scene when FaNee returned from a concert in a condition that Leo Cooper knew had
to be the result of marijuana. JoAnn Cooper, who ordinarily
strikes people as too gentle to raise her voice, found herself losing her temper regularly. Finally, Leo Cooper asked a counsellor
he knew, Jim Griffin, to stop in at Halls High School and have a
talk with FaNee — unofficially.

Griffin — a young man with a warm, informal manner —   8
worked for the Juvenile Court of Knox County. He had a reputation for being able to reach teenagers who wouldn't talk to
their parents or to school administrators. One Friday in March
of 1977, he spent an hour and a half talking to FaNee Cooper.
As Griffin recalls the interview, FaNee didn't seem alarmed by

his presence. She seemed to him calm and controlled — Griffin thought it was something like talking to another adult — and, unlike most of the teenagers he dealt with, she looked him in the eye the entire time. Griffin, like some of FaNee's friends, found her eyes unsettling — "the coldest, most distant, but, at the same time, the most knowing eyes I'd ever seen." She expressed affection for her parents, but she didn't seem interested in exploring ways of getting along better with them. The impression she gave Griffin was that they were who they were, and she was who she was, and there didn't happen to be any connection. Several times, she made the same response to Griffin's suggestions: "It's too late."

That weekend, neither FaNee nor her parents brought up   9
the subject of Griffin's visit. Leo Cooper has spoken of the weekend as being particularly happy; a friend of FaNee's who stayed over remembers it as particularly strained. FaNee stayed home from school on Monday because of a bad headache — she often had bad headaches — but felt well enough on Monday evening to drive to the library. She was to be home at nine. When she wasn't, Mrs. Cooper began to phone her friends. Finally, around ten, Leo Cooper got into his other car and took a swing around Halls — past the teenage hangouts like the Exxon station and the Pizza Hut and the Smoky Mountain Market. Then he took a second swing. At eleven, FaNee was still not home.

She hadn't gone to the library. She had picked up two girl   10
friends and driven to the home of a third, where everyone took five Valium tablets. Then the four girls drove over to the Exxon station, where they met four boys from their crowd. After a while, the group bought some beer and some marijuana and reassembled at Charlie Stevens's trailer. Charlie Stevens was five or six years older than everyone else in the group — a skinny, slow-thinking young man with long black hair and a sparse beard. He was married and had a child, but he and his wife had separated; she was back in Union County with the baby. Stevens had remained in their trailer — parked in the yard near his mother's house, in a back-road area of Knox County dominated by decrepit, unpainted sheds and run-down trailers and

rusted-out automobiles. Stevens had picked up FaNee at home once or twice — apparently, more as a driver for the group than as a date — and the Coopers, having learned that his unsuitability extended to being married, had asked her not to see him.

In Charlie's trailer, which had no heat or electricity, the   11 group drank beer and passed around joints, keeping warm with blankets. By eleven or so, FaNee was what one of her friends has called "super-messed-up." Her speech was slurred. She was having trouble keeping her balance. She had decided not to go home. She had apparently persuaded herself that her parents intended to send her away to some sort of home for incorrigibles. "It's too late," she said to one of her friends. "It's just too late." It was decided that one of the boys, David Munsey, who was more or less the leader of the group, would drive the Coopers' car to FaNee's house, where FaNee and Charlie Stevens would pick him up in Stevens's car — a worn Pinto with four bald tires, one light, and a dragging muffler. FaNee wrote a note to her parents, and then, perhaps because her handwriting was suffering the effects of beer and marijuana and Valium, asked Stevens to rewrite it on a large piece of paper, which would be left on the seat of the Coopers' car. The Stevens version was just about the same as FaNee's, except that Stevens left out a couple of sentences about trying to work things out ("I'm willing to try") and, not having won any spelling championships himself, he misspelled a few words, like "tomorrow." The note said, "Dear Mom and Dad. Sorry I'm late. Very late. I left your car because I thought you might need it tomorrow. I love you all, but this is something I just had to do. The man talked to me privately for one and a half hours and I was really scared, so this is something I just had to do, but don't worry, I'm with a very good friend. Love you all. FaNee. P.S. Please try to understand I love you all very much, really I do. Love me if you have a chance."

At eleven-thirty or so, Leo Cooper was sitting in his living   12 room, looking out the window at his driveway — a long gravel road that runs almost four hundred feet from the house to Brown Gap Road. He saw the car that FaNee had been driving pull into the driveway. "She's home," he called to his wife, who had just left the room. Cooper walked out on the deck over the garage. The car had stopped at the end of the driveway, and the lights had gone out. He got into his other car and drove to the end of the driveway. David Munsey had already joined Charlie Stevens and FaNee, and the Pinto was just leaving, travelling at a normal rate of speed. Leo Cooper pulled out on the road behind them.

Stevens turned left on Crippen Road, a road that has a field   13 on one side and two or three small houses on the other, and there Cooper pulled his car in front of the Pinto and stopped, blocking the way. He got out and walked toward the Pinto. Suddenly, Stevens put the car in reverse, backed into a driveway a hundred yards behind him, and sped off. Cooper jumped in his car and gave chase. Stevens raced back to Brown Gap Road, ran a stop sign there, ran another stop sign at Maynardville Highway, turned north, veered off onto the old Andersonville Pike, a nearly abandoned road that runs parallel to the highway, and then crossed back over the highway to the narrow, dark country roads on the other side. Stevens sometimes drove with his lights out. He took some of the corners by suddenly applying his hand brake to make the car swerve around in a ninety-degree turn. He was in familiar territory — he actually passed his trailer — and Cooper had difficulty keeping up. Past the trailer, Stevens swept down a hill into a sharp left turn that took him onto Foust Hollow Road, a winding, hilly road not much wider than one car.

At a fork, Cooper thought he had lost the Pinto. He started   14 to go right, and then saw what seemed to be a spark from Stevens's dragging muffler off to the left, in the darkness. Cooper took the left fork, down Salem Church Road. He went down a hill, and then up a long, curving hill to a crest, where he saw the Stevens car ahead. "I saw the car airborne. Up in the air," he later testified. "It was up in the air. And then it completely rolled over one more time. It started to make another flip forward, and just as it started to flip to the other side it flipped back this way, and my daughter's body came out."

Cooper slammed on his brakes and skidded to a stop up   15 against the Pinto. "Book!" Stevens shouted — the group's equivalent of "Scram!" Stevens and Munsey disappeared into the darkness. "It was dark, no one around, and so I started yelling for FaNee," Cooper has testified. "I thought it was an eternity before I could find her body, wedged under the back end of that car. . . . I tried everything I could, and saw that I couldn't get her loose. So I ran to a trailer back up to the top of the hill back up there to try to get that lady to call to get me some help, and then apparently she didn't think that I was serious. . . . I took the jack out of my car and got under, and it was dark, still couldn't see too much what was going on . . . and started prying and got her loose, and I don't know how. And then I dragged her over to the side, and, of course, at the time I felt reasonably assured that she was gone, because her head was completely — on one side just as if you had taken a sledgehammer and just hit it and bashed it in. And I did have the pleasure of one thing. I had the pleasure of listening to her breathe about the last three times she ever breathed in her life."

David Munsey did not return to the wreck that night, but   16
Charlie Stevens did. Leo Cooper was kneeling next to his daughter's body. Cooper insisted that Stevens come close enough to see FaNee. "He was kneeling down next to her," Stevens later testified. "And he said, 'Do you know what you've done? Do you really know what you've done?' Like that. And I just looked at her, and I said, 'Yes,' and just stood there. Because I couldn't say nothing." There was, of course, a legal decision to be made about who was responsible for FaNee Cooper's death. In a deposition, Stevens said he had been fleeing for his life. He testified that when Leo Cooper blocked Crippen Road, FaNee had said that her father had a gun and intended to hurt them. Stevens was bound over and eventually indicted for involuntary manslaughter. Leo Cooper testified that when he approached the Pinto on Crippen Road, FaNee had a strange expression that he had never seen before. "It wasn't like FaNee, and I knew something was wrong," he said. "My concern was to get FaNee out of the car." The district attorney's office asked that Cooper be bound over for reckless driving, but the judge declined to do so. "Any father would have done what he did," the judge said. "I can see no criminal act on the part of Mr. Cooper."

Almost two years passed before Charlie Stevens was   17
brought to trial. Part of the problem was assuring the presence
of David Munsey, who had joined the Navy but seemed inclined
to assign his own leaves. In the meantime, the Coopers went to
court with a civil suit — they had "uninsured-motorist coverage," which requires their insurance company to cover any de-
fendant who has no insurance of his own — and they won a
judgment. There were ways of assigning responsibility, of
course, which had nothing to do with the law, civil or criminal.
A lot of people in Knoxville thought that Leo Cooper had, in
the words of his lawyer, "done what any daddy worth his salt
would have done." There were others who believed that FaNee
Cooper had lost her life because Leo Cooper had lost his temper. Leo Cooper was not among those who expressed any
doubts about his actions. Unlike his wife, whose eyes filled with
tears at almost any mention of FaNee, Cooper seemed able,
even eager to go over the details of the accident again and again.
With the help of a school-board security man, he conducted his
own investigation. He drove over the route dozens of times.
"I've thought about it every day, and I guess I will the rest of my
life," he said as he and his lawyer and the prosecuting attorney
went over the route again the day before Charlie Stevens's trial
finally began. "But I can't tell any alternative for a father. I simply wanted her out of that car. I'd have done the same thing
again, even at the risk of losing her."

Tennessee law permits the family of a victim to hire a special   18
prosecutor to assist the district attorney. The lawyer who acted
for the Coopers in the civil case helped prosecute Charlie
Stevens. Both he and the district attorney assured the jurors
that the presence of a special prosecutor was not to be construed
to mean that the Coopers were vindictive. Outside the courtroom, Leo Cooper said that the verdict was of no importance to
him — that he felt sorry, in a way, for Charlie Stevens. But
there were people in Knoxville who thought Cooper had a lot
riding on the prosecution of Charlie Stevens. If Stevens was not
guilty of FaNee Cooper's death — found so by twelve of his
peers — who was?

At the trial, Cooper testified emotionally and remarkably   19
graphically about pulling FaNee out from under the car and
watching her die in his arms. Charlie Stevens had shaved his
beard and cut his hair, but the effort did not transform him into
an impressive witness. His lawyer — trying to argue that it
would have been impossible for Stevens to concoct the story
about FaNee's having mentioned a gun, as the prosecution
strongly implied — said, "His mind is such that if you ask him a
question you can hear his mind go around, like an old mill
creaking." Stevens did not deny the recklessness of his driving
or the sorry condition of his car. It happened to be the only car
he had available to flee in, he said, and he had fled in fear for his
life.

The prosecution said that Stevens could have let FaNee out   20
of the car when her father stopped them, or could have gone to
the commercial strip on the Maynardville Highway for protection. The prosecution said that Leo Cooper had done what he
might have been expected to do under the circumstances —
alone, late at night, his daughter in danger. The defense said
precisely the same about Stevens: he had done what he might
have been expected to do when being pursued by a man he had
reason to be afraid of. "I don't fault Mr. Cooper for what he did,
but I'm sorry he did it," the defense attorney said. "I'm sorry the
girl said what she said." The jury deliberated for eighteen minutes. Charlie Stevens was found guilty. The jury recommended
a sentence of from two to five years in the state penitentiary. At
the announcement, Leo Cooper broke down and cried. JoAnn
Cooper's eyes filled with tears; she blinked them back and continued to stare straight ahead.

In a way, the Coopers might still strike a casual visitor as an   21
ideal family — handsome parents, a bright and bubbly teenage
daughter, a little boy learning the hook shot from his father, a
warm house with some land around it. FaNee's presence is
there, of course. A picture of her, with a small bouquet of
flowers over it, hangs in the living room. One of her poems is
displayed in a frame on a table. Even if Leo Cooper continues to
think about that night for the rest of his life, there are questions

he can never answer. Was there a way that Leo and JoAnn Cooper could have prevented FaNee from choosing the path she chose? Would she still be alive if Leo Cooper had not jumped into his car and driven to the end of the driveway to investigate? Did she in fact tell Charlie Stevens that her father would hurt them — or even that her father had a gun? Did she want to get away from her family even at the risk of tearing around dark country roads in Charlie Stevens's dismal Pinto? Or did she welcome the risk? The poem of FaNee's that the Coopers have displayed is one she wrote a week before her death:

> I think I'm going to die
> And I really don't know why.
> But look in my eye
> When I tell you good-bye.
> I think I'm going to die.

QUESTIONS ON MEANING AND PURPOSE

1. Which appears to be the dominant PURPOSE of Trillin's essay: to report a death, to tell why it happened, or to tell a revealing story?
2. How would you characterize Leo and JoAnn Cooper?
3. Of all the people who talk about FaNee and her problems, who seems to understand her best?
4. In paragraph 18, Trillin hints that Leo Cooper might have felt threatened had Charlie Stevens won acquittal. What, exactly, is the threat?
5. What do the samples of FaNee's writing that appear in Trillin's essay (paragraphs 2, 4, 5, 11, 21) contribute to your understanding of her behavior?

QUESTIONS ON WRITING STRATEGY

1. In paragraph 5, Trillin talks about the Jocks in a Knox County high school. What makes this material more than mere digression?

2. What do the direct quotations — from Leo and JoAnn Cooper; the friend called Marcia; the counsellor, Jim Griffin; FaNee herself; Charlie Stevens; Cooper's lawyer — contribute to Trillin's narrative, other than local color?

3. Does Trillin seem to be biased against or in favor of anyone in his narrative? Or does he conceal all bias? Muster EVIDENCE for your answer.

4. In his final paragraph, Trillin asks a series of questions. Do they provide a satisfactory CONCLUSION to his narrative? Discuss.

5. In his introduction to *Killings*, Trillin recalls that local newspaper reporters he met while working on the story of FaNee Cooper did not understand his interest in the case. "They couldn't imagine why I had come all the way from New York to write about a death that probably hadn't even made their front page. Only one person had died, and she had not been an important person." How might the AUDIENCE of *The New Yorker*, a nationally circulated magazine of fiction, poetry, humor, and general commentary, read about a killing with expectations different from those of readers of a local newspaper?

6. In an interview on how he writes, Trillin has remarked that in setting down the story of a violent death, which "has within it its own narrative line — its own beginning, middle, and end," he tries to make his laborious reporting invisible:

> Then what I try to do when I write is get out of the way and just let the story tell itself. I try to get as many of the details as cleanly as possible into the story and try to get all the marks of writing off of the story. Sometimes I think of it as trying to change clothes in a tiny closet.[1]

In what ways does "It's Just Too Late" reflect this method of storytelling? To what extent does the writer himself remain invisible? Does his research show? Does he make you forget that the story required note taking, legwork, and extensive conversations with people?

QUESTIONS ON LANGUAGE

1. Consult your dictionary if you need help defining the following: introspective, errant, magnanimous, gentility (paragraph 1); afflic-

---

[1]"A Writer's Process: A Conversation with Calvin Trillin," by Alice Trillin, *Journal of Basic Writing* (Fall/Winter 1981), pp. 5–18.

tion (2); decrepit (10); incorrigibles (11); deposition, indicted (16); construed, vindictive (18).

2. What do the Jocks mean when they "talk about having a real good Christian witness" (paragraph 5)?

3. What do you infer about the author's feelings toward Leo Cooper when he describes Cooper as having "a manner that may come from years of trying to leave errant junior-high-school students with the impression that a responsible adult is magnanimous, even humble, about invariably being in the right" (paragraph 1)?

SUGGESTIONS FOR WRITING

1. Suppose that Mr. Cooper had been able to stop Charlie Stevens's car before FaNee was killed — and that you, as the reporter, beginning after paragraph 13 in "It's Just Too Late," have to tell what happened next. Imagine and write a new, briefer ending for Trillin's narrative.

2. As objectively as you can, narrate the experience of a high-school acquaintance who committed a rebellious act that had dire (but not necessarily fatal) consequences.

· Maxine Hong Kingston ·

Among contemporary writers, surely MAXINE HONG KINGS-
TON is our foremost interpreter of Chinese-American life. She
was born in 1940, the daughter of Tom and Ying Lan (Chew)
Hong, proprietors of a laundry in Stockton, California. (In
1963 she extended her name by marriage to Earll Kingston, a
professional actor.) For Chinese-Americans in the San
Joaquin Valley, the Hong family's laundry served as a social
center where stories were told aloud. In time, Kingston was to
write down many remembered tales and histories she had
heard as a child. Following her graduation from the University of California, Berkeley, she taught English in high schools
and colleges and for several years was visiting writer at the
University of Hawaii. An author of widely varied skills,
Kingston has contributed articles, short stories, and poems to
magazines including *The New Yorker, Ms., American Heritage,
New West, English Journal,* and the *New York Times Magazine.*
Her highly praised autobiography, *The Woman Warrior: Memoirs of a Girlhood among Ghosts* (1976), received the National
Book Critics Circle Award for nonfiction. *China Men* (1980)
won an American Book Award. She now lives in Studio City,
California.

My Legal Father Enters America

Among the many Chinese eager to settle on Gold Mountain
(their name for the United States — a name that probably
grew out of old tales of the gold rush), there must have been
some who entered illegally, others who faced the "white demons" manning the immigration office. In *China Men,* Maxine Hong Kingston includes differing versions of how her
scholarly immigrant father entered the United States in the
1920s. In one of her accounts, he stows away on a ship from
Cuba to New York and enters the country illegally. The
equally convincing version given here, in which Kingston
calls him "the legal father," has him suffering in approved
fashion through the immigration process in San Francisco.
Nowhere does Kingston say unequivocally which route her father really took. Like her other versions of the story, this one,
alive with the ring of truth, seems rooted in family legend.

Arriving in San Francisco Bay, the legal father was detained   1
for an indefinite time at the Immigration Station on Angel Island, almost within swimming distance of San Francisco. In a
wooden house, a white demon physically examined him, poked
him in the ass and genitals, looked in his mouth, pulled his eye-
lids with a hook. This was not the way a father ought to have
been greeted. A cough tickled his chest and throat, but he held
it down. The doctor demon pointed to a door, which he entered
to find men and boys crowded together from floor to ceiling in
bunkbeds and on benches; they stood against the walls and at
the windows. These must be the hundred China Men who
could enter America, he thought. But the quota was one hundred a year, not one hundred per day, and here were packed
more than one hundred, nearer two hundred or three. A few
people made room for him to set down his suitcases. "A newcomer. Another newcomer," they called out. A welcome party
made its way to him. "I'm the president of the Self-Governing
Association," one of them was telling him in a dialect almost
like his. "The most important rule we have here is that we guard
one another's chances for immigration." He also asked for dues;
the father gave a few dimes toward buying newspapers and phonograph records, an invention that he had never heard before.
"Now you're eligible to vote," said the president, who then said
that he had won his office by having been on the island the
longest, three and a half years. The legal father's heart sank, and
rose again; there must be something wrong with this man, not a
good man, a criminal to be jailed for so long. "Do you want to
spend money on a rubber ball? Vote Yes or No." The legal father voted No. How odd it would be to say to these men, "Play
ball. Go ahead. Play with it," as if they were boys and could
play. Even the boys wouldn't play. Who can be that light-
hearted? He wasn't really going to stay here for more than a day
or two, was he? He made his way across the room. Some of the
men were gambling, others exercising, cutting one another's
hair, staring at their feet or folded hands or the floor. He saw
two men handcuffed to each other. Readers chanted San Francisco newspapers, *Young China* and *Chinese World*. The legal father, who was skillful and lucky, joined a game and won forty

silver dollars, and gave away one for the rubber ball. He learned who was being deported and who was serving a year's sentence before deportation.

A bell went off like a ship's alarm, but it was a dinner bell. The father followed the others to a dining hall. About ten women were coming out. They were the first women he had seen since China, and they already belonged to husbands. He did not know that he had come to a country with no women. The husbands and wives talked quickly as the guards pushed them past one another. The father saw the man ahead of him hold hands with a woman for a moment and — he saw it — pass her a note. She dropped it. She knelt and, fixing her shoe with one hand, snatched the piece of paper with the other. A big white matron grabbed her arm and took the paper. Though these people were all strangers, the father joined the men who surrounded the matron. They wrested the paper from her and tore it up. The legal father ate some of the shreds. That was the last time the men's and women's mealtimes overlapped. There seemed to be no other immediate consequences; perhaps denial of entry would be the punishment.

The China Men who worked in the kitchen brought food cooked and served in buckets. "Poison," the prisoners grumbled. "A couple of years ago," said the president of the Self-Governing Association, "the demons tried to starve us to death. They were taking the food money for themselves. If it weren't for us rioting, you newcomers wouldn't be eating so much today. We faced bayonets for this food." The legal father wasn't sure he would've wanted any more of the slop they were eating.

The men spent the long days rehearsing what they would say to the Immigration Demon. The forgetful men fingered their risky notes. Those who came back after being examined told what questions they had been asked. "I had to describe all the streets in my village." "They'll ask, 'Do you have any money?' and 'Do you have a job?'" "They've been asking those questions all this week," the cooks and janitors confirmed. "What's the right answer?" asked the legal fathers. "Well, last week they liked 'No job' because it proves you were an aristocrat. And they liked 'No money' because you showed a willingness to work. But this week, they like 'Yes job' and 'Yes money' because you wouldn't be taking jobs away from white workers." The men groaned, "Some help." The demons did not treat people of any other race the way they did Chinese. The few Japanese left in a day or two. It was because their emperor was strong.

Footsteps walked across the ceiling, and bedsprings   5
squeaked above their heads. So there were more of them locked on the second floor. "The women are up there," the father was told. Diabolical, inauspicious beginning — to be trodden over by women. "Living under women's legs," said the superstitious old-fashioned men from the backward villages. "Climbed over by women." It was bad luck even to walk under women's pants on clotheslines. No doubt the demons had deliberately planned this humiliation. The legal father decided that for a start in the new country, he would rid himself of Chinese superstitions; this curse would not count.

He read the walls, which were covered with poems. Those   6
who could write protested this jailing, this wooden house (*wood* rhyming with *house*), the unfair laws, the emperor too weak to help them. They wrote about the fog and being lonely and afraid. The poets had come to a part of the world not made for honor, where "a hero cannot use his bravery." One poet was ready to ride his horse to do mighty American deeds but instead here he sat corraled, "this wooden house my coffin." The poets must have stayed long to carve the words so well. The demons were not going to free him, a scholar, then. Some were not poems exactly but statements. "This island is not angelic." "It's not true about the gold." One man blamed "the Mexican Exclusion Laws" for his imprisonment. The writers were anonymous; no official demon could trace them and penalize them. Some signed surname and village, but they were still disguised; there were many of that name from that village, many men named Lee from Toi Sahn, many a Hong of Sun Woi, and many a Three District Man and Four District No Such Man. There were dates of long stays.

Night fell quickly; at about four o'clock the fog poured   7
down the San Francisco hillsides, covered the bay, and clouded

the windows. Soon the city was gone, held fast by black sea and sky. The fog horns mourned. San Francisco might have been a figment of Gold Mountain dreams.

The legal father heard cries and thumps from someone 8 locked in a separate shed. Words came out of the fog, the wind whipping a voice around the Island. "Let me land. Let me out. Let me land. I want to come home."

In the middle of one night when he was the only man 9 awake, the legal father took out his Four Valuable Things,[1] and using spit and maybe tears to mix the ink, he wrote a poem on the wall, just a few words to observe his stay. He wrote about wanting freedom. He did not sign his name; he would find himself a new American name when he landed. If the U.S. government found out his thoughts on freedom, it might not let him land. The next morning the readers sang the new poem for the others to hear. "Who wrote this wonderful poem during the night?" they asked, but the father modestly did not say.

For one another's entertainment, the men rehearsed and 10 staged skits, puppet shows, and heroic parts of operas. They juggled fruit, bottles, and the new rubber ball. The father, who was traveling with the adventures of Yüeh Fei, the Patriot, in six volumes, read aloud the part where Yüeh Fei's mother carved on his back four words: FIRST — PROTECT MY NATION. He held up for all to see the illustrations of warriors in battle. He also carried the poems of Li Po, the best poet, the Heavenly Poet, the Great White Light, Venus. The father sang about a sentry stopping Li Po from entering a city. Li Po was drunk as usual and riding a mule. He refused to give his name to the sentry, but wrote a daring poem that he was a man from whose mouth the emperor had wiped the drool; the emperor's favorite wife had held his inkslab. The impressed sentry granted him entrance. This poem heartened the men; they laughed and clapped at Li Po's cleverness and the sentry's recognition of him and poetry.

"What is a poem exactly?" asked an illiterate man, a Gold 11 Mountain Sojourner who had spent twenty years in America

[1]Writing brushes, ink, inkslab, and paper. — EDS.

and was on his way back to his family. "Let me give it a try," he said. "A short poem: 'On the Gold Mountain, I met black men black like coal.' Is that a poem?" The literate men were delighted. "Marvelous," they said. "Of course, it's a poem." "A simile. A simile. Yes, a poem." The legal father liked it so much, he remembered it forever.

The legal father learned many people's thoughts because he   12 wrote their letters. They told their wives and mothers how wonderful they found the Gold Mountain. "The first place I came to was The Island of Immortals," they told him to write. "The foreigners clapped at our civilized magnificence when we walked off the ship in our brocades. A fine welcome. They call us 'Celestials.'" They were eating well; soon they would be sending money. Yes, a magical country. They were happy, not at all frightened. The Beautiful Nation was glorious, exactly the way they had heard it would be. "I'll be seeing you in no time." "Today we ate duck with buns and plum sauce," which was true on days when the China Men in San Francisco sent gifts.

Every day at intervals men were called out one by one. The   13 legal father kept himself looking presentable. He wore his Western suit and shined shoes, constantly ready.

One morning the barracks awoke to find a man had hanged   14 himself. He had done it from a railing. At first he looked as if he had been tortured, his legs cut off. He had tied his legs bent at the knees like an actor or beggar playing a man with no legs, and hung himself by pushing over his chair. His body had elongated from hanging all night. The men looked through his papers and found X's across them. When new arrivals looked for beds, nobody told them that a dead, hung man had slept in that one.

Also, the rumor went, a woman upstairs had killed herself   15 by sharpening a chopstick and shoving it through her ear. Her husband had sent for her, and she did not understand why he did not come to take her home.

At last came the legal father's turn to be interrogated. He   16 combed his hair again. He said his good-byes. Inside the interrogation room were several white demons in formal wear; the legal father gauged by the width of lapels and ties that his own suit was not quite stylish. Standing beside the table was a Chinese-looking soldier in American uniform and a demon soldier in the same uniform. This Chinese American was the interpreter. The legal father sat opposite the interrogators, who asked his name, his village, where he was born, his birth date — easy questions.

"Can you read and write?" the white demon asked in English and the Chinese American asked in Cantonese.   17

"Yes," said the legal father.   18

But the secretary demon was already writing No since he obviously couldn't, needing a translator.   19

"When did you cut off your pigtail?" asked the translator.   20

"In 1911," said the legal father. It was a safe answer, the year   21
he would have picked anyway, not too early before the Republic nor too late, not too revolutionary nor too reactionary. Most people had cut their hair in 1911. He might have cut it for fashion as much as for revolution.

"Do you have relatives who are American citizens?"   22

The janitor, a China Man, who just then entered the room   23
with dustpan and broom, nodded.

"Yes."   24

"Who?"   25

"My grandfather is an American. My father is an American.   26
So I'm an American, also my three older brothers and three uncles — all Americans."

Then came the trap questions about how many pigs did   27
they own in 1919, whether the pig house was made out of bricks or straw, how many steps on the back stoop, how far to the out-house, how to get to the market from the farm, what were the addresses of the places his grandfather and father and brothers and uncles had lived in America. The interrogators liked asking questions with numbers for answers. Numbers seemed true to them. "How many times did your grandfather return to the United States?" "Twice." "Twice?" "Yes, twice. He was here once and returned twice. He was here three times altogether. He spent half his life in America and half in China." They looked into his eyes for lies. Even the Chinese American looked into his eyes, and they repeated his answers, as if doubting them. He

squelched an urge to change the answers, elaborate on them. "Do you have any money?" "Yes." "How much?" He wondered if they would charge him higher fees the more money he reported. He decided to tell the truth; lying added traps. Whether or not he spoke the truth didn't matter anyway; demons were capricious. It was up to luck now.

They matched his answers to the ones his relatives and fellow villagers gave. He watched the hands with yellow hair on their backs turn the copies of his grandfather's and father's papers.   28

They told him to go back to the jail, where he waited for more weeks. The next time he was called to be examined — *searched* the Chinese word — they asked again, "What American relatives do you have?"   29

"My grandfather and father," he said again, "and also my three brothers and three uncles."   30

"Your grandfather's papers are illegal," the Chinese American translated. "And your father is also an illegal alien." One by one the demons outlawed his relatives and ancestors, including a Gold Rush grandfather, who had paid a bag of gold dust to an American Citizenship Judge for papers. "There are no such things as Citizenship Judges," said the Immigration Demon and put an X across the paper that had been in the family for seventy-five years. He moved on to ask more trap questions, the directions the neighbors' houses faced and the number of water buffaloes in 1920, and sent him back to the barracks.   31

He waited again. He was examined again, and since he had an accurate memory, he told them the same number of pigs as the last two times, the same number of water buffaloes (one), the same year of cutting his queue, and at last they said, "You may enter the United States of America." He had passed the American examination; he had won America. He was not sure on what basis they let him in — his diploma, his American lineage (which may have turned out to be good after all), his ability to withstand jailing, his honesty, or the skill of his deceits.   32

This legal father then worked his way across the continent to New York, the center of America.   33

QUESTIONS ON MEANING AND PURPOSE

1. What does Kingston mean when she says, "He did not know that he had come to a country with no women" (paragraph 2)?
2. Explain the old men's curious belief that the demons had set out to humiliate them by locating the women's room above the men's (paragraph 5).
3. Explain the IRONY in paragraph 19.
4. In what ways do the legal father and his fellow immigrants cope with the Immigration Demon? What do they fear most?
5. What PURPOSE other than to entertain do you find in Kingston's essay?

QUESTIONS ON WRITING STRATEGY

1. In what PERSON does Kingston narrate the legal father's experiences on Angel Island? What devices does the author use to convince you that the POINT OF VIEW is chiefly that of an educated Chinese man who does not, however, speak English?
2. Point to some places in the essay where the point of view shifts from the legal father's to the author's.
3. For whom does Kingston seem to be writing? Herself? Her fellow Chinese-Americans? Her family? The general public? To what extent does her sense of an AUDIENCE seem to have influenced her writing?
4. From this essay, what do you infer about Kingston's attitude toward the U.S. Immigration Service? How is it revealed?

QUESTIONS ON LANGUAGE

1. If necessary, look up the following words in a dictionary: diabolical, inauspicious (paragraph 5); figment (7); brocades (12); capricious (27); queue, deceits (32).
2. Explain what is meant by "risky notes" (paragraph 4).
3. Comment on Kingston's use of the loaded word *demon* to describe Americans not of Chinese descent.
4. What does the author mean by "*wood* rhyming with *house*" (paragraph 6)?

SUGGESTIONS FOR WRITING

1. Write a paragraph in which you comment on the treatment the legal father and his countrymen received from the immigration people.
2. Narrate some bit of the history that is part of your family lore. It might be the story of how a relative first came to America. Include specific details. Where facts are thin you may have to rely, as perhaps Kingston did, on your own conjectures about what happened.

—— POSTSCRIPT ON PROCESS ——

Maxine Hong Kingston

From the following comment by Maxine Hong Kingston on her story of the legal father, you'll see that her narrative style would be hard to imitate. Few of us grow up in families that place such importance on storytelling; few of us can trace ourselves back through twenty-five generations of storytellers. Yet the author has liberating advice for anyone who seeks to capture the past in words. Don't worry if, before you begin to write, you search out and discover "too much truth." Your own memory, you may find, is an excellent editor.

You probably think that when a writer uses a real-life situation in a story, she has to fill in undramatic gaps with made-up dialogue and car chases and helicopter crashes. It is certainly true that real life does seem to have stretches when you eat by yourself, then you take your dirty clothes to the Laundromat, where you meet nobody interesting, and then you eat again, watch TV, and go to bed by yourself. At first glance, you would think that such a day — such a life — would not make much of a story, but what I have just given you is an outline of a big section of my next book. When the action is particularly uninteresting — that is exactly when you can go wild with the rich inner life and complex thoughts of your hero. His way of seeing the world will paint the walls of his apartment and the streets of the city with atmosphere. Whatever the people in the Laundromat say will sound with a loud, perhaps meaningful, noise. 1

But what about writing about real people who have adventures and who confront one another in secret dialogues? I am lucky in that I am one in a long line of storytellers. Our family can now trace ourselves name by name back twenty-five generations, and, before that, mythologically, to prehistoric, pre-Han times. We also have a habit of telling our dreams at breakfast and, after work, telling what happened at the office. When I went to Singapore, my aunt asked after my mother: "And what does she dream about?" I was able to tell her. Even in the United 2

States, we haven't lost the ability to talk-story. In fact, I think we have become even more adept at it out of necessity. The story about the Legal/Illegal Father is typical of immigrants, who have at least one true story to tell the immigration officials, and other true stories to tell when entertaining, or advising, or archiving. As a writer, after getting over the idea that I had to know only one truth, I realized that my problem is that I have too much truth to tell rather than too little. My task, like gardening in Hawaii, is cutting and pruning and hacking back, rather than planting. The difficult writing came when I decided that I would find ways to give all the versions of stories. Incidentally, giving "good" versions and "bad" versions freed me to tell the stories that might make my family angry at me.

Young writers who come from families that do not talk-story   3
need not feel at a disadvantage. There is an abundance of phenomena in life itself, and it is the writer's task to choose artfully what to set down.

Well, then. Are there rules for choosing? As the years go by,   4
I have become aware of what an interesting point of view I have, and so I rely on my sense of curiosity and on my memory. If I am bored by somebody or some event, and if I forget them, then there has been a weeding out, and what remains is the unforgettable.

1. Write a narrative with one of the following as your subject. It may be (as your instructor may advise) either a first-person memoir, or a story written in the third person, observing the experience of someone else. Decide before you begin whether you are writing (1) an anecdote; (2) an essay consisting mainly of a single narrative; or (3) an essay that includes more than one story.

   A memorable experience from your early life
   A lesson you learned the hard way
   A trip into unfamiliar territory
   An embarrassing moment that taught you something
   A brush with death
   A monumental misunderstanding
   An accident
   An unexpected encounter
   A story about a famous person, or someone close to you
   A conflict or contest
   An assassination attempt
   A historic event of significance

2. Tell a true story of your early or recent school days, either humorous or serious, showing what a struggle school or college has been for you. (For comparable stories, see Thurber's "University Days" or, in Chapter 10, Richard Rodriguez's "Aria.")

· 2 ·

DESCRIPTION

Writing with Your Senses

THE METHOD

Like narration, description is a familiar method of expression, already a working part of you. In any talk-fest with friends, you probably do your share of describing. You depict in words someone you've met by describing her clothes, the look on her face, the way she walks. You describe somewhere you've been, something you admire, something you just can't abide. In a diary or in a letter to a friend, you describe your college (cast concrete buildings, crowded walks, pigeons rattling their wings); or perhaps you describe your brand-new secondhand car, from the snakelike glitter of its hubcaps to the odd antiques in its trunk, bequeathed by its previous owner. You hardly can live a day without describing something or hearing something described. Small wonder that, in written discourse, description is almost as indispensable as paper.

73

Description reports the testimony of your senses. It invites your readers to imagine that they too not only see, but perhaps also hear, taste, smell, and touch the subject you describe. Usually, you write a description for either of two purposes: (1) to convey information without bias or emotion; or (2) to convey it with feeling.

In writing with the first purpose in mind, you write an *objective* (or *impartial, public,* or *functional*) description. You describe your subject so clearly and exactly that your reader will understand it, or recognize it, and you leave your emotions out. Technical or scientific descriptive writing is usually objective: a manual detailing the parts of an internal combustion engine, a biologist's report of a previously unknown species of frog. You write this kind of description in sending a friend directions for finding your house ("Look for the green shutters on the windows and a new garbage can at the front door"). Although in a personal letter describing your house, you might very well become emotionally involved with it (and call it, perhaps, a "fleabag"), in writing an objective description your purpose is not to convey your feelings. You are trying to make the house easily recognized.

The other type of descriptive writing is *subjective* (or *emotional, personal,* or *impressionistic*) description. This is the kind included in a magazine advertisement for a new car. It's what you write in your letter to a friend setting forth what your college is like — whether you are pleased or displeased with it. In this kind of description, you may use biases and personal feelings — in fact, they are essential. Let us consider a splendid example: a subjective description of a storm at sea. Charles Dickens, in his memoir *American Notes,* conveys his passenger's-eye view of an Atlantic steamship on a morning when the ocean is wild:

> Imagine the ship herself, with every pulse and artery of her huge body swollen and bursting . . . sworn to go on or die. Imagine the wind howling, the sea roaring, the rain beating; all in furious array against her. Picture the sky both dark and wild, and the clouds in fearful sympathy with the waves, making another ocean in the air. Add to all this the clattering on deck and down below; the tread of hurried feet; the loud

hoarse shouts of seamen; the gurgling in and out of water through the scuppers; with every now and then the striking of a heavy sea upon the planks above, with the deep, dead, heavy sound of thunder heard within a vault; and there is the head wind of that January morning.

I say nothing of what may be called the domestic noises of the ship; such as the breaking of glass and crockery, the tumbling down of stewards, the gambols, overhead, of loose casks and truant dozens of bottled porter, and the very remarkable and far from exhilarating sounds raised in their various staterooms by the seventy passengers who were too ill to get up to breakfast.

Notice how many *sounds* are included in this primarily ear-minded description. We can infer how Dickens feels about the storm. It is a terrifying event that reduces the interior of the vessel to chaos; and yet the writer (in hearing the loose barrels and beer bottles merrily *gambol*, in finding humor in the seasick passengers' plight) apparently delights in it. Writing subjectively, he intrudes his feelings. Think of what a starkly different description of the very same storm the captain might set down — *objectively* — in the ship's log: "At 0600 hours, watch reported a wind from due north of 70 knots. Whitecaps were noticed, in height two ells above the bow. Below deck, much gear was reported adrift, and ten casks of ale were broken and their staves strewn about. Mr. Liam Jones, chief steward, suffered a compound fracture of the left leg. . . . " But Dickens, not content simply to record information, strives to ensure that the mind's eye is dazzled and the mind's ear regaled.

Description is usually found in the company of other methods of writing. Often, for instance, it will enliven narration and make the people in the story and the setting unmistakably clear. Writing an argument in his essay "Why Don't We Complain?", William F. Buckley begins with a description of eighty suffering commuters perspiring in an overheated train; the description makes the argument more powerful. Description will help a writer in examining the effects of a flood, or in comparing and contrasting two towns. Keep the method of description in mind when you come to try expository and argumentative writing.

THE PROCESS

Understand, first of all, your purpose in writing a description. Are you going to write a subjective description, expressing your personal feelings? Or, instead, do you want to write an objective description, trying only to see and report, leaving out your emotions and biases?

Give a little thought to your audience. What do your readers need to be told, if they are to share the feelings you would have them share, if they are clearly to behold what you want them to? If, let's say, you are describing a downtown street on a Saturday night for an audience of fellow students who live in the same city and know it well, then you need not dwell on the street's familiar geography. What must you tell? Only those details that make the place different on a Saturday night. But if you are remembering your home city, and writing for readers who don't know it, you'll need to establish a few central landmarks in order to sketch (in their minds) an unfamiliar street on a Saturday night.

Before you begin to write a description, go look at your subject. If that is not possible, your next best course is to spend a few minutes imagining the subject until, in your mind's eye, you can see every flyspeck on it.

Then, having fixed your subject in mind, ask yourself which of its features you'll need to report to your particular audience, for your particular purpose. If you plan to write a subjective description of an old house, laying weight on its spooky atmosphere for readers you wish to make shiver, then you might mention its squeaking bats and its shadowy halls, leaving out any reference to its busy swimming pool and the stomping disco music that billows from its interior. If, however, you are describing the house in a classified ad, for an audience of possible buyers, you might focus instead on its eat-in kitchen, working fireplace, and proximity to public transportation. Details have to be carefully selected. Too many will blur the effect and only confuse your reader.

Let your description, as a whole, convey one dominant impression. (The swimming pool and the disco music might be details useful in a description meant to convey that the house is full of merriment.) Perhaps many details will be worth noticing; if so, you will want to arrange them so that your reader will see which matter most. In his description of the storm at sea — a subjective description — Charles Dickens sorts out the pandemonium for us. He groups the various sounds into two classes: those of sea and sailors, and the "domestic noises" of the ship's passengers — their smashing dishes, their rolling bottles, the crashing of stewards who wait on them. Like many effective descriptions, this one clearly reveals a principle of organization.

In organizing your description, you may find it helpful to be aware of your *point of view* — the physical angle from which you're perceiving and describing. In the previous chapter, on narration, we spoke of point of view: how essential it is for a story to have a narrator — one who, from a certain position, reports what takes place. A description, too, needs a consistent point of view: that of an observer who stays put and observes steadily. For instance, when describing a landscape as seen from the air, do not swoop suddenly to earth.

You can organize a description in several ways. Some writers, as they describe something, make a carefully planned inspection tour of its details, moving spatially (from left to right, from near to far, from top to bottom, from center to periphery), or perhaps moving from prominent objects to tiny ones, from dull to bright, from commonplace to extraordinary — or vice versa. The plan you choose is the one that best fulfills your purpose. If you were to describe, for instance, a chapel in the middle of a desert, you might begin with the details of the lonely terrain. Then, as if approaching the chapel with the aid of a zoom lens, you might detail its exterior and then go on inside. That might be a workable method to write a description *if* your purpose were to emphasize the sense that the chapel is an island of beauty and warmth in the midst of desolation. Say, however, that your purpose was quite different: to emphasize the interior design of the chapel. You might then begin your description inside the structure, perhaps with its most prominent feature, the stained glass windows. You might mention the surrounding desert later in your description, but only incidentally. An effective

description makes a definite impression. The writer arranges details so that the reader is firmly left with the feeling the writer intends to convey.

Whatever method you follow in arranging details, stick with
it all the way through. Don't start out describing a group of cats
by going from old cats to kittens, then switch in the middle of
your description and line up the cats according to color. If your
arrangement would cause any difficulty for the reader, you need
to rearrange your details. If a writer, in describing a pet shop,
should skip about wildly from clerks to cats to customers to catfood to customers to catfood to clerks, the reader may quickly
be lost. Instead, the writer might group clerks together with customers, and cats together with catfood (or in some other clear
order). But suppose (the writer might protest) it's a wildly confused pet shop I'm trying to describe? No matter — the writer
nevertheless has to write in an orderly manner, if the reader is to
understand. Dickens describes a scene of shipboard chaos, yet
his prose is orderly.

Feel no grim duty to include every perceptible detail. To do
so would only invite chaos — or perhaps, for the reader, mere
tedium. Pick out the features that matter most. One revealing,
hard-to-forget detail (such as Dickens's truant porter bottles) is,
like a single masterly brush stroke, worth a whole coat of dull
paint. In selecting or discarding details, ask, What am I out to
accomplish? What main impression of my subject am I trying to
give?

Luckily, to write a memorable description, you don't need a
storm at sea or any other awe-inspiring subject. As E. B. White
demonstrates in his essay in this chapter, "Once More to the
Lake," you can write about a summer cabin on a lake as effectively as you can write about a tornado. Although we tend to
think of description as referring to a single object, you can describe an abstraction or a general type. You can, for instance,
describe a new style of dress, or the identifying features of Italian
sports cars, or a typical turnpike food-and-fuel plaza. Here is humorist S. J. Perelman using metaphor to convey the garish
brightness of a certain low-rent furnished house. Notice how he
makes clear the abstract spirit of the place: "After a few days, I

could have sworn that our faces began to take on the hue of Kodachromes, and even the dog, an animal used to bizarre surroundings, developed a strange, off-register look, as if he were badly printed in overlapping colors."[1] The subject of a description may even be as intangible as a disease, or an interior sensation — as Joan Didion shows us in her feelingful essay on migraine, "In Bed."

When you, too, write an effective description, you'll convey your sensory experience as exactly as possible. Find vigorous, specific words, and you will enable your reader to behold with the mind's eye — and to feel with the mind's fingertips.

DESCRIPTION IN A PARAGRAPH

At 2:59 this Monday afternoon, a thick hush settles like cigarette smoke inside the sweat-scented TV room of Harris Hall. First to arrive, freshman Lee Ann squashes down into the catbird seat in front of the screen. Soon she is flanked by roommates Lisa and Kate, silent, their mouths straight lines, their upturned faces lit by the nervous flicker of a detergent ad. To the left and right of the couch, Pete and Anse crouch on the floor, leaning forward like runners awaiting a starting gun. Behind them, stiff standees line up at attention. Farther back still, English majors and jocks compete for an unobstructed view. Fresh from class, shirttail flapping, arm crooking a bundle of books, Dave barges into the room demanding, "Has it started? Has it started yet?" He is shushed. Somebody shushes a popped-open can of Dr. Pepper whose fizz is distractingly loud. What do these students so intently look forward to — the announcement of World War III? A chord of music climbs and the screen dissolves to a title: "General Hospital."

Comment. Although in the end the anticipated mindblower turns out to be merely an installment of a gripping soap opera, the purpose of this description is to build one definite impression: that something vital is about to arrive. Details are se-

---

[1]"The Marx Brothers," in *The Last Laugh* (New York: Simon and Schuster, 1981), p. 152.

lected accordingly: *thick hush, nervous flicker*, people jostling one another for a better view. The watchers are portrayed as tense and expectant, their mouths straight lines, their faces upturned, the men on the floor crouching forward. The chief appeal is to our visual imaginations, but a few details address our auditory imaginations (the fizz of a can of soda, people saying *Shhh-h-h!*) and our olfactory imaginations (*sweat-scented*) besides.

In organizing this description, the writer's scrutiny moves outward from the television screen: first to the students immediately in front of it, then to those on either side, next to the second row, then to the third, and finally to the last anxious arrival. By this arrangement, the writer presents the details to the reader in a natural order. The main impression is enforced, since the TV screen is the center for all eyes.

· Joan Didion ·

A writer whose fame is fourfold — as novelist, essayist, journalist, and screenwriter — JOAN DIDION was born in 1934 in California, where her family has lived for five generations. After graduation from the University of California, Berkeley, she spent a few years in New York, working as a feature editor for *Vogue*, a fashion magazine. She now lives in Los Angeles. Didion has written four much-discussed novels: *River Run* (1963), *Play It As It Lays* (1971), *A Book of Common Prayer* (1977), and *Democracy* (1984). Recently, *Salvador* (1983), her book-length essay based on a visit to war-torn El Salvador, also received wide attention. With her husband, John Gregory Dunne, she has coauthored screenplays, notably for *True Confessions* (1981) and for the Barbra Streisand film *A Star Is Born* (1976).

In Bed

"In Bed," an essay from Joan Didion's collection *The White Album* (1979), describes migraine headaches in general and her own in particular. She demonstrates without a doubt that feelings, as well as people, places, and things, are fit subjects for description. Any migraine victim will acknowledge that the author knows whereof she speaks. Even nonsufferers are likely to wince under the spell of Didion's vivid, sensuous prose.

Three, four, sometimes five times a month, I spend the day in bed with a migraine headache, insensible to the world around me. Almost every day of every month, between these attacks, I feel the sudden irrational irritation and flush of blood into the cerebral arteries which tell me that migraine is on its way, and I take certain drugs to avert its arrival. If I did not take the drugs, I would be able to function perhaps one day in four. The physiological error called migraine is, in brief, central to the given of my life. When I was 15, 16, even 25, I used to think that I could

81

rid myself of this error by simply denying it, character over chemistry. "Do you have headaches *sometimes? frequently? never?*" the application forms would demand. "Check one." Wary of the trap, wanting whatever it was that the successful circumnavigation of that particular form could bring (a job, a scholarship, the respect of mankind and the grace of God), I would check one. "*Sometimes*," I would lie. That in fact I spent one or two days a week almost unconscious with pain seemed a shameful secret, evidence not merely of some chemical inferiority but of all my bad attitudes, unpleasant tempers, wrongthink.

For I had no brain tumor, no eyestrain, no high blood pres-   2 sure, nothing wrong with me at all: I simply had migraine headaches, and migraine headaches were, as everyone who did not have them knew, imaginary. I fought migraine then, ignored the warnings it sent, went to school and later to work in spite of it, sat through lectures in Middle English and presentations to advertisers with involuntary tears running down the right side of my face, threw up in washrooms, stumbled home by instinct, emptied ice trays onto my bed and tried to freeze the pain in my right temple, wished only for a neurosurgeon who would do a lobotomy on house call, and cursed my imagination.

It was a long time before I began thinking mechanistically   3 enough to accept migraine for what it was: something with which I would be living, the way some people live with diabetes. Migraine is something more than the fancy of a neurotic imagination. It is an essentially hereditary complex of symptoms, the most frequently noted but by no means the most unpleasant of which is a vascular headache of blinding severity, suffered by a surprising number of women, a fair number of men (Thomas Jefferson had migraine, and so did Ulysses S. Grant, the day he accepted Lee's surrender), and by some unfortunate children as young as two years old. (I had my first when I was eight. It came on during a fire drill at the Columbia School in Colorado Springs, Colorado. I was taken first home and then to the infirmary at Peterson Field, where my father was stationed. The Air Corps doctor prescribed an enema.) Almost anything can trigger a specific attack of migraine: stress, allergy, fatigue, an abrupt change in barometric pressure, a contretemps over a parking ticket. A flashing light. A fire drill. One inherits, of course, only the predisposition. In other words I spent yesterday in bed with a headache not merely because of my bad attitudes, unpleasant tempers and wrongthink, but because both my grandmothers had migraine, my father has migraine and my mother has migraine.

No one knows precisely what it is that is inherited. The   4 chemistry of migraine, however, seems to have some connection with the nerve hormone named serotonin, which is naturally present in the brain. The amount of serotonin in the blood falls sharply at the onset of migraine, and one migraine drug, methysergide, or Sansert, seems to have some effect on serotonin. Methysergide is a derivative of lysergic acid (in fact Sandoz Pharmaceuticals first synthesized LSD-25 while looking for a migraine cure), and its use is hemmed about with so many contraindications and side effects that most doctors prescribe it only in the most incapacitating cases. Methysergide, when it is prescribed, is taken daily, as a preventive; another preventive which works for some people is old-fashioned ergotamine tartrate, which helps to constrict the swelling blood vessels during the "aura," the period which in most cases precedes the actual headache.

Once an attack is under way, however, no drug touches it.   5 Migraine gives some people mild hallucinations, temporarily blinds others, shows up not only as a headache but as a gastrointestinal disturbance, a painful sensitivity to all sensory stimuli, an abrupt overpowering fatigue, a strokelike aphasia, and a crippling inability to make even the most routine connections. When I am in a migraine aura (for some people the aura lasts fifteen minutes, for others several hours), I will drive through red lights, lose the house keys, spill whatever I am holding, lose the ability to focus my eyes or frame coherent sentences, and generally give the appearance of being on drugs, or drunk. The actual headache, when it comes, brings with it chills, sweating, nausea, a debility that seems to stretch the very limits of endurance. That no one dies of migraine seems, to someone deep into an attack, an ambiguous blessing.

My husband also has migraine, which is unfortunate for   6 him but fortunate for me: perhaps nothing so tends to prolong an attack as the accusing eye of someone who has never had a headache. "Why not take a couple of aspirin," the unafflicted will say from the doorway, or "I'd have a headache, too, spending a beautiful day like this inside with all the shades drawn." All of us who have migraine suffer not only from the attacks themselves but from this common conviction that we are perversely refusing to cure ourselves by taking a couple of aspirin, that we are making ourselves sick, that we "bring it on ourselves." And in the most immediate sense, the sense of why we have a headache this Tuesday and not last Thursday, of course we often do. There certainly is what doctors call a "migraine personality," and that personality tends to be ambitious, inward, intolerant of error, rather rigidly organized, perfectionist. "You don't look like a migraine personality," a doctor once said to me. "Your hair's messy. But I suppose you're a compulsive housekeeper." Actually my house is kept even more negligently than my hair, but the doctor was right nonetheless: perfectionism can also take the form of spending most of a week writing and rewriting and not writing a single paragraph.

But not all perfectionists have migraine, and not all migrain- 7
ous people have migraine personalities. We do not escape heredity. I have tried in most of the available ways to escape my own migrainous heredity (at one point I learned to give myself two daily injections of histamine with a hypodermic needle, even though the needle so frightened me that I had to close my eyes when I did it), but I still have migraine. And I have learned now to live with it, learned when to expect it, how to outwit it, even how to regard it, when it does come, as more friend than lodger. We have reached a certain understanding, my migraine and I. It never comes when I am in real trouble. Tell me that my house is burned down, my husband has left me, that there is gunfighting in the streets and panic in the banks, and I will not respond by getting a headache. It comes instead when I am fighting not an open but a guerrilla war with my own life, during weeks of small household confusions, lost laundry, unhappy help, canceled appointments, on days when the telephone rings too much and I get no work done and the wind is coming up. On days like that my friend comes uninvited.

And once it comes, now that I am wise in its ways, I no 8
longer fight it. I lie down and let it happen. At first every small

apprehension is magnified, every anxiety a pounding terror. Then the pain comes, and I concentrate only on that. Right there is the usefulness of migraine, there in that imposed yoga, the concentration on the pain. For when the pain recedes, ten or twelve hours later, everything goes with it, all the hidden resentments, all the vain anxieties. The migraine has acted as a circuit breaker, and the fuses have emerged intact. There is a pleasant convalescent euphoria. I open the windows and feel the air, eat gratefully, sleep well. I notice the particular nature of a flower in a glass on the stair landing. I count my blessings.

QUESTIONS ON MEANING AND PURPOSE

1. According to the author, how do migraines differ from ordinary headaches? What are their distinctive traits?
2. What once made Didion ashamed to admit that she suffered from migraines?
3. While imparting facts about migraine, what does Didion simultaneously reveal about her own personality?
4. Sum up in your own words the tremendous experience that Didion describes in the final paragraph.

QUESTIONS ON WRITING STRATEGY

1. Didion's essay draws upon both subjective personal experience and objective medical knowledge. How does she signal her TRANSITIONS from impressionistic to impartial description, and from impartial back to impressionistic?
2. Point to a few examples of sensuous detail in Didion's writing. What do such IMAGES contribute to her essay's EFFECT?
3. In paragraph 2 when Didion declares that she "wished only for a neurosurgeon who would do a lobotomy on house call," do you take her literally? What do you make of her remark in paragraph 5: "That no one dies of migraine seems, to someone deep into an attack, an ambiguous blessing"? (See *Hyperbole* under *Figures of Speech* in Useful Terms.)
4. What similarity do you find between the subject of "In Bed" and that of Lewis Thomas's "On Smell" (page 9)? What differences do you find between the two authors' treatments of their subjects?

QUESTIONS ON LANGUAGE

1. Consult a dictionary if you need help in defining the following: vascular, contretemps, predisposition (paragraph 3); synthesized, contraindications (4); aphasia, aura (5).
2. Speaking in paragraph 1 of the *circumnavigation* of an application form, Didion employs a METAPHOR. In paragraph 7 she introduces another: a *guerrilla war*. In paragraph 8 she uses a SIMILE: "The migraine has acted as a circuit breaker." Comment on the aptness of these FIGURES OF SPEECH.
3. In the title of Didion's essay, what arrests you? Is this title a shameless teaser, a curiosity-rousing phrase that has nothing to do with the essay, or does it fit?

SUGGESTIONS FOR WRITING

1. Write a paragraph in which, by means of impartial description, you familiarize your reader with an illness you know intimately. (If you have never had such an illness, pick an unwelcome mood you know: the blues, for instance, or an irresistible desire to giggle during a solemn ceremony.)
2. Then write, on the same subject, a second paragraph: this time, an impressionistic description of the same malady or mood.

· E. B. White ·

ELWYN BROOKS WHITE, born in 1899, lives on a farm in North Brooklin, Maine. From there he keeps an eye on the rest of the country. From 1926 until lately, he was a regular contributor to *The New Yorker*, and his essays, editorials, anonymous features for "The Talk of the Town," and fillers helped build the magazine a reputation for wit and good writing. If as a child you read *Charlotte's Web* (1952), you have met E.B. White before. His *Letters* were collected in 1976, his *Essays* in 1977, and his *Poems and Sketches* in 1981. On July 4, 1963, President Kennedy named White in the first group of Americans to receive the Presidential Medal for Freedom, with a citation that called him "an essayist whose concise comment on men and places has revealed to yet another age the vigor of the English sentence."

Once More to the Lake

"The essayist," says White in a foreword to his *Essays*, "is a self-liberated man, sustained by the childish belief that everything he thinks about, everything that happens to him, is of general interest." In White's case this belief is soundly justified. Perhaps if a duller writer had written "Once More to the Lake," or an essay by that title, we wouldn't much care about it, for at first its subject seems as personal, flat, and ordinary as a letter home. White's loving and exact description, however, brings this lakeside camp to life for us. In the end, the writer arrives at an awareness that shocks him — shocks us, too, by a familiar sensory detail in the last line.

August 1941

One summer, along about 1904, my father rented a camp on   1 a lake in Maine and took us all there for the month of August. We all got ringworm from some kittens and had to rub Pond's Extract on our arms and legs night and morning, and my father rolled over in a canoe with all his clothes on; but outside of that the vacation was a success and from then on none of us ever thought there was any place in the world like that lake in Maine. We returned summer after summer — always on August 1 for one month. I have since become a salt-water man, but sometimes in summer there are days when the restlessness of the tides and the fearful cold of the sea water and the incessant wind that blows across the afternoon and into the evening make me wish for the placidity of a lake in the woods. A few weeks ago this feeling got so strong I bought myself a couple of bass hooks and a spinner and returned to the lake where we used to go, for a week's fishing and to revisit old haunts.

I took along my son, who had never had any fresh water up   2 his nose and who had seen lily pads only from train windows. On the journey over to the lake I began to wonder what it would be like. I wondered how time would have marred this unique, this holy spot — the coves and streams, the hills that the sun set behind, the camps and the paths behind the camps. I was sure that the tarred road would have found it out, and I wondered in what other ways it would be desolated. It is strange how much you can remember about places like that once you allow your mind to return into the grooves that lead back. You remember one thing, and that suddenly reminds you of another thing. I guess I remembered clearest of all the early mornings, when the lake was cool and motionless, remembered how the bedroom smelled of the lumber it was made of and of the wet woods whose scent entered through the screen. The partitions in the camp were thin and did not extend clear to the top of the rooms, and as I was always the first up I would dress softly so as not to wake the others, and sneak out into the sweet outdoors and start out in the canoe, keeping close along the shore in the long shadows of the pines. I remembered being very careful never to rub my paddle against the gunwale for fear of disturbing the stillness of the cathedral.

The lake had never been what you would call a wild lake.   3 There were cottages sprinkled around the shores, and it was in farming country although the shores of the lake were quite heavily wooded. Some of the cottages were owned by nearby farmers, and you would live at the shore and eat your meals at the farmhouse. That's what our family did. But although it wasn't wild, it was a fairly large and undisturbed lake and there were places in it that, to a child at least, seemed infinitely remote and primeval.

I was right about the tar: it led to within half a mile of the shore. But when I got back there, with my boy, and we settled into a camp near a farmhouse and into the kind of summertime I had known, I could tell that it was going to be pretty much the same as it had been before — I knew it, lying in bed the first morning smelling the bedroom and hearing the boy sneak quietly out and go off along the shore in a boat. I began to sustain the illusion that he was I, and therefore, by simple transposition, that I was my father. This sensation persisted, kept cropping up all the time we were there. It was not an entirely new feeling, but in this setting it grew much stronger. I seemed to be living a dual existence. I would be in the middle of some simple act, I would be picking up a bait box or laying down a table fork, or I would be saying something and suddenly it would be not I but my father who was saying the words or making the gesture. It gave me a creepy sensation.

We went fishing the first morning. I felt the same damp moss covering the worms in the bait can, and saw the dragonfly alight on the tip of my rod as it hovered a few inches from the surface of the water. It was the arrival of this fly that convinced me beyond any doubt that everything was as it always had been, that the years were a mirage and that there had been no years. The small waves were the same, chucking the rowboat under the chin as we fished at anchor, and the boat was the same boat, the same color green and the ribs broken in the same places, and under the floorboards the same fresh water leavings and débris — the dead hellgrammite, the wisps of moss, the rusty discarded fishhook, the dried blood from yesterday's catch. We stared silently at the tips of our rods, at the dragonflies that came and went. I lowered the tip of mine into the water, tentatively, pensively dislodging the fly, which darted two feet away, poised, darted two feet back, and came to rest again a little farther up the rod. There had been no years between the ducking of this dragonfly and the other one — the one that was part of memory. I looked at the boy, who was silently watching his fly, and it was my hands that held his rod, my eyes watching. I felt dizzy and didn't know which rod I was at the end of.

We caught two bass, hauling them in briskly as though they   6
were mackerel, pulling them over the side of the boat in a businesslike manner without any landing net, and stunning them with a blow on the back of the head. When we got back for a swim before lunch, the lake was exactly where we had left it, the same number of inches from the dock, and there was only the merest suggestion of a breeze. This seemed an utterly enchanted sea, this lake you could leave to its own devices for a few hours and come back to, and find that it had not stirred, this constant and trustworthy body of water. In the shallows, the dark, water-soaked sticks and twigs, smooth and old, were undulating in clusters on the bottom against the clean ribbed sand, and the track of the mussel was plain. A school of minnows swam by, each minnow with its small individual shadow, doubling the attendance, so clear and sharp in the sunlight. Some of the other campers were in swimming, along the shore, one of them with a cake of soap, and the water felt thin and clear and unsubstantial. Over the years there had been this person with the cake of soap, this cultist, and here he was. There had been no years.

Up to the farmhouse to dinner through the teeming dusty   7
field, the road under our sneakers was only a two-track road. The middle track was missing, the one with the marks of the hooves and the splotches of dried, flaky manure. There had always been three tracks to choose from in choosing which track to walk in; now the choice was narrowed down to two. For a moment I missed terribly the middle alternative. But the way led past the tennis court, and something about the way it lay there in the sun reassured me; the tape had loosened along the backline, the alleys were green with plantains and other weeds, and the net (installed in June and removed in September) sagged in the dry noon, and the whole place steamed with midday heat and hunger and emptiness. There was a choice of pie for dessert, and one was blueberry and one was apple, and the waitresses were the same country girls, there having been no passage of time, only the illusion of it as in a dropped curtain — the waitresses were still fifteen; their hair had been washed, that was the

only difference — they had been to the movies and seen the pretty girls with the clean hair.

Summertime, oh, summertime, pattern of life indelible with fade-proof lake, the wood unshatterable, the pasture with the sweetfern and the juniper forever and ever, summer without end; this was the background, and the life along the shore was the design, the cottages with their innocent and tranquil design, their tiny docks with the flagpole and the American flag floating against the white clouds in the blue sky, the little paths over the roots of the trees leading from camp to camp and the paths leading back to the outhouses and the can of lime for sprinkling, and at the souvenir counters at the store the miniature birchbark canoes and the postcards that showed things looking a little better than they looked. This was the American family at play, escaping the city heat, wondering whether the newcomers in the camp at the head of the cove were "common" or "nice," wondering whether it was true that the people who drove up for Sunday dinner at the farmhouse were turned away because there wasn't enough chicken. 8

It seemed to me, as I kept remembering all this, that those times and those summers had been infinitely precious and worth saving. There had been jollity and peace and goodness. The arriving (at the beginning of August) had been so big a business in itself, at the railway station the farm wagon drawn up, the first smell of the pine-laden air, the first glimpse of the smiling farmer, and the great importance of the trunks and your father's enormous authority in such matters, and the feel of the wagon under you for the long ten-mile haul, and at the top of the last long hill catching the first view of the lake after eleven months of not seeing this cherished body of water. The shouts and cries of the other campers when they saw you, and the trunks to be unpacked, to give up their rich burden. (Arriving was less exciting nowadays, when you sneaked up in your car and parked it under a tree near the camp and took out the bags and in five minutes it was all over, no fuss, no loud wonderful fuss about trunks.) 9

Peace and goodness and jollity. The only thing that was wrong now, really, was the sound of the place, an unfamiliar nervous sound of the outboard motors. This was the note that 10 jarred, the one thing that would sometimes break the illusion and set the years moving. In those other summertimes all motors were inboard; and when they were at a little distance, the noise they made was a sedative, an ingredient of summer sleep. They were one-cylinder and two-cylinder engines, and some were make-and-break and some were jump-spark, but they all made a sleepy sound across the lake. The one-lungers throbbed and fluttered, and the twin-cylinder ones purred and purred, and that was a quiet sound, too. But now the campers all had outboards. In the daytime, in the hot mornings, these motors made a petulant, irritable sound; at night in the still evening when the afterglow lit the water, they whined about one's ears like mosquitoes. My boy loved our rented outboard, and his great desire was to achieve single-handed mastery over it, and authority, and he soon learned the trick of choking it a little (but not too much), and the adjustment of the needle valve. Watching him I would remember the things you could do with the old one-cylinder engine with the heavy flywheel, how you could have it eating out of your hand if you got really close to it spiritually. Motorboats in those days didn't have clutches, and you would make a landing by shutting off the motor at the proper time and coasting in with a dead rudder. But there was a way of reversing them, if you learned the trick, by cutting the switch and putting it on again exactly on the final dying revolution of the flywheel, so that it would kick back against compression and begin reversing. Approaching a dock in a strong following breeze, it was difficult to slow up sufficiently by the ordinary coasting method, and if a boy felt he had complete mastery over his motor, he was tempted to keep it running beyond its time and then reverse it a few feet from the dock. It took a cool nerve, because if you threw the switch a twentieth of a second too soon you would catch the flywheel when it still had speed enough to go up past center, and the boat would leap ahead, charging bull-fashion at the dock.

We had a good week at the camp. The bass were biting well 11 and the sun shone endlessly, day after day. We would be tired at night and lie down in the accumulated heat of the little bedrooms after the long hot day and the breeze would stir almost imperceptibly outside and the smell of the swamp drift in through the rusty screens. Sleep would come easily and in the morning the red squirrel would be on the roof, tapping out his gay routine. I kept remembering everything, lying in bed in the mornings — the small steamboat that had a long rounded stern like the lip of a Ubangi, and how quietly she ran on the moonlight sails, when the older boys played their mandolins and the girls sang and we ate doughnuts dipped in sugar, and how sweet the music was on the water in the shining night, and what it had felt like to think about girls then. After breakfast we would go up to the store and the things were in the same place — the minnows in a bottle, the plugs and spinners disarranged and pawed over by the youngsters from the boys' camp, the Fig Newtons and the Beeman's gum. Outside, the road was tarred and cars stood in front of the store. Inside, all was just as it had always been, except there was more Coca-Cola and not so much Moxie and root beer and birch beer and sarsaparilla. We would walk out with the bottle of pop apiece and sometimes the pop would backfire up our noses and hurt. We explored the streams, quietly, where the turtles slid off the sunny logs and dug their way into the soft bottom; and we lay on the town wharf and fed worms to the tame bass. Everywhere we went I had trouble making out which was I, the one walking at my side, the one walking in my pants.

One afternoon while we were at that lake a thunderstorm 12 came up. It was like the revival of an old melodrama that I had seen long ago with childish awe. The second-act climax of the drama of the electrical disturbance over a lake in America had not changed in any important respect. This was the big scene, still the big scene. The whole thing was so familiar, the first feeling of oppression and heat and a general air around camp of not wanting to go very far away. In midafternoon (it was all the same) a curious darkening of the sky, and a lull in everything that had made life tick; and then the way the boats suddenly swung the other way at their moorings with the coming of a breeze out of the new quarter, and the premonitory rumble. Then the kettle drum, then the snare, then the bass drum and cymbals, then crackling light against the dark, and the gods grinning and licking their chops in the hills. Afterward the calm, the rain steadily rustling in the calm lake, the return of light and hope and spirits, and the campers running out in joy and relief to go swimming in the rain, their bright cries perpetuating the deathless joke about how they were getting simply drenched, and the children screaming with delight at the new sensation of bathing in the rain, and the joke about getting drenched linking the generations in a strong indestructible chain. And the comedian who waded in carrying an umbrella.

When the others went swimming my son said he was going   13
in, too. He pulled his dripping trunks from the line where they had hung all through the shower and wrung them out. Languidly, and with no thought of going in, I watched him, his hard little body, skinny and bare, saw him wince slightly as he pulled up around his vitals the small, soggy, icy garment. As he buckled the swollen belt, suddenly my groin felt the chill of death.

QUESTIONS ON MEANING AND PURPOSE

1. When E. B. White takes his son to the summer place he himself had loved as a child, what changes does he find there? What things have stayed the same?
2. How do you account for the distortions that creep into the author's sense of time?
3. What does the discussion of inboard and outboard motors (paragraph 10) have to do with the author's divided sense of time?
4. What do you take to be White's main PURPOSE in this essay? At what point do you become aware of it?

QUESTIONS ON WRITING STRATEGY

1. To what degree does White make us aware of the impression that this trip to the lake makes on his son?
2. In paragraph 4, the author first introduces his confused feeling that he has gone back in time to his own childhood, an idea that he repeats and expands throughout his account. What is the function of these repetitions?

3. Try to describe the impact of the essay's final paragraph. By what means is it achieved?
4. To what extent is this essay written to appeal to any but middle-aged readers? Is it comprehensible to anyone whose vacations were never spent at a Maine summer cottage?
5. What is the TONE of White's essay?

QUESTIONS ON LANGUAGE

1. Be sure you know the meanings of the following words: incessant, placidity (paragraph 1); gunwale (2); primeval (3); transposition (4); hellgrammite (5); undulating, cultist (6); indelible, tranquil (8); petulant (10); imperceptibly (11); premonitory (12); languidly (13).
2. Comment on White's DICTION in his reference to the lake as "this unique, this holy spot" (paragraph 2).
3. Explain what White is describing in the sentence that begins, "Then the kettle drum . . . " (paragraph 12). Where else does the author use METAPHORS?
4. Where in his essay does White use IMAGES effectively?

SUGGESTIONS FOR WRITING

1. In a descriptive paragraph, try to appeal to each of your reader's five senses.
2. Describe in a brief essay a place you loved as a child. Or, if you have ever returned to a favorite old haunt, describe the experience. Was it pleasant or painful — or both? What, exactly, made it so?

· George Orwell ·

GEORGE ORWELL was the pen name of Eric Blair (1903-1950), born in Bengal, India, the son of an English civil servant. After attending Eton on a scholarship, he joined the British police in Burma, where he acquired a distrust for the methods of the empire. Then followed years of tramping, odd jobs, and near-starvation — recalled in *Down and Out in Paris and London* (1933). From living on the fringe of society and from his reportorial writing about English miners and factory workers, Orwell deepened his sympathy with underdogs.

Severely wounded while fighting in the Spanish Civil War, he wrote a memoir, *Homage to Catalonia* (1938), voicing disillusionment with Loyalists who, he claimed, sought not to free Spain but to exterminate their political enemies. A socialist by conviction, Orwell kept pointing to the dangers of a collective state run by totalitarians. In *Animal Farm* (1945), he satirized Soviet bureaucracy; and in his famous novel *1984* (1949) he foresaw a regimented England whose government perverts truth and spies on citizens by two-way television. (The motto of the state and its leader: "BIG BROTHER IS WATCHING YOU.")

The Moon under Water

"The Moon under Water" first appeared on February 9, 1946, in the *Evening Standard*, a London newspaper. In his essay, Orwell spells out the pleasures — from Victorian fittings and motherly barmaids to draught stout and pink china mugs — that make The Moon under Water his favorite pub in all London. Who wouldn't like a place so redolent with charm, comfort, and good company? You might head for it when you visit London — but there's one obstacle in your way.

My favorite public house, "The Moon under Water," is only   1
two minutes from a bus stop, but it is on a side-street, and drunks and rowdies never seem to find their way there, even on Saturday nights.

Its clientèle, though fairly large, consists mostly of regulars   2
who occupy the same chair every evening and go there for conversation as much as for the beer.

If you are asked why you favor a particular public house, it   3
would seem natural to put the beer first, but the thing that most
appeals to me about "The Moon under Water" is what people
call its "atmosphere."

To begin with, its whole architecture and fittings are un-   4
compromisingly Victorian. It has no glass-topped tables or other
modern miseries, and, on the other hand, no sham roof-beams,
ingle-nooks or plastic panels masquerading as oak. The grained
woodwork, the ornamental mirrors behind the bar, the cast-
iron fireplaces, the florid ceiling stained dark yellow by tobacco-
smoke, the stuffed bull's head over the mantelpiece — everything has the solid comfortable ugliness of the nineteenth
century.

In winter there is generally a good fire burning in at least   5
two of the bars, and the Victorian lay-out of the place gives one
plenty of elbow-room. There are a public bar, a saloon bar, a
ladies' bar, a bottle-and-jug for those who are too bashful to buy
their supper beer publicly, and upstairs, a dining-room.

Games are only played in the public, so that in the other   6
bars you can walk about without constantly ducking to avoid
flying darts.

In "The Moon under Water" it is always quiet enough to   7
talk. The house possesses neither a radio nor a piano, and even
on Christmas Eve and such occasions the singing that happens
is of a decorous kind.

The barmaids know most of their customers by name, and   8
take a personal interest in everyone. They are all middle-aged
women — two of them have their hair dyed in quite surprising
shades — and they call everyone "dear," irrespective of age or
sex. ("Dear," not "Ducky": pubs where the barmaid calls you
"Ducky" always have a disagreeable raffish atmosphere.)

Unlike most pubs, "The Moon under Water" sells tobacco   9
as well as cigarettes, and it also sells aspirins and stamps, and is
obliging about letting you use the telephone.

You cannot get dinner at "The Moon under Water," but   10
there is always the snack counter where you can get liver-sau-

sage sandwiches, mussels (a speciality of the house), cheese, pickles and those large biscuits with caraway seeds in them which only seem to exist in public houses.

Upstairs, six days a week, you can get a good, solid lunch —   11
for example, a cut off the joint, two vegetables and boiled jam roll — for about three shillings.

The special pleasure of this lunch is that you can have   12
draught stout with it. I doubt whether as many as ten per cent of London pubs serve draught stout, but "The Moon under Water" is one of them. It is a soft, creamy sort of stout, and it goes better in a pewter pot.

They are particular about their drinking vessels at "The   13
Moon under Water" and never, for example, make the mistake of serving a pint of beer in a handleless glass. Apart from glass and pewter mugs, they have some of those pleasant strawberry-pink china ones which are now seldom seen in London. China mugs went out about thirty years ago, because most people like their drink to be transparent, but in my opinion beer tastes better out of china.

The great surprise of "The Moon under Water" is its garden.   14
You go through a narrow passage leading out of the saloon, and find yourself in a fairly large garden with plane trees under which there are little green tables with iron chairs round them. Up at one end of the garden there are swings and a chute for the children.

On summer evenings there are family parties, and you sit   15
under the plane trees having beer or draught cider to the tune of delighted squeals from children going down the chute. The prams with the younger children are parked near the gate.

Many as are the virtues of "The Moon under Water" I think   16
that the garden is its best feature, because it allows whole families to go there instead of Mum having to stay at home and mind the baby while Dad goes out alone.

And though, strictly speaking, they are only allowed in the   17
garden, the children tend to seep into the pub and even to fetch drinks for their parents. This, I believe, is against the law, but it is a law that deserves to be broken, for it is the puritanical nonsense of excluding children — and therefore to some extent,

women — from pubs that has turned these places into mere boozing-shops instead of the family gathering-places that they ought to be.

"The Moon under Water" is my ideal of what a pub should 　18 be — at any rate, in the London area. (The qualities one expects of a country pub are slightly different.)

But now is the time to reveal something which the discern- 　19 ing and disillusioned reader will probably have guessed already. There is no such place as "The Moon under Water."

That is to say, there may well be a pub of that name, but I 　20 don't know of it, nor do I know any pub with just that combina- tion of qualities.

I know pubs where the beer is good but you can't get meals, 　21 others where you can get meals but which are noisy and crowded, and others which are quiet but where the beer is gen- erally sour. As for gardens, offhand I can only think of three London pubs that possess them.

But, to be fair, I do know of a few pubs that almost come up 　22 to "The Moon under Water." I have mentioned above ten quali- ties that the perfect pub should have, and I know one pub that has eight of them. Even there, however, there is no draught stout and no china mugs.

And if anyone knows of a pub that has draught stout, open 　23 fires, cheap meals, a garden, motherly barmaids and no radio, I should be glad to hear of it, even though its name were some- thing as prosaic as "The Red Lion" or "The Railway Arms."

QUESTIONS ON MEANING AND PURPOSE

1. How would you reply to the student who said, "What this essay is about is hardly earthshaking. I can't imagine why Orwell wrote it, or why I should read it"?

2. From Orwell's essay, what do you learn about life in London in the late 1940s?

3. In what ways does The Moon under Water differ from a typical American bar?

4. To what extent, do you think, is Orwell's ideal pub based on reality? Cite EVIDENCE for your answer.

QUESTIONS ON WRITING STRATEGY

1. Even if you didn't know that "The Moon under Water" first appeared in a London daily, which details would suggest that Orwell's essay was aimed at a British newspaper AUDIENCE?
2. How do you account for the fact that many American readers remain unaware until paragraph 19 that Orwell is describing an ideal rather than a real pub?
3. Look closely at paragraphs 4, 8, 10, and 14. What lends Orwell's details their flavor of realism?
4. Describe the TONE of Orwell's essay. How serious does the writer feel about his ideal pub and its imagined proprietors?

QUESTIONS ON LANGUAGE

1. Be sure you know how to define the following: public house (paragraph 1); uncompromisingly, florid (4); decorous (7); irrespective, raffish (8); joint, shillings (11); transparent (13); saloon, chute (14); prams (15); discerning, disillusioned (19); prosaic (23).
2. Which words in Orwell's essay reflect British rather than American usage? (If you need help, see your desk dictionary.)
3. What suggestions lurking in the name The Moon under Water make it appropriate for the pub Orwell describes?

SUGGESTIONS FOR WRITING

1. Not all readers would endorse every one of the amenities Orwell wants in The Moon under Water. Write a short reply to the author, telling him which of his preferences you take exception to, and what you would put in their place.
2. In a brief essay, describe *your* ideal place: an apartment, a bookstore, a dorm room, a vacation spot, a classroom, a restaurant, a gym, a supermarket or convenience store, a garden, a golf course. With concrete details, try to make the ideal seem actual.

· Annie Dillard ·

ANNIE DILLARD is accomplished as a prose writer, poet, and literary critic. Born in 1945, she earned a B.A. (1967) and an M.A. (1968) from Hollins College in Virginia. She is now a contributing editor for *Harper's* and Adjunct Professor at Wesleyan University in Middletown, Connecticut. The author of six books of poetry and prose, she won a general nonfiction Pulitzer Prize for *Pilgrim at Tinker Creek* (1974), a work alive with close, intense, and poetic descriptions of the natural world. *Encounters with Chinese Writers* (1984), narrative nonfiction, is her latest book.

Lenses

Looking at pond life through a microscope and observing a pair of whistling swans through binoculars may strike you as pursuits having little to do with each other, but in putting together her essay Annie Dillard discovered that the two activities were more alike than she had ever suspected. The author included "Lenses" in a recent collection of essays, *Teaching a Stone to Talk* (1982).

You get used to looking through lenses; it is an acquired   1
skill. When you first look through binoculars, for instance, you can't see a thing. You look at the inside of the barrel; you blink and watch your eyelashes; you play with the focus knob till one eye is purblind.

The microscope is even worse. You are supposed to keep   2
both eyes open as you look through its single eyepiece. I spent my childhood in Pittsburgh trying to master this trick: seeing through one eye, with both eyes open. The microscope also teaches you to move your hands wrong, to shove the glass slide to the right if you are following a creature who is swimming off to the left — as if you were operating a tiller, or backing a trailer, or performing any other of those paradoxical maneuvers which

101

require either sure instincts or a grasp of elementary physics, neither of which I possess.

A child's microscope set comes with a little five-watt lamp.   3
You place this dim light in front of the microscope's mirror; the mirror bounces the light up through the slide, through the magnifying lenses, and into your eye. The only reason you do not see everything in silhouette is that microscopic things are so small they are translucent. The animals and plants in a drop of pond water pass light like pale stained glass; they seem so soaked in water and light that their opacity has leached away.

The translucent strands of algae you see under a micro-   4
scope — Spirogyra, Oscillatoria, Cladophora — move of their own accord, no one knows how or why. You watch these swaying yellow, green, and brown strands of algae half mesmerized; you sink into the microscope's field forgetful, oblivious, as if it were all a dream of your deepest brain. Occasionally a zippy rotifer comes barreling through, black and white, and in a tremendous hurry.

My rotifers and daphniae and amoebae were in an especially   5
tremendous hurry because they were drying up. I burnt out or broke my little five-watt bulb right away. To replace it, I rigged an old table lamp laid on its side; the table lamp carried a seventy-five-watt bulb. I was about twelve, immortal and invulnerable, and did not know what I was doing; neither did anyone else. My parents let me set up my laboratory in the basement, where they wouldn't have to smell the urine I collected in test tubes and kept in the vain hope it would grow something horrible. So in full, solitary ignorance I spent evenings in the basement staring into a seventy-five-watt bulb magnified three hundred times and focused into my eye. It is a wonder I can see at all. My eyeball itself would start drying up; I blinked and blinked.

But the pond water creatures fared worse. I dropped them   6
on a slide, floated a cover slip over them, and laid the slide on the microscope's stage, which the seventy-five-watt bulb had heated like a grill. At once the drop of pond water started to evaporate. Its edges shrank. The creatures swam among algae in a diminishing pool. I liked this part. The heat worked for me as a

centrifuge, to concentrate the biomass. I had about five minutes to watch the members of a very dense population, excited by the heat, go about their business until — as I fancied sadly — they all caught on to their situation and started making out wills.

I was, then, not only watching the much-vaunted wonders   7 in a drop of pond water; I was also, with mingled sadism and sympathy, setting up a limitless series of apocalypses. I set up and staged hundreds of ends-of-the-world and watched, enthralled, as they played themselves out. Over and over again, the last trump sounded, the final scroll unrolled, and the known world drained, dried, and vanished. When all the creatures lay motionless, boiled and fried in the positions they had when the last of their water dried completely, I washed the slide in the sink and started over with a fresh drop. How I loved that deep, wet world where the colored algae waved in the water and the rotifers swam!

But oddly, this is a story about swans. It is not even a story;   8 it is a description of swans. This description of swans includes the sky over a pond, a pair of binoculars, and a mortal adult who had long since moved out of the Pittsburgh basement.

In the Roanoke valley of Virginia, rimmed by the Blue   9 Ridge Mountains to the east and the Allegheny Mountains to the west, is a little semi-agricultural area called Daleville. In Daleville, set among fallow fields and wooded ridges, is Daleville Pond. It is a big pond, maybe ten acres; it holds a lot of sky. I used to haunt the place because I loved it; I still do. In winter it had that airy scruffiness of deciduous lands; you greet the daylight and the open space, and spend the evening picking burrs out of your pants.

One Valentine's Day, in the afternoon, I was crouched   10 among dried reeds at the edge of Daleville Pond. Across the pond from where I crouched was a low forested mountain ridge. In every other direction I saw only sky, sky crossed by the reeds which blew before my face whichever way I turned.

I was looking through binoculars at a pair of whistling   11 swans. Whistling swans! It is impossible to say how excited I was to see whistling swans in Daleville, Virginia. The two were a pair, mated for life, migrating north and west from the Atlantic coast to the high arctic. They had paused to feed at Daleville Pond. I had flushed them, and now they were flying and circling the pond. I crouched in the reeds so they would not be afraid to come back to the water.

Through binoculars I followed the swans, swinging where   12
they flew. All their feathers were white; their eyes were black. Their wingspan was six feet; they were bigger than I was. They flew in unison, one behind the other; they made pass after pass at the pond. I watched them change from white swans in front of the mountain to black swans in front of the sky. In clockwise ellipses they flew, necks long and relaxed, alternately beating their wide wings and gliding.

As I rotated on my heels to keep the black frame of the   13
lenses around them, I lost all sense of space. If I lowered the binoculars I was always amazed to learn in which direction I faced — dazed, the way you emerge awed from a movie and try to reconstruct, bit by bit, a real world, in order to discover where in it you might have parked the car.

I lived in that circle of light, in great speed and utter silence.   14
When the swans passed before the sun they were distant — two black threads, two live stitches. But they kept coming, smoothly, and the sky deepened to blue behind them and they took on light. They gathered dimension as they neared, and I could see their ardent, straining eyes. Then I could hear the brittle blur of their wings, the blur which faded as they circled on, and the sky brightened to yellow behind them and the swans flattened and darkened and diminished as they flew. Once I lost them behind the mountain ridge; when they emerged they were flying suddenly very high, and it was like music changing key.

I was lost. The reeds in front of me, swaying and out of focus   15
in the binoculars' circular field, were translucent. The reeds were strands of color passing light like cells in water. They were those yellow and green and brown strands of pond algae I had watched so long in a light-soaked field. My eyes burned; I was watching algae wave in a shrinking drop; they crossed each other and parted wetly. And suddenly into the field swam two

whistling swans, two tiny whistling swans. They swam as fast as rotifers: two whistling swans, infinitesimal, beating their tiny wet wings, perfectly formed.

QUESTIONS ON MEANING AND PURPOSE

1. What does Dillard's title have to do with her essay's PURPOSE as stated in paragraph 8? What further information concerning the author's purpose does the POSTSCRIPT supply?
2. What difficulties did Dillard, as a child, encounter when she tried to look through a microscope? What is the author's point in mentioning them?
3. Exactly what connection did the author find between watching swans through binoculars and studying pond water under a microscope? At what points in her essay does she emphasize the connection?
4. What does Dillard mean, in her final paragraph, when she says, "I was lost"?

QUESTIONS ON WRITING STRATEGY

1. How much knowledge of science and nature does Dillard expect of her AUDIENCE? How much did Dillard herself need in order to write "Lenses"?
2. By what means does the author make her TRANSITIONS from pond life to swans and then back again? Do you find the transitions effective, or too abrupt?
3. With what sensuous details does Dillard indicate that the swans are near to her? Far away?
4. Where, in Dillard's essay, do you find touches of humor?

QUESTIONS ON LANGUAGE

1. If necessary, look up the following words in your dictionary: purblind (paragraph 1); paradoxical (2); translucent, opacity, leached (3); mesmerized, rotifer (4); daphniae, amoebae, invulnerable (5); centrifuge, biomass (6); apocalypses (7); fallow, deciduous (9); flushed (11); ellipses (12); ardent (14); infinitesimal (15).

2. How could the swans Dillard describes "change from white swans in front of the mountain to black swans in front of the sky" (paragraph 12)? How could they have "tiny wet wings" (paragraph 15)?
3. Point to passages in which the author makes effective use of SIMILE and METAPHOR.
4. What do the IMAGES in paragraph 14 contribute to Dillard's description?

SUGGESTIONS FOR WRITING

1. In a paragraph or two, detail your struggles with some instrument or gadget you had to use before you understood fully how it worked: a telescope, a household appliance, a pinball machine, a chain saw, a lawn mower, a computer, a video game, a pitching machine, a bicycle pump, a self-service gasoline pump. Your TONE need not be serious.
2. Using at least one simile, one metaphor, and one image, describe one of the following: a pair of cardinals, a mother cat, a crow, a butterfly, a tank full of goldfish, a sunrise or sunset, or any other manifestation of the natural world. Load your description with closely observed details.

—— POSTSCRIPT ON PROCESS ——

Annie Dillard

To read Annie Dillard's comment about writing "Lenses" is to see at once how valuable a habit journal keeping can be for the professional writer. More surprising to most of us, perhaps, is what we learn from this postscript about the importance of revising. Although the author declares that writing "Lenses" was "easy," it soon becomes apparent that, by most standards, good writers tend to be hard on themselves.

I wrote "Lenses" to see if I could evoke in the reader the [1] same switcheroo that caught me when, looking through binoculars, I seemed suddenly to be looking through a microscope. I wrote it a few years after the event, working from a journal entry.

The key passage in the journal entry reads: [2]

> And the weeds in front of me, as I faced the light, were translucent, out-of-focus, crossed and waving; they looked in the circle of light through the binoculars just like algae strands in pond water, and it was very easy to see the field of vision as pond water, algae strands, flat on a microscope's stage — and in it, among the strands, two tiny flying whistling swans.

The rest of the journal entry was full of details I could use. [3] The swans changed like Escher birds from white in front of the mountain to black in front of the sky. (I disliked invoking Escher, who isn't much of an artist, but I thought the simile would communicate quickly the effect I wanted.) The swans flew in unison, clockwise, in ellipses; I lost all sense of space; the swans were like stitches; I lived in that circle of light; I could hear their wings; the sky changed color behind them; when I lost them behind a ridge and they emerged flying high, it was like music changing key.

In order to work this enthusiastic, personal description into [4] what I hoped would be an interesting essay, everything had to push towards a punch line, towards the moment when the binoculars' field turns into a microscope's field, and the swans appear as small as rotifers. In order for *that* to work, I'd have to lay in a lot of background about looking at pond water through a microscope — so the microscope would be in the reader's "experience," as it were, just as it had been in my experience when the swans came along.

So I began a draft of roughly the same form as the final essay. It started with a long-winded, generalized description (or complaint) about looking at things through lenses, and continued with a description of children's microscope kits, and of my childhood forays with the microscope, looking at pond water. In writing this draft I indulged in some perhaps extraneous reminiscing: because my makeshift light was so strong, my specimens dried up as I watched. I hoped this would be amusing enough and self-deprecating enough to justify its inclusion. By the end of the draft I had hopes of returning to this drying-up business to suggest a general apocalypse — to suggest that the big, real world might be somebody's overheated drop, or to suggest, at any rate, a feeling of mortality and immanent loss. (Alas, I had to abandon this; a friend convinced me it was phony.) To return the reader to the subject at hand, and to get off the joking tone (the creatures lay boiled and fried), I added a sentence at the end of the microscope section: "How I loved that deep, wet world where the colored algae waved in the water and the rotifers swam!" I was distant enough from that feeling to state it baldly, I hoped; the point of the sentence was not the feeling — my love for the wet world — but a restatement of the image I wanted the reader to bear in mind — the waving algae and swimming rotifers.

Then I had a nasty problem. How could I change the subject? How could I change the subject, and with it the setting in both time and space? I was so afraid that readers would feel they'd been had that in the first draft I addressed them directly: "Perhaps I should break it to you gently that this is a story about swans. It is not even a story; it is a description of swans. Like the creatures in pond water, you have been heartlessly set up for an unsuspected end." Later I thought that this frontal assault would only reinforce the readers' sense of being had. I tried instead to brazen it out, with as much authority and as little fear

5

6

as I could muster, throwing only to readers the sympathetic word "oddly."

And so I plowed through the first draft, leaning heavily on   7
the journal entry for data. I took pains to lay in the Virginia setting, so the reader would have time to catch his breath and accustom himself to the new time and place. I tried to keep the
swans visible and the verbs interesting and matter-of-fact.

I had a devil of a time with the paragraph about losing a   8
sense of space — where should it go? Logically it didn't fit anywhere; it was loose. Therefore, I should take it out. But I left it
in, hoping its bringing up my dazedness would prepare for the
perceptual switch at the essay's end. Really I left it in because I
was ridiculously fond of the simile about emerging from a movie.
"Lenses" is, I think, a slight essay; I collected it in a book only
because I still liked that bit about coming out of a movie and trying to reconstruct, bit by bit, a real world, in order to discover
where in it you might have parked the car.

The first draft ended: 9

> And suddenly into the field swam two whistling swans, two
> tiny whistling swans. They swam as fast as rotifers: two whis-
> tling swans, infinitesimal, beating their tiny wet wings, per-
> fectly formed.
>   How much time, I wondered, do we have?

In a subsequent draft I tried, very delicately, to expand this   10
last notion. In one phrase, and one phrase only, I described a
shrinking sky. I wanted some idea of mortality. The joking of
the first part, when the microscopic creatures' drop shrank,
would now become quickly serious. It would stun, I fondly
hoped, the reader with a rushing sense of death, a sense of the
beauty of human life and its swift loss. It would be a premoni-
tion, a pang; the essay would contract to that moment and expand to that meaning. I myself had lost those days — both my
innocent childhood days at the microscope, and those grand
days in my twenties on Daleville Pond. Now Daleville Pond was
drained and developed, and I no longer lived in Virginia.

But I couldn't do it. Every six months or so I looked at the   11
"finished" piece. The ending always seemed forced; my friend
had been right. (She's my best critic.) I'd write another version,

look at it again later, and write yet another version. Finally after several years I decided to cut my losses and give up what had been my brightest hopes for the piece. Even now, after the piece has been published several times, I can't help but think: couldn't I still do it? The groundwork's all there. Just a few strong sentences, right at the end, could mean so much, and make it all so much more interesting.

There were, of course, many more changes from the first   12
draft to the published version. I was happy to have so many things to look up. Whenever you get to look something up, you find all sorts of information you can use to give your writing substance. As I write, I mark queries in the page's margin: Check plural *daphnia*. Do swans pair for life? Migrating from where to where? Don't they fly at night?

I looked up all the algae, to check color and spelling; I   13
looked up whistling swans and learned where they were going and the span of their wings (six feet). I called Virginia to learn the size of Daleville Pond (ten acres).

Rewriting, I also condensed, of course. Of the heated drop,   14
I'd said, "Its contours pulled together." Waking up to the tortured abstraction of the phrase, I changed it to "Its edges shrank." I like short sentences. They're forceful, and they can get you out of big trouble. I changed the order of some paragraphs, sentences, and phrases. I had, for instance, a seventy-five-watt bulb focused into my eye and magnified three hundred times; I changed it to "magnified three hundred times and focused into my eye." I took out many self-indulgent references to myself and my feelings.

I condensed the opening a lot. I always have to condense or   15
toss openings; I suspect most writers do. When you begin something, you're so grateful to have begun you'll write down anything, just to prolong the sensation. Later, when you've learned what the writing is really about, you go back and throw away the beginning and start over.

"Lenses" was easy to write; it had only six or seven versions,   16
and most of those were fiddlings with the last few paragraphs. I

sent the book version to the publisher seven years after the journal entry. I'm not entirely sure I'm done with it yet. It was easy only because I abandoned my far-fetched ambition for it, and settled for pure description. Description's not too hard if you mind your active verbs, keep ticking off as many sense impressions as you can, and omit feelings.

· ADDITIONAL WRITING TOPICS ·
DESCRIPTION

1. This is an in-class writing experiment. Describe another person in the room so clearly and unmistakably that when you read your description aloud, your subject will be recognized. (Be objective. No insulting descriptions, please!)
2. Write four paragraphs describing one subject from *each* of the following categories. It will be up to you to make the general subject refer to a particular person, place, thing or event, feeling or abstraction. Write at least one paragraph as an *objective* description and at least one as a *subjective* description. (Identify your method in each case, so that your instructor can see how well you carry it out.)

Person

A friend or roommate
A typical high-school student
One of your parents
An elderly person you know
A prominent politician
A historic figure

Place

A classroom
A college campus
A vacation spot
A hospital emergency room
A snow scene
A forest

Thing or Event

A dentist's drill
A foggy day
A season of the year
A walk on the beach or in the snow
An auction
A block party
A fire or a drowning

A day at the fair
A birthday celebration
A dramatic performance

Feeling or Abstraction

The symptoms of an illness
Love
Rage
Fear
Frustration
Patriotism
Success
Justice

NARRATION AND DESCRIPTION

3. Use a combination of narration and description to develop any one of the following topics:

   My first day on the job
   My first day at college
   Returning to an old neighborhood
   Getting lost
   A brush with a celebrity
   Delivering bad (or good) news

EXAMPLE

Pointing to Instances

THE METHOD

"There are many women runners of distinction," a writer begins, and quickly goes on, "among them Joan Benoit, Zola Budd, Mary Decker, Grete Waitz. . . ."

You have just seen examples at work. An example (from the Latin *exemplum*: "one thing selected from among many") is an instance that reveals a whole type. By selecting an example, a writer shows the nature or character of the group from which it is taken. In a written essay, an example will often serve to illustrate a general statement. For example, here is film critic Pauline Kael, making a point about the work of a veteran actor, Cary Grant:

> The romantic male stars aren't necessarily sexually aggressive. Henry Fonda wasn't; neither was James Stewart, or,

later, Marcello Mastroianni. The foursquare Clark Gable, with his bold, open challenge to women, was more the exception than the rule, and Gable wasn't romantic, like Grant. Gable got down to brass tacks; his advances were basic, his unspoken question was "Well, sister, what do you say?" If she said no, she was failing what might almost be nature's test. She'd become overcivilized, afraid of her instincts — afraid of being a woman. There was a violent, primal appeal in Gable's sex scenes; it was all out front — in the way he looked at her, man to woman. Cary Grant doesn't challenge a woman that way. (When he tried, as the frontiersman in *The Howards of Virginia*, he looked thick and stupid.)[1]

Kael might have allowed the opening sentence of her paragraph — the topic sentence — to remain a vague generalization. Instead, she follows it immediately with the names of three male movie stars who gently charm, not sexually challenge, their women audiences. Then, to show the style of acting she *doesn't* mean, she gives the example of Clark Gable. Her main purpose (in her paragraph, and in fact, in her whole essay) is to set forth the style of Cary Grant. That is why she adds an example of a film in which, when Grant tried to play a sexually aggressive character, he failed miserably. By all of these examples, Kael not only explains and supports her generalization, she lends life to it.

The method of giving examples — of illustrating what you're saying with a "for instance" — is not merely helpful to practically all kinds of writing, it is indispensable. Bad writers — those who bore us, or lose us completely — often have an ample supply of ideas; their trouble is that they never pull their ideas down out of the clouds. A dull writer, for instance, might declare, "The true romantic film star is a man of gentle style"; but, instead of giving examples, the writer might go on, "Romantic film stars thus strike nonaggressive blows for the dignity of womankind," or something — adding still another large, unillustrated idea. Specific examples are *needed* elements in good prose. Not only do they make ideas understandable, but they also keep

[1]"The Man from Dream City," in *When the Lights Go Down* (New York: Holt, Rinehart and Winston, 1980), p. 4.

Example **117**

readers awake. (The previous paragraphs have tried — by giving examples from Pauline Kael and from "a dull writer" — to illustrate this point.)

Although examples may be given as briefly and numerously as in the sentence about women runners of distinction (which simply lists names), examples also may be extended, treated at some length and in ample detail. In a funny and incisive essay in this chapter, Andrew Ward portrays a run-down gas station, with its unlovable owner and its mean watchdog. Ward offers the portrait as an example of a type of American business that is rapidly vanishing, and he spends most of his essay in developing this example — and in making his point unforgettable.

THE PROCESS

Where do you find examples? In anything you know — or care to learn. Start close to home. Seek examples in your own immediate knowledge and experience. When assigned an elephant-sized subject that you think you know nothing about — ethical dilemmas, for instance — rummage your memory and you may discover that you know more than you thought. In what ethical dilemmas have you ever found yourself? Deciding whether or not to date your best friend's fiancé (or fiancée) when your best friend is out of town? Being tempted to pilfer from the jelly jar of a small boy's Kool-Aid stand when you need a quarter for a bus? No doubt you can supply your own examples. It is the method — exemplifying — that matters. To bring some huge and ethereal concept down to earth may just set your expository faculties galloping over the plains of your own life to the sound of "hi-yo, Silver!" For different examples, you can explore your conversations with others, your studies, and the storehouse of information you have gathered from books, newspapers, magazines, radio and TV, and from popular hearsay: proverbs and sayings, bits of wisdom you've heard voiced in your family, folklore, popular song.

Now and again, you may feel an irresistible temptation to make up an example out of thin air. This procedure is risky, but can work wonderfully — if, that is, you have a wonder-working imagination. When Henry David Thoreau, in *Walden*, attacks Americans' smug pride in the achievements of nineteenth-century science and industry, he wants to illustrate that kind of invention or discovery "which distracts our attention from serious things." And so he makes up the examples — farfetched, but pointed — of a transatlantic speaking tube and what it might convey: "We are eager to tunnel under the Atlantic and bring the Old World some weeks nearer to the New; but perchance the first news that will leak through into the broad, flapping American ear will be that the Princess Adelaide has the whooping cough."

These examples (and the sarcastic phrase about the American ear) bespeak genius; but, of course, not every writer can be a Thoreau — or needs to be. A hypothetical example may well be better than no example at all; yet, as a rule, an example from fact or experience is likely to carry more weight. Suppose you have to write about the benefits — any benefits — that recent science has conferred upon the nation. You might imagine one such benefit: the prospect of one day being able to vacation in outer space and drift about in free-fall like a soap bubble. That imagined benefit would be all right, but it is obviously a conjecture that you dreamed up without going to the library. Do a little digging in recent books and magazines (for the latter, with the aid of the *Readers' Guide to Periodical Literature*). Your reader will feel better informed to be told that science — specifically, the NASA space program — has produced useful inventions. You add:

> Among these are the smoke detector, originally developed as Skylab equipment; the inflatable air bag to protect drivers and pilots, designed to cushion astronauts in splashdowns; a walking chair that enables paraplegics to mount stairs and travel over uneven ground, derived from the moonwalkers' surface buggy; the technique of cryosurgery, the removal of cancerous tissue by fast freezing.

By using specific examples like these, you render the idea of "benefits to society" more concrete and more definite. Such examples are not prettifications of your essay; they are necessary if you are to hold your readers' attention and convince them that you are worth listening to.

Example 119

In illustrating a point, how many examples do you give? As many as you need to make your point clear to the reader you're writing for. One is enough for Andrew Ward, who gives us a typical old-fashioned gas station of a kind most of us will recognize. (His essay, by the way, goes on to make a second point with the aid of a second example.) But for Banesh Hoffmann in his memoir of Einstein (another essay in this chapter), a whole array of brief examples — facts, anecdotes, remembered conversation — seems needed to show the personality and character of a man whom few readers can have known so intimately.

When giving examples, you'll find the methods of *narration* (Chapter 1) and *description* (Chapter 2) particularly useful. Sometimes an example takes the form of a narrative: a brief story, an anecdote, or a case history. Sometimes it embodies a vivid description of a person, place, or thing. Still another method, *analogy*, dealt with in Chapter 7, is sometimes invaluable. It uses a familiar, simple example to make an unfamiliar or complicated thing clear.

Lazy writers think, "Oh well, I can't come up with any example here — I'll just leave it to the reader to find one." The flaw in this assumption is that the reader may be as lazy as the writer. As a result, a perfectly good idea may be left suspended in the stratosphere. S. I. Hayakawa tells the story of a professor who, in teaching a philosophy course, spent a whole semester on the theory of beauty. When students asked him for a few examples of beautiful paintings, symphonies, or works of nature, he refused, saying, "We are interested in principles, not in particulars." The professor himself may well have been interested in principles, but it is a safe bet that his classroom resounded with snores. In written exposition, it is undoubtedly the particulars — the pertinent examples — that keep a reader awake and having a good time, and taking in the principles besides.

EXAMPLE IN A PARAGRAPH

Though a television sitcom may claim to take place in Fargo, or Seattle, or Houston, it will homogenize its locale, removing everything distinctive and regional. Consider a classic example: the Wisconsin of "Happy Days" and its spin-off "Laverne & Shirley," two shows that now, in reruns, have attained immortality. When has any patron of Arnold's hang-out been heard to order a bratwurst? Arthur Fonzarelli, it would seem, is an old-time Brooklyn motorcycle fancier, accent and all. Like no known Milwaukee is the backdrop of "Laverne & Shirley." Supposedly typical Milwaukee working women, the two heroines are named DeFazio and Feeney. To be sure, Italian-Americans and Irish-Americans may be found in Milwaukee, with difficulty; but had the scriptsmiths been true to the ethnic composition of the city, they would have christened the pair Schmidt and Kosnowski. True, Laverne and Shirley work in a brewery, and now and again they go bowling. Still, Milwaukee viewers must think it odd that nei-ther woman ever visits Mitchell Park, lolls on the lakefront, buys cream puffs at the Wisconsin State Fair, or reads the comics in the *Journal* and the *Sentinel*.

Comment. This writer's opening statement — the thesis sentence — might have been harder to grasp without examples. By referring in detail to situation comedies, the writer illustrates a creative liberty to be noticed in TV shows: that of wiping away all distinctive local features and life-styles from wherever the show is supposed to take place. The programs might have just been mentioned by name as examples of sitcoms that all-Ameri-canize their locales. Mere mentions, though, probably would be less interesting, and, hence, less effective. To ask *why* TV come-dies homogenize their settings and to guess at an answer would call for another paragraph — one that might be written by the method of *cause and effect* (dealt with in Chapter 8), rather than by the method of example.

· Arthur R. Miller ·

ARTHUR R. MILLER, born in 1934, is familiar to many viewers of his TV series, "Miller's Court." A professor of law at the Harvard Law School, he is known also for his work on court procedure and the right of privacy, areas in which he has helped draft legislation. Miller has served the public as a member of the U.S. Commission on New Technological Uses of Copyrighted Works, and as the reporter for the Advisory Committee on Civil Rules for the U.S. Supreme Court. He has appeared weekly as the legal expert on "Good Morning, America" and as a guest on "Phil Donahue." The author of more than twenty books, Miller writes an occasional column for *USA Today*.

Self-Defense: Can You Protect Yourself and Avoid the Slammer?

"Self-Defense: Can You Protect Yourself and Avoid the Slammer?" is taken from the chapter by that name in *Miller's Court* (1982). Miller's title poses a question of interest to everyone concerned about violent crime. Some of what the law says regarding your right to defend yourself may surprise you. What happens to you, for instance, if the assailant you bop in panic falls, hits his head, and dies?

Self-defense flourishes in periods and places in which the law is weak or nonexistent. In ancient China, Buddhist monks, harried by bandits beyond the control of the central government, developed the techniques that were to become karate and kung fu as a means of unarmed self-defense. And in the American Old West, where the law stopped at least one town back toward the east, men wore Colt forty-fives strapped to their sides as part of their normal dress.

The right of self-defense, however, becomes severely re-

121

stricted as civilization closes in. In a modern, law-abiding society, you do not have the right to "settle affairs" for yourself; rather you must look to the official organs of the government — the police and the courts — for protection from the lawless behavior of others. Indeed, Thomas Hobbes, one of the more morose English political philosophers (in a line worthy of comic Rodney Dangerfield, Hobbes once wrote that life is "poor, nasty, brutish, and short"), conceived the formation of the state as taking place when each man relinquishes his sword to the king, who then becomes the sole possessor of power and the source of justice and safety for all.

Unfortunately, as we all know, the cops can't be everywhere   3
at once. So the law will let you take certain measures to protect yourself. . . . Just what you can do — without ending up in the slammer — is the subject of this essay.

Imagine you're a woman living alone in a big city. Lately, a   4
number of people in your apartment building have been mugged right in the neighborhood — the worst place is an unlighted section of street near where you get off the bus from work. Since you often stay late at the office, you have no choice but to walk there after dark. A neighborhood committee has approached the police about getting more protection, but the police say that they already are spread thin and can't spare the manpower. To make matters worse, the city is in financial trouble and will be laying off officers, so in the future you can count on even less protection.

It's becoming clear to you that the neighborhood isn't going   5
to get any safer, so you begin thinking about what you can do to protect yourself. Your thoughts grow more serious when you learn that the woman who lives across the hall was badly beaten by a mugger near the bus stop. Now you're really determined, but what's the first move? Should you learn karate, or buy a gun or a can of Mace? Are any of these measures illegal — will they get you into trouble? Now that you're actually considering self-defense, you realize you really don't know what you're allowed to do.

So the first thing you do is ask a lawyer friend what your   6
rights are. He tells you that the law differs from state to state,

but that the basic rule is that you can use reasonable force to repel a real or apparent attack. The amount of force that is "reasonable" differs according to the circumstances, but you're generally justified in using the same amount of force against your assailant as he is using, or proposes to use, against you. And you are allowed to use deadly force (which is force likely to kill, even if it doesn't succeed) against an attack that could kill you or cause you serious bodily harm.

In some states, however, there is a duty to retreat before resorting to deadly force: You must make an effort to escape, if it appears that you can do so safely, before you are entitled to use it. The classic case is the fight at the local saloon, in which the aggressor pulls a knife on the other man, who responds by pulling out a gun. Can he shoot if the knife wielder advances upon him? Not in a duty-to-retreat state if there's a back door to the saloon and he can safely run away. As you can see, the duty to retreat places a higher premium on human life than on human dignity. Thus it is not surprising that the states that allow you to "stand your ground" are generally found in the South and West — regions where the notion of "a man's right to be a man" is more deeply rooted than it is in the East.

Even in states that require you to retreat before using deadly force, there's an exception to the rule: You're generally entitled to stand your ground in your own home if you are menaced by an intruder. This stems from the old idea that your home is your castle, and that you should not have to retreat from the one place that is indisputably yours. But even in this context, society's desire to preserve life and discourage "frontier justice" has led a few courts to limit the defense of the home by force.

So now that you know the rules, what do you do next? You enroll in a self-defense class given especially for women. You learn how to chop throats and gouge eyes and stomp insteps and throw all sorts of exotic punches and kicks. You work out diligently, practice hard, and after eight weeks you're given your diploma, which officially declares you a mistress of unarmed combat.

Now, let's suppose a week after graduation from self-defense school, you get off the bus late one night and start walking home. Suddenly a man comes up and grabs you and starts to

wrestle you to the ground. You use your newly acquired expertise to knock him flat on his back. Obviously you can't be convicted of assault. This is a clear case of self-defense, since you
acted to protect yourself from physical attack. A court most
likely would conclude that you used reasonable force to repel
the attacker, especially since you did not employ deadly force.

Let's say that when you knock him down he hits his head   11
on the pavement and dies. Does that change anything? The answer is that it probably doesn't, since his death was not a result
that could reasonably have been expected to follow from the
amount of force you used in the course of legitimate self-defense.
In other words, you did not use deadly force, even if death in
fact resulted. Assuming that your use of force was justified, the
law won't hold you responsible for any unforeseen injury to
your opponent.

But what if the man hadn't actually gotten close enough to   12
grab you? What if he had suddenly emerged from the shadows,
and without waiting for more, you had delivered a kick that sent
him sprawling? Suppose it turns out he's a perfectly respectable
citizen who just wanted to ask you for directions?

The rule is that you can use force against what reasonably   13
appears to be an attack, even if you were mistaken and weren't
really being threatened. For example, if someone points a fake
gun at you as a practical joke, you can use force, in this case
even deadly force, if under the circumstances you reasonably believed that the gun was real and that the person was about to
shoot you. Similarly, if you reasonably believed that the man
approaching you was about to attack you, then you would be
entitled to protect yourself, even if it turned out that your "assailant" only wanted directions. The key, of course, is whether
you were reasonable in believing you were under attack. You are
not allowed to let fly every time someone comes near you, or
bumps you, or says something unpleasant.

So what happens when you flatten the man who wanted di-   14
rections? If he did no more than walk toward you, you probably
were not justified in using force. He would have had to have
done more for you to say you believed he was about to attack
you — for example, if he had said something, or had made a

threatening gesture, or followed you for a ways before approaching you. But unless you can supply some reason for your "belief"
that you were under attack, you can be charged with the crime
of assault, and also can be sued by the man you knocked down
for money damages to compensate him for his injuries.

How do you react to that? Not surprisingly, you might say   15
that you are an unarmed woman and that if you wait for a potential assailant to make his intentions clear, it may well be too
late for you to defend yourself. There may be some truth to your
argument, but in addition to your safety, the law has to consider
the well-being of innocent people who might want to use the
city streets. Suppose that you weren't the woman who was approached on the street, but were the wife or close friend of the
man who wanted directions. How would you feel about his being clobbered by someone who was so jumpy she struck him before even attempting to find out what he wanted?

Thus far we've considered unarmed resistance. But what   16
about weapons? And under what conditions can you use deadly
force?

Let's say you've been going to self-defense school for eight   17
weeks, but so far the most you can break with your mighty chop
is a Hershey bar. Worse yet, your instructor tells you that it
takes up to two years before most people can be considered proficient in unarmed combat, and that in your case he thinks
that's an extremely optimistic projection. You begin to doubt
you'll ever be a mistress of unarmed combat. So you decide
you'd better get a weapon. There's an old penknife under the
sink; it's rusty and the blade just falls open, but it's the best
you've got, so you drop it into your handbag.

The next night you have to work late at the office, and it's   18
past midnight when you get off the bus and have to walk
through the same dark stretch of street. A man comes out of the
darkness toward you. You increase your pace, but he keeps coming. He grabs you by the hair and neck and starts to drag you
into a vacant lot. In a panic you reach into your bag, pull out
the knife, which drops open, and stab blindly at the man. He
lets go and staggers away. You run to the nearest telephone and

call the police. When they come, you lead them back to the vacant lot, where your assailant is found lying dead of knife wounds. At the police station he's identified as a convicted rapist, out on parole, who is suspected of having attacked two other women in the past month.

Justified self-defense? The answer is not absolutely clear. 19 There's no question that you were entitled to defend yourself from the attack, but the question is whether you were justified in using deadly force. As stated earlier, the general rule is that you can resort to deadly force only if you reasonably fear your attacker will kill you or cause you serious bodily harm. In our imaginary case, it is not definite what he intended to do, since you killed him before he got very far. It's possible that he only intended to rob you, which would not have justified your using deadly force unless he threatened serious harm to you in the course of the robbery.

You argue that if you wait for him to prove he's making a 20 deadly attack, it may be too late for you to make any defense at all. You say it's one thing to require you to wait to see if he means to attack you, but quite another to expect you to "evaluate" the seriousness of an assault that's under way. You point out that as a woman confronted on a dark street by a man, who usually will be significantly stronger than you are, you don't have the luxury of testing out the ferocity of his attack — you have to act forcefully and quickly if you are going to have any sort of chance. You also point out that the man's history indicates that rape, not robbery, was his purpose.

Maybe so, but the law treats the use of deadly force as a very 21 serious matter and permits it only in extremely limited circumstances. Your relative physical weakness does not automatically justify a quick resort to deadly force, although it can be a factor in determining if you acted "reasonably" under the circumstances. One difficulty with your case is that you responded with deadly force to an unarmed attack, and there is an old rule that an attack with fists or hands threatens only an "ordinary assault," and thus does not justify a defense with a weapon.

By now you may be a bit annoyed at the law's concern 22 about the attacker rather than the victim. How do you respond?

Well, you might say, (1) a man can do serious harm to a woman with just his fists, and (2) the man's prior record, plus the nature of the attack, indicate he was going to rape you. But let's face it, you didn't know anything about that record. Should that make a difference? Unfortunately — for you — it does. The attacker's history of rape technically cannot help you, since the question of whether you used excessive force has to be determined according to what you knew at the time of the attack. This is the other side of the rule that an apparent attack, even if not real, justifies resistance: Only appearances seem to count. Thus you cannot claim to be exonerated on the basis of facts you didn't know at the time.

Of course, his being a convicted rapist may help you in that the prosecutor probably will not bring a criminal action against you. The prosecutor is not obliged to charge everyone he thinks might have committed a crime; he uses what is called "prosecutorial discretion" to select which of the many potential cases should be taken to criminal court. Indeed, this discretion may be the reason why there have been relatively few cases in which a woman has been prosecuted for killing a man who tried to rape her. One result is that there is very little law on the question of whether rape constitutes serious bodily injury for purposes of allowing defense with deadly force. Although it's generally assumed that it does, there can't be a definite answer until more cases are decided (thus establishing clear precedent to be followed in other cases) or statutes are enacted to codify this assumption. Of course, even if it were determined that rape alone doesn't justify resistance with deadly force, the victim usually could claim she had no way of knowing her assailant wouldn't go beyond the sexual assault and seriously injure her. 23

But enough theory — let's get back to your case. What would happen if the prosecutor decided to bring you to trial? There's a good chance you'd be acquitted. In light of all the circumstances — a woman alone at night in a dangerous part of the city, the superior strength of your attacker, and the violence of the assault — a jury could easily conclude that you were justified in using deadly force. But be warned: Juries are notoriously unpredictable; moreover, they probably won't be told about the 24 man's rape record, since it's not relevant to how you reacted. Thus there's a chance they might decide that you were too quick to resort to deadly force, since the assailant was never definitely shown to have threatened you with death or serious bodily harm, and you could end up convicted of manslaughter.

Keep in mind that in only slightly different circumstances   25
you would not be entitled to use deadly force — for example, if the man had threatened only to take your purse or knock you down or even to molest you. These assaults may be met with force, but not force likely to kill. Remember also that in many states you have a duty to retreat, if it appears you can do so in safety, before using deadly force. In an urban environment, the duty to retreat, which is really a duty to avoid deadly confrontation regardless of right or wrong, might take a different form from fleeing the scene of the commotion. Thus if the attack we've been considering had taken place in daytime on a crowded street, a court might say that you had an obligation to yell for help or physically resist before stabbing your assailant, since it is likely that someone would have helped you or that he would have been frightened off.

Finally, the use of deadly force is particularly risky in cases   26
in which the assailant's acts are ambiguous. Earlier we concluded that you could be charged with assault if you knocked down a man who just wanted directions. Your case would be much worse if you had stabbed him, not only because you would be up for manslaughter — or perhaps murder — instead of assault, but also because you would have a harder time justifying your apprehension as excusing your acts. If the law hesitates to let you assume that a man who walks up to you at night on a deserted street means to assault you, it will be even less inclined to let you assume he was going to kill you or cause you serious bodily harm. The fact of life is that if you're going to use a weapon, you'd better be sure you really have to.

The imaginary case illustrates the problems in applying the   27
traditional law of self-defense to cases involving women. The law has grown up around quarrels between men, and assumes the defender and his assailant to be of roughly equal size and strength. It also assumes that an attack without a weapon is not

likely to result in death or serious bodily injury, which has given rise to the rule, already mentioned, that deadly force usually is not justified against an unarmed attack.

All this ignores the fact that a woman may be unable effec- 28 tively to resist an attack by even an unarmed man without resort to weapons, and that she may be seriously injured by a man using only his fists. Still, the policy of severely restricting the use of deadly force makes changes in the law unlikely, although it is possible that the disparity in strength between attacker and defender will be considered more carefully in the future in deciding what was "reasonable" resistance under the circumstances.

Indeed, one recent case suggests that women should not be 29 held to the same standard as men in deciding if they responded too quickly or with too much force, on the theory that they are prone to be fearful of attack because of the passive role traditionally assigned to them. It is questionable, however, that courts will accept this subjective analysis, since the law feels more comfortable with objective standards, which often rely on notions of "reasonableness."

Moreover, pressure to establish a separate standard for 30 women is seen by some as inconsistent, at least psychologically, with the current movement to secure a constitutional amendment guaranteeing equal rights for women. It's somewhat analogous to the ambivalent reaction that greeted the United States Supreme Court's decision upholding the constitutionality of male-only draft registration.

Let's go back to the point at which you had just returned to 31 the vacant lot with the police and found your assailant lying dead of knife wounds. Let's say that everyone agrees you acted in justified self-defense. Are you free to go home? Not necessarily. You could find yourself charged with carrying a concealed weapon. Every state regulates the possession or carrying of certain weapons. In New York, for example, it is illegal to own a gravity knife — one that opens by the weight of the blade. Since that old knife of yours opens that way, in New York you could be charged with a crime.

But everyone agrees that you used the knife in justified self- 32 defense, so how can you be charged with breaking the law? The answer is that the law considers defending yourself and carrying the knife to be "severable transactions," which means they are looked at separately in judging whether you have committed a crime. As to stabbing your attacker, you acted in justified self-defense. But carrying the knife, whether you use it or not, is illegal, and you can be prosecuted even if it's agreed that you needed the knife to protect yourself.

The law on what weapons are illegal to possess or carry differs from state to state; local governments, such as cities and towns, may impose additional restrictions. In general, weapons such as gravity knives, switchblades, blackjacks, and especially firearms, are prohibited or strictly regulated. And you can't count on soft treatment just because you're a law-abiding citizen — at least one state has passed a law making a minimum jail term of one year *mandatory* for anyone caught with an unlicensed firearm. So be careful — before you acquire any sort of weapon, you should find out if owning it is a crime or if it must be licensed.   33

QUESTIONS ON MEANING AND PURPOSE

1. Where in Miller's essay does the author state his PURPOSE?
2. Sum up the legal difference between *force* and *deadly force*. When are you justified in using each? When are you not justified?
3. How would you explain Miller's assertion that "the notion of 'a man's right to be a man' is more deeply rooted" in the West and South than in the East (paragraph 7)?
4. What important points does the author make about the laws of self-defense as they apply to women?

QUESTIONS ON WRITING STRATEGY

1. What contrast does the author set up in his first two paragraphs? What do these paragraphs contribute to the essay as a whole?
2. What impact is Miller's use of the first and second PERSON likely to have on his readers?
3. Describe the AUDIENCE for whom Miller seems to be writing. How might his essay be different had he directed it to his fellow law professionals?

4. Where in his essay does Miller use RHETORICAL QUESTIONS to good effect?
5. What function do Miller's many examples perform in "Self-Defense"?

QUESTIONS ON LANGUAGE

1. Where in his essay does Miller use colloquial, even slangy DICTION? Is it appropriate, or not? In general, would you call Miller's explanation of the law heavy or light on legalese?
2. Look up the following words in the dictionary if you don't know what they mean: relinquishes (paragraph 2); repel (6); indisputably (8); expertise (10); potential (15); proficient, projection (17); ferocity (20); exonerated (22); codify (23); confrontation (25); ambiguous, apprehension (26); analogous, ambivalent (30).
3. What is a gravity knife?

SUGGESTIONS FOR WRITING

1. Consider Miller's hypothetical example in which a frightened person reacts with violence to an innocent pedestrian's request for directions (paragraphs 12–14). Write a newspaper editorial in which you comment on the incident and call for action.
2. Ask yourself a question: Am I a lark (an early riser) or an owl (someone who goes to bed and gets up late)? Which visitors throw hospital patients into depression? What are the ingredients for a successful (or unsuccessful) evening out? What makes my roommate so hard to live with? Can a jock enjoy life with a bookworm? Better questions may occur to you. Then write an answer containing at least two vivid examples.

· Andrew Ward ·

Born in Chicago in 1946, ANDREW WARD attended Oberlin and the Rhode Island School of Design. After graduation from college, he worked as a photographer for the Ford Foundation in New Delhi, India, then for two years taught art at the Marvelwood School in Cornwall, Connecticut. His work has appeared in *American Heritage, The Atlantic, Fantasy & Science Fiction, Horizon, Inquiry,* and other magazines; in the annual *Best American Short Stories of 1973*; and in two collections, *Fits and Starts: The Posthumous Memoirs of Andrew Ward* (1978) and *Bits and Pieces* (1980). For children, Ward has written *Baby Bear and the Long Sleep* (1980). He has remarked, "I consider myself a humorist — a designation which performs the function of forcing my intentions out into the open. My work must pass a simple test: if it fails to get a laugh or raise a smile from my readers (meaning my wife and brother), then it fails to justify itself."

They Also Wait Who Stand and Serve Themselves

"They Also Wait Who Stand and Serve Themselves" was first published in *The Atlantic*. Detailing in two extended examples a gas station as it was and as it is, the essay seems to prove that, with the passage of time, a bad scene can be counted on to worsen. There is more here, though, than simple nostalgia for a vanishing institution.

Anyone interested in the future of American commerce   1
should take a drive sometime to my neighborhood gas station. Not that it is or ever was much of a place to visit. Even when I first moved here, five years ago, it was shabby and forlorn: not at all like the garden spots they used to feature in the commercials, where trim, manicured men with cultivated voices tipped their visors at your window and asked what they could do for you.

Sal, the owner, was a stocky man who wore undersized,   2
popped-button shirts, sagging trousers, and oil-spattered work
shoes with broken laces. "Gas stinks" was his motto, and every
gallon he pumped into his customers' cars seemed to take something out of him. "Pumping gas is for morons," he liked to say,
leaning indelibly against my rear window and watching the digits fly on the pump register. "One of these days I'm gonna dump
this place on a Puerto Rican, move to Florida, and get into
something nice, like hero sandwiches."

He had a nameless, walleyed assistant who wore a studded   3
denim jacket and, with his rag and squeegee, left a milky film on
my windshield as my tank was filling. There was a fume-crazed,
patchy German shepherd, which Sal kept chained to the air
pump, and if you followed Sal into his cluttered, overheated office next to the service bays, you ran a gauntlet of hangers-on,
many of them Sal's brothers and nephews, who spent their time
debating the merits of the driving directions he gave the bewil-
dered travelers who turned into his station for help.

"I don't know," one of them would say, pulling a bag of po-   4
tato chips off the snack rack, "I think I would have put 'em onto
91, gotten 'em off at Willow, and then — bango! — straight
through to Hamden."

Sal guarded the rest room key jealously and handed it out   5
with reluctance, as if something in your request had betrayed
some dismal aberration. The rest room was accessible only
through a little closet littered with tires, fan belts, and cases of
oil cans. Inside, the bulb was busted and there were never any
towels, so you had to dry your hands on toilet paper — if Sal
wasn't out of toilet paper, too.

The soda machine never worked for anyone except Sal,   6
who, when complaints were lodged, would give it a contemptuous kick as he trudged by, dislodging warm cans of grape soda
which, when their pop-tops were flipped, gave off a fine purple
spray. There was, besides the snack rack in the office, a machine
that dispensed peanuts on behalf of the Sons of Garibaldi. The
metal shelves along the cinderblock wall were sparsely stocked
with cans of cooling system cleaner, windshield de-icer, anti-
freeze, and boxed head lamps and oil filters. Over the battered
yellow wiper case, below the Coca-Cola clock, and half hidden

by a calendar from a janitorial supply concern, hung a little brass plaque from the oil company, awarded in recognition of Salvatore A. Castallano's ten-year business association.

I wish for the sake of nostalgia that I could say Sal was a   7
craftsman, but I can't. I'm not even sure he was an honest man. I suspect that when business was slow he may have cheated me, but I never knew for sure because I don't know anything about cars. If I brought my Volvo in because it was behaving strangely, I knew that as far as Sal was concerned it could never be a simple matter of tightening a bolt or re-attaching a hose. "Jesus," he'd wearily exclaim after a look under the hood. "Mr. Ward, we got problems." I usually let it go at that and simply asked him when he thought he could have it repaired, because if I pressed him for details he would get all worked up. "Look, if you don't want to take my word for it, you can go someplace else. I mean, it's a free country, you know? You got spalding on your caps, which means your dexadrometer isn't charging, and pretty soon you're gonna have hairlines in your flushing drums. You get hairlines in your flushing drums and you might as well forget it. You're driving junk."

I don't know what Sal's relationship was with the oil com-   8
pany. I suppose it was pretty distant. He was never what they call a "participating dealer." He never gave away steak knives or NFL tumblers or stuffed animals with his fill-ups, and never got around to taping company posters on his windows. The map rack was always empty, and the company emblem, which was supposed to rotate thirty feet above the station, had broken down long before I first laid eyes on it, and had frozen at an angle that made it hard to read from the highway.

If, outside of television, there was ever such a thing as an oil   9
company service station inspector, he must have been appalled by the grudging service, the mad dog, the sepulchral john. When there was supposed to have been an oil shortage a few years ago, Sal's was one of the first stations to run out of gas. And several months ago, during the holiday season, the company squeezed him out for good.

I don't know whether Sal is now happily sprinkling olive oil   10
over salami subs somewhere along the Sun Belt. I only know

that one bleak January afternoon I turned into his station to find him gone. At first, as I idled by the no-lead pump, I thought the station had been shut down completely. Plywood had been nailed over the service bays, Sal's name had been painted out above the office door, and all that was left of his dog was a length of chain dangling from the air pump's vacant mast.

But when I got out of the car I spotted someone sitting in   11 the office with his boots up on the counter, and at last caught sight of the "Self-Service Only" signs posted by the pumps. Now, I've always striven for a degree of self-sufficiency. I fix my own leaky faucets and I never let the bellboy carry my bags. But I discovered as I squinted at the instructional sticker by the nozzle that there are limits to my desire for independence. Perhaps it was the bewilderment with which I approach anything having to do with the internal combustion engine; perhaps it was my conviction that fossil fuels are hazardous; perhaps it was the expectation of service, the sense of helplessness, that twenty years of oil company advertising had engendered, but I didn't want to pump my own gas.

A mongrel rain began to fall upon the oil-slicked tarmac as I   12 followed the directions spelled out next to the nozzle. But somehow I got them wrong. When I pulled the trigger on the nozzle, no gas gushed into my fuel tank, no digits flew on the gauge.

"Hey, buddy," a voice sounded out of a bell-shaped speaker   13 overhead. "Flick the switch."

I turned toward the office and saw someone with Wild Bill   14 Hickok hair leaning over a microphone.

"Right. Thanks," I answered, and turned to find the switch.   15 There wasn't one. There was a bolt that looked a little like a switch, but it wouldn't flick.

"The switch," the voice crackled in the rain. "Flick the   16 switch."

I waved back as if I'd finally understood, but I still couldn't   17 figure out what he was talking about. In desperation, I stuck the nozzle back into my fuel tank and pulled the trigger. Nothing.

In the office I could see that the man was now angrily pull-   18 ing on a slicker. "What the hell's the matter with you?" he asked, storming by me. "All you gotta do is flick the switch."

"I couldn't find the switch," I told him.   19

"Well, what do you call this?" he wanted to know, pointing   20
to a little lever near the pump register.

"A lever," I told him.   21

"Christ," he muttered, flicking the little lever. The digits on   22
the register suddenly formed neat rows of zeros. "All right, it's
set. Now you can serve yourself," the long-haired man said,
ducking back to the office.

As the gas gushed into my fuel tank and the fumes rose to   23
my nostrils, I thought for a moment about my last visit to Sal's.
It hadn't been any picnic: Sal claimed to have found something
wrong with my punting brackets, the German shepherd
snapped at my heels as I walked by, and nobody had change for
my ten. But the transaction had dimension to it: I picked up
some tips about color antennas, entered into the geographical
debate in the office, and bought a can of windshield wiper sol-
vent (to fill the gap in my change). Sal's station had been a dime
a dozen, but it occurred to me, as the nozzle began to balk and
shudder in my hand, that gas stations of its kind were going the
way of the village smithy and the corner grocer.

I got a glob of grease on my glove as I hung the nozzle back   24
on the pump, and it took more than a minute to satisfy myself
that I had replaced the gas cap properly. I tried to whip up a feeling of accomplishment as I headed for the office, but I could not
forget Sal's dictum: Pumping gas is for morons.

The door to the office was locked, but a sign directed me to   25
a stainless steel teller's drawer which had been installed in the
plate glass of the front window. I stood waiting for a while with
my money in hand, but the long-haired man sat inside with his
back to me, so at last I reached up and hesitantly knocked on
the glass with my glove.

The man didn't hear me or had decided, in retaliation for   26
our semantic disagreement, to ignore me for a while. I reached
up to knock again, but noticed that my glove had left a greasy
smear on the window. Ever my mother's son, I reflexively
reached into my pocket for my handkerchief and was about to
wipe the grease away when it hit me: at last the oil industry had
me where it wanted me — standing in the rain and washing its
windshield.

QUESTIONS ON MEANING AND PURPOSE

1. What makes this essay something more than simple nostalgia? What mixture of feelings toward Sal's gas station does Ward express?
2. For what reason does Ward prefer the gas station of the past over what it has become?
3. How would you characterize the author's relationship with the oil industry?
4. What is the central PURPOSE of this essay: to describe two methods of running a gas station, or to show through two extended examples a certain profound change? Exactly what in the essay indicates its purpose?

QUESTIONS ON WRITING STRATEGY

1. In what parts of this essay does the writer make particularly good use of the method of description (explained in Chapter 2)?
2. How effectively do the essay's two extended examples illustrate Ward's THESIS?
3. Where in his essay does Ward use IRONY?
4. Of what advantage is it to the writer that his AUDIENCE is familiar with gas stations? Where does the essay tell you things you already know? Where does it tell you something you might not have realized before?

QUESTIONS ON LANGUAGE

1. Figure out, from context or from the dictionary, the meanings of the following: walleyed, ran a gauntlet (paragraph 3); reluctance, aberration, accessible (5); contemptuous (6); sepulchral (9); retaliation, semantic (26).
2. What do you make of the words in Sal's diagnosis (paragraph 7): "spalding on your caps," "your dexadrometer isn't charging," "hairlines in your flushing drums"? Is Sal feeding the author a line of double talk, or is Ward showing his audience how the language of auto mechanics sounded to him?
3. What is a *mongrel rain* (paragraph 12)? Is *mongrel* an effective modifier here? Why, or why not?
4. Draw on your knowledge of the Old West to explain *Wild Bill Hickok hair* (paragraph 14).

5. The title of Ward's essay is an ALLUSION to a sonnet by the English poet John Milton, beginning "When I consider how my light is spent," and ending with the insight that those who serve God passively (like Milton, who was blind and could no longer take an active role in the Puritan cause) "also serve who only stand and wait." How does this allusion serve Ward?

SUGGESTIONS FOR WRITING

1. In a lighthearted essay, agree or disagree with Ward's insight that "progress" is not necessarily synonymous with improvement.
2. Try to describe in a brief essay some familiar institution of contemporary life: supermarkets, drive-in movies, game arcades, or whatever else interests you. Be sure to include at least one extended example.
3. Discuss in an essay full of examples: To what extent does the current trend toward depersonalization in retailing extend beyond gas stations?

· Banesh Hoffmann ·

Born in Richmond, England, in 1906, BANESH HOFFMANN has pursued a distinguished career as mathematician and physicist, author and teacher. After taking his B.A. from Oxford, he crossed the Atlantic to study at Princeton, where he completed his Ph.D. Later, as a member of Princeton's Institute for Advanced Study, he became a colleague of Albert Einstein. For more than forty years (1937–77), Hoffmann was a professor of mathematics at Queens College in Flushing, New York. Among his several books are *The Strange Story of the Quantum* (1959), *The Tyranny of Testing* (1978) and, in collaboration with Helen Dukas, Einstein's personal secretary, two highly praised studies: *Albert Einstein: Creator and Rebel* (1973), a biography that centers on Einstein the theoretical physicist, and *Albert Einstein: The Human Side* (1979). Hoffmann also has written for magazines as diverse as the *American Scholar* and the *Baker Street Journal* (for fans of Sherlock Holmes).

My Friend, Albert Einstein

Most of us know Einstein as the brilliant mathematician and scientist who propounded the theory of relativity and the quantum theory of light. To Banesh Hoffmann, the great thinker was also a friend. He writes about Einstein with respect and affection, and some of what the author says about Einstein may surprise you. The essay appeared first in *Reader's Digest* and was reprinted later in *Unforgettable Characters* (1980), a volume compiled by the magazine's editors.

He was one of the greatest scientists the world has ever   1
known, yet if I had to convey the essence of Albert Einstein in a single word, I would choose *simplicity*. Perhaps an anecdote will help. Once, caught in a downpour, he took off his hat and held it under his coat. Asked why, he explained, with admirable logic, that the rain would damage the hat, but his hair would be none the worse for its wetting. This knack for going instinctively

to the heart of a matter was the secret of his major scientific discoveries — this and his extraordinary feeling for beauty.

I first met Albert Einstein in 1935, at the famous Institute for Advanced Study in Princeton, N.J. He had been among the first to be invited to the Institute, and was offered *carte blanche* as to salary. To the director's dismay, Einstein asked for an impossible sum: it was far too *small*. The director had to plead with him to accept a larger salary.

I was in awe of Einstein, and hesitated before approaching him about some ideas I had been working on. When I finally knocked on his door, a gentle voice said, "Come" — with a rising inflection that made the single word both a welcome and a question. I entered his office and found him seated at a table, calculating and smoking his pipe. Dressed in ill-fitting clothes, his hair characteristically awry, he smiled a warm welcome. His utter naturalness at once set me at ease.

As I began to explain my ideas, he asked me to write the equations on the blackboard so he could see how they developed. Then came the staggering — and altogether endearing — request: "Please go slowly. I do not understand things quickly." This from Einstein! He said it gently, and I laughed. From then on, all vestiges of fear were gone.

Einstein was born in 1879 in the German city of Ulm. He had been no infant prodigy; indeed, he was so late in learning to speak that his parents feared he was a dullard. In school, though his teachers saw no special talent in him, the signs were already there. He taught himself calculus, for example, and his teachers seemed a little afraid of him because he asked questions they could not answer. At the age of 16, he asked himself whether a light wave would seem stationary if one ran abreast of it. From that innocent question would arise, ten years later, his theory of relativity.

Einstein failed his entrance examinations at the Swiss Federal Polytechnic School, in Zurich, but was admitted a year later. There he went beyond his regular work to study the masterworks of physics on his own. Rejected when he applied for academic positions, he ultimately found work, in 1902, as a patent examiner in Berne, and there in 1905 his genius burst into fabulous flower.

Among the extraordinary things he produced in that memorable year were his theory of relativity, with its famous offshoot, $E = mc^2$ (energy equals mass times the speed of light squared), and his quantum theory of light. These two theories were not only revolutionary, but seemingly contradictory: the former was intimately linked to the theory that light consists of waves, while the latter said it consists somehow of particles. Yet this unknown young man boldly proposed both at once — and he was right in both cases, though how he could have been is far too complex a story to tell here. 7

Collaborating with Einstein was an unforgettable experience. In 1937, the Polish physicist Leopold Infeld and I asked if we could work with him. He was pleased with the proposal, since he had an idea about gravitation waiting to be worked out in detail. Thus we got to know not merely the man and the friend, but also the professional. 8

The intensity and depth of his concentration were fantastic. When battling a recalcitrant problem, he worried it as an animal worries its prey. Often, when we found ourselves up against a seemingly insuperable difficulty, he would stand up, put his pipe on the table, and say in his quaint English, "I will a little tink" (he could not pronounce "th"). Then he would pace up and down, twirling a lock of his long, graying hair around his forefinger. 9

A dreamy, faraway and yet inward look would come over his face. There was no appearance of concentration, no furrowing of the brow — only a placid inner communion. The minutes would pass, and then suddenly Einstein would stop pacing as his face relaxed into a gentle smile. He had found the solution to the problem. Sometimes it was so simple that Infeld and I could have kicked ourselves for not having thought of it. But the magic had been performed invisibly in the depths of Einstein's mind, by a process we could not fathom. 10

When his wife died he was deeply shaken, but insisted that now more than ever was the time to be working hard. I remem- 11 ber going to his house to work with him during that sad time. His face was haggard and grief-lined, but he put forth a great effort to concentrate. To help him, I steered the discussion away from routine matters into more difficult theoretical problems, and Einstein gradually became absorbed in the discussion. We kept at it for some two hours, and at the end his eyes were no longer sad. As I left, he thanked me with moving sincerity. "It was a fun," he said. He had had a moment of surcease from grief, and then groping words expressed a deep emotion.

Although Einstein felt no need for religious ritual and be-   12
longed to no formal religious group, he was the most deeply religious man I have known. He once said to me, "Ideas come from God," and one could hear the capital "G" in the reverence with which he pronounced the word. On the marble fireplace in the mathematics building at Princeton University is carved, in the original German, what one might call his scientific credo: "God is subtle, but he is not malicious." By this Einstein meant that scientists could expect to find their task difficult, but not hopeless: the Universe was a Universe of law, and God was not confusing us with deliberate paradoxes and contradictions.

Einstein was an accomplished amateur musician. We used to   13
play duets, he on the violin, I at the piano. One day he surprised me by saying Mozart was the greatest composer of all. Beethoven "created" his music, but the music of Mozart was of such purity and beauty one felt he had merely "found" it — that it had always existed as part of the inner beauty of the Universe, waiting to be revealed.

It was this very Mozartean simplicity that most character-   14
ized Einstein's methods. His 1905 theory of relativity, for example, was built on just two simple assumptions. One is the so-called principle of relativity, which means, roughly speaking, that we cannot tell whether we are at rest or moving smoothly. The other assumption is that the speed of light is the same no matter what the speed of the object that produces it. You can see how reasonable this is if you think of agitating a stick in a lake to create waves. Whether you wiggle the stick from a stationary pier, or from a rushing speedboat, the waves, once gen-

erated, are on their own, and their speed has nothing to do with that of the stick.

Each of these assumptions, by itself, was so plausible as to seem primitively obvious. But together they were in such violent conflict that a lesser man would have dropped one or the other and fled in panic. Einstein daringly kept both — and by so doing he revolutionized physics. For he demonstrated they could, after all, exist peacefully side by side, provided we gave up cherished beliefs about the nature of time. 15

Science is like a house of cards, with concepts like time and space at the lowest level. Tampering with time brought most of the house tumbling down, and it was this that made Einstein's work so important — and controversial. At a conference in Princeton in honor of his 70th birthday, one of the speakers, a Nobel Prize winner, tried to convey the magical quality of Einstein's achievement. Words failed him, and with a shrug of helplessness he pointed to his wristwatch, and said in tones of awed amazement, "It all came from this." His very ineloquence made this the most eloquent tribute I have heard to Einstein's genius. 16

Although fame had little effect on Einstein as a person, he could not escape it; he was, of course, instantly recognizable. One autumn Saturday, I was walking with him in Princeton discussing some technical matters. Parents and alumni were streaming excitedly toward the stadium, their minds on the coming football game. As they approached us, they paused in sudden recognition, and a momentary air of solemnity came over them as if they had been reminded of a different world. Yet Einstein seemed totally unaware of this effect and went on with the discussion as though they were not there. 17

We think of Einstein as one concerned only with the deepest aspects of science. But he saw scientific principles in everyday things to which most of us would give barely a second thought. He once asked me if I had ever wondered why a man's feet will sink into either dry or completely submerged sand, while sand that is merely damp provides a firm surface. When I could not answer, he offered a simple explanation. 18

It depends, he pointed out, on *surface tension*, the elastic-skin 19 effect of a liquid surface. This is what holds a drop together, or causes two small raindrops on a windowpane to pull into one big drop the moment their surfaces touch.

When sand is damp, Einstein explained, there are tiny   20
amounts of water between grains. The surface tensions of these tiny amounts of water pull all the grains together, and friction then makes them hard to budge. When the sand is dry, there is obviously no water between grains. If the sand is fully immersed, there is water between grains, but no water *surface* to pull them together.

This is not as important as relativity; yet there is no telling   21
what seeming trifle will lead an Einstein to a major discovery. And the puzzle of the sand does give us an inkling of the power and elegance of his mind.

Einstein's work, performed quietly with pencil and paper,   22
seemed remote from the turmoil of everyday life: But his ideas were so revolutionary they caused violent controversy and irrational anger. Indeed, in order to be able to award him a belated Nobel Prize, the selection committee had to avoid mentioning relativity, and pretend the prize was awarded primarily for his work on the quantum theory.

Political events upset the serenity of his life even more.   23
When the Nazis came to power in Germany, his theories were officially declared false because they had been formulated by a Jew. His property was confiscated, and it is said a price was put on his head.

When scientists in the United States, fearful that the Nazis   24
might develop an atomic bomb, sought to alert American authorities to the danger, they were scarcely heeded. In desperation, they drafted a letter which Einstein signed and sent directly to President Roosevelt. It was this act that led to the fateful decision to go all-out on the production of an atomic bomb — an endeavor in which Einstein took no active part. When he heard of the agony and destruction that his $E = mc^2$ had wrought, he was dismayed beyond measure, and from then on there was a look of ineffable sadness in his eyes.

There was something elusively whimsical about Einstein. It 25
is illustrated by my favorite anecdote about him. In his first year
in Princeton, on Christmas Eve, so the story goes, some children
sang carols outside his house. Having finished, they knocked on
his door and explained they were collecting money to buy
Christmas presents. Einstein listened, then said, "Wait a moment." He put on his scarf and overcoat, and took his violin
from its case. Then, joining the children as they went from door
to door, he accompanied their singing of "Silent Night" on his
violin.

How shall I sum up what it meant to have known Einstein 26
and his works? Like the Nobel Prize winner who pointed helplessly at his watch, I can find no adequate words. It was akin to
the revelation of great art that lets one see what was formerly
hidden. And when, for example, I walk on the sand of a lonely
beach, I am reminded of his ceaseless search for cosmic simplicity — and the scene takes on a deeper, sadder beauty.

QUESTIONS ON MEANING AND PURPOSE

1. Which of the following do you find Hoffmann doing: writing a biography, reminiscing, entertaining his readers, explaining relativity, illustrating some point about Einstein? Which PURPOSE
   seems to predominate?
2. What qualities did Einstein possess that gave him a permanent
   place in the author's affections?
3. From his essay, what are you able to learn about the author himself?
4. What connections between Einstein the scientist and Einstein the
   man does Hoffmann's essay reveal to us?

QUESTIONS ON WRITING STRATEGY

1. If Hoffmann were to rewrite "My Friend, Albert Einstein," addressing himself only to an AUDIENCE of scientists, what
   changes in his essay might result?

2. What is Hoffmann's THESIS? Where does he state it?
3. Study three or four of the examples Hoffmann includes in his essay. What is the function of each?
4. How do paragraphs 5–7 and 14–15 differ from most of the others in Hoffmann's essay? Does the material in these paragraphs contribute something of value to the essay? If so, what?
5. Where in his essay does Hoffmann use physical description? (See Chapter 2.) Where does he include a brief analogy? (See Chapter 7.)

QUESTIONS ON LANGUAGE

1. Look up the following words if you do not know what they mean: essence (paragraph 1); *carte blanche* (2); inflection, awry (3); vestiges (4); prodigy (5); recalcitrant, insuperable (9); placid (10); surcease (11); paradoxes (12); ineffable (24); elusively, whimsical (25).
2. In his essay, the author more than once uses the word *anecdote*. Is an anecdote the same as an example? Explain.

SUGGESTIONS FOR WRITING

1. Write a reply to the student who said, "If Einstein had never lived, the world would be a better place because the atomic bomb would never have been invented."
2. Write an essay about someone whose behavior you can illustrate with vivid examples. Your subject need not be a famous person, merely someone you know fairly well: a relative, teacher, or friend; a colorful town character; a leader, or a zealous follower. If possible, choose examples that will highlight the one or two traits that seem to you most worth noticing.

· Malcolm Cowley ·

MALCOLM COWLEY, born in 1898, a boyhood friend of Kenneth Burke (Chapter 6), has had a long and distinguished career as translator, critic, poet, lecturer, editor, and literary historian. He has served as visiting professor of English at many universities and as literary editor of *The New Republic* (1930–40). Cowley's books include *Exile's Return* (1934), *The Literary Situation* (1954), and *The Flower and the Leaf* (1984), a volume of essays. He now works and, apparently, grows old gracefully at home in Connecticut.

Vices and Pleasures: The View from 80

With serene good humor, the author of "Vices and Pleasures: The View from 80" (editors' title) looks at old age and discovers that, while it has its disadvantages, life's closing chapter also offers compensations to those who can appreciate them. Though the work of an octogenarian, Cowley's writing is frank, fresh, and full of pertinent examples. This essay is the beginning of Cowley's book *The View from Eighty* (1981).

Even before he or she is 80, the aging person may undergo 1 another identity crisis like that of adolescence. Perhaps there had also been a middle-aged crisis, the male or the female menopause, but for the rest of adult life he had taken himself for granted, with his capabilities and failings. Now, when he looks in the mirror, he asks himself, "Is this really me?" — or he avoids the mirror out of distress at what it reveals, those bags and wrinkles. In his new makeup he is called upon to play a new role in a play that must be improvised. André Gide, that long-lived man of letters, wrote in his journal, "My heart has remained so young that I have the continual feeling of playing a part, the part of the 70-year-old that I certainly am; and the infirmities and weaknesses that remind me of my age act like a prompter, reminding me of my lines when I tend to stray. Then, like the good actor I want to be, I go back into my role, and I pride myself on playing it well."

In his new role the old person will find that he is tempted by 2 new vices, that he receives new compensations (not so widely known), and that he may possibly achieve new virtues. Chief among these is the heroic or merely obstinate refusal to surrender in the face of time. One admires the ships that go down with all flags flying and the captain on the bridge.

Among the vices of age are avarice, untidiness, and vanity, 3 which last takes the form of a craving to be loved or simply admired. Avarice is the worst of those three. Why do so many old persons, men and women alike, insist on hoarding money when they have no prospect of using it and even when they have no heirs? They eat the cheapest food, buy no clothes, and live in a single room when they could afford better lodging. It may be that they regard money as a form of power; there is a comfort in watching it accumulate while other powers are dwindling away. How often we read of an old person found dead in a hovel, on a mattress partly stuffed with bankbooks and stock certificates! The bankbook syndrome, we call it in our family, which has never succumbed.

Untidiness we call the Langley Collyer syndrome. To ex- 4 plain, Langley Collyer was a former concert pianist who lived alone with his 70-year-old brother in a brownstone house on upper Fifth Avenue. The once fashionable neighborhood had become part of Harlem. Homer, the brother, had been an admiralty lawyer, but was now blind and partly paralyzed; Langley played for him and fed him on buns and oranges, which he thought would restore Homer's sight. He never threw away a daily paper because Homer, he said, might want to read them all. He saved other things as well and the house became filled with rubbish from roof to basement. The halls were lined on both sides with bundled newspapers, leaving narrow passageways in which Langley had devised booby traps to catch intruders.

On March 21, 1947, some unnamed person telephoned the 5 police to report that there was a dead body in the Collyer house. The police broke down the front door and found the hall impassable, then they hoisted a ladder to a second-story window. Behind it Homer was lying on the floor in a bathrobe; he had starved to death. Langley had disappeared. After some delay, the police broke into the basement, chopped a hole in the roof, and began throwing junk out of the house, top and bottom. It was 18 days before they found Langley's body, gnawed by rats. Caught in one of his own booby traps, he had died in a hallway just outside Homer's door. By that time the police had collected, and the Department of Sanitation had hauled away, 120 tons of rubbish, including besides the newspapers, 14 grand pianos and the parts of a dismantled Model T Ford.

Why do so many old people accumulate junk, not on the   6 scale of Langley Collyer, but still in a dismaying fashion? Their tables are piled high with it, their bureau drawers are stuffed with it, their closet rods bend with the weight of clothes not worn for years. I suppose that the piling up is partly from lethargy and partly from the feeling that everything once useful, including their own bodies, should be preserved. Others, though not so many, have such a fear of becoming Langley Collyers that they strive to be painfully neat. Every tool they own is in its place, though it will never be used again; every scrap of paper is filed away in alphabetical order. At last their immoderate neatness becomes another vice of age, if a milder one.

The vanity of older people is an easier weakness to explain,   7 and to condone. With less to look forward to, they yearn for recognition of what they have been: the reigning beauty, the athlete, the soldier, the scholar. It is the beauties who have the hardest time. A portrait of themselves at twenty hangs on the wall, and they try to resemble it by making an extravagant use of creams, powders, and dyes. Being young at heart, they think they are merely revealing their essential persons. The athletes find shelves for their silver trophies, which are polished once a year. Perhaps a letter sweater lies wrapped in a bureau drawer. I remember one evening when a no-longer athlete had guests for dinner and tried to find his sweater. "Oh, that old thing," his wife said. "The moths got into it and I threw it away." The athlete sulked and his guests went home early.

Often the yearning to be recognized appears in conversation   8 as an innocent boast. Thus, a distinguished physician, retired at 94, remarks casually that a disease was named after him. A former judge bursts into chuckles as he repeats bright things that he said on the bench. Aging scholars complain in letters (or one of them does), "As I approach 70 I'm becoming avid of honors, and such things — medals, honorary degrees, etc. — are only passed around among academics on a *quid pro quo* basis (one hood capping another)." Or they say querulously, "Bill Underwood has ten honorary doctorates and I have only three. Why didn't they elect me to . . . ?" and they mention the name of some learned society. That search for honors is a harmless passion, though it may lead to jealousies and deformations of character, as with Robert Frost in his later years. Still, honors cost little. Why shouldn't the very old have more than their share of them?

To be admired and praised, especially by the young, is an 9 autumnal pleasure enjoyed by the lucky ones (who are not always the most deserving). "What is more charming," Cicero observes in his famous essay *De Senectute*, "than an old age surrounded by the enthusiasm of youth! . . . Attentions which seem trivial and conventional are marks of honor — the morning call, being sought after, precedence, having people rise for you, being escorted to and from the forum. . . . What pleasures of the body can be compared to the prerogatives of influence?" But there are also pleasures of the body, or the mind, that are enjoyed by a greater number of older persons.

Those pleasures include some that younger people find hard 10 to appreciate. One of them is simply sitting still, like a snake on a sun-warmed stone, with a delicious feeling of indolence that was seldom attained in earlier years. A leaf flutters down; a cloud moves by inches across the horizon. At such moments the older person, completely relaxed, has become a part of nature — and a living part, with blood coursing through his veins. The future does not exist for him. He thinks, if he thinks at all, that life for younger persons is still a battle royal of each against each, but that now he has nothing more to win or lose. He is not so much above as outside the battle, as if he had assumed the uniform of some small neutral country, perhaps Liechtenstein or Andorra. From a distance he notes that some of the combatants, men or women, are jostling ahead — but why do they fight so hard when the most they can hope for is a longer obituary? He can watch the scrounging and gouging, he can hear the shouts of exultation, the moans of the gravely wounded, and meanwhile he feels secure; nobody will attack him from ambush.

Age has other physical compensations besides the nirvana of dozing in the sun. A few of the simplest needs become a pleasure to satisfy. When an old woman in a nursing home was asked what she really liked to do, she answered in one word: "Eat." She might have been speaking for many of her fellows. Meals in a nursing home, however badly cooked, serve as climactic moments of the day. The physical essence of the pensioners is being renewed at an appointed hour; now they can go back to meditating or to watching TV while looking forward to the next meal. They can also look forward to sleep, which has become a definite pleasure, not the mere interruption it once had been.

Here I am thinking of old persons under nursing care. Others ferociously guard their independence, and some of them suffer less than one might expect from being lonely and impoverished. They can be rejoiced by visits and meetings, but they also have company inside their heads. Some of them are busiest when their hands are still. What passes through the minds of many is a stream of persons, images, phrases, and familiar tunes. For some that stream has continued since childhood, but now it is deeper; it is their present and their past combined. At times they conduct silent dialogues with a vanished friend, and these are less tiring — often more rewarding — than spoken conversations. If inner resources are lacking, old persons living alone may seek comfort and a kind of companionship in the bottle. I should judge from the gossip of various neighborhoods that the outer suburbs from Boston to San Diego are full of secretly alcoholic widows. One of those widows, an old friend, was moved from her apartment into a retirement home. She left behind her a closet in which the floor was covered wall to wall with whiskey bottles. "Oh, those empty bottles!" she explained. "They were left by a former tenant."

Not whiskey or cooking sherry but simply giving up is the

greatest temptation of age. It is something different from a stoi-
cal acceptance of infirmities, which is something to be admired.
At 63, when he first recognized that his powers were failing,
Emerson wrote one of his best poems, "Terminus":

> It is time to be old,
> To take in sail: —
> The god of bounds,
> Who sets to seas a shore,
> Came to me in his fatal rounds,
> And said: "No more!
> No farther shoot
> Thy broad ambitious branches, and thy root.
> Fancy departs: no more invent;
> Contract thy firmament
> To compass of a tent."

Emerson lived in good health to the age of 79. Within his   14
narrowed firmament, he continued working until his memory
failed; then he consented to having younger editors and collabo-
rators. The givers-up see no reason for working. Sometimes they
lie in bed all day when moving about would still be possible, if
difficult. I had a friend, a distinguished poet, who surrendered in
that fashion. The doctors tried to stir him to action, but he
refused to leave his room. Another friend, once a successful artist, stopped painting when his eyes began to fail. His doctor
made the mistake of telling him that he suffered from a fatal disease. He then lost interest in everything except the splendid
Rolls-Royce, acquired in his prosperous days, that stood in the
garage. Daily he wiped the dust from its hood. He couldn't drive
it on the road any longer, but he used to sit in the driver's seat,
start the motor, then back the Rolls out of the garage and drive
it in again, back twenty feet and forward twenty feet; that was
his only distraction.

I haven't the right to blame those who surrender, not being   15
able to put myself inside their minds or bodies. Often they must
have compelling reasons, physical or moral. Not only do they
suffer from a variety of ailments, but also they are made to feel
that they no longer have a function in the community. Their
families and neighbors don't ask them for advice, don't really lis-

ten when they speak, don't call on them for efforts. One notes
that there are not a few recoveries from apparent senility when
that situation changes. If it doesn't change, old persons may decide that efforts are useless. I sympathize with their problems,
but the men and women I envy are those who accept old age as a
series of challenges.

For such persons, every new infirmity is an enemy to be out-   16
witted, an obstacle to be overcome by force of will. They enjoy
each little victory over themselves, and sometimes they win a
major success. Renoir was one of them. He continued painting,
and magnificently, for years after he was crippled by arthritis;
the brush had to be strapped to his arm. "You don't need your
hand to paint," he said. Goya was another of the unvanquished.
At 72 he retired as an official painter of the Spanish court and
decided to work only for himself. His later years were those of
the famous "black paintings" in which he let his imagination
run (and also of the lithographs, then a new technique). At 78
he escaped a reign of terror in Spain by fleeing to Bordeaux. He
was deaf and his eyes were failing; in order to work he had to
wear several pairs of spectacles, one over another, and then use
a magnifying glass; but he was producing splendid work in a totally new style. At 80 he drew an ancient man propped on two
sticks, with a mass of white hair and beard hiding his face and
with the inscription "I am still learning."

Giovanni Papini said when he was nearly blind, "I prefer   17
martyrdom to imbecility." After writing sixty books, including
his famous *Life of Christ*, he was at work on two huge projects
when he was stricken with a form of muscular atrophy. He lost
the use of his left leg, then of his fingers, so that he couldn't hold
a pen. The two big books, though never to be finished, moved
forward slowly by dictation; that in itself was a triumph.
Toward the end, when his voice had become incomprehensible,
he spelled out a word, tapping on the table to indicate letters of
the alphabet. One hopes never to be faced with the need for
such heroic measures.

"Eighty years old!" the great Catholic poet Paul Claudel   18
wrote in his journal. "No eyes left, no ears, no teeth, no legs, no
wind! And when all is said and done, how astonishingly well
one does without them!"

QUESTIONS ON MEANING AND PURPOSE

1. According to Cowley, what causes the "identity crisis" that aging people are likely to undergo?
2. List the vices, the compensations, and the virtues the author says many old people have in common.
3. Which virtue of old age does Cowley regard as the most admirable? Which temptation of old age seems to him the most prevalent?
4. "Cowley's purpose is simply to claim that all the sugar is in the bottom of the cup." How accurate is this remark? In a sentence, how would *you* sum up Cowley's apparent PURPOSE in writing?

QUESTIONS ON WRITING STRATEGY

1. What do Cowley's illustrative examples contribute to his insights about old people? In particular, what point is made by the quotation from Emerson's poem "Terminus"?
2. What examples does Cowley take from his own experience? Upon what other sources of examples does he draw?
3. Where in his essay does the author capitalize on the fact that he is himself an old man? To what extent does his age heighten his credibility?
4. What RHETORICAL QUESTIONS does Cowley pose in paragraphs 1, 8, 9, and 10? What do they contribute?
5. Take a close look at paragraph 16. In what sentence or sentences do you find the main idea? What two examples serve to illustrate it?
6. In the next paragraph (17), the example of Giovanni Papini seems to illustrate the same general truth; for what possible reason does Cowley make it a separate paragraph?
7. What final EFFECT does Cowley achieve by his quotation from Paul Claudel? From the essay as a whole, do you have the sense that Cowley approves or disapproves of Claudel's observation?

QUESTIONS ON LANGUAGE

1. Consult your dictionary for definitions of these words: succumbed (paragraph 3); lethargy (6); querulously (8); precedence, prerogatives (9); indolence (10); nirvana, climactic (11); stoical (13); firmament (14); unvanquished (16); atrophy (17).

2. Cowley says of the aging person, "In his new makeup he is called upon to play a new role in a play that must be improvised" (paragraph 1). What is his "new makeup"? What is the "play that must be improvised"?

SUGGESTIONS FOR WRITING

1. In your own essay, concoct a recipe for growing old gracefully.
2. Using examples to illustrate, as Cowley does, write an essay about the virtues, vices, and compensations of people your own age.

· Roger Rosenblatt ·

ROGER ROSENBLATT, born in 1940, received his Ph.D. from Harvard and served from 1970 to 1973 as director of the expository writing program there. Deciding to leave the academic world, he moved to Washington, D.C., where he became literary editor of *The New Republic* and a columnist and member of the editorial board of the Washington *Post*. Now a senior writer for *Time* magazine, he has written one book of literary criticism, *Black Fiction* (1974), and *Children of War* (1983), a survey of the effects of political violence on children around the world.

Oops! How's That Again?

For the past few years *Time* has been printing a weekly essay on a large and significant general subject. "Oops! How's That Again?", a contribution to this series, appeared in 1981. Rosenblatt, despite a space limit imposed on him, manages to enrich his discussion with memorable examples; and although, as befits its subject, the tone of his essay is humorous, Rosenblatt is concerned with the psychological causes of bloopers. The essay is funny, but it is much more.

"That is not what I meant at all. That is not it, at all."
— T. S. Eliot, "The Love Song of J. Alfred Prufrock"

At a royal luncheon in Glasgow last month, Businessman   1
Peter Balfour turned to the just-engaged Prince Charles and wished him long life and conjugal happiness with Lady Jane. The effect of the sentiment was compromised both by the fact that the Prince's betrothed is Lady Diana (Spencer) and that Lady Jane (Wellesley) is one of his former flames. "I feel a perfect fool," said Balfour, who was unnecessarily contrite. Slips of the tongue occur all the time. In Chicago recently, Governor James Thompson was introduced as "the mayor of Illinois," which was a step

down from the time he was introduced as "the Governor of the United States." Not all such fluffs are so easy to take, however. During the primaries, Nancy Reagan telephoned her husband as her audience listened in, to say how delighted she was to be looking at all "the beautiful white people." And France's Prime Minister Raymond Barre, who has a reputation for putting his *pied* in his *bouche*, described last October's bombing of a Paris synagogue as "this odious attack that was aimed at Jews and that struck at innocent Frenchmen" — a crack that not only implied Jews were neither innocent nor French but also suggested that the attack would have been less odious had it been more limited.

One hesitates to call Barre sinister, but the fact is that verbal errors can have a devastating effect on those who hear them and on those who make them as well. Jimmy Carter never fully recovered from his reference to Polish lusts for the future in a mistranslated speech in 1977, nor was Chicago's Mayor Daley ever quite the same after assuring the public that "the policeman isn't there to create disorder, the policeman is there to preserve disorder." Dwight Eisenhower, John Kennedy, Spiro Agnew, Gerald Ford, all made terrible gaffes, with Ford perhaps making the most unusual ("Whenever I can I always watch the Detroit Tigers on radio"). Yet this is no modern phenomenon. The term *faux pas* goes back at least as far as the seventeenth century, having originally referred to a woman's lapse from virtue. Not that women lapse more than men in this regard. Even Marie Antoinette's fatal remark about cake and the public, if true, was due to poor translation.

In fact, mistranslation accounts for a great share of verbal errors. The slogan "Come Alive with Pepsi" failed understandably in German when it was translated: "Come Alive out of the Grave with Pepsi." Elsewhere it was translated with more precision: "Pepsi Brings Your Ancestors Back from the Grave." In 1965, prior to a reception for Queen Elizabeth II outside Bonn, Germany's President Heinrich Lübke, attempting an English translation of *"Gleich geht es los"* (It will soon begin), told the Queen: "Equal goes it loose." The Queen took the news well, but no better than the President of India, who was greeted at an airport in 1962 by Lübke, who, intending to ask, "How are you?" instead said: "Who are you?" To which his guest answered responsibly: "I am the President of India."

The most prodigious collector of modern slips was Kermit   4
Schafer, whose "blooper" records of mistakes made on radio and television consisted largely of toilet jokes, but were nonetheless a great hit in the 1950s. Schafer was an avid self-promoter and something of a blooper himself, but he did have an ear for such things as the introduction by Radio Announcer Harry von Zell of President "Hoobert Heever," as well as the interesting message: "This portion of *Women on the Run* is brought to you by Phillips' Milk of Magnesia." Bloopers are the lowlife of verbal error, but spoonerisms are a different fettle of kitsch. In the early 1900s the Rev. William Archibald Spooner caused a stir at New College, Oxford, with his famous spoonerisms, most of which were either deliberate or apocryphal. But a real one — his giving out a hymn in chapel as "Kinquering Kongs Their Titles Take" — is said to have brought down the house of worship, and to have kicked off the genre. After that, spoonerisms got quite elaborate. Spooner once reportedly chided a student: "You have hissed all my mystery lectures. In fact, you have tasted the whole worm, and must leave by the first town drain."

Such missteps, while often howlingly funny to ignorami like   5
us, are deadly serious concerns to psychologists and linguists. Victoria Fromkin of the linguistics department at U.C.L.A. regards slips of the tongue as clues to how the brain stores and articulates language. She believes that thought is placed by the brain into a grammatical framework before it is expressed — this in spite of the fact that she works with college students. A grammatical framework was part of Walter Annenberg's trouble when, as the newly appointed U.S. Ambassador to Britain, he was asked by the Queen how he was settling in to his London residence. Annenberg admitted to "some discomfiture as a result of a need for elements of refurbishing." Either he was overwhelmed by the circumstance or he was losing his mind.

When you get to that sort of error, you are nearing a psy-   6
chological abyss. It was Freud who first removed the element of accident from language with his explanation of "slips," but lately

others have extended his theories. Psychiatrist Richard Yazmajian, for example, suggests that there are some incorrect words that exist in associative chains with the correct ones for which they are substituted, implying a kind of "dream pair" of elements in the speaker's psyche. The nun who poured tea for the Irish bishop and asked, "How many lords, my lump?" might therefore have been asking a profound theological question.

On another front, Psychoanalyst Ludwig Eidelberg made   7
Freud's work seem childishly simple when he suggested that a slip of the tongue involves the entire network of id, ego and superego. He offers the case of the young man who entered a restaurant with his girlfriend and ordered a room instead of a table. You probably think that you understand that error. But just listen to Eidelberg: "All the wishes connected with the word 'room' represented a countercathexis mobilized as a defense. The word 'table' had to be omitted, because it would have been used for infantile gratification of a repressed oral, aggressive and scopophilic wish connected with identification with the preoedipal mother." Clearly, this is no laughing matter.

Why then do we hoot at these mistakes? For one thing, it   8
may be that we simply find conventional discourse so predictable and boring that any deviation comes as a delightful relief. In his deeply unfunny *Essay on Laughter* the philosopher Henri Bergson theorized that the act of laughter is caused by any interruption of normal human fluidity or momentum (a pie in the face, a mask, a pun). Slips of the tongue, therefore, are like slips on banana peels; we crave their occurrence if only to break the monotonies. The monotonies run to substance. When that announcer introduced Hoobert Heever, he may also have been saying that the nation had had enough of Herbert Hoover.

Then too there is the element of pure meanness in such   9
laughter, both the meanness of enjoyment in watching an embarrassed misspeaker's eyes roll upward as if in prayer — his hue turn magenta, his hands like homing larks fluttering to his mouth — and the mean joy of discovering his hidden base motives and critical intent. At the 1980 Democratic National Convention, Jimmy Carter took a lot of heat for referring to Hubert Humphrey as Hubert Horatio Hornblower because it was in-

stantly recognized that Carter thought Humphrey a windbag.
David Hartman of *Good Morning America* left little doubt about
his feelings for a sponsor when he announced: "We'll be right
back after this word from General Fools." At a conference in
Berlin in 1954, France's Foreign Minister Georges Bidault was
hailed as "that fine little French tiger, Georges Bidet," thus belit-
tling the tiger by the tail. When we laugh at such stuff, it is the
harsh and bitter laugh, the laugh at the disclosure of inner con-
demning truth.

Yet there is also a more kindly laugh that occurs when a   10
blunderer does not reveal his worst inner thoughts, but his most
charitable or optimistic. Gerald Ford's famous error in the 1976
presidential debate, in which he said that Poland was not under
Soviet domination, for instance. In a way, that turned out to
contain a grain of truth, thanks to Lech Walesa and the strikes;
in any case it was a nice thing to wish. As was U.N. Ambassador
Warren Austin's suggestion in 1948 that Jews and Arabs resolve
their differences "in a true Christian spirit." Similarly, Nebras-
ka's former Senator Kenneth Wherry might have been thinking
dreamily when, in an hour-long speech on a country in Southeast Asia, he referred throughout to "Indigo-China." One has to
be in the mood for such a speech.

Of course, the most interesting laugh is the one elicited by   11
the truly bizarre mistake, because such a mistake seems to dis-
close a whole new world of logic and possibility, a deranged double for the life that is. What Lewis Carroll displayed through the
looking glass, verbal error also often displays by conjuring up
ideas so supremely nutty that the laughter it evokes is sublime.
The idea that Pepsi might actually bring one back from the
grave encourages an entirely new view of experience. In such a
view it is perfectly possible to lust after the Polish future, to
watch the Tigers on the radio, to say "Equal goes it loose" with
resounding clarity.

Still, beyond all this is another laugh entirely, that neither   12
condemns, praises, ridicules nor conspires, but sees into the essential nature of a slip of the tongue and consequently sympa-
thizes. After all, most human endeavor results in a slip of the
something — the best-laid plans gone suddenly haywire by nat-

ural blunder: the chair, cake or painting that turns out not exactly as one imagined; the kiss or party that falls flat; the life that
is not quite what one had in mind. Nothing is ever as dreamed.

So we laugh at each other, perfect fools all, flustered by the   13
mistake of our mortality.

QUESTIONS ON MEANING AND PURPOSE

1. In which paragraphs of Rosenblatt's essay do you find any of these
   PURPOSES: to illustrate different kinds of verbal errors, to probe
   why they happen, to explain why we laugh at them, or simply to
   entertain us? Which seems Rosenblatt's main purpose?
2. Quote the famous remark by Marie Antoinette to which Rosenblatt refers in paragraph 2.
3. What explanations does Rosenblatt advance for the human tendency to make verbal errors? Is the reader meant to regard all of
   the theories with equal seriousness?
4. What relationship does Rosenblatt discover between verbal errors
   and the work of Lewis Carroll?
5. What examples of verbal error (public blunders, memorable mis-
   translations, "bloopers," spoonerisms) have you heard or read
   about recently? When you cite one that seems particularly revealing, take a guess at its possible cause.

QUESTIONS ON WRITING STRATEGY

1. What is the TOPIC SENTENCE in paragraph 2? In illustrating
   this general statement, how many examples does Rosenblatt give?
   Where does he draw them from?
2. Into what groups has Rosenblatt organized his numerous examples
   of verbal missteps?
3. What EFFECT does the author achieve by using the first PER-
   SON plural in his CONCLUSION?
4. Recall the fact that this essay first appeared in *Time*, a news magazine whose AUDIENCE largely consists of people in business and
   in the professions (medicine, law, teaching, media, technology).
   Why would you expect such readers to find verbal errors a subject
   of personal interest?

QUESTIONS ON LANGUAGE

1. Rosenblatt occasionally uses French words. Be sure you know the meanings of *pied, bouche* (paragraph 1), and *faux pas* (2); and you will more fully appreciate the humor in paragraph 9 if you know what a *bidet* is.
2. Look up *bar sinister* in the dictionary. Then explain Rosenblatt's play on words when he says, "One hesitates to call Barre sinister. . . ." (paragraph 2).
3. From examples that the author gives in paragraph 4, explain what a *spoonerism* is. What is *kitsch*?

SUGGESTIONS FOR WRITING

1. If you have ever had the experience of putting your *pied* in your *bouche*, recount it and its consequences. You might, as an alternative, tell how this fate befell someone else.
2. Examine some other variety of verbal behavior for which you can collect enough examples. (Some possibilities: nicknames, sportswriters' colorful figures of speech, coined words, slang, the invented names of fast foods, the special vocabulary of a subculture such as runners or poker players, dialect and regional speech.) Like Rosenblatt, give examples and then try to account for the phenomenon they exemplify.

─── POSTSCRIPT ON PROCESS ───

Roger Rosenblatt

Writers don't always know when they sit down to write what direction their words will take. Roger Rosenblatt got his essay started by doing the easy part first. As he wrote, ideas surfaced and took shape. And throughout the process, the author managed to keep one eye on his audience.

How did I write this essay? You never know the whole answer to that question. But I can swear to one thing: I had no idea when I started out that the piece would end up where it did. All I had in the beginning was the slip of the tongue concerning Prince Charles. That led to recollections of similar slips. Then I consulted books (there are collections of such things), and asked friends and colleagues what bloopers they could recall. Soon I had a pile of quite funny material, the breadth and variety of which suggested a possible subject for an essay. But an essay, unlike an article, requires both the identification of a phenomenon and some explanation of it. My essay, then, had to be about the why and what of verbal errors. Not having considered the matter before — and suspecting that my readers had not either — I decided to present most of my examples within the opening paragraphs, and to proceed from there. Indeed, the first third of the essay consists almost entirely of examples covering the range of the subject.

When dealing with a humorous subject, there are two advantages in spreading out one's examples as early as possible. For one thing, the examples warm up the audience; even before knowing what the essay is going to be about, people will feel kindly toward it. (Readers are impatient animals, and as a general rule I find that it helps to win their interest or affection within the first couple of sentences.) Second, by spilling most of my beans in the beginning I was able to tell the readers in effect: Let's lap up this material, but let's also put it behind us, since we may be getting to more serious business later on. In other words, if the readers get most of the horse laughs out of their systems at the outset, they may sooner, on their own, arrive at the question, "What am I laughing at?" which is also the central question of the essay.

To get to that question, I felt the need of a bridge, thus the   3
three paragraphs in the middle of the piece about psychological analyses. It is always unfair to call upon psychologists in a humorous essay (psychologists being clownish figures in American culture), but their function here was not merely as goats. They allowed me to make a transition between an atmosphere of jokes and one of contemplation while retaining a sense of fun ("Clearly, this is no laughing matter"). They also allowed me to keep the readers on my side, for by making the psychologists run interference for me, I was able to go beyond the explanations offered by the experts and ask, "Why do *we* laugh at verbal errors?" By such devices an essayist can assume a just-plain-folks voice, which is a very good voice for lecturing.

A note on voice. I found it tricky to control the tone of the   4
essay, and I'm still not sure that I got it right. What I sought was a voice that was at once superior to the people making the verbal errors (since laughter usually derives from feelings of superiority) and, at the same time, sympathetic. Perhaps subconsciously I was anticipating the essay's final point, long before it actually occurred to me, by creating a tone that would be consistent with it. Why I punned so often, I cannot explain. Punning cools a tone, and I may have wanted to avoid any hint of warmth in the piece until the very end.

The "lecture" or substance of the essay occurs in the final six   5
paragraphs, where five discrete explanations are offered for why we laugh at slips of the tongue. By the time I got to this point in the writing, I had begun to brood on the subject and was able to come up with some definite reasons for the phenomenon. The process of this sort of thinking is always mysterious to me; you hit upon idea after idea, all of which stay fairly close to the subject. Then suddenly something strikes you that is much wider and deeper than the matter at hand, but is nonetheless connected to it. Technically one calls this a generalization, but it seems much more. In a way it is a leap of faith, a taking-off from

a small particular into everything that is most wonderful and terrible about our lives.

Whenever this happens, I wonder if the thought was always   6
there in the first place, lying hidden, waiting for some event to spring it free. No discussion of process will explain such things satisfactorily.

1. Select one of the following general statements, or set forth a general statement of your own that one of these inspires. Making it your central idea (or THESIS), maintain it in an essay full of examples. Draw your examples from your reading, your studies, your conversation, or your own experience.

   People one comes to admire don't always at first seem likable.
   Fashions this year are loonier than ever before.
   Bad habits are necessary to the nation's economy.
   Each family has its distinctive life-style.
   Certain song lyrics, closely inspected, will prove obscene.
   Comic books are going to the dogs.
   At some point in life, most people triumph over crushing difficulties.
   Churchgoers aren't perfect.
   TV commercials suggest: Buy this product and your love life will improve like crazy.
   Home cooking can't win over fast food.
   Ordinary lives sometimes give rise to legends.
   Some people I know are born winners (or losers).
   Books can change our lives.
   Certain machines *do* have personalities.
   Some road signs lead drivers astray.

2. In a brief essay, make some GENERALIZATION about either the terrors or the joys that ethnic minorities seem to share. To illustrate your generalization, draw examples from personal experience, from outside reading, or from two or three of the following *Bedford Reader* essays: Maya Angelou's "Champion of the World" and Maxine Hong Kingston's "My Legal Father Enters America" in Chapter 1; A. M. Rosenthal's "No News from Auschwitz" in Chapter 4; Dick Gregory's "If You Had To Kill Your Own Hog" in Chapter 7; Martin Luther King, Jr.'s "I Have A Dream" and Richard Rodriguez's "Aria" in Chapter 10.

4

COMPARISON
AND CONTRAST

Setting Things Side by Side

THE METHOD

Should we pass laws to regulate pornography, or just let pornography run wild? Which team do you place your money on, the Dolphins or the Colts? To go to school full-time or part-time: what are the rewards and drawbacks of each way of life? How do the Republican and the Democratic platforms stack up against each other? How is the work of Picasso like or unlike that of Matisse? These are questions that may be addressed by the dual method of *comparison and contrast*. In comparing, you point to similarities; in contrasting, to differences. Together, the two strategies use one subject to explain or clarify another by setting the two side by side.

With the aid of this method, you can show why you prefer one thing to another, one course of action to another, one idea to another. In an argument in which you support one of two possible choices, a careful and detailed comparison and contrast of the choices may be extremely convincing. In an expository essay, it can demonstrate that you understand your subjects thoroughly. That is why, on exams that call for essay answers, often you will be asked to compare and contrast. Sometimes the examiner will come right out and say, "Compare and contrast nineteenth-century methods of treating drug addiction with those of the present day." Sometimes, however, comparison and contrast won't even be mentioned by name; instead, the examiner will ask, "What resemblances and differences do you find between John Updike's short story 'A & P' and the Grimm fairy tale 'Godfather Death'?" Or, "Evaluate the relative desirability of holding a franchise as against going into business as an independent proprietor." But those — as you realize when you begin to plan your reply — are just other ways of asking you to compare and contrast.

In practice, the two methods are usually inseparable. A little reflection will show you why you need both. Say you intend to write a portrait-in-words of two people. No two people are in every respect exactly the same, or entirely dissimilar. Simply to compare them, or to contrast them, would not be true to life. To set them side by side and portray them accurately, you must consider both similarities and differences.

A good essay in comparing and contrasting serves a purpose. Most of the time, the writer of such an essay has one of two purposes in mind:

1. *The purpose of showing each of two subjects distinctly by considering both side by side.* Writing with such a purpose, the writer doesn't necessarily find one of the subjects better than the other. In "The Black and White Truth about Basketball" in this chapter, Jeff Greenfield details two styles of playing the game; and his conclusion is not that either black or white basketball is the more beautiful, but that the two styles can complement each other on the same court.

2. *The purpose of evaluating, or judging between two things.* In daily life, we often compare and contrast two possibilities to choose between them: which college course to elect, which

movie to see, which luncheon special to take — chipped beef over green noodles or fried smelt on a bun? Our thinking on a matter such as the last is quick and informal: "Hmmmm, the smelt *looks* better. Red beef, green noodles — ugh, what a sight! Smelt has bones, but the beef is rubbery. Still, I don't like the smell of that smelt. I'll go for the beef (or maybe just grab a hamburger after class)." In essays, too, a writer, by comparing points, decides which of two things is more admirable: "Organic Gardening, Yes; Gardening with Chemical Fertilizers, No!" — or "Skydiving versus the Safe, Sane Life." In writing, as in thinking, you need to consider the main features of both subjects, the positive features and the negative, and to choose the subject whose positive features more clearly predominate.

THE PROCESS

The first step in comparing and contrasting is to select subjects that will display a clear basis for comparison. In other words, you have to pick two subjects that have enough in common to be worth placing side by side. You'll have the best luck if you choose two of a kind: two California wines, two mystery writers, two schools of political thought. You can't readily compare and contrast, say, bowling in America with teacher training in Sweden, because the basis for comparison isn't apparent. You'll need to show your reader a valid reason for bringing the two together. From the title of his essay "Grant and Lee," Bruce Catton leads us to expect insights into the characters of the two Civil War generals. But in an essay called "General Grant and Mick Jagger," you would be hard-pressed to find any real basis for comparison. Although the writer might wax ingenious and claim, "Like Grant, Jagger has posed a definite threat to Nashville," the ingenuity would wear thin and soon the yoking together of general and rock star would fall apart.

The basis for comparison has to be carefully limited. You would be overly ambitious to try to compare and contrast the Soviet way of life with the American way of life in 500 words; you probably couldn't include all the important similarities and differences. In a brief paper, you would be wise to select a single point: to show, for instance, how day care centers in Russia and the United States are both alike and dissimilar.

Students occasionally groan when asked to compare and contrast things; but, in fact, this method isn't difficult. You have only to plan your paper carefully, make an outline (in your head or on paper), and then follow it. Here are two usual ways to compare and contrast:

1. *Subject by subject.* Set forth all your facts about Subject A, then do the same for Subject B. Next, sum up their similarities and differences. In your conclusion, state what you think you have shown. This procedure works for a paper of a couple of paragraphs, but for a longer one, it has a built-in disadvantage. Readers need to remember all the facts about Subject A while they read about Subject B. If the essay is long and lists many facts, this procedure may burden the reader.

2. *Point by point.* Usually more workable in writing a long paper than the first method, a different method is to compare and contrast as you go. You consider one point at a time, taking up your two subjects alternately. In this way, you continually bring the subjects together, perhaps in every paragraph. Your outline might look like this:

TITLE: "Jed and Jake: Two Bluegrass Banjo-pickers"

PURPOSE: To show the distinct identities of the two musicians

INTRODUCTION: Who are Jed and Jake?

1. *Training*
    Jed: studied under Scruggs
    Jake: studied under Segovia

2. *Choice of material*
    Jed: traditional
    Jake: innovative

3. *Technical dexterity*
    Jed: highly skilled
    Jake: highly skilled

4. *Playing style*
    Jed: likes to show off
    Jake: keeps work simple

5. *On-stage manner*
    Jed: theatrical
    Jake: cool and reserved

CONCLUSION

And your conclusion might be: Although similar in degree of skill, the two differ greatly in aims and in personalities. Jed is better suited to the Grand Ol' Opry; Jake, to a concert hall. Now, this is a more extensive outline than you would need for a brief (say, 250-word) essay; but it might be fine for an essay of seven substantial paragraphs. (If you were writing only 250 words, you might not need any formal outline at all. You might just say your say about Jed, then do the same for Jake, briefly sum up the differences and similarities between the two, and then conclude.) Another way to organize a longer paper would be to group together all the similarities, then group together all the differences. No matter how you group your points, they have to balance; you can't discuss Jed's on-stage manner without discussing Jake's too. If you have nothing to say about Jake's on-stage manner, then you might as well omit the point.

As you write, an outline will help you see the shape of your paper, and keep your procedure in mind. A sure-fire loser is the paper that proposes to compare and contrast two subjects and then proceeds to discuss quite different elements in each: Jed's playing style and Jake's choice of material, Jed's fondness for smelt on a bun and Jake's hobby of antique car collecting. The writer of such a paper doesn't compare and contrast the two musicians at all, but provides two quite separate discussions.

By the way, comparison and contrast works most efficiently for a *pair* of subjects. If you want to write about *three* banjo-pickers, you might first consider Jed and Jake, then Jake and Josh, then Josh and Jed — but it would probably be easiest to compare and contrast all three point by point.

In writing an essay of this variety, you may find an outline your firmest friend, but don't be the simple tool of your outline. Few essays are more boring to read than the long comparison-and-contrast written mechanically. The reader comes to feel like a weary tennis spectator, whose head has to swivel from side to side: now Jed, now back to Jake; now Jed again, now back to Jake again. No law decrees that an outline has to be followed in lock-step order, nor that a list of similarities and a list of differences must be of the same length, nor that if you spend fifty words discussing Jed's banjo-picking skill, you are obliged to give Jake his fifty, too. Your essay, remember, doesn't need to be as symmetrical as a pair of salt and pepper shakers. What is your outline but a simple means to organize your account of a complicated reality? As you write, keep casting your thoughts upon a living, particular world — not twisting and squeezing that world into a rigid scheme, but moving through it with open senses, being patient and faithful and exact in your telling of it.

COMPARISON AND CONTRAST
IN A PARAGRAPH

Seen on aged 16-millimeter film, the original production of Paddy Chayevsky's "Marty" makes clear the differences between television drama of 1953 and that of today. Today there's no weekly Goodyear Playhouse to showcase original one-hour plays; most scriptwriters write serials about familiar characters. "Marty" features no car chases, no bodice ripping, no "Dallas" mansion. Instead, it simply shows the awakening of love between a heavyset butcher and a mousy high-school teacher: both single, lonely, and shy, never twice dating the same person. Unlike the writer of today, Chayevsky couldn't set scenes outdoors or on location. In one small studio, in slow lingering takes (some five minutes long — not eight to twelve seconds, as we now expect), the camera probes the faces of two seated characters as Marty and his pal Angie plan Saturday night ("What do you want to do?" — "I dunno, what do *you*?") Oddly, the effect is spellbinding. To bring such scenes to life, the actors must project with vigor; and like the finer actors of today, Rod Steiger as Marty exploits each moment. In 1953, plays were telecast live. Today, well-edited videotape may eliminate blown lines, but a chill slickness prevails. Technically, "Marty" is primitive, yet it probes souls. Most televised drama today displays a physically larger world — only to nail a box around it.

Comment. The writer of this closely knit paragraph compares and contrasts televised drama of today with drama of television's so-called Golden Age — in particular, "Marty," an outstanding example. Most of his paragraph is taken up with differences. That both eras of television have actors who make the most of their time on screen is the one similarity he notices. In building his paragraph, the writer followed this outline:

1. *Today*: mostly serials
   Then: Goodyear Playhouse, weekly series of new plays
2. *Today*: violence, sex, luxury
   Then: simplicity
3. *Today*: scenes outdoors, on location
   Then: one small studio
4. *Today*: brief takes
   Then: long, slow takes
5. *Today*: good acting
   Then: good acting
6. *Today*: plays videotaped
   Then: plays telecast live
7. *Conclusion*: TV drama today shows a more limited world.

In fulfilling this outline, the writer didn't proceed in a rigid, mechanical alternation of *Today* and *Then*, but took each point in whatever order came naturally. This is a long outline, as a paragraph so full and meaty required, and it might have sufficed for a whole essay had the writer wanted to develop his comparison at greater length with the aid of other examples.

· Bruce Catton ·

BRUCE CATTON (1899–1978) was a Michigan-born newspaper-man who became one of America's leading historians of the Civil War. His book *A Stillness at Appomattox* (1953) earned him both the Pulitzer Prize for the writing of history and the National Book Award. In addition, Catton's many works include *Mr. Lincoln's Army* (1951), *The Hallowed Ground* (1956), *Waiting for the Morning Train: An American Boyhood* (1972), and *Gettysburg: The Final Fury* (1974).

Grant and Lee:
A Study in Contrasts

"Grant and Lee: A Study in Contrasts" first appeared in *The American Story*, a book of essays written by eminent historians. In his discussion of the two great Civil War generals, Catton contrasts not only two very different men, but the conflicting traditions they represented. Catton's essay builds toward the conclusion that, in one outstanding way, the two leaders were more than a little alike.

When Ulysses S. Grant and Robert E. Lee met in the parlor   1
of a modest house at Appomattox Court House, Virginia, on
April 9, 1865, to work out the terms for the surrender of Lee's
Army of Northern Virginia, a great chapter in American life
came to a close, and a great new chapter began.

These men were bringing the Civil War to its virtual finish.   2
To be sure, other armies had yet to surrender, and for a few days
the fugitive Confederate government would struggle desperately
and vainly, trying to find some way to go on living now that its
chief support was gone. But in effect it was all over when Grant
and Lee signed the papers. And the little room where they wrote
out the terms was the scene of one of the poignant, dramatic
contrasts in American history.

They were two strong men, these oddly different generals,   3 and they represented the strengths of two conflicting currents that, through them, had come into final collision.

Back of Robert E. Lee was the notion that the old aristo-   4
cratic concept might somehow survive and be dominant in American life.

Lee was tidewater Virginia, and in his background were   5
family, culture, and tradition . . . the age of chivalry trans-
planted to a New World which was making its own legends and its own myths. He embodied a way of life that had come down through the age of knighthood and the English country squire. America was a land that was beginning all over again, dedicated to nothing much more complicated than the rather hazy belief that all men had equal rights, and should have an equal chance in the world. In such a land Lee stood for the feeling that it was somehow of advantage to human society to have a pronounced inequality in the social structure. There should be a leisure class, backed by ownership of land; in turn, society itself should be keyed to the land as the chief source of wealth and influence. It would bring forth (according to this ideal) a class of men with a strong sense of obligation to the community; men who lived not to gain advantage for themselves, but to meet the solemn obliga-
tions which had been laid on them by the very fact that they were privileged. From them the country would get its leadership; to them it could look for the higher values — of thought, of con-
duct, of personal deportment — to give it strength and virtue.

Lee embodied the noblest elements of this aristocratic ideal.   6
Through him, the landed nobility justified itself. For four years, the Southern states had fought a desperate war to uphold the ideals for which Lee stood. In the end, it almost seemed as if the Confederacy fought for Lee; as if he himself was the Confederacy . . . the best thing that the way of life for which the Confed-
eracy stood could ever have to offer. He had passed into legend before Appomattox. Thousands of tired, underfed, poorly clothed Confederate soldiers, long-since past the simple enthusi-
asm of the early days of the struggle, somehow considered Lee the symbol of everything for which they had been willing to die. But they could not quite put this feeling into words. If the Lost Cause, sanctified by so much heroism and so many deaths, had a living justification, its justification was General Lee.

Grant, the son of a tanner on the Western frontier, was ev-   7
erything Lee was not. He had come up the hard way, and embodied nothing in particular except the eternal toughness and
sinewy fiber of the men who grew up beyond the mountains. He
was one of a body of men who owed reverence and obeisance to
no one, who were self-reliant to a fault, who cared hardly anything for the past but who had a sharp eye for the future.

These frontier men were the precise opposites of the tidewa-   8
ter aristocrats. Back of them, in the great surge that had taken
people over the Alleghenies and into the opening Western country, there was a deep, implicit dissatisfaction with a past that
had settled into grooves. They stood for democracy, not from
any reasoned conclusion about the proper ordering of human
society, but simply because they had grown up in the middle of
democracy and knew how it worked. Their society might have
privileges, but they would be privileges each man had won for
himself. Forms and patterns meant nothing. No man was born
to anything, except perhaps to a chance to show how far he
could rise. Life was competition.

Yet along with this feeling had come a deep sense of belong-   9
ing to a national community. The Westerner who developed a
farm, opened a shop or set up in business as a trader, could hope
to prosper only as his own community prospered — and his
community ran from the Atlantic to the Pacific and from Canada down to Mexico. If the land was settled, with towns and
highways and accessible markets, he could better himself. He
saw his fate in terms of the nation's own destiny. As its horizons
expanded, so did his. He had, in other words, an acute dollars-
and-cents stake in the continued growth and development of his
country.

And that, perhaps, is where the contrast between Grant   10
and Lee becomes most striking. The Virginia aristocrat, inevitably, saw himself in relation to his own region. He lived in a static
society which could endure almost anything except change. Instinctively, his first loyalty would go to the locality in which that
society existed. He would fight to the limit of endurance to defend it, because in defending it he was defending everything that
gave his own life its deepest meaning.

The Westerner, on the other hand, would fight with an 11 equal tenacity for the broader concept of society. He fought so because everything he lived by was tied to growth, expansion, and a constantly widening horizon. What he lived by would survive or fall with the nation itself. He could not possibly stand by unmoved in the face of an attempt to destroy the Union. He would combat it with everything he had, because he could only see it as an effort to cut the ground out from under his feet.

So Grant and Lee were in complete contrast, representing 12 two diametrically opposed elements in American life. Grant was the modern man emerging; beyond him, ready to come on the stage, was the great age of steel and machinery, of crowded cities and a restless, burgeoning vitality. Lee might have ridden down from the old age of chivalry, lance in hand, silken banner fluttering over his head. Each man was the perfect champion of his cause, drawing both his strengths and his weaknesses from the people he led.

Yet it was not all contrast, after all. Different as they were — 13 in background, in personality, in underlying aspiration — these two great soldiers had much in common. Under everything else, they were marvelous fighters. Furthermore, their fighting qualities were really very much alike.

Each man had, to begin with, the great virtue of utter tenac- 14 ity and fidelity. Grant fought his way down the Mississippi Valley in spite of acute personal discouragement and profound military handicaps. Lee hung on in the trenches at Petersburg after hope itself had died. In each man there was an indomitable quality . . . the born fighter's refusal to give up as long as he can still remain on his feet and lift his two fists.

Daring and resourcefulness they had, too; the ability to 15 think faster and move faster than the enemy. These were the qualities which gave Lee the dazzling campaigns of Second Manassas and Chancellorsville and won Vicksburg for Grant.

Lastly, and perhaps greatest of all, there was the ability, at 16 the end, to turn quickly from war to peace once the fighting was over. Out of the way these two men behaved at Appomattox came the possibility of a peace of reconciliation. It was a possibility not wholly realized, in the years to come, but which did, in

the end, help the two sections to become one nation again . . .
after a war whose bitterness might have seemed to make such a
reunion wholly impossible. No part of either man's life became
him more than the part he played in their brief meeting in the
McLean house at Appomattox. Their behavior there put all succeeding generations of Americans in their debt. Two great
Americans, Grant and Lee — very different, yet under everything very much alike. Their encounter at Appomattox was one
of the great moments of American history.

QUESTIONS ON MEANING AND PURPOSE

1. What is Bruce Catton's PURPOSE in writing: to describe the
   meeting of two generals in a famous moment in history; to explain
   how the two men stood for opposing social forces in America; or
   to show how the two differed in personality?
2. Summarize the background and the way of life that produced Robert E. Lee; then do the same for Ulysses S. Grant. According to
   Catton, what ideals did each man represent?
3. In the historian's view, what essential traits did the two men have
   in common? Which trait does Catton think most important of all?
   For what reason?
4. How does this essay help you understand why Grant and Lee were
   such determined fighters?
5. Although slavery, along with other issues, helped precipitate the
   Civil War, Catton in this particular essay does not deal with it. If
   he had recalled the facts of slavery, would he have destroyed his
   thesis that Lee had a "strong sense of obligation to the community"? (*What* community?)

QUESTIONS ON WRITING STRATEGY

1. From the content of this essay, and from knowing where it first appeared, what can you infer about Catton's original AUDIENCE?
   At what places in his essay does the writer expect of his readers a
   great familiarity with United States history?
2. What effect does the writer achieve by setting both his INTRO-
   DUCTION and his CONCLUSION in Appomattox?

3. For what reasons does Catton contrast the two generals *before* he compares them? Suppose he had reversed his outline, and had dealt first with Grant and Lee's mutual resemblances. Why would his essay have been less effective?

4. Pencil in hand, draw a single line down the margin of every paragraph in which you find the method of contrast. Then draw a *double* line next to every paragraph in which you find the method of comparison. How much space does Catton devote to each method? Why didn't he give comparison and contrast equal time?

5. Closely read the first sentence of every paragraph and underline each word or phrase in it that serves as a TRANSITION. Then review your underlinings. How much COHERENCE has Catton given his essay?

6. What is the TONE of this essay — that is, what is the writer's attitude toward his two subjects? Is Catton poking fun at Lee by imagining the Confederate general as a knight of the Middle Ages, "lance in hand, silken banner fluttering over his head" (paragraph 12)?

7. Does Catton's treatment of the two generals as SYMBOLS obscure the reader's sense of them as individuals? (Lee, at least, is called a symbol in paragraph 6.) Discuss this question, keeping in mind what you decided to be Catton's purpose in writing his essay.

QUESTIONS ON LANGUAGE

1. In his opening paragraph, Catton uses a METAPHOR: American life is a book containing chapters. Find other FIGURES OF SPEECH in his essay. What do they contribute?

2. Look up *poignant* in the dictionary. Why is it such a fitting word in paragraph 2? Why wouldn't *touching*, *sad*, or *teary* have been as good?

3. What information do you glean from the sentence, "Lee was tidewater Virginia" (paragraph 5)?

4. Define *aristocratic* as Catton uses it in paragraphs 4 and 6.

5. Define obeisance (paragraph 7); indomitable (14).

SUGGESTIONS FOR WRITING

1. Compare and contrast two other figures of American history with whom you are familiar: Franklin D. Roosevelt and John F. Kennedy, Lincoln and Douglas, or Susan B. Anthony and Elizabeth Cady Stanton — to suggest only a few.

2. In a brief essay full of specific examples, discuss: Do the "two diametrically opposed elements in American life" (as Catton calls them) still exist in the country today? Are there still any "landed nobility"?

3. In your thinking and your attitudes, whom do you more closely resemble — Grant or Lee? Compare and contrast your outlook with that of one famous American or the other. (A serious tone for this topic isn't required.)

· John Updike ·

Born in 1932 in Shillingford, Pennsylvania, JOHN UPDIKE received his A.B. degree from Harvard in 1954, then spent a year in England at Oxford University's Ruskin School of Drawing and Fine Art. From 1955 to 1957 he worked on the staff of *The New Yorker*, a magazine to which he has long contributed. The author of more than two dozen books — including short stories, serious poetry and light verse for both adults and children, book reviews, critical writing, and essays — Updike is best known as a novelist of great variety and dazzling skill. *The Centaur* (1963) received the National Book Award; more recently, *Rabbit Is Rich* (1982) garnered the Pulitzer Prize and the American Book Award for fiction and a National Book Critics Circle award. *The Witches of Eastwick* (1984) also has been much talked about.

Venezuela for Visitors

Updike has included "Venezuela for Visitors," first published in *The New Yorker*, in *Hugging the Shore: Essays and Criticism* (1983). In this richly detailed essay, the author calls attention to some surprising similarities between the rich in Venezuela and the poor, who are Indians. As Updike details them, however, the similarities have the curious, inside-out effect of heightening our sense of the stark contrasts between the two groups. How accurate, we wonder, are the observations of any "visitor" in a foreign country? How seriously are we meant to take what Updike says?

All Venezuela, except for the negligible middle class, is divided between the Indians *(los indios)* and the rich *(los ricos)*. The Indians are mostly to be found in the south, amid the muddy tributaries of the Orinoco and the god-haunted *tepuys* (mesas) that rear their fearsome mile-high crowns above the surrounding jungle, whereas the rich tend to congregate in the north, along the sunny littoral, in the burgeoning metropolis of Caracas, and on the semi-circular shores of Lake Maracaibo, from which their sumptuous black wealth is drawn. The negligible middle class occupies a strip of arid savanna in the center of the nation and a few shunned enclaves on the suburban slopes of Monte Avila.

The Indians, who range in color from mocha to Dentyne, are generally under five feet tall. Their hair style runs to page-boys and severe bangs, with some tonsures in deference to lice. Neither sex is quite naked: the males wear around their waists a thong to which their foreskins are tied, pulling their penises taut upright; the females, once out of infancy, suffer such adornments as three pale sticks symmetrically thrust into their lower faces. The gazes of both sexes are melting, brown, alert, canny. The visitor, standing among them with his Nikon FE and L. L. Bean fannypack,[1] is shy at first, but warms to their inquisitive touches, which patter and rub across his person with a soft, sandy insistence unlike both the fumblings of children and the caresses one Caucasian adult will give another. There is an infectious, wordless ecstasy in their touches, and a blank eagerness with yet some parameters of tact and irony. *These are human presences*, the visitor comes to realize.

The rich, who range in color from porcelain to mocha, are generally under six feet tall. Their hair style runs to chignons and blow-dried trims. Either sex is elegantly clad: the males favor dark suits of medium weight (nights in Caracas can be cool), their close English cut enhanced by a slight Latin flare, and shirts with striped bodies but stark-white collars and French cuffs held by agates and gold; the females appear in a variety of gowns and mock-military pants suits, Dior and de la Renta originals flown in from Paris and New York. The gazes of both sexes are melting, brown, alert, canny. The visitor, standing among them in his funky Brooks Brothers suit and rumpled blue button-down, is shy at first, but warms to their excellent English, acquired at colleges in London or "the States," and to their impeccable manners, which conceal, as their fine clothes conceal their skins, rippling depths of Spanish and those dark thoughts that the mind phrases to itself in its native language. They tell

[1]Japanese camera and portable sack from a Maine supplier of outdoor clothes and equipment. — Eds.

anecdotes culled from their rich international lives; they offer, as the evening deepens, confidences, feelers, troubles. These, too, are human presences.

The Indians live in *shabonos* — roughly circular lean-tos 4 woven beautifully of palm thatch in clearings hacked and burned out of the circumambient rain forest. A *shabono* usually rots and is abandoned within three years. The interiors are smoky, from cooking fires, and eye diseases are common among the Indians. They sleep, rest, and die in hammocks (*cinchorros*) hung as close together as pea pods on a vine. Their technology, involving in its pure state neither iron nor the wheel, is yet highly sophisticated: the chemical intricacies of curare have never been completely plumbed, and with their blowpipes of up to sixteen feet in length the Indians can bring down prey at distances of over thirty meters. They fish without hooks, by employing nets and thrashing the water with poisonous lianas. All this sounds cheerier than it is. It is depressing to stand in the gloom of a *shabono*, the palm thatch overhead infested with giant insects, the Indians drooping in their hammocks, their eyes diseased, their bellies protuberant, their faces and limbs besmirched with the same gray-brown dirt that composes the floor, their possessions a few brown baskets and monkey skins. Their lives are not paradise but full of anxiety — their religion a matter of fear, their statecraft a matter of constant, nagging war. To themselves, they are "the people" (*Yanomami*); to others, they are "the killers" (*Waikás*).

The rich dwell in *haciendas* — airy long ranch houses whose 5 roofs are of curved tile and, surprisingly, dried sugar-cane stalks. Some *haciendas* surviving in Caracas date from the sixteenth century, when the great valley was all but empty. The interiors are smoky, from candlelit dinners, and contact lenses are common among the rich. The furniture is solid, black, polished by generations of servants. Large paintings by Diebenkorn, Stella, Baziotes, and Botero[2] adorn the white plaster walls, along with

[2]Modern or contemporary painters whose work has recently had large New York exhibitions: three Americans (Richard Diebenkorn, born in 1922; Frank Stella, born in 1936; William Baziotes, 1912–1963) and a Colombian, Fernando Botero, born in 1932. — EDS.

lurid religious pictures in the colonial Spanish style. The appliances are all modern and paid for; even if the oil in Lake Maracaibo were to give out, vast deposits of heavy crude have been discovered in the state of Bolívar. All this sounds cheerier than it is. The rich wish they were in Paris, London, New York. Many have condominiums in Miami. *Haute couture* and abstract painting may not prove bulwark enough. Constitutional democracy in Venezuela, though the last dictator fled in 1958, is not so assured as may appear. Turbulence and tyranny are traditional. Che Guevara[3] is still idealized among students. To themselves, the rich are good, decent, amusing people; to others, they are "*reaccionarios.*"

Missionaries, many of them United States citizens, move   6
among the Indians. They claim that since Western civilization, with all its diseases and detritus, must come, it had best come through them. Nevertheless, Marxist anthropologists inveigh against them. Foreign experts, many of them United States citizens, move among the rich. They claim they are just helping out, and that anyway the oil industry was nationalized five years ago. Nevertheless, Marxist anthropologists are not mollified. The feet of the Indians are very broad in front, their toes spread wide for climbing avocado trees. The feet of the rich are very narrow in front, their toes compressed by pointed Italian shoes. The Indians seek relief from tension in the use of *ebene*, or *yopo*, a mind-altering drug distilled from the bark of the *ebene* tree and blown into the user's nose through a hollow cane by a colleague. The rich take cocaine through the nose, and frequent mind-altering discotheques, but more customarily imbibe cognac, *vino blanco*, and Scotch, in association with colleagues.

These and other contrasts and comparisons between the Indians and the rich can perhaps be made more meaningful by the   7
following anecdote: A visitor, after some weeks in Venezuela, was invited to fly to the top of a *tepuy* in a helicopter, which crashed. As stated, the *tepuys* are supposed by the Indians to be the forbidden haunts of the gods; and, indeed, they present an

---

[3]Argentine-born guerrilla leader, revolutionary theorist, and exponent of Cuban communism (1928–1967). — EDS.

exotic, attenuated vegetation and a craggy geology to the rare intruder. The crash was a minor one, breaking neither bones nor bottles (a lavish picnic, including *mucho vino blanco*, had been packed). The bottles were consumed, the exotic vegetation was photographed, and a rescue helicopter arrived. In the Cessna back to Caracas, the survivors couldn't get enough of discussing the incident and their survival, and the red-haired woman opposite the visitor said, "I *love* the way you pronounce *'tepuy.'"* She imitated him: *tupooey.* "Real zingy," she said. The visitor slowly realized that he was being flirted with, and that therefore *this woman was middle-class.* In Venezuela, only the negligible middle class flirts. The Indians kidnap or are raped; the rich commandeer, or languorously give themselves in imperious surrender.

The Indians tend to know only three words of Spanish: 8 "*¿Cómo se llama?*" ("What is your name?"). In Indian belief, to give one's name is to place oneself in the other's power. And the rich, when one is introduced, narrow their eyes and file one's name away in their mysterious depths. Power among them flows along lines of kinship and intimacy. After an imperious surrender, a rich female gazes at her visitor with new interest out of her narrowed, brown, melting, kohl-ringed eyes. He has become someone to be reckoned with, if only as a potential source of financial embarrassment. "Again, what is your name?" she asks.

Los indios and *los ricos* rarely achieve contact. When they do, 9 *mestizos* result, and the exploitation of natural resources. In such lies the future of Venezuela.

QUESTIONS ON MEANING AND PURPOSE

1. "In this essay Updike, as usual, uses words brilliantly and says nothing." How would you reply to this statement?
2. Is Updike's main PURPOSE to compare and contrast rich and poor Venezuelans, to write a travelogue, to castigate Americans who in one way or another exploit the Venezuelans, to make fun

of foreigners, to entertain, or to impart information about a South American country? Discuss.

3. What points of similarity does the author find between the rich and the Indians in Venezuela? What lends IRONY to the similarities?

4. In his last sentence, Updike says, "In such lies the future of Venezuela." To what does *such* refer?

QUESTIONS ON WRITING STRATEGY

1. What does Updike's title contribute to your understanding of his essay?

2. In both paragraph 2 and paragraph 3 Updike writes, "The gazes of both sexes are melting, brown, alert, canny." What is the EFFECT of this repetition? What other repetitions are used to similar effect?

3. What is the TONE of the last sentence in paragraph 2? Is Updike there condescending to the Indians?

4. What is the tone of the entire essay? What does Updike accomplish with his tone?

5. Point to a few passages of description in Updike's essay. Does the author favor objective or subjective description? (See Chapter 2, Description.)

6. What in his essay might Updike have changed had he written it for an AUDIENCE of Venezuelans?

QUESTIONS ON LANGUAGE

1. Use a dictionary if you need help defining the following words: negligible, littoral, burgeoning, sumptuous, savanna, enclaves (paragraph 1); parameters (2); chignons, enhanced, impeccable, culled (3); circumambient, curare, plumbed, lianas, protuberant, besmirched (4); lurid, bulwark (5); detritus, inveigh, mollified, imbibe (6); exotic, attenuated, commandeer, languorously, imperious (7); kohl-ringed (8).

2. Find definitions for the French and Spanish words Updike uses: *haute couture, reaccionarios* (paragraph 5); *vino blanco* (6); *mucho* (7); *mestizos* (9).

3. What is meant by "sumptuous black wealth" (paragraph 1)?

4. What synonyms could you substitute for *mocha* and *Dentyne* (paragraph 2)? for *porcelain* (3)?

5. What, exactly, does Updike mean by the following phrases: "the negligible middle class" (paragraph 1); "some tonsures in deference to lice," "with yet some parameters of tact and irony" (2)?

SUGGESTIONS FOR WRITING

1. Recall a visit you have made to some new place. What struck you about the area and its people? Sum up your observations in a paragraph. Be as accurate as you can.

2. Write two paragraphs, one pointing out similarities and one pointing out differences between two groups of people: children and adults; students and teachers; blue-collar workers and white-collar workers; runners and football players; readers and TV watchers. Other possible topics may occur to you. In your final sentence, make some judgment about your comparison. Which group do you favor? Why?

· A. M. Rosenthal ·

ABRAHAM MICHAEL ROSENTHAL, born in 1922 in Ontario, Canada, came to the United States when he was four. His long association with the *New York Times* began in 1944: Since then, he has served the newspaper as correspondent at the United Nations and in India, Poland, Switzerland, and Japan; as managing editor; and, currently, as executive editor. The author of *38 Witnesses* (1964), Rosenthal also has written articles for the *New York Times Magazine*, *Saturday Evening Post*, and *Foreign Affairs*. In 1960 his reporting of international news won him a Pulitzer Prize.

No News from Auschwitz

"No News from Auschwitz" was first published in the *New York Times* on August 31, 1958, when Rosenthal was a correspondent assigned to Warsaw, Poland. At the time, mention of the holocaust had practically disappeared from American newspapers and periodicals — as though Hitler's murder of six million Jews and countless other victims seemed too horrendous to recall. Rosenthal's article served in 1958 as a powerful reminder. It still does.

BRZEZINKA, POLAND — The most terrible thing of all, some- 1
how, was that at Brzezinka the sun was bright and warm, the rows of graceful poplars were lovely to look upon and on the grass near the gates children played.

It all seemed frighteningly wrong, as in a nightmare, that at 2
Brzezinka the sun should ever shine or that there should be light and greenness and the sound of young laughter. It would be fitting if at Brzezinka the sun never shone and the grass withered, because this is a place of unutterable terror.

And yet, every day, from all over the world, people come to 3
Brzezinka, quite possibly the most grisly tourist center on earth. They come for a variety of reasons — to see if it could really have been true, to remind themselves not to forget, to pay hom-

age to the dead by the simple act of looking upon their place of suffering.

Brzezinka is a couple of miles from the better-known south- 4 ern Polish town of Oswiecim. Oswiecim has about 12,000 inhabitants, is situated about 171 miles from Warsaw and lies in a damp, marshy area at the eastern end of the pass called the Moravian Gate. Brzezinka and Oswiecim together formed part of that minutely organized factory of torture and death that the Nazis called Konzentrationslager Auschwitz.

By now, fourteen years after the last batch of prisoners was 5 herded naked into the gas chambers by dogs and guards, the story of Auschwitz has been told a great many times. Some of the inmates have written of those memories of which sane men cannot conceive. Rudolf Franz Ferdinand Hoess, the superintendent of the camp, before he was executed wrote his detailed memoirs of mass exterminations and the experiments on living bodies. Four million people died here, the Poles say.

And so there is no news to report about Auschwitz. There is 6 merely the compulsion to write something about it, a compulsion that grows out of a restless feeling that to have visited Auschwitz and then turned away without having said or written anything would somehow be a most grievous act of discourtesy to those who died here.

Brzezinka and Oswiecim are very quiet places now; the 7 screams can no longer be heard. The tourist walks silently, quickly at first to get it over with and then, as his mind peoples the barracks and the chambers and the dungeons and flogging posts, he walks draggingly. The guide does not say much either, because there is nothing much for him to say after he has pointed.

For every visitor, there is one particular bit of horror that he 8 knows he will never forget. For some it is seeing the rebuilt gas chamber at Oswiecim and being told that this is the "small one." For others it is the fact that at Brzezinka, in the ruins of the gas chambers and the crematoria the Germans blew up when they retreated, there are daisies growing.

There are visitors who gaze blankly at the gas chambers and 9 the furnaces because their minds simply cannot encompass them, but stand shivering before the great mounds of human hair behind the plate-glass window or the piles of babies' shoes or the brick cells where men sentenced to death by suffocation were walled up.

One visitor opened his mouth in a silent scream simply at   10
the sight of boxes — great stretches of three-tiered wooden boxes in the women's barracks. They were about six feet wide, about three feet high, and into them from five to ten prisoners were shoved for the night. The guide walks quickly through the barracks. Nothing more to see here.

A brick building where sterilization experiments were car-   11
ried out on women prisoners. The guide tries the door — it's locked. The visitor is grateful that he does not have to go in, and then flushes with shame.

A long corridor where rows of faces stare from the walls.   12
Thousands of pictures, the photographs of prisoners. They are all dead now, the men and women who stood before the cameras, and they all knew they were to die.

They all stare blank-faced, but one picture, in the middle of   13
a row, seizes the eye and wrenches the mind. A girl, 22 years old, plumply pretty, blond. She is smiling gently, as at a sweet, treasured thought. What was the thought that passed through her young mind and is now her memorial on the wall of the dead at Auschwitz?

Into the suffocation dungeons the visitor is taken for a mo-   14
ment and feels himself strangling. Another visitor goes in, stumbles out and crosses herself. There is no place to pray at Auschwitz.

The visitors look pleadingly at each other and say to the   15
guide, "Enough."

There is nothing new to report about Auschwitz. It was a   16
sunny day and the trees were green and at the gates the children played.

QUESTIONS ON MEANING AND PURPOSE

1. What reason does Rosenthal give for having written this essay?
2. What do the responses of his fellow tourists contribute to your understanding of the author's own reactions?
3. If Rosenthal had gone into greater detail about each of the horrors his pilgrimage revealed, do you think his essay would have been stronger or weaker? Explain.

QUESTIONS ON WRITING STRATEGY

1. Comment on the IRONY implicit in Rosenthal's choice of a title.
2. In paragraph 6, the author writes, "And so there is no news to report about Auschwitz"; and he begins paragraph 16 by declaring, "There is nothing new to report about Auschwitz." What do these two echoes of the title lend to the essay's impact?
3. On what aspect of the contrast between past and present does Rosenthal focus his attention? By what means does he lay EMPHASIS on the contrast?

QUESTIONS ON LANGUAGE

1. Comment on Rosenthal's choice of words in his assertion that sunshine, light, greenness, and young laughter seem "wrong." With what justification can daisies growing in the ruins be called "horrible"?
2. Explain the author's use of the word *shame* in paragraph 11.

SUGGESTIONS FOR WRITING

1. In a brief essay convey your personal responses to some historic site you have visited or to a moving historic event you have read about. To help the reader share your reactions, include precise, carefully chosen details in your writing rather than merely venting your feelings in a general way. Show what you felt through your description of what you saw or read.
2. Choose an old building in your town, a park, a ghost town, a converted schoolhouse, or any other place with a past. Write an essay in which you compare and contrast the place as it is now and as it once was.

· Jeff Greenfield ·

JEFF GREENFIELD, born in 1943, was graduated from Yale University School of Law; he became a sportswriter, a humorist, a media commentator for CBS-TV, and (at present) political and media analyst for ABC News. Earlier in his career, he served as a staff aide and writer of speeches for both John V. Lindsay, former mayor of New York City, and the late attorney general Robert F. Kennedy. His books include *A Populist Manifesto* (1972), *Where Have You Gone, Joe DiMaggio?* (1973), *The World's Greatest Team* (a history of the Boston Celtics, 1976), *Television: The First 50 Years* (1977), *Playing to Win: An Insider's Guide to Politics* (1980), and *The Real Campaign* (1982).

The Black and White Truth
about Basketball

When Jeff Greenfield's survey of "black" and "white" basketball, subtitled "A Skin-Deep Theory of Style," was first published in *Esquire* magazine in 1975, it provoked immediate interest and controversy. For this edition of *The Bedford Reader*, Greenfield again revised his essay and brought it up to date. (His thesis in this 1984 version is essentially unchanged.)

The dominance of black athletes over professional basket- 1
ball is beyond dispute. Two thirds of the players are black, and the number would be greater were it not for the continuing practice of picking white bench warmers for the sake of balance. The Most Valuable Player award of the National Basketball Association has gone to blacks for twenty-three of the last twenty-five years. The NBA was the first pro sports league of any stature to hire a black coach (Bill Russell of the Celtics) and the first black general manager (Wayne Embry of the Bucks). What discrimination remains — lack of opportunity for lucrative benefits such as speaking engagements and product endorsements — has more to do with society than with basketball.

This dominance reflects a natural inheritance; basketball is 2

192

a pastime of the urban poor. The current generation of black athletes are heirs to a tradition half a century old: in a neighborhood without the money for bats, gloves, hockey sticks, tennis rackets, or shoulder pads, basketball is accessible. "Once it was the game of the Irish and Italian Catholics in Rockaway and the Jews on Fordham Road in the Bronx," writes David Wolf in his brilliant book, *Foul!* "It was recreation, status, and a way out." But now the ethnic names are changed; instead of Red Holzmans, Red Auerbachs, and McGuire brothers, there are Julius Ervings and Darryl Dawkins and Kareem Abdul-Jabbars. And professional basketball is a sport with a national television contract and million-dollar salaries.

But the mark on basketball of today's players can be measured by more than money or visibility. It is a question of style. For there is a clear difference between "black" and "white" styles of play that is as clear as the difference between 155th Street at Eighth Avenue and Crystal City, Missouri. Most simply (remembering we are talking about culture, not chromosomes), "black" basketball is the use of superb athletic skill to adapt to the limits of space imposed by the game. "White" ball is the pulverization of that space by sheer intensity.

It takes a conscious effort to realize how constricted the space is on a basketball court. Place a regulation court (ninety-four by fifty feet) on a football field, and it will reach from the back of the end zone to the twenty-one-yard line; its width will cover less than a third of the field. On a baseball diamond, a basketball court will reach from home plate to just beyond first base. Compared to its principal indoor rival, ice hockey, basketball covers about one-fourth the playing area. And during the normal flow of the game, most of the action takes place on about the third of the court nearest the basket. It is in this dollhouse space that ten men, each of them half a foot taller than the average man, come together to battle each other.

There is, thus, no room; basketball is a struggle for the edge: the half step with which to cut around the defender for a lay-up, the half second of freedom with which to release a jump shot, the instant a head turns allowing a pass to a teammate breaking for the basket. It is an arena for the subtlest of skills: the head fake, the shoulder fake, the shift of body weight to the right and the sudden cut to the left. Deception is crucial to success; and to young men who have learned early and painfully that life is a battle for survival, basketball is one of the few games in which the weapon of deception is a legitimate rule and not the source of trouble.

If there is, then, the need to compete in a crowd, to battle   6
for the edge, then the surest strategy is to develop the *unexpected*; to develop a shot that is simply and fundamentally different from the usual methods of putting the ball in the basket. Drive to the hoop, but go under it and come up the other side; hold the ball at waist level and shoot from there instead of bringing the ball up to eye level; leap into the air and fall away from the basket instead of toward it. All these tactics take maximum advantage of the crowding on a court; they also stamp uniqueness on young men who may feel it nowhere else.

"For many young men in the slums," David Wolf writes,   7
"the school yard is the only place they can feel true pride in what they do, where they can move free of inhibitions and where they can, by being spectacular, rise for the moment against the drabness and anonymity of their lives. Thus, when a player develops extraordinary 'school yard' moves and shots . . . [they] become his measure as a man."

So the moves that begin as tactics for scoring soon become   8
calling cards. You don't just lay the ball in for an uncontested basket; you take the ball in both hands, leap as high as you can, and slam the ball through the hoop. When you jump in the air, fake a shot, bring the ball back to your body, and throw up a shot, all without coming back down, you have proven your worth in uncontestable fashion.

This liquid grace is an integral part of "black" ball, almost   9
exclusively the province of the playground player. Some white stars like Bob Cousy, Billy Cunningham, Doug Collins, and Paul Westphal had it: the body control, the moves to the basket, the free-ranging mobility. They also had the surface ease that is integral to the "black" style; an incorporation of the ethic of mean streets — to "make it" is not just to have wealth, but to have it without strain. Whatever the muscles and organs are doing, the face of the "black" star almost never shows it. George

Gervin of the San Antonio Spurs can drive to the basket with two men on him, pull up, turn around, and hit a basket without the least flicker of emotion. The Knicks' former great Walt Frazier, flamboyant in dress, cars, and companions, displayed nothing but a quickly raised fist after scoring a particularly important basket. (Interestingly, the black coaches in the NBA exhibit far less emotion on the bench than their white counterparts; Al Attles and K. C. Jones are statuelike compared with Jack Ramsey or Dick Motta or Kevin Loughery.)

If there is a single trait that characterizes "black" ball it is leaping agility. Bob Cousy, ex-Celtic great and former pro coach, says that "when coaches get together, one is sure to say, 'I've got the one black kid in the country who can't jump.' When coaches see a white boy who can jump or who moves with extraordinary quickness, they say, 'He should have been born black, he's that good.'"

Don Nelson, former Celtic and coach of the Milwaukee Bucks, recalls that in 1970, Dave Cowens, then a relatively unknown Florida State graduate, prepared for his rookie season by playing in the Rucker League, an outdoor Harlem competition that pits pros against playground stars and college kids. So ferocious was Cowens' leaping power, Nelson says, that "when the summer was over, everyone wanted to know who the white son of a bitch was who could jump so high." That's another way to overcome a crowd around the basket — just go over it.

Speed, mobility, quickness, acceleration, "the moves" — all of these are catch-phrases that surround the "black" playground style of play. So does the most racially tinged of attributes, "rhythm." Yet rhythm is what the black stars themselves talk about; feeling the flow of the game, finding the tempo of the dribble, the step, the shot. It is an instinctive quality, one that has led to difficulty between systematic coaches and free-form players. "Cats from the street have their own rhythm when they play," said college dropout Bill Spivey, onetime New York high-school star. "It's not a matter of somebody setting you up and you shooting. You *feel* the shot. When a coach holds you back, you lose the feel and it isn't fun anymore."

Connie Hawkins, the legendary Brooklyn playground star,

said of Laker coach Bill Sharman's methodical style of teaching, "He's systematic to the point where it begins to be a little too much. It's such an action-reaction type of game that when you have to do everything the same way, I think you lose something."

There is another kind of basketball that has grown up in America. It is not played on asphalt playgrounds with a crowd of kids competing for the court; it is played on macadam driveways by one boy with a ball and a backboard nailed over the garage; it is played in Midwestern gyms and on Southern dirt courts. It is a mechanical, precise development of skills (when Don Nelson was an Iowa farm boy his incentive to make his shots was that an errant rebound would land in the middle of chicken droppings), without frills, without flow, but with effectiveness. It is "white" basketball: jagged, sweaty, stumbling, intense. A "black" player overcomes an obstacle with finesse and body control; a "white" player reacts by outrunning or outpowering the obstacle. 14

By this definition, the Boston Celtics are a classically "white" team. The Celtics almost never use a player with dazzling moves; that would probably make Red Auerbach swallow his cigar. Instead, the Celtics wear you down with execution, with constant running, with the same play run again and again. The rebound triggers the fast break, with everyone racing downcourt; the ball goes to Larry Bird, who pulls up and takes the jump shot, or who fakes the shot and passes off to the man following, the "trailer," who has the momentum to go inside for a relatively easy shot. 15

Perhaps the most classically "white" position is that of the quick forward, one without great moves to the basket, without highly developed shots, without the height and mobility for rebounding effectiveness. What does he do? He runs. He runs from the opening jump to the last horn. He runs up and down the court, from base line to base line, back and forth under the basket, looking for the opening, for the pass, for the chance to take a quick step and the high-percentage shot. To watch San Antonio's Mark Olberding, a player without speed or moves, is to wonder what he is doing in the NBA — until you see him swing free and throw up a shot that, without demanding any ap- 16 parent skill, somehow goes in the basket more frequently than the shots of any of his teammates. To watch Kurt Rambis of the Los Angeles Lakers, an ungainly collection of arms, legs, and elbows, thumping up and down the court at half-speed is to wonder whether the NBA has begun a hire-the-handicapped program — until you see Rambis muscling aside an opponent to grab a rebound, or watch him trail the fast-break to steer an errant shot into the basket. And to have watched Boston Celtic immortal John Havlicek is to have seen "white" ball at its best.

Havlicek stands in dramatic contrast to Julius Erving of the Philadelphia 76ers. Erving has the capacity to make legends come true; leaping from the foul line and slam-dunking the ball on his way down; going up for a lay-up, pulling the ball to his body and throwing under and up the other side of the rim, defying gravity and probability with moves and jumps. Havlicek looked like the living embodiment of his small-town Ohio background. He would bring the ball downcourt, weaving left, then right, looking for the path. He would swing the ball to a teammate, cut behind a pick, take the pass and release the shot in a flicker of time. It looked plain, unvarnished. But there are not half a dozen players in the league who can see such possibilities for a free shot, then get that shot off as quickly and efficiently as Havlicek. 17

To former pro Jim McMillian, a black with "white" attributes, himself a quick forward, "it's a matter of environment. Julius Erving grew up in a different environment from Havlicek — John came from a very small town in Ohio. There everything was done the easy way, the shortest distance between two points. It's nothing fancy, very few times will he go one-on-one; he hits the lay-up, hits the jump shot, makes the free throw, and after the game you look up and you say, 'How did he hurt us that much?'" 18

"White" ball, then, is the basketball of patience and method. "Black" ball is the basketball of electric self-expression. One player has all the time in the world to perfect his skills, the other a need to prove himself. These are slippery categories, because a poor boy who is black can play "white" and a white boy of middle-class parents can play "black." Jamaal Wilkes and Paul Westphal are athletes who seem to defy these categories. And 19 what makes basketball the most intriguing of sports is how these styles do not necessarily clash; how the punishing intensity of "white" players and the dazzling moves of the "blacks" can fit together, a fusion of cultures that seems more and more difficult in the world beyond the out-of-bounds line.

QUESTIONS ON MEANING AND PURPOSE

1. According to Greenfield, how did black athletes come to dominate professional basketball?
2. What differences does the author discern between "black" and "white" styles of play? How do exponents of the two styles differ in showing emotion?
3. How does Greenfield account for these differences? Sum up in your own words the author's point about school yards (paragraph 7) and his point about macadam driveways, gyms, and dirt courts (paragraph 14). Explain "the ethic of mean streets" (paragraph 9).
4. Does Greenfield stereotype black and white players? Where in his essay does he admit there are players who don't fit neatly into his two categories?
5. Do you agree with the author's observations about playing style? Can you think of any EVIDENCE to the contrary?

QUESTIONS ON WRITING STRATEGY

1. How much do we have to know about professional basketball to appreciate Greenfield's essay? Is it written only for basketball fans, or for a general AUDIENCE?
2. In what passage in his essay does Greenfield begin comparing and contrasting? What has been the function of the paragraphs that have come before this passage?
3. In paragraph 4 the author compares a basketball court to a football field, a baseball diamond, and an ice hockey arena. What is the basis for his comparison?
4. Where in his essay does Greenfield concentrate on "black" basketball? Where does he explain what "white" basketball is? To which of the two styles does he devote more space? Where does he illustrate both together?
5. Revising his essay for *The Bedford Reader,* Greenfield changed

many of his examples. In paragraph 2, for instance, the Julius Ervings, Darryl Dawkins, and Kareem Abdul-Jabbars were, in the
1975 version of the essay, "Earl Monroes and Connie Hawkins
and Nate Archibalds." In paragraph 9, George Gervin of the San
Antonio Spurs replaced Bob McAdoo of the Buffalo Braves. In 15,
Larry Bird was substituted for John Havlicek. In 16, San Antonio's Mark Olberding was originally "Boston's Don Nelson." In
the same paragraph, Havlicek is now dubbed a "Boston Celtic immortal," and a brief description of Kurt Rambis of the Los Angeles
Lakers is now added. Why did Greenfield make these and other
similar changes? How do they make the essay more effective?

QUESTIONS ON LANGUAGE

1. Consult the dictionary if you need help in defining the following
   words: lucrative (paragraph 1); ethnic (2); pulverization (3); constricted (4); inhibitions, anonymity (7); uncontestable (8); flamboyant (9); errant, finesse (14); execution (15); ungainly (16); embodiment (17).
2. Talk to someone who knows basketball if you need help in understanding the head fake, the shoulder fake (paragraph 5); fast break,
   jump shot, "trailer" (15); high-percentage shot (16); a pick (17).
   What kind of DICTION do you find in these instances?
3. When Greenfield says, "We are talking about culture, not chromosomes" (paragraph 3), how would you expect him to define these
   terms?
4. Explain the author's reference to the word *rhythm* as "the most racially tinged of attributes" (paragraph 12).

SUGGESTIONS FOR WRITING

1. In a paragraph or two, discuss how well you think Greenfield has
   surmounted the difficulties facing any writer who makes generalizations about people.
2. Compare and contrast college basketball and professional basketball (or, for a narrower subject, a college team and a pro team).
3. Write a brief essay in which you compare and contrast the styles of
   any two athletes who play the same game.
4. Compare and contrast the styles of two people in the same line of
   work, showing how their work is affected by their different personalities. You might take, for instance, two singers, two taxidrivers,
   two bank tellers, two evangelists, two teachers, or two symphony
   orchestra conductors.

—— POSTSCRIPT ON PROCESS ——

Jeff Greenfield

In this candid recollection, Jeff Greenfield reveals how the thesis he sets forth in "The Black and White Truth about Basketball" first came to him. He tells how he gathered his information from basketball professionals, how he tried to compare and contrast the two styles of play with humor and good will.

Writing for a living offers a smorgasbord of anxieties and rewards. The uncertainty of where the next paycheck is coming from; the still, small voice that tells you that you are missing the point of a story; the disposition of an editor whose marital spat of the night before may blind him to the virtues of your writing today — all of these make writing a craft not recommended to those in need of civil service security.

On the other side of the ledger — apart from the rush of ego when your name appears in print — is the excitement triggered by an intriguing, perhaps original, bit of speculation. This is what happened to me when I came to write "The Black and White Truth about Basketball."

In the early 1970s, I was spending a good deal of time playing hookey from my work as a political consultant writing books and magazine articles; and no writing was more enjoyable than sports reporting. Thanks to Dick Schaap, then editor of *Sport* and a knowledgeable political journalist, I was in effect taking little paid vacations: going to hockey and basketball games, interviewing athletes, getting free tickets to the best seats in the house, and getting paid to write about the games.

Coming from the world of politics where everything was debatable — who would win, whose position was right, who was engaging in "desperation smear tactics" — I relished the world of sports, where winners and losers were clearly identifiable, where the best and the worst were universally recognized (except for the endless debates about whether Bill Russell or Wilt

200

Chamberlain was the greatest basketball player of all time),
where passion and exultation were nightly occurrences.

It was while writing about various star basketball players of
the time — men like the New York Knicks' Willis Reed, the Boston Celtics' Dave Cowens — that I first began noticing how often off-hand, utterly unmalicious racial references were being
thrown about.

A white player in practice would miss a rebound, and a
black teammate would joke, "Come on, man, jump like a
brother." A black player would lose a footrace for a ball, and
someone would quip, "Looks black, plays white." It slowly became clear to me that many of those in the basketball world
freely acknowledged that there were different styles of play that
broke down, roughly speaking, into black and white characteristics.

At first, it did not even occur to me that this would make a
publishable magazine piece. For one thing, I came from a typical
post-war liberal family, repulsed by the racial stereotypes which
still dominated "respectable" conversation. In a time when
black Americans were heavily portrayed as happy-go-lucky,
shiftless, childlike adults, consigned to success as athletes and
tap-dancers, the idea that there was anything like a "black" or
"white" way to play basketball would have seemed something
out of a segregationist manifesto.

For another, I have always been an enthusiastic follower of
the sports pages and had never seen any such analysis in the
many newspapers I read. Apparently, most sportswriters felt
equally uncomfortable with a foray into race; it had, after all,
taken baseball more than a half a century to admit blacks into
its ranks. Indeed, one of the more common assertions of bigots
in the 1930s and 1940s was that blacks could not be great athletes because "they couldn't take the pressure." It is easy to understand why race was not a comfortable basis on which to analyze athletic grace.

In the end, I decided to write about "black" and "white"
basketball because it made the game more enjoyable to me.
Clearly, there *were* different ways to play the game; clearly the
kind of self-assertion represented by the spectacular moves of

black schoolyard ball was a reflection of how important the game was to an inner-city kid, for whom the asphalt court was the cheapest — maybe the only — release from a nasty, sometimes brutish, existence. And books such as Pete Axthelm's *The City Game* and David Wolf's *Foul* had brilliantly explored the significance of basketball in the urban black world of modern America.

I talked with players and sportswriters alike when I wrote the article; without exception, they approached the subject as I did: with humor, unself-consciously. Perhaps it is a measure of the progress we have made in racial matters that no one — black or white — thought it insulting or offensive to remark on the different styles of play, to note that the gravity-defying slam-dunks of a Julius Erving and the carefully-calibrated shots of a Kevin McHale are two facets of the same game.   10

Perhaps the most important lesson I learned from "The Black and White Truth about Basketball" is to listen — really listen — to the comments of people engaged in an enterprise, whether it's sports or business or politics. By listening to the commonly-accepted assumptions of people on the inside, you may find something intriguing worth explaining to people on the outside.   11

· ADDITIONAL WRITING TOPICS ·
COMPARISON AND CONTRAST

1. In an essay replete with examples, compare and contrast any of the following pairs:

   Women and men as consumers
   The styles of two runners
   The personality of a dog and the personality of a cat
   Alexander Hamilton and Thomas Jefferson: their opposing views of central government
   How city dwellers and country dwellers spend their leisure time
   The presentation styles of two television news commentators

2. Approach a comparison and contrast essay on one of the following general subjects by explaining why you prefer one thing to the other:

   Two football teams
   German-made cars and Detroit-made cars
   Two horror movies
   Television when you were a child and television today
   City life and small-town or rural life
   Malls and main streets
   Two neighborhoods
   Two sports

3. Write an essay in which you compare a reality with an ideal, such as:

   The house you live in and the house of your dreams
   A real vacation and an ideal one
   Your present schedule and the one you'd prefer
   The job you have and the job you dream of
   The car you own and the car you'd love to own
   Some present ability and some ideal ability

· 5 ·

PROCESS ANALYSIS

Explaining Step by Step

THE METHOD

A chemist working for a soft-drink firm is handed a six-pack of a competitor's product: Orange Quench. "Find out what this bellywash is," he is told. First, perhaps, he smells the stuff and tastes it. Then he boils a sample, examines the powdery residue, and tests for sugar and acid. At last, he draws up a list of the mysterious drink's ingredients: water, corn syrup, citric acid, sodium benzoate, coloring. Methodically, the chemist has performed an analysis. The nature of Orange Quench stands revealed.

Analysis, also called *division*, is the separation of something into its parts, the better to understand it. An action, or a series of actions, may be analyzed, too. Writing a report to his boss, the soft-drink chemist might tell how he went about learning the ingredients of Orange Quench. Perhaps, if the company wanted to imitate the competitor's product, he might provide instructions for making something just like Orange Quench out of the same ingredients. Writing with either of those purposes, the chemist would be using the method of *process analysis*: explaining step by step how something is done or how to do something.

Like any type of analysis, process analysis divides a subject into its components. It divides a continuous action into stages. Processes much larger and more involved than the making of Orange Quench also may be analyzed. When a news commentator reports the overthrow of a government by armed rebels — a process that may have taken years — she may point out how the fighting began and how it spread, how the capital city was surrounded, how the national television station was seized, how the former president was taken prisoner, and how a general was proclaimed the new president. Exactly what does the commentator do? She takes a complicated event and divides it into parts. She explains what happened first, second, third, and finally. Others, to be sure, may analyze the event differently, but the commentator gives us one good interpretation of what took place, and of how it came about.

Because it is useful in explaining what is complicated, process analysis is a favorite method of news commentators — and of scientists who explain how atoms behave when split, or how to go about splitting them. The method, however, may be useful to anybody. Two kinds of process analysis are very familiar to you. The first (or *directive*) kind tells a reader how to do something, or make something. You meet it when you read a set of instructions for assembling newly purchased stereo components, or follow the directions to a stereo store ("Turn right at the blinker and follow Patriot Boulevard for 2.4 miles. . . . "). The second (or *informative*) kind of process analysis tells us how something is done, or how it takes place. This is the kind we often read out of curiosity. Such an essay may tell of events beyond our control: how the Grand Canyon was formed, how lions hunt, how a fertilized egg develops into a child. In this chapter, you will find examples of both kinds of process analysis

— both the "how to" and the "how." In a practical directive, Peter Elbow tells you how to write when a deadline looms and you absolutely have to produce. Jessica Mitford, in a spellbinding informative essay, explains how corpses are embalmed; but, clearly, she doesn't expect you to rush down to your basement and give her instructions a try.

Sometimes the method is used very imaginatively. Foreseeing that the sun eventually will cool, the earth shrink, the oceans freeze, and all life perish, an astronomer who cannot possibly behold the end of the world nevertheless can write a process analysis of it. An exercise in learned guesswork, such an essay divides a vast and almost inconceivable event into stages that, taken one at a time, become clearer and more readily imaginable.

Whether it is useful or useless (but fun to imagine), a good essay in process analysis holds a certain fascination. Leaf through a current issue of a newsstand magazine, and you will find that process analysis abounds in it. You may meet, for instance, articles telling you how to tenderize cuts of meat, sew homemade designer jeans, lose fat, cut hair, play the money markets, arouse a bored mate, and program a computer. Less practical, but not necessarily less interesting, are the informative articles: how brain surgeons work, how diamonds are formed, how cities fight crime. Readers, it seems, have an unslakable thirst for process analysis. In a recent *New York Times Book Review*, we find a list of best-selling "how to" books, all taking apart processes. The most popular are "how to eat" books: *Eat to Win* (how to feed yourself and become a better athlete), *The James Coco Diet* (how, according to an actor-comedian, to slim down healthily). High on the list, too, are a cookbook (and what, after all, are recipes but step-by-step directives for making things?), a book to help increase your productivity on the job, and *Nothing Down*: "How to buy real estate with little or no money." Elsewhere in the book review, other possibly helpful titles are advertised: *Honoring the Self*, or how to raise the level of your self-esteem; *101 Do-It-Yourself Projects* ("How to build 101 objects you can point to with pride and that add beauty and value to your home"); and *How to Make Love to a Woman*. Evidently, if anything will still make an American crack a book, it is a step-by-step explanation of how he or she, too, can be successful — whether as a lover, a loser of weight, or a cabinet-maker.

THE PROCESS

Here are suggestions for writing an effective process analysis of your own. (In fact, what you are about to read is itself a process analysis.)

1. Understand clearly the process you are about to analyze. Think it through. This preliminary survey will make the task of writing far easier for you.

2. If you are giving a set of detailed instructions, ask yourself: Are there any preparatory steps a reader ought to take? If there are, list them. (These might include: "Remove the packing from the components," or, "First, lay out three eggs, one pound of Sheboygan bratwurst. . . . ")

3. List the steps or stages in the process. Try setting them down in chronological order, one at a time — if this is possible. Some processes, however, do not happen in an orderly sequence, but occur all at once. If, for instance, you are writing an account of a typical earthquake, what do you mention first? The shifting of underground rock strata? Cracks in the earth? Falling houses? Bursting water mains? Toppling trees? Mangled cars? Casualties? (Here is a subject for which the method of *classification*, to be discussed in Chapter 6, may come to your aid. You might sort out apparently simultaneous events into categories: injury to people; damage to homes, to land, to public property.)

4. Now glance back over your list, making sure you haven't omitted anything or instructed your reader to take the steps in the wrong order. Sometimes a stage of a process may contain a number of smaller stages. Make sure none has been left out. If any seems particularly tricky or complicated, underline it on your list to remind yourself when you write your essay to slow down and detail it with extra care.

5. Ask yourself, Will I use any specialized or technical terms? If you will, be sure to define them. You'll sympathize with your

reader if you have ever tried to work a Hong Kong–made short-wave radio that comes with an instruction booklet written in translatorese, full of unexplained technical jargon; or if you have ever tried to assemble a plastic tricycle according to a directive that reads, "Position sleeve casing on wheel center in fork with shaft in tong groove, and gently but forcibly tap in medium pal nut head. . . . "

6. Use time-markers. That is, indicate *when* one stage of a process stops and the next begins. By doing so, you will greatly aid your reader in following you. Here, for example, is a paragraph of plain medical prose that makes good use of helpful time-markers. (In this passage, the time-markers are the words in *italics*.)

> In the human, *thirty-six hours after* the egg is fertilized, a two-cell egg appears. A twelve-cell development takes place *in seventy-two hours*. The egg is still round and has increased little in diameter. In this respect it is like a real estate development. *At first* a road bisects the whole area; *then* a cross road divides it into quarters, and *later* other roads divide it into eighths and twelfths. This happens without the taking of any more land, simply by subdivision of the original tract. *On the third or fourth day*, the egg passes from the Fallopian tube into the uterus. *By the fifth day* the original single large cell has subdivided into sixty small cells and floats about the slitlike uterine cavity *a day or two longer, then* adheres to the cavity's inner lining. *By the twelfth day* the human egg is already firmly implanted. Impregnation is *now* completed, *as yet* unbeknown to the woman. *At present*, she has not even had time to miss her first menstrual period, and other symptoms of pregnancy are *still several days distant*.[1]

Brief as these time-markers are, they define each stage of the human egg's journey. Note how the writer, after declaring in the second sentence that the egg forms twelve cells, backtracks for a moment and retraces the process by which the egg has subdivided, comparing it (by a brief analogy) to a piece of real estate. (For more examples of *analogy*, see Chapter 7.) By showing your

---

[1] Adapted from *Pregnancy and Birth* by Alan F. Guttmacher, M.D. (New York: New American Library, 1970).

reader how one event follows another, time-markers serve as transitions. Vary them so that they won't seem mechanical. If you can, avoid the monotonous repetition of a fixed phrase (*In the fourteenth stage . . . , In the fifteenth stage . . .*). Even boring time-markers, though, are better than none at all. As in any chronological narrative, words and phrases such as *in the beginning, first, second, next, after that, three seconds later, at the same time,* and *finally* can help a process to move smoothly in the telling and lodge firmly in the reader's mind.

7. When you begin writing a first draft, state your analysis in generous detail, even at the risk of being wordy. When you revise, it will be easier to delete than to amplify.

8. Finally, when your essay is finished, reread it carefully. If it is a simple *directive* ("How to Eat an Ice Cream Cone without Dribbling"), ask a friend to try it out. See if somebody else can follow your instructions without difficulty. If you have written an *informative* process analysis ("How the Dinosaurs Perished"), however, ask others to read your essay and tell you whether the process unfolds as clearly in their minds as it does in yours.

PROCESS ANALYSIS IN A PARAGRAPH

Everyone has heard of the Nielsen ratings, but how many people know how the A. C. Nielsen Company learns which television programs are the most popular with American viewers? Arnold Becker explains in "The Network Ratings Business" (written for Judy Fireman's *TV Book*) just how the process works. First, a meter is installed in each of about 1,200 households chosen by Nielsen as representative samples. In each sample household, the meter registers whenever the television set is turned on and to what channel the dial is tuned. In the middle of every night, a computer automatically dials a phone number connected to each meter, and the meter transfers into the computer the data it has gathered. The computer records which channels are switched on and at what times in all the sample households. With this information in hand, Nielsen matches the computer data with each network's daily schedule of programs. The company is then able to tell the networks exactly how many households in the sample are tuned in to each TV show. The process is beautifully simple. What Becker fails to mention is that the rating system, ingenious though it may be, is not entirely foolproof. So far, Nielsen's computers are incapable of recording one crucial fact: Is the turned-on TV set in each sample household playing to an audience — or merely to an empty room?

Comment. Briefly and straightforwardly, this writer sums up four principal steps by which the Nielsen Company samples the habits of TV viewers. Time-markers indicate the stages: (1) *First*; (2) *In the middle of every night*; (3) *With this information in hand*; and (4) *then*. Note how valuable that last *then* is in the paragraph, indicating that Nielsen has at last arrived at a result. The two concluding sentences aren't strictly part of the process analysis; still, they seem essential in that they point to crucial facts that this whole efficient, computerized process actually leaves out. Incidentally, rather than wrestling repeatedly with some awkward phrase ("The A. C. Nielsen Company," "The Nielsen surveyors"), the writer elected simply to say Nielsen. This paragraph illustrates the kind of writing you often do in a research paper: summing up in your own words, and in a shorter space, evidence found in a book.

· Jessica Mitford ·

JESSICA MITFORD was born in Batsford Mansion, England, in 1917, the daughter of Lord and Lady Redesdale. In her autobiography, *Daughters and Rebels* (1960), she tells how she received a genteel schooling at home, then as a young woman left England for America and became a naturalized citizen. She also has become one of her adopted country's most distinguished muckrakers. Exposing with her typewriter what she regards as corruption, abuse, and absurdity in our society, she has written *The American Way of Death* (1963); *Kind and Unusual Punishment: The Prison Business* (1973); and *Poison Penmanship* (1979), a collection of her articles from *The Atlantic*, *Harper's*, and other periodicals. *A Fine Old Madness* (1977) is a second volume of her autobiography.

Behind the Formaldehyde Curtain

The most famous (or notorious) thing Jessica Mitford has written is *The American Way of Death*. The following essay is a self-contained selection from it. In the book, Mitford criticizes the mortuary profession; and when her work landed on bestseller lists, the author was the subject of bitter attacks from funeral directors all over North America. To finish reading the essay, you will need a stable stomach as well as an awareness of Mitford's outrageous sense of humor. "Behind the Formaldehyde Curtain" is a clear, painstaking process analysis, written with masterly style.

The drama begins to unfold with the arrival of the corpse at the mortuary. 1

Alas, poor Yorick! How surprised he would be to see how his counterpart of today is whisked off to a funeral parlor and is in short order sprayed, sliced, pierced, pickled, trussed, trimmed, creamed, waxed, painted, rouged and neatly dressed — transformed from a common corpse into a Beautiful Memory 2

Picture. This process is known in the trade as embalming and restorative art, and is so universally employed in the United States and Canada that the funeral director does it routinely, without consulting corpse or kin. He regards as eccentric those few who are hardy enough to suggest that it might be dispensed with. Yet no law requires embalming, no religious doctrine commends it, nor is it dictated by considerations of health, sanitation, or even of personal daintiness. In no part of the world but in Northern America is it widely used. The purpose of embalming is to make the corpse presentable for viewing in a suitably costly container; and here too the funeral director routinely, without first consulting the family, prepares the body for public display.

Is all this legal? The processes to which a dead body may be   3
subjected are after all to some extent circumscribed by law. In most states, for instance, the signature of next of kin must be obtained before an autopsy may be performed, before the deceased may be cremated, before the body may be turned over to a medical school for research purposes; or such provision must be made in the decedent's will. In the case of embalming, no such permission is required nor is it ever sought. A textbook, *The Principles and Practices of Embalming*, comments on this: "There is some question regarding the legality of much that is done within the preparation room." The author points out that it would be most unusual for a responsible member of a bereaved family to instruct the mortician, in so many words, to "*embalm*" the body of a deceased relative. The very term "embalming" is so seldom used that the mortician must rely upon custom in the matter. The author concludes that unless the family specifies otherwise, the act of entrusting the body to the care of a funeral establishment carries with it an implied permission to go ahead and embalm.

Embalming is indeed a most extraordinary procedure, and   4
one must wonder at the docility of Americans who each year pay hundreds of millions of dollars for its perpetuation, blissfully ignorant of what it is all about, what is done, how it is done. Not one in ten thousand has any idea of what actually takes place. Books on the subject are extremely hard to come by. They are not to be found in most libraries or bookshops.

In an era when huge television audiences watch surgical op-   5
erations in the comfort of their living rooms, when, thanks to
the animated cartoon, the geography of the digestive system has
become familiar territory even to the nursery school set, in a
land where the satisfaction of curiosity about almost all matters
is a national pastime, the secrecy surrounding embalming can,
surely, hardly be attributed to the inherent gruesomeness of the
subject. Custom in this regard has within this century suffered a
complete reversal. In the early days of American embalming,
when it was performed in the home of the deceased, it was almost mandatory for some relative to stay by the embalmer's side
and witness the procedure. Today, family members who might
wish to be in attendance would certainly be dissuaded by the funeral director. All others, except apprentices, are excluded by
law from the preparation room.

A close look at what does actually take place may explain in   6
large measure the undertaker's intractable reticence concerning
a procedure that has become his major *raison d'être*. Is it possible
he fears that public information about embalming might lead
patrons to wonder if they really want this service? If the funeral
men are loath to discuss the subject outside the trade, the reader
may, understandably, be equally loath to go on reading at this
point. For those who have the stomach for it, let us part the formaldehyde curtain. . . .

The body is first laid out in the undertaker's morgue — or   7
rather, Mr. Jones is reposing in the preparation room — to be
readied to bid the world farewell.

The preparation room in any of the better funeral establish-   8
ments has the tiled and sterile look of a surgery, and indeed the
embalmer-restorative artist who does his chores there is beginning to adopt the term "dermasurgeon" (appropriately cor-
rupted by some mortician-writers as "demi-surgeon") to describe
his calling. His equipment, consisting of scalpels, scissors, augers, forceps, clamps, needles, pumps, tubes, bowls and basins, is
crudely imitative of the surgeon's, as is his technique, acquired
in a nine- or twelve-month post-high-school course in an embalming school. He is supplied by an advanced chemical industry with a bewildering array of fluids, sprays, pastes, oils, pow-

ders, creams, to fix or soften tissue, shrink or distend it as needed, dry it here, restore the moisture there. There are cosmetics, waxes and paints to fill and cover features, even plaster of Paris to replace entire limbs. There are ingenious aids to prop and stabilize the cadaver: a Vari-Pose Head Rest, the Edwards Arm and Hand Positioner, the Repose Block (to support the shoulders during the embalming), and the Throop Foot Positioner, which resembles an old-fashioned stocks.

Mr. John H. Eckels, president of the Eckels College of Mortuary Science, thus describes the first part of the embalming procedure: "In the hands of a skilled practitioner, this work may be done in a comparatively short time and without mutilating the body other than by slight incision — so slight that it scarcely would cause serious inconvenience if made upon a living person. It is necessary to remove the blood, and doing this not only helps in the disinfecting, but removes the principal cause of disfigurements due to discoloration."   9

Another textbook discusses the all-important time element: 10
"The earlier this is done, the better, for every hour that elapses between death and embalming will add to the problems and complications encountered. . . . " Just how soon should one get going on the embalming? The author tells us, "On the basis of such scanty information made available to this profession through its rudimentary and haphazard system of technical research, we must conclude that the best results are to be obtained if the subject is embalmed before life is completely extinct — that is, before cellular death has occurred. In the average case, this would mean within an hour after somatic death." For those who feel that there is something a little rudimentary, not to say haphazard, about this advice, a comforting thought is offered by another writer. Speaking of fears entertained in early days of premature burial, he points out, "One of the effects of embalming by chemical injection, however, has been to dispel fears of live burial." How true; once the blood is removed, chances of live burial are indeed remote.

To return to Mr. Jones, the blood is drained out through   11
the veins and replaced by embalming fluid pumped in through the arteries. As noted in *The Principles and Practices of Embalm-*

ing, "every operator has a favorite injection and drainage point
— a fact which becomes a handicap only if he fails or refuses to
forsake his favorites when conditions demand it." Typical favorites are the carotid artery, femoral artery, jugular vein, subclavian vein. There are various choices of embalming fluid. If Flex-
tone is used, it will produce a "mild, flexible rigidity. The skin
retains a velvety softness, the tissues are rubbery and pliable.
Ideal for women and children." It may be blended with B. and
G. Products Company's Lyf-Lyk tint, which is guaranteed to reproduce "nature's own skin texture . . . the velvety appearance
of living tissue." Suntone comes in three separate tints: Suntan;
Special Cosmetic Tint, a pink shade "especially indicated for female subjects"; and Regular Cosmetic Tint, moderately pink.

About three to six gallons of a dyed and perfumed solution   12
of formaldehyde, glycerin, borax, phenol, alcohol and water is
soon circulating through Mr. Jones, whose mouth has been
sewn together with a "needle directed upward between the upper lip and gum and brought out through the left nostril," with
the corners raised slightly "for a more pleasant expression." If he
should be bucktoothed, his teeth are cleaned with Bon Ami and
coated with colorless nail polish. His eyes, meanwhile, are closed
with flesh-tinted eye caps and eye cement.

The next step is to have at Mr. Jones with a thing called a   13
trocar. This is a long, hollow needle attached to a tube. It is
jabbed into the abdomen, poked around the entrails and chest
cavity, the contents of which are pumped out and replaced with
"cavity fluid." This done, and the hole in the abdomen sewn up,
Mr. Jones's face is heavily creamed (to protect the skin from
burns which may be caused by leakage of the chemicals), and he
is covered with a sheet and left unmolested for a while. But not
for long — there is more, much more, in store for him. He has
been embalmed, but not yet restored, and the best time to start
the restorative work is eight to ten hours after embalming, when
the tissues have become firm and dry.

The object of all this attention to the corpse, it must be re-   14
membered, is to make it presentable for viewing in an attitude of
healthy repose. "Our customs require the presentation of our

dead in the semblance of normality . . . unmarred by the ravages of illness, disease or mutilation," says Mr. J. Sheridan Mayer in his *Restorative Art.* This is rather a large order since few people die in the full bloom of health, unravaged by illness and unmarked by some disfigurement. The funeral industry is equal to the challenge: "In some cases the gruesome appearance of a mutilated or disease-ridden subject may be quite discouraging. The task of restoration may seem impossible and shake the confidence of the embalmer. This is the time for intestinal fortitude and determination. Once the formative work is begun and affected tissues are cleaned or removed, all doubts of success vanish. It is surprising and gratifying to discover the results which may be obtained."

The embalmer, having allowed an appropriate interval to   15
elapse, returns to the attack, but now he brings into play the skill and equipment of sculptor and cosmetician. Is a hand missing? Casting one in plaster of Paris is a simple matter. "For replacement purposes, only a cast of the back of the hand is necessary; this is within the ability of the average operator and is quite adequate." If a lip or two, a nose or an ear should be missing, the embalmer has at hand a variety of restorative waxes with which to model replacements. Pores and skin texture are simulated by stippling with a little brush, and over this cosmetics are laid on. Head off? Decapitation cases are rather routinely handled. Ragged edges are trimmed, and head joined to torso with a series of splints, wires and sutures. It is a good idea to have a little something at the neck — a scarf or a high collar — when time for viewing comes. Swollen mouth? Cut out tissue as needed from inside the lips. If too much is removed, the surface contour can easily be restored by padding with cotton. Swollen necks and cheeks are reduced by removing tissue through vertical incisions made down each side of the neck. "When the deceased is casketed, the pillow will hide the suture incisions . . . as an extra precaution against leakage, the suture may be painted with liquid sealer."

The opposite condition is more likely to present itself —   16
that of emaciation. His hypodermic syringe now loaded with

massage cream, the embalmer seeks out and fills the hollowed and sunken areas by injection. In this procedure the backs of the hands and fingers and the under-chin area should not be neglected.

Positioning the lips is a problem that recurrently challenges   17
the ingenuity of the embalmer. Closed too tightly, they tend to give a stern, even disapproving expression. Ideally, embalmers feel, the lips should give the impression of being ever so slightly parted, the upper lip protruding slightly for a more youthful appearance. This takes some engineering, however, as the lips tend to drift apart. Lip drift can sometimes be remedied by pushing one or two straight pins through the inner margin of the lower lip and then inserting them between the two front upper teeth. If Mr. Jones happens to have no teeth, the pins can just as easily be anchored in his Armstrong Face Former and Denture Replacer. Another method to maintain lip closure is to dislocate the lower jaw, which is then held in its new position by a wire run through holes which have been drilled through the upper and lower jaws at the midline. As the French are fond of saying, *il faut souffrir pour être belle.*[1]

If Mr. Jones has died of jaundice, the embalming fluid will   18
very likely turn him green. Does this deter the embalmer? Not if he has intestinal fortitude. Masking pastes and cosmetics are heavily laid on, burial garments and casket interiors are color-correlated with particular care, and Jones is displayed beneath rose-colored lights. Friends will say "How *well* he looks." Death by carbon monoxide, on the other hand, can be rather a good thing from the embalmer's viewpoint: "One advantage is the fact that this type of discoloration is an exaggerated form of a natural pink coloration." This is nice because the healthy glow is already present and needs but little attention.

The patching and filling completed, Mr. Jones is now   19
shaved, washed and dressed. Cream-based cosmetic, available in pink, flesh, suntan, brunette and blond, is applied to his hands and face, his hair is shampooed and combed (and, in the case of

---

[1]You have to suffer to be beautiful. — Eds.

Mrs. Jones, set), his hands manicured. For the horny-handed son of toil special care must be taken; cream should be applied to remove ingrained grime, and the nails cleaned. "If he were not in the habit of having them manicured in life, trimming and shaping is advised for better appearance — never questioned by kin."

Jones is now ready for casketing (this is the present participle of the verb "to casket"). In this operation his right shoulder should be depressed slightly "to turn the body a bit to the right and soften the appearance of lying flat on the back." Positioning the hands is a matter of importance, and special rubber positioning blocks may be used. The hands should be cupped slightly for a more lifelike, relaxed appearance. Proper placement of the body requires a delicate sense of balance. It should lie as high as possible in the casket, yet not so high that the lid, when lowered, will hit the nose. On the other hand, we are cautioned, placing the body too low "creates the impression that the body is in a box." 20

Jones is next wheeled into the appointed slumber room where a few last touches may be added — his favorite pipe placed in his hand or, if he was a great reader, a book propped into position. (In the case of little Master Jones a Teddy bear may be clutched.) Here he will hold open house for a few days, visiting hours 10 A.M. to 9 P.M. 21

All now being in readiness, the funeral director calls a staff conference to make sure that each assistant knows his precise duties. Mr. Wilber Kriege writes: "This makes your staff feel that they are a part of the team, with a definite assignment that must be properly carried out if the whole plan is to succeed. You never heard of a football coach who failed to talk to his entire team before they go on the field. They have drilled on the plays they are to execute for hours and days, and yet the successful coach knows the importance of making even the bench-warming third-string substitute feel that he is important if the game is to be won." The winning of *this* game is predicated upon glass-smooth handling of the logistics. The funeral director has notified the pallbearers whose names were furnished by the family, 22

has arranged for the presence of clergyman, organist, and solo-
ist, has provided transportation for everybody, has organized
and listed the flowers sent by friends. In *Psychology of Funeral Service* Mr. Edward A. Martin points out: "He may not always do
as much as the family thinks he is doing, but it is his helpful
guidance that they appreciate in knowing they are proceeding as
they should. . . . The important thing is how well his services
can be used to make the family believe they are giving unlimited
expression to their own sentiment."

The religious service may be held in a church or in the   23
chapel of the funeral home; the funeral director vastly prefers
the latter arrangement, for not only is it more convenient for
him but it affords him the opportunity to show off his beautiful
facilities to the gathered mourners. After the clergyman has had
his say, the mourners queue up to file past the casket for a last
look at the deceased. The family is *never* asked whether they
want an open-casket ceremony; in the absence of their instruction to the contrary, this is taken for granted. Consequently
well over 90 per cent of all American funerals feature the open
casket — a custom unknown in other parts of the world. Foreigners are astonished by it. An English woman living in San
Francisco described her reaction in a letter to the writer:

> I myself have attended only one funeral here — that of an
> elderly fellow worker of mine. After the service I could not un-
> derstand why everyone was walking towards the coffin (sorry,
> I mean casket), but thought I had better follow the crowd. It
> shook me rigid to get there and find the casket open and poor
> old Oscar lying there in his brown tweed suit, wearing a sun-
> tan makeup and just the wrong shade of lipstick. If I had not
> been extremely fond of the old boy, I have a horrible feeling
> that I might have giggled. Then and there I decided that I
> could never face another American funeral — even dead.

The casket (which has been resting throughout the service   24
on a Classic Beauty Ultra Metal Casket Bier) is now transferred
by a hydraulically operated device called Porto-Lift to a balloon-
tired, Glide Easy casket carriage which will wheel it to yet an-

other conveyance, the Cadillac Funeral Coach. This may be lavender, cream, light green — anything but black. Interiors, of course, are color-correlated, "for the man who cannot stop short of perfection."

At graveside, the casket is lowered into the earth. This of- 25 fice, once the prerogative of friends of the deceased, is now performed by a patented mechanical lowering device. A "Lifetime Green" artificial grass mat is at the ready to conceal the sere earth, and overhead, to conceal the sky, is a portable Steril Chapel Tent ("resists the intense heat and humidity of summer and the terrific storms of winter . . . available in Silver Grey, Rose or Evergreen"). Now is the time for the ritual scattering of earth over the coffin, as the solemn words "earth to earth, ashes to ashes, dust to dust" are pronounced by the officiating cleric. This can today be accomplished "with a mere flick of the wrist with the Gordon Leak-Proof Earth Dispenser. No grasping of a handful of dirt, no soiled fingers. Simple, dignified, beautiful, reverent! The modern way!" The Gordon Earth Dispenser (at $5) is of nickel-plated brass construction. It is not only "attractive to the eye and long wearing"; it is also "one of the 'tools' for building better public relations" if presented as "an appropriate non-commercial gift" to the clergyman. It is shaped something like a saltshaker.

Untouched by human hand, the coffin and the earth are 26 now united.

It is in the function of directing the participants through this 27 maze of gadgetry that the funeral director has assigned to himself his relatively new role of "grief therapist." He has relieved the family of every detail, he has revamped the corpse to look like a living doll, he has arranged for it to nap for a few days in a slumber room, he has put on a well-oiled performance in which the concept of *death* has played no part whatsoever — unless it was inconsiderately mentioned by the clergyman who conducted the religious service. He has done everything in his power to make the funeral a real pleasure for everybody concerned. He and his team have given their all to score an upset victory over death.

QUESTIONS ON MEANING AND PURPOSE

1. What was your emotional response to this essay? Can you analyze your feelings?
2. To what does the author attribute the secrecy that surrounds the process of embalming?
3. What, according to Mitford, is the mortician's intent? What common obstacles to fulfilling it must be surmounted?
4. What do you understand from Mitford's remark in paragraph 10, on dispelling fears of live burial: "How true; once the blood is removed, chances of live burial are indeed remote"?
5. Do you find any implied PURPOSE in this essay? Does Mitford seem primarily out to rake muck, or does she offer any positive suggestions to Americans?

QUESTIONS ON WRITING STRATEGY

1. What is Mitford's TONE? In her opening two paragraphs, exactly what shows her attitude toward her subject?
2. Why do you think Mitford goes into so much grisly detail? How does it serve her purpose?
3. What is the effect of calling the body Mr. Jones (or Master Jones)?
4. Paragraph by paragraph, what time-markers does the author employ? (If you need a refresher on this point, see the discussion of time-markers on page 211.)
5. Into what stages has the author divided the embalming process?
6. To whom does Mitford address her process analysis? How do you know she isn't writing for an AUDIENCE of professional morticians?
7. Consider one of the quotations from the journals and textbooks of professionals and explain how it serves the author's general purpose.
8. Of what value to the essay is the letter from the English woman in San Francisco (paragraph 23)?

QUESTIONS ON LANGUAGE

1. Explain the ALLUSION to Yorick in paragraph 2.
2. What IRONY do you find in Mitford's statement in paragraph 7, "The body is first laid out in the undertaker's morgue — or rather,

Mr. Jones is reposing in the preparation room"? Pick out any other words or phrases in the essay that seem ironic. Comment especially on those you find in the essay's last two sentences.

3. Why is it useful to Mitford's purpose that she cites the brand names of morticians' equipment and supplies (the Edwards Arm and Hand Positioner, Lyf-Lyk tint)? List all the brand names in the essay that are memorable.

4. Define counterpart (paragraph 2); circumscribed, autopsy, cremated, decedent, bereaved (3); docility, perpetuation (4); inherent, mandatory (5); intractable, reticence, *raison d'être*, formaldehyde (6); "dermasurgeon," augers, forceps, distend, stocks (8); somatic (10); carotid artery, femoral artery, jugular vein, subclavian vein, pliable (11); glycerin, borax, phenol, bucktoothed (12); trocar, entrails (13); stippling, sutures (15); emaciation (16); jaundice (18); predicated (22); queue (23); hydraulically (24); cleric (25); therapist (27).

SUGGESTIONS FOR WRITING

1. Defend the ritual of the American funeral, or of the mortician's profession, against Mitford's sarcastic attack.

2. Compare and contrast the custom of embalming the corpse for display, as described by Mitford, with a possible alternative way of dealing with the dead.

3. With the aid of the *Readers' Guide to Periodical Literature*, find information about the recent phenomenon of quick-freezing the dead. Set forth this process, including its hoped-for result of reviving the corpses in the far future.

4. Analyze some other process whose operations may not be familiar to everyone. (Have you ever held a job, or helped out in a family business, that has taken you behind the scenes? How is fast food prepared? How are cars serviced? How is a baby sat? How is a house constructed?) Detail it step by step in an essay that includes time-markers.

· Alexander Petrunkevitch ·

Russian-born ALEXANDER PETRUNKEVITCH (1875–1964) was one of the world's foremost zoologists. Educated in Russia and Germany, he came to the United States in 1903 and taught at several universities. From 1910 to his retirement in 1944 he was a popular member of the faculty at Yale. He wrote two books hailed as classics in their field: *Index Catalogue of Spiders of North, Central, and South America* (1911) and *An Inquiry into the Natural Classification of Spiders* (1933). Petrunkevitch was also a poet and translator, a photographer, a historian of the Russian revolution, and a philosopher. Among his later books were *Choice and Responsibility* (1947) and *Principles of Classification* (1952).

The Spider and the Wasp

In "The Spider and the Wasp" Petrunkevitch details the process by which digger wasps provide food for their young, who thrive on paralyzed tarantulas. What makes the essay interesting even to nonscientists is the author's explanation of why, in her struggle with the tarantula, the wasp always wins. What built-in advantage does she have? And how do her victims manage to survive as a species? Petrunkevitch, who spent years observing the behavior of spiders and wasps, advances some convincing theories.

To hold its own in the struggle for existence, every species of 1 animal must have a regular source of food, and if it happens to live on other animals, its survival may be very delicately balanced. The hunter cannot exist without the hunted; if the latter should perish from the earth, the former would, too. When the hunted also prey on some of the hunters, the matter may become complicated.

This is nowhere better illustrated than in the insect world. 2 Think of the complexity of a situation such as the following: There is a certain wasp, *Pimpla inquisitor*, whose larvae feed on the larvae of the tussock moth. *Pimpla* larvae in turn serve as food for the larvae of a second wasp, and the latter in their turn nourish still a third wasp. What subtle balance between fertility and mortality must exist in the case of each of these four species to prevent the extinction of all of them! An excess of mortality over fertility in a single member of the group would ultimately wipe out all four.

This is not a unique case. The two great orders of insects, Hymenoptera and Diptera, are full of such examples of interrelationship. And the spiders (which are not insects but members of a separate order of arthropods) also are killers and victims of insects. 3

The picture is complicated by the fact that those species which are carnivorous in the larval stage have to be provided with animal food by a vegetarian mother. The survival of the young depends on the mother's correct choice of a food which she does not eat herself. 4

In the feeding and safeguarding of their progeny the insects and spiders exhibit some interesting analogies to reasoning and some crass examples of blind instinct. The case I propose to describe here is that of the tarantula spiders and their arch-enemy, the digger wasps of the genus *Pepsis*. It is a classic example of what looks like intelligence pitted against instinct—a strange situation in which the victim, though fully able to defend itself, submits unwittingly to its destruction. 5

Most tarantulas live in the Tropics, but several species occur in the temperate zone and a few are common in the southern U.S. Some varieties are large and have powerful fangs with which they can inflict a deep wound. These formidable-looking spiders do not, however, attack man; you can hold one in your hand, if you are gentle, without being bitten. Their bite is dangerous only to insects and small mammals such as mice; for a man it is no worse than a hornet's sting. 6

Tarantulas customarily live in deep cylindrical burrows, from which they emerge at dusk and into which they retire at dawn. Mature males wander about after dark in search of females and occasionally stray into houses. After mating, the male dies in a few weeks, but a female lives much longer and can mate 7

several years in succession. In a Paris museum is a tropical speci-
men which is said to have been living in captivity for 25 years.

A fertilized female tarantula lays from 200 to 400 eggs at a   8
time; thus it is possible for a single tarantula to produce several
thousand young. She takes no care of them beyond weaving a
cocoon of silk to enclose the eggs. After they hatch, the young
walk away, find convenient places in which to dig their burrows
and spend the rest of their lives in solitude. Tarantulas feed
mostly on insects and millipedes. Once their appetite is appeased, they digest the food for several days before eating again.
Their sight is poor, being limited to sensing a change in the intensity of light and to the perception of moving objects. They
apparently have little or no sense of hearing, for a hungry tarantula will pay no attention to a loudly chirping cricket placed in
its cage unless the insect happens to touch one of its legs.

But all spiders, and especially hairy ones, have an extremely   9
delicate sense of touch. Laboratory experiments prove that tarantulas can distinguish three types of touch: pressure against
the body wall, stroking of the body hair, and riffling of certain
very fine hairs on the legs called trichobothria. Pressure against
the body, by a finger or the end of a pencil, causes the tarantula
to move off slowly for a short distance. The touch excites no defensive response unless the approach is from above, where the
spider can see the motion, in which case it rises on its hind legs,
lifts its front legs, opens its fangs and holds this threatening pos-
ture as long as the object continues to move. When the motion
stops, the spider drops back to the ground, remains quiet for a
few seconds, and then moves slowly away.

The entire body of a tarantula, especially its legs, is thickly   10
clothed with hair. Some of it is short and woolly, some long and
stiff. Touching this body hair produces one of two distinct reactions. When the spider is hungry, it responds with an immediate
and swift attack. At the touch of a cricket's antennae the tarantula seizes the insect so swiftly that a motion picture taken at the
rate of 64 frames per second shows only the result not the process of capture. But when the spider is not hungry, the stimulation of its hair merely causes it to shake the touched limb. An
insect can walk under its hairy belly unharmed.

The trichobothria, very fine hairs growing from disklike   11
membranes of the legs, were once thought to be the spider's
hearing organs, but we now know that they have nothing to do
with sound. They are sensitive only to air movement. A light
breeze makes them vibrate slowly without disturbing the common hair. When one blows gently on the trichobothria, the tarantula reacts with a quick jerk of its four front legs. If the front
and hind legs are stimulated at the same time, the spider makes a
sudden jump. This reaction is quite independent of the state of
its appetite.

These three tactile responses — to pressure on the body   12
wall, to moving of the common hair, and to flexing of the trichobothria — are so different from one another that there is no
possibility of confusing them. They serve the tarantula ade-
quately for most of its needs and enable it to avoid most annoyances and dangers. But they fail the spider completely when it
meets its deadly enemy, the digger wasp *Pepsis*.

These solitary wasps are beautiful and formidable creatures.   13
Most species are either a deep shiny blue all over, or deep blue
with rusty wings. The largest have a wing span of about four
inches. They live on nectar. When excited, they give off a pungent odor — a warning that they are ready to attack. The sting
is much worse than that of a bee or common wasp, and the pain
and swelling last longer. In the adult stage the wasp lives only a
few months. The female produces but a few eggs, one at a time
at intervals of two or three days. For each egg the mother must
provide one adult tarantula, alive but paralyzed. The tarantula
must be of the correct species to nourish the larva. The mother
wasp attaches the egg to the paralyzed spider's abdomen. Upon
hatching from the egg, the larva is many hundreds of times
smaller than its living but helpless victim. It eats no other food
and drinks no water. By the time it has finished its single gargantuan meal and become ready for wasphood, nothing remains of
the tarantula but its indigestible chitinous skeleton.

The mother wasp goes tarantula-hunting when the egg in   14
her ovary is almost ready to be laid. Flying low over the ground
late on a sunny afternoon, the wasp looks for its victim or for
the mouth of a tarantula burrow, a round hole edged by a bit of

silk. The sex of the spider makes no difference, but the mother is highly discriminating as to species. Each species of *Pepsis* requires a certain species of tarantula, and the wasp will not attack the wrong species. In a cage with a tarantula which is not its normal prey the wasp avoids the spider, and is usually killed by it in the night.

Yet when a wasp finds the correct species, it is the other way 15 about. To identify the species the wasp apparently must explore the spider with her antennae. The tarantula shows an amazing tolerance to this exploration. The wasp crawls under it and walks over it without evoking any hostile response. The molestation is so great and so persistent that the tarantula often rises on all eight legs, as if it were on stilts. It may stand this way for several minutes. Meanwhile the wasp, having satisfied itself that the victim is of the right species, moves off a few inches to dig the spider's grave. Working vigorously with legs and jaws, it excavates a hole 8 to 10 inches deep with a diameter slightly larger than the spider's girth. Now and again the wasp pops out of the hole to make sure that the spider is still there.

When the grave is finished, the wasp returns to the taran- 16 tula to complete her ghastly enterprise. First she feels it all over once more with her antennae. Then her behavior becomes more aggressive. She bends her abdomen, protruding her sting, and searches for the soft membrane at the point where the spider's leg joins its body — the only spot where she can penetrate the horny skeleton. From time to time, as the exasperated spider slowly shifts ground, the wasp turns on her back and slides along with the aid of her wings, trying to get under the tarantula for a shot at the vital spot. During all this maneuvering, which can last for several minutes, the tarantula makes no move to save itself. Finally the wasp corners it against some obstruction and grasps one of its legs in her powerful jaws. Now at last the harassed spider tries a desperate but vain defense. The two contestants roll over and over on the ground. It is a terrifying sight and the outcome is always the same. The wasp finally manages to thrust her sting into the soft spot and holds it there for a few seconds while she pumps in the poison. Almost immediately the tarantula falls paralyzed on its back. Its legs stop twitching; its heart stops beating. Yet it is not dead, as is shown by the fact that if taken from the wasp it can be restored to some sensitivity by being kept in a moist chamber for several months.

After paralyzing the tarantula, the wasp cleans herself by dragging her body along the ground and rubbing her feet, sucks the drop of blood oozing from the wound in the spider's abdomen, then grabs a leg of the flabby, helpless animal in her jaws and drags it down to the bottom of the grave. She stays there for many minutes, sometimes for several hours, and what she does all that time in the dark we do not know. Eventually she lays her egg and attaches it to the side of the spider's abdomen with a sticky secretion. Then she emerges, fills the grave with soil carried bit by bit in her jaws, and finally tramples the ground all around to hide any trace of the grave from prowlers. Then she flies away, leaving her descendant safely started in life. 17

In all this the behavior of the wasp evidently is qualitatively different from that of the spider. The wasp acts like an intelligent animal. This is not to say that instinct plays no part or that she reasons as man does. But her actions are to the point; they are not automatic and can be modified to fit the situation. We do not know for certain how she identifies the tarantula — probably it is by some olfactory or chemo-tactile sense — but she does it purposefully and does not blindly tackle a wrong species. 18

On the other hand, the tarantula's behavior shows only confusion. Evidently the wasp's pawing gives it no pleasure, for it tries to move away. That the wasp is not simulating sexual stimulation is certain, because male and female tarantulas react in the same way to its advances. That the spider is not anesthetized by some odorless secretion is easily shown by blowing lightly at the tarantula and making it jump suddenly. What, then, makes the tarantula behave as stupidly as it does? 19

No clear, simple answer is available. Possibly the stimulation by the wasp's antennae is masked by a heavier pressure on the spider's body, so that it reacts as when prodded by a pencil. But the explanation may be much more complex. Initiative in attack 20 is not in the nature of tarantulas; most species fight only when cornered so that escape is impossible. Their inherited patterns of behavior apparently prompt them to avoid problems rather than attack them. For example, spiders always weave their webs in three dimensions, and when a spider finds that there is insufficient space to attach certain threads in the third dimension, it leaves the place and seeks another, instead of finishing the web in a single plane. This urge to escape seems to arise under all circumstances, in all phases of life, and to take the place of reasoning. For a spider to change the pattern of its web is as impossible as for an inexperienced man to build a bridge across a chasm obstructing his way.

In a way the instinctive urge to escape is not only easier but   21
more efficient than reasoning. The tarantula does exactly what is most efficient in all cases except in an encounter with a ruthless and determined attacker dependent for the existence of her own species on killing as many tarantulas as she can lay eggs. Perhaps in this case the spider follows its usual pattern of trying to escape, instead of seizing and killing the wasp, because it is not aware of its danger. In any case, the survival of the tarantula species as a whole is protected by the fact that the spider is much more fertile than the wasp.

QUESTIONS ON MEANING AND PURPOSE

1. State in your own words the THESIS of Petrunkevitch's essay.
2. Of what importance to your understanding of the relationship between the tarantula and the digger wasp is the information in paragraphs 6, 7, 10, and 14?
3. In their encounters, what is the basic difference between the behavior of the tarantula and that of the digger wasp? What is the effect of this difference?
4. What reasons does Petrunkevitch set forth for the tarantula's "stupid" behavior (paragraphs 20–21)? On what EVIDENCE does the author base his explanation?

5. Explain the "balance between fertility and mortality" that is maintained between the tarantula and the digger wasp. Of what importance is this balance?

QUESTIONS ON WRITING STRATEGY

1. How would you characterize the *Scientific American* AUDIENCE for whom this essay was first written? (Look at a copy of the magazine for clues.) How extensive a knowledge of science does Petrunkevitch seem to expect of his readers?
2. What function do paragraphs 2–4 perform?
3. Where in the essay does the analysis of a process begin?
4. Exactly what process does Petrunkevitch analyze? What function does the process analysis serve in this essay?
5. Where in his essay does the author make particularly good use of description? (See Chapter 2.)

QUESTIONS ON LANGUAGE

1. Consult your dictionary if you need to know what any of the following words mean: larvae, subtle, mortality (paragraph 2); unique, arthropods (3); carnivorous (4); progeny, unwittingly (5); formidable (6); millipedes, appeased, intensity (8); riffling (9); nectar, pungent, abdomen, gargantuan, chitinous (13); discriminating (14); evoking, molestation, excavates (15); protruding, maneuvering, harassed (16); secretion, descendant (17); qualitatively, olfactory, chemo-tactile (18); simulating, anesthetized (19); chasm (20).
2. To what extent is the author's use of technical language a stumbling block for the ordinary reader? Where in the essay do you find evidence that the author may be trying to help the reader understand?
3. Point to a few sentences that contain words more commonly used in connection with people than with spiders and wasps. Do such words affect your response to the essay? If so, how?
4. Describe the important difference between "exhibit some interesting analogies to reasoning" (paragraph 5) and "exhibit reasoning ability." Why do you think Petrunkevitch chose the former phrase rather than the latter?

SUGGESTIONS FOR WRITING

1. Write a paragraph in which you explain the difference between instinctual and intelligent behavior. Include an example of each.
2. In what ways does a human mother's concern for her baby resemble that of the digger wasp? In what important ways do the two behaviors differ? Present your conclusions in a brief essay, written by the method of comparison and contrast (discussed in Chapter 4).
3. Drawing on written information or on your observations, write an essay in which you describe a process by which any creature supports or nourishes its young.

· Peter Elbow ·

PETER ELBOW is well known as a director of writing programs for community groups and for college students. Born in 1935, he received his education at Williams College and at Brandeis, Harvard, and Oxford. He has taught at Wesleyan University, M.I.T., Franconia College, and the Harvard Graduate School of Education, as well as at Evergreen State College in Olympia, Washington. Most recently he started the highly acclaimed "Workshop in Language and Thinking" at Bard College. Currently Director of the Writing Programs at the State University of New York at Stony Brook, he is the author of many articles and of the influential *Writing without Teachers* (1973) and *Writing with Power* (1981).

Desperation Writing

What do you do when you have a paper due but can't think of a word to say about the assigned subject? This is a problem faced by most college students at one time or another. But take heart. Peter Elbow has come up with a solution. What's more, if you try to follow his advice, you will find it much less painful than you expected. "Desperation Writing" has offered solace and help to thousands since it first appeared in *Writing without Teachers*.

I know I am not alone in my recurring twinges of panic that   1
I won't be able to write something when I need to, I won't be able to produce coherent speech or thought. And that lingering doubt is a great hindrance to writing. It's a constant fog or static that clouds the mind. I never got out of its clutches till I discovered that it was possible to write something — not something great or pleasing but at least something usable, workable — when my mind is out of commission. The trick is that you have to do all your cooking out on the table: your mind is incapable of doing any inside. It means using symbols and pieces of paper not as a crutch but as a wheel chair.

The first thing is to admit your condition: because of some   2
mood or event or whatever, your mind is incapable of anything
that could be called thought. It can put out a babbling kind of
speech utterance, it can put a simple feeling, perception, or sort-
of-thought into understandable (though terrible) words. But it is
incapable of considering anything in relation to anything else.
The moment you try to hold that thought or feeling up against
some other to see the relationship, you simply lose the picture —
you get nothing but buzzing lines or waving colors.

So admit this. Avoid anything more than one feeling, per-   3
ception, or thought. Simply write as much as possible. Try simply to steer your mind in the direction or general vicinity of the
thing you are trying to write about and start writing and keep
writing.

Just write and keep writing. (Probably best to write on only   4
one side of the paper in case you should want to cut parts out
with scissors — but you probably won't.) Just write and keep
writing. It will probably come in waves. After a flurry, stop and
take a brief rest. But don't stop too long. Don't think about
what you are writing or what you have written or else you will
overload the circuit again. Keep writing as though you are
drugged or drunk. Keep doing this till you feel you have a lot of
material that might be useful; or, if necessary, till you can't
stand it any more — even if you doubt that there's anything useful there.

Then take a pad of little pieces of paper — or perhaps 3×5 5
cards — and simply start at the beginning of what you were
writing, and as you read over what you wrote, every time you
come to any thought, feeling, perception, or image that could be
gathered up into one sentence or one assertion, do so and write
it by itself on a little sheet of paper. In short, you are trying to
turn, say, ten or twenty pages of wandering mush into twenty or
thirty hard little crab apples. Sometimes there won't be many
on a page. But if it seems to you that there are none on a page,
you are making a serious error — the same serious error that put
you in this comatose state to start with. You are mistaking
lousy, stupid, second-rate, wrong, childish, foolish, worthless
ideas for no ideas at all. Your job is not to pick out *good* ideas

but to pick out ideas. As long as you were conscious, your words will be full of things that could be called feelings, utterances, ideas — things that can be squeezed into one simple sentence. This is your job. Don't ask for too much.

After you have done this, take those little slips or cards, 6 read through them a number of times — not struggling with them, simply wandering and mulling through them; perhaps shifting them around and looking through them in various sequences. In a sense these are cards you are playing solitaire with, and the rules of this particular game permit shuffling the unused pile.

The goal of this procedure with the cards is to get them to 7 distribute themselves in two or three or ten or fifteen different piles on your desk. You can get them to do this almost by themselves if you simply keep reading through them in different orders; certain cards will begin to feel like they go with other cards. I emphasize this passive, thoughtless mode because I want to talk about desperation writing in its pure state. In practice, almost invariably at some point in the procedure, your sanity begins to return. It is often at this point. You actually are moved to have thoughts or — and the difference between active and passive is crucial here — to *exert* thought; to hold two cards together and *build* or *assert* a relationship. It is a matter of bringing energy to bear.

So you may start to be able to do something active with 8 these cards, and begin actually to think. But if not, just allow the cards to find their own piles with each other by feel, by drift, by intuition, by mindlessness.

You have now engaged in the two main activities that will 9 permit you to get something cooked out on the table rather than in your brain: writing out into messy words, summing up into single assertions, and even sensing relationships between assertions. You can simply continue to deploy these two activities.

If, for example, after that first round of writing, assertion- 10 making, and pile-making, your piles feel as though they are useful and satisfactory for what you are writing — paragraphs or sections or trains of thought — then you can carry on from there. See if you can gather each pile up into a single assertion.

When you can, then put the subsidiary assertions of that pile
into their best order to fit with that single unifying one. If you
can't get the pile into one assertion, then take the pile as the basis for doing some more writing out into words. In the course of
this writing, you may produce for yourself the single unifying assertion you were looking for; or you may have to go through the
cycle of turning the writing into assertions and piles and so
forth. Perhaps more than once. The pile may turn out to want
to be two or more piles itself; or it may want to become part of a
pile you already have. This is natural. This kind of meshing into
one configuration, then coming apart, then coming together
and meshing into a different configuration — this is growing
and cooking. It makes a terrible mess, but if you can't do it in
your head, you have to put up with a cluttered desk and a lot of
confusion.

   If, on the other hand, all that writing *didn't* have useful ma-   11
terial in it, it means that your writing wasn't loose, drifting,
quirky, jerky, associative enough. This time try especially to let
things simply remind you of things that are seemingly crazy or
unrelated. Follow these odd associations. Make as many metaphors as you can — be as nutty as possible — and explore the
metaphors themselves — open them out. You may have all your
energy tied up in some area of your experience that you are leaving out. Don't refrain from writing about whatever else is on
your mind: how you feel at the moment, what you are losing
your mind over, randomness that intrudes itself on your consciousness, the pattern on the wallpaper, what those people you
see out the window have on their minds — though keep coming
back to the whateveritis you are supposed to be writing about.
Treat it, in short, like ten-minute writing exercises. Your best
perceptions and thoughts are always going to be tied up in whatever is really occupying you, and that is also where your energy
is. You may end up writing a love poem — or a hate poem — in
one of those little piles while the other piles will finally turn into
a lab report on data processing or whatever you have to write
about. But you couldn't, in your present state of having your
head shot off, have written that report without also writing the

poem. And the report will have some of the juice of the poem in it and vice versa.

QUESTIONS ON MEANING AND PURPOSE

1. On what assumptions does Elbow base his advice?
2. Where in his essay does the author reveal his PURPOSE?
3. What value does Elbow discern in "lousy, stupid, second-rate, wrong, childish, foolish, worthless ideas" (paragraph 5)?
4. In your own words, describe the role of the unconscious in the process Elbow analyzes. Where in the process does the conscious mind have to do its part?
5. How does the author justify writing a poem when the assignment is to write a lab report?

QUESTIONS ON WRITING STRATEGY

1. What effect does the author achieve by opening his essay in the first PERSON?
2. At what AUDIENCE does Elbow direct his advice?
3. Into how many steps does the author break down the process he analyzes? What are they?
4. Point to effective samples of time-markers in this essay. (Time-markers are discussed on page 211.)
5. Point to phrases or sentences in the essay that seem to you designed to offer encouragement and comfort.

QUESTIONS ON LANGUAGE

1. Where in his essay does the author make good use of FIGURES OF SPEECH?
2. Using a dictionary if necessary, define the following words: coherent, hindrance (paragraph 1); assertion, comatose (5); configuration (10).

SUGGESTIONS FOR WRITING

1. Approach a writing assignment for any one of your classes by following Peter Elbow's advice. Write steadily in the manner prescribed for at least ten minutes; then sort out any ideas you may have brought forth. If you have no class assignment that involves writing, work instead on a journal entry about some recent event, book, idea, or experience that impressed you. When your exercise has been completed, write a paragraph in which you evaluate how well Elbow's method succeeded for you. Did it lead to any good results? Any surprises?

2. In a brief essay, explain how to tackle any job you're not in the mood for: researching a paper, preparing a speech, performing a lab experiment, studying for a test, cleaning your house, washing your car, getting up in the morning. The process should involve at least three steps.

· John Train ·

JOHN TRAIN, writer, humorist, and professional investment adviser, was born in 1928 in New York City. After completing undergraduate and graduate degrees at Harvard, he studied at the Sorbonne. In Paris, he helped found and edit a distinguished literary magazine, *The Paris Review*. Now president of Train Smith Counsel, a New York investment firm, he has written columns for *Forbes*, a leading business magazine, and for *Harvard Magazine* and the *Wall Street Journal*. Train's *The Money Masters* (1980), a best-seller, has been much admired for its incisive, behind-the-scenes portraits of financiers. Lighter in weight are his "remarkable" books: collections of hilarious facts. This popular series, beginning with *Remarkable Names* (1977), reached a fifth volume with *Remarkable Relatives* (1981). Train, who has been decorated for humanitarian service by the governments of Italy and France, recently has worked on behalf of Afghan refugees.

For the Adventurous Few: How to Get Rich

This essay appears as a chapter in John Train's *Preserving Capital and Making It Grow* (1983), which explains the processes of money management. As Train notes in his postscript, an earlier version of the book was written at the suggestion of one of his clients, a publisher: *The Dance of the Money Bees* (1973). Success as we generally perceive it, according to Train, is a pale substitute for the hard but useful and exciting life of the entrepreneur, the venturer — who might become rich enough to endow a museum. What's the secret? Read on.

The first step is to stop thinking the way people do who don't get rich. 1

Almost none of my "successful" friends in the East are getting rich: They either started out that way or else just have good jobs, as law partners, bankers, company vice-presidents (plus a few presidents), or whatever. 2

These friends of mine become respectable, but they don't   3
get *rich*, not the way people did in the old days or still do out
West or in places like Mexico, Brazil, Spain, the Middle East, or
Taiwan, with palaces in town, yachts, ranches here and there,
and collections they eventually give to museums. My friends in
New York, Boston, and Washington have a dismal commute to
work every day, stay in the office late, pay huge taxes, work
around the house on weekends, and divorce their wives, when
with a little more money, they could maintain a jolly girl in a
penthouse full of antiques on a live-and-let-live basis like real big
shots . . . everybody would be happier.

It is all just as the Cassandras in Newport and the Union   4
Club[1] prophesied when Roosevelt got in.

It needn't be, however. You can still get rich, although, as I   5
say, you have to change your thinking.

All these successful but non-rich friends of mine have mod-   6
est, conventional points of view. They went to the right schools
and colleges, they joined the right law firms, brokerage houses,
or banks; they appear in the right clubs; they have deliberately
turned themselves into professionals or corporate functionaries.
After federal, state, and city income taxes, capital gains taxes,
real estate and inheritance taxes, and the salary ceilings imposed
by the threshold of pain of the clients of the law firms or the
shareholders of the banks or corporations, they can't possibly
do well. Furthermore, the few dollars they can snatch from all
these shark-infested waters aren't worth much. The law partner
who has to live in New York will also send his three children to
private schools: $12,000 each, counting the extras, which in a
top tax bracket means he has to earn about $90,000 before taxes
just for tuition. Let's not talk about house repairs or medical
bills.

The worst of it is that the lawyer or brokerage house vice-   7
president knows that he isn't needed. Other countries get along

---

[1]Those who, like the Trojan princess Cassandra of Greek legend, uttered
predictions of doom, but in gathering places of the rich after Franklin D.
Roosevelt's 1933 inauguration. — EDS.

splendidly with almost no lawyers. A lawyer in Paris, for instance, is quite an exotic figure, and the Japanese resist the arrival of American law firms, saying they want less lawyering and more conscience. (Per capita, Japan has a twentieth of the lawyers — and crime — of America.)

The New York lawyers are like the clerics who made Europe run for centuries: highly trained, often dedicated, and given wide responsibilities because they renounce great personal advantage. Professionals, in a word, not tycoons. New York and Boston are the Vatican of such people: the trust officers, auditors, and investment counselors in their modest habits of charcoal gray. 8

So step number one is to abandon the entire Eastern respectable point of view, which prizes a safe seat in the shadow of the throne more than the magnificent reality. You have to think like an Elizabethan, an adventurer; like the American of a century ago, not his clerkish descendant of today. You must think as a builder, a conqueror. 9

Second, you must ask yourself: Where am I needed enough so that I can really get paid for it if I'm able to stand some risk and discomfort? 10

The answer is, in the developing countries with idle resources — specifically, the ones that have sufficiently overcome their political hangups to be able to welcome capital and entrepreneurship for what it's worth to them, not what envious professors think should suffice in another kind of world. 11

Much of the world's surface is lying fallow, useless to its population, for lack of entrepreneurs. If you are clever and energetic enough to make the grade in a good law firm, you probably have multiples of what it takes to play a role in building up a developing country. Never fear, the countries themselves know the score — they have investment codes, tax rates, and labor unions, not to speak of anti-free-enterprise intellectuals; but the needs and opportunities are still so great that a trained and able man can reasonably expect to build an interest in something really valuable during his career. 12

In such places it is taken for granted that one works hard, 13

takes risks, creates something, and is well rewarded for it, now
an almost lost idea in the respectable Eastern Seaboard circles,
where "new money" is mentioned in whispers.

Young friends of mine have developed a minerals empire in   14
British Columbia; created the principal agricultural-equipment
distribution company in Central America; organized the Hong
Kong television station; started a bottling company in Thailand;
developed a large petrochemical venture in the south of Spain;
organized a major investment bank in Madrid; put together a
fertilizer complex in Korea; organized vineyards in Australia. I
can cite dozens of such cases. Most of these people live magnificently, with swarms of servants who are delighted to have the
work. It's expected: They're merchant princes. That also gives
them a chance to exercise a benevolent influence if they're so inclined: To give the public the Morgan Library or the Frick Museum, the founders first had to make the money.

Mind you, the way the world is going I'm not sure that my   15
friends' grandchildren will see much of what they've earned.
The governments are likely to pick most of it up along the way.
That, however, may well be a good thing for the grandchildren.
My father's opinion was that if you loved your children you
should not leave them so much that they wouldn't have to do
something themselves . . . just the equivalent of a family farm or
a professional practice: a place to work, or a little nest egg. The
rest should be up to them.

Let me describe the actual process. In the first place, you will   16
have a much easier time if you know something valuable before
you set off. A good grasp of investment banking (more precisely,
the "deal business") would suffice, or a degree in engineering
plus a few years operating in a manufacturing company, or field
and money-raising experience in oil or hard-rock geology, or a
thorough knowledge of some aspect of finance, such as consumer credit or leasing, or of a consumer business, such as bottling or mail order sales. You must have a business sense and en-
trepreneurial flair. Ask a seasoned friend how he sizes you up.
You also need six months' or a year's eating money, preferably
borrowed from older family members.

After you arrive in Vancouver or Caracas or São Paolo or   17

Lisbon or Sydney or Denver or Singapore (one hopes that the place has been chosen rationally, a high growth rate being indispensable), ask around about the young Americans who are doing interesting things. Visit them. Call on a couple of banks and lawyers (preferably with letters of introduction from your own) and take soundings. Everybody will give you lunch. Write it all down. Then visit the local development bank and whatever the ministry of development is called, and then the people who run the local and the U.S. Chambers of Commerce.

If you push right along following up leads, within a couple of   18
months you will have found three or four projects in search of an entrepreneur, including, with luck, one or two where your expertise is applicable. There will be no fast-food franchise, for instance; or a group will want to put up a chemical plant or open a mine and doesn't know which is the correct foreign know-how partner; or the local beer tastes terrible and the development bank would be glad to put money into a joint venture with local investors and a European beer company, but they don't know who to go to; or a hotel site is available but Intercontinental has said no. Who should be next? If an investment bank is operating in the area, the manager can tell you of a dozen such projects that look good but which he is too busy to do more than lend to when they mature. (Make sure the manager is a moneymaker himself, though. Usually they aren't.)

In a month you will have five telephone calls waiting for you   19
each time you get back to your hotel, and after three months you can decide to work on two or three of these projects for a piece of the action and expenses — but no salary.

If you are always honest, energetic, and careful, then even if   20
the first project doesn't score, you will get a reputation for being serious, and after a while the solid groups will seek you out with something really worthwhile.

The obvious function for the technically competent young   21
American in this situation is writing the feasibility study in English, using a variety of assumptions and with the figures really worked out, and then helping raise the foreign capital.

When you have got the study in adequate form, go home   22
and ask the uncle who grub-staked you who the foreign corpo-

rate know-how and financial partner should be. He won't know, but one of his cronies in a management consulting firm will give you introductions to three or four.

Present the deal to the most likely company last. The first 23 presentations will reveal so many shortcomings in your feasibility study that you will be partially discredited. By the last one or two you should have thought of almost everything.

It's easier to put this sort of thing together than you'd think. 24 Have yourself cut in for a free 5 percent interest and a part-time job as assistant managing director.

After two or three years and a couple of small deals ($1 mil- 25 lion or so) you can try for the brass ring of a $5-million hotel or bottling company or a $10-million manufacturing plant. If you do it from scratch, you can cut yourself in for some free stock, and you'll be on your way.

Why can't all this be done in the States? It can, but the com- 26 petition is much tougher. Any number of large corporations are constantly sifting through stacks of self-generated expansion possibilities. There are hundreds of competent deal makers in even provincial centers, and the real G.N.P.[2] growth in sectors where individual entrepreneurs can function is more limited.

In the United States you haven't got the comfortable mar- 27 gin for error that you have in the developing country, where you have more opportunities, less competing talent, and a chance to look up the answers in the back of the book, so to speak, by bringing in foreign know-how.

Of course, we do have internal frontiers. A lot of entrepre- 28 neurs prospered in Silicon Valley, and it's probably not too late to get in on the Western energy play; if you are hungry enough and have the right background, you can start a successful new service business in any rapidly growing area.

Anyway, it only takes one 10 percent free slice (or even your 29 third of the free slice) of a $10-million project and you are off to the races. If the enterprise succeeds and after five or ten years is worth three or four times as much, you've made it. The chances may be better than you think, although by no means certain: I

---

[2]Gross National Product, the value of goods and services produced in a nation during the year. — EDS.

have other Elizabethan friends who went to the wrong countries or who weren't all that able and who *haven't* become tycoons, or even successful. But even they seem to me to exude a sense of life more fully experienced than most of my country-club professional friends.

I am not talking about putting money into foreign ventures   30 without going there. It will be lost. I am talking about going and staying, of committing your working life to a place that needs your energy, talent, and knowledge of a more advanced economy and will reward it. I can't guarantee that this prescription will make you rich, but it probably won't happen any other way.

And when your former classmate turns up — now a post-   31 doctoral student in neo-Hegelian dialectics — and asks you about the contrast between your elegant existence and that of the poorer citizens, don't bother to tell him about the hundreds of people you created jobs for or the thousands who eat because you made the desert bloom. Just seize him by the seat of his pants and collar and propel him into your (heated) swimming pool.

Learned Hand[3] put it better, as usual: ". . . in establishing a   32 business, or in excavating an ancient city, or in rearing a family, or in writing a play, or in observing an epidemic, or in splitting up an atom, or in learning the nature of space, or even in divining the structure of this giddy universe, in all chosen jobs the craftsman must be at work, and the craftsman, as Stevenson says, gets his hire as he goes. . . . If it be selfishness to work on the job one likes, because one likes it and for no other end, let us accept the odium."

QUESTIONS ON MEANING AND PURPOSE

1. Where does the author indicate his main PURPOSE in writing this essay? What additional purposes do you discern?
2. What preparatory steps does Train advise his readers to take if they wish to follow his advice?

[3]Noted American jurist (1872–1961), author of *The Spirit of Liberty.*—Eds.

3. What personal traits does a person need to pursue the course Train outlines?
4. How does the author counter the objection he seems to expect from his readers: that to get rich in a developing country would be to exploit its populace?

QUESTIONS ON WRITING STRATEGY

1. What function do the first eight paragraphs of Train's essay perform?
2. Where in his essay does Train make good use of time-markers? (Time-markers are discussed on page 211.)
3. Where does the author make outrageous statements? What is their function?
4. Describe the general TONE of Train's remarks. How seriously are we to take his advice?
5. Comment on Train's omission of women in the AUDIENCE he addresses. Is this a sexist fault on his part? Can you suggest what reasons he might set forth for directing his remarks at young men only?

QUESTIONS ON LANGUAGE

1. What does the author mean by "their modest habits of charcoal gray" (paragraph 8)? What CONNOTATIONS lurk in that phrase?
2. Explain the METAPHOR in "these shark-infested waters" (paragraph 6). Where else in the essay do you find metaphors? Where does the author use SIMILES?
3. What is "new money" (paragraph 13)? What does Train mean when he says that it is "mentioned in whispers" in "respectable Eastern Seaboard circles"?
4. Be sure you know what Train means by the following: functionaries (paragraph 6); exotic (7); renounce (8); entrepreneurship, suffice (11); fallow (12); petrochemical, benevolent (14); indispensable (17); expertise, applicable (18); grub-staked (22); provincial (26); dialectics (31); odium (32).

SUGGESTIONS FOR WRITING

1. Write a brief essay in which you explore whether, or how, any of Train's suggestions might apply to women as well as men.

2. Write a directive process analysis of your own in which you offer advice to someone who wants to enjoy a more exciting life-style. Possible topics: how to marry money; how to be president; how to win a beauty contest; how to write a best-seller; how to be an all-star athlete; how to become a rock star. Express yourself with confidence if not with utter seriousness.

─── POSTSCRIPT ON PROCESS ───

John Train

Readers of John Train's essay may ask to what extent it is based on firsthand experience; in the following comment, the writer supplies an answer. After recalling briefly how he departed from his early path toward teaching, he tells how his book *Preserving Capital* (from which the essay is taken) grew out of his work as an investment counselor. Train knows the joys and problems of being a writer while practicing a profession; and his closing words underline the link between knowing the world from having made a living in it and then writing about what you have learned.

After emerging from Harvard with a B.A. in history and literature and an M.A. in comparative literature, I moved to Paris to think things over and perhaps seek a doctorate. I did enlist at the Sorbonne, but after a while realized that comp. lit. was not, for me, a good field. In case you don't know, the *comparatiste* does not compare one author against another, which could be interesting, but one school against another: essentially one compares literary theories, not literary works. How does the neoclassic conception of the hero compare with the Aristotelian conception, for instance; or, what is an epic? 1

Unfortunately, you are not analyzing innate distinctions, like a taxonomist contemplating birds and fish, but rather you're inventing a category and then deciding what you want to put into it. In any event, you are drifting away from the juicy prime matter and into the realm of cobwebs. Goethe said it in a memorably garbled metaphor: "*Grau, lieber Freund . . .*": "Gray, dear friend, is all theory; but green is life's golden tree." So true! 2

I came to suspect that I was setting about life in reverse: drawing the conclusions before experiencing the data. My eyes were opened by Bernard Berenson,[1] whom my family knew 3

---

[1]Lithuanian-born American art critic and historian (1865–1959), authority on Italian art, particularly that of the Renaissance. For much of his long life, Berenson made his home in Italy.—EDS.

quite well, and with whom I was staying at Vallombrosa. One day we took a tiny walk. I use that term because B.B., rug over immaculately tailored forearm, would creep along a few steps, halt, seize your elbow, swinging you around in front, and then say something. We were tottering along in this way when B.B. asked me, "What will you be doing next year?" "I may work on a doctorate in comp. lit.," I replied. His face clouded slightly. "What do you think of comp. lit.?" I inquired anxiously. He stopped, seized my elbow, swinging me around in front, and bayed hoarsely, "*Comp. lit. is as dead as cold mutton!*"[2] Since he always said he had gone astray in his own life in becoming an art "expert," he was glad to set young men straight.

Back in Paris, I realized that for me, at least, he was right. So   4
I banded together with some friends and started a literary magazine called *The Paris Review*, of which I became managing editor. It was a "little" magazine: that is, we tried to discover new writers. I was now wandering away from literature, though: not writing, not even directly handling too much text, but helping a machine to run. I was halfway into business. And it was great fun! Much more so than comp. lit., I'm sorry to say.

Although the *Review* meant a lot of work for little or no pay,   5
it was a wonderful time to be young and in Paris. Alas, my agreeable life ended when, as a sergeant in the Army Reserve, I was called to the colors during the Korean War. At this sign that America really was drawing the sword, the enemy's will faltered and the war tapered off, but that did not get me out of the Army. On emerging I discovered with interest that the *Review*, although a *succès d'estime*,[3] was scarcely enriching its backers (who had put up a total of $7,000), but that another little project I had launched, a French-Swiss finance company, was, on the contrary, buzzing along at a great rate. I had not known what I

---

[2]The same term was used by Oscar Wilde, when some companions sent him to a brothel in Calais, while they waited in a café. "How was it, Oscar?" they asked when he returned. "Uh!" replied the lord of language, sitting down heavily, "just like cold mutton. Still, tell them in London, and my reputation will be completely restored." [Wilde (1854–1900), Dublin-born British author and playwright famed for his wit and his command of words, had been convicted of having had homosexual relations with a minor.—EDS.]

[3]A critical success, rather than a popular or a financial one.—EDS.

was doing in starting it, and it wasn't well run, but the opportunity had been authentic. I even stood to make quite a lot of money.

So I descended yet another step down the ivory tower and   6
entered the financial world, in due course organizing a European-American oil royalty company, which prospered wonderfully; a French paper pulp engineering firm, which didn't; what is now the leading Greek financial services company; the Guinean national tire retreading company; mining ventures in Canada and Mexico; several agricultural projects (a very tough life indeed); and many other ventures. All this evolved into the profession of investment counsel, which I've been practicing for very many years now, in New York.

One wants one's clients to understand what one is trying to   7
do, so I would send them little explanatory essays from time to time. After a few years, one of my clients, Cass Canfield, Sr., formerly head of Harper & Row, urged me to assemble them into a book, which he published.[4] It's mostly quite straightforward stuff: stocks, bonds, good and bad businesses, why the market goes up and down. But at the very end I couldn't resist adding an *envoi*, out of nostalgia for my earlier venturesome life, even though it had little to do with the real subject of the volume. I wrote it on a plane, as I'm writing this explanatory note.

Like my father, who as a lawyer-turned-author wrote forty   8
or fifty books, I find myself writing more as I get older—both books on subjects ranging from finance to etymology, and columns, most recently on foreign and military matters for the *Wall Street Journal*. As a good Gemini, I'm happy only when riding both horses: the everyday work of the world, involved with people—knitted into life, as Yeats said—and the life of the mind. They're complementary.

[4]One technical hint to writers: *ferret* out the exciting verb, in the active voice. Many Americans will say *He is supportive* instead of *He supports*, or *The statue will be placed* instead of *The statue will stand*. Shun the likes of *is, has, does*, and the passive voice. A strong verb *rows* the sentence along.

· ADDITIONAL WRITING TOPICS ·
PROCESS ANALYSIS

1. Write a *directive* process analysis (a "how to" essay) in which, drawing on your own knowledge, you instruct someone in doing or making something. Divide the process into steps and be sure to detail each step thoroughly. Some possible subjects (any of which may be modified or narrowed with the approval of your instructor):

How to enlist people's confidence
How to bake bread
How to meditate
How to teach a child to swim
How to select a science fiction novel
How to make money playing football pools
How to drive a car
How to prepare yourself to take an intelligence test
How to tell a fish story
How to compose a photograph
How to judge cattle
How to buy a used motorcycle
How to enjoy an opera
How to organize your own rock group
How to eat an artichoke
How to groom a horse
How to bellydance
How to make a movie
How to build (or fly) kites
How to start lifting weights
How to aid a person who is choking
How to behave on a first date
How to get your own way
How to kick a habit
How to lose weight
How to win at poker
How to make an effective protest or complaint

Or, if you don't like any of those topics, what else do you know that others might care to learn from you?

2. Step by step, working in chronological order, write a careful *in-formative* analysis of any one of the following processes. (This is not to be a "how to" essay, but an essay that explains how something happens.) Make use of description wherever necessary, and be sure to include frequent time-markers. If one of these topics should give you a better idea for a paper, discuss your choice of subject with your instructor.

How a student is processed during orientation or registration
How you found living quarters
How you decided what to major in
How a professional umpire (or an insurance underwriter, or some other professional) does his or her job
How an amplifier works
How a political candidate runs for office
How a fire company responds to a fire
How birds teach their young (or some other process in the natural world: how sharks feed, how a snake swallows an egg)
How the Appalachian Trail was blazed
How a Rubik's cube functions (or how it drives people crazy)
How police control crowds
How people usually make up their minds when shopping for new cars (or new clothes)
How an idea has come to be accepted

3. Write a directive process analysis in which you use a light tone. Although you do not take your subject in deadly earnest, your humor will probably be effective only if you take the method of process analysis seriously. Make clear each stage of the process and explain it in sufficient detail.

How to get through the month of November (or March)
How to flunk out of college swiftly and efficiently
How to sleep through a class with open eyes
How to outwit a pinball machine
How to choose a mate
How to go broke
How to dump a girl- or boyfriend
How to sell something that nobody wants

· 6 ·

DIVISION AND CLASSIFICATION

Slicing into Parts, Sorting into Kinds

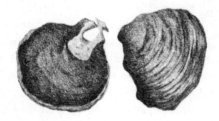

THE METHODS

If you have read the previous chapter about process analysis, you'll recall that *division* (also called *analysis*) is the separation of something into its parts. It is the method by which a chemist breaks down an unfamiliar substance into its components; and, as a method in writing, *division* is often used to explain some action or operation. A writer may divide such a subject into its chronological stages: telling us step by step how a fertilized human egg grows, or how the Nielsen Company determines the popularity of a TV show, or how a desperate writer generates ideas to write about.

Think of the method of division, then, as an instrument ready to use and gleaming in your hand. With its aid, you can slice up a large and complicated subject into smaller parts that you more easily can deal with — and that your reader more readily can grasp. At this point, kindly underline the following two sentences, because they're essential. You can apply the method of division not only to processes, but also to other subjects. In so doing, you take a thing and — much as you do with a process — separate it into its component parts. If, for example, your subject were fried chicken, you could divide it into breast, thighs, wings, drumsticks, and the part that goes over the fence last; and you could write an essay discussing each part and its respective merits. In their guidebook *New York on $20 a Day*, Joan Hamburg and Norma Ketay divide the city into sections: Midtown East, Midtown West, Pennsylvania Station and Chelsea, Little Italy, and so on. In reality, New York is not a distinctly different place from one street to the next; but by dividing New York into neighborhoods, the writers have organized their book in a way that will help the reader-tourist more easily take in the city's complicated geography.

Useful for tangible things such as chicken and cities, the method of division may suit a more abstract subject as well. In "I Want a Wife," an essay in this chapter, Judy Syfers divides the role of a wife into its various functions or services. In an essay called "Teacher," Robert Francis divides the knowledge of poetry he imparts to his class into six pie sections. The first slice is what he told his students that they knew already.

> The second slice is what I told them that they could have found out just as well or better from books. What, for instance, is a sestina?
> The third slice is what I told them that they refused to accept. I could see it on their faces, and later I saw the evidence in their writing.
> The fourth slice is what I told them that they were willing to accept and may have thought they accepted but couldn't accept since they couldn't fully understand. This also I saw in their faces and in their work. Here, no doubt, I was mostly to blame.
> The fifth slice is what I told them that they discounted as whimsy or something simply to fill up time. After all, I was being paid to talk.

> The sixth slice is what I didn't tell them, for I didn't try to
> tell them all I knew. Deliberately I kept back something — a
> few professional secrets, a magic formula or two.[1]

There are always multiple ways to divide a subject, just as there
are many ways to slice a pie. Francis could have divided his
knowledge of poetry into knowledge of English poetry, knowledge of American poetry, and so forth; or the writers of the New
York guidebook could have divided the city into historic landmarks, centers of entertainment, shopping districts, and so on.
(Incidentally, Francis's account of slicing his pie is also an *analogy*, a method of illustrating a difficult idea by comparing it to
something familiar. See Chapter 7 for more examples.)

Half-brother to division is the method of *classification*, the
sorting out of things into categories. The method of classification is familiar to us from everyday life. Preparing to can
peaches, we might begin by classifying the peaches on hand into
three groups: firm, soft, and rotten. In classification, your subject is a *number* of things. Say, for instance, you're going to write
an essay explaining that people have widely different sleep
habits. Your subject is people as sleepers; and you might classify
them into late sleepers, midmorning sleepers, and early risers.

Like division, classification is done for a purpose. In the case
of the peaches, we would sort them out in order to see which to
can at once, which to can later, and which to throw away. Writers, too, classify things for reasons. In their guide to New York,
Hamburg and Ketay arrange their discussion of the city's low-
priced hotels into categories: Rooms for Singles and Students,
Rooms for Families, Rooms for Servicemen, and Rooms for
General Occupancy. Their purpose is to match up the visitor
with a suitable kind of room. Their subject, remember, is multiple: hundreds of hotels. This is how you can tell classification
from division. In division, your subject is a *single* thing: one pie,
one city. If you were applying the method of division to a peach,
you might take a knife and separate your subject into skin, a pit,

---

[1]*Pot Shots at Poetry* (Ann Arbor: University of Michigan Press, 1980).

and two halves. The essay you could write about a certain peach by the method of division might interest a botanist, a farmer, or a cannery owner. Writing an essay by the method of division, you might divide a certain hotel into its component parts: lobby, rooms, coffee shop, restaurant, bar, ballroom, kitchen, laundry, parking garage, and offices.

Just as you can divide a pie in many ways, you can classify a subject according to many principles. A different New York guidebook might classify hotels according to price: grand luxury class, luxury class, commercial class, budget class, fleabag, and flophouse. The purpose of this classification would be to match visitors to hotels fitting their pocketbooks. The principle you use in classifying things depends on your purpose. A linguist might write an essay classifying the languages of the world according to their origins (Romance languages, Germanic languages, Coptic languages . . .), but a student battling with a college language requirement might write a humorous essay classifying them into three groups: hard to learn, harder to learn, and unlearnable. (Either way of sorting languages would be classification and not division, because the subject would be many languages, not one language. You could, of course, write an essay *dividing* the English language into British English, North American English, Australian English, and so on — *if* your purpose were to show regional varieties of English around the world.)

The simplest method of classification is *binary (or two-part) classification*, in which you sort things out into (1) those with a certain distinguishing feature and (2) those without it. You might classify a group of people, for example, into smokers and nonsmokers, blind people and sighted people, runners and non-runners, believers and nonbelievers. Binary classification is most useful when your subject is easily divisible into positive and negative categories.

Classification is a method particularly favored by writers who evaluate things. In a survey of current movies, a newspaper critic might classify the films into categories: "Don't Miss," "Worth Seeing," "So-So," and "Never Mind." This kind of classifying is the method of the magazine *Consumer Reports* in its comments on different brands of stereo speakers or canned tuna. Products are sorted into groups (excellent, good, fair, poor, and not acceptable), and the merits of each are discussed by the method of description. (Of a frozen pot pie: "Bottom crust gummy, meat spongy when chewed, with nondescript old-poultry and stale-flour flavor.")

As the writer of an anonymous jingle reminds us,

> Big fleas have little fleas, and these
> Have littler fleas to bite 'em,
> And these have fleas, and these have fleas,
> And on *ad infinitum*.

In being faithful to reality, you will sometimes find that you have to slice parts into smaller parts, or sort out the members of categories into subcategories. Writing about the varieties of English spoken around the world, a writer could subclassify them into regional dialects: breaking North American English into British Columbian English, Southern Appalachian English, and so on. To be more exact, a guidebook to New York might subdivide Midtown West into the Bryant Park area, Times Square, and the West Side.

As readers, we all enjoy watching a writer cleverly sort things out into categories, or break things into their elements; for we love to see whether the writer's classifications or divisions are familiar to us. This may account for the appeal of popular magazine articles such as "The Seven Common Garden Varieties of Moocher," "The Five Embarrassing Types of Social Blunder," or "The Eleven Components of a Kiss" (an essay in division).

Simple as division and classification are, both methods help us make sense of complex realities. Both separate a subject into smaller, more comprehensible units. Division takes one thing for its subject and answers the question, What are its parts? Classification, on the other hand, takes two or more things for its subject and answers the question, Into what groups or families can these be sorted? Both methods make large ideas more easily graspable, for both writer and reader.

THE PROCESS

In writing by either division or classification, having an outline at your elbow is a help. When dividing a subject into parts,
you'll want to make sure you don't omit any. When classifying
the members of a group into various pigeonholes, you'll probably need to glance at your outline from time to time, to keep
your pigeonholes straight.

In writing her brief essay "I Want a Wife," Judy Syfers must
have needed an outline to work out the different activities of a
wife carefully before she began, so that she clearly knew where
to draw her distinctions between them. Making a valid division
is chiefly a matter of giving your subject thought, but for the division to seem useful and convincing to your reader, it will have
to refer to the world of the senses. The method requires not only
cogitation, but open eyes and a willingness to provide examples
and evidence.

In a workable classification, make sure that the categories
you choose don't overlap. If you were writing a survey of popular magazines for adults and you were sorting your subject into
categories that included women's magazines and sports magazines, you might soon run into trouble. Into which category
would you place *Women's Sports?* The trouble is that both categories take in the same item. To avoid this problem, you'll need
to reorganize your classification on a different principle. You
might sort out the magazines by their audiences: magazines for
women, magazines for men, magazines for women and men. Or
you might group them according to subject matter: sports magazines, literary magazines, astrology magazines, fashion magazines, TV fan magazines, trade journals, and so on. *Women's
Sports* would fit into either of those classification schemes.

Things may be classified into categories that reveal truth, or
into categories that don't tell us a damned thing. To sort out ten
U.S. cities according to their relative freedom from air pollu-
tion, or their cost of living, or the degree of progress they have
made in civil rights might prove highly informative and useful.
Such a classification might even tell us where we'd want to live.
But to sort out the cities according to a superficial feature such

as the relative size of their cat and dog populations wouldn't interest anyone, probably, except a veterinarian looking for a job. Let your reader in on the basis for classification that you choose, and explain why you have chosen it.

When you draw up a scheme of classification, be sure you include all essential categories. Omitting an important category can weaken the effect of your essay, no matter how well-written it is. It would be a major oversight, for example, if you were to classify the student body of a state university according to religious affiliations and not include a category for the numerous nonaffiliated. Your reader might wonder if your sloppiness in forgetting a category extended to your thinking about the topic as well.

For both division and classification, show your reader *why* you went to all the work of dividing or classifying, anyway, and what you have learned by it. In making your division or classification did you come to any conclusion? If so, state it. ("After dividing San Francisco into neighborhoods, and then classifying the neighborhoods, I feel sure that Minneapolis is the place for me after all.")

DIVISION AND CLASSIFICATION
IN TWO PARAGRAPHS

A canned laugh, whatever its style, is made up of three elements. The first is intensity, for a laugh machine can deliver a product of any desired volume, whether mild, medium, or ear splitting. Duration is the second ingredient, for a laugh may be short, medium, or long. By jiggling keys, the machine operator supplies a third ingredient: a fixed number of laughers. Any number is on tap, from a handful of titterers to a roaring throng. Should a producer desire a laugh from one sex or another, these may be subdivided into women or men. When John Ritter accidentally reveals his polka-dotted boxer shorts on the "Three's Company" show, the shrill merriment of women will predominate. A ripped dress, however, will be greeted with the guffaws of men. At the dubbing session, furiously working the keys and tromping the footpedals, the machine operator blends these ingredients like a maestro weaving a symphony out of brass, woodwinds, percussion, and strings.

Though the machine will supply thirty-two different styles of laughter, most laughs fall into one of five reliable types. There is the *titter*, a light vocal laugh with which an imaginary audience responds to a comedian's least wriggle or grimace. Some producers rely heavily on the *chuckle*, a deeper, more chesty response. Most profound of all, the *belly laugh* is summoned to acclaim broader jokes and sexual innuendos. When provided at full level of sound and in longest duration, the belly laugh becomes the Big Boffola. There is also the *wild howl* or *screamer*, an extreme response used not more than three times per show, lest it seem fake. These are crowd laughs, and yet the machine also offers the *freaky laugh*, the piercing, eccentric screech of a solitary kook. With it, a producer affirms that even a canned audience may include one thorny individualist.

Comment. The laugh machine, as you may have gathered, is used to fill a moment of silence in the soundtrack of a comedy program. Most televised comedies, even some that boast they have live audiences, rely on it. According to rumor (for its exact workings are a secret), the machine contains a bank of thirty-two tapes, which the operator turns on singly or in combination. In these two paragraphs, the writer first proceeded by the method of division, taking a single subject — a machine-made laugh — and breaking it into its components. The second paragraph groups laughs into five categories. Like anything else written by the method of classification, the paragraph takes as its subject a *number* of things, which it then sorts out.

· Judy Syfers ·

JUDY SYFERS, born in 1937 in San Francisco, where she now lives, earned a B.F.A. in painting from the University of Iowa in 1962. Drawn into political action by her work in the feminist movement, she went to Cuba in 1973, where she studied class relationships as a way of understanding change in a society. "I am not a 'writer,' " Syfers declares, "but really am a disenfranchised (and fired) housewife, now secretary. I have published other articles in various types of publications (one on abortion, one on union organizing, for instance) and have written for, edited, and produced a newsletter for school paraprofessionals in San Francisco."

I Want a Wife

"I Want a Wife" first appeared in the December 1971 issue of *Ms.* magazine. It has since become one of the best-known manifestos in popular feminist writing, and it has been reprinted widely. In her essay, Syfers trenchantly divides the work of a wife into five parts, explains each part, and comes to an inescapable conclusion.

I belong to that classification of people known as wives. I am A Wife. And, not altogether incidentally, I am a mother.

Not too long ago a male friend of mine appeared on the scene fresh from a recent divorce. He had one child, who is, of course, with his ex-wife. He is looking for another wife. As I thought about him while I was ironing one evening, it suddenly occurred to me that I, too, would like to have a wife. Why do I want a wife?

I would like to go back to school so that I can become economically independent, support myself, and, if need be, support those dependent upon me. I want a wife who will work and send me to school. And while I am going to school I want a wife to take care of my children. I want a wife to keep track of the children's doctor and dentist appointments. And to keep track of

mine, too. I want a wife to make sure my children eat properly
and are kept clean. I want a wife who will wash the children's
clothes and keep them mended. I want a wife who is a good nurturant attendant to my children, who arranges for their schooling, makes sure that they have an adequate social life with their
peers, takes them to the park, the zoo, etc. I want a wife who
takes care of the children when they are sick, a wife who arranges to be around when the children need special care, because, of course, I cannot miss classes at school. My wife must
arrange to lose time at work and not lose the job. It may mean a
small cut in my wife's income from time to time, but I guess I can
tolerate that. Needless to say, my wife will arrange and pay for
the care of the children while my wife is working.

I want a wife who will take care of my physical needs. I want   4
a wife who will keep my house clean. A wife who will pick up after my children, a wife who will pick up after me. I want a wife
who will keep my clothes clean, ironed, mended, replaced when
need be, and who will see to it that my personal things are kept
in their proper place so that I can find what I need the minute I
need it. I want a wife who cooks the meals, a wife who is a good
cook. I want a wife who will plan the menus, do the necessary
grocery shopping, prepare the meals, serve them pleasantly, and
then do the cleaning up while I do my studying. I want a wife
who will care for me when I am sick and sympathize with my
pain and loss of time from school. I want a wife to go along when
our family takes a vacation so that someone can continue to
care for me and my children when I need a rest and change of
scene.

I want a wife who will not bother me with rambling com-   5
plaints about a wife's duties. But I want a wife who will listen to
me when I feel the need to explain a rather difficult point I have
come across in my course of studies. And I want a wife who will
type my papers for me when I have written them.

I want a wife who will take care of the details of my social   6
life. When my wife and I are invited out by my friends, I want a
wife who will take care of the babysitting arrangements. When I
meet people at school that I like and want to entertain, I want a
wife who will have the house clean, will prepare a special meal,
serve it to me and my friends, and not interrupt when I talk

about things that interest me and my friends. I want a wife who will have arranged that the children are fed and ready for bed before my guests arrive so that the children do not bother us. I want a wife who takes care of the needs of my guests so that they feel comfortable, who makes sure that they have an ashtray, that they are passed the hors d'oeuvres, that they are offered a second helping of the food, that their wine glasses are replenished when necessary, that their coffee is served to them as they like it. And I want a wife who knows that sometimes I need a night out by myself.

I want a wife who is sensitive to my sexual needs, a wife who   7
makes love passionately and eagerly when I feel like it, a wife who makes sure that I am satisfied. And, of course, I want a wife who will not demand sexual attention when I am not in the mood for it. I want a wife who assumes the complete responsibility for birth control, because I do not want more children. I want a wife who will remain sexually faithful to me so that I do not have to clutter up my intellectual life with jealousies. And I want a wife who understands that *my* sexual needs may entail more than strict adherence to monogamy. I must, after all, be able to relate to people as fully as possible.

If, by chance, I find another person more suitable as a wife   8
than the wife I already have, I want the liberty to replace my present wife with another one. Naturally, I will expect a fresh, new life; my wife will take the children and be solely responsible for them so that I am left free.

When I am through with school and have a job, I want my   9
wife to quit working and remain at home so that my wife can more fully and completely take care of a wife's duties.

My God, who *wouldn't* want a wife?   10

QUESTIONS ON MEANING AND PURPOSE

1. Sum up the duties of a wife as Syfers sees them.
2. To what inequities in the roles traditionally assigned to men and to women does "I Want a Wife" call attention?

3. What is the THESIS of this essay? Is it stated or implied?
4. Is Syfers unfair to men?

QUESTIONS ON WRITING STRATEGY

1. What EFFECT does Syfers obtain with the title "I Want a Wife"?
2. What do the first two paragraphs accomplish?
3. What is the TONE of this essay?
4. How do you explain the fact that Syfers never uses the pronoun *she* to refer to a wife? Does this make her prose unnecessarily awkward?
5. In what order or sequence does the author arrange her paragraphs? (To see it, try rearranging them.)
6. Knowing that this essay was first published in *Ms.* magazine in 1971, what can you guess about its intended readers? Does "I Want a Wife" strike a college AUDIENCE today as revolutionary?
7. In her first sentence, Syfers says she belongs "to that classification of people known as wives"; but she develops her essay by division. In what way would the essay be different if the author had used classification?

QUESTIONS ON LANGUAGE

1. What is achieved by the author's frequent repetition of the phrase *I want a wife*?
2. Be sure you know how to define the following words as Syfers uses them: nurturant (paragraph 3); replenished (6); adherence, monogamy (7).
3. In general, how would you describe the DICTION of this essay? How well does it suit the essay's intended audience?

SUGGESTIONS FOR WRITING

1. Write a brief essay entitled "I Want a Husband" in which, using examples as Syfers does, you enumerate the stereotyped roles traditionally assigned to men in our society.
2. Classify types of husbands, or types of wives.
3. Imagining that you want to employ someone to do a specific job, divide the task into two or three parts. Then, guided by your divisions, write an accurate job description in essay form.

· Gail Sheehy ·

GAIL SHEEHY was born in 1937. She earned her B.S. degree from the University of Vermont in 1958 and was a fellow in Columbia University's Journalism School in 1970. A contributor to the *New York Times Magazine, Esquire, McCall's, Ms., Cosmopolitan, Rolling Stone,* and other magazines, she has also written a novel, *Lovesounds* (1970), and several popular studies of contemporary life: *Speed Is of the Essence* (1971), *Panthermania* (1971), *Hustling* (1973), *Passages* (1976), and *Pathfinders* (1981).

Predictable Crises
of Adulthood

"Predictable Crises of Adulthood" is adapted from the second chapter of the best-selling *Passages*. In it, Sheehy identifies and describes six predictable stages that people pass through between the ages of eighteen and fifty. Not everyone, of course, goes through the stages at the prescribed time; but see whether any of these crises are familiar to you.

We are not unlike a particularly hardy crustacean. The lobster grows by developing and shedding a series of hard, protective shells. Each time it expands from within, the confining shell must be sloughed off. It is left exposed and vulnerable until, in time, a new covering grows to replace the old.

With each passage from one stage of human growth to the next we, too, must shed a protective structure. We are left exposed and vulnerable — but also yeasty and embryonic again, capable of stretching in ways we hadn't known before. These sheddings may take several years or more. Coming out of each passage, though, we enter a longer and more stable period in which we can expect relative tranquility and a sense of equilibrium regained. . . .

265

As we shall see, each person engages the steps of develop-   3
ment in his or her own characteristic *step-style*. Some people
never complete the whole sequence. And none of us "solves"
with one step — by jumping out of the parental home into a job
or marriage, for example — the problems in separating from the
caregivers of childhood. Nor do we "achieve" autonomy once
and for all by converting our dreams into concrete goals, even
when we attain those goals. The central issues or tasks of one period are never fully completed, tied up, and cast aside. But when
they lose their primacy and the current life structure has served
its purpose, we are ready to move on to the next period.

Can one catch up? What might look to others like listless-   4
ness, contrariness, a maddening refusal to face up to an obvious
task may be a person's own unique detour that will bring him
out later on the other side. Developmental gains won can later
be lost — and rewon. It's plausible, though it can't be proven,
that the mastery of one set of tasks fortifies us for the next period and the next set of challenges. But it's important not to
think too mechanistically. Machines work by units. The bureaucracy (supposedly) works step by step. Human beings, thank
God, have an individual inner dynamic that can never be precisely coded.

Although I have indicated the ages when Americans are   5
likely to go through each stage, and the differences between men
and women where they are striking, do not take the ages too seriously. The stages are the thing, and most particularly the sequence.

Here is the briefest outline of the developmental ladder.   6

Pulling Up Roots

Before 18, the motto is loud and clear: "I have to get away   7
from my parents." But the words are seldom connected to
action. Generally still safely part of our families, even if away at
school, we feel our autonomy to be subject to erosion from moment to moment.

After 18, we begin Pulling Up Roots in earnest. College, mil-   8
itary service, and short-term travels are all customary vehicles

our society provides for the first round trips between family and a base of one's own. In the attempt to separate our view of the world from our family's view, despite vigorous protestations to the contrary — "I know exactly what I want!" — we cast about for any beliefs we can call our own. And in the process of testing those beliefs we are often drawn to fads, preferably those most mysterious and inaccessible to our parents.

Whatever tentative memberships we try out in the world,   9
the fear haunts us that we are really kids who cannot take care of ourselves. We cover that fear with acts of defiance and mimicked confidence. For allies to replace our parents, we turn to our contemporaries. They become conspirators. So long as their perspective meshes with our own, they are able to substitute for the sanctuary of the family. But that doesn't last very long. And the instant they diverge from the shaky ideals of "our group," they are seen as betrayers. Rebounds to the family are common between the ages of 18 and 22.

The tasks of this passage are to locate ourselves in a peer   10
group role, a sex role, an anticipated occupation, an ideology or world view. As a result, we gather the impetus to leave home physically and the identity to *begin* leaving home emotionally.

Even as one part of us seeks to be an individual, another   11
part longs to restore the safety and comfort of merging with another. Thus one of the most popular myths of this passage is: We can piggyback our development by attaching to a Stronger One. But people who marry during this time often prolong financial and emotional ties to the family and relatives that impede them from becoming self-sufficient.

A stormy passage through the Pulling Up Roots years will   12
probably facilitate the normal progression of the adult life cycle. If one doesn't have an identity crisis at this point, it will erupt during a later transition, when the penalties may be harder to bear.

The Trying Twenties

The Trying Twenties confront us with the question of how   13
to take hold in the adult world. Our focus shifts from the inte-

rior turmoils of late adolescence — "Who am I?" "What is
truth?" — and we become almost totally preoccupied with working out the externals. "How do I put my aspirations into effect?"
"What is the best way to start?" "Where do I go?" "Who can
help me?" "How did *you* do it?"

In this period, which is longer and more stable compared   14
with the passage that leads to it, the tasks are as enormous as
they are exhilarating: To shape a Dream, that vision of ourselves
which will generate energy, aliveness, and hope. To prepare for
a lifework. To find a mentor if possible. And to form the capacity for intimacy, without losing in the process whatever consistency of self we have thus far mustered. The first test structure
must be erected around the life we choose to try.

Doing what we "should" is the most pervasive theme of the   15
twenties. The "shoulds" are largely defined by family models,
the press of the culture, or the prejudices of our peers. If the prevailing cultural instructions are that one should get married and
settle down behind one's own door, a nuclear family is born. If
instead the peers insist that one should do one's own thing, the
25-year-old is likely to harness himself onto a Harley-Davidson
and burn up Route 66 in the commitment to have no commitments.

One of the terrifying aspects of the twenties is the inner con-   16
viction that the choices we make are irrevocable. It is largely a
false fear. Change is quite possible, and some alteration of our
original choices is probably inevitable.

Two impulses, as always, are at work. One is to build a firm,   17
safe structure for the future by making strong commitments, to
"be set." Yet people who slip into a ready-made form without
much self-examination are likely to find themselves *locked in.*

The other urge is to explore and experiment, keeping any   18
structure tentative and therefore easily reversible. Taken to the
extreme, these are people who skip from one trial job and one
limited personal encounter to another, spending their twenties
in the *transient* state.

Although the choices of our twenties are not irrevocable,   19
they do set in motion a Life Pattern. Some of us follow the lock-
in pattern, others the transient pattern, the wunderkind pat-

tern, the caregiver pattern, and there are a number of others. Such patterns strongly influence the particular questions raised for each person during each passage. . . .

Buoyed by powerful illusions and belief in the power of the will, we commonly insist in our twenties that what we have chosen to do is the one true course in life. Our backs go up at the merest hint that we are like our parents, that two decades of parental training might be reflected in our current actions and attitudes.   20

"Not me," is the motto, "I'm different."   21

Catch-30

Impatient with devoting ourselves to the "shoulds," a new vitality springs from within as we approach 30. Men and women alike speak of feeling too narrow and restricted. They blame all sorts of things, but what the restrictions boil down to are the outgrowth of career and personal choices of the twenties. They may have been choices perfectly suited to that stage. But now the fit feels different. Some inner aspect that was left out is striving to be taken into account. Important new choices must be made, and commitments altered or deepened. The work involves great change, turmoil, and often crisis — a simultaneous feeling of rock bottom and the urge to bust out.   22

One common response is the tearing up of the life we spent most of our twenties putting together. It may mean striking out on a secondary road toward a new vision or converting a dream of "running for president" into a more realistic goal. The single person feels a push to find a partner. The woman who was previously content at home with children chafes to venture into the world. The childless couple reconsiders children. And almost everyone who is married, especially those married for seven years, feels a discontent.   23

If the discontent doesn't lead to a divorce, it will, or should, call for a serious review of the marriage and of each partner's aspirations in their Catch-30 condition. The gist of that condition was expressed by a 29-year-old associate with a Wall Street law firm: 24

"I'm considering leaving the firm. I've been there four years   25
now; I'm getting good feedback, but I have no clients of my own.
I feel weak. If I wait much longer, it will be too late, too close to
that fateful time of decision on whether or not to become a partner. I'm success-oriented. But the concept of being 55 years old
and stuck in a monotonous job drives me wild. It drives me
crazy now, just a little bit. I'd say that 85 percent of the time I
thoroughly enjoy my work. But when I get a screwball case, I
come away from court saying, 'What am I doing here?' It's a *visceral* reaction that I'm wasting my time. I'm trying to find some
way to make a social contribution or a slot in city government. I
keep saying, 'There's something more.' "

Besides the push to broaden himself professionally, there is a   26
wish to expand his personal life. He wants two or three more
children. "The concept of a home has become very meaningful
to me, a place to get away from troubles and relax. I love my son
in a way I could not have anticipated. I never could live alone."

Consumed with the work of making his own critical life-   27
steering decisions, he demonstrates the essential shift at this age:
an absolute requirement to be more self-concerned. The self has
new value now that his competency has been proved.

His wife is struggling with her own age-30 priorities. She   28
wants to go to law school, but he wants more children. If she is
going to stay home, she wants him to make more time for the
family instead of taking on even wider professional commitments. His view of the bind, of what he would most like from his
wife, is this:

"I'd like not to be bothered. It sounds cruel, but I'd like not   29
to have to worry about what she's going to do next week. Which
is why I've told her several times that I think she should do
something. Go back to school and get a degree in social work or
geography or whatever. Hopefully that would fulfill her, and
then I wouldn't have to worry about her line of problems. I want
her to be decisive about herself."

The trouble with his advice to his wife is that it comes out of   30
concern with *his* convenience, rather than with *her* development. She quickly picks up on this lack of goodwill: He is trying
to dispose of her. At the same time, he refuses her the same latitude to be "selfish" in making an independent decision to

broaden her horizons. Both perceive a lack of mutuality. And that is what Catch-30 is all about for the couple.

Rooting and Extending

Life becomes less provisional, more rational and orderly in 31 the early thirties. We begin to settle down in the full sense. Most of us begin putting down roots and sending out new shoots. People buy houses and become very earnest about climbing career ladders. Men in particular concern themselves with "making it." Satisfaction with marriage generally goes downhill in the thirties (for those who have remained together) compared with the highly valued, vision-supporting marriage of the twenties. This coincides with the couple's reduced social life outside the family and the in-turned focus on raising their children.

The Deadline Decade

In the middle of the thirties we come upon a crossroads. We 32 have reached the halfway mark. Yet even as we are reaching our prime, we begin to see there is a place where it finishes. Time starts to squeeze.

The loss of youth, the faltering of physical powers we have 33 always taken for granted, the fading purpose of stereotyped roles by which we have thus far identified ourselves, the spiritual dilemma of having no absolute answers — any or all of these shocks can give this passage the character of crisis. Such thoughts usher in a decade between 35 and 45 that can be called the Deadline Decade. It is a time of both danger and opportunity. All of us have the chance to rework the narrow identity by which we defined ourselves in the first half of life. And those of us who make the most of the opportunity will have a full-out authenticity crisis.

To come through this authenticity crisis, we must reexam- 34 ine our purposes and reevaluate how to spend our resources from now on. "Why am I doing all this? What do I really believe in?" No matter what we have been doing, there will be parts of ourselves that have been suppressed and now need to find expression. "Bad" feelings will demand acknowledgment along with the good.

It is frightening to step off onto the treacherous footbridge   35
leading to the second half of life. We can't take everything with us on this journey through uncertainty. Along the way, we discover that we are alone. We no longer have to ask permission because we are the providers of our own safety. We must learn to give ourselves permission. We stumble upon feminine or masculine aspects of our natures that up to this time have usually been masked. There is grieving to be done because an old self is dying. By taking in our suppressed and even our unwanted parts, we prepare at the gut level for the reintegration of an identity that is ours and ours alone — not some artificial form put together to please the culture or our mates. It is a dark passage at the beginning. But by disassembling ourselves, we can glimpse the light and gather our parts into a renewal.

Women sense this inner crossroads earlier than men do.   36
The time pinch often prompts a woman to stop and take an all-points survey at age 35. Whatever options she has already played out, she feels a "my last chance" urgency to review those options she has set aside and those that aging and biology will close off in the *now foreseeable* future. For all her qualms and confusion about where to start looking for a new future, she usually enjoys an exhilaration of release. Assertiveness begins rising. There are so many firsts ahead.

Men, too, feel the time push in the mid-thirties. Most men   37
respond by pressing down harder on the career accelerator. It's "my last chance" to pull away from the pack. It is no longer enough to be the loyal junior executive, the promising young novelist, the lawyer who does a little *pro bono* work on the side. He wants now to become part of top management, to be recognized as an established writer, or an active politician with his own legislative program. With some chagrin, he discovers that he has been too anxious to please and too vulnerable to criticism. He wants to put together his own ship.

During this period of intense concentration on external ad-   38
vancement, it is common for men to be unaware of the more difficult, gut issues that are propelling them forward. The survey

that was neglected at 35 becomes a crucible at 40. Whatever rung of achievement he has reached, the man of 40 usually feels stale, restless, burdened, and unappreciated. He worries about his health. He wonders, "Is this all there is?" He may make a series of departures from well-established lifelong base lines, including marriage. More and more men are seeking second careers in midlife. Some become self-destructive. And many men in their forties experience a major shift of emphasis away from pouring all their energies into their own advancement. A more tender, feeling side comes into play. They become interested in developing an ethical self.

Renewal or Resignation

Somewhere in the mid-forties, equilibrium is regained. A   39
new stability is achieved, which may be more or less satisfying.

If one has refused to budge through the midlife transition,   40
the sense of staleness will calcify into resignation. One by one,
the safety and supports will be withdrawn from the person who
is standing still. Parents will become children; children will become
strangers; a mate will grow away or go away; the career
will become just a job — and each of these events will be felt as
an abandonment. The crisis will probably emerge again around
50. And although its wallop will be greater, the jolt may be just
what is needed to prod the resigned middle-ager toward seeking
revitalization.

On the other hand . . .   41

If we have confronted ourselves in the middle passage and   42
found a renewal of purpose around which we are eager to build a
more authentic life structure, these may well be the best years.
Personal happiness takes a sharp turn upward for partners who
can now accept the fact: "I cannot expect *anyone* to fully understand
me." Parents can be forgiven for the burdens of our childhood.
Children can be let go without leaving us in collapsed silence.
At 50, there is a new warmth and mellowing. Friends
become more important than ever, but so does privacy. Since it
is so often proclaimed by people past midlife, the motto of this
stage might be "No more bullshit."

QUESTIONS ON MEANING AND PURPOSE

1. In your own words, describe each of Sheehy's six predictable stages of adult life.
2. According to the author, what happens to people who fail to experience a given stage of growth at the usual time?
3. How would you characterize Sheehy's attitude toward growth and change in adult life?
4. For what PURPOSE does Sheehy employ the method of division? How does it serve her readers, too?

QUESTIONS ON WRITING STRATEGY

1. How apt, do you think, is the opening METAPHOR: the comparison between a lobster periodically shedding its shell and a person entering each new phase of growth?
2. What, if anything, does the author gain by writing her essay in the first PERSON plural?
3. What difficulties go along with making GENERALIZATIONS about human beings? To what extent does Sheehy surmount these difficulties?
4. How much knowledge of psychology does Sheehy expect of her AUDIENCE?

QUESTIONS ON LANGUAGE

1. Consult your dictionary if you need help in defining the following words: crustacean (paragraph 1); embryonic, tranquility, equilibrium (2); autonomy, primacy (3); plausible (4); inaccessible (8); sanctuary (9); impetus (10); exhilarating, mentor (14); pervasive (15); irrevocable (16); tentative (18); wunderkind (19); visceral (25); mutuality (30); dilemma (33); *pro bono*, chagrin, vulnerable (37); crucible (38); calcify (40).
2. What is a "nuclear family" (paragraph 15)?
3. The author coins a few phrases of her own. Refer to the context in which they appear to help you define the following: *step-style* (paragraph 3); Stronger One (11); *locked in* (17); Catch-30 (24); authenticity crisis (33).

SUGGESTIONS FOR WRITING

1. From your experience, observation, or reading, test the accuracy of one of Sheehy's accounts of a typical period of crisis.
2. Inspired by Sheehy's division of life after eighteen into phases, look back on your own earlier life or that of a younger person you know, and detail a series of phases in it. Invent names for the phases.

· Kenneth Burke ·

Born in Pittsburgh in 1897, KENNETH BURKE is most often labeled a literary critic. "My aim," he says of his life's work, "is to develop a theory of language in general, with emphasis upon its application to specific texts." Yet Burke's highly original thinking neatly fits no categories, and as a critic he delights in bringing together areas of knowledge ordinarily separated. A writer of broad range (author not only of criticism but also of a novel, short stories, poems, and translations from the German), he has held varied jobs: music critic for *The Dial* and *The Nation*, visiting professor of sociology at Harvard. Of late, some of his ideas have been increasingly applied to the teaching of composition, notably "Burke's Pentad," a series of questions with which to explore before beginning to write (see page 346). Burke's major critical works include (and we list only the dates of revised editions) *Permanence and Change* (1954), *Attitudes toward History* (1959), *The Philosophy of Literary Form* (1967), *A Grammar of Motives* and *A Rhetoric of Motives* (1969), and *The Rhetoric of Religion* (1970). Though he studied at Ohio State and Columbia, Burke never earned a degree; his eight doctorates are honorary. Still lecturing occasionally, he continues to live and work, as he has done for many years, on a farm in Andover, New Jersey.

Classifying Proverbs

Kenneth Burke seems to have regarded many of his published books as early drafts. With zeal, he has later revised them, sometimes greatly changing them. Perhaps his most widely read book, *The Philosophy of Literary Form: Studies in Symbolic Action*, first appeared in 1941. In 1957 Burke revised and abridged it; he later reissued it, unabridged, in 1967. A collection of miscellaneous essays, it escorts us on a difficult but dazzling journey through psychoanalysis, magic, religion, Shakespeare's plays, semantics, literary theory, the rise of Nazism, and the music of poetry. For the following lively illustration of a first-rate writer dividing and classifying, we have gone to the abridged edition. What follows is only Section 1 of a much longer essay, "Literature as Equipment for Living." Burke sorts out English proverbs according to their purposes. (After so doing, he will go on to suggest, "Why not extend such analysis of proverbs to encompass the whole field of literature?")

Examine random specimens in *The Oxford Dictionary of English Proverbs*. You will note, I think, that there is no "pure" literature here. Everything is "medicine." Proverbs are designed for consolation or vengeance, for admonition or exhortation, for foretelling.   1

Or they name typical, recurrent situations. That is, people find a certain social relationship recurring so frequently that they must "have a word for it." The Eskimos have special names for many different kinds of snow (fifteen, if I remember rightly) because variations in the quality of snow greatly affect their living. Hence, they must "size up" snow much more accurately than we do. And the same is true of social phenomena. Social structures give rise to "type" situations, subtle subdivisions of the relationships involved in competitive and cooperative acts. Many proverbs seek to chart, in more or less homey and picturesque ways, these "type" situations. I submit that such naming is done, not for the sheer glory of the thing, but because of its bearing upon human welfare. A different name for snow implies a different kind of hunt. Some names for snow imply that one should not hunt at all. And similarly, the names for typical, recurrent social situations are not developed out of "disinterested curiosity," but because the names imply a command (what to expect, what to look out for).   2

To illustrate with a few representative examples: 3

Proverbs designed for consolation: "The sun does not shine on both sides of the hedge at once." "Think of ease, but work on." "Little troubles the eye, but far less the soul." "The worst luck now, the better another time." "The wind in one's face makes one wise." "He that hath lands hath quarrels." "He knows how to carry the dead cock home." "He is not poor that hath little, but he that desireth much."   4

For vengeance: "At length the fox is brought to the furrier." "Shod in the cradle, barefoot in the stubble." "Sue a beggar and   5 get a louse." "The higher the ape goes, the more he shows his tail." "The moon does not heed the barking of dogs." "He measures another's corn by his own bushel." "He shuns the man who knows him well." "Fools tie knots and wise men loose them."

Proverbs that have to do with foretelling (the most obvious   6
are those to do with the weather): "Sow peas and beans in the wane of the moon, Who soweth them sooner, he soweth too soon." "When the wind's in the north, the skillful fisher goes not forth." "When the sloe tree is as white as a sheet, sow your barley whether it be dry or wet." "When the sun sets bright and clear, An easterly wind you need not fear. When the sun sets in a bank, A westerly wind we shall not want."

In short: "Keep your weather eye open": be realistic about   7
sizing up today's weather, because your accuracy has bearing upon tomorrow's weather. And forecast not only the meteorological weather, but also the social weather: "When the moon's in the full, then wit's in the wane." "Straws show which way the wind blows." "When the fish is caught, the net is laid aside." "Remove an old tree, and it will wither to death." "The wolf may lose his teeth, but never his nature." "He that bites on every weed must needs light on poison." "Whether the pitcher strikes the stone, or the stone the pitcher, it is bad for the pitcher." "Eagles catch no flies." "The more laws, the more offenders."

In this foretelling category we might also include the recipes   8
for wise living, sometimes moral, sometimes technical: "First thrive, and then wive." "Think with the wise but talk with the vulgar." "When the fox preacheth, then beware your geese." "Venture a small fish to catch a great one." "Respect a man, he will do the more."

In the class of "typical, recurrent situations" we might put   9
such proverbs and proverbial expressions as: "Sweet appears sour when we pay." "The treason is loved but the traitor is hated." "The wine in the bottle does not quench thirst." "The sun is never the worse for shining on a dunghill." "The lion kicked by an ass." "The lion's share." "To catch one napping." "To smell a rat." "To cool one's heels."

By all means, I do not wish to suggest that this is the only 10
way in which the proverbs could be classified. For instance, I
have listed in the "foretelling" group the proverb, "When the
fox preacheth, then beware your geese." But it could obviously
be "taken over" for vindictive purposes. Or consider a proverb
like "Virtue flies from the heart of a mercenary man." A poor
man might obviously use it either to console himself for being
poor (the implication being, "Because I am poor in money I am
rich in virtue") or to strike at another (the implication being,
"When he got money, what else could you expect of him but de-
terioration?"). In fact, we could even say that such symbolic
vengeance would itself be an aspect of solace. And a proverb like
"The sun is never the worse for shining on a dunghill" (which I
have listed under "typical recurrent situations") might as well be
put in the vindictive category.

The point of issue is not to find categories that "place" the 11
proverbs once and for all. What I want is categories that suggest
their active nature. Here is no "realism for its own sake." Here is
realism for promise, admonition, solace, vengeance, foretelling,
instruction, charting, all for the direct bearing that such acts
have upon matters of welfare. . . .

Proverbs are *strategies* for dealing with *situations*. In so far as 12
situations are typical and recurrent in a given social structure,
people develop names for them and strategies for handling
them. Another name for strategies might be *attitudes*.

People have often commented on the fact that there are *con-* 13
trary proverbs. But I believe that the above approach to proverbs suggests a necessary modification of that comment. The apparent contradictions depend upon differences in *attitude*,
involving a correspondingly different choice of *strategy*. Consider, for instance, the *apparently* opposite pair: "Repentance
comes too late" and "Never too late to mend." The first is admonitory. It says in effect: "You'd better look out, or you'll get
yourself too far into this business." The second is consolatory,
saying in effect: "Buck up, old man, you can still pull out of
this."

QUESTIONS ON MEANING AND PURPOSE

1. In his INTRODUCTION (paragraph 1), Burke contends that proverbs aren't "pure" literature, but "medicine." What do you understand him to mean?
2. What are some apparent PURPOSES (according to Burke) for which people make up proverbs? What general function and usefulness do proverbs serve?
3. Explain what you understand by these English proverbs that Burke cites: "Little troubles the eye, but far less the soul," "The wind in one's face makes one wise" (paragraph 4); "Sue a beggar and get a louse," "The higher the ape goes, the more he shows his tail" (5); "He that bites on every weed must needs light on poison," "Eagles catch no flies" (7); "The treason is loved but the traitor is hated" (9).
4. How does Burke defend proverbs against the charge that their makers contradict one another (and so, presumably, don't have much wisdom to give us after all)?

QUESTIONS ON WRITING STRATEGY

1. On what basis does Burke classify proverbs? What determines the categories in which he places them?
2. Why does Burke admit (in paragraph 10) that it would be possible to classify certain proverbs in quite different ways? What possible objection does he anticipate from his AUDIENCE?
3. "This so-called essay is nothing but a bare-bones list." Do you agree? What, besides list making, did its writer need to put into it?

QUESTIONS ON LANGUAGE

1. Some of the proverbs Burke cites have been around for hundreds of years; some are still part of living speech. To what do you attribute this long life? What do you find in their language that makes them memorable?
2. Define *admonition* and *exhortation* (paragraph 1). Burke doesn't draw up a category of proverbs that admonish or exhort us; but from among the proverbs he gives us, find one or two exhortative examples and one or two admonitory examples.

SUGGESTIONS FOR WRITING

1. Gather together several examples of some other kind of brief discourse that interests you — jokes, insults, nicknames, names of sports teams or rock groups, graffiti, children's skip-rope jingles, advertising slogans, comic strip exclamations (OOF!, AWKKKK!, EEEEEK!). Sort out your specimens into at least three categories. Then write an essay on your subject, illustrating each category with examples.

2. Write eight or ten new, original proverbs. Each of your proverbs should have a purpose: one of the ones Burke cites, or some other. You may find it helpful to cast your thoughts upon typical situations people get into that you might give them advice about. Try thinking like a proverb maker: in terms of sun and moon; trees, birds, and animals; bottles, money, dunghills, and other common objects; eating, sleeping, tying knots, and other everyday acts. If you need inspiration, browse in Burke's source, *The Oxford Dictionary of English Proverbs*, or other compilations. Harold Courlander's *Treasury of Afro-American Folklore* (New York, 1976) has sections of proverbs from Haiti, Surinam, and the United States—samples: "Talking about fire doesn't boil the pot," "You can't dance till dawn with a borrowed drum," and (from Creole Louisiana) "Don't tie up a dog with a chain of sausages."

   After you get your proverbs down on paper in rough form, make sure your choice of words is not ABSTRACT but CONCRETE. Strive for concision. Bring your proverbs to class, prepared to read them aloud. See if you have made up any proverb that others will want to quote. This assignment won't be easy, but it could make you immortal. All you have to do is put a pointed thought into the right words — like whoever first said "Sweet appears sour when we pay."

PAUL FUSSELL, literary critic and cultural historian, was born in Pasadena, California, in 1924. After taking his Ph.D. at Harvard, he taught English at Connecticut College, then at Rutgers for twenty-eight years. Earlier in his career, Fussell won high repute for his *Poetic Meter and Poetic Form* (1965, revised in 1979) and for his studies in the British eighteenth century. In 1975, with *The Great War and Modern Memory*, a study of World War I and its literature, his work reached a wider audience and gained him a National Book Award, an award from the National Book Critics Circle, and the Ralph Waldo Emerson Award of Phi Beta Kappa. Some of Fussell's knowledge of war was personal: As an infantry officer in World War II, he had received the Bronze Star and twice had been wounded in combat. He now serves as contributing editor for *The New Republic* and as Donald T. Regan Professor of English at the University of Pennsylvania. His recent books include *Abroad: British Literary Traveling between the Wars* (1980) and *Class: A Guide through the American Status System* (1983).

Notes on Class

This lively, debatable partitioning of American society first appeared in 1980 in *The New Republic*, a serious but not solemn magazine of comment on the nation and the world. Later, Fussell reprinted it in a varied gathering of his essays from American and British magazines, *The Boy Scout Handbook and Other Observations* (1982). "Notes on Class" contains premises and scaffolding on which Fussell was to build later in *Class*. More amply in that whole book, he sets forth his analysis, devoting chapters to indicators such as personal appearance and clothing, houses and cars, consumption (drinking, eating out, traveling, catalog shopping), education and reading (if any), and choice of words. He also makes sharp remarks about both social climbing and social sinking; if these short "Notes" intrigue you, don't miss the book.

The task of dividing American society into levels is clearly formidable. In a new postscript that follows his essay, Fussell tells us how he first went about it. Class isn't a subject that most Americans talk about much; one great value of Fussell's essay may be to help us face matters that often worry us more than we admit.

If the dirty little secret used to be sex, now it is the facts   1
about social class. No subject today is more likely to offend.
Over thirty years ago Dr. Kinsey generated considerable alarm
by disclosing that despite appearances one-quarter of the male
population had enjoyed at least one homosexual orgasm. A similar alarm can be occasioned today by asserting that despite the
much-discussed mechanism of "social mobility" and the constant redistribution of income in this country, it is virtually impossible to break out of the social class in which one has been
nurtured. Bad news for the'ambitious as well as the bogus, but
there it is.

Defining class is difficult, as sociologists and anthropologists   2
have learned. The more data we feed into the machines, the less
likely it is that significant formulations will emerge. What follows here is based not on interviews, questionnaires, or any kind
of quantitative technique but on perhaps a more trustworthy
method — perception. Theory may inform us that there are
three classes in America, high, middle, and low. Perception will
tell us that there are at least nine, which I would designate and
arrange like this:

> Top Out-of-Sight
> Upper
> Upper Middle
>
> ---
>
> Middle
> High-Proletarian
> Mid-Proletarian
> Low-Proletarian
>
> ---
>
> Destitute
> Bottom Out-of-Sight

In addition, there is a floating class with no permanent location
in this hierarchy. We can call it Class X. It consists of well-to-do

hippies, "artists," "writers" (who write nothing), floating bohe-
mians, politicians out of office, disgraced athletic coaches, resid-
ers abroad, rock stars, "celebrities," and the shrewder sort of
spies.

The quasi-official division of the population into three eco-   3
nomic classes called high-, middle-, and low-income groups
rather misses the point, because as a class indicator the amount
of money is not as important as the source. Important distinctions at both the top and bottom of the class scale arise less from
degree of affluence than from the people or institutions to whom
one is beholden for support. For example, the main thing distinguishing the top three classes from each other is the amount of
money inherited in relation to the amount currently earned.
The Top Out-of-Sight Class (Rockefellers, du Ponts, Mellons,
Fords, Whitneys) lives on inherited capital entirely. Its money is
like the hats of the Boston ladies who, asked where they got
them, answer, "Oh, we *have* our hats." No one whose money,
no matter how ample, comes from his own work, like film stars,
can be a member of the Top Out-of-Sights, even if the size of his
income and the extravagance of his expenditure permit him
temporary social access to it.

Since we expect extremes to meet, we are not surprised to   4
find the very lowest class, Bottom Out-of-Sight, similar to the
highest in one crucial respect: it is given its money and kept sort
of afloat not by its own efforts but by the welfare machinery or
the prison system. Members of the Top Out-of-Sight Class
sometimes earn some money, as directors or board members of
philanthropic or even profitable enterprises, but the amount
earned is laughable in relation to the amount already possessed.
Membership in the Top Out-of-Sight Class depends on the ability to flourish without working at all, and it is this that suggests
a curious brotherhood between those at the top and the bottom
of the scale.

It is this also that distinguishes the Upper Class from its bet-   5
ters. It lives on both inherited money and a salary from attractive, if usually slight, work, without which, even if it could survive and even flourish, it would feel bored and a little ashamed.
The next class down, the Upper Middle, may possess virtually as

much as the two above it. The difference is that it has earned most of it, in law, medicine, oil, real-estate, or even the more honorific forms of trade. The Upper Middles are afflicted with a bourgeois sense of shame, a conviction that to live on the earnings of others, even forebears, is not entirely nice.

The Out-of-Sight Classes at top and bottom have something 6 else in common: they are literally all but invisible (hence their name). The façades of Top Out-of-Sight houses are never seen from the street, and such residences (like Rockefeller's upstate New York premises) are often hidden away deep in the hills, safe from envy and its ultimate attendants, confiscatory taxation and finally expropriation. The Bottom Out-of-Sight Class is equally invisible. When not hidden away in institutions or claustrated in monasteries, lamaseries, or communes, it is hiding from creditors, deceived bail-bondsmen, and merchants intent on repossessing cars and furniture. (This class is visible briefly in one place, in the spring on the streets of New York City, but after this ritual yearly show of itself it disappears again.) When you pass a house with a would-be impressive façade addressing the street, you know it is occupied by a mere member of the Upper or Upper Middle Class. The White House is an example. Its residents, even on those occasions when they are Kennedys, can never be classified as Top Out-of-Sight but only Upper Class. The house is simply too conspicuous, and temporary residence there usually constitutes a come-down for most of its occupants. It is a hopelessly Upper- or Upper-Middle-Class place.

Another feature of both Top and Bottom Out-of-Sight 7 Classes is their anxiety to keep their names out of the papers, and this too suggests that socially the President is always rather vulgar. All the classes in between Top and Bottom Out-of-Sight slaver for personal publicity (monograms on shirts, inscribing one's name on lawn-mowers and power tools, etc.), and it is this lust to be known almost as much as income that distinguishes them from their Top and Bottom neighbors. The High- and Mid-Prole Classes can be recognized immediately by their pride in advertising their physical presence, a way of saying, "Look! We pay our bills and have a known place in the community, and you can find us there any time." Thus hypertrophied house-numbers on the front, or house numbers written "Two Hundred Five" ("Two Hundred and Five" is worse) instead of 205, or flamboyant house or family names blazoned on façades, like "The Willows" or "The Polnickis."

(If you go behind the façade into the house itself, you will   8
find a fairly trustworthy class indicator in the kind of wood visible there. The top three classes invariably go in for hardwoods for doors and panelling; the Middle and High-Prole Classes, pine, either plain or "knotty." The knotty-pine "den" is an absolute stigma of the Middle Class, one never to be overcome or disguised by temporarily affected higher usages. Below knotty pine there is plywood.)

Façade study is a badly neglected anthropological field. As   9
we work down from the (largely white-painted) bank-like façades of the Upper and Upper Middle Classes, we encounter such Middle and Prole conventions as these, which I rank in order of social status:

Middle	1.	A potted tree on either side of the front door, and the more pointy and symmetrical the better.
	2.	A large rectangular picture-window in a split-level "ranch" house, displaying a table-lamp between two side curtains. The cellophane on the lampshade must be visibly inviolate.
	3.	Two chairs, usually metal with pipe arms, disposed on the front porch as a "conversation group," in stubborn defiance of the traffic thundering past.
High-Prole	4.	Religious shrines in the garden, which if small and understated, are slightly higher class than
Mid-Prole	5.	Plaster gnomes and flamingos, and blue or lavender shiny spheres supported by fluted cast-concrete pedestals.
Low-Prole	6.	Defunct truck tires painted white and enclosing flower beds. (Auto tires are a grade higher.)
	7.	Flower-bed designs worked in dead light bulbs or the butts of disused beer bottles.

The Destitute have no façades to decorate, and of course the Bottom Out-of-Sights, being invisible, have none either, although both these classes can occasionally help others decorate theirs — painting tires white on an hourly basis, for example, or even watering and fertilizing the potted trees of the Middle Class. Class X also does not decorate its façades, hoping to stay loose and unidentifiable, ready to re-locate and shape-change the moment it sees that its cover has been penetrated.

In this list of façade conventions an important principle   10
emerges. Organic materials have higher status than metal or plastic. We should take warning from Sophie Portnoy's[1] aluminum venetian blinds, which are also lower than wood because the slats are curved, as if "improved," instead of classically flat. The same principle applies, as *The Preppy Handbook*[2] has shown so effectively, to clothing fabrics, which must be cotton or wool, never Dacron or anything of that prole kind. In the same way, yachts with wood hulls, because they must be repaired or replaced (at high cost) more often, are classier than yachts with fiberglass hulls, no matter how shrewdly merchandised. Plastic hulls are cheaper and more practical, which is precisely why they lack class.

As we move down the scale, income of course decreases, but   11
income is less important to class than other seldom-invoked measurements: for example, the degree to which one's work is supervised by an omnipresent immediate superior. The more free from supervision, the higher the class, which is why a dentist ranks higher than a mechanic working under a foreman in a large auto shop, even if he makes considerably more money than the dentist. The two trades may be thought equally dirty: it is the dentist's freedom from supervision that helps confer class upon him. Likewise, a high-school teacher obliged to file weekly "lesson plans" with a principal or "curriculum co-ordinator" thereby occupies a class position lower than a tenured professor, who reports to no one, even though the high-school teacher may be richer, smarter, and nicer. (Supervisors and Inspectors are titles that go with public schools, post offices, and

[1]Mother of the central character in *Portnoy's Complaint* (1969), a comic novel by Philip Roth. — EDS.

[2]Popular humor book (1980), purportedly a guide to the looks, dress, tastes, and habits of students and ex-students of private preparatory schools. — EDS.

police departments: the student of class will need to know no more.) It is largely because they must report that even the highest members of the naval and military services lack social status: they all have designated supervisors — even the Chairman of the Joint Chiefs of Staff has to report to the President.

Class is thus defined less by bare income than by constraints 12 and insecurities. It is defined also by habits and attitudes. Take television watching. The Top Out-of-Sight Class doesn't watch at all. It owns the companies and pays others to monitor the thing. It is also entirely devoid of intellectual or even emotional curiosity: it *has* its ideas the way it has its money. The Upper Class does look at television but it prefers Camp[3] offerings, like the films of Jean Harlow or Jon Hall. The Upper Middle Class regards TV as vulgar except for the highminded emissions of National Educational Television, which it watches avidly, especially when, like the Shakespeare series, they are the most incompetently directed and boring. Upper Middles make a point of forbidding children to watch more than an hour a day and worry a lot about violence in society and sugar in cereal. The Middle Class watches, preferring the more "beautiful" kinds of non-body-contact sports like tennis or gymnastics or figure-skating (the music is a redeeming feature here). With High-, Mid-, and Low-Proles we find heavy viewing of the soaps in the daytime and rugged body-contact sports (football, hockey, boxing) in the evening. The lower one is located in the Prole classes the more likely one is to watch "Bowling for Dollars" and "Wonder Woman" and "The Hulk" and when choosing a game show to prefer "Joker's Wild" to "The Family Feud," whose jokes are sometimes incomprehensible. Destitutes and Bottom Out-of-Sights have in common a problem involving choice. Destitutes usually "own" about three color sets, and the problem is which three programs to run at once. Bottom Out-of-Sights exercise no choice at all, the decisions being made for them by correctional or institutional personnel.

---

[3]This term may be applied to anything cutesy, banal, inappropriate, artificial but not artistic, and in spectacularly bad taste: plastic statues of the Venus de Milo, for example, with alarm clocks where their navels ought to be. — Eds.

The time when the evening meal is consumed defines class   13
better than, say, the presence or absence on the table of ketchup
bottles and ashtrays shaped like little toilets enjoining the diners
to "Put Your Butts Here." Destitutes and Bottom Out-of-Sights
eat dinner at 5:30, for the Prole staff on which they depend must
clean up and be out roller-skating or bowling early in the evening. Thus Proles eat at 6:00 or 6:30. The Middles eat at 7:00,
the Upper Middles at 7:30 or, if very ambitious, at 8:00. The
Uppers and Top Out-of-Sights dine at 8:30 or 9:00 or even later,
after nightly protracted "cocktail" sessions lasting usually
around two hours. Sometimes they forget to eat at all.

Similarly, the physical appearance of the various classes de-   14
fines them fairly accurately. Among the top four classes thin is
good, and the bottom two classes appear to ape this usage, although down there thin is seldom a matter of choice. It is the
three Prole classes that tend to fat, partly as a result of their use
of convenience foods and plenty of beer. These are the classes
too where anxiety about slipping down a rung causes nervous
overeating, resulting in fat that can be rationalized as advertising the security of steady wages and the ability to "eat out" often. Even "Going Out for Breakfast" is not unthinkable for
Proles, if we are to believe that they respond to the McDonald's
TV ads as they're supposed to. A recent magazine ad for a diet
book aimed at Proles stigmatizes a number of erroneous assumptions about body weight, proclaiming with some inelegance that
"They're all a crock." Among such vulgar errors is the proposition that "All Social Classes Are Equally Overweight." This the
ad rejects by noting quite accurately:

> Your weight is an advertisement of your social standing. A
> century ago, corpulence was a sign of success. But no more.
> Today it is the badge of the lower-middle-class, where obesity
> is *four times* more prevalent than it is among the upper-middle
> and middle classes.

It is not just four times more prevalent. It is at least four times
more visible, as any observer can testify who has witnessed Prole
women perambulating shopping malls in their bright, very tight
jersey trousers. Not just obesity but the flaunting of obesity is
the Prole sign, as if the object were to give maximum aesthetic

offense to the higher classes and thus achieve a form of revenge.

Another physical feature with powerful class meaning is the   15
wearing of plaster casts on legs and ankles by members of the top
three classes. These casts, a sort of white badge of honor, be-
token stylish mishaps with frivolous but costly toys like horses,
skis, snowmobiles, and mopeds. They signify a high level of conspicuous waste in a social world where questions of unpayable
medical bills or missed working days do not apply. But in the
matter of clothes, the Top Out-of-Sight is different from both
Upper and Upper Middle Classes. It prefers to appear in new
clothes, whereas the class just below it prefers old clothes. Likewise, all three Prole classes make much of new garments, with
the highest possible polyester content. The question does not
arise in the same form with Destitutes and Bottom Out-of-
Sights. They wear used clothes, the thrift shop and prison supply room serving as their Bonwit's and Korvette's.

This American class system is very hard for foreigners to   16
master, partly because most foreigners imagine that since America was founded by the British it must retain something of British institutions. But our class system is more subtle than the
British, more a matter of gradations than of blunt divisions, like
the binary distinction between a gentleman and a cad. This
seems to lack plausibility here. One seldom encounters in the
United States the sort of absolute prohibitions which (half-comi-
cally, to be sure) one is asked to believe define the gentleman in
England. Like these:

> A gentleman never wears brown shoes in the city, or
> A gentleman never wears a green suit, or
> A gentleman never has soup at lunch, or
> A gentleman never uses a comb, or
> A gentleman never smells of anything but tar, or
> "No gentleman can fail to admire Bellini." — W. H. Auden[4]

---

[4]Vincenzo Bellini (1801–1835) was the Italian composer of *Norma* and
other operas; Auden (1903–1973), an English-born American poet, critic, and
translator of opera librettos. — EDS.

In America it seems to matter much less the way you present yourself — green, brown, neat, sloppy, scented — than what your backing is — that is, where your money comes from. What the upper orders display here is no special uniform but the kind of psychological security they derive from knowing that others recognize their freedom from petty anxieties and trivial prohibitions.

"Language most shows a man," Ben Jonson used to say. 17 "Speak, that I may see thee." As all acute conservatives like Jonson know, dictional behavior is a powerful signal of a firm class line. Nancy Mitford so indicated in her hilarious essay of 1955, "The English Aristocracy," based in part on Professor Alan S. C. Ross's more sober study "Linguistic Class-Indicators in Present-Day English." Both Mitford and Ross were interested in only one class demarcation, the one dividing the English Upper Class ("U," in their shorthand) from all below it ("non-U"). Their main finding was that euphemism and genteelism are vulgar. People who are socially secure risk nothing by calling a spade a spade, and indicate their top-dog status by doing so as frequently as possible. Thus the U-word is *rich*, the non-U *wealthy*. What U-speakers call *false teeth* non-U's call *dentures*. The same with *wigs* and *hairpieces*, *dying* and *passing away* (or *over*).

For Mitford, linguistic assaults from below are sometimes so 18 shocking that the only kind reaction of a U-person is silence. It is "the only possible U-response," she notes, "to many embarrassing modern situations: the ejaculation of 'cheers' before drinking, for example, or 'It was so nice seeing you' after saying goodbye. In silence, too, one must endure the use of the Christian name by comparative strangers. . . ." In America, although there are more classes distinguishable here, a linguistic polarity is as visible as in England. Here U-speech (or our equivalent of it) characterizes some Top Out-of-Sights, Uppers, Upper Middles, and Class X's. All below is a waste land of genteelism and jargon and pretentious mispronunciation, pathetic evidence of the upward social scramble and its hazards. Down below, the ear is bad and no one has been trained to listen. Culture words especially are the downfall of the aspiring. Sometimes it is diphthongs that invite disgrace, as in *be-yóu-ti-ful*. Sometimes the aspirant rushes full-face into disaster by flourishing those secret class indicators, the words *exquisite* and *despicable*, which, like another secret sign, *patina*, he (and of course she as often) stresses on the middle syllable instead of the first. High-class names from cultural history are a frequent cause of betrayal, especially if they are British, like Henry Purcell.[5] In America non-U speakers are fond of usages like "Between he and I." Recalling vaguely that mentioning oneself last, as in "He and I were there," is thought gentlemanly, they apply that principle uniformly, to the entire destruction of the objective case. There's also a problem with *like*. They remember something about the dangers of illiteracy its use invites, and hope to stay out of trouble by always using *as* instead, finally saying things like "He looks as his father." These contortions are common among young (usually insurance or computer) trainees, raised on Leon Uris,[6] and *Playboy*, most of them Mid- or High-Proles pounding on the firmly shut door of the Middle Class. They are the careful, dark-suited first-generation aspirants to American respectability and (hopefully, as they would put it) power. Together with their deployment of the anomalous nominative case on all occasions goes their preference for jargon (you can hear them going at it on airplanes) like *parameters* and *guidelines* and *bottom lines* and *funding, dialogue, interface,* and *lifestyles*. Their world of language is one containing little more than smokescreens and knowing innovations. "Do we gift the Johnsons, dear?" the corporate wife will ask the corporate husband at Christmas time.

Just below these people, down among the Mid- and Low-   19
Proles, the complex sentence gives trouble. It is here that we get sentences beginning with elaborate pseudo-genteel participles

---

[5]English composer and organist (1659–1695), whose name the English pronounce like *purse'll* in "Your purse'll be stolen if you don't watch it" (not "pur-*sell*"). — Eds.

[6]American novelist of war and strife, author of *Battle Cry* (1953), *Exodus* (1957), *Trinity* (1976), and other best-sellers. — Eds.

like "Being that it was a cold day, the furnace was on." All classes below those peopled by U-speakers find the gerund out of reach and are thus forced to multiply words and say, "The people in front of him at the theater got mad due to the fact that he talked so much" instead of "His talking at the theater annoyed the people in front." (But *people* is not really right: *individuals* is the preferred term with non-U speakers. Grander, somehow.) It is also in the domain of the Mid- and Low-Prole that the double negative comes into its own as well as the superstitious avoidance of *lying* because it may be taken to imply telling untruths. People are thus depicted as always *laying* on the beach, the bed, the grass, the sidewalk, and without the slightest suggestion of their performing sexual exhibitions. A similar unconscious inhibition determines that *set* replace *sit* on all occasions, lest low excremental implications be inferred. The ease with which *sit* can be interchanged with the impolite word is suggested in a Second World War anecdote told by General Matthew Ridgway. Coming upon an unidentifiable head and shoulders peeping out of a ditch near the German border, he shouted, "Put up your hands, you son of a bitch!", to be answered, so he reports, "Aaah, go sit in your hat."

All this is evidence of a sad fact. A deep class gulf opens between two current generations: the older one that had some Latin at school or college and was taught rigorous skeptical "English," complete with the diagramming of sentences; and the younger one taught to read by the optimistic look-say method and encouraged to express itself — as the saying goes — so that its sincerity and well of ideas suffer no violation. This new generation is unable to perceive the number of syllables in a word and cannot spell and is baffled by all questions of etymology (it thinks *chauvinism* has something to do with gender aggressions). It cannot write either, for it has never been subjected to tuition in the sort of English sentence structure which resembles the sonata in being not natural but artificial, not innate but mastered. Because of its misspent, victimized youth, this generation is already destined to fill permanently the middle-to-low slots in the corporate society without ever quite understanding what devilish mechanism has prevented it from ascending. The disappear-

20

ance of Latin as an adjunct to the mastery of English can be
measured by the rapid replacement of words like *continuing* by
solecisms like *ongoing*. A serious moment in cultural history occurred a few years ago when gasoline trucks changed the warning word on the rear from *Inflammable* to *Flammable*. Public education had apparently produced a population which no longer
knew *In-* as an intensifier. That this happened at about the moment when every city was rapidly running up a "Cultural Center" might make us laugh, if we don't cry first. In another few
generations Latinate words will be found only in learned writing, and the spoken language will have returned to the state it
was in before the revival of learning. Words like *intellect* and *curiosity* and *devotion* and *study* will have withered away together
with the things they denote.

There's another linguistic class-line, dividing those who per- 21
sist in honoring the nineteenth-century convention that advertising, if not commerce itself, is reprehensible and not at all to be
cooperated with, and those proud to think of themselves not as
skeptics but as happy consumers, fulfilled when they can image
themselves as functioning members of a system by responding to
advertisements. For U-persons a word's succeeding in an ad is a
compelling reason never to use it. But possessing no other
source of idiom and no extra-local means of criticizing it, the
subordinate classes are pleased to appropriate the language of
advertising for personal use, dropping brand names all the time
and saying things like "They have some lovely fashions in that
store." In the same way they embrace all sub-professional euphemisms gladly and employ them proudly, adverting without
irony to hair stylists, sanitary engineers, and funeral directors in
complicity with the consumer world which cynically casts them
as its main victims. They see nothing funny in paying a high
price for an article and then, after a solemn pause, receiving part
of it back in the form of a "rebate." Trapped in a world wholly
defined by the language of consumption and the hype, they har-
bor restively, defending themselves against actuality by calling
habitual drunkards *people with alcohol problems*, madness *mental
illness*, drug use *drug abuse*, building lots *homesites*, houses *homes*
("They live in a lovely $250,000 home"), and drinks *beverages*.

Those delighted to employ the vacuous commercial "Have a   22
nice day" and those who wouldn't think of saying it belong
manifestly to different classes, no matter how we define them,
and it is unthinkable that those classes will ever meld. Calvin
Coolidge said that the business of America is business. Now apparently the business of America is having a nice day. Tragedy?
Don't need it. Irony? Take it away. Have a nice day. Have a nice
day. A visiting Englishman of my acquaintance, a U-speaker if
there ever was one, has devised the perfect U-response to "Have
a nice day": "Thank you," he says, "but I have other plans."
The same ultimate divide separates the two classes who say respectively when introduced, "How do you do?" and "Pleased to
meet you." There may be comity between those who think *pres-
tigious* a classy word and those who don't, but it won't survive
much strain, like relations between those who think *momentarily*
means in a moment (airline captain over loudspeaker: "We'll be
taking off momentarily, folks") and those who know it means
for a moment. Members of these two classes can sit in adjoining
seats on the plane and get along fine (although there's a further
division between those who talk to their neighbors in planes
and elevators and those who don't), but once the plane has emptied, they will proceed toward different destinations. It's the
same with those who conceive that *type* is an adjective ("He's a
very classy type person") and those who know it's only a noun
or verb.

The pretence that either person can feel at ease in the pres-   23
ence of the other is an essential element of the presiding American fiction. Despite the lowness of the metaphor, the idea of the
melting pot is high-minded and noble enough, but empirically it
will be found increasingly unconvincing. It is our different language habits as much as anything that make us, as the title of
Richard Polenberg's book puts it, *One Nation Divisible.*

Some people invite constant class trouble because they be-   24
lieve the official American publicity about these matters. The official theory, which experience is constantly disproving, is that
one can earn one's way out of his original class. Richard Nixon's
behavior indicates dramatically that this is not so. The sign of
the Upper Class to which he aspired is total psychological secu-

rity, expressed in loose carriage, saying what one likes, and imperviousness to what others think. Nixon's vast income from law and politics — his San Clemente property aped the style of the Upper but not the Top Out-of-Sight Class, for everyone knew where it was, and he wanted them to know — could not alleviate his original awkwardness and meanness of soul or his nervousness about the impression he was making, an affliction allied to his instinct for cunning and duplicity. Hammacher Schlemmer might have had him specifically in mind as the consumer of their recently advertised "Champagne Recork": "This unusual stopper keeps 'bubbly' sprightly, sparkling after uncorking ceremony is over. Gold electro-plated." I suspect that it is some of these same characteristics that make Edward Kennedy often seem so inauthentic a member of the Upper Class. (He's not Top Out-of-Sight because he chooses to augment his inheritance by attractive work.)

What, then, marks the higher classes? Primarily a desire for   25
privacy, if not invisibility, and a powerful if eccentric desire for freedom. It is this instinct for freedom that may persuade us that inquiring into the American class system this way is an enterprise not entirely facetious. Perhaps after all the whole thing has something, just something, to do with ethics and aesthetics. Perhaps a term like *gentleman* still retains some meanings which are not just sartorial and mannerly. Freedom and grace and independence: it would be nice to believe those words still mean something, and it would be interesting if the reality of the class system — and everyone, after all, hopes to rise — should turn out to be a way we pay those notions a due if unwitting respect.

QUESTIONS ON MEANING AND PURPOSE

1. What is Fussell's main PURPOSE in "Notes on Class"?
2. Why does he reject the usual division of Americans into high-, middle-, and low-income groups? In his own nine-part division, what several factors determine class?

3. What interesting similarities does Fussell discover between people at the very top of his class ladder and those at the very bottom?
4. What do you have to do to belong to Class X?
5. In Fussell's CONCLUSION (paragraph 25), what does he see the "higher classes" trying to achieve? Explain his remark, "Perhaps a term like *gentleman* still retains some meanings which are not just sartorial and mannerly."

QUESTIONS ON WRITING STRATEGY

1. Do Fussell's sympathies appear to lie with any particular class or classes? Does he scorn anyone? What is the general TONE of his essay? Does he seem to be kidding, or serious?
2. How heavily does Fussell use examples? Where did he obtain his EVIDENCE?
3. In paragraph 3, how does he distinguish the three top classes from one another?
4. For readers of what class or classes did Fussell originally write? What evidence of his awareness of his AUDIENCE do you find in his essay?

QUESTIONS ON LANGUAGE

1. According to Fussell, how important is language in placing a person in the class structure? Where do you place if you say "between he and I"? Explain Fussell's remark about the younger generation in paragraph 20: "Because of its misspent, victimized youth, this generation is already destined to fill permanently the middle-to-low slots in the corporate society without ever quite understanding what devilish mechanism has prevented it from ascending." Discuss.
2. Look up in your dictionary the preferred pronunciations of "those secret class indicators" that Fussell cites in paragraph 18: *exquisite*, *despicable*, and *patina*. (What, by the way, is a patina?) How would you guess Fussell expects a non-upper-class speaker to mispronounce these words? What is wrong with the statement, "We'll be taking off *momentarily*, folks" (22)?
3. Note Fussell's discussion of JARGON (at the end of paragraph 18). How do you define this term? What other people use jargon besides air travelers in business suits? What other gems of jargon have you seen or heard lately?

4. How extensive is Fussell's own vocabulary? Define proletarian, bo-
   hemians (paragraph 2); façades, confiscatory, expropriation, claustrated (6); hypertrophied (7); stigmatizes (14); dictional behavior,
   euphemism, genteelism (17); a linguistic polarity, diphthongs,
   anomalous (18); chauvinism (20); idiom, adverting, complicity
   (21); vacuous, comity (22); imperviousness (24); sartorial (25).

SUGGESTIONS FOR WRITING

1. Pointing to specifics in "Notes on Class," attack or defend this
   proposition: "Paul Fussell is a snob."
2. In paragraph 9 Fussell offers a detailed list, classifying people according to the outsides of their homes. Write a similar list classifying people according to some other principle: the cars they drive
   (and how they equip and decorate them), the movies or the snack
   foods they favor, their attitudes toward women's liberation. If you
   need more information about the classes and their preferences, do
   some digging first: talk with friends, take a walk through different
   neighborhoods with your senses open. Be prepared to read your
   list aloud and to justify your classifications.
3. Analyze an issue of one of these magazines: *The New Yorker,
   Vogue, Town & Country, The Atlantic, Gourmet, National Enquirer*
   (in appearance, a tabloid newspaper), *Good Housekeeping, Hustler,*
   or some other periodical suggested by your instructor. Try to determine the Fussellian class or classes of its audience. (You can usually tell who reads a magazine by closely inspecting its advertisements.) In an essay of 500–700 words, report your findings, giving
   evidence and illustrating your paper with a few clippings from the
   magazine (or, if it's the library's, photocopies).
4. Write a two- or three-paragraph essay under one of these titles
   (which you can modify to suit yourself):

   Don't Dump on Us Top Out-of-Sighters
   A Defense of My Own Good Old Middle Class
   I'm a Prole and Proud of It — Want to Fight?

── POSTSCRIPT ON PROCESS ──

Paul Fussell

Prewriting can take many forms. For "Notes on Class," Paul Fussell found inspiration in an old party game called "Categories." But of course that was just the beginning. The path from "Categories" to "Notes on Class" was strewn with challenges. The first of them was to decide how many classes make up contemporary American society. Then, where does one class end and the next begin?

An old party game called "Categories" is what provided a large part of the inspiration for "Notes on Class." Here, each player marks squares on paper and agrees on certain categories to occupy the left-hand squares. Categories like

> Automobiles
> Countries
> Drinks
> Composers
> Colleges

Then the players agree on a key word that will run across the top of the sheet, one letter per square. Like *second*. Then, working against time, you fill each square with an appropriate thing, thus: in the first, or *S*, column,

> Saab
> Spain
> Sauterne
> Sibelius
> Stanford

The player filling in all the squares first wins.

To play my game of "Class," I made a large chart out of cardboard, listing across the top the nine classes as I'd distinguished them and, along the left side, entering a series of social class indicators like clothes, house fronts, food, drink, dining hours, body weight, TV habits, language, reading, and the like. Then I filled in the squares, and in writing the essay I proceeded down and across. I would hope that the method and atmosphere of *game* would suggest to the reader that the essay belongs more to the world of *play* than to the world of *responsible study*.

Why did I come up with nine classes, instead of the customary three, or five? Because by that extra subdivision I could indicate important distinctions at top and bottom, distinctions arising less from sheer income than from something like *morale*. Near the top, people with lots of money differ from one another by exuding satisfaction or apology about the source of their riches. Thus distinctions had to be drawn there between those who'd worked for their cash and those who'd inherited it, for they tend to think of themselves as different kinds of people. Again, lower down, an important distinction between strata of working people is the security and self-respect they feel in their jobs, almost regardless of income. In calling those near the bottom *proles*, by the way, I intended not to be contemptuous but to allude ironically to that class in George Orwell's novel *1984*, as a way of suggesting that they were being treated as uninteresting and predictable creatures by society, not by me.

In one unguarded moment Walt Whitman termed *Leaves of Grass* "only a language experiment," and that designation applies in some degree to any piece of writing lucky enough to work, regardless of its artistic, social, or philosophic ambitions. In "Notes on Class" part of the fun for me was managing language so as to generate an ironic tone of mock-pedantry. (The pompous phrase *façade study* is an example.) By this tone I hoped to signal that my approach to the topic — although in part serious, as in the last paragraph — was at bottom satiric and comic. By invoking a "high" word like *enjoining* close to a "low" word like *butts*, one sets in motion a comedy of conscious inappropriateness. That method of straight-faced surprise, and sometimes shock, is what the essay depends on. Sometimes the surprise results from the speaker's mock-aristocratic, breezy, totally self-assured tone, as when he stigmatizes all ocupants of the White House as rather common because of their visibility, or indicates

that he conceives dentistry to be quite dirty work because it involves sticking your fingers in other people's mouths.

Every essay that functions owes a lot to a tradition, which it   5
merely advances further, for an essay that was totally original
would be so far out that the reader wouldn't even recognize the
literary form as *an essay.* "Notes on Class" echoes Susan Son-
tag's essay "Notes on Camp." My piece is more ironic than hers,
but my method owes a great deal to her example. Both of us
have made our essays by the act of unmasking facts or appearances that are commonly taken at face value.

The big problem in writing "Notes on Class" was to keep my   6
annoyance — at the sight of ugly fat people or the sound of pretentious euphemisms — under control, to prevent its perverting
the comedy into solemnity or anger. I'm not sure I've succeeded
in sustaining the perfect balance between the ludicrous and the
serious that satire requires.

1. Write an essay by the method of division, in which you analyze one of the following subjects. In breaking your subject into its component parts, explain or describe each part in some detail; try to indicate how each part functions, or how it contributes to the whole. If you have to subdivide any parts into smaller ones, go ahead, but clearly indicate to your reader what you are doing.

   An event to remember
   A year in the life of a student
   A paycheck at your disposal
   Your favorite sonnet
   A short story, a play, or a dramatic film that made you think
   The government of your community
   The most popular bookstore (or other place of business) in town
   The Bible
   A band or orchestra
   The public school system of your town or city

2. Write an essay by the method of classification, in which you sort out the following subjects into categories. Make clear your purpose in classifying things, and the basis of your classification. This essay shouldn't turn out to be a disconnected list, but should break down the subject into groups. You may find it helpful to make up a name for each group, or otherwise clearly identify it. One way to approach this assignment would be to build qualifiers into your introduction. Let your audience know that of all the types there are, you plan to write, say, about those that are "among the best" or "among the worst"; "the outstanding" or "the most ridiculous."

The records you own	Comic strips
Families	Movie monsters
Sports cars	Sports announcers
Stand-up comedians	Inconsiderate people
Present-day styles of marriage	Radio stations
Vacations	Mall millers (people who mill
College students today	around malls)
Paperback novels	
Waiter you'd never tip	

· 7 ·

ANALOGY

Drawing a Parallel

THE METHOD

The photography instructor is perspiring. He is trying to explain the workings of a typical camera to people who barely know how to pop a film cartridge into an Instamatic. "Let me give you an analogy," he offers — and from that moment, the faces of his class start coming alive. They understand him. What helps is his *analogy*: a point-by-point comparison that explains something unknown in terms of something familiar.

"Like the pupil in the human eye," the instructor begins, "the aperture of a camera — that's the opening in front — is adjustable. It contracts or it widens, letting in a lesser or a greater amount of light. The film in the camera is like the retina at the back of the eye — it receives an image. . . ." And the instructor continues, taking up one point at a time, working out the similarities between camera and eye.

To make clear his explanation, the instructor uses an analogy often found in basic manuals of photography. The inner workings of a Konica FS-1 may be mysterious to a beginning student of photography, but the parts of the eye are familiar to anyone who has looked in a mirror, or has had to draw and label the parts of the eye in sixth grade. Not every time you write an essay, but once in a while, analogy will be a wonderfully useful method. With its help you can explain a subject that is complicated, unfamiliar, or intangible. You can put it into terms as concrete and understandable as nuts and nutcrackers.

Like comparison and contrast, analogy is a method of explanation that sets things side by side. But the former is a way to explain two obviously similar things, to consider both their differences and their similarities. You might show, in writing a comparison and contrast, how San Francisco is quite unlike Boston in history, climate, and predominant life-styles, but like it in being a seaport and a city proud of its own (and neighboring) colleges. That isn't the way an analogy works. In an analogy you yoke together two apparently unlike things (eye and camera, the task of navigating a spacecraft and the task of sinking a putt), and all you care about is their major similarities.

If the photography instructor had said, "The human eye is a kind of camera," he would have stated a *metaphor*. As you may recall from having read any poetry, a metaphor is a figure of speech that declares one thing to be another — even though it isn't, in a strictly literal sense — for the purpose of making us aware of similarity. "Hope," says the poet Emily Dickinson, "is the thing with feathers / That perches in the soul" — thus pointing to the similarity between a feeling and a bird (also between the human soul and a tree that birds light in). By its very nature, an analogy is a kind of extended metaphor: *extended*, because usually it goes on longer than a line of poetry and it touches on a number of similarities. Here is an example. In August 1981, after *Voyager 2* transmitted to Earth its spectacular pictures of Saturn, NASA scientists held a news briefing. They wanted to explain to the public the difficulty of what they had achieved. They realized, however, that most people have no clear idea of the distance from Earth to Saturn, nor of the complexities of space navigation; and so they used an analogy. To bring *Voyager 2* within close range of Saturn, they explained, was analogous to sinking a putt from 500 miles away. Extending the metaphor, one scientist added, "Of course, you should allow the golfer to run alongside the ball and make trajectory corrections by blowing on it."[1] A listener can immediately grasp the point: such a feat is colossally hard.

Scientists explaining their work to nonscientists are particularly fond of such analogies because they deal with matters that an audience without technical training may find difficult. But the method is a favorite, too, of preachers and philosophers, because it can serve to make things beyond the experience of our senses vivid and graspable. We see this happening in one of the most famous passages in medieval literature. It is an analogy given by the eighth-century English historian Bede, who tells how in the year 627 King Edwin of Northumbria summoned a council to decide whether to accept the strange new religion of Christianity. Said one counselor:

> Your Majesty, when we compare the present life of man on earth with that time of which we have no knowledge, it seems to me like the swift flight of a single sparrow through the banqueting-hall where you are sitting at dinner on a winter's day with your thanes and counselors. In the midst there is a comforting fire to warm the hall; outside, the storms of winter rain or snow are raging. This sparrow flies swiftly in through one door of the hall, and out through another. While he is inside, he is safe from the winter storms; but after a few moments of comfort, he vanishes from sight into the wintry world from which he came. Even so, man appears on earth for a little while; but of what went before this life or of what follows, we know nothing. Therefore, if this new teaching has brought any more certain knowledge, it seems only right that we should follow it.[2]

[1]Quoted by Robert Cooke in a news story, "Voyager Sends a Surprise Package," Boston *Globe*, August 27, 1981.

[2]*A History of the English Church and People*, trans. Leo Sherley-Price, rev. R. E. Latham (Baltimore: Penguin Books, 1968), p. 127.

Why, after twelve centuries, has this analogy remained un-forgotten? Our minds cannot grasp infinite time, and we hardly can comprehend humankind's relation to it. But we can readily visualize a winter's snow and rain and a sparrow's flight through a banquet hall.

Like a poet, who also discovers metaphors, the writer who draws an analogy gives pleasure by making a comparison that offers a reader a little surprise. In setting forth vigorous, con-crete, and familiar examples, an analogy strikes us with poem-like force. For this reason, it is sometimes used by a writer who wishes to sway and arouse an audience, to engrave a message in memory. In his celebrated speech, "I Have a Dream," Martin Luther King, Jr., draws a remarkable analogy to express the an-ger and disappointment of American blacks that, one hundred years after Lincoln's Emancipation Proclamation, their full free-dom has yet to be achieved. "It is obvious today," declares Dr. King, "that America has defaulted on this promissory note"; and he compares the founding fathers' written guarantee — of the rights of life, liberty, and the pursuit of happiness — to a bad check returned for insufficient funds. Yet his speech ends on a different note, and with a different analogy. He prays that the "jangling discords of our nation" will become in time a "sym-phony of brotherhood." (For the entire speech, see Chapter 10.)

Dr. King does not pretend to set forth a logical argument. There may be logic in his poetic words, but his purpose is to rouse his listeners and inspire them to fight on. Sometimes, however, you find the method of analogy used in an argument that pretends to be carefully reasoned, but really isn't logical at all. (For more about this misuse of analogy, see *Argument from Analogy* in the list of logical fallacies on page 447.)

THE PROCESS

When you set forth a subject that you believe will be unfa-miliar to your readers, then analogy may come to your aid. In explaining some special knowledge, the method is most likely to be valuable. Did you ever play some unusual sport? Are you ex-pert in a particular skill, or knowledgeable in some hobby? Did you ever travel to some place your readers may not have visited? Have you ever learned the workings of some specialized machine (a mechanical potato peeler, say, or an automatic pinsetter)? Have you had any experience that most people haven't? Is your family background, perhaps, unusual? You may then have a subject that will be made clearer by the method of analogy.

With subject in hand, consider: exactly what will your analogy be? A bright idea has to dawn on you. If none *does* dawn, then it's far better to write your essay by some other method than to contrive a laborious, forced analogy. "Death is a dollar bill," one writer began — but the analogy that followed seemed a counterfeit. Remember: An effective analogy points to real similarities, not manufactured ones. (The author of the dollar bill essay went on: "Death is a cold condition, like cold, hard cash. . . ." — inflating an already weak currency.)

An analogy likens its subject to something more familiar than itself — as space navigation is likened to a game of golf. Your subject may be an abstraction or a feeling, but in analogy you can't use another abstraction or feeling to explain it. Were a scientist, for instance, to liken the steering of *Voyager 2* to the charting of a person's spiritual course through life, the result might be a fascinating essay, but it wouldn't explain the steering of the spacecraft. (If the scientist's main *subject* were the charting of a spiritual course, and if he were writing for an audience of technicians to whom the steering of *Voyager 2* was familiar, then indeed, he could write an analogy.)

There's one more preliminary test of your idea. Like all good metaphors, an analogy sets forth a writer's fresh discovery. The reader ought to think, "Look at that! Those two things are a lot alike! Who would have thought so?" (You, the writer — that's who.) That is why the analogy of a camera to the human eye (if you haven't heard it before) is striking; and why Bede's comparison of a life to the flight of a sparrow through a warm room is effective. You could write an essay likening toothpaste to bar soap, and remark that both make suds and float dirt away; but the result would probably put the reader to sleep, and anyhow, it wouldn't be an analogy. Both things would be simple and familiar, and too similar. You wouldn't be using one to explain the other. Dissimilarity, as well as similarity, has to be present to make a metaphor. And so, before you write, make sure that your subject and what you explain it with are noticeably *unlike* each other.

You now have your bright idea. Next you make a brief outline, listing your subject, what you'll use to explain it, and their similarities. Most analogies begin by likening the two, then go on to work through the similarities one point at a time. Never mind the differences. If your analogy is to form only a part of your essay, then later, perhaps, you will want to mention the differences — but wait until you have completed your analogy.

At last, with your outline before you, you are ready to write. As you work, visualize your subject (*if* it can be visualized — Bede's subject, the brevity of life, can't). Be sure to hold in your mind's eye the thing with which you explain your subject. Try for the most exact, concrete words you can find. An effective analogy is definite. It makes something swing wide, as a key unlocks a door.

ANALOGY IN A PARAGRAPH

Fred Silverman ran a network's TV schedule with all the self-assurance of a man writing menus for a truck stop. You could find him, as a rule, in the kitchen — for he insisted on tasting the cooking. If the woof of a dog didn't sound right in a cartoon, the producer had to be told how a dog barks. Like the proprietor of a diner who had to watch how much salt and pepper went into everything, Silverman worried and fussed, first as head programmer for CBS and then for ABC (the once sleepy joint that his menus transformed into the busiest, shiniest eatery around), later as president of NBC. Silverman worried according to a principle: "In putting together a schedule, the first thing you have to do is maintain a certain audience level." That meant ratings. With a universal bill of fare, Silverman set out to please all comers: truckers, teenagers, families with kids, retirees. He liked what they liked, and it wasn't pheasant under glass. He noted which items moved and which didn't. He'd cancel an exotic *Pink Lady* show (featuring two Japanese singers, sensations in their country, but duds here) the way the menu-man might cross out a slow-selling sukiyaki. Was a situation comedy unappealing to the Nielsen appetite? In went a dash of sex, like A-1 sauce sloshed on the baconburger. People wanted to know what they were eating; they wanted none of this subtle stuff. In a police drama, the ingredients had to be recognizable types: cops, robbers, good guys, nasties, tall heroes, feminine flames. It was Silverman who introduced block programming: the method of scheduling popular shows in a sequence, which the viewers consumed in a lump — like the Tuesday night $2.79 soup–spaghetti–salad combination. For the decade of the seventies, more successfully than any competitor's, Silverman's menus gave people what they wanted. But somehow, the customers drifted. The kitchen lights went out.

Comment. How the chief programmer of a television network decides what shows reach the screen (and survive) is a process with which most of us aren't familiar. The writer of this analogy set out to offer a rough sense of it. She decided to concentrate on the methods of Fred Silverman, probably the most famous of programmers, the man who had the deepest effect on prime-time viewing in the 1970s. Silverman's successful touch was the marvel of his competitors and peers in the television industry. To try to explain it, the writer drew insights from Sally Bedell's book *Up the Tube: Prime-Time TV and the Silverman Years* (New York: Viking Press, 1981), a detailed history of Silverman's career. (When NBC ratings dropped in the spring of 1981, Silverman was replaced as the network's president.) At first, the writer was going to compare Silverman to a cook, but that comparison seemed less accurate than to compare him to a menu writer who kept taking part in the cooking. In a paragraph, only a few points about Silverman's methods could be included; and so, before she began, the writer jotted them down in this simple outline form: Silverman

1. involved himself in production
2. tried to please a mass audience
3. shared tastes of that audience
4. canceled what didn't prove popular
5. kept programs simple, characters typical
6. introduced block programming.

The next step was to find what corresponded to these activities in a restaurant. The writer added to each point of her outline another comparable activity: The proprietor of a diner

1. superintended use of salt and pepper
2. tried to please truckers, teenagers, families
3. shunned pheasant under glass
4. crossed out an item too exotic
5. kept food simple
6. offered a combination special.

Following this enlarged outline, she wrote the paragraph. (It had to be rewritten three times before she liked it.) As this example demonstrates, an analogy likens its subject to a concrete term or terms — to things as definite as salt and pepper.

· Dick Gregory ·

Comedian, writer, and civil rights activist DICK GREGORY was born in Saint Louis in 1932. An outstanding athlete at Southern Illinois University, Gregory twice won the Missouri state championship for running the mile. Entering show business as a stand-up comic in a Chicago nightclub, he became famous from guest appearances on television and from his record albums of comedy routines. But Gregory's seriousness, too, is evident in his frequent appearances in cities and on campuses as an advocate of black rights. In 1968 he was nominated for president by the Peace and Freedom Party. Gregory has written a dozen books, including *Dick Gregory's Political Primer* (1971) and *Dick Gregory's Natural Diet for Folks Who Eat* (1973), his autobiography *Nigger* (1964) and its sequel *Up from Nigger* (1976), and (with Mark Lane) an account of the assassination of Martin Luther King, Jr., *Code Name Zorro* (1977).

If You Had to Kill Your Own Hog

This powerful essay in analogy comes from Gregory's *The Shadow That Scares Me* (1971), a book of comment on politics and how America lives. Beginning with a memory of conversations with his mother, Gregory goes on to draw an extended analogy that forcefully argues its point. Actually, you will find Gregory arguing on behalf of not one but two causes close to his heart.

My momma could never understand how white folks could   1
twist the words of the Bible around to justify racial segregation. Yet she could read the Ten Commandments, which clearly say, "Thou shalt not kill," and still justify eating meat. Momma couldn't read the newspaper very well, but she sure could interpret the Word of God. "God meant you shouldn't kill people," she used to say. But I insisted, "Momma, He didn't say that. He said, 'Thou shalt not kill.' If you leave that statement alone, a

whole lot of things would be safe from killing. But if you are going to twist the words about killing to mean what you want them to mean, then let white folks do the same thing with justifying racial segregation."

"You can't live without eating meat," Momma would persist. "You'd starve." I couldn't buy that either. You get milk from a cow without killing it. You do not have to kill an animal to get what you need from it. You get wool from the sheep without killing it. Two of the strongest animals in the jungle are vegetarians — the elephant and the gorilla. The first two years are the most important years of a man's life, and during that period he is not involved with eating meat. If you suddenly become very ill, there is a good chance you will be taken off a meat diet. So it is a myth that killing is necessary for survival. The day I decide that I must have a piece of steak to nourish my body, I will also give the cow the same right to nourish herself on human beings.

There is so little basic difference between animals and humans. The process of reproduction is the same for chickens, cattle, and humans. If suddenly the air stopped circulating on the earth, or the sun collided with the earth, animals and humans would die alike. A nuclear holocaust will wipe out all life. Life in the created order is basically the same and should be respected as such. It seems to me the Bible says it is wrong to kill — period.

If we can justify *any* kind of killing in the name of religion, the door is opened for all kinds of other justifications. The fact of killing animals is not as frightening as our human tendency to justify it — to kill and not even be aware that we are taking life. It is sobering to realize that when you misuse one of the least of Nature's creatures, like the chicken, you are sowing the seed for misusing the highest of Nature's creatures, man.

Animals and humans suffer and die alike. If you had to kill your own hog before you ate it, most likely you would not be able to do it. To hear the hog scream, to see the blood spill, to see the baby being taken away from its momma, and to see the look of death in the animal's eye would turn your stomach. So you get the man at the packing house to do the killing for you.

In like manner, if the wealthy aristocrats who are perpetrating conditions in the ghetto actually heard the screams of ghetto suffering, or saw the slow death of hungry little kids, or witnessed the strangulation of manhood and dignity, they could not continue the killing. But the wealthy are protected from such horror. They have people to do the killing for them. The wealthy profit from the daily murders of ghetto life but they do not see them. Those who immerse themselves in the daily life of the ghetto see the suffering — the social workers, the police, the local merchants, and the bill collectors. But the people on top never really see.

By the time you see a piece of meat in the butcher shop window, all the blood and suffering have been washed away. When you order a steak in a restaurant, the misery has been forgotten and you see the finished product. You see a steak with butter and parsley on it. It looks appetizing and appealing and you are pleased enough to eat it. You never even consider the suffering which produced your meal or the other animals killed that day in the slaughterhouse. In the same way, all the wealthy aristocrats ever see of the black community is the finished product, the window dressing, the steak on the platter — Ralph Bunche and Thurgood Marshall[1]. The United Nations or the Supreme Court bench is the restaurant and the ghetto street corner is the slaughterhouse.

Life under ghetto conditions cuts short life expectancy. The Negro's life expectancy is shorter than the white man's. The oppressor benefits from continued oppression financially; he makes more money so that he can eat a little better. I see no difference between a man killing a chicken and a man killing a human being, by overwork and forcing ghetto conditions upon him, both so that he can eat a little better. If you can justify killing to eat meat, you can justify the conditions of the ghetto. I cannot justify either one.

6

7

---

[1]Bunche (1904–1971) was a black American statesman, diplomat, and undersecretary of the United Nations, who received the Nobel Peace Prize in 1950; Marshall (born in 1908), the first black to be appointed justice of the Supreme Court.— EDS.

Every time the white folks made my momma mad, she   8
would grab the Bible and find something bitter in it. She would
come home from the rich white folks' house, after they had just
called her "nigger" or patted her on the rump or caught her
stealing some steaks, open her Bible and read aloud, "It is easier
for a camel to pass through the eye of a needle than for a rich
man to get into Heaven." When you get involved with distort-
ing the words of the Bible, you don't have to be bitter. The same
tongue can be used to bless and curse men.

QUESTIONS ON MEANING AND PURPOSE

1. What causes does Gregory argue for? What particular belief about
   food and eating does he hold?
2. What do you take to be the central PURPOSE of this essay?
   Which THESIS does the essay as a whole most emphatically support?
3. What other useful purpose is served by the appearances of Gregory's mother? With which of her attitudes does the writer disagree?
   What IRONY do you find in her bitterly quoting the Bible after
   being caught "stealing some steaks"?
4. What do you understand from Gregory's ALLUSIONS to Ralph
   Bunche and Thurgood Marshall, calling them "the window dressing, the steak on the platter" (paragraph 6)?
5. Is or is not Gregory a fundamentalist — one who believes in inter-
   preting the Bible literally? Point to statements in the essay to support your reply. Consider in particular the CONCLUSION.
6. "I see no difference between a man killing a chicken and a man
   killing a human being" (paragraph 7). Does Gregory here fall into
   the logical fallacy of oversimplification? (If you need to know about
   this fallacy, see page 446 in Chapter 10.) Or does his remark follow
   from his stated belief about human and animal life (paragraph 4)?

QUESTIONS ON WRITING STRATEGY

1. What is Gregory's central analogy? What is likened to what?
   Which is the more familiar thing used to explain the less familiar?

2. For what AUDIENCE does Gregory appear primarily to write? Who is the *you* in the essay's title?
3. What do Gregory's specific references to meat, steaks, blood, "the look of death in the animal's eye" contribute to the effectiveness of his analogy?

QUESTIONS ON LANGUAGE

1. "Momma couldn't read the newspaper very well, but she sure could interpret the Word of God" (paragraph 1). Does the COLLOQUIAL EXPRESSION *sure could* strike you as a blemish or an asset here?
2. Comment on Gregory's use of ABSTRACT and CONCRETE language. Skim back through the essay and point to effective examples of both.

SUGGESTIONS FOR WRITING

1. Write a brief essay entitled "A Carnivore's Rebuttal," differing with Dick Gregory about meat eating — or, if you prefer:
2. Instead, write a brief essay beginning with this thesis sentence: "Eating our fellow creatures is a mistake" (or "a great wrong").

Whichever topic you take, try — in one paragraph of your essay — to illustrate a point by inventing a fresh analogy.

· James C. Rettie ·

The quiet, hard-working life of JAMES C. RETTIE (1904–1969), an economist by profession, has rendered him a man of mystery about whom few facts are known. Although he wrote many scholarly articles and reports, Rettie is mainly remembered as the author of a single famous work: the following essay, often reprinted in textbooks and anthologies. Rettie completed it in 1948 while working at an experimental station of the National Forest Service in Upper Darby, Pennsylvania. Later, during the presidencies of John F. Kennedy and Lyndon B. Johnson, he served as an advisor to the U.S. Department of the Interior.

"But a Watch in the Night": A Scientific Fable

In writing his essay, Rettie apparently drew some of his ideas from a U.S. government pamphlet, "To Hold This Soil," prepared by the Department of Agriculture. In it, we are given a relatively matter-of-fact account of soil erosion. But Rettie had a flash of genius, and converted the pamphlet's statistics into a remarkable analogy, couched in a science fiction narrative.

Out beyond our solar system there is a planet called Copernicus. It came into existence some four or five billion years before the birth of our Earth. In due course of time it became inhabited by a race of intelligent men. 1

About 750 million years ago the Copernicans had developed the motion picture machine to a point well in advance of the stage that we have reached. Most of the cameras that we now use in motion picture work are geared to take twenty-four pictures per second on a continuous strip of film. When such film is run through a projector, it throws a series of images on 2 the screen and these change with a rapidity that gives the visual impression of normal movement. If a motion is too swift for the human eye to see it in detail, it can be captured and artificially slowed down by means of the slow-motion camera. This one is geared to take many more shots per second — ninety-six or even more than that. When the slow motion film is projected at the normal speed of twenty-four pictures per second, we can see just how the jumping horse goes over a hurdle.

What about motion that is too slow to be seen by the human eye? That problem has been solved by the use of the time-lapse camera. In this one, the shutter is geared to take only one shot per second, or one per minute, or even one per hour — depending upon the kind of movement that is being photographed. When the time-lapse film is projected at the normal speed of twenty-four pictures per second, it is possible to see a bean sprout growing up out of the ground. Time-lapse films are useful in the study of many types of motion too slow to be observed by the unaided, human eye.

The Copernicans, it seems, had time-lapse cameras some 757 million years ago and they also had superpowered telescopes that gave them a clear view of what was happening upon this Earth. They decided to make a film record of the life history of Earth and to make it on the scale of one picture per year. The photography has been in progress during the last 757 million years.

In the near future, a Copernican interstellar expedition will arrive upon our Earth and bring with it a copy of the time-lapse film. Arrangements will be made for showing the entire film in one continuous run. This will begin at midnight of New Year's Eve and continue day and night without a single stop until midnight of December 31. The rate of projection will be twenty-four pictures per second. Time on the screen will thus seem to move at the rate of twenty-four years per second; 1440 years per minute; 86,400 years per hour; approximately two million years per day; and sixty-two million years per month. The normal life-span of individual man will occupy about three seconds. The full period of earth history that will be unfolded on the screen (some 757 million years) will extend from what the geologists call Pre-Cambrian times up to the present. This will, by no means, cover

the full time-span of the earth's geological history but it will embrace the period since the advent of living organisms.

During the months of January, February, and March the   6
picture will be desolate and dreary. The shape of the land masses
and the oceans will bear little or no resemblance to those that
we know. The violence of geological erosion will be much in evidence. Rains will pour down on the land and promptly go
booming down to the seas. There will be no clear streams anywhere except where the rains fall upon hard rock. Everywhere
on the steeper ground the stream channels will be filled with
boulders hurled down by rushing waters. Raging torrents and
dry stream beds will keep alternating in quick succession. High
mountains will seem to melt like so much butter in the sun. The
shifting of land into the seas, later to be thrust up as new mountains, will be going on at a grand scale.

Early in April there will be some indication of the presence   7
of single-celled living organisms in some of the warmer and shel-
tered coastal waters. By the end of the month it will be noticed
that some of these organisms have become multicellular. A few
of them, including the Trilobites, will be encased in hard shells.

Toward the end of May, the first vertebrates will appear,   8
but they will still be aquatic creatures. In June about 60 per cent
of the land area that we know as North America will be under
water. One broad channel will occupy the space where the
Rocky Mountains now stand. Great deposits of limestone will
be forming under some of the shallower seas. Oil and gas deposits will be in process of formation — also under shallow seas.
On land there will still be no sign of vegetation. Erosion will be
rampant, tearing loose particles and chunks of rock and grinding them into sand and silt to be spewed out by the streams into
bays and estuaries.

About the middle of July the first land plants will appear   9
and take up the tremendous job of soil building. Slowly, very
slowly, the mat of vegetation will spread, always battling for its
life against the power of erosion. Almost foot by foot, the plant
life will advance, lacing down with its root structures whatever
pulverized rock material it can find. Leaves and stems will be
giving added protection against the loss of the soil foothold. The

increasing vegetation will pave the way for the land animals that
will live upon it.

Early in August the seas will be teeming with fish. This will
be what geologists call the Devonian period. Some of the races
of these fish will be breathing by means of lung tissue instead of
through gill tissues. Before the month is over, some of the lung
fish will go ashore and take on a crude lizard-like appearance.
Here are the first amphibians.

In early September the insects will put in their appearance.
Some will look like huge dragonflies and will have a wing spread
of 24 inches. Large portions of the land masses will now be covered with heavy vegetation that will include the primitive spore-
propagating trees. Layer upon layer of this plant growth will
build up, later to appear as the coal deposits. About the middle
of this month, there will be evidence of the first seed-bearing
plants and the first reptiles. Heretofore, the land animals will
have been amphibians that could reproduce their kind only by
depositing a soft egg mass in quiet waters. The reptiles will be
shown to be freed from the aquatic bond because they can reproduce by means of a shelled egg in which the embryo and its
nurturing liquids are sealed and thus protected from destructive
evaporation. Before September is over, the first dinosaurs will be
seen — creatures destined to dominate the animal realm for
about 140 million years and then to disappear.

In October there will be series of mountain uplifts along
what is now the eastern coast of the United States. A creature
with feathered limbs — half bird and half reptile in appearance
— will take itself into the air. Some small and rather unpretentious animals will be seen to bring forth their young in a form
that is a miniature replica of the parents and to feed these young
on milk secreted by mammary glands in the female parent. The
emergence of this mammalian form of animal life will be recognized as one of the great events in geologic time. October will
also witness the high water mark of the dinosaurs — creatures
ranging in size from that of the modern goat to monsters like
Brontosaurus that weighed some 40 tons. Most of them will be
placid vegetarians, but a few will be hideous-looking carnivores,
like Allosaurus and Tyrannosaurus. Some of the herbivorous di-

10

11

12

nosaurs will be clad in bony armor for protection against their flesh-eating comrades.

November will bring pictures of a sea extending from the   13
Gulf of Mexico to the Arctic in space now occupied by the
Rocky Mountains. A few of the reptiles will take to the air on
bat-like wings. One of these, called Pteranodon, will have a
wingspread of 15 feet. There will be a rapid development of the
modern flowering plants, modern trees, and modern insects.
The dinosaurs will disappear. Toward the end of the month
there will be a tremendous land disturbance in which the Rocky
Mountains will rise out of the sea to assume a dominating place
in the North American landscape.

As the picture runs on into December it will show the mam-   14
mals in command of the animal life. Seed-bearing trees and
grasses will have covered most of the land with a heavy mantle
of vegetation. Only the areas newly thrust up from the sea will
be barren. Most of the streams will be crystal clear. The turmoil
of geologic erosion will be confined to localized areas. About December 25 will begin the cutting of the Grand Canyon of the
Colorado River. Grinding down through layer after layer of sedimentary strata, this stream will finally expose deposits laid
down in Pre-Cambrian times. Thus in the walls of that canyon
will appear geological formations dating from recent times to the
period when the Earth had no living organisms upon it.

The picture will run on through the latter days of December   15
and even up to its final day with still no sign of mankind. The
spectators will become alarmed in the fear that man has somehow been left out. But not so; sometime about noon on December 31 (one million years ago) will appear a stooped, massive
creature of man-like proportions. This will be Pithecanthropus,
the Java ape man. For tools and weapons he will have nothing
but crude stone and wooden clubs. His children will live a precarious existence threatened on the one side by hostile animals
and on the other by tremendous climatic changes. Ice sheets —
in places 4000 feet deep — will form in the northern parts of
North America and Eurasia. Four times this glacial ice will push
southward to cover half the continents. With each advance the
plant and animal life will be swept under or pushed southward.

With each recession of the ice, life will struggle to reestablish itself in the wake of the retreating glaciers. The woolly mammoth, the musk ox, and the caribou all will fight to maintain themselves near the ice line. Sometimes they will be caught and put into cold storage — skin, flesh, blood, bones and all.

The picture will run on through supper time with still very little evidence of man's presence on the earth. It will be about 11 o'clock when Neanderthal man appears. Another half hour will go by before the appearance of Cro-Magnon man living in caves and painting crude animal pictures on the walls of his dwelling. Fifteen minutes more will bring Neolithic man, knowing how to chip stone and thus produce sharp cutting edges for spears and tools. In a few minutes more it will appear that man has domesticated the dog, the sheep and, possibly, other animals. He will then begin the use of milk. He will also learn the arts of basket weaving and the making of pottery and dugout canoes. 16

The dawn of civilization will not come until about five or six minutes before the end of the picture. The story of the Egyptians, the Babylonians, the Greeks, and the Romans will unroll during the fourth, the third, and the second minute before the end. At 58 minutes and 43 seconds past 11:00 P.M. (just 1 minute and 17 seconds before the end) will come the beginning of the Christian era. Columbus will discover the new world 20 seconds before the end. The Declaration of Independence will be signed just 7 seconds before the final curtain comes down. 17

In those few moments of geologic time will be the story of all that has happened since we became a nation. And what a story it will be! A human swarm will sweep across the face of the continent and take it away from the . . . red men. They will change it far more radically than it has ever been changed before in a comparable time. The great virgin forests will be seen going down before ax and fire. The soil, covered for eons by its protective mantle of trees and grasses, will be laid bare to the ravages of water and wind erosion. Streams that had been flowing clear will, once again, take up a load of silt and push it toward the seas. Humus and mineral salts, both vital elements of productive soil, will be seen to vanish at a terrifying rate. The railroads and highways and cities that will spring up may divert attention, but 18

TOOK a long time to create and we are destroying it so so fast.

they cannot cover up the blight of man's recent activities. In great sections of Asia, it will be seen that man must utilize cow dung and every scrap of available straw or grass for fuel to cook his food. The forests that once provided wood for this purpose will be gone without a trace. The use of these agricultural wastes for fuel, in place of returning them to the land, will be leading to increasing soil impoverishment. Here and there will be seen a dust storm darkening the landscape over an area a thousand miles across. Man-creatures will be shown counting their wealth in terms of bits of printed paper representing other bits of a scarce but comparatively useless yellow metal that is kept buried in strong vaults. Meanwhile, the soil, the only real wealth that can keep mankind alive on the face of this earth is savagely being cut loose from its ancient moorings and washed into the seven seas.

We have just arrived upon this earth. How long will we stay?   19

QUESTIONS ON MEANING AND PURPOSE

1. What is the subject of Rettie's analogy? To what does he liken it?
2. For what reason does the writer include this analogy: to give us a sense of the vast extent of time, to show us how humankind would appear to alien beings, to demonstrate how much has gone into the growth and development of the earth and living things, or what?
3. Sum up the PURPOSE of the essay as a whole. What is Rettie's THESIS?
4. Why does the writer end with a RHETORICAL QUESTION? What answer does he expect us to supply?

QUESTIONS ON WRITING STRATEGY

1. Do you have any trouble accepting Rettie's notion of a movie whose screening takes a year? What commonplace, practical objections to such a movie occur to you? Is Rettie's analogy silly, or does it serve him well?

2. What is the writer's POINT OF VIEW? How does the inclusion of the Copernicans help establish it?
3. If Rettie had been asked to omit his analogy, what paragraphs would he have had to cut? Could his essay survive without the analogy? What would be lost?
4. What other environmental problems might Rettie have mentioned in his CONCLUSION? Why doesn't he discuss such problems? (Suggestion: What would this have done to his plot summary of the movie?)
5. What kinds of TRANSITIONS are most numerous at the start of paragraphs? Why are they essential in this essay?
6. In what section of the essay does the method of process analysis appear? Into what main stages does the writer divide the history of the earth?
7. Can Rettie, in his conclusion, be accused of SENTIMENTALITY?

QUESTIONS ON LANGUAGE

1. The title of Rettie's essay is an ALLUSION to Psalms 90:4 in the King James Version of the Bible: "For a thousand years in Thy sight are but as yesterday when it is past, and as a watch in the night." Can you explain this quotation? What light does it cast on the essay?
2. What is the value of the essay's subtitle, "A Scientific Fable"? What is a fable?
3. What terms from the vocabulary of science (Pre-Cambrian, for example) occur in this essay? Is Rettie writing for an AUDIENCE of trained specialists? Do you think he could have done without such terms?
4. Make sure the following words and phrases are part of your vocabulary: hurdle (paragraph 2); time-lapse camera (3); interstellar, geological, advent (5); desolate, erosion, torrents (6); multicellular (7); vertebrates, aquatic, rampant, spewed, estuaries (8); pulverized (9); spore-propagating, reptiles, amphibians, realm (11); unpretentious, replica, mammary, mammalian, carnivores, herbivorous (12); mantle, sedimentary (14); precarious, Eurasia, recession (15); domesticated (16); eons, silt, humus, impoverishment, moorings (18).

SUGGESTIONS FOR WRITING

1. In a paragraph or two, respond to Rettie's essay, and give reasons for your reaction.

2. Write an essay in which you discuss the effects on the environment of some human activity: for instance, manufacturing; the disposal of chemical wastes; the production of nuclear energy; the commercial taking of seals, whales, or other wild animals. Decide whether to take an OBJECTIVE or a SUBJECTIVE attitude toward your material. If possible, choose some situation that you know from reading or experience.

3. Continue the plot summary of Rettie's movie into the future, showing the consequences of forces at work in the world today. (Will you supply the movie with a happy or an unhappy ending?)

· Henry David Thoreau ·

HENRY DAVID THOREAU (1817–1862) was born in Concord, Massachusetts, where, except for short excursions, he remained for the whole of his life. After his graduation from Harvard College, he taught school briefly, worked sometimes as surveyor and house painter, and for a time worked in his father's pencil factory (and greatly improved the product). The small sales of his first, self-published book, *A Week on the Concord and Merrimac Rivers* (1849), led him to remark, "I have now a library of nearly nine hundred volumes, over seven hundred of which I wrote myself."

The philosopher Ralph Waldo Emerson befriended his neighbor Thoreau; but although the two agreed that a unity exists between man and nature, they did not always see eye to eye on matters of politics. Unlike Emerson, Thoreau was an activist. He helped escaped slaves flee to Canada; he went to jail rather than pay his poll tax to a government that made war against Mexico. He recounts this brush with the law in his essay "Civil Disobedience" (1849), in which later readers (including Mahatma Gandhi of India and Martin Luther King, Jr.) have found encouragement for their own nonviolent resistance. One other book appeared in Thoreau's lifetime: *Walden* (1854), a searching account of his life in (and around, and beyond) the one-room cabin he built for himself at Walden Pond near Concord. When Thoreau lay dying, an aunt asked whether he had made his peace with God. "I did not know we had quarreled," he replied.

The Battle of the Ants

At Walden Pond, Thoreau mercilessly simplified his needs. Making himself almost self-sustaining, he proved to his own satisfaction that he could write, read Plato, grow beans, and observe in minute detail the natural world. In the following famous section of *Walden*, Thoreau reports a war he happened to observe while going to fetch wood. It is artful reporting, for Thoreau wrote with care: like a craftsman lovingly joining wood to make a cabinet. To revise *Walden*, a relatively short book, took him seven years. Thoreau's is a style marked

by a New England Yankee tightness of lip — indeed, there are
no useless words — and by an evident delight in setting forth
an analogy.

One day when I went out to my wood-pile, or rather my pile   1
of stumps, I observed two large ants, the one red, the other
much larger, nearly half an inch long, and black, fiercely contending with one another. Having once got hold they never let
go, but struggled and wrestled and rolled on the chips inces-
santly. Looking farther, I was surprised to find that the chips
were covered with such combatants, that it was not a *duellum*,
but a *bellum*,[1] a war between two races of ants, the red always
pitted against the black, and frequently two red ones to one
black. The legions of these Myrmidons[2] covered all the hills and
vales in my wood-yard, and the ground was already strewn with
the dead and dying, both red and black. It was the only battle
which I have ever witnessed, the only battle-field I ever trod
while the battle was raging; internecine war; the red republicans
on the one hand, and the black imperialists on the other. On
every side they were engaged in deadly combat, yet without any
noise that I could hear, and human soldiers never fought so resolutely. I watched a couple that were fast locked in each other's
embraces, in a little sunny valley amid the chips, now at noon-
day prepared to fight till the sun went down, or life went out.
The smaller red champion had fastened himself like a vice to his
adversary's front, and through all the tumblings on that field
never for an instant ceased to gnaw at one of his feelers near the
root, having already caused the other to go by the board; while
the stronger black one dashed him from side to side, and, as I
saw on looking nearer, had already divested him of several of his
members. They fought with more pertinacity than bulldogs.
Neither manifested the least disposition to retreat. It was evi-

---

[1]Not a hand-to-hand combat, but a whole war.— EDS.

[2]Fierce warriors, originally not men but a tribe of ants. In Homer's *Iliad*
the god Zeus, transforming them, sends them to help fight the war against
Troy.— EDS.

dent that their battle-cry was "Conquer or die." In the meanwhile there came along a single red ant on the hillside of this valley, evidently full of excitement, who either had dispatched his foe, or had not yet taken part in the battle; probably the latter, for he had lost none of his limbs; whose mother had charged him to return with his shield or upon it. Or perchance he was some Achilles, who had nourished his wrath apart, and had now come to avenge or rescue his Patroclus.[3] He saw this unequal combat from afar — for the blacks were nearly twice the size of the red — he drew near with rapid pace till he stood on his guard within half an inch of the combatants; then, watching his opportunity, he sprang upon the black warrior, and commenced his operations near the root of his right foreleg, leaving the foe to select among his own members; and so there were three united for life, as if a new kind of attraction had been invented which put all other locks and cements to shame. I should not have wondered by this time to find that they had their respective musical bands stationed on some eminent chip, and playing their national airs the while, to excite the slow and cheer the dying combatants. I was myself excited somewhat even as if they had been men. The more you think of it, the less the difference. And certainly there is not the fight recorded in Concord history, at least, if in the history of America, that will bear a moment's comparison with this, whether for the numbers engaged in it, or for the patriotism and heroism displayed. For numbers and for carnage it was an Austerlitz or Dresden.[4] Concord Fight! Two killed on the patriots' side, and Luther Blanchard wounded! Why here every ant was a Buttrick — "Fire! for God's sake fire!" — and thousands shared the fate of Davis and Hosmer.[5] There was not one hireling there. I have no doubt that it was a principle they fought for, as much as our ancestors, and not to avoid a three-penny tax on their tea; and the results of

---

[3]In the *Iliad* again, the Greek hero Achilles and his slain comrade-in-arms.— EDS.

[4]Battles that Napoleon waged with great loss of life.— EDS.

[5]Minutemen who fought the British redcoats in the Battle of Concord Bridge, 1775.— EDS.

this battle will be as important and memorable to those whom it concerns as those of the battle of Bunker Hill, at least.

I took up the chip on which the three I have particularly described were struggling, carried it into my house, and placed it under a tumbler on my window-sill, in order to see the issue. Holding a microscope to the first-mentioned red ant, I saw that, though he was assiduously gnawing at the near fore leg of his enemy, having severed his remaining feeler, his own breast was all torn away, exposing what vitals he had there to the jaws of the black warrior, whose breastplate was apparently too thick for him to pierce; and the dark carbuncles of the sufferer's eyes shone with ferocity such as war only could excite. They struggled half an hour longer under the tumbler, and when I looked again the black soldier had severed the heads of his foes from their bodies, and the still living heads were hanging on either side of him like ghastly trophies at his saddle-bow, still apparently as firmly fastened as ever, and he was endeavoring with feeble struggles, being without feelers, and with only the remnant of a leg, and I know not how many other wounds, to divest himself of them, which at length, after half an hour more, he accomplished. I raised the glass, and he went off over the window-sill in that crippled state. Whether he finally survived that combat, and spent the remainder of his days in some Hôtel des Invalides,[6] I do not know; but I thought that his industry would not be worth much thereafter. I never learned which party was victorious, nor the cause of the war, but I felt for the rest of that day as if I had my feelings excited and harrowed by witnessing the struggle, the ferocity and carnage, of a human battle before my door.

Kirby and Spence tell us that the battles of ants have long been celebrated and the date of them recorded, though they say that Huber[7] is the only modern author who appears to have witnessed them. "Aeneas Sylvius," say they, "after giving a very circumstantial account of one contested with great obstinacy by a great and small species on the trunk of a pear tree," adds that

2

3

---

[6]In Paris, a home for old soldiers.— Eds.

[7]Three leading entomologists (or zoologists specializing in insects) of Thoreau's day: Kirby and Spence in America, Huber in Switzerland.— Eds.

"'this action was fought in the pontificate of Eugenius the Fourth, in the presence of Nicholas Pistoriensis, an eminent lawyer, who related the whole history of the battle with the greatest fidelity.' A similar engagement between great and small ants is recorded by Olaus Magnus, in which the small ones, being victorious, are said to have buried the bodies of their own soldiers, but left those of their giant enemies a prey to the birds. This event happened previous to the expulsion of the tyrant Christian the Second from Sweden." The battle which I witnessed took place in the Presidency of Polk, five years before the passage of Webster's Fugitive-Slave Bill.

QUESTIONS ON MEANING AND PURPOSE

1. In finding the Battle of Concord Bridge a minor skirmish when compared to the battle of the ants, in crediting the ant soldiers with greater heroism (paragraph 1), is Thoreau putting down patriotism? Does he hint that the American Revolution didn't matter? What is his point?
2. For what PURPOSE (or purposes) does Thoreau seem to write such a detailed account of so trifling a war?

QUESTIONS ON WRITING STRATEGY

1. "Human soldiers," says Thoreau in paragraph 1, "never fought so resolutely." With what specific examples and observations does he support his GENERALIZATION? Point to memorable details that make us see the ant soldiers' inhuman determination.
2. In drawing his analogy, does Thoreau seek to explain the behavior of ants by comparing it to human war, or to explain human war by comparing it to the behavior of ants? (Which of the two kinds of warfare — ant or human — does Thoreau appear to regard as strange and unfamiliar, and therefore in greater need of explaining?)
3. What is the TONE of this essay? In his attitude toward the ant war (and human war), does Thoreau seem grim, amused, appalled, disgusted, mocking, or what? How can you tell?
4. Do Thoreau's ALLUSIONS to history and to Greek literature

seem decorations meant to show off his knowledge? What do they add to the essay? Look closely at one or two of them.

5. In many anthologies, you will find this selection with paragraph 3 shaved off. Why is Thoreau's CONCLUSION so effective? If it is omitted, what is lost?

QUESTIONS ON LANGUAGE

1. What is an *internecine war* (paragraph 1)?
2. Define any of these other words you may have doubts about: perchance, eminent (paragraph 1); assiduously, carbuncles, saddlebow, carnage (2); circumstantial, obstinacy (3).
3. In noting that the black ant has a *breastplate* (paragraph 2), Thoreau sees the ant soldier as wearing armor like a man. What other examples of PERSONIFICATION do you find?
4. Is this essay written in the technical vocabulary of a professional entomologist (like Alexander Petrunkevitch)? Glance again at Thoreau's microscopic description of the ants (paragraph 2): How specialized are its words?

SUGGESTIONS FOR WRITING

1. In a paragraph draw an analogy between some *typical* person, whose general sort you've observed, and some animal, bird, or insect. You might consider someone bursting with energy; someone who takes until eleven o'clock in the morning to wake up; a belligerent sort; a talkative scold; a ravenous eater; or — what kind of person interests you?
2. Describe some phenomenon or some creature in the natural world that has fascinated you. If, as you write, an analogy occurs to you, put it in; but don't force one if it doesn't come naturally.
3. Like Thoreau, the ancient Greek writer Aesop was fond of likening animals to persons. Some of his *Fables* may be familiar to you: the one about the hare and the tortoise (with the slow, persistent plodder winning the race), the tale of the fox and the grapes (about the fox who, when he couldn't reach the tempting fruit, decided that it must be sour anyway), and that of the mice who wanted to bell the cat (but who couldn't get one of their number to volunteer). An Aesop fable usually sums up the point of a story in a closing moral ("Slow and steady is sure to win," "There is comfort in pretending that the unattainable is not worth having," "It is easier to plan than to fulfill"). Read or reread a few of Aesop's fables, then try writing one of your own.

· X. J. Kennedy ·

X. J. KENNEDY (who pasted an X to his real name, Joe, to be less readily confused with the sire of the famous Kennedys), was born in 1929 in Dover, New Jersey. A graduate of Seton Hall and Columbia, he served in the Navy as a white hat, then attended the universities of Paris and Michigan. He has taught freshman writing and other courses at Michigan, North Carolina (Greensboro), and Tufts; and poetry work-shops at Tufts, Wellesley, and California (Irvine). Now a writer full-time, he frequently visits colleges to talk and to meet students and faculty. Like Gaul, his writing is divisible into four parts: poems, collected first in *Nude Descending a Staircase* (1961) and recently in *Cross Ties: Selected Poems* (1985); criticism and reviews; children's books, among them a novel *The Owlstone Crown* (1983) and a verse collection *The Forgetful Wishing Well* (1985); and textbooks, including this one. Dorothy M. Kennedy and he have also collaborated on *Knock at a Star: A Child's Introduction to Poetry*, cited as a 1983 Teacher's Choice Book by the National Council of Teachers of English.

Writing with a DECmate II: Building Sand Castles

Eight months before attempting this essay, Kennedy discarded his typewriter for a word processor. In an analogy, he tries to explain to any reader not yet familiar with word processing what writing with electronic help is like. He had planned to sign his essay with another name, not out of modesty but to escape the reader's charge: "Look at that egotist! A textbook editor who uses his own stuff!" But he has taken a by-line on the publisher's insistence that *The Bedford Reader* will have no Postscript on Process by a writer in false whiskers. This essay has not been printed before.

"Oh, you'll take to it," said my teacher with a farewell smile. 1 "You'll see. In a few days it will be just like driving a car with an automatic shift."

For two mornings, at the Digital Equipment Corporation's   2
business center, she had been training me. The lessons came
with the word processor I'd bought after months of trepidation.
They had been humbling. I had felt hurled back to kindergarten, a kid who couldn't shape a letter of the alphabet by himself
without a teacher guiding his hand.

The first morning had been nerve-racking. Out of control,   3
words scooted across the monitor's screen like speed-freaked
cockroaches. But my teacher was patient. A former English major, she forgave poet-types whose lines kept trying to extend out
beyond the edge of the screen and take off into space. By the
close of the second morning the ends of the lines stayed visible.
Now she was dismissing me. From now on I'd have to solo.

I drove home. Ever since, I've been writing everything — let-   4
ters, poems, limericks, stray ideas — on the DECmate. After a
few tense initial days, my teacher's good cheer proved justified.
Oh, it was hard at first to set a margin without any margin stop,
as on a typewriter. Not to put words directly on paper, but
merely to arrange electrons — not to be hammering away at the
old sheet of wood pulp, but to be drawing up an intangible set of
orders for a separate robot, a printer, to follow — made me feel
slightly disembodied and removed from earth. But by and by
the prose started to flow. Soon I felt a heady new freedom to do
what I most love: to fool around with the choices and places of
words.

Some computer buffs, the kind who even write their own   5
programs, heap scorn on buyers of dedicated word processors.
Dedicated means built for a purpose — unlike personal computers, with which you can do almost anything: balance your
checkbook, chart your biorhythms, play a fast game of Chop-
lifter in full color. PCs are for the imaginative, who want to
tackle an infinite number of tasks and one day decode the se-
crets of the universe. Users of dedicated word processors (or
"small office systems"), who just want to write or keep accounts,
are seen by comparison as just ape-browed Neanderthals.

From such computer buffs, the universe-decoding kind, the   6
keyboard of my DECmate II provokes a sneer. It is disgustingly
simple to operate. For every ordinary move you make in writing,

it has a special key with a readable label on it. Hit the key labeled DELETE WORD and — *zap!* — out goes that superfluous adjective. A few zaps will cut out a whole block of a few hundred words and paste it in elsewhere. You don't have to learn a secret code in order to move a paragraph or to underline something. That complexity is the drawback of most word-processing programs I've seen that run on personal computers.

But I'm not here to trumpet the wonders of my contraption.   7
I want to try to explain what it's like to write with a word processor. The nearest thing to it is an experience you may have had as a kid: building sand castles. Sand castles are best built on perilous oceanfronts, not on safe lakefronts. To erect a sand castle under the threat of the waves gives you a delectable sense of defying devastation. A similar foreboding of doom hovers over the writer who uses a word processor. What if there's a power failure and your work is wiped away? At least every half-hour, superstitiously, I tell the computer to save what I've written; and often I make a copy of it.

And yet despite this fear, to see your castle of words start to   8
rise fills you with an odd sense of freedom and playfulness. The experience is like whomping together some piles of wet sand that you want to develop into towers. First you just stack up that sand any old sloppy way, just to indicate roughly the shape of your superstructure. You get the piles to stand up straight, then you pat them smooth, then you take your shovel and tool them to a finely detailed finish. That is much like what you do in producing an essay on a word processor. You gather your material into a rough preliminary shape, then you work on smoothing it. You can jot down ideas, arrange them into an outline, then gradually tool them into a finished form. The whole process completes itself before your eyes.

Soul-satisfying, too, is the ease with which you can lift one   9
portion of your work and move it elsewhere. Like the castle builder who grasps two seashells for a forklift and picks up an unwanted tower and moves it someplace else on the structure where she thinks it belongs, you make a couple of cursor moves and pick up a paragraph. You set it down on a different page. Then you step back and see if it looks connected. If you don't

like it there after all you can move it back, or smash it flat with a couple of key pushes.

I never knew a sand castle architect who didn't, toward the 10
end of his work, cast about for some nice scallop shell or hand-some hunk of driftwood to top off his turrets with. For such a builder, it is a closing ritual to take up shovel and carve his ini-tials or other motto in the seafront wall. I think writers do some-thing like that. When the thing is nearly done and standing there, they step back to look for any finishing touches they can add: an image, a nice-sounding line, an apt quotation. A word processor, because it eliminates the need to retype, makes add-ing last-minute doodads easy.

At last, in building a castle, your deliberations are done. 11
Moat is dug, drawbridge (a clamshell) set in place. Your edifice stands there shimmering. You fix your work in more or less last-ing form by ever so carefully shaking or dribbling water on it. Having wetted the surfaces of your towers and minarets and walls, you let the hot sun dry them. The result, if you've applied the moisture properly, is a hard and substantial castle with a crust on the order of cement. It may even stand up to the tides for several hours. With a dedicated word processor, to lock your work into shape is much easier than that. All you need do is press GOLD FILE, and your essay is stored on a disk. There it will last for years, unless you forgetfully lay a magnet on it.

John Keats wished this epitaph cut on his stone: "Here lies 12
one whose words are writ in water." Now, Keats wasn't putting himself down; he knew who he was — "one of the English po-ets" — and most likely he was thinking of the poet's transitory and runny medium, the English language. Words shift, erode, change. Chaucer grows difficult to read. Already, only a short while since Bob Dylan wrote his "Subterranean Homesick Blues," certain words in that lyric call for explanatory footnotes in a textbook.

I think of language not as water, but as sand: a crumbling, 13
temporary medium. Oh, you can hang on to a vestige of your work, it's true: and for the sand castle builder this means getting there before the tide rises and clicking a photograph of it. When you write with computer assistance it is even simpler to click a

picture to save. You have the negative — the whole thing filed on a disk — and from that negative you can readily make a print — or rather a printout. Like the sand castle builder, you have something lasting to show for all your toil, though all the while the fingers of water keep fumbling higher and higher up the beach and circling what you've made; though nearby, from the edge of its domain, the sea continues booming and seething ominously.

QUESTIONS ON MEANING AND PURPOSE

1. "Kennedy's PURPOSE is obviously to sell DECmate IIs, so rhapsodic does he wax about them." Test this accusation.
2. What main points of comparison between castle building and computer-aided writing make up this analogy?

QUESTIONS ON WRITING STRATEGY

1. This essay has a long INTRODUCTION. At what point does the writer start setting forth his analogy? Do you find the information in the opening paragraphs helpful and needed, or is there too much of it?
2. What is the TONE of this essay? Is it entirely serious?
3. In the CONCLUSION (paragraph 13), do you suspect the writer of doing anything further than drawing a simple analogy?

QUESTIONS ON LANGUAGE

1. In paragraph 5, what definition is given for a dedicated word processor?
2. Do you approve, in paragraph 6, of the writer's use of *zap*, a comic-book word for what ray guns do? What does it add, if anything?
3. What is the writer's view of language in paragraphs 12 and 13?
4. Define with the aid of your dictionary any of the following words you need to know better: buffs, biorhythms, Neanderthals (paragraph 5); contraption (7); superstructure (8); forklift (9); hunk (10); minarets (11).

SUGGESTIONS FOR WRITING

1. In a brief personal essay, detail your own first encounter with a computer, a word processor, a hi-fi system, or some other product of technology.

2. In one meaty paragraph, set forth an analogy between practicing some sport you know well (playing basketball, climbing a mountain, running, sailing, or whatever) and some other activity familiar to most people. Your purpose is to explain the nature of the sport to a reader unfamiliar with it. You might show, for example, how trying to sink a basket on a crowded court is like trying to buy a gift on Christmas Eve in a furiously busy department store, or how mountain climbing is like climbing many flights of cluttered (and therefore dangerous) stairs. If you like, you might explain instead of a sport some physical task you are well acquainted with (driving a car, taking a photograph, diapering a baby, getting up in the morning).

— POSTSCRIPT ON PROCESS —

X. J. Kennedy

In these remarks on how he wrote the preceding essay, Kennedy calls attention to a powerful force that, when you write, you can have going for you. It is worth remembering, perhaps, whenever you find writing a dry and cerebral activity.

Whenever I have to write, I start by thinking aimlessly. I stretch out flat on an old couch, to make it easier for any ideas to roll uphill. At this early stage I don't care what order these ideas come in. All I think about is what I want to say. When a few notions gather, I get up and hastily write whatever parts of my project I most keenly feel like writing. Then I tool over these parts, buffing and polishing each separate fragment until it looks good enough to print.

As a whole, of course, the article is still far from readable. In truth it isn't even an article yet, but just a bunch of polished scraps. Next I shuffle all these disconnected parts into some order that seems reasonable. (Formerly, I worked with a stack of paper, dealing sheets and scraps into piles like a man dealing cards; now I shuffle and sort right on the screen of the DEC.) I group together ideas that look like blood relatives. A design for the whole article will emerge, though gaping holes appear in it — places where parts are missing because I didn't feel like writing them. At these points, I scribble brief notes to myself, indicating roughly what ought to be said. With heroic effort I fill in all the missing parts. Then I tool over the whole thing, putting in transitions to hoodwink a reader into thinking he or she is following a steadily and consistently unfolding process of thought.

Some such order is a must. Were I to leave the ideas in the helter-skelter order they first came in, a reader would get lost and give up on me. Their arrangement would have no more logic than the arrangement of a grasshopper's footprints. In "Writing with a DECmate II," the last paragraph was the first to

337

arrive. When it was done, by the way, I felt greatly relieved. No matter how wildly the rest of the article might hop around, at least it had somewhere to land.

Mine is a wasteful way of writing. If you always write under   4
the pressure of a deadline, don't try it; it will slow you down. (If you have to budget your time, you want to outline before you write.) Sometimes, like an amateur fixer of clocks, I'll finish a job with parts to spare, some of them nicely polished parts. Junking these brassy leftovers can be painful. There will be some paragraph I really like that just won't fit in anywhere. Of course, it has to go. In the "DECmate" essay, three such paragraphs that cost much time and effort ended up being scrapped — decomposed back to electrons. My method (if it is one) may be less brisk and efficient than outlining before you write, but it is more enjoyable. For me at least, it produces more satisfying results. In every job I complete, there are at least a few lines that came of their own free wills.

After I had polished three or four paragraphs to go into   5
"Writing with a DECmate II," I noticed some obviously missing parts. A true analogy makes point-by-point comparisons. And so I filled in the point about finishing touches: about sticking in an image or a quotation like a bit of driftwood or a shell for decoration. I put in the part about wiping out what you have written — how it's like smashing a sand castle flat.

In much the same way as I used to work on paper, I pro-   6
duced a lumpy, uneven draft — most of it naked outline, some of it decent prose. Here is one advantage of writing on a screen instead of on paper. Without endless retyping, you can add to your outline, plunking sentences and paragraphs right in where they belong. Your emerging essay is like a thin stew bubbling on a burner. Perhaps it already has a few lumps of meat in it, but it needs more substance. All right, you add more meat and vegetables. You simmer the concoction until its texture is thick and smooth. When it smells done all the way through, you spoon it onto a plate — that is, you print it out. In this way, outline grows into essay. The process saves clean-up time, because from basic ingredients to savory product, your stew all gets cooked in one pot.

To write readably, it helps to get het up about something. 7
For me the crucial need is to build up, before I write, a head of
emotional steam. "Hunger is the best sauce," declares a proverb;
and in like fashion, desire to say something is the best aid to saying it. To interest a reader, first interest yourself. In a sense,
most prewriting strategies — brainstorming, freewriting, reading
around in a subject, conversing with people, rummaging your
memory — help you become interested. They're ways to build
up not only a supply of things to say but also emotional steam to
start your pistons turning. Another way to fan your fire is to
reach back into childhood for your inspiration. First memories
are deeply etched, and full of feeling. I guess the writing of
"Writing with a DECmate II" really began about forty-six summers ago in Ocean Grove, New Jersey.

Develop one of these topics by the method of analogy. (You might consider several of these topics, until one of them blooms into a bright idea for an analogy.)

The training of a professional writer
The body's circulatory system
The way a rumor spreads
Succeeding in whatever you do
The way a child learns to walk and talk
What it's like to get behind in your schoolwork
The presence of God in your life
Becoming sure of yourself in a new situation
Trying to understand a difficult concept
Getting the job done through cooperation instead of competition
Teaching worthwhile values to a child
How violent crime intrudes on our lives
Competition between the sexes
Building character
A crushing failure
The brightest spot in your day
Learning a new skill
How your body fights germs
Being a nonconformist
Trying to get by without sufficient preparation
Going into debt
An allergic reaction
The experience of unexpected happiness

· 8 ·

CAUSE AND EFFECT

Asking Why

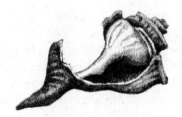

THE METHOD

Press the button of a doorbell and, inside the house or apartment, chimes sound. Why? Because the touch of your finger on the button closed an electrical circuit. But why did you ring the doorbell? Because you were sent by your dispatcher: you are a bill collector calling on a customer whose payments are three months overdue.

The touch of your finger on the button is the *immediate cause* of the chimes: the event that precipitates another. That you were ordered by your dispatcher to go ring the doorbell is a *remote cause*: an underlying, more basic reason for the event, not apparent to an observer. Probably, ringing the doorbell will lead to some results: the door will open, and you may be given a check — or a kick in the teeth.

To divide the flow of events into reasons and results: this is the kind of analysis you make when you write by the method of *cause and effect*. You try to answer the question, Why did something happen? or the question, What were the consequences?

Seeking causes, you can ask, for example, Why did guerrilla warfare erupt in El Salvador? For what reason or reasons do birds migrate? What has caused sales of Detroit-made cars to pick up lately? Looking for effects, you can ask, What have been the effects of the birth-control pill on the typical American family? What impact has the personal computer had on the nursing profession? You can look to a possible future and ask, Of what use might a course in psychology be to me if I become an office manager? Suppose a new comet the size of Halley's were to strike Philadelphia — what would be the probable consequences? Essay exams in history and economics courses tend often to ask for either causes or effects: What were the principal causes of America's involvement in the war in Vietnam? What were the immediate effects on the world monetary system of Franklin D. Roosevelt's removing the United States from the gold standard?

Don't, by the way, confuse cause and effect with the method of process analysis. Some process analysis essays, too, deal with happenings; but they ask the question, *How* (not why) did something happen? If you were explaining the process by which the doorbell rings, you might break the happening into stages — (1) the finger presses the button; (2) the circuit closes; (3) the current travels the wire; (4) the chimes make music — and you'd set forth the process in detail. But why did the finger press the button? What happened because the doorbell rang? To answer those questions, you need cause and effect.

Sometimes one event will appear to trigger another, and it in turn will trigger yet another, and another still, in an order we call a *causal chain*. A classic example of such a chain is set forth in a Mother Goose rhyme:

> For want of a nail the shoe was lost,
> For want of a shoe the horse was lost,
> For want of a horse the rider was lost,
> For want of a rider the battle was lost,
> For want of a battle the kingdom was lost—
> And all for the want of a nail.

In reality, causes are seldom so easy to find as that missing nail: they tend to be many and complicated. A battle may be lost for more than one reason. Perhaps the losing general had fewer soldiers, and had a blinding hangover the morning he mapped out his battle strategy. Perhaps winter set in, expected reinforcements failed to arrive, and a Joan of Arc inspired the winning army. The downfall of a kingdom is not to be explained as though it were the toppling of the last domino in a file. Still, one event precedes another in time, and in discerning causes you don't ignore chronological order; you pay attention to it.

In trying to account for some public event (a strike, say, or the outcome of an election), in trying to explain a whole trend in today's society (toward nonsmoking, or late marriage), you can expect to find a whole array of causes — interconnected, perhaps, like the strands of a spiderweb. You'll want to do an honest job of unraveling. This may take time. For a jury to decide why an accused slayer acted as he did, weeks of testimony from witnesses, detectives, and psychiatrists may be required, then days of deliberation. It took a great historian, Jakob Burckhardt, most of his lifetime to set forth a few reasons for the dawn of the Italian Renaissance. To be sure, juries must take great care when a life hangs in the balance; and Burckhardt, after all, was writing an immense book. To produce a college essay, you don't have forty years; but before you start to write, you will need to devote extra time and thought to seeing which facts are the causes, and which matter most.

To answer the questions Why? and What followed as a result? may sometimes be hard, but it can be satisfying — even illuminating. Indeed, to seek causes and effects is one way for the mind to discover order in a reality that otherwise might seem (as life came to seem to Macbeth) a tale told by an idiot, full of sound and fury, signifying nothing.

THE PROCESS

In writing an essay that seeks causes or one that seeks effects, first make sure that your subject is manageable. Choose a subject you can get to the bottom of, given the time and information you have. For a 500-word essay due Thursday, the causes of teenage rebellion would be a topic less wieldy than why a certain thirteen-year-old you know ran away from home. Excellent papers may be written on large subjects, and yet they may be written on smaller, more personal subjects as well. You can ask yourself, for instance, why you behaved in a certain way at a certain moment. You can examine the reasons for your current beliefs and attitudes. Such a paper might be rewarding: you might happen upon a truth you hadn't realized before. In fact, both you and your reader may profit from an essay that seeks causes along the lines of these: "Why I Espouse Nudism," or "Why I Quit College and Why I Returned." Such a paper, of course, takes thought. It isn't easy to research your own motivations. A thoughtful, personal paper that discerns *effects* might follow from a topic such as "Where Nudism Led Me" or "What Happened When I Quit College."

When seeking remote causes, look only as far back as necessary. Explaining why a small town has fallen on hard times, you might confine yourself to the immediate cause of the hardship: the closing of a factory. You might explain what caused the shutdown: a dispute between union and management. You might even go back to the cause of the dispute (announced firings) and the cause of the firings (loss of sales to a Japanese competitor). For a short essay, that might be far enough back in time to go; but if you were writing a whole book (*Putzville 1985: Its Glorious Past and Its Present Agony*), you might look to causes still more remote. You could trace the beginning of the decline of Putzville back to the discovery, in Kyoto in 1845, of a better carrot grater. A manageable short paper showing *effect* might work in the other direction, moving from the factory closing to its impact on the town: unemployment, the closing of stores and the only movie house, people packing up and moving away.

When you can see a number of apparent causes, weigh them and assign each a relative importance. Which do you find matter most? Often, you will see that causes are more important or less so: *major* or *minor*. If Judd acquires a heavy drug habit and also takes up video game playing, and as a result finds himself penniless, it is probably safe to assume that the drug habit is the major cause of his going broke and his addiction to Frogger a minor one. If you were writing about his sad case, you'd probably emphasize the drug habit by giving it most of your space, perhaps touching on video games in a brief sentence.

You can plan out an essay by arranging events in chronological order (or in reverse order: from a recent event back to past events that cause it). If Judd drops out of college, the most immediate cause might be his inability to meet a tuition payment. But his lack of money might have a cause, too: his having earlier acquired a heavy drug habit. The cause of his addiction might be traced back further still: to a period of depression he suffered, and to an even earlier, more remote cause — the death of a friend in a car accident. In writing about him, you might begin with the accident, and then step by step work out its consequences; or you could begin with Judd's withdrawal from school, and trace a causal chain back to the accident.

In so doing beware of the logical fallacy "after this, therefore because of this" (in Latin, *post hoc, ergo propter hoc*) — that is, don't expect Event A to cause Event B just because A happened before B. This is the error of the superstitious man who decides that he lost his job because a black cat walked in front of him. Another error is to oversimplify the causal chain to two links (when it has many links and several connected lengths) — to claim, say, that violent crime is simply a result of "all these gangster shows on TV." Avoid such wrong turns in reasoning by patiently looking for evidence before you write, and by giving it careful thought. (For a fuller list of such *logical fallacies* or errors in reasoning, see pages 446–447.)

To understand the deep-down causes of a person's act takes thought. Before you write, you can ask yourself a few searching questions. These have been suggested by the work of literary critic Kenneth Burke (author of "Classifying Proverbs" in Chapter 6). Burke asks (and answers) the questions in a complicated way, but for most practical purposes, before you write about the cause of a human act, ask yourself these five questions:

1. What act am I trying to explain?
2. What is the character, personality, or mental state of whoever acted?
3. In what scene or location did the act take place, and in what circumstances?

4. What instruments or means did the person use?
5. For what purpose did he or she act?

Burke calls these elements a *pentad* (or set of five): the *act*, the *actor*, the *scene*, the *agency*, and the *purpose*. If you are trying to explain, for instance, why a person burned down a liquor shop, it will be revealing to ask about his character and mental state. Was the act committed by the shop's worried, debt-ridden owner? A mentally disturbed antialcohol crusader? A drunk who had been denied a purchase? The scene of the burning, too, might tell you something. Was the shop near a church, a mental hospital, or a fireworks factory? And what was the agency (or means of the act): a flaming torch or a flipped-away cigarette butt? To learn the purpose might be illuminating, whether it was to collect insurance on the shop, to get revenge, or to work what the actor believed to be the will of the Lord.

You can further deepen your inquiry by seeing relationships between the terms of the pentad. Ask, for instance, what does the actor have to do with this scene? (Is he or she the preacher in the church across the street, who has been staring at the liquor shop resentfully for the past twenty years?) If you are interested and care to explore the possibilities of Burke's pentad, you can pair up its five terms in ten different ways.[1]

You can use Burke's pentad to help explain the acts of groups as well as those of individuals. Why, for instance, did the sophomore class revel degenerate into a brawl? Here are some possible answers:

1. *Act*: the brawl
2. *Actors*: the sophs were letting off steam after exams, and a mean, tense spirit prevailed
3. *Scene*: a keg-beer party outdoors in the quad at midnight on a sticky and hot May night
4. *Agencies*: fists and beer bottles
5. *Purpose*: the brawlers were seeking to punish whoever kicked over the keg

---

[1]Act to actor, actor to scene, actor to agency, actor to purpose, act to scene, act to agency, act to purpose, scene to agency, scene to purpose, agency to purpose. This approach can go profoundly deep; if you truly wish to explore it, we suggest you try writing ten questions in the form What does act have to do with actor? for each pair, and ask them of some act you'd like to explain.

Don't worry if not all the questions apply, if not all the answers are immediately forthcoming. Bring the pentad to bear on the sad case of Judd, and probably only the question about his character and mental state would help you much. Even a single hint, though, can help you write. Burke's pentad isn't meant to be a grim rigmarole; it is a means of discovery, to generate a lot of possible material for you — insights, observations, hunches to pursue. It won't solve each and every human mystery, but sometimes it will helpfully deepen your thought.

In stating what you believe to be causes and effects, don't be afraid to voice a well-considered hunch. Your instructor doesn't expect you to write, in a short time, a *definitive* account of the causes of an event or a belief or a phenomenon — only to write a coherent and reasonable one. To discern all causes — including remote ones — and all effects is beyond the power of any one human mind. Still, admirable and well-informed writers on matters such as politics, economics, and world and national affairs are often canny guessers and brave drawers of inferences. At times, even the most cautious and responsible writer has to leap boldly over a void to strike firm ground on the far side. Consider your evidence. Think about it hard. Look well before leaping. Then take off.

CAUSE AND EFFECT IN A PARAGRAPH

Why is it that, despite a growing interest in soccer among American athletes, and despite its ranking as the most popular sport in the world, commercial television ignores it? To see a televised North American Soccer League game, you have to tune at odd hours to public TV. Part of the reason stems from the basic nature of network television, which exists not to inform and entertain but to sell. During most major sporting events on television — football, baseball, basketball, boxing — producers can take advantage of natural interruptions in the action to broadcast sales pitches; or, if the natural breaks occur too infrequently, the producers can contrive time-outs for the sole purpose of airing lucrative commercials. But soccer is played in two solid halves of forty-five minutes each; not even injury to a player is cause for a time-out. How, then, to

insert the requisite number of commercial breaks without resorting to false fouls or other questionable tactics? After CBS
aired a soccer match on May 27, 1967, players reported, according to Stanley Frank, that before the game the referee
had instructed them "to stay down every nine minutes." The
resulting hue and cry rose all the way to the House Communications Subcommittee. From that day to this, no one has
been able to figure out how to screen advertising jingles during a televised soccer game. The result is that the commercial
networks have to treat the North American Soccer League as
if it didn't exist.

Comment. In this paragraph, the writer seeks a cause, and
in her opening sentence poses the "Why?" question she will answer. The middle portion of the paragraph explains that soccer,
unlike other sports, is difficult to adapt to commercial television.
In mentioning the famous case reported by Frank, she shows
what happened when, for a change, a soccer game was telecast,
but was artificially orchestrated so as to allow blank moments
for commercials. There is only one cause to be found, and it is
stated (together with its effect) in the concluding two sentences.
Note how the writer illustrates her generalizations with examples. The only unillustrated one is the statement that network
TV exists for the purpose of selling things; and this seems an apparent truth we all know already.

· Gore Vidal ·

Gore Vidal was born in 1925 at the U.S. Military Academy at West Point, where his father was an instructor. At the age of nineteen, he wrote his first novel, *Williwaw* (1946), while serving as a warrant officer aboard an army supply ship. Among the later (and more popular) of his nineteen novels are *Burr* (1973), *1876* (1976), *Kalki* (1978), *Creation* (1981), *Duluth* (1983), and *Lincoln* (1984). He has also written mysteries under the pen name Edgar Box. As a playwright, he is best known for *Visit to a Small Planet* (1957), which was made into a film. The grandson of Senator T. P. Gore, who represented Oklahoma for thirty years, Vidal himself entered politics in 1960 as a Democratic-Liberal candidate for the House of Representatives. In 1982 he ran again: as a candidate for the Senate in the California Democratic primary. A frequent contributor of brilliant, opinionated essays to *The New York Review of Books*, Vidal divides his time between Italy and America. *The Second American Revolution* (1982) is his most recent essay collection.

Drugs

Vidal, whom some critics have called America's finest living essayist, first published "Drugs" on the "op ed" page of the *New York Times* (the page opposite the editorial page, reserved for diverse opinions). Vidal included it in *Homage to Daniel Shays: Collected Essays 1952-1972*. In the essay, he suggests some generally unrecognized causes for the nation's problems with drug addiction, and proposes a radical solution. See if you think it might work.

It is possible to stop most drug addiction in the United   1
States within a very short time. Simply make all drugs available and sell them at cost. Label each drug with a precise description of what effect — good and bad — the drug will have on the

taker. This will require heroic honesty. Don't say that marijuana is addictive or dangerous when it is neither, as millions of
people know — unlike "speed," which kills most unpleasantly,
or heroin, which is addictive and difficult to kick.

For the record, I have tried — once — almost every drug   2
and liked none, disproving the popular Fu Manchu theory that
a single whiff of opium will enslave the mind. Nevertheless many
drugs are bad for certain people to take and they should be told
why in a sensible way.

Along with exhortation and warning, it might be good for   3
our citizens to recall (or learn for the first time) that the United
States was the creation of men who believed that each man has
the right to do what he wants with his own life as long as he
does not interfere with his neighbor's pursuit of happiness.
(That his neighbor's idea of happiness is persecuting others does
confuse matters a bit.)

This is a startling notion to the current generation of Ameri   4
cans. They reflect a system of public education which has made
the Bill of Rights, literally, unacceptable to a majority of high
school graduates (see the annual Purdue reports) who now form
the "silent majority" — a phrase which that underestimated wit
Richard Nixon took from Homer who used it to describe the
dead.

Now one can hear the warning rumble begin: if everyone is   5
allowed to take drugs everyone will and the GNP will decrease,
the Commies will stop us from making everyone free, and we
shall end up a race of zombies, passively murmuring "groovy" to
one another. Alarming thought. Yet it seems most unlikely that
any reasonably sane person will become a drug addict if he
knows in advance what addiction is going to be like.

Is everyone reasonably sane? No. Some people will always   6
become drug addicts just as some people will always become alcoholics, and it is just too bad. Every man, however, has the
power (and should have the legal right) to kill himself if he
chooses. But since most men don't, they won't be mainliners either. Nevertheless, forbidding people things they like or think
they might enjoy only makes them want those things all the

more. This psychological insight is, for some mysterious reason, perennially denied our governors.

It is a lucky thing for the American moralist that our country has always existed in a kind of time-vacuum: we have no public memory of anything that happened before last Tuesday. No one in Washington today recalls what happened during the years alcohol was forbidden to the people by a Congress that thought it had a divine mission to stamp out Demon Rum — launching, in the process, the greatest crime wave in the country's history, causing thousands of deaths from bad alcohol, and creating a general (and persisting) contempt among the citizenry for the laws of the United States.

The same thing is happening today. But the government has learned nothing from past attempts at prohibition, not to mention repression.

Last year when the supply of Mexican marijuana was slightly curtailed by the Feds, the pushers got the kids hooked on heroin and deaths increased dramatically, particularly in New York. Whose fault? Evil men like the Mafiosi? Permissive Dr. Spock? Wild-eyed Dr. Leary? No.

The Government of the United States was responsible for those deaths. The bureaucratic machine has a vested interest in playing cops and robbers. Both the Bureau of Narcotics and the Mafia want strong laws against the sale and use of drugs because if drugs are sold at cost there would be no money in it for anyone.

If there was no money in it for the Mafia, there would be no friendly playground pushers, and addicts would not commit crimes to pay for the next fix. Finally, if there was no money in it, the Bureau of Narcotics would wither away, something they are not about to do without a struggle.

Will anything sensible be done? Of course not. The American people are as devoted to the idea of sin and its punishment as they are to making money — and fighting drugs is nearly as big a business as pushing them. Since the combination of sin and money is irresistible (particularly to the professional politician), the situation will only grow worse.

QUESTIONS ON MEANING AND PURPOSE

1. How readily do you accept Vidal's implicit assumption that a person with easy access to drugs would be unlikely to "interfere with his neighbor's pursuit of happiness"?
2. Spend enough time in the library to learn more about the era of Prohibition in the United States. To what extent do the facts support Vidal's contention that Prohibition was a bad idea?
3. For what reasons, according to Vidal, is it unlikely that our drug laws will be eased? Can you suggest other possible reasons why the Bureau of Narcotics favors strict drug laws?
4. Vidal's essay was first published in 1970. Do you find the views expressed in it still timely, or hopelessly out of date?
5. What do you take to be Vidal's main PURPOSE in writing this essay? How well does he accomplish it?

QUESTIONS ON WRITING STRATEGY

1. How would you characterize Vidal's humor? Find some examples of it.
2. In paragraphs 3 and 4, Vidal summons our founding fathers and the Bill of Rights to his support. Is this tactic fair or unfair? Explain.
3. In paragraph 10, Vidal asserts that the government of the United States is the cause of heroin deaths among the young in New York. By what steps does he reach this judgment? Is the author guilty of oversimplification? (See the discussion of *oversimplification* on page 446).
4. Where in the essay does Vidal appear to anticipate the response of his AUDIENCE? How can you tell?
5. What function do the essay's RHETORICAL QUESTIONS perform?

QUESTIONS ON LANGUAGE

1. Know the definitions of the following terms: exhortation (paragraph 3); GNP (5); mainliners, perennially (6); curtailed (9).
2. How do you interpret Vidal's use of the phrase *underestimated wit* to describe Richard Nixon?

SUGGESTIONS FOR WRITING

1. Write a paragraph in which you try to predict both the good and the ill effects you think might result from following Vidal's advice to "make all drugs available and sell them at cost."
2. In a short essay, evaluate Vidal's suggestion that every drug be labeled with a description of its probable effect on the taker. How likely does it seem to you that the warnings printed on containers of addictive or dangerous drugs would be heeded?

· Carl Sagan ·

Known widely as an interpreter of science to common readers (and television viewers), CARL SAGAN is himself a noted astronomer. For his leading role in the *Mariner*, *Viking*, and *Voyager* expeditions to other planets, he has received medals from the National Aeronautics and Space Administration. His work was vital in establishing the surface temperatures of Venus and in understanding the seasonal changes on Mars, and he has been responsible for four messages addressed to intelligent extraterrestrials, carried into space by *Pioneer 10* and *11* and *Voyager 1* and *2*. Born in New York City in 1934, Sagan completed four degrees at the University of Chicago. He now directs the Laboratory for Planetary Studies and holds a professorship of astronomy and space sciences at Cornell. Active in the Union of Concerned Scientists, Sagan in 1983 co-authored a petition whose signers, forty leading scientists, called for an international treaty to ban all weapons from space. Among his books are several best-sellers: *The Dragons of Eden* (1977), winner of the Pulitzer Prize for literature; *Broca's Brain: Reflections on the Romance of Science* (1979); and *Cosmos* (1980), based on Sagan's PBS television series of the same title, in which he appeared as narrator.

The Nuclear Winter

Sagan has written more than 400 articles for popular magazines and for professional journals. Of all of them, the following essay may be of most immediate concern. Citing scientific findings, it shows how a nuclear war might affect our earth and its people. Sagan first published the essay in the Sunday newspaper supplement *Parade* on October 30, 1983, perhaps in the hope of alerting and alarming that popular weekly's millions of readers. "The Nuclear Winter" happens to be a memorable study in cause and effect; but, more important, it states an urgent, even frightening thesis. This is one essay we urge you to read, reread, and remember.

Into the eternal darkness, into fire, into ice.
— Dante, *The Inferno*

Except for fools and madmen, everyone knows that nuclear   1
war would be an unprecedented human catastrophe. A more or
less typical strategic warhead has a yield of 2 megatons, the explosive equivalent of 2 million tons of TNT. But 2 million tons
of TNT is about the same as all the bombs exploded in World
War II — a single bomb with the explosive power of the entire
Second World War but compressed into a few seconds of time
and an area 30 or 40 miles across . . .

In a 2-megaton explosion over a fairly large city, buildings   2
would be vaporized, people reduced to atoms and shadows, out-
lying structures blown down like matchsticks and raging fires ig-
nited. And if the bomb were exploded on the ground, an enormous crater, like those that can be seen through a telescope on
the surface of the Moon, would be all that remained where midtown once had been. There are now more than 50,000 nuclear
weapons, more than 13,000 megatons of yield, deployed in the
arsenals of the United States and the Soviet Union — enough
to obliterate a million Hiroshimas.

But there are fewer than 3000 cities on the Earth with popu-   3
lations of 100,000 or more. You cannot find anything like a million Hiroshimas to obliterate. Prime military and industrial targets that are far from cities are comparatively rare. Thus, there
are vastly more nuclear weapons than are needed for any plausible deterrence of a potential adversary.

Nobody knows, of course, how many megatons would be   4
exploded in a real nuclear war. There are some who think that a
nuclear war can be "contained," bottled up before it runs away
to involve many of the world's arsenals. But a number of detailed analyses, war games run by the U.S. Department of Defense and official Soviet pronouncements, all indicate that this
containment may be too much to hope for: Once the bombs begin exploding, communications failures, disorganization, fear,
the necessity of making in minutes decisions affecting the fates
of millions and the immense psychological burden of knowing
that your own loved ones may already have been destroyed are
likely to result in a nuclear paroxysm. Many investigations, including a number of studies for the U.S. government, envision

the explosion of 5000 to 10,000 megatons — the detonation of tens of thousands of nuclear weapons that now sit quietly, inconspicuously, in missile silos, submarines and long-range bombers, faithful servants awaiting orders.

The World Health Organization, in a recent detailed study   5 chaired by Sune K. Bergstrom (the 1982 Nobel laureate in physiology and medicine), concludes that 1.1 billion people would be killed outright in such a nuclear war, mainly in the United States, the Soviet Union, Europe, China and Japan. An additional 1.1 billion people would suffer serious injuries and radiation sickness, for which medical help would be unavailable. It thus seems possible that more than 2 billion people — almost half of all the humans on Earth — would be destroyed in the immediate aftermath of a global thermonuclear war. This would represent by far the greatest disaster in the history of the human species and, with no other adverse effects, would probably be enough to reduce at least the Northern Hemisphere to a state of prolonged agony and barbarism. Unfortunately, the real situation would be much worse.

In technical studies of the consequences of nuclear weapons   6 explosions, there has been a dangerous tendency to underestimate the results. This is partly due to a tradition of conservatism which generally works well in science but which is of more dubious applicability when the lives of billions of people are at stake. In the Bravo test of March 1, 1954, a 15-megaton thermonuclear bomb was exploded on Bikini Atoll. It had about double the yield expected, and there was an unanticipated last-minute shift in the wind direction. As a result, deadly radioactive fallout came down on Rongelap in the Marshall Islands, more than 200 kilometers away. Almost all the children on Rongelap subsequently developed thyroid nodules and lesions, and other long-term medical problems, due to the radioactive fallout.

Likewise, in 1973, it was discovered that high-yield airbursts   7 will chemically burn the nitrogen in the upper air, converting it into oxides of nitrogen; these, in turn, combine with and destroy the protective ozone in the Earth's stratosphere. The surface of the Earth is shielded from deadly solar ultraviolet radiation by a layer of ozone so tenuous that, were it brought down to sea level, it would be only 3 millimeters thick. Partial destruction of this ozone layer can have serious consequences for the biology of the entire planet.

These discoveries, and others like them, were made by 8 chance. They were largely unexpected. And now another consequence — by far the most dire — has been uncovered, again more or less by accident.

The U.S. Mariner 9 spacecraft, the first vehicle to orbit another planet, arrived at Mars in late 1971. The planet was enveloped in a global dust storm. As the fine particles slowly fell out, we were able to measure temperature changes in the atmosphere and on the surface. Soon it became clear what had happened:

The dust, lofted by high winds off the desert into the upper 10 Martian atmosphere, had absorbed the incoming sunlight and prevented much of it from reaching the ground. Heated by the sunlight, the dust warmed the adjacent air. But the surface, enveloped in partial darkness, became much chillier than usual. Months later, after the dust fell out of the atmosphere, the upper air cooled and the surface warmed, both returning to their normal conditions. We were able to calculate accurately, from how much dust there was in the atmosphere, how cool the Martian surface ought to have been.

Afterwards, I and my colleagues, James B. Pollack and Brian 11 Toon of NASA's Ames Research Center, were eager to apply these insights to the Earth. In a volcanic explosion, dust aerosols are lofted into the high atmosphere. We calculated by how much the Earth's global temperature should decline after a major volcanic explosion and found that our results (generally a fraction of a degree) were in good accord with actual measurements. Joining forces with Richard Turco, who has studied the effects of nuclear weapons for many years, we then began to turn our attention to the climatic effects of nuclear war. [The scientific paper, "Global Atmospheric Consequences of Nuclear War," is written by R. P. Turco, O. B. Toon, T. P. Ackerman, J. B. Pollack and Carl Sagan. From the last names of the authors, this work is generally referred to as "TTAPS."]

We knew that nuclear explosions, particularly ground- 12 bursts, would lift an enormous quantity of fine soil particles into the atmosphere (more than 100,000 tons of fine dust for every megaton exploded in a surface burst). Our work was further spurred by Paul Crutzen of the Max Planck Institute for Chemistry in Mainz, West Germany, and by John Birks of the University of Colorado, who pointed out that huge quantities of smoke would be generated in the burning of cities and forests following a nuclear war.

Groundbursts — at hardened missile silos, for example — generate fine dust. Airbursts — over cities and unhardened military installations — make fires and therefore smoke. The amount of dust and soot generated depends on the conduct of the war, the yields of the weapons employed and the ratio of groundbursts to airbursts. So we ran computer models for several dozen different nuclear war scenarios. Our baseline case, as in many other studies, was a 5000-megaton war with only a modest fraction of the yield (20 percent) expended on urban or industrial targets. Our job, for each case, was to follow the dust and smoke generated, see how much sunlight was absorbed and by how much the temperatures changed, figure out how the particles spread in longitude and latitude, and calculate how long before it all fell out of the air back onto the surface. Since the radioactivity would be attached to these same fine particles, our calculations also revealed the extent and timing of the subsequent radioactive fallout.

Some of what I am about to describe is horrifying. I know, because it horrifies me. There is a tendency — psychiatrists call it "denial" — to put it out of our minds, not to think about it. But if we are to deal intelligently, wisely, with the nuclear arms race, then we must steel ourselves to contemplate the horrors of nuclear war.

The results of our calculations astonished us. In the baseline case, the amount of sunlight at the ground was reduced to a few percent of normal — much darker, in daylight, than in a heavy overcast and too dark for plants to make a living from photosynthesis. At least in the Northern Hemisphere, where the great preponderance of strategic targets lies, an unbroken and deadly gloom would persist for weeks.

Even more unexpected were the temperatures calculated. In the baseline case, land temperatures, except for narrow strips of coastline, dropped to minus 25° Celsius (minus 13° Fahrenheit) and stayed below freezing for months — even for a summer war. (Because the atmospheric structure becomes much more stable as the upper atmosphere is heated and the lower air is cooled, we may have severely *under*estimated how long the cold and the dark would last.) The oceans, a significant heat reservoir, would not freeze, however, and a major ice age would probably not be triggered. But because the temperatures would drop so catastrophically, virtually all crops and farm animals, at least in the Northern Hemisphere, would be destroyed, as would most varieties of uncultivated or undomesticated food supplies. Most of the human survivors would starve.

In addition, the amount of radioactive fallout is much more than expected. Many previous calculations simply ignored the intermediate time-scale fallout. That is, calculations were made for the prompt fallout — the plumes of radioactive debris blown downwind from each target — and for the long-term fallout, the fine radioactive particles lofted into the stratosphere that would descend about a year later, after most of the radioactivity had decayed. However, the radioactivity carried into the upper atmosphere (but not as high as the stratosphere) seems to have been largely forgotten. We found for the baseline case that roughly 30 percent of the land at northern midlatitudes could receive a radioactive dose greater than 250 rads, and that about 50 percent of northern midlatitudes could receive a dose greater than 100 rads. A 100-rad dose is the equivalent of about 1000 medical X-rays. A 400-rad dose will, more likely than not, kill you.

The cold, the dark and the intense radioactivity, together lasting for months, represent a severe assault on our civilization and our species. Civil and sanitary services would be wiped out. Medical facilities, drugs, the most rudimentary means for relieving the vast human suffering, would be unavailable. Any but the most elaborate shelters would be useless, quite apart from the question of what good it might be to emerge a few months later. Synthetics burned in the destruction of the cities would produce a wide variety of toxic gases, including carbon monoxide, cyanides, dioxins and furans. After the dust and soot settled out, the solar ultraviolet flux would be much larger than its present value. Immunity to disease would decline. Epidemics and pandemics would be rampant, especially after the billion or so unburied bodies began to thaw. Moreover, the combined influence of these severe and simultaneous stresses on life are likely to produce even more adverse consequences — biologists call them synergisms — that we are not yet wise enough to foresee.

So far, we have talked only of the Northern Hemisphere. But it now seems — unlike the case of a single nuclear weapons test — that in a real nuclear war, the heating of the vast quantities of atmospheric dust and soot in northern midlatitudes will transport these fine particles toward and across the Equator. We see just this happening in Martian dust storms. The Southern Hemisphere would experience effects that, while less severe than in the Northern Hemisphere, are nevertheless extremely ominous. The illusion with which some people in the Northern Hemisphere reassure themselves — catching an Air New Zealand flight in a time of serious international crisis, or the like — is now much less tenable, even on the narrow issue of personal survival for those with the price of a ticket.   19

But what if nuclear wars *can* be contained, and much less than 5000 megatons is detonated? Perhaps the greatest surprise in our work was that even small nuclear wars can have devastating climatic effects. We considered a war in which a mere 100 megatons were exploded, less than one percent of the world arsenals, and only in low-yield airbursts over cities. This scenario, we found, would ignite thousands of fires, and the smoke from these fires alone would be enough to generate an epoch of cold and dark almost as severe as in the 5000-megaton case. The threshold for what Richard Turco has called the Nuclear Winter is very low.   20

Could we have overlooked some important effect? The carrying of dust and soot from the Northern to the Southern Hemisphere (as well as more local atmospheric circulation) will certainly thin the clouds out over the Northern Hemisphere. But, in many cases, this thinning would be insufficient to render the climatic consequences tolerable — and every time it got better in the Northern Hemisphere, it would get worse in the Southern.   21

Our results have been carefully scrutinized by more than 22
100 scientists in the United States, Europe and the Soviet Union. There are still arguments on points of detail. But the overall
conclusion seems to be agreed upon: There are severe and previously unanticipated global consequences of nuclear war — sub-
freezing temperatures in a twilit radioactive gloom lasting for
months or longer.

Scientists initially underestimated the effects of fallout, were 23
amazed that nuclear explosions in space disabled distant satel-
lites, had no idea that the fireballs from high-yield thermonuclear explosions could deplete the ozone layer and missed altogether the possible climatic effects of nuclear dust and smoke.
What else have we overlooked?

Nuclear war is a problem that can be treated only theoreti- 24
cally. It is not amenable to experimentation. Conceivably, we
have left something important out of our analysis, and the effects are more modest than we calculate. On the other hand, it
is also possible — and, from previous experience, even likely —
that there are further adverse effects that no one has yet been
wise enough to recognize. With billions of lives at stake, where
does conservatism lie — in assuming that the results will be better than we calculate, or worse?

Many biologists, considering the nuclear winter that these 25
calculations describe, believe they carry somber implications for
life on Earth. Many species of plants and animals would become
extinct. Vast numbers of surviving humans would starve to
death. The delicate ecological relations that bind together organisms on Earth in a fabric of mutual dependency would be torn,
perhaps irreparably. There is little question that our global civilization would be destroyed. The human population would be
reduced to prehistoric levels, or less. Life for any survivors
would be extremely hard. And there seems to be a real possibility of the extinction of the human species.

It is now almost 40 years since the invention of nuclear 26
weapons. We have not yet experienced a global thermonuclear
war — although on more than one occasion we have come tremulously close. I do not think our luck can hold forever. Men and
machines are fallible, as recent events remind us. Fools and

madmen do exist, and sometimes rise to power. Concentrating always on the near future, we have ignored the long-term consequences of our actions. We have placed our civilization and our species in jeopardy.

Fortunately, it is not yet too late. We can safeguard the 27 planetary civilization and the human family if we so choose. There is no more important or more urgent issue.

QUESTIONS ON MEANING AND PURPOSE

1. Evaluate the reasons Sagan gives for his skepticism about the possibility of "contained nuclear war."
2. "Nuclear war is a problem that can be treated only theoretically" (paragraph 24). To what extent does this fact affect the author's credibility?
3. According to the author, what is the chief effect of a nuclear airburst?
4. What similarities exist between the effects of a volcanic eruption and those of a nuclear groundburst? What is the most important difference between the two?
5. From what sources does Sagan draw EVIDENCE for his conviction that a "nuclear winter" would follow a nuclear war? What difference would it make to the climate if the conflict were a "contained nuclear war"?
6. Where in the essay do you find support for the idea that Sagan has a PURPOSE other than merely to frighten his readers?

QUESTIONS ON WRITING STRATEGY

1. How does Sagan's capsule history of the Bravo test help support his essay's central THESIS?
2. In paragraphs 9 and 10, Sagan details the results of a dust storm on Mars. What connection does this material have with the main body of the essay? Does its inclusion impair the essay's UNITY?
3. Where in his essay does Sagan make effective use of RHETORICAL QUESTIONS?
4. What sentences or passages effectively serve as TRANSITIONS?

5. What constraints or limitations would an AUDIENCE of *Parade* magazine readers have placed on Sagan? How well has he triumphed over these limitations?

QUESTIONS ON LANGUAGE

1. Be sure you understand, from context or with the aid of your dictionary, what the following words mean: unprecedented (paragraph 1); obliterate (2); plausible, adversary (3); paroxysm (4); barbarism (5); applicability, nodules, lesions (6); oxides, tenuous (7); photosynthesis, preponderance (15); catastrophically (16); rudimentary, flux, pandemics, rampant (18); ominous, tenable (19); epoch (20); deplete (23); amenable (24); somber, irreparably (25); tremulously, fallible, jeopardy (26).
2. Where in his essay does the author lapse into scientific JARGON? Could he have substituted plainer words? To what extent does Sagan's use of jargon interfere with the average reader's understanding?
3. In paragraphs 2, 4, 7, and 25 Sagan uses vivid SIMILES, METAPHORS, and IMAGES. What do these FIGURES OF SPEECH contribute to the essay's impact?
4. Twice in his essay (in paragraphs 1 and 26) Sagan employs the phrase *fools and madmen*. In each case, how does the context affect the image conjured up by the phrase?

SUGGESTIONS FOR WRITING

1. In his final paragraph Sagan writes, "We can safeguard the planetary civilization and the human family if we so choose." Write a brief process analysis (see Chapter 5) in which you suggest how this might be accomplished.
2. Compare and contrast Sagan's essay with Russell Baker's "Universal Military Motion" (Chapter 10). Pay special attention to the TONE of both authors.
3. Write an essay in which you detail some effects of the nuclear buildup other than possible all-out holocaust. How, for instance, has the buildup affected our national budget? What is its psychological effect on the populace? To what extent is the buildup a deterrent to war? What effect does government secrecy about nuclear warheads have on the American people? How does our stockpile of nuclear arms affect our image abroad? Be sure to back up your assertions with evidence.

· Sheila Tobias ·

SHEILA TOBIAS, born in 1935, is a Radcliffe graduate and has
an M.A. in history from Columbia University. She has been
a university teacher and administrator, most recently at Wesleyan University in Connecticut. One of the founding members of the National Organization of Women (NOW) and a
"math avoider," she published *Overcoming Math Anxiety* in
1978. Shortly afterward, in Washington, D.C., she and two
colleagues founded Overcoming Math Anxiety, a consulting
and training service that runs math clinics for adults. Recently she has written (with Peter Goudinoff) *What Kinds of
Guns Are They Buying for Your Butter? A Beginner's Guide to
Defense, Weaponry, and Military Spending* (1982).

*Who's Afraid of Math,
and Why?*

In "Who's Afraid of Math, and Why?," an excerpt from *Overcoming Math Anxiety*, Tobias attacks the myth of the "mathematical mind" and examines some of the hang-ups people
have about learning math. Math avoiders, it seems, are
mostly — but not solely — women. Tobias explains why.

The first thing people remember about failing at math is
that it felt like sudden death. Whether the incident occurred
while learning "word problems" in sixth grade, coping with
equations in high school, or first confronting calculus and statistics in college, failure came suddenly and in a very frightening
way. An idea or a new operation was not just difficult, it was impossible! And, instead of asking questions or taking the lesson
slowly, most people remember having had the feeling that they
would never go any further in mathematics. If we assume that
the curriculum was reasonable, and that the new idea was but
the next in a series of learnable concepts, the feeling of utter defeat was simply not rational; yet "math anxious" college stu-

dents and adults have revealed that no matter how much the teacher reassured them, they could not overcome that feeling.

A common myth about the nature of mathematical ability 2 holds that one either has or does not have a mathematical mind. Mathematical imagination and an intuitive grasp of mathematical principles may well be needed to do advanced research, but why should people who can do college-level work in other subjects not be able to do college-level math as well? Rates of learning may vary. Competency under time pressure may differ. Certainly low self-esteem will get in the way. But where is the evidence that a student needs a "mathematical mind" in order to succeed at learning math?

Consider the effects of this mythology. Since only a few peo- 3 ple are supposed to have this mathematical mind, part of what makes us so passive in the face of our difficulties in learning mathematics is that we suspect all the while we may not be one of "them," and we spend our time waiting to find out when our nonmathematical minds will be exposed. Since our limit will eventually be reached, we see no point in being methodical or in attending to detail. We are grateful when we survive fractions, word problems, or geometry. If that certain moment of failure hasn't struck yet, it is only temporarily postponed.

Parents, especially parents of girls, often expect their chil- 4 dren to be nonmathematical. Parents are either poor at math and had their own sudden-death experiences, or, if math came easily for them, they do not know how it feels to be slow. In either case, they unwittingly foster the idea that a mathematical mind is something one either has or does not have.

Mathematics and Sex

Although fear of math is not a purely female phenomenon, 5 girls tend to drop out of math sooner than boys, and adult women experience an aversion to math and math-related activities that is akin to anxiety. A 1972 survey of the amount of high school mathematics taken by incoming freshmen at Berkeley revealed that while 57 percent of the boys had taken four years of high school math, only 8 percent of the girls had had the same amount of preparation. Without four years of high school math, students at Berkeley, and at most other colleges and universities, are ineligible for the calculus sequence, unlikely to attempt chemistry or physics, and inadequately prepared for statistics and economics.

Unable to elect these entry-level courses, the remaining 92   6
percent of the girls will be limited, presumably, to the career choices that are considered feminine: the humanities, guidance and counseling, elementary school teaching, foreign languages, and the fine arts.

Boys and girls may be born alike with respect to math, but   7
certain sex differences in performance emerge early according to several respected studies, and these differences remain through adulthood. They are:

1. Girls compute better than boys (elementary school and on).
2. Boys solve word problems better than girls (from age thirteen on).
3. Boys take more math than girls (from age sixteen on).
4. Girls learn to hate math sooner and possibly for different reasons.

Why the differences in performance? One reason is the   8
amount of math learned and used at play. Another may be the difference in male-female maturation. If girls do better than boys at all elementary school tasks, then they may compute better for no other reason than that arithmetic is part of the elementary school curriculum. As boys and girls grow older, girls become, under pressure, academically less competitive. Thus, the falling off of girls' math performance between ages ten and fifteen may be because:

1. Math gets harder in each successive year and requires more work and commitment.
2. Both boys and girls are pressured, beginning at age ten, not to excel in areas designated by society to be outside their sex-role domains.
3. Thus girls have a good excuse to avoid the painful struggle with math; boys don't.

Such a model may explain girls' lower achievement in math   9
overall, but why should girls even younger than ten have diffi-

culty in problem-solving? In her review of the research on sex differences, psychologist Eleanor Maccoby noted that girls are generally more conforming, more suggestible, and more dependent upon the opinion of others than boys (all learned, not innate, behaviors). Being so, they may not be as willing to take risks or to think for themselves, two behaviors that are necessary in solving problems. Indeed, in one test of third-graders, girls were found to be not nearly as willing to estimate, to make judgments about "possible right answers," or to work with systems they had never seen before. Their very success at doing what is expected of them up to that time seems to get in the way of their doing something new.

If readiness to do word problems, to take one example, is as much a function of readiness to take risks as it is of "reasoning ability," then mathematics performance certainly requires more than memory, computation, and reasoning. The differences in math performance between boys and girls — no matter how consistently those differences show up — cannot be attributed simply to differences in innate ability. 10

Still, if one were to ask the victims themselves, they would probably disagree: they would say their problems with math have to do with the way they are "wired." They feel they are somehow missing something — one ability or several — that other people have. Although women want to believe they are not mentally inferior to men, many fear that, where math is concerned, they really are. Thus, we have to consider seriously whether mathematical ability has a biological basis, not only because a number of researchers believe this to be so, but because a number of victims agree with them. 11

The Arguments from Biology

The search for some biological basis for math ability or disability is fraught with logical and experimental difficulties. Since not all math underachievers are women, and not all women are mathematics-avoidant, poor performance in math is unlikely to be due to some genetic or hormonal difference between the sexes. Moreover, no amount of research so far has unearthed a 12 "mathematical competency" in some tangible, measurable substance in the body. Since "masculinity" cannot be injected into women to test whether or not it improves their mathematics, the theories that attribute such ability to genes or hormones must depend for their proof on circumstantial evidence. So long as about 7 percent of the Ph.D.'s in mathematics are earned by women, we have to conclude either that these women have genes, hormones, and brain organization different from those of the rest of us, or that certain positive experiences in their lives have largely undone the negative fact that they are female, or both.

Genetically, the only difference between males and females   13
(albeit a significant and pervasive one) is the presence of two chromosomes designated X in every female cell. Normal males exhibit an X-Y combination. Because some kinds of mental retardation are associated with sex-chromosomal anomalies, a number of researchers have sought a converse linkage between specific abilities and the presence or absence of the second X. But the linkage between genetics and mathematics is not supported by conclusive evidence.

Since intensified hormonal activity commences at adoles-   14
cence, a time during which girls seem to lose interest in mathematics, much more has been made of the unequal amounts in females and males of the sex-linked hormones androgen and estrogen. Biological researchers have linked estrogen — the female hormone — with "simple repetitive tasks," and androgen — the male hormone — with "complex restructuring tasks." The assumption here is not only that such specific talents are biologically based (probably undemonstrable) but also that one cannot be good at *both* repetitive and restructuring kinds of assignments.

Sex Roles and Mathematics Competence

The fact that many girls tend to lose interest in math at the   15
age they reach puberty (junior high school) suggests that puberty might in some sense cause girls to fall behind in math. Several explanations come to mind: the influence of hormones,

more intensified sex-role socialization, or some extracurricular learning experience exclusive to boys of that age.

One group of seventh-graders in a private school in New England gave a clue as to what children themselves think about all of this. When asked why girls do as well as boys in math until the sixth grade, while sixth-grade boys do better from that point on, the girls responded: "Oh, that's easy. After sixth grade, we have to do real math." The answer to why "real math" should be considered to be "for boys" and not "for girls" can be found not in the realm of biology but only in the realm of ideology of sex differences. 16

Parents, peers, and teachers forgive a girl when she does badly in math at school, encouraging her to do well in other subjects instead. " 'There, there,' my mother used to say when I failed at math," one woman says. "But I got a talking-to when I did badly in French." Lynn Fox, who directs a program for mathematically gifted junior high boys and girls on the campus of Johns Hopkins University, has trouble recruiting girls and keeping them in her program. Some parents prevent their daughters from participating altogether for fear that excellence in math will make them too different. The girls themselves are often reluctant to continue with mathematics, Fox reports, because they fear social ostracism. 17

Where do these associations come from? 18

The association of masculinity with mathematics sometimes extends from the discipline to those who practice it. Students, asked on a questionnaire what characteristics they associate with a mathematician (as contrasted with a "writer"), selected terms such as rational, cautious, wise, and responsible. The writer, on the other hand, in addition to being seen as individualistic and independent, was also described as warm, interested in people, and altogether more compatible with a feminine ideal. 19

As a result of this psychological conditioning, a young woman may consider math and math-related fields to be inimical to femininity. In an interesting study of West German teenagers, Erika Schildkamp-Kuendiger found that girls who identified themselves with the feminine ideal underachieved in mathematics, that is, did less well than would have been ex- 20 pected of them based on general intelligence and performance in other subjects.

Street Mathematics: Things, Motion, Scores

Not all the skills that are necessary for learning mathematics   21
are learned in school. Measuring, computing, and manipulating objects that have dimensions and dynamic properties of their own are part of the everyday life of children. Children who miss out on these experiences may not be well primed for math in school.

Feminists have complained for a long time that playing with   22
dolls is one way of convincing impressionable little girls that they may only be mothers or housewives — or, as in the case of the Barbie doll, "pinup girls" — when they grow up. But doll-playing may have even more serious consequences for little girls than that. Do girls find out about gravity and distance and shapes and sizes playing with dolls? Probably not.

A curious boy, if his parents are tolerant, will have taken   23
apart a number of household and play objects by the time he is ten, and, if his parents are lucky, he may even have put them back together again. In all of this he is learning things that will be useful in physics and math. Taking parts out that have to go back in requires some examination of form. Building something that stays up or at least stays put for some time involves working with structure.

Sports is another source of math-related concepts for chil-   24
dren which tends to favor boys. Getting to first base on a not very well hit grounder is a lesson in time, speed, and distance. Intercepting a football thrown through the air requires some rapid intuitive eye calculations based on the ball's direction, speed, and trajectory. Since physics is partly concerned with velocities, trajectories, and collisions of objects, much of the math taught to prepare a student for physics deals with relationships and formulas that can be used to express motion and acceleration.

What, then, can we conclude about mathematics and sex? If   25
math anxiety is in part the result of math avoidance, why not re-

quire girls to take as much math as they can possibly master? If being the only girl in "trig" is the reason so many women drop math at the end of high school, why not provide psychological counseling and support for those young women who wish to go on? Since ability in mathematics is considered by many to be unfeminine, perhaps fear of success, more than any bodily or mental dysfunction, may interfere with girls' ability to learn math.

QUESTIONS ON MEANING AND PURPOSE

1. According to Tobias, what effect does the myth of the "mathematical mind" have on the ordinary person's performance in math?
2. To what does the author attribute the fact that girls tend to compute better than boys? How does Tobias account for boys' superior problem-solving ability?
3. Of the probable causes Tobias cites for the fact that girls as they mature generally perform less well in math than boys, which one does the author rule out? On what basis? Are you satisfied that she is justified in doing so?
4. According to the author, what differences exist between the play patterns of little boys and those of little girls? In what way do these differences favor boys and handicap girls in their later efforts to acquire math skills?
5. In what additional ways, according to Tobias, does gender influence math performance? Of these, which does the author rank as the most important?
6. How would you expect a math avoider to react to this essay?

QUESTIONS ON WRITING STRATEGY

1. At what point in her essay does Tobias shift her EMPHASIS from math anxiety in general to math anxiety as a special problem for girls?
2. What do the statistics quoted in paragraphs 5, 6, and 7 contribute to the essay's EFFECT?
3. What, if anything, does Tobias gain by putting her "arguments from biology" ahead of the other possible causes of poor math performance?

4. Do you think this essay would have been as effective if Tobias had written it as a first-person narrative of her own experiences with math? Why or why not? (See PERSON in Useful Terms.)

QUESTIONS ON LANGUAGE

1. How would you characterize Tobias's prose: terse, poetic, utilitarian, or persuasive?
2. In paragraph 11, Tobias twice refers to "victims." Comment on her word choice.
3. The title of this essay contains an ALLUSION. What is its source?
4. What does Tobias mean by "wired" (paragraph 11)?
5. Be sure you can define the following words: albeit, anomalies (paragraph 13); socialization (15); ideology (16); ostracism (17); trajectory (24); dysfunction (25).

SUGGESTIONS FOR WRITING

1. Write a brief description or narrative in which math panic (or stage fright, or final exam panic) strikes you or someone you know. A little exaggeration, you will find, just might add zest to your account.
2. Identify a few differences between men and women that, like differences in mathematical ability, seem the result not of biology but of cultural conditioning. Then, in a paragraph or two, trace the causes of one such difference. Or attempt to show, as some researchers do, that mathematical ability really is an inborn, sex-linked trait.

· Marie Winn ·

MARIE WINN was born in Czechoslovakia in 1936. As a child she emigrated with her family to New York City, where she attended the public schools. She was graduated from Radcliffe College and went on to Columbia University for further study. A regular contributor to the *New York Times Magazine*, she is the author of eleven books for both adults and children, including *The Fireside Book of Fun and Game Songs* (1974). *The Plug-In Drug: Television, Children and the Family* (1977) attracted a great deal of attention when it was published; so did *Children without Childhood* (1983).

The End of Play

A few years ago "What Became of Childhood Innocence?" by Marie Winn appeared as a cover story in the *New York Times Magazine*. The article was the seed from which *Children without Childhood* grew. To put together her book, Winn interviewed hundreds of parents and children. The interviews revealed that since the 1960s American children have changed markedly, and so has society's attitude — not only toward children but toward the whole idea of childhood as a golden age of protected innocence. *Children without Childhood* documents those changes. "The End of Play," a chapter from the book, outlines one of them and examines some of its causes.

Of all the changes that have altered the topography of childhood, the most dramatic has been the disappearance of childhood play. Whereas a decade or two ago children were easily distinguished from the adult world by the very nature of their play, today children's occupations do not differ greatly from adult diversions.

Infants and toddlers, to be sure, continue to follow certain timeless patterns of manipulation and exploration; adolescents, too, have not changed their free-time habits so very much, turning as they ever have towards adult pastimes and amusements in

1

2

their drive for autonomy, self-mastery, and sexual discovery. It is among the ranks of school-age children, those six-to-twelve-year-olds who once avidly filled their free moments with childhood play, that the greatest change is evident. In the place of traditional, sometimes ancient childhood games that were still popular a generation ago, in the place of fantasy and make-believe play — "You be the mommy and I'll be the daddy" — doll play or toy-soldier play, jump-rope play, ball-bouncing play, today's children have substituted television viewing and, most recently, video games.

Many parents have misgivings about the influence of television. They sense that a steady and time-consuming exposure to passive entertainment might damage the ability to play imaginatively and resourcefully, or prevent this ability from developing in the first place. A mother of two school-age children recalls: "When I was growing up, we used to go out into the vacant lots and make up week-long dramas and sagas. This was during third, fourth, fifth grades. But my own kids have never done that sort of thing, and somehow it bothers me. I wish we had cut down on the TV years ago, and maybe the kids would have learned how to play."

The testimony of parents who eliminate television for periods of time strengthens the connection between children's television watching and changed play patterns. Many parents discover that when their children don't have television to fill their free time, they resort to the old kinds of imaginative, traditional "children's play." Moreover, these parents often observe that under such circumstances "they begin to seem more like children" or "they act more childlike." Clearly, a part of the definition of childhood, in adults' minds, resides in the nature of children's play.

Children themselves sometimes recognize the link between play and their own special definition as children. In an interview about children's books with four ten-year-old girls, one of them said: "I read this story about a girl my age growing up twenty years ago — you know, in 1960 or so — and she seemed so much younger than me in her behavior. Like she might be playing with dolls, or playing all sorts of children's games, or jump-roping or something." The other girls all agreed that they had noticed a similar discrepancy between themselves and fictional children in books of the past: those children seemed more like children. "So what do *you* do in your spare time, if you don't play with dolls or play make-believe games or jump rope or do things kids did twenty years ago?" they were asked. They laughed and answered, "We watch TV."

But perhaps other societal factors have caused children to give up play. Children's greater exposure to adult realities, their knowledge of adult sexuality, for instance, might make them more sophisticated, less likely to play like children. Evidence from the counterculture communes of the sixties and seventies adds weight to the argument that it is television above all that has eliminated children's play. Studies of children raised in a variety of such communes, all television-free, showed the little communards continuing to fill their time with those forms of play that have all but vanished from the lives of conventionally reared American children. And yet these counterculture kids were casually exposed to all sorts of adult matters — drug taking, sexual intercourse. Indeed, they sometimes incorporated these matters into their play: "We're mating," a pair of six-year-olds told a reporter to explain their curious bumps and grinds. Nevertheless, to all observers the commune children preserved a distinctly childlike and even innocent demeanor, an impression that was produced mainly by the fact that they spent most of their time playing. Their play defined them as belonging to a special world of childhood.

Not all children have lost the desire to engage in the old-style childhood play. But so long as the most popular, most dominant members of the peer group, who are often the most socially precocious, are "beyond" playing, then a common desire to conform makes it harder for those children who still have the drive to play to go ahead and do so. Parents often report that their children seem ashamed of previously common forms of play and hide their involvement with such play from their peers. "My fifth-grader still plays with dolls," a mother tells, "but she keeps them hidden in the basement where nobody will see them." This social check on the play instinct serves to hasten the end of childhood for even the least advanced children.

What seems to have replaced play in the lives of great num- 8 bers of preadolescents these days, starting as early as fourth grade, is a burgeoning interest in boy-girl interactions — "going out" or "going together." These activities do not necessarily involve going anywhere or doing anything sexual, but nevertheless are the first stage of a sexual process that used to commence at puberty or even later. Those more sophisticated children who are already involved in such manifestly unchildlike interests make plain their low opinion of their peers who still *play*. "Some of the kids in the class are real weird," a fifth-grade boy states. "They're not interested in going out, just in trucks and stuff, or games pretending they're monsters. Some of them don't even *try* to be cool."

Video Games versus Marbles

Is there really any great difference, one might ask, between 9 that gang of kids playing video games by the hour at their local candy store these days and those small fry who used to hang around together spending equal amounts of time playing marbles? It is easy to see a similarity between the two activities: each requires a certain amount of manual dexterity, each is almost as much fun to watch as to play, each is simple and yet challenging enough for that middle-childhood age group for whom time can be so oppressive if unfilled.

One significant difference between the modern pre-teen fad 10 of video games and the once popular but now almost extinct pastime of marbles is economic: playing video games costs twenty-five cents for approximately three minutes of play; playing marbles, after a small initial investment, is free. The children who frequent video-game machines require a considerable outlay of quarters to subsidize their fun; two, three, or four dollars is not an unusual expenditure for an eight- or nine-year-old spending an hour or two with his friends playing Asteroids or Pac-Man or Space Invaders. For most of the children the money comes from their weekly allowance. Some augment this amount by enterprising commercial ventures — trading and selling comic books, or doing chores around the house for extra money.

But what difference does it make *where* the money comes from? Why should that make video games any less satisfactory as an amusement for children? In fact, having to pay for the entertainment, whatever the source of the money, and having its duration limited by one's financial resources changes the nature of the game, in a subtle way diminishing the satisfactions it offers. Money and time become intertwined, as they so often are in the adult world and as, in the past, they almost never were in the child's world. For the child playing marbles, meanwhile, time has a far more carefree quality, bounded only by the requirements to be home by suppertime or by dark.

But the video-game-playing child has an additional burden — a burden of choice, of knowing that the money used for playing Pac-Man could have been saved for Christmas, could have been used to buy something tangible, perhaps something "worthwhile," as his parents might say, rather than being "wasted" on video games. There is a certain sense of adultness that spending money imparts, a feeling of being a consumer, which distinguishes a game with a price from its counterparts among the traditional childhood games children once played at no cost.

There are other differences as well. Unlike child-initiated and child-organized games such as marbles, video games are adult-created mechanisms not entirely within the child's control, and thus less likely to impart a sense of mastery and fulfillment: the coin may get jammed, the machine may go haywire, the little blobs may stop eating the funny little dots. Then the child must go to the storekeeper to complain, to get his money back. He may be "ripped off" and simply lose his quarter, much as his parents are when they buy a faulty appliance. This possibility of disaster gives the child's play a certain weight that marbles never imposed on its light-hearted players.

Even if a child has a video game at home requiring no coin outlay, the play it provides is less than optimal. The noise level

of the machine is high — too high, usually, for the child to conduct a conversation easily with another child. And yet, according to its enthusiasts, this very noisiness is a part of the game's
attraction. The loud whizzes, crashes, and whirrs of the video-
game machine "blow the mind" and create an excitement that is
quite apart from the excitement generated simply by trying to
win a game. A traditional childhood game such as marbles, on
the other hand, has little built-in stimulation; the excitement of
playing is generated entirely by the players' own actions. And
while the pace of a game of marbles is close to the child's natural
physiological rhythms, the frenzied activities of video games
serve to "rev up" the child in an artificial way, almost in the way
a stimulant or an amphetamine might. Meanwhile the perceptual impact of a video game is similar to that of watching television — the action, after all, takes place on a television screen —
causing the eye to defocus slightly and creating a certain
alteration in the child's natural state of consciousness.

Parents' instinctive reaction to their children's involvement   15
with video games provides another clue to the difference between this contemporary form of play and the more traditional
pastimes such as marbles. While parents, indeed most adults, derive open pleasure from watching children at play, most parents
today are not delighted to watch their kids flicking away at the
Pac-Man machine. This does not seem to them to be real play.
As a mother of two school-age children anxiously explains, "We
used to do real childhood sorts of things when I was a kid. We'd
build forts and put on crazy plays and make up new languages,
and just generally we *played.* But today my kids don't play that
way at all. They like video games and of course they still go in
for sports outdoors. They go roller skating and ice skating and
skiing and all. But they don't seem to really *play.*"

Some of this feeling may represent a certain nostalgia for the   16
past and the old generation's resistance to the different ways of
the new. But it is more likely that most adults have an instinctive understanding of the importance of play in their own childhood. This feeling stokes their fears that their children are being
deprived of something irreplaceable when they flip the levers on

the video machines to manipulate the electronic images rather than flick their fingers to send a marble shooting towards another marble.

Play Deprivation

In addition to television's influence, some parents and 17
teachers ascribe children's diminished drive to play to recent changes in the school curriculum, especially in the early grades.

"Kindergarten, traditionally a playful port of entry into for- 18
mal school, is becoming more academic, with children being taught specific skills, taking tests, and occasionally even having homework," begins a report on new directions in early childhood education. Since 1970, according to the United States census, the proportion of three- and four-year-olds enrolled in school has risen dramatically, from 20.5 percent to 36.7 percent in 1980, and these nursery schools have largely joined the push towards academic acceleration in the early grades. Moreover, middle-class nursery schools in recent years have introduced substantial doses of academic material into their daily programs, often using those particular devices originally intended to help culturally deprived preschoolers in compensatory programs such as Headstart to catch up with their middle-class peers. Indeed, some of the increased focus on academic skills in nursery schools and kindergartens is related to the widespread popularity among young children and their parents of *Sesame Street*, a program originally intended to help deprived children attain academic skills, but universally watched by middle-class toddlers as well.

Parents of the *Sesame Street* generation often demand a "seri- 19
ous," skill-centered program for their preschoolers in school, afraid that the old-fashioned, play-centered curriculum will bore their alphabet-spouting, number-chanting four- and five-year-olds. A few parents, especially those whose children have not attended television classes or nursery school, complain of the high-powered pace of kindergarten these days. A father whose five-year-old daughter attends a public kindergarten declares: "There's a lot more pressure put on little kids these days than

when we were kids, that's for sure. My daughter never went to nursery school and never watched *Sesame,* and she had a lot of trouble when she entered kindergarten this fall. By October, just a month and a half into the program, she was already flunking. The teacher told us our daughter couldn't keep up with the other kids. And believe me, she's a bright kid! All the other kids were getting gold stars and smiley faces for their work, and every day Emily would come home in tears because she didn't get a gold star. Remember when we were in kindergarten? We were *children* then. We were allowed just to play!"

A kindergarten teacher confirms the trend towards early ac-   20
ademic pressure. "We're expected by the dictates of the school system to push a lot of curriculum," she explains. "Kids in our kindergarten can't sit around playing with blocks any more. We've just managed to squeeze in one hour of free play a week, on Fridays."

The diminished emphasis on fantasy and play and imagina-   21
tive activities in early childhood education and the increased fo-cus on early academic-skill acquisition have helped to change childhood from a play-centered time of life to one more closely resembling the style of adulthood: purposeful, success-centered, competitive. The likelihood is that these preschool "workers" will not metamorphose back into players when they move on to grade school. This decline in play is surely one of the reasons why so many teachers today comment that their third- or fourth-graders act like tired businessmen instead of like chil-dren.

What might be the consequences of this change in children's   22
play? Children's propensity to engage in that extraordinary se-ries of behaviors characterized as "play" is perhaps the single great dividing line between childhood and adulthood, and has probably been so throughout history. The make-believe games anthropologists have recorded of children in primitive societies around the world attest to the universality of play and to the uniqueness of this activity to the immature members of each so-ciety. But in those societies, and probably in Western society be-fore the middle or late eighteenth century, there was always a certain similarity between children's play and adult work. The

child's imaginative play took the form of imitation of various aspects of adult life, culminating in the gradual transformation of the child's play from make-believe work to *real* work. At this point, in primitive societies or in our own society of the past, the child took her or his place in the adult work world and the distinctions between adulthood and childhood virtually vanished. But in today's technologically advanced society there is no place for the child in the adult work world. There are not enough jobs, even of the most menial kind, to go around for adults, much less for children. The child must continue to be dependent on adults for many years while gaining the knowledge and skills necessary to become a working member of society.

This is not a new situation for children. For centuries children have endured a prolonged period of dependence long after the helplessness of early childhood is over. But until recent years children remained childlike and playful far longer than they do today. Kept isolated from the adult world as a result of deliberate secrecy and protectiveness, they continued to find pleasure in socially sanctioned childish activities until the imperatives of adolescence led them to strike out for independence and self-sufficiency.

Today, however, with children's inclusion in the adult world both through the instrument of television and as a result of a deliberately preparatory, integrative style of child rearing, the old forms of play no longer seem to provide children with enough excitement and stimulation. What then are these so-called children to do for fulfillment if their desire to play has been vitiated and yet their entry into the working world of adulthood must be delayed for many years? The answer is precisely to get involved in those areas that cause contemporary parents so much distress: addictive television viewing during the school years followed, in adolescence or even before, by a search for similar oblivion via alcohol and drugs; exploration of the world of sensuality and sexuality before achieving the emotional maturity necessary for altruistic relationships.

Psychiatrists have observed among children in recent years a marked increase in the occurrence of depression, a state long considered antithetical to the nature of childhood. Perhaps this phenomenon is at least somewhat connected with the current sense of uselessness and alienation that children feel, a sense that play may once upon a time have kept in abeyance.

QUESTIONS ON MEANING AND PURPOSE

1. How many causes does the author find for the decline of play among children today? What are they?
2. What similarities exist, according to Winn, between playing marbles and playing video games? Sum up the important differences between the two activities.
3. Does Winn's essay seem to you to reveal any PURPOSE other than to inform? Give EVIDENCE for your answer.
4. For discussion: Are there factors in addition to those Winn mentions that divert today's children from spontaneous play? If so, what are they?

QUESTIONS ON WRITING STRATEGY

1. Winn opens her essay with a startling GENERALIZATION. What is the strongest evidence she includes in support of it? What is the weakest?
2. At the start of paragraph 6 Winn suggests and then dismisses one explanation for the decline of play. What reason does she give for dismissing this second explanation? Does its inclusion strengthen or weaken her THESIS?
3. What does the essay gain from direct quotation?
4. How might Winn's essay be different had she written it for an AUDIENCE of child development experts rather than for an audience of general readers?
5. Would you call Winn's writing OBJECTIVE or SUBJECTIVE?

QUESTIONS ON LANGUAGE

1. Consult your dictionary if you need to look up definitions for the following words: topography (paragraph 1); autonomy (2); discrepancy (5); societal, demeanor (6); precocious (7); burgeoning, puberty (8); augment (10); tangible (12); optimal, perceptual (14); nos-

talgia (16); compensatory (18); metamorphose (21); propensity, culminating (22); imperatives (23); vitiated, altruistic (24); antithetical, abeyance (25).
2. What seems to be the author's rationale for enclosing certain words and short phrases in quotation marks?
3. How well is Winn's DICTION tailored to the audience she aims to reach? To what extent, for instance, does she use occupational JARGON? Unfamiliar words?

SUGGESTIONS FOR WRITING

1. Write a paragraph in which you describe and evaluate the view of the world you think television imparts to children.
2. Write from the POINT OF VIEW of a child today, complaining either that you are being hurried to grow up, or that you are being held back from maturity.

—— POSTSCRIPT ON PROCESS ——

Marie Winn

If you tend to think of professional writers as extraordinary men and women "whose words flow trippingly from their head onto the page," what Marie Winn reveals about the hard work involved in putting together a book — or even a chapter — will be an eye-opener. Does she enjoy doing it? Well, yes and no.

"I hate and I love," begins a poem by Catullus, perfectly 1 summing up my feelings about writing. Let me start with the good part. There's nothing I like better than improving a piece of writing. I love spending an hour or two with a dictionary and a thesaurus looking for a more nearly perfect word than the one I have used, or taking my pen and ruthlessly pruning all the unnecessary adjectives (a practice I can wholeheartedly recommend to you), or fooling around with the rhythm of a sentence or a paragraph by changing a verb into a participle, or making any number of little changes that a magazine editor I work with ruefully calls "mouse milking." Unfortunately, if I were to guess at the proportion of time of the days or months or sometimes years that go into the writing of an article or book spent at this delightful occupation, I would say that it is a very small percentage.

This doesn't mean that of the three years I worked on *Chil-* 2 *dren without Childhood* I wrote for two years and eleven months and then enjoyed a month polishing and refining the prose. For me, the pleasure and pain of writing go on simultaneously. Once I have finally forced myself to bite the bullet and get to work, as soon as the flow of writing stops, after a few sentences or paragraphs or, if I am extraordinarily lucky, a few pages, then, as a little reward for having actually written something, and also as a procrastinating measure to delay the painful necessity of having to write something again, I play with the words and sentences on the page.

That's the trouble, of course: there have to be words and sentences on the page before I can enjoy the pleasures of playing with them. Somehow I have to transform the vague and confused tangle of ideas in my head into an orderly and logical sequence on a blank piece of paper. That's the real hell of writing: the inescapable need to think clearly. Most of the time I don't think clearly. It's too hard — why bother? But to write you cannot avoid clear thinking. You have to figure it out, make it all hang together, consider the implications, the alternatives, eliminate the contradictions, the extraneous thoughts, the illogical conclusions. I *hate* that part of writing, and I have a feeling that you know perfectly well what I'm talking about. You just may not realize that the agonies you go through when you have to write something, a paper for a school course, for instance, are universal. You may have imagined that writers are some sort of special creatures whose words flow trippingly from their heads onto the page. This is certainly not true. Just about all the writers I know are miserable most of the time they have to write, and the tiny group that claim to feel otherwise are lying through their teeth to make the rest of us feel bad.

There's another phase of each writing project, however, that falls somewhere between the pain of actual writing and the pure pleasures of polishing: the time spent gathering together the material about which to write. For the chapter included here, "The End of Play," the research phase lasted almost a year. During that time I interviewed parents in three geographically diverse communities about the kinds of play they remembered from their own childhoods and how these resembled or differed from their children's play patterns today. I talked to teachers about their perceptions of change in children's play and about changes in school curricula that have affected play. I observed and talked to many children at their homes, at school, at playgrounds and video arcades, among other places. And I spent many hours in the library, reading books and scholarly papers about children's play in other cultures and at other historical times. All this may sound quite enjoyable — talking to people, reading books — and indeed it would be, if it weren't for the fact that one has to write about it afterwards. When interviewing parents or teachers or children, I cannot sit back and simply enjoy a conversation, listening and reacting, going back and forth the way one usually does. Though it is often difficult, I must suppress my own thoughts and reactions during an interview and focus entirely on what the other person is saying, and, especially, what she or he is *not* saying. I have to devise strategies at getting those crucial, unsaid thoughts out into the open, even when they are obviously painful or embarrassing. Since this goes against so many deeply ingrained social instincts, it takes away much of the enjoyment I might normally feel when talking to another person. But here is the most distressing thing of all: as I gather material for an article or book, as I interview people, as I read books and papers on my subject, I have to concentrate on what I am reading or hearing or seeing with all the intensity I can muster. In fact, I have to *think*.

This does not mean that I spend most of the time I am working on a piece of writing engaged in real thinking. Actually, most of my efforts go into *avoiding* thinking. My daily struggle as a writer is to take the untidy mind that hates to think, that wants to dream and imagine and, often, simply to vegetate and force it to stop resisting and face the task at hand. William Butler Yeats once wrote a short poem called "The Balloon of the Mind" which reads:

> Hands, do what you're bid:
> Bring the balloon of the mind
> That bellies and drags in the wind
> Into its narrow shed.

I believe that anybody who writes understands immediately what Yeats was talking about in that poem. I have those lines on the wall in front of my typewriter, and my eye sometimes falls on them as my mind bellies and drags in the wind. Sometimes it helps.

1. In a short essay, explain *either* the causes *or* the effects of a situation that concerns you. Narrow your topic enough to treat it in some detail, and provide more than a mere list of causes or effects. If seeking causes, you will have to decide carefully how far back to go in your search for remote causes. If stating effects, fill your essay with examples. Here are some topics to consider:

The scarcity of jobs for teenagers

Friction between two roommates, or two friends

The pressure on students to get good grades

The fact that important sports events are often televised on holidays

Some quirk in your personality, or a friend's

The increasing need for more than one breadwinner per family

The temptation to do something dishonest to get ahead

The popularity of a particular television program, comic strip, rock group, or popular singer

The steady increase in college costs

The scarcity of people in training for employment as skilled workers: plumbers, tool and die makers, electricians, masons, carpenters, to name a few

A decision to enter the ministry or a religious order

The fact that cigarette advertising has been banned from television

The installation of seat belts in all new cars

The absence of a peacetime draft

The fact that more couples are choosing to have only one child, or none

The growing popularity of private elementary and high schools

The fact that most Americans can communicate in no language other than English

Being "born again"

The grim tone of recent novels for young people (such as Robert Cormier's *I Am the Cheese* and other best-selling juvenile fiction dealing with violence, madness, and terror)

The fact that women increasingly are training for jobs formerly regarded as men's only

The pressure on young people to conform to the standards of their peers

The emphasis on competitive sports in high school and college

Children's watching soft-core pornography on cable television

2. In *Blue Highways* (1982), an account of his rambles around America, William Least Heat Moon asserts why Americans, and not the British, settled the vast tract of northern land that lies between the Mississippi and the Rockies. He traces what he believes to be the major cause in this paragraph:

> Were it not for a web-footed rodent and a haberdashery fad in eighteenth-century Europe, Minnesota might be a Canadian province today. The beaver, almost as much as the horse, helped shape the course of early American history. Some *Mayflower* colonists paid their passage with beaver pelts; and a good fur could bring an Indian three steel knifes or a five-foot stack could bring a musket. But even more influential were the trappers and fur traders penetrating the great Northern wilderness between the Mississippi River and the Rocky Mountains, since it was their presence that helped hold the Near West against British expansion from the north; and it was their explorations that opened the heart of the nation to white settlement. These men, by making pelts the currency of the wilds, laid the base for a new economy that quickly overwhelmed the old. And all because European men of mode simply had to wear a beaver hat.

In a Least Heat Moon–like paragraph of your own, explain how a small cause produced a large effect. You might generate ideas by browsing in a history book — where you might find, for instance, that a cow belonging to Mrs. Patrick O'Leary is believed to have started the Great Chicago Fire of 1871 by kicking over a lighted lantern — or in a collection of *Ripley's Believe It or Not*. If some small event in your life has had large consequences, you might care to write instead from personal experience.

9

DEFINITION

Establishing a Boundary

THE METHOD

As a rule, when we hear the word *definition*, we immediately think of a dictionary. In that helpful storehouse — a writer's best friend — we find the literal and specific meaning (or meanings) of a word. The dictionary supplies this information concisely: in a sentence, in a phrase, or even in a synonym — a single word that means the same thing ("**narrative** [năr - ə - tĭv] *n.* **1:** story . . .").

To state such a definition is often an excellent way for the writer of an essay to begin. A short definition may clarify your subject to your reader, and perhaps help you to limit what you have to say. If, for instance, you are going to discuss a demolition derby, explaining such a spectacle to readers who may

never have seen one, you might offer at the outset a short definition of *demolition derby*, your subject and your key term.

In constructing a short definition, a usual procedure is this.
First, you state the general class to which your subject belongs;
then you add any particular features that distinguish it. You
could say: "A demolition derby is a contest" — that is its general
class — "in which drivers ram old cars into one another until
only one car is left running." Short definitions may also be useful at *any* moment in your essay. If you introduce a technical
term, you'll want to define it briefly: "As the derby proceeds,
there's many a broken manifold — that's the fitting that con-
nects the openings of a car engine's exhaust."

In this chapter, however, we are mainly concerned with another sort of definition. It is *extended definition*, a kind of expository writing that relies on a variety of other methods. Suppose
you wanted to write an essay to make clear what *poetry* means.
You'd cite poems as examples. You might compare and contrast
poetry with prose. You could analyze (or divide) poetry by speci-
fying its elements: rhythm, metaphor and other figures of
speech, imagery, and so on. You could distinguish it from prose
by setting forth its effects on the reader. (Emily Dickinson, a
poet herself, once stated the effect that reading a poem had
upon her: "I feel as if the top of my head were taken off.") In
fact, extended definition, unlike other methods of writing discussed in this book, is perhaps less a method in itself than the
application of a variety of methods to clarify a purpose. Like description, extended definition tries to *show* a reader its subject. It
does so by establishing boundaries, for its writer tries to differen-
tiate a subject from anything that might be confused with it.
When Tom Wolfe, in his essay in this chapter, seeks to define a
certain trend he has noticed in newspapers, books, and television, he describes exactly what he sees happening, so that we,
too, will understand what he calls "the pornography of violence." In an extended definition, a writer studies the nature of a
subject, carefully sums up its chief characteristics, and strives to
answer the question, What is this? — or What makes this what
it is, not something else?

An extended definition can *define* (from the Latin, "to set bounds to") a word, or it can define a thing (a laser beam), a concept (male chauvinism), or a general phenomenon (the popularity of the demolition derby). Unlike a sentence definition, or any you would find in a standard dictionary, an extended definition takes room: at least a paragraph, perhaps an entire volume. The subject may be as large as the concepts of *superstition* and *vulgarity* — as essays in this chapter will indicate.

Outside an English course, how is this method of writing used? In a newspaper feature, a sports writer defines what makes a "great team" great. In a journal article, a physician defines the nature of a previously unknown syndrome or disease. In a written opinion, a judge defines not only a word but a concept, *obscenity*. In a book review, a critic defines a newly prevalent kind of poem. In a letter to a younger brother or sister contemplating college, a student might define a *gut course* and how to recognize one.

Unlike a definition in a dictionary that sets forth the literal meaning of a word in an unimpassioned manner, some definitions imply biases. In defining *patron* to the earl of Chesterfield, who had tried to befriend him after ignoring his petitions for aid during his years of grinding poverty, Samuel Johnson wrote scornfully: "Is not a Patron, my Lord, one who looks with unconcern on a man struggling for life in the water, and, when he has reached the ground, encumbers him with help?" Irony, metaphor, and short definition have rarely been wielded with such crushing power. (*Encumbers*, by the way, is a wonderfully physical word in its context: it means "to burden with dead weight.") In his extended definition of *pornoviolence*, Tom Wolfe is biased, even jaundiced, in his view of American media. In having many methods of writing at their disposal, writers of extended definitions have ample freedom and wide latitude.

THE PROCESS

Writing an extended definition, you'll want to employ whatever method or methods of writing can best answer the question, What is the nature of this subject? You will probably find yourself making use of much that you have earlier learned from this book. If your subject is the phenomenon of the demolition derby, you might wish to begin by giving a short definition, like the definition of *demolition derby* on page 390. Feel no duty, however, to place a dictionaryish definition in the introduction of every essay you write. In explaining a demolition derby, you might decide that your readers already have at least a vague idea of the meaning of the term and that they need no short, formal definition of it. You might open your extended definition with the aid of *narration*. You could relate the events at a typical demolition derby, starting with the lineup of old, beat-up vehicles. Following the method of *description*, you might begin:

> One hundred worthless cars — everything from a 1940 Cadillac to a Dodge Dart to a recently wrecked Thunderbird — their glass removed, their radiators leaking, assemble on a racetrack or an open field. Their drivers, wearing crash helmets, buckle themselves into their seats, some pulling at beer cans to soften the blows to come.

You might proceed by *example*, listing demolition derbies you have known ("The great destruction of 184 vehicles took place at the Orleans County Fair in Barton, Vermont, in the summer of '81. . . ."). If you have enough examples, you might wish to *classify* them; or perhaps you might *divide* a demolition derby into its components — cars, drivers, judges, first-aid squad, and spectators — discussing each. You could *compare and contrast* a demolition derby with that amusement park ride known as Bumper Cars or Dodge-'ems, in which small cars with rubber bumpers bash one another head-on, but (unlike cars in the derby) harmlessly. A *process analysis* of a demolition derby might help your readers understand the nature of the spectacle: how in round after round cars are eliminated until one remains. You might ask: What causes the owners of old cars to want to smash them? Or perhaps: What causes people to watch the destruction? Or: What are the consequences? To answer such questions in an essay, you would apply the method of *cause and effect*. Perhaps an *analogy* might occur to you, one that would explain the demolition derby to someone unfamiliar with it: "It is like a birthday party in which every kid strives to have the last un-popped balloon."

Say you're preparing to write an extended definition of any-thing living or in motion (a basketball superstar, for instance, or a desert or a comet). To discover points about your subject worth noticing, you may find it useful to ask yourself a series of questions. These questions may be applied both to individual subjects, such as the superstar, and to collective subjects — insti-tutions (like the American family, a typical savings bank, a uni-versity, the Church of Jesus Christ of Latter-Day Saints) and or-ganizations (IBM, the Mafia, a punk rock group, a Little League baseball team). To illustrate how the questions might work, at least in one instance, let's say you plan to write a paper defining a male chauvinist.[1]

1. *Is this subject unique, or are there others of its kind? If it re-sembles others, in what ways? How is it different?* As you can see, these last two questions invite you to compare and contrast. Ap-plied to the concept of a male chauvinist, these questions might remind you that male chauvinists come in different varieties: middle-aged and college-aged, for instance, and you might care to compare and contrast the two kinds.

2. *In what different forms does it occur, while keeping its own identity?* Specific examples might occur to you: your Uncle George, who won't hire any "damned females" in his auto repair shop; some college-age male acquaintance who regards women as nothing but *Penthouse* centerfolds. Each form — Uncle George and the would-be stud — might rate a description.

3. *When and where do we find it? Under what circumstances and in what situations?* Well, where have you been lately? At any parties where male chauvinism reared its ugly head? In any class-

---

[1]The six questions that follow are very freely adapted from those first stated by Richard E. Young, Alton L. Becker, and Kenneth L. Pike, who have applied insights from psychology and linguistics to the writing process. Their procedure for generating ideas and discovering information is called *tagmemics*. To investigate subjects in greater depth, their own six questions may be used in nine possible combinations, as they explain in detail in *Rheto-ric: Discovery and Change* (New York: Harcourt Brace Jovanovich, 1970).

room discussions? Consider other areas of your experience: Did you meet any such male pigs while holding a part-time or summer job?

4. *What is it at the present moment?* Perhaps you might make the point that a few years ago male chauvinists used to be blatant tyrants and harsh critics of women. Today, wary of being recognized, they appear as ordinary citizens who now and then slip in a little tyranny, or make a nasty remark. You might care to draw examples from life.

5. *What does it do? What are its functions and activities?* Male chauvinism tries to keep women in what it imagines to be their place. These questions might even invite you to reply with a process analysis. You might show how some actual male chauvinist you know goes about implementing his views: How a personnel director you met, who determines pay scales, systematically eliminates women from better-paying jobs. How the *Penthouse* reader plots a seduction.

6. *How is it put together? What parts make it up? What holds these parts together?* You could apply analysis to the various beliefs and assumptions that, all together, make up a male chauvinist's attitude. This question might work well in writing about some organization: the personnel director's company, for instance, with its unfair hiring policies.

Not all these questions will fit every subject under the sun, and some may lead nowhere, but you will usually find them well worth asking. They can make you aware of points to notice, remind you of facts you already know. They can also suggest interesting points you need to find out more about.

In defining something, you need not try to forge a definition so absolute that it will stand till the mountains turn to plains. Like a mapmaker, the writer of an extended definition draws approximate boundaries, takes in only some of what lies within them, and ignores what lies outside. The boundaries, of course, may be wide; and for this reason, the writing of an extended definition sometimes tempts a writer to sweep across a continent airily and to soar off into abstract clouds. Like any other method of expository writing, though, definition will work only

for the writer who remembers the world of the senses and supports every generalization with concrete evidence.

There may be no finer illustration of the perils of definition
than, in Charles Dickens's novel *Hard Times*, the scene of the
grim schoolroom of a teacher named Gradgrind, who insists on
facts but who completely ignores living realities. When a girl
whose father is a horse trainer is unable to define a horse, Gradgrind blames her for not knowing what a horse is; and he praises
the definition of a horse supplied by a pet pupil: "Quadruped.
Graminivorous. Forty teeth, namely twenty-four grinders, four
eye-teeth, and twelve incisive. Sheds coat in the spring; in
marshy countries, sheds hoofs, too. Hoofs hard, but requiring to
be shod with iron. Age known by marks in mouth." To anyone
who didn't already know what a horse is, this enumeration of
statistics would prove of little help. In writing an extended definition, never lose sight of the reality you are attempting to
bound, even if its frontiers are as inclusive as those of *psychological burnout* or *human rights*. Give your reader examples, tell an illustrative story, use an analogy, bring in specific description —
in whatever method you use, keep coming down to earth.
Without your eyes on the world, you will define no reality. You
might define *animal husbandry* till the cows come home, and
never make clear what it means.

DEFINITION IN A PARAGRAPH

In "The Dukes of Hazzard," who is a villain? What character, saturated with evil, is a true menace? At first, the prime
candidate might seem pudgy Jefferson Davis Hogg, political
boss of the territory. Two desires smolder in Boss Hogg's
heart: to make money, and to jail Bo and Luke Duke, the
show's young Galahads. Hogg lies, cheats, deceives, steals,
forges signatures — even rewrites the law. Yet he stops short
of wholehearted villainy. He will not kill. Being a native of
Hazzard County, he can't quite escape the goodness that
springs from its soil. And so he runs the Boar's Head Tavern
like a jolly master of revels, affording Daisy, cousin of the
Duke boys, the job of dispensing tap beer. His blithering
henchman, Sheriff Rosco P. Coltraine, who can't even set up

a roadblock without ramming his own cruiser into it, is
hardly a villain, either. Each week Hogg and his stooge are
outclassed by sharks more deadly and purposeful: racketeers,
dealers in poisonous moonshine, widow swindlers, kidnap-
pers, counterfeiters, escaped public enemies. Unlike the lo-
cals, these grim professionals are eager to kill. We sense that
Hazzard County stands alone against the world, its natives
surrounded by a sea of inscrutable evil whose waves keep
breaking against the county line. Once in a while an outsider
who isn't a villain strays into Hazzard, but such harmless visitors are never total strangers. They're bluegrass music stars
whose faces and songs every soul in the county knows. On
"The Dukes," the nature of villainy is simple. A villain is any
new face in town.

Comment. In this one-paragraph essay, the writer begins
with a short definition of a villain: a character saturated with
evil; a true menace. This short definition given, the writer's next
step is to demonstrate (by the method of description) that it
doesn't apply to Boss Hogg. On "The Dukes of Hazzard," there
are characters more sinister, and the writer discerns their traits:
(1) they are killers; and (2) they are outsiders. Still another
method of exposition may be seen in the paragraph: example.
Hogg's likable traits are illustrated; and we are given examples,
too, of the various, more sinister enemies the Dukes must face
(racketeers, and so on). Although the paragraph doesn't fully
compare and contrast Hazzard County natives with outsiders,
its final statement makes clear that such a distinction can be
drawn. The TV show, implies the writer, gives us a crudely simplified world.

· Tom Wolfe ·

Tom Wolfe, author, journalist, and cartoonist, was born in 1931 in Richmond, Virginia, and went to Washington and Lee University. After taking a Ph.D. in American studies at Yale, he decided against an academic career and instead worked as a reporter for the Springfield (Massachusetts) *Union*, then as a correspondent for the Washington *Post* in Latin America. Early in the 1960s, Wolfe began writing his electrifying satiric articles on the American scene (with special, mocking attention to subcultures and trend-setters), which have enlivened *New York*, *Esquire*, *Rolling Stone*, *Harper's*, and other sophisticated magazines. Among his books are *The Electric Kool-Aid Acid Test*, a memoir of LSD-spaced-out hippies (1965); *The Kandy-Kolored Tangerine-Flake Streamline Baby*, glimpses of popular follies and foibles, and *The Pump House Gang*, a study of California surfers (both 1968); *Radical Chic and Mau-Mauing the Flak Catchers*, an unflattering view of New York artists and literati (1970); *From Bauhaus to Our House* (1981), a complaint against modern architecture; a retrospective selection of essays, *The Purple Decades* (1983); and a novel, *The Bonfire of the Vanities* (1985). Recently, *The Right Stuff* (1979), a chronicle of America's first astronauts, became a movie.

Pornoviolence

This essay, from a collection raking over the 1970s, *Mauve Gloves & Madmen, Clutter & Vine* (1976), is vintage Tom Wolfe. He played a large part in the invention of "the new journalism" (a brand of reporting that tells the truth excitedly, as if it were fiction), and his essay is marked by certain breathless features of style: long sentences full of parenthetical asides, ellipses (. . .), generous use of italics. (For a sampling of lively reporting by Wolfe and others, see the anthology Wolfe edited with E. W. Johnson, *The New Journalism*, 1973.) In the following essay Wolfe coins a term to fit the blend of pornography and pandering to bloodlust that he finds creeping into the media. His remarks have dated little since they first appeared.

"Keeps His Mom-in-law in Chains, meet *Kills Son and Feeds*   1
Corpse to Pigs."

"Pleased to meet you."   2

"Teenager Twists Off Corpse's Head . . . to Get Gold Teeth,   3
meet *Strangles Girl Friend, Then Chops Her to Pieces."*

"How you doing?"   4

"Nurse's Aide Sees Fingers Chopped Off in Meat Grinder, meet   5
I Left My Babies in the Deep Freeze."

"It's a pleasure."   6

It's a pleasure! No doubt about that! In all these years of   7
journalism I have covered more conventions than I care to remember. Podiatrists, theosophists, Professional Budget Finance
dentists, oyster farmers, mathematicians, truckers, dry cleaners,
stamp collectors, Esperantists, nudists, and newspaper editors —
I have seen them all, together, in vast assemblies, sloughing
through the wall-to-wall of a thousand hotel lobbies (the nudists
excepted) in their shimmering gray-metal suits and pajama-stripe
shirts with white Plasti-Coat name cards on their chests, and I
have sat through their speeches and seminars (the nudists included) and attentively endured ear baths such as you wouldn't
believe. And yet none has ever been quite like the convention of
the stringers for *The National Enquirer.*

The Enquirer is a weekly newspaper that is probably known   8
by sight to millions more than know it by name. No one who
ever came face-to-face with *The Enquirer* on a newsstand in its
wildest days is likely to have forgotten the sight: a tabloid with
great inky shocks of type all over the front page saying something on the order of *Gouges Out Wife's Eyes to Make Her Ugly,*
Dad Hurls Hot Grease in Daughter's Face, Wife Commits Suicide
after 2 Years of Poisoning Fails to Kill Husband . . .

The stories themselves were supplied largely by stringers,   9
i.e., correspondents, from all over the country, the world, for
that matter, mostly copy editors and reporters on local newspapers. Every so often they would come upon a story, usually via
the police beat, that was so grotesque the local sheet would discard it or run it in a highly glossed form rather than offend or
perplex its readers. The stringers would preserve them for *The*
Enquirer, which always rewarded them well and respectfully.

One year *The Enquirer* convened and feted them at a hotel   10 in Manhattan. This convention was a success in every way. The only awkward moment was at the outset when the stringers all pulled in. None of them knew each other. Their hosts got around the problem by introducing them by the stories they had supplied. The introductions went like this:

"Harry, I want you to meet Frank here. Frank did that   11
story, you remember that story, *Midget Murderer Throws Girl Off Cliff after She Refuses to Dance with Him.*"

"Pleased to meet you. That was some story."   12

"And Harry did the one about *I Spent Three Days Trapped at*   13
Bottom of Forty-Foot-Deep Mine Shaft and Was Saved by a Swarm of Flies."

"Likewise, I'm sure."   14

And *Midget Murderer Throws Girl Off Cliff* shakes hands   15
with *I Spent Three Days Trapped at Bottom of Forty-Foot-Deep Mine Shaft*, and *Buries Her Baby Alive* shakes hands with *Boy, Twelve, Strangles Two-Year-Old Girl*, and *Kills Son and Feeds Corpse to Pigs* shakes hands with *He Strangles Old Woman and Smears Corpse with Syrup, Ketchup, and Oatmeal* . . . and . . .

. . . There was a great deal of esprit about the whole thing.   16
These men were, in fact, the avant-garde of a new genre that since then has become institutionalized throughout the nation without anyone knowing its proper name. I speak of the new pornography, the pornography of violence.

Pornography comes from the Greek word "*porne*," meaning   17
harlot, and pornography is literally the depiction of the acts of harlots. In the new pornography, the theme is not sex. The new pornography depicts practitioners acting out another, murkier drive: people staving teeth in, ripping guts open, blowing brains out, and getting even with all those bastards . . .

The success of *The Enquirer* prompted many imitators to en-   18
ter the field, *Midnight, The Star Chronicle, The National Insider, Inside News, The National Close-up, The National Tattler, The National Examiner.* A truly competitive free press evolved, and soon a reader could go to the newspaper of his choice for *Kill the Retarded! (Won't You Join My Movement?)* and *Unfaithful Wife? Burn Her Bed!, Harem Master's Mistress Chops Him with Machete, Babe Bites Off Boy's Tongue,* and *Cuts Buddy's Face to Pieces for Stealing His Business and Fiancée.*

And yet the last time I surveyed the Violence press, I no-   19
ticed a curious thing. These pioneering journals seem to have
pulled back. They seem to be regressing to what is by now the
Redi-Mix staple of literate Americans, mere sex. *Ecstasy and Me
(by Hedy Lamarr)*,[1] says *The National Enquirer*. *I Run a Sex Art
Gallery*, says *The National Insider*. What has happened, I think,
is something that has happened to avant-gardes in many fields,
from William Morris and the Craftsmen to the Bauhaus group.[2]
Namely, their discoveries have been preempted by the Establishment and so thoroughly dissolved into the mainstream they no
longer look original.

Robert Harrison, the former publisher of *Confidential*, and   20
later publisher of the aforementioned *Inside News*, was perhaps
the first person to see it coming. I was interviewing Harrison
early in January 1964 for a story in *Esquire* about six weeks after
the assassination of President Kennedy, and we were in a cab in
the West Fifties in Manhattan, at a stoplight, by a newsstand,
and Harrison suddenly pointed at the newsstand and said,
"Look at that. They're doing the same thing *The Enquirer* does."

There on the stand was a row of slick-paper, magazine-size   21
publications, known in the trade as one-shots, with titles like
Four Days That Shook the World, *Death of a President*, *An American Tragedy*, or just *John Fitzgerald Kennedy (1921–1963)*. "You
want to know why people buy those things?" said Harrison.
"People buy those things to see a man get his head blown off."

And, of course, he was right. Only now the publishers were   22
in many cases the pillars of the American press. Invariably,
these "special coverages" of the assassination bore introductions
piously commemorating the fallen President, exhorting the
American people to strength and unity in a time of crisis, urging
greater vigilance and safeguards for the new President, and even

---

[1]*Ecstasy*, an early, European-made Hedy Lamarr film, was notorious for
its scenes of soft-core lovemaking. Later, paired with Charles ("Come with me
to the Casbah") Boyer, she rose to Hollywood stardom in *Algiers* (1938). —
EDS.

[2]Morris (1834–1896), English artist, poet, printer, and socialist, founded a
company of craftspeople to bring tasteful design to furniture (the Morris chair)
and other implements of everyday life. The Bauhaus, an influential art school
in Germany (1919–1933), taught crafts and brought new ideas of design to architecture and to goods produced in factories. — EDS.

raising the nice metaphysical question of collective guilt in "an age of violence."

In the years since then, of course, there has been an incessant replay, with every recoverable clinical detail, of those less than five seconds in which a man got his head blown off. And throughout this deluge of words, pictures, and film frames, I have been intrigued with one thing: The point of view, the vantage point, is almost never that of the victim, riding in the Presidential Lincoln Continental. What you get is . . . the view from Oswald's rifle. You can step right up here and look point-blank right through the very hairline cross in Lee Harvey Oswald's Optics Ordnance in weaponry four-power Japanese telescope sight and watch, frame by frame by frame by frame, as that man there's head comes apart. Just a little History there before your very eyes.

The television networks have schooled us in the view from Oswald's rifle and made it seem a normal pastime. The TV viewpoint is nearly always that of the man who is going to strike. The last time I watched *Gunsmoke*, which was not known as a very violent Western in TV terms, the action went like this: The Wellington agents and the stagecoach driver pull guns on the badlands gang leader's daughter and Kitty, the heart-of-gold saloonkeeper, and kidnap them. Then the badlands gang shoots two Wellington agents. Then they tie up five more and talk about shooting them. Then they desist because they might not be able to get a hotel room in the next town if the word got around. Then one badlands gang gunslinger attempts to rape Kitty while the gang leader's younger daughter looks on. Then Kitty resists, so he slugs her one in the jaw. Then the gang leader slugs him. Then the gang leader slugs Kitty. Then Kitty throws hot stew in a gang member's face and hits him over the back of the head with a revolver. Then he knocks her down with a rock. Then the gang sticks up a bank. Here comes the marshal, Matt Dillon. He shoots a gang member and breaks it up. Then the gang leader shoots the guy who was guarding his daughter and the woman. Then the marshal shoots the gang leader. The final exploding bullet signals The End.

It is not the accumulated slayings and bone crushings that make this pornoviolence, however. What makes it porno-

23

24

25

violence is that in almost every case the camera angle, therefore the viewer, is with the gun, the fist, the rock. The pornography of violence has no point of view in the old sense that novels do. You do not live the action through the hero's eyes. You live with the aggressor, whoever he may be. One moment you are the hero. The next you are the villain. No matter whose side you may be on consciously, you are in fact with the muscle, and it is you who disintegrate all comers, villains, lawmen, women, anybody. On the rare occasions in which the gun is emptied into the camera — i.e., into your face — the effect is so startling that the pornography of violence all but loses its fantasy charm. There are not nearly so many masochists as sadists among those little devils whispering into one's ears.

In fact, sex — "sadomasochism" — is only a part of the por-   26
nography of violence. Violence is much more wrapped up, simply, with status. Violence is the simple, ultimate solution for problems of status competition, just as gambling is the simple, ultimate solution for economic competition. The old pornography was the fantasy of easy sexual delights in a world where sex was kept unavailable. The new pornography is the fantasy of easy triumph in a world where status competition has become so complicated and frustrating.

Already the old pornography is losing its kick because of   27
overexposure. In the late thirties, Nathanael West published his last and best-regarded novel, *The Day of the Locust*, and it was a terrible flop commercially, and his publisher said if he ever published another book about Hollywood it would "have to be *My Thirty-nine Ways of Making Love by Hedy Lamarr*." He thought he was saying something that was funny because it was beyond the realm of possibility. Less than thirty years later, however, Hedy Lamarr's *Ecstasy and Me* was published. Whether she mentions thirty-nine ways, I'm not sure, but she gets off to a flying start: "The men in my life have ranged from a classic case history of impotence, to a whip-brandishing sadist who enjoyed sex only after he tied my arms behind me with the sash of his robe. There was another man who took his pleasure with a girl in my own bed, while he thought I was asleep in it."

Yet she was too late. The book very nearly sank without a   28 trace. The sin itself is wearing out. Pornography cannot exist without certified taboo to violate. And today Lust, like the rest of the Seven Deadly Sins — Pride, Sloth, Envy, Greed, Anger, and Gluttony — is becoming a rather minor vice. The Seven Deadly Sins, after all, are only sins against the self. Theologically, the idea of Lust — well, the idea is that if you seduce some poor girl from Akron, it is not a sin because you are ruining her, but because you are wasting your time and your energies and damaging your own spirit. This goes back to the old work ethic, when the idea was to keep every able-bodied man's shoulder to the wheel. In an age of riches for all, the ethic becomes more nearly: Let him do anything he pleases, as long as he doesn't get in my way. And if he does get in my way, or even if he doesn't . . . well . . . we have *new* fantasies for that. *Put hair on the walls.*

"Hair on the walls" is the invisible subtitle of Truman Capote's book *In Cold Blood*. The book is neither a who-done-it nor a will-they-be-caught, since the answers to both questions are known from the outset. It does ask why-did-they-do-it, but the answer is soon as clear as it is going to be. Instead, the book's suspense is based largely on a totally new idea in detective stories: the promise of gory details, and the withholding of them until the end. Early in the game one of the two murderers, Dick, starts promising to put "plenty of hair on them-those walls" with a shotgun. So read on, gentle readers, and on and on; you are led up to the moment before the crime on page 60 — yet the specifics, what happened, the gory details, are kept out of sight, in grisly dangle, until page 244. ²⁹

But Dick and Perry, Capote's killers, are only a couple of Low Rent bums. With James Bond the new pornography reached a dead center, the bureaucratic middle class. The appeal of Bond has been explained as the appeal of the lone man who can solve enormously complicated, even world problems through his own bravery and initiative. But Bond is not a lone man at all, of course. He is not the Lone Ranger. He is much easier to identify than that. He is a salaried functionary in a bureaucracy. He is a sport, but a believable one; not a millionaire, but a bureaucrat on an expense account. He is not even a high-level bureaucrat. He is an operative. This point is carefully and ³⁰

repeatedly made by having his superiors dress him down for violations of standard operating procedure. Bond, like the Lone Ranger, solves problems with guns and fists. When it is over, however, the Lone Ranger leaves a silver bullet. Bond, like the rest of us, fills out a report in triplicate.

Marshall McLuhan[3] says we are in a period in which it will   31
become harder and harder to stimulate lust through words and pictures — i.e., the old pornography. In the latest round of pornographic movies the producers have found it necessary to introduce violence, bondage, torture, and aggressive physical destruction to an extraordinary degree. The same sort of bloody escalation may very well happen in the pure pornography of violence. Even such able craftsmen as Truman Capote, Ian Fleming, NBC, and CBS may not suffice. Fortunately, there are historical models to rescue us from this frustration. In the latter days of the Roman Empire, the Emperor Commodus became jealous of the celebrity of the great gladiators. He took to the arena himself, with his sword, and began dispatching suitably screened cripples and hobbled fighters. Audience participation became so popular that soon various *illuminati* of the Commodus set, various boys and girls of the year, were out there, suited up, gaily cutting a sequence of dwarfs and feebles down to short ribs. Ah, swinging generations, what new delights await?

QUESTIONS ON MEANING AND PURPOSE

1. Which of these statements comes closest to summing up Tom Wolfe's main PURPOSE in writing "Pornoviolence"?

   Wolfe writes to define a word.
   Wolfe writes to define a trend in society.

[3]Canadian English professor (1911–1980); author of *The Medium Is the Message* (1967), *War and Peace in the Global Village* (1968), and other books, McLuhan analyzed the effects on world society of television and other electronic media. — EDS.

Wolfe writes to define a trend in the media that reflects a trend in society.

Wolfe writes to explain how John F. Kennedy was assassinated.

Wolfe writes to entertain us by mocking Americans' latest foolishness.

(If you don't find any of these statements adequate, compose your own.)

2. If you have ever read *The National Enquirer* or any of its imitators, test the accuracy of Wolfe's reporting. What is the purpose of a featured article in the *Enquirer*?

3. According to Wolfe, what POINT OF VIEW does the writer or producer of pornoviolence always take? What other examples of this point of view (in violent incidents on films or TV shows) can you supply? (Did you ever see a replay on TV news of Jack Ruby's shooting of Oswald, for instance?)

4. "Violence is the simple, ultimate solution for problems of status competition" (paragraph 26). What does Wolfe mean? (If you have read Paul Fussell's "Notes on Class" in Chapter 6, recall what Fussell has to say about status and competition for it.)

5. Wolfe does not explicitly pass judgment on Truman Capote's book *In Cold Blood*. But what is his opinion of it? How can you tell?

6. "No advocate of change for the sake of change, Tom Wolfe writes as a conservative moralist who, like Jonathan Swift, rankles with savage indignation." Does this critical remark fit this particular essay? What, in Wolfe's view, appears to be happening to America and Americans?

QUESTIONS ON WRITING STRATEGY

1. On first reading, what did you make of Wolfe's opening sentence, "*Keeps His Mom-in-Law in Chains*, meet *Kills Son and Feeds Corpse to Pigs*"? At what point did you first tumble to what the writer was doing? What IRONY do you find in the convention hosts' introducing people by the headlines of their gory stories? What advantage is it to Wolfe's essay that his INTRODUCTION (with its odd introductions) keeps you guessing for a while?

2. What is Wolfe's point in listing (in paragraph 7) some of the other conventions he has reported — gatherings of nudists, oyster farmers, and others?

3. At what moment does Wolfe give us his short definition of *porno-violence*, or the new pornography? Do you think he would have done better to introduce his short definition of the word in paragraph 1? Why or why not?
4. What rhetorical method does Wolfe employ in paragraph 30 to set James Bond and the Lone Ranger side by side?
5. What is the TONE or attitude of Wolfe's CONCLUSION (paragraph 31)? Note in particular the closing line.

QUESTIONS ON LANGUAGE

1. What help to the reader does Wolfe provide by noting the source of the word *pornography* (paragraph 17)?
2. "The television networks have schooled us in the view from Oswald's rifle" (paragraph 24). What CONNOTATIONS enlarge the meaning of *schooled*?
3. Define *masochist* and *sadist* (paragraph 25). What kind of DICTION do you find in these terms? In "plenty of hair on them-those walls" (29)?
4. How much use does Wolfe make of COLLOQUIAL EXPRESSIONS? Point to examples.
5. What does Wolfe mean in noting that the fighters slain by the Emperor Commodus were *hobbled* and the cripples were *suitably screened* (paragraph 31)? What unflattering connotations does this emperor's very name contain? (If you don't get this, look up *commode* in your desk dictionary.)

SUGGESTIONS FOR WRITING

1. In a paragraph, narrate or describe some recent example of porno-violence you have seen in the movies or on television, or observed. In a second paragraph, comment on it.
2. Write an essay defining some current trend you've noticed in films or TV, popular music, sports, consumer buying, or some other large arena of life. Like Wolfe, invent a name for it. Use plenty of examples to make your definition clear.

· Margaret Mead ·

Anthropologist MARGARET MEAD won early acclaim for going to live among primitive peoples and writing about their culture in *Coming of Age in Samoa* (1928), *Growing Up in New Guinea* (1930), and *Sex and Temperament in Three Primitive Societies* (1935). She also studied the cultures of the United States and of the Soviet Union and held several advisory positions for the U.S. government during and after World War II. Born in Philadelphia in 1901, she was graduated from Barnard College and received her Ph.D. from Columbia University, where she taught for many years. From 1926 to 1969 she served as a curator of anthropology at the American Museum of Natural History in New York City. One of the most recent of her more than twenty books was *Culture and Commitment, a Study of the Generation Gap* (1970). Although since her death in 1978 some of the anthropologist's early work has come under attack, Mead's impressive reputation as a pioneer in her field lives on.

New Superstitions for Old

Most of us probably wouldn't admit to being superstitious. After all, we live in the 1980s. We know there isn't any sensible evidence that will convict black cats crossing our path or umbrellas opened in the house of bringing bad luck. And yet, how many of us find ourselves now and then throwing spilled salt over our left shoulder, or taking extra steps to avoid walking under a ladder? How is it that, in spite of the advance of scientific knowledge, superstitions live on? What, exactly, is a superstition? In this essay, one of a series she wrote for *Redbook*, Mead defines superstitions old and new. She and her fellow anthropologist Rhoda Metraux included the essay in *A Way of Seeing* (1970), one of three volumes they co-authored. In the book's foreword, Mead reports that before she wrote an essay for the series, she and Metraux would heatedly discuss its subject. Thus Mead calls this and her other *Redbook* essays "in a very real sense, a co-operative venture."

Once in a while there is a day when everything seems to run   1
smoothly and even the riskiest venture comes out exactly right.
You exclaim, "This is my lucky day!" Then as an afterthought
you say, "Knock on wood!" Of course, you do not really believe
that knocking on wood will ward off danger. Still, boasting
about your own good luck gives you a slightly uneasy feeling —
and you carry out the little protective ritual. If someone challenged you at that moment, you would probably say, "Oh,
that's nothing. Just an old superstition."

But when you come to think about it, what is a superstition?   2

In the contemporary world most people treat old folk beliefs   3
as superstitions — the belief, for instance, that there are lucky
and unlucky days or numbers, that future events can be read
from omens, that there are protective charms or that what happens can be influenced by casting spells. We have excluded
magic from our current world view, for we know that natural
events have natural causes.

In a religious context, where truths cannot be demon-   4
strated, we accept them as a matter of faith. Superstitions, however, belong to the category of beliefs, practices and ways of
thinking that have been discarded because they are inconsistent
with scientific knowledge. It is easy to say that other people are
superstitious because they believe what we regard to be untrue.
"Superstition" used in that sense is a derogatory term for the beliefs of other people that we do not share. But there is more to it
than that. For superstitions lead a kind of half life in a twilight
world where, sometimes, we partly suspend our disbelief and act
as if magic worked.

Actually, almost every day, even in the most sophisticated   5
home, something is likely to happen that evokes the memory of
some old folk belief. The salt spills. A knife falls to the floor.
Your nose tickles. Then perhaps, with a slightly embarrassed
smile, the person who spilled the salt tosses a pinch over his left
shoulder. Or someone recites the old rhyme, "Knife falls, gentleman calls." Or as you rub your nose you think, That means a
letter. I wonder who's writing? No one takes these small responses very seriously or gives them more than a passing
thought. Sometimes people will preface one of these ritual acts

— walking around instead of under a ladder or hastily closing an umbrella that has been opened inside a house — with such a remark as "I remember my great-aunt used to . . ." or "Germans used to say you ought not . . ." And then, having placed the belief at some distance away in time or space, they carry out the ritual.

Everyone also remembers a few of the observances of childhood — wishing on the first star; looking at the new moon over the right shoulder; avoiding the cracks in the sidewalk on the way to school while chanting, "Step on a crack, break your mother's back"; wishing on white horses, on loads of hay, on covered bridges, on red cars; saying quickly, "Bread-and-butter" when a post or a tree separated you from the friend you were walking with. The adult may not actually recite the formula "Star light, star bright . . ." and may not quite turn to look at the new moon, but his mood is tempered by a little of the old thrill that came when the observance was still freighted with magic.

Superstition can also be used with another meaning. When I discuss the religious beliefs of other peoples, especially primitive peoples, I am often asked, "Do they really have a religion, or is it all just superstition?" The point of contrast here is not between a scientific and a magical view of the world but between the clear, theologically defensible religious beliefs of members of civilized societies and what we regard as the false and childish views of the heathen who "bow down to wood and stone." Within the civilized religions, however, where membership includes believers who are educated and urbane and others who are ignorant and simple, one always finds traditions and practices that the more sophisticated will dismiss offhand as "just superstition" but that guide the steps of those who live by older ways. Mostly these are very ancient beliefs, some handed on from one religion to another and carried from country to country around the world.

Very commonly, people associate superstition with the past, with very old ways of thinking that have been supplanted by modern knowledge. But new superstitions are continually coming into being and flourishing in our society. Listening to mothers in the park in the 1930's, one heard them say, "Now, don't you run out into the sun, or Polio will get you." In the 1940's elderly people explained to one another in tones of resignation, "It was the Virus that got him down." And every year the cosmetics industry offers us new magic — cures for baldness, lotions that will give every woman radiant skin, hair coloring that will restore to the middle-aged the charm and romance of youth — results that are promised if we will just follow the simple directions. Families and individuals also have their cherished, private superstitions. You must leave by the back door when you are going on a journey, or you must wear a green dress when you are taking an examination. It is a kind of joke, of course, but it makes you feel safe.

These old half-beliefs and new half-beliefs reflect the keenness of our wish to have something come true or to prevent something bad from happening. We do not always recognize new superstitions for what they are, and we still follow the old ones because someone's faith long ago matches our contemporary hopes and fears. In the past people "knew" that a black cat crossing one's path was a bad omen, and they turned back home. Today we are fearful of taking a journey and would give anything to turn back — and then we notice a black cat running across the road in front of us.   9

Child psychologists recognize the value of the toy a child holds in his hand at bedtime. It is different from his thumb, with which he can close himself in from the rest of the world, and it is different from the real world, to which he is learning to relate himself. Psychologists call these toys — these furry animals and old, cozy baby blankets — "transitional objects"; that is, objects that help the child move back and forth between the exactions of everyday life and the world of wish and dream.   10

Superstitions have some of the qualities of these transitional objects. They help people pass between the areas of life where what happens has to be accepted without proof and the areas where sequences of events are explicable in terms of cause and effect, based on knowledge. Bacteria and viruses that cause sickness have been identified; the cause of symptoms can be diagnosed and a rational course of treatment prescribed. Magical   11 charms no longer are needed to treat the sick; modern medicine has brought the whole sequence of events into the secular world. But people often act as if this change had not taken place. Laymen still treat germs as if they were invisible, malign spirits, and physicians sometimes prescribe antibiotics as if they were magic substances.

Over time, more and more of life has become subject to the controls of knowledge. However, this is never a one-way process. Scientific investigation is continually increasing our knowledge. But if we are to make good use of this knowledge, we must not only rid our minds of old, superseded beliefs and fragments of magical practice, but also recognize new superstitions for what they are. Both are generated by our wishes, our fears and our feeling of helplessness in difficult situations.   12

Civilized peoples are not alone in having grasped the idea of superstitions — beliefs and practices that are superseded but that still may evoke compliance. The idea is one that is familiar to every people, however primitive, that I have ever known. Every society has a core of transcendent beliefs — beliefs about the nature of the universe, the world and man — that no one doubts or questions. Every society also has a fund of knowledge related to practical life — about the succession of day and night and of the seasons; about correct ways of planting seeds so that they will germinate and grow; about the processes involved in making dyes or the steps necessary to remove the deadly poison from manioc roots so they become edible. Island peoples know how the winds shift and they know the star toward which they must point the prow of the canoe exactly so that as the sun rises they will see the first fringing palms on the shore toward which they are sailing.   13

This knowledge, based on repeated observations of reliable sequences, leads to ideas and hypotheses of the kind that underlie scientific thinking. And gradually as scientific knowledge, once developed without conscious plan, has become a great self-corrective system and the foundation for rational planning and action, old magical beliefs and observances have had to be discarded.   14

But it takes time for new ways of thinking to take hold, and   15 often the transition is only partial. Older, more direct beliefs live on in the hearts and minds of elderly people. And they are learned by children who, generation after generation, start out life as hopefully and fearfully as their forebears did. Taking their first steps away from home, children use the old rituals and invent new ones to protect themselves against the strangeness of the world into which they are venturing.

So whatever has been rejected as no longer true, as limited,   16
provincial and idolatrous, still leads a half life. People may say, "It's just a superstition," but they continue to invoke the ritual's protection or potency. In this transitional, twilight state such beliefs come to resemble dreaming. In the dream world a thing can be either good or bad; a cause can be an effect and an effect can be a cause. Do warts come from touching toads, or does touching a toad cure the wart? Is sneezing a good omen or a bad omen? You can have it either way — or both ways at once. In the same sense, the half-acceptance and half-denial accorded superstitions give us the best of both worlds.

Superstitions are sometimes smiled at and sometimes   17
frowned upon as observances characteristic of the old-fashioned, the unenlightened, children, peasants, servants, immigrants, foreigners or backwoods people. Nevertheless, they give all of us ways of moving back and forth among the different worlds in which we live — the sacred, the secular and the scientific. They allow us to keep a private world also, where, smiling a little, we can banish danger with a gesture and summon luck with a rhyme, make the sun shine in spite of storm clouds, force the stranger to do our bidding, keep an enemy at bay and straighten the paths of those we love.

QUESTIONS ON MEANING AND PURPOSE

1. How does the author distinguish superstition from religious faith? Is the distinction clear? Try to give examples of each to match Mead's definitions.

2. According to Mead's essay, what do superstitions have in common with "transitional objects": the stuffed animals or blankets that children take to bed with them?
3. How does Mead account for the fact that, despite our ever-increasing knowledge, superstitions live on?
4. Mead seems to hold opposing views of the value of superstition. Cite EVIDENCE from the essay to support each view.
5. What further PURPOSE, beyond defining a difficult concept, do you find in Mead's essay?

QUESTIONS ON WRITING STRATEGY

1. In what paragraphs does Mead define superstition by telling us what it is *not*?
2. Where in her essay does the author make effective use of example? (See Chapter 3.) Of the methods of comparison and contrast (Chapter 4), process analysis (Chapter 5), and cause and effect (Chapter 8)?
3. On what basis can we assume that Mead's essay was written for a general AUDIENCE?
4. What sentences or passages effectively serve as TRANSITIONS?
5. To which of the points she has made in the body of her essay does the author return in her final paragraph? What suggestions are new to the CONCLUSION?

QUESTIONS ON LANGUAGE

1. From context or with the aid of your dictionary, define the following words: derogatory (paragraph 4); urbane (7); malign (11); superseded (12); transcendent (13); rational (14); provincial, idolatrous (16); secular (17).
2. What does the author mean by *protective ritual* (paragraph 1)? By a *half life* (4)?
3. How do the CONNOTATIONS of *faith* and *ritual* differ from those of *superstition*? What new and different connotations does Mead appear to suggest?

SUGGESTIONS FOR WRITING

1. In a paragraph, draw on your reading or experience to evaluate Mead's statement (in paragraph 11): "Magical charms no longer are needed to treat the sick."

2. Do you or your family members have any "cherished, private superstitions"? If so, explain in a brief essay how such superstitions
   help or hinder you.
3. Write a definition of something "magical" that many people flirt
   with in spite of its having little or no scientific support: astrology,
   palm reading, fortune-telling, numerology, spiritualism, ESP.
   What seems to you to give these phenomena their popular appeal?

· Mark Twain ·

MARK TWAIN (1835–1910), born Samuel Langhorne Clemens, grew up in Hannibal, Missouri, the town his books made famous. In the course of his life, the brilliant creator of Huck Finn and Tom Sawyer was a steamboat pilot, a newspaperman, a gold miner, a world traveler, a writer, and a lecturer. Full of contradictions, Twain was a humorist whose view of life grew more and more bitter as he grew old. His reputation as one of America's finest writers is firmly established. Ernest Hemingway said that American literature "begins with *Huckleberry Finn.*"

Corn-Pone Opinions

"Corn-Pone Opinions" was first published years after Twain's death: in *Europe and Elsewhere* (1923), a collection of essays and travel writings. Probably Twain wrote the essay late in life. In it, drawing on the oratory of a slave he knew and admired when he was a boy, Twain names and defines one aspect of human behavior as he perceives it. His view is not overly kind. See if you agree with Twain's assessment of human nature and the opinions that his fellow mortals hold dear.

Fifty years ago, when I was a boy of fifteen and helping to inhabit a Missourian village on the banks of the Mississippi, I had a friend whose society was very dear to me because I was forbidden by my mother to partake of it. He was a gay and impudent and satirical and delightful young black man — a slave — who daily preached sermons from the top of his master's woodpile, with me for sole audience. He imitated the pulpit style of the several clergymen of the village, and did it well, and with fine passion and energy. To me he was a wonder. I believed he was the greatest orator in the United States and would some day be heard from. But it did not happen; in the distribution of rewards he was overlooked. It is the way, in this world.

415

He interrupted his preaching, now and then, to saw a stick   2
of wood; but the sawing was a pretense — he did it with his
mouth; exactly imitating the sound the bucksaw makes in
shrieking its way through the wood. But it served its purpose; it
kept his master from coming out to see how the work was getting along. I listened to the sermons from the open window of a
lumber room at the back of the house. One of his texts was this:

"You tell me whar a man gits his corn pone, en I'll tell you   3
what his 'pinions is."

I can never forget it. It was deeply impressed upon me. By   4
my mother. Not upon my memory, but elsewhere. She had
slipped in upon me while I was absorbed and not watching. The
black philosopher's idea was that a man is not independent, and
cannot afford views which might interfere with his bread and
butter. If he would prosper, he must train with the majority; in
matters of large moment, like politics and religion, he must
think and feel with the bulk of his neighbors, or suffer damage
in his social standing and in his business prosperities. He must
restrict himself to corn-pone opinions — at least on the surface.
He must get his opinions from other people; he must reason out
none for himself; he must have no first-hand views.

I think Jerry was right, in the main, but I think he did not go   5
far enough.

1. It was his idea that a man conforms to the majority view   6
of his locality by calculation and intention.

This happens, but I think it is not the rule.   7

2. It was his idea that there is such a thing as a first-hand   8
opinion; an original opinion; an opinion which is coldly reasoned out in a man's head, by a searching analysis of the facts
involved, with the heart unconsulted, and the jury room closed
against outside influences. It may be that such an opinion has
been born somewhere, at some time or other, but I suppose it
got away before they could catch it and stuff it and put it in the
museum.

I am persuaded that a coldly-thought-out and independent   9
verdict upon a fashion in clothes, or manners, or literature, or
politics, or religion, or any other matter that is projected into
the field of our notice and interest, is a most rare thing — if it
has indeed ever existed.

A new thing in costume appears — the flaring hoopskirt, for   10
example — and the passers-by are shocked, and the irreverent
laugh. Six months later everybody is reconciled; the fashion has
established itself; it is admired, now, and no one laughs. Public
opinion resented it before, public opinion accepts it now, and is
happy in it. Why? Was the resentment reasoned out? Was the
acceptance reasoned out? No. The instinct that moves to conformity did the work. It is our nature to conform; it is a force
which not many can successfully resist. What is its seat? The inborn requirement of self-approval. We all have to bow to that;
there are no exceptions. Even the woman who refuses from first
to last to wear the hoopskirt comes under that law and is its
slave; she could not wear the skirt and have her own approval;
and that she *must* have, she cannot help herself. But as a rule
our self-approval has its source in but one place and not elsewhere—the approval of other people. A person of vast consequences can introduce any kind of novelty in dress and the general world will presently adopt it — moved to do it, in the first
place, by the natural instinct to passively yield to that vague
something recognized as authority, and in the second place by
the human instinct to train with the multitude and have its approval. An empress introduced the hoopskirt, and we know the
result. A nobody introduced the bloomer, and we know the
result. If Eve should come again, in her ripe renown, and rein-
troduce her quaint styles — well, we know what would happen.
And we should be cruelly embarrassed, along at first.

The hoopskirt runs its course and disappears. Nobody rea-   11
sons about it. One woman abandons the fashion; her neighbor
notices this and follows her lead; this influences the next
woman; and so on and so on, and presently the skirt has vanished out of the world, no one knows how nor why, nor cares,
for that matter. It will come again by and by and in due course
will go again.

Twenty-five years ago, in England, six or eight wine glasses   12
stood grouped by each person's plate at a dinner party, and they
were used, not left idle and empty; today there are but three or
four in the group, and the average guest sparingly uses about
two of them. We have not adopted this new fashion yet, but we
shall do it presently. We shall not think it out; we shall merely

conform, and let it go at that. We get our notions and habits and opinions from outside influences; we do not have to study them out.

Our table manners, and company manners, and street man-   13
ners change from time to time, but the changes are not reasoned out; we merely notice and conform. We are creatures of outside influences; as a rule we do not think, we only imitate. We cannot invent standards that will stick; what we mistake for standards are only fashions, and perishable. We may continue to admire them, but we drop the use of them. We notice this in literature. Shakespeare is a standard, and fifty years ago we used to write tragedies which we couldn't tell from — from somebody else's; but we don't do it any more, now. Our prose standard, three quarters of a century ago, was ornate and diffuse; some authority or other changed it in the direction of compactness and simplicity, and conformity followed, without argument. The historical novel starts up suddenly, and sweeps the land. Everybody writes one, and the nation is glad. We had historical novels before; but nobody read them, and the rest of us conformed — without reasoning it out. We are conforming in the other way, now, because it is another case of everybody.

The outside influences are always pouring in upon us, and   14
we are always obeying their orders and accepting their verdicts. The Smiths like the new play; the Joneses go to see it, and they copy the Smith verdict. Morals, religions, politics, get their following from surrounding influences and atmospheres, almost entirely; not from study, not from thinking. A man must and will have his own approval first of all, in each and every moment and circumstance of his life — even if he must repent of a self-approved act the moment after its commission, in order to get his self-approval *again*: but, speaking in general terms, a man's self-approval in the large concerns of life has its source in the approval of the peoples about him, and not in a searching personal examination of the matter. Mohammedans are Mohammedans because they are born and reared among that sect, not because they have thought it out and can furnish sound reasons for being Mohammedans; we know why Catholics are Catholics; why Presbyterians are Presbyterians; why Baptists are Baptists; why

Mormons are Mormons; why thieves are thieves; why monarchists are monarchists; why Republicans are Republicans and Democrats, Democrats. We know it is a matter of association and sympathy, not reasoning and examination; that hardly a man in the world has an opinion upon morals, politics, or religion which he got otherwise than through his associations and sympathies. Broadly speaking, there are none but corn-pone opinions. And broadly speaking, corn-pone stands for self-approval. Self-approval is acquired mainly from the approval of other people. The result is conformity. Sometimes conformity has a sordid business interest — the bread-and-butter interest — but not in most cases, I think. I think that in the majority of cases it is unconscious and not calculated; that it is born of the human being's natural yearning to stand well with his fellows and have their inspiring approval and praise — a yearning which is commonly so strong and so insistent that it cannot be effectually resisted, and must have its way.

A political emergency brings out the corn-pone opinion in fine force in its two chief varieties — the pocketbook variety, which has its origin in self-interest, and the bigger variety, the sentimental variety — the one which can't bear to be outside the pale; can't bear to be in disfavor; can't endure the averted face and the cold shoulder; wants to stand well with his friends, wants to be smiled upon, wants to be welcome, wants to hear the precious words, "*He's* on the right track!" Uttered, perhaps by an ass, but still an ass of high degree, an ass whose approval is gold and diamonds to a smaller ass, and confers glory and honor and happiness, and membership in the herd. For these gauds many a man will dump his life-long principles into the street, and his conscience along with them. We have seen it happen. In some millions of instances. 15

Men think they think upon great political questions, and they do; but they think with their party, not independently; they read its literature, but not that of the other side; they arrive at convictions, but they are drawn from a partial view of the matter in hand and are of no particular value. They swarm with their party, they feel with their party, they are happy in their party's approval; and where the party leads they will follow, 16 whether for right and honor, or through blood and dirt and a mush of mutilated morals.

In our late canvass half of the nation passionately believed that in silver lay salvation, the other half as passionately believed that that way lay destruction. Do you believe that a tenth part of the people, on either side, had any rational excuse for having an opinion about the matter at all? I studied that mighty question to the bottom — came out empty. Half of our people passionately believe in high tariff, the other half believe otherwise. Does this mean study and examination, or only feeling? The latter, I think. I have deeply studied that question, too — and didn't arrive. We all do no end of feeling, and we mistake it for thinking. And out of it we get an aggregation which we consider a boon. Its name is Public Opinion. It is held in reverence. It settles everything. Some think it the Voice of God.

QUESTIONS ON MEANING AND PURPOSE

1. What do you learn from Twain's essay about American life in the nineteenth century? How is it different from life today? What, if anything, remains the same?
2. How does the narrative in the INTRODUCTION of Twain's essay serve the author's PURPOSE? (Narration is discussed in Chapter 1.)
3. How does Twain's definition of "corn-pone opinions" differ from the view of the slave who coined the phrase? What attitude toward humanity does Twain's view seem to reflect?
4. Twain says that corn-pone opinions come in two varieties. What are they? What brings about each variety?
5. What criticisms might a feminist of today direct toward this essay? What do you find in the essay to support the criticisms or to defend Twain?

QUESTIONS ON WRITING STRATEGY

1. What evidence of Twain's famous sense of humor do you find? What does it contribute to the TONE of his essay?

2. Do Twain's RHETORICAL QUESTIONS strengthen or weaken his essay? Point them out.
3. What is the function of paragraph 9?
4. In paragraph 10 and twice in paragraph 14, Twain makes the same point in almost the same words. What is it? Does the repetition help or hurt his essay?
5. Where does "Corn-Pone Opinions" benefit from Twain's use of lively examples? (See Chapter 3, Example.)
6. In Twain's essay, what references to matters of common knowledge at the turn of the century might lead a modern AUDIENCE to consult a history book?

QUESTIONS ON LANGUAGE

1. Consult your dictionary if you need help defining the following words: irreverent, bloomer (paragraph 10); ornate, diffuse (13); sordid (14); gauds (15); aggregation (17).
2. What is corn-pone? What does Twain mean by "outside the pale" (paragraph 15); "ripe renown" and "quaint styles" (10)?
3. Where does the author use HYPERBOLE? To what extent do his exaggerations cause you to doubt the validity of his opinions?
4. Pick out those words or phrases in which Twain expresses himself most colorfully. What IMAGES does he give us? What CONCRETE language?
5. Point to other FIGURES OF SPEECH. What do they contribute?

SUGGESTIONS FOR WRITING

1. Twain finds corn-pone opinions prevalent in five areas: clothes, manners, literature, politics, and religion. In a paragraph, show how much you think people today are ruled by corn-pone opinions in any one of these areas or in any other (music, movies, or television, for instance).
2. Take a direction opposite Twain's. Give a name to the opinions held not by a conformist but by a rebel. Then, using plenty of examples, write a definition that will give your reader a clear understanding of what motivates the nonconformist to behave as he or she does toward clothes, manners, literature, politics, and religion.

· Joseph Epstein ·

JOSEPH EPSTEIN, author, critic, and editor of *The American Scholar*, teaches writing and literature at Northwestern University. He was born in Chicago in 1937. A graduate of the University of Chicago, he served in the army from 1958 to 1960. His lively and incisive essays have appeared from time to time in such places as the *New York Times Book Review*, *Commentary*, *The New Criterion*, the *New York Times Magazine*, and *Harper's*. He is the author of *Divorce in America* (1975); *Familiar Territory* (1980); *Ambition* (1981); *The Middle of My Tether* (1983); and *Plausible Prejudices* (1985).

What Is Vulgar?

Epstein wrote "What Is Vulgar?" for *The American Scholar*, the magazine published by Phi Beta Kappa (the oldest American honor society for college students). Later he included it in *The Middle of My Tether*. In the essay Epstein seems to have a rollicking good time deciding what vulgarity is. He examines the history of both word and concept. He speculates about what vulgarity is *not*. He relishes colorful examples. Some aspects of his definition may surprise you; others may give you a jolt. We're sure they won't bore you.

What's vulgar? Some people might say that the contraction   1
of the words *what* and *is* itself is vulgar. On the other hand, I remember being called a stuffed shirt by a reviewer of a book of mine because I used almost no contractions. I have forgotten the reviewer's name but I have remembered the criticism. Not being of that category of writers who never forget a compliment, I also remember being called a racist by another reviewer for observing that failure to insist on table manners in children was to risk dining with Apaches. The larger criticisms I forget, but, oddly, these goofy little criticisms stick in the teeth like sesame seeds. Yet that last trope — is it, too, vulgar? Ought I really to be picking my teeth in public, even metaphorically?

What, to return to the question in uncontractioned form, is   2
vulgar? Illustrations, obviously, are wanted. Consider a relative
of mine, long deceased, my father's Uncle Jake and hence my
grand-uncle. I don't wish to brag about bloodlines, but my Uncle Jake was a bootlegger during Prohibition who afterward went
into the scrap-iron — that is to say, the junk — business. Think
of the archetypal sensitive Jewish intellectual faces: of Spinoza,
of Freud, of Einstein, of Oppenheimer.[1] In my uncle's face you
would not have found the least trace of any of them. He was
completely bald, weighed in at around two hundred fifty
pounds, and had a complexion of clear vermilion. I loved him,
yet even as a child I knew there was about him something a bit
— how shall I put it? — outsized, and I refer not merely to his
personal tonnage. When he visited our home he generally
greeted me by pressing a ten- or twenty-dollar bill into my hand
— an amount of money quite impossible, of course, for a boy of
nine or ten, when what was wanted was a quarter or fifty-cent
piece. A widower, he would usually bring a lady-friend along;
here his tastes ran to Hungarian women in their fifties with operatic bosoms. These women wore large diamond rings, possibly
the same rings, which my uncle may have passed from woman
to woman. A big spender and a high roller, my uncle was an
immigrant version of the sport, a kind of Diamond Chaim
Brodsky.

But to see Uncle Jake in action you had to see him at table.   3
He drank whiskey with his meal, the bottle before him on the
table along with another of seltzer water, both of which he supplied himself. He ate and drank like a character out of Rabelais.[2]
My mother served him his soup course, not in a regular bowl,
but in a vessel more on the order of a tureen. He would eat hot
soup and drink whiskey and sweat — my Uncle Jake did not, de-

---

[1]Benedict (or Baruch) Spinoza (1632–1677) was a Dutch philosopher;
Sigmund Freud (1856–1939), the Austrian founder of psychoanalysis; J. Robert Oppenheimer (1904–1967), an American physicist who opposed the government's decision to develop the hydrogen bomb. For more about Albert
Einstein (1879–1955), see the essay by Banesh Hoffmann in Chapter 3. — Eds.

[2]François Rabelais (1494?–1553?), French humorist who in *Gargantua and
Pantagruel* (1532–1534) depicts two giants with tremendous appetites. — Eds.

cidedly, do anything so delicate as perspire — and sometimes it seemed that the sweat rolled from his face right into his soup dish, so that, toward the end, he may well have been engaged in an act of liquid auto-cannibalism, consuming his own body fluids with a whiskey chaser.

He was crude, certainly, my Uncle Jake; he was coarse, of   4 course; gross, it goes without saying; uncouth, beyond question. But was he vulgar? I don't think he was. For one thing, he was good-hearted, and it somehow seems wrong to call anyone vulgar who is good-hearted. But more to the point, I don't think that if you had accused him of being vulgar, he would have known what the devil you were talking about. To be vulgar requires at least a modicum of pretension, and this Uncle Jake sorely lacked. "Wulgar," he might have responded to the accusation that he was vulgar, "so vat's dis wulgar?"

To go from persons to things, and from lack of pretension to   5 a mountain of it, let me tell you about a house I passed one night, in a neighborhood not far from my own, that so filled me with disbelief that I took a hard right turn at the next corner and drove round the block to make certain I had actually seen what I thought I had. I had, but it was no house — it was a bloody edifice!

The edifice in question totally fills its rather modest lot,   6 leaving no backyard at all. It is constructed of a white stone, sanded and perhaps even painted, with so much gray-colored mortar that, even though it may be real, the stone looks fake. The roof is red. It has two chimneys, neither of which, I would wager, functions. My confidence here derives from the fact that nothing much else in the structure of the house seems to function. There is, for example, a balcony over a portico — a portico held up by columns — onto which the only possible mode of entry is by pole vault. There is, similarly, over the attached garage, a sun deck whose only access appears to be through a bathroom window. The house seems to have been built on the aesthetic formula of functionlessness follows formlessness.

But it is in its details that the true spirit of the house   7 emerges. These details are not minuscule, and neither are they subtle. For starters, outside the house under the portico, there is a chandelier. There are also two torch-shaped lamps on either side of the front door, which is carved in a scallop pattern, giving it the effect of seeming the back door to a much larger house. Along the short walk leading up to this front door stand, on short pillars, two plaster of paris lions — gilded. On each pillar, in gold and black, appears the owner's name. A white chain fence, strung along poles whose tops are painted gold, spans the front of the property; it is the kind of fence that would be more appropriate around, say, the tomb of Lenin. At the curb are two large cars, sheets of plastic covering their grills; there is also a trailer; and, in the summer months, a boat sits in the short driveway leading up to the garage. The lawn disappoints by being not Astro-Turf but, alas, real grass. However, closer inspection reveals two animals, a skunk and a rabbit, both of plastic, in petrified play upon the lawn — a nice, you might almost say a finishing, touch. Sometimes, on long drives or when unable to sleep at night, I have pondered upon the possible decor of this extraordinary house's den and upon the ways of man, which are various beyond imagining.

You want vulgar, I am inclined to exclaim, I'll show you vul-   8
gar: the house I have just described is vulgar, patently, palpably, pluperfectly vulgar. Forced to live in it for more than three hours, certain figures of refined sensibility — Edith Wharton or Harold Acton or Wallace Stevens[3] — might have ended as suicides. Yet as I described that house, I noted two contradictory feelings in myself: how pleasant it is to point out someone else's vulgarity, and yet the fear that calling someone else vulgar may itself be slightly vulgar. After all, the family that lives in this house no doubt loves it; most probably they feel that they have a real showplace. Their house, I assume, gives them a large measure of happiness. Yet why does my calling their home vulgar also give me such a measure of happiness? I suppose it is because vulgarity can be so amusing — other people's vulgarity, that is.

[3]Edith Wharton (1862–1937), American novelist, who frequently wrote of well-to-do society; Harold Acton (1904–), British art critic, historian, and student of Chinese culture, author of *Memoirs of an Aesthete* (1948) and other works; Wallace Stevens (1879–1955), American poet and insurance company executive, who wrote with a philosopher's sensibility. — EDS.

Here I must insert that I have invariably thought that the   9
people who have called me vulgar were themselves rather vulgar. So far as I know I have been called vulgar three times, once
directly, once behind my back, and once by association. In each
instance the charge was intellectual vulgarity: on one occasion a
contributor to a collection of essays on contemporary writing
that I once reviewed called me vulgar because I didn't find anything good to say about this book of some six hundred pages;
once an old friend, an editor with whom I had had a falling out,
over politics, told another friend of mine that an article I had
written seemed to him vulgar; and, finally, having patched
things up with this friend and having begun to write for his magazine again, yet a third friend asked me why I allowed my writing to appear in that particular magazine, when it was so patently — you guessed her, Chester — vulgar.

None of these accusations stung in the least. In intellectual   10
and academic life, vulgar is something one calls people with
whom one disagrees. Like having one's ideas called reductionist,
it is nothing to get worked up about — certainly nothing to take
personally. What would wound me, though, is if word got back
to me that someone had said that my manners at table were so
vulgar that it sickened him to eat with me, or that my clothes
were laughable, or that taste in general wasn't exactly my strong
point. In a novel whose author or title I can no longer remember, I recall a female character who was described as having vulgar thumbs. I am not sure I have a clear picture of vulgar
thumbs, but if it is all the same, I would just as soon not have
them.

I prefer not to be thought vulgar in any wise. When not long   11
ago a salesman offered to show me a winter coat that, as he put
it, "has been very popular," I told him to stow it — if it has been
popular, it is not for me. I comb my speech, as best I am able, of
popular phrases: you will not hear an unfundamental "basically" or a flying "whatever" from these chaste lips. I do not utter "bottom line"; I do not mutter "trade-off." I am keen to cut
myself out from the herd, at least when I can. In recent years
this has not been difficult. Distinction has lain in plain speech,
plain dress, clean cheeks. The simple has become rococo, the ro-

coco simple. But now I see that television anchormen, hair-dressers, and other leaders in our society have adopted this plainer look. This is discomfiting news. Vulgar is, after all, as vulgar does.

Which returns us yet again to the question: What is vulgar? 12 *The Oxford English Dictionary*, which provides more than two pages on the word, is rather better at telling us what vulgar was than what it is. Its definitions run from "1. The common or usual language of a country; the vernacular. *Obs.*" to "13. Having a common and offensively mean character; coarsely commonplace; lacking in refinement or good taste; uncultured, ill-bred." Historically, the word vulgar was used in fairly neutral description up to the last quarter of the seventeenth century to mean and describe the common people. Vulgar was common but not yet contemned. I noted such a neutral usage as late as a William Hazlitt essay of 1818, "On the Ignorance of the Learned," in which Hazlitt writes: "The vulgar are in the right when they judge for themselves; they are wrong when they trust to their blind guides." Yet, according to the *OED*, in 1797 the *Monthly Magazine* remarked: "So the word *vulgar* now implies something base and groveling in actions."

From the early nineteenth century on, then, vulgar has 13 been purely pejorative, a key term in the lexicon of insult and invective. Its currency as a term of abuse rose with the rise of the middle class; its spread was tied to the spread of capitalism and democracy. Until the rise of the middle class, until the spread of capitalism and democracy, people perhaps hadn't the occasion or the need to call one another vulgar. The rise of the middle class, the spread of capitalism and democracy, opened all sorts of social doors; social classes commingled as never before; plutocracy made possible almost daily strides from stratum to stratum. Still, some people had to be placed outside the pale, some doors had to be locked — and the cry of vulgarity, properly intoned, became a most effective Close Sesame.

Such seems to me roughly the social history of the word vul- 14 gar. But the history of vulgarity, the thing itself even before it had a name, is much longer. According to the French art historian Albert Dasnoy, aesthetic vulgarity taints Greek art of the

fourth and third centuries B.C. "An exhibition of Roman portraits," Dasnoy writes, "shows that, between the Etruscan style
of the earliest and the Byzantine style of the latest, vulgarity
made its first full-blooded appearance in the academic realism of
imperial Rome." Vulgarity, in Dasnoy's view, comes of the
shock of philosophic rationalism, when humankind divests itself
of belief in the sacred. "Vulgarity seems to be the price of man's
liberation," he writes, "one might even say, of his evolution. It is
unquestionably the price of the freeing of the individual personality." Certainly it is true that one would never think to call a
savage vulgar; a respectable level of civilization has to have been
reached to qualify for the dubious distinction of being called
vulgar.

"You have surely noticed the curious fact," writes Valéry,[4]   15
"that a certain *word*, which is perfectly clear when you hear or
use it in *everyday* speech, and which presents no difficulty when
caught up in the rapidity of an ordinary sentence, becomes mys-
teriously cumbersome, offers a strange resistance, defeats all efforts at definition, the moment you withdraw it from circulation
for separate study and try to find its meaning after taking away
its temporary function." Vulgar presents special difficulties,
though: while vulgarity has been often enough on display —
may even be a part of the human soul that only the fortunate
and the saintly are able to root out — every age has its own notion of what constitutes the vulgar. Riding a bicycle at Oxford in
the 1890s, Max Beerbohm reports, "was the earmark of vulgarity." Working further backward, we find that Matthew Arnold
frequently links the word vulgar with the word hideous and
hopes that culture "saves the future, as one may hope, from being vulgarized, even if it cannot save the present." "In Jane Austen's novels," Lionel Trilling writes, "vulgarity has these elements: smallness of mind, insufficiency of awareness, assertive
self-esteem, the wish to devalue, especially to devalue the human
worth of other people." Hazlitt found vulgarity in false feeling
among "the herd of pretenders to what they do not feel and to
what is not natural to them, whether in high or low life."

[4]Paul Valéry (1871–1945), French poet and literary critic. — EDS.

Vulgarity, it begins to appear, is often in the eye of the be- 16
holder. What is more, it comes in so many forms. It is so multiple and so complex — so multiplex. There are vulgarities of
taste, of manner, of mind, of spirit. There are whole vulgar ages
— the Gilded Age in the United States, for one, at least to hear
Mark Twain and Henry Adams tell it. (Is our own age another?)
To compound the complication there is even likeable vulgarity.
This is vulgarity of the kind that Cyril Connolly must have had
in mind when he wrote, "Vulgarity is the garlic in the salad of
life." In the realm of winning vulgarity are the novels of Balzac,
the paintings of Frans Hals, some of the music of Tchaikovsky
(excluding the cannon fire in the 1812 Overture, which is vulgarity of the unwinning kind).

Rightly used, profanity, normally deemed the epitome of 17
vulgar manners, can be charming. I recently moved to a new
apartment, and the person I dealt with at the moving company
we employed, a woman whose voice had an almost strident mat-
ter-of-factness, instructed me to call back with an inventory of
our furniture. When I did, our conversation, starting with my
inventory of our living room, began:

"One couch." 18

"One couch." 19

"Two lamp tables, a coffee table, a small gateleg table." 20

"Four tables." 21

"Two wing chairs and an occasional chair." 22

"Three chairs." 23

"One box of bric-a-brac." 24

"One box of shit." 25

Heavy garlic of course is not to every taste; but then again 26
some people do not much care for endive. I attended city
schools, where garlic was never in short supply and where profanity, in proper hands, could be a useful craft turned up to the
power of fine art. I have since met people so well-mannered, so
icily, elegantly correct, that with a mere glance across the table
or a word to a waiter they could put a chill on the wine and indeed on the entire evening. Some people have more, some less,
in the way of polish, but polish doesn't necessarily cover vulgarity. As there can be diamonds in the rough, so can there be
sludge in the smooth.

It would be helpful in drawing a definitional bead on the   27
word vulgar if one could determine its antonym. But I am not
sure that it has an antonym. Refined? I think not. Sophisticated? Not really. Elegant? Nope. Charming? Close, but I can
think of charming vulgarians — M. Rabelais, please come forth
and take a bow. Besides, charm is nearly as difficult to define as
vulgarity. Perhaps the only safe thing to be said about charm is
that if you think you have it, you can be fairly certain that you
don't.

If vulgarity cannot be defined by its antonym, from the rear   28
so to say, examples may be more to the point. I once heard a
friend describe a woman thus: "Next to Sam Jensen's prose,
she's the vulgarest thing in New York." From this description, I
had a fairly firm sense of what the woman was like. Sam Jensen
is a writer for one of the newsmagazines; each week on schedule
he makes a fresh cultural discovery, writing as if every sentence
will be his last, every little movie or play he reviews will change
our lives — an exhibitionist with not a great deal to exhibit.
Sam Jensen is a fictitious name — made up to protect the guilty
— but here are a few sentences that he, not I, made up:

> The great Victorian William Morris combined a practical so-
> cialism with a love for the spirit of the King Arthur legends.
> What these films show is the paradox democracy has forgot-
> ten — that the dream of Camelot is the ultimate dream of
> freedom and order in a difficult but necessary balance.

> The screenplay by Michael Wilson and Richard Maibaum is
> not from an Ian Fleming novel; it's really a cookbook that
> throws Roger Moore as Bond into these action recipes like a
> cucumber tossed into an Osterizer. Osterization is becoming
> more and more necessary for Moore; he's beginning to look a
> bit puckered, as if he's been bottled in Bond.

From these sentences — with their false paradoxes, muffed metaphors, obvious puns, and general bloat — I think I can extrapolate the woman who, next to this prose, is the vulgarest thing
in New York. I see teeth, I see elaborate hairdo, much jewelry,
flamboyant dress, a woman requiring a great deal of attention,
who sucks up most of the mental oxygen in any room she is in
— a woman, in sum, vastly overdone.

Coming at things from a different angle, I imagine myself in   29
session with a psychologist, playing the word association game.
"Vulgar," he says, "quick, name ten items you associate with the
word vulgar." "Okay," I say, "here goes:

1. Publicity
2. The Oscar awards
3. The Aspen Institute for Humanistic Studies
4. Talk shows
5. Pulitzer Prizes
6. Barbara Walters
7. Interviews with writers
8. Lauren Bacall
9. Dialogue as an ideal
10. Psychology."

This would not, I suspect, be everyone's list. Looking it over, I
see that, of the ten items, several are linked with one another.
But let me inquire into what made me choose the items I did.

Ladies first. Barbara Walters seems to me vulgar because for   30
a great many years now she has been paid to ask all the vulgar
questions, and she seems to do it with such cheerfulness, such
competence, such amiable insincerity. "What did you think
when you first heard your husband had been killed?" she will
ask, just the right hush in her voice. "What went on in your
mind when you learned that you had cancer, now for the third
time?" The questions that people with imagination do not need
to ask, the questions that people with good hearts know they
have no right to ask, these questions and others Barbara Walters
can be depended upon to ask. "Tell me, Holy Father, have you
never regretted not having children of your own?"

Lauren Bacall has only recently graduated to vulgarity, or at   31
least she has only in the past few years revealed herself vulgar.
Hers is a double vulgarity: the vulgarity of false candor — the
woman who, presumably, tells it straight — and the vulgarity
provided by someone who has decided to cash in her chips. In
her autobiography, Miss Bacall has supposedly told all her se-
crets; when interviewed on television — by, for example, Barbara Walters — the tack she takes is that of the ringwise babe
over whose eyes no one, kiddo, is going to pull the cashmere.
Yet turn the channel or page, and there is Miss Bacall in a com-

mercial or advertisement doing her best to pull the cashmere over ours. Vulgar stuff.

Talk shows are vulgar for the same reason that Pulitzer   32
Prizes and the Aspen Institute for Humanistic Studies are vulgar. All three fail to live up to their pretensions, which are extravagant: talk shows to being serious, Pulitzer Prizes to rewarding true merit, the Aspen Institute to promoting "dialogue" (see
item 9), "the bridging of cultures," "the interdisciplinary approach," and nearly every other phony shibboleth that has
cropped up in American intellectual life over the past three decades.

Publicity is vulgar because those who seek it — and even   33
those who are sought by it — tend almost without exception to
be divested of their dignity. You have to sell yourself, the sales
manuals used to advise, in order to sell your product. With publicity, though, one is selling only oneself, which is different.
Which is a bit vulgar, really.

The Oscar awards ceremony is the single item on my list   34
least in need of explanation, for it seems vulgar prima facie. It is
the air of self-congratulation — of, a step beyond, self-adulation
— that is so splendidly vulgar about the Oscar awards ceremony. Self-congratulation, even on good grounds, is best concealed; on no grounds whatever, it is embarrassing. But then,
for vulgarity, there's no business like show business.

Unless it be literary business. The only thing worse than   35
false modesty is no modesty at all, and no modesty at all is what
interviews with writers generally bring out. "That most vulgar of
all crowds the literary," wrote Keats presciently — that is, before
the incontestable evidence came in with the advent and subsequent popularity of what is by now that staple of the book review and little magazine and talk show, the interview with the
great author. What these interviews generally come down to is
an invitation to writers to pontificate upon things for which it is
either unseemly for them to speak (the quality of their own
work) or upon which they are unfit to judge (the state of the cosmos). Roughly a decade ago I watched Isaac Bashevis Singer,[5]

[5]Singer (born in 1904), Polish-born American writer of fiction in Yiddish,
received the Nobel Prize for Literature in 1978. — EDS.

when asked on a television talk show what he thought of the Vietnam War, answer, "I am a writer, and that doesn't mean I have to have an opinion on everything. I'd rather discuss literature." Still, how tempting it is, with an interviewer chirping away at your feet, handing you your own horn and your own drum, to blow it and beat it. As someone who has been interviewed a time or two, I can attest that never have I shifted spiritual gears so quickly from self-importance to self-loathing as during and after an interview. What I felt was, well, vulgar.

Psychology seems to me vulgar because it is too often overbearing in its confidence. Instead of saying, "I don't know," it readily says, "unresolved Oedipus complex" or "manic-depressive syndrome" or "identity crisis." As with other intellectual discoveries before (Marxism) and since (structuralism), psychology acts as if it is holding all the theoretical keys, but then in practice reveals that it doesn't even know where the doors are. As an old *Punch* cartoon once put it, "It's worse than wicked, my dear, it's vulgar."

Reviewing my list and attempting to account for the reasons why I have chosen the items on it, I feel I have a firmer sense of what I think vulgar. Exhibitionism, obviousness, pretentiousness, self-congratulation, self-importance, hypocrisy, overconfidence — these seem to me qualities at the heart of vulgarity in our day. It does, though, leave out common sense, a quality which, like clarity, one might have thought one could never have in overabundance. (On the philosophy table in my local bookstore, a book appeared with the title *Clarity Is Not Enough*; I could never pass it without thinking, "Ah, but it's a start.") Yet too great reliance on common sense can narrow the mind, make meager the imagination. Strict common sense abhors mystery, seldom allows for the attraction of tradition, is intolerant of questions that haven't any answers. The problem that common sense presents is knowing the limits of common sense. The too commonsensical man or woman grows angry at anything that falls outside his or her common sense, and this anger seems to me vulgar.

Vulgarity is not necessarily stupid but it is always insensitive. Its insensitivity invariably extends to itself: the vulgar person seldom knows that he is vulgar, as in the old joke about the young woman whose fiancé reports to her that his parents found her vulgar, and who, enraged, responds, "What's this vulgar crap?" Such obvious vulgarity can be comical, like a nouveau riche man bringing opera glasses to a porno film, or the Chicago politician who, while escorting the then ruling British monarch through City Hall, supposedly introduced him to the assembled aldermen by saying, "King, meet the boys." But such things are contretemps merely, not vulgarity of the insidious kind.

In our age vulgarity does not consist in failing to recognize 39 the fish knife or to know the wine list but in the inability to make distinctions. Not long ago I heard a lecture by a Harvard philosophy professor on a Howard Hawks movie, and thought, as one high reference after another was made in connection with this low subject, "Oh, Santayana,[6] 'tis better you are not alive to see this." A vulgar performance, clearly, yet few people in the audience of professors and graduate students seemed to notice.

A great many people did notice, however, when, in an act of 40 singular moral vulgarity, a publisher, an editor, and a novelist recently sponsored a convicted murderer for parole, and the man, not long after being paroled, murdered again. The reason for these men speaking out on behalf of the convict's parole, they said, was his ability as a writer: his work appeared in the editor's journal; he was to have a book published by the publisher's firm; the novelist had encouraged him from the outset. Distinctions — crucial distinctions — were not made: first, that the man was not a very good writer, but a crudely Marxist one, whose work was filled with hatreds and half-truths; second, and more important, that, having killed before, he might kill again — might just be a pathological killer. Not to have made these distinctions is vulgarity at its most vile. But to adopt a distinction new to our day, the publisher, the editor, and the novelist took responsibility for what they had done — responsibility but no real blame.

Can an entire culture grow vulgar? Matthew Arnold feared 41 such might happen in "the mechanical and material civilisation" of the England of his day. Vladimir Nabokov felt it already had

[6]George Santayana (1863–1952) was a Spanish-born American poet and philosopher. — Eds.

happened in the Soviet Union, a country, as he described it, "of moral imbeciles, of smiling slaves and poker-faced bullies," without, as in the old days, "a Gogol, a Tolstoy, a Chekhov in quest of that simplicity of truth [who] easily distinguished the vulgar side of things as well as the trashy systems of pseudo-thought." Moral imbeciles, smiling slaves, poker-faced bullies — the curl of a sneer in those Nabokovian phrases is a sharp reminder of the force that the charge of "vulgar" can have as an insult — as well as a reminder of how deep and pervasive vulgarity can become.

But American vulgarity, if I may put it so, is rather more refined. It is also more piecemeal than pervasive, and more insidious. Creeping vulgarity is how I think of it, the way Taft Republicans[7] used to think of creeping socialism. The insertion of a science fiction course in a major university curriculum, a television commercial by a once-serious actor for a cheap wine, an increased interest in gossip and trivia that is placed under the rubric Style in our most important newspapers: so the vulgar creeps along, while everywhere the third- and fourth-rate — in art, in literature, in intellectual life — is considered good enough, or at any rate highly interesting. 42

Yet being refined — or at least sophisticated — American vulgarity is vulnerable to the charge of being called vulgar. "As long as war is regarded as wicked," said Oscar Wilde, "it will always have its fascination. When it is looked upon as vulgar, it will cease to be popular." There may be something to this, if not for war then at least for designer jeans, French literary criticism, and other fashions. The one thing the vulgar of our day do not like to be called is vulgar. So crook your little finger, purse your lips, distend your nostrils slightly as you lift your nose in the air the better to look down it, and repeat after me: *Vulgar! Vulgar! Vulgar!* The word might save us all. 43

[7]Robert A. Taft (1889–1953), U.S. senator from Ohio from 1939 to 1953, was a leading spokesperson for Republican conservatives. — EDS.

QUESTIONS ON MEANING AND PURPOSE

1. On what basis does the author conclude that the house with the portico is vulgar and Uncle Jake is not?
2. To what events in history does Epstein attribute the growth of unfavorable CONNOTATIONS around the word *vulgar*?
3. What are the key words in Epstein's definition of vulgarity? Where does he list them? Which one seems at first glance the most surprising?
4. In which paragraph does the author most succinctly sum up his definition of vulgarity?
5. What points does Epstein make in paragraph 4 and in paragraph 38? Does he contradict himself? Explain.
6. Look up *vulgar* and *vulgarity* in your desk dictionary. In his essay, what liberties has Epstein taken with the dictionary definition? To what extent are these liberties justified? Do they hint at any PURPOSE besides definition?

QUESTIONS ON WRITING STRATEGY

1. Epstein uses the example of Uncle Jake to perform several functions in his essay. What are they?
2. What does Epstein's TONE contribute to his essay?
3. What proportion of Epstein's essay is devoted to illustrating what vulgarity is *not*? Of what value is this material to the essay as a whole?
4. What devices does Epstein use to give his long essay COHERENCE?
5. What segments of Epstein's AUDIENCE might be expected to enjoy his essay the most? Whom might it offend?

QUESTIONS ON LANGUAGE

1. Be sure you know what the following words mean as Epstein uses them: archetypal, vermilion, sport (paragraph 2); modicum, pretension (4); edifice (5); portico (6); minuscule (7); patently, palpably, pluperfectly, sensibility (8); reductionist (10); rococo, discomfiting (11); contemned (12); pejorative, lexicon, invective, commingled, plutocracy, stratum (13); aesthetic, rationalism, divests (14); epitome (17); extrapolate (28); shibboleth (32); prima facie (34); presciently, incontestable, advent, pontificate (35); theo-

1

retical (36); abhors (37); nouveau riche, contretemps, insidious (38); singular, pathological (40); pervasive (41); piecemeal, insidious (42).
2. What does the author mean by "operatic bosoms" (paragraph 2); "in petrified play" (7); "outside the pale" (13); "diamonds in the rough" (26); "drawing a definitional bead" (27)?
3. What ALLUSION do you find in the name "Diamond Chaim Brodsky" (paragraph 2)? In the phrases "functionlessness follows formlessness" (6); "Vulgar is . . . as vulgar does" (11); "Close Sesame" (13); and "pull the cashmere" (31)?
4. Where in the essay does Epstein use COLLOQUIAL EXPRESSIONS? Where does his word choice inject humor into the essay?
5. Identify the METAPHORS in paragraph 26. Do they have any function other than as word play? If so, what?

SUGGESTIONS FOR WRITING

1. Write your own definition of some quality other than vulgarity. Possible subjects might be refinement, prudishness, generosity, classiness, sensitivity, dishonesty, or snobbishness. One approach might be to tell what the quality is *not* as well as what it is. Load your essay with examples.
2. In paragraph 29, Epstein lists ten items he associates with the word *vulgar*. Paul Fussell, author of "Notes on Class" (Chapter 6), is another distinguished writer to ponder the subject of vulgarity. In his book *Class*, in a section of imaginary (and very funny) letters from his readers, he answers the request, "To settle a bet, would you indicate some things that are Vulgar?":

> I'd say these are vulgar, but in no particular order: Jerry Lewis's TV telethon; any "Cultural Center"; beef Wellington; cute words for drinks like *drinky-poos* or *nightcaps*; dinner napkins with high polyester content; colored wineglasses; oil paintings depicting members of the family; display of laminated diplomas.

(Old clothes and paper napkins, he adds, aren't vulgar; neither are fireworks on the Fourth of July.) In a paragraph, nominate a few other "vulgar" things and tell why you think each deserves its label.

—— POSTSCRIPT ON PROCESS ——

Joseph Epstein

One of the most fearsome things writers face is a blank piece of paper; but for the author of "What Is Vulgar?" forewarned is forearmed. Well in advance of his deadline, Joseph Epstein accumulates a folder full of ideas about his subject. Then, when he faces that sheet of paper, he is seldom at a loss for words.

As a professional writer, I have this in common with the student writer: like him or her, I cannot sit around and wait for inspiration to arrive. Much of what I write is written under the pressure of deadlines, just as students write under the pressure of the deadlines assigned them by their teachers. Some people are driven bonkers by deadline pressure; after working under it for many years now, I have come not to mind it. Without it, my guess is, I would probably not have written as much as I have been able to write.

The essay "What Is Vulgar?" was written under a deadline. It is one of a series of four essays I write every year for the *The American Scholar* magazine. Knowing I have to produce an essay of this kind every three months, I am able to plan for it somewhat in advance. The way I plan is perhaps idiosyncratic but not complicated, and I wonder if it can't be used to good effect by student writers. Once I have chosen a topic for my essay, I set aside a folder on which I write the title of the essay, if I have decided on a title, or at least the essay's general subject. Into this folder, usually on index cards though sometimes on odd scraps of paper, I note everything I can think of that has some connection with the subject of my essay: apposite quotations, anecdotes, other books and articles on the same subject that I ought to look into, notions of my own, curious contradictions — in sum, anything and everything I can think of that pertains to the subject or is even tangential to it.

438

I may begin this folder weeks before I actually begin writing   3
my essay. As the days pass, I add to the stock of items in the
folder whenever anything further on the subject occurs to me,
either from my reading, my random observations, or fugitive
thoughts that come in the shower, before falling asleep, or at
other inopportune times. Sometimes, while shopping, or driving
around, I will think up possible opening sentences for my essay.
These, too, go into the folder. The point of the folder is that,
when I finally do sit down to the writing of my essay, I don't sit
down empty-handed — or, perhaps more precisely, empty-
minded. I have a store of material before me, which I find a very
great aid to composition. It beats sitting around waiting for inspiration, which, in my experience, is usually even tardier than
Godot.[1]

Here I must say that I am one of those writers who never use   4
an outline. I am not opposed to outlines in logic or on principle
but by temperament. I have never felt comfortable with them. I
wonder if many serious essayists do use outlines. Aldous Huxley
once described the method of the great French essayist Mon-
taigne as "free association artistically controlled." I know something similar occurs in my own writing. We all free-associate easily enough; the trick is in the artistic control. But I know I have
given up on outlines because I have discovered that there is no
way I can know what will be in the second paragraph of something I write until I have written the first paragraph. My first
paragraph may contain a phrase or end on a point I hadn't anticipated, and this phrase or point may send me off into an entirely unexpected direction in my second paragraph.

For example, my having written in my previous paragraph   5
that I cannot know what my second paragraph will include until
I have written my first paragraph reminds me that E. M. Forster,
the English novelist and essayist, used to say that he didn't
know what he truly thought about a subject until he wrote
about it. (My guess is that Forster was not an outline man, ei-

---

[1]In *Waiting for Godot* (1952), a play by Irish-born French writer Samuel
Beckett, two tramps linger in a barren wasteland, looking forward to the coming of Godot, a mysterious redeemer who does not arrive. — EDS.

ther.) So, too, for me. When I set out to write the essay "What Is Vulgar?" I had only a vague notion of what would go into it (apart from some of the scraps in that folder). Certainly, I was not yet clear about my thoughts on vulgarity. The chief point of the essay, for me, was to find out what I really did think about it. The essay itself, now that it is done, shows a writer in the act of thinking.

Which is a roundabout way of saying that, for me, writing is 6 foremost a mode of thinking and, when it works well, an act of discovery. I write to find out what I believe, what seems logical and sensible to me, what notions, ideas, and views I can live with. I don't mean to say that, when I begin an essay, I don't have some general views or feeling about my subject. I mean instead that, when I begin, I am never altogether sure how I am going to end. Robert Frost once said that whenever he knew how one of his poems was going to end, it almost invariably turned out to be a bad poem. I believe him. Writing for discovery, to find out what one truly thinks of things, may be a bit riskier than writing knowing one's conclusion in advance, but it figures to be much more interesting, more surprising, and, once one gets over one's early apprehension at the prospect of winging it, more fun.

· ADDITIONAL WRITING TOPICS ·
DEFINITION

1. Write an essay in which you define an institution, a trend, a phenomenon, or an abstraction. Following are some suggestions designed to stimulate ideas. Before you begin, limit your subject as far as possible, and illustrate your essay with specific examples.

Education
Progress
Advertising
Happiness
Overpopulation
Personality
Fads
Women's liberation
Reaganomics
Marriage
A Fascist
Sportsmanship
Politics
Leadership
Leisure
Originality
Character
Imagination
Democracy
A smile
A classic (of music, literature, art, or film)
Dieting
Meditation
A friend

2. In a brief essay, define one of the following. In each instance, you have a choice of something good or something bad to talk about.

A good or bad boss
A good or bad parent
A good or bad host
A good or bad TV newscaster

A good or bad physician
A good or bad nurse
A good or bad dentist
A good or bad minister, priest, or rabbi
A good or bad roommate
A good or bad driver
A good or bad disk jockey

3. In a paragraph define for someone who has never heard the word one of the following: nerd, wimp, free spirit, preppie, "dog," "turkey," druggie, snob, freak, winner, loser, loner, freeloader, burnout, soul, mellowing out, quack, deadbeat, "bomb," pig-out, grossout, winging it.

· 10 ·

ARGUMENT AND PERSUASION

Appealing to Reason and Emotion

THE METHOD

Some people love to argue for the joy of doing so, the way some people love to take part in a brawl. The knockdown, drag-out kind of argument, however, is not the kind we are concerned with. In this chapter we will be dealing with a form of expression that, in ancient Athens, could be heard in speeches in a public forum. Today we find it in excellent newspaper editorials, thoughtful magazine articles, and other effective statements of a writer's view.

Argument is one of the four varieties of prose writing — along with narration, description, and exposition — already familiar to you. (Exposition is that sort of writing whose several methods have been set forth in Chapters 3 through 9.) The method of argument is to make an appeal to reason or feelings (or both). The end of argument is *persuasion*: to move readers to accept the writer's view — even to act on it.

Without being aware that we follow any special method, we try daily to persuade our listeners — including ourselves. We talk ourselves into doing something ("Time for that visit to the dentist. Don't want to get cavities, right?"); we try to convince mate or roommate to buy a new rug ("Look at this dump!"). A lawyer presents one side of a case; a marketing executive urges the launching of a new product; a candidate appeals to voters to go to the polls. Advertisers bombard us with their urgings. Ministers, priests, and rabbis implore us to lead better lives. Small wonder, then, that persuasion — and, when necessary, how to resist persuasion — may be among the most useful skills you can acquire.

How do you write an argument? You set forth an assertion (sometimes called a *proposition*): a statement of what you believe, and sometimes, too, a course of action you recommend. Usually, but not always, you make such an assertion at the beginning of your essay: "Welfare funds need to be trimmed from our state budget," or, "To cut back welfare funds now would be a mistake."

In argument, you will probably draw on the methods of writing you have previously learned. You might give *examples* of wasteful welfare spending, or of areas where welfare funds are needed. You might foresee the probable *effects* of cutting welfare programs or retaining them. You might *compare and contrast* one course of action with the other. You might use *narration* to tell a pointed anecdote; you might *describe* (whether you are for or against the funding) certain welfare recipients and their lives. You might employ several methods in one argument.

When we say that an argument appeals to the reason *or* to the emotions of a reader, we make only a rough distinction between the two. In fact, no argument is ever purely reasonable or purely emotional, for people can't be divided neatly into thinking parts and feeling parts. A kind of argument that *seems* almost wholly rational — certainly it tries hard to be — is a newspaper column of advice to investors. On the basis of evidence and reasoning, the columnist urges the purchase of stocks and commodities; but probably investors and their advisers are, like everyone else, subject to excitement and given to fear and greed. Perhaps the nearest thing to purely emotional argument is found in advertising that seeks to arouse our desires to buy a new car or a roll-on deodorant — not to awaken our minds. But generally, the arguments we read will mingle thought and feelings, in greater or lesser proportion. The most forcefully written appeal to reason is the one that supports an assertion the writer deeply cares about; and in the most effective appeal to emotion the writer doesn't just froth wildly and passionately, but makes sense and considers evidence. Though H. L. Mencken's "The Penalty of Death" (in this chapter) is written with feeling and touches the feelings of an audience, it is mainly a reasoned argument. In Martin Luther King's inspiring "I Have a Dream" (also in this chapter), the heart of the hearer matters more than the mind.

Sometimes the writer of an appeal to reason will follow a formal method of *logic*, the science of orderly thinking. We find such a method in a *syllogism*, a three-step form of reasoning:

> All men are mortal.
> Socrates is a man.
> Therefore, Socrates is mortal.

The first statement is the *major premise*, the second the *minor premise*, and the third the *conclusion*. Few people today argue in this strict, three-part form; yet many writers argue by using the thinking behind the syllogism — *deductive reasoning*. Beginning with a statement of truth, this kind of logic moves to a statement of truth about an individual or particular. If you observe that conservative Republicans desire less government regulation of business and that William F. Buckley is a conservative Republican, and conclude that Buckley may be expected to desire less government regulation of business, then you employ deductive reasoning. If, on the other hand, you were to interview Buckley and a hundred other conservative Republicans, find that they were unanimous in their views, and then conclude that conservative Republicans favor less government regulation of business, you would be using the opposite method: *inductive reasoning.* Inductive reasoning is essential to the method of scientists, who collect many observations of individuals and then venture a general statement that applies to them all. Writing in *Zen and the Art of Motorcycle Maintenance*, Robert M. Pirsig gives examples of deductive and inductive reasoning:

> If the cycle goes over a bump and the engine misfires, and then goes over another bump and the engine misfires, and then goes over another bump and the engine misfires, and then goes over a long smooth stretch of road and there is no misfiring, and then goes over a fourth bump and the engine misfires again, one can logically conclude that the misfiring is caused by the bumps. That is induction: reasoning from particular experiences to general truths.
>
> Deductive inferences do the reverse. They start with general knowledge and predict a specific observation. For example if, from reading the hierarchy of facts about the machine, the mechanic knows the horn of the cycle is powered exclusively by electricity from the battery, then he can logically infer that if the battery is dead the horn will not work. That is deduction.[1]

Either method of reasoning is only as accurate as the observations on which it is based. In arguments we read and hear, we often meet *logical fallacies*, errors of reasoning that lead to the wrong conclusions. You'll need to watch out for them, from the time when you're first thinking about your subject and planning your paper. To help you recognize them when you see them or hear them, and so guard against them when you write, here is a list of the most common ones.

Non sequitur (from the Latin, "it does not follow"): stating a conclusion that doesn't follow from the first premise or premises. "I've lived in this town a long time — why, my grandfather was the first mayor — so I'm against putting fluoride in the drinking water."

Oversimplification: supplying neat and easy explanations for large and complicated phenomena. "These scientists are always

[1]*Zen and the Art of Motorcycle Maintenance* (New York: William Morrow, 1974), p. 107.

messing around with the moon and the planets; that's why the climate is changing nowadays." Oversimplified solutions are also popular: "All these teenage kids that get in trouble with the law — why, they ought to ship 'em over to Russia. That would straighten 'em out!"

Either/or reasoning: assuming that a reality may be divided into only two parts or extremes; assuming that a given problem has only one of two possible solutions. "What do we do about these sheiks who keep jacking up oil prices? Either we kowtow to 'em, or we bomb 'em off the face of the earth, right?" Obviously, either/or reasoning is another kind of extreme oversimplication.

Argument from doubtful or unidentified authority: "Certainly we ought to castrate all sex offenders; Uncle Oswald says we should." Or: "According to reliable sources, my opponent is lying."

Argumentation ad hominem (from the Latin, "argument to the man"): attacking a person's views by attacking his or her character. "Mayor Burns was seen with a prostitute on Taylor Street. How can we listen to his plea for a city nursing home?"

Begging the question: taking for granted from the start what you set out to demonstrate. When you reason in a *logical* way, you state that because something is true, then, as a result, some other truth follows. When you beg the question, however, you repeat that what is true is true. If you argue, for instance, that dogs are a menace to people because they are dangerous, you don't prove a thing, since the idea that dogs are dangerous is already assumed in the statement that they are a menace. Beggars of questions often just repeat what they already believe, only in different words. This fallacy sometimes takes the form of *arguing in a circle*, or demonstrating a premise by a conclusion and a conclusion by a premise: "I should go to college because that is the right thing to do. Going to college is the right thing to do because it is expected of me."

Post hoc, ergo propter hoc (from the Latin, "after this, therefore because of this"): confusing cause and effect. See page 345.

Argument from analogy: using an extended metaphor (discussed in Chapter 7) as though it offers evidence. Pierre Berton, a Canadian journalist, once wrote a clever article "Is There a

Teacher in the House?" satirizing opponents of public health care. In it Berton writes in the voice of an after-dinner speaker alarmed by the idea of establishing a public school system — which in fact, of course, already exists:

> Under this foreign system each one of us would be forced by government edict, and under penalty of imprisonment, to send our children to school until each reaches the age of sixteen — whether we wish to or not. . . . Ask yourself, gentlemen, if it is economically sane to hand a free education, no strings attached, to everybody in the nation between the ages of six and sixteen!

Berton's speaker doesn't even mention free public health care, but he echoes accusations made familiar by its opponents. He calls the whole idea "foreign" and too costly; he complains that its advocates are "pie-in-the-sky idealists." We realize that we have heard these accusations before, but directed against another idea. Free clinics, Berton suggests, are just like free schools — a system we all take for granted. By this analogy, Berton implies that because public health care and public education are similar, they are equally practicable and desirable. If Berton were writing a serious, reasoned argument, then an opponent might protest that clinics and schools aren't quite alike and that Berton omits all their important differences. This is the central weakness in most arguments by analogy. Dwelling only on similarities, a writer doesn't consider *dissimilarities* — since to admit them might weaken the analogy.

Often, in appealing to reason, a writer brings readers new facts. In appealing to emotion, however, the writer sometimes just restates what readers already know well. Editorials in publications for special audiences (members of ethnic groups or religious denominations, also people whose political views are far to the left or right), tend to contain few factual surprises for their subscribers, who presumably read to be reassured or reinspired. In spoken discourse, this kind of appeal to emotion may be heard in the commencement day speech or the Fourth of July oration; or, to give an impressive example, in Dr. King's speech "I Have a Dream." This speech did not tell its audience anything new to them, for the listeners were mostly blacks disappointed in the American dream. Dr. King appeals not primarily to reason, but to emotions — and to the willingness of his audience to be inspired.

Emotional argument can, of course, be cynical manipulation. It can entail selling a sucker a bill of shoddy goods by appealing to pride ("Don't you want the best for your children?") in the fashion of unscrupulous advertisers, con artists, and hard-sell pushers. But argument can stir readers to constructive action by fair means, recognizing that we are not intellectual robots, but creatures with feelings, and that our feelings matter. Indeed, sometimes the readers' feelings must be engaged, or they may reply to an argument, "True, but who cares?" Argument, when it is effective, makes us feel that the writer's views must also be our own.

An appeal to emotion makes its case in definite, concrete, and memorable terms. It may proceed by using clear and colorful examples, description, metaphor and analogy, narrative. Concreteness of diction, including figures of speech, marks the writing of revolutionary war patriot Thomas Paine. Attempting to persuade the colonists to rise against the king, Paine begins his pamphlet *The Crisis*: "These are the times that try men's souls. The summer soldier and the sunshine patriot will, in this crisis, shrink from the service of their countrymen. . . . Tyranny, like Hell, is not easily conquered." Paine's phrase *the summer soldier and the sunshine patriot* is something more than mere name-calling. By splendid metaphors the pamphleteer points to a recognizable form of hypocrisy: some soldiers and patriots are faithful to their cause only when the cause is easy to uphold. Paine selects words that carry powerful suggestions: *tyranny*, *Hell*. Writers whose purpose is to sway an audience are fond of such language. To take an example of a different kind, a writer of advertising for a restaurant, in trying to describe the Wednesday night special so that the reader's mouth waters, may write — choosing words rich in favorable connotations — "Sizzling prime cut of charcoal-broiled sirloin garnished with fresh sautéed mushrooms." (A flat, objective description might instead read: "U.S. choice grade sirloin steak with fried mushrooms.")

At the other extreme, a different writer, perhaps arguing in favor of vegetarianism, might describe the same meal as "hot slab of dead steer buried under fungus." (That description, however, might seem to the reader a little too heavily biased.)

Recklessly employed, such strongly connotative words may only thwart the writer's appeal. *Name-calling* (or *mud-slinging*) is often self-defeating. In this sort of verbal abuse, one's opponents become "mere pantywaist liberals and stooges of Moscow," or "rabid gold bugs and royalists-come-lately" (to give examples of unfair names for political thinkers on the left and on the right). Any cause the writer opposes is defined in emotionally loaded terms. Prison reform becomes "the mollycoddling of cutthroats and child molesters," and proposed equal rights legislation "the flinging open of ladies' rest rooms to Peeping Toms." But the reader who hasn't completely dispensed with reason will not be swayed.

The responsible writer, to be sure, will gladly argue with the aid of richly connotative words. Consider the varied (and variously useful) meanings, for instance, of the words *idea, concept,* and *notion*. A writer might choose any one of them to refer to a thought, but the thought would sound more impressive if called an idea. Calling it a concept would glorify it: a concept, according to William Safire, "is an idea with big ideas." To downgrade the thought, the writer might call it a notion — a word conveying suggestions of bargain stores with "notions counters." Different words can't help having sharply different connotations, as every sensitive writer is aware.

Still another resource in argument is *ethical appeal*: impressing your reader that you are a well-informed person of good will, good sense, and good moral character — therefore, to be believed. You make such an appeal mainly by reasoning carefully, collecting ample evidence, and writing well. You can also cite or quote respected authorities.

In argument, you do not prove your assertion in the same irrefutable way a chemist can prove that hydrogen will burn. If you assert, "The cost-of-living index should be recalculated because it now gives disproportionate weight to housing costs," that is not the kind of assertion that is either true or false. Argument exists precisely because it deals with matters about which more than one opinion is possible. When you write an argument, you try to help your reader behold and understand just one open-eyed and open-minded view of reality.

THE PROCESS

In writing an argument, your main concern is to maintain an assertion you believe. You may find such an assertion by thinking and feeling, by scanning a newspaper, by listening to a discussion of some problem or controversy.

State clearly, if possible at the beginning of your essay, the assertion you intend to defend. If you like, you can explain why it is worth upholding, showing, perhaps, that it concerns many of your readers, perhaps the whole country. (You may wish to set forth at the start of your paper some solution or course of action; or you may prefer to save this element for your conclusion.)

Introduce your least important point first and build in a crescendo to the strongest point you have. This structure will lend emphasis to your essay, and perhaps make your chain of ideas more persuasive as the reader continues to follow it.

For every point, give evidence: facts, figures, or observations. If you introduce statistics, make sure that they are up to date and fairly represented. In an essay advocating a law against smoking, it would be unfair to declare that "in Pottsville, Illinois, last year, 50 percent of all deaths were caused by lung cancer," if only two people died in Pottsville last year — one of them struck by a car.

Provided you can face potential criticisms fairly, and give your critics due credit, you might want to recognize the objections you expect your assertion will meet. This is the strategy H. L. Mencken uses in "The Penalty of Death," and he introduces it in his essay near the beginning.

In your conclusion, briefly restate your basic assertion, if possible in a fresh, pointed way. (For example, see the concluding sentence in the essay in this chapter by William F. Buckley.) In emotionally persuasive writing, you will probably want to end in one final, strong appeal. (See "I Have a Dream.")

Finally, don't forget the power of humor in argument. You don't have to crack gratuitous jokes, but there is often an advantage in having a reader or listener who laughs on your side. When Abraham Lincoln debated Stephen Douglas, he triumphed in his reply to Douglas's snide remark that Lincoln had once been a bartender. "I have long since quit my side of the bar," Lincoln declared, "while Mr. Douglas clings to his as tenaciously as ever."

Here are two short examples of argument and persuasion. In the first paragraph, the writer tries mainly to appeal to your reason, and, in the second, to your feelings. Do these appeals at all succeed?

APPEAL TO REASON
IN A PARAGRAPH

In the offices of public television these days, nervousness prevails. Congress has slashed by 20 percent the 1983 budget for the Public Broadcasting System; Exxon and other once-generous corporations have pared down their gift lists; and now the very audience on whom the 277 PBS stations depend for contributions — educated people with high incomes — is being courted by cable television with promises of Broadway plays and live ballet. Should PBS expire, some believe, the nation will suffer no great loss. Won't commercial networks pick up "Nova," "Great Performances," and other relatively popular public television programs? Let those who don't like commercials subscribe to pay TV. In defense of PBS, we might argue that a "Sesame Street" packed with cereal commercials would be a less effective teaching instrument. Besides, for millions of Americans, cable TV is priced out of reach. In most areas, installation costs currently run from $30 to $60, followed by monthly viewing charges. But, skeptics retort, if low-income viewers must keep watching commercial television, what will change? PBS is elitist. Its audience contains less than 2 percent of the populace. Although it may be elitist to claim that no taxi driver watches opera or Shakespearean plays on PBS, public television is strongly oriented toward affluent upper middlebrows. Yet, that this orientation need be permanent is questionable.

APPEAL TO EMOTION
IN A PARAGRAPH

If public television is to serve in the future those whom it now serves only in token fashion — working people, the old, adolescents, inner-city black and Hispanic adults — it will need to increase both the variety and the quantity of its offerings. How? ask the skeptics. By pumping in more government money? The result will be pork barreling. Give PBS producers fatter funding and soon their office rugs will be as deep as those in the executive suites of ABC, NBC, and CBS. This objection, however, seems trivial. So little government money is spent on any of the arts today that it seems miserly to deny PBS a slightly increased measure of support. The power of the cathode tube to nourish or starve the mind is undeniable. Let PBS be subsidized as generously as museums and parks, public schools, state colleges. Let it be supported even more generously, for most of us spend more hours with television. If the cost seems high, we have only to ponder the alternative. It is to sentence lower-income viewers to keep watching whatever will pry their slim paychecks away from them. Should public television fold, it is safe to predict, spot commercials, bandit chases, and witless situation comedies will smother to intellectual death an audience unable to escape from them.

Comment. The first of these paragraphs (the one that primarily appeals to reason) is relatively calm and objective. It gives a few general facts about the current plight of public television; cites arguments against worrying over this plight; and offers arguments in rebuttal. In the second paragraph (the one that primarily appeals to feelings), the tone becomes more emotional — both in the skeptics' charges (including words loaded with unfavorable connotations — *pork barreling, fatter* — and the reference to deep office rugs, suggesting lavish spending) and in the counterarguments. The rhetorical device of parallelism is invoked in the two sentences that begin "Let . . . ," and the conclusion pulls out the emotional restraints — especially with the phrase *smother to intellectual death.* The writer tries to arouse the sympathies of the reader toward the underprivileged, who (she argues) will be the greatest losers if public television expires. The writer might have introduced more facts in the second paragraph. The contention that few government funds are spent on the arts, for instance, could have been bolstered with the report that about one-fortieth of one percent of the previous federal budget was devoted to the arts. But the main purpose of the second paragraph is to arouse an emotional response. The paragraph is reasonable, but not (like paragraph 1) a factual, reasoned argument.

· William F. Buckley, Jr. ·

WILLIAM FRANK BUCKLEY, JR., was born in 1925, the son of a millionaire. Soon after his graduation from Yale he wrote *God and Man at Yale* (1951), a memoir with a bias in favor of conservative political values and traditional Christian principles. With the publication of *McCarthy and His Enemies* (1954), a defense of the late Senator Joseph McCarthy and his crusade against Communists, Buckley and his coauthor L. Brent Bozell, infuriated liberals. He has continued to outrage them ever since, in many other books (including *Up from Liberalism*, 1959), in a syndicated newspaper column, and in the conservatively oriented magazine he founded and still edits, *The National Review*. A man of a certain wry charm, Buckley has been a successful television talk-show host on the program "Firing Line." In 1965 he ran for mayor of New York as a candidate of the Conservative Party. Lately he has written *Atlantic High*, a celebration of sailing (1983), and a series of novels about the exploits of Blackford Oakes, an urbane spy for the CIA.

Why Don't We Complain?

Most people, riding in an overheated commuter train, would perspire quietly. For Buckley, this excess of warmth sparks an indignant essay in which he takes to task both himself and his fellow Americans. Does the essay appeal mainly to reason or to emotion? And what would happen if everyone were to do as Buckley urges?

It was the very last coach and the only empty seat on the entire train, so there was no turning back. The problem was to breathe. Outside, the temperature was below freezing. Inside the railroad car the temperature must have been about 85 degrees. I took off my overcoat, and a few minutes later my jacket, and noticed that the car was flecked with the white shirts of the passengers. I soon found my hand moving to loosen my tie. From one end of the car to the other, as we rattled through Westchester County, we sweated; but we did not moan.

I watched the train conductor appear at the head of the car. 2 "Tickets, all tickets, please!" In a more virile age, I thought, the passengers would seize the conductor and strap him down on a seat over the radiator to share the fate of his patrons. He shuffled down the aisle, picking up tickets, punching commutation cards. *No one addressed a word to him.* He approached my seat, and I drew a deep breath of resolution. "Conductor," I began with a considerable edge to my voice. . . . Instantly the doleful eyes of my seatmate turned tiredly from his newspaper to fix me with a resentful stare: what question could be so important as to justify my sibilant intrusion into his stupor? I was shaken by those eyes. I am incapable of making a discreet fuss, so I mumbled a question about what time we were due in Stamford (I didn't even ask whether it would be before or after dehydration could be expected to set in), got my reply, and went back to my newspaper and to wiping my brow.

The conductor had nonchalantly walked down the gauntlet 3 of eighty sweating American freemen, and not one of them had asked him to explain why the passengers in that car had been consigned to suffer. There is nothing to be done when the temperature *outdoors* is 85 degrees, and indoors the air conditioner has broken down; obviously when that happens there is nothing to do, except perhaps curse the day that one was born. But when the temperature outdoors is below freezing, it takes a positive act of will on somebody's part to set the temperature *indoors* at 85. Somewhere a valve was turned too far, a furnace overstocked, a thermostat maladjusted: something that could easily be remedied by turning off the heat and allowing the great outdoors to come indoors. All this is so obvious. What is not obvious is what has happened to the American people.

It isn't just the commuters, whom we have come to visualize 4 as a supine breed who have got on to the trick of suspending their sensory faculties twice a day while they submit to the creeping dissolution of the railroad industry. It isn't just they who have given up trying to rectify irrational vexations. It is the American people everywhere.

A few weeks ago at a large movie theatre I turned to my wife 5 and said, "The picture is out of focus." "Be quiet," she answered. I obeyed. But a few minutes later I raised the point again, with mounting impatience. "It will be all right in a minute," she said apprehensively. (She would rather lose her eyesight than be around when I make one of my infrequent scenes.) I waited. It was *just* out of focus — not glaringly out, but out. My vision is 20-20, and I assume that is the vision, adjusted, of most people in the movie house. So, after hectoring my wife throughout the first reel, I finally prevailed upon her to admit that it *was* off, and very annoying. We then settled down, coming to rest on the presumption that: a) someone connected with the management of the theatre must soon notice the blur and make the correction; or b) that someone seated near the rear of the house would make the complaint in behalf of those of us up front; or c) that — any minute now — the entire house would explode into cat-calls and foot stamping, calling dramatic attention to the irksome distortion.

What happened was nothing. The movie ended, as it had   6
begun *just* out of focus, and as we trooped out, we stretched our faces in a variety of contortions to accustom the eye to the shock of normal focus.

I think it is safe to say that everybody suffered on that occa-   7
sion. And I think it is safe to assume that everyone was expecting someone else to take the initiative in going back to speak to the manager. And it is probably true even that if we had supposed the movie would run right through the blurred image, someone surely would have summoned up the purposive indignation to get up out of his seat and file his complaint.

But notice that no one did. And the reason no one did is be-   8
cause we are all increasingly anxious in America to be unobtrusive, we are reluctant to make our voices heard, hesitant about claiming our rights; we are afraid that our cause is unjust, or that if it is not unjust, that it is ambiguous; or if not even that, that it is too trivial to justify the horrors of a confrontation with Authority; we will sit in an oven or endure a racking headache before undertaking a head-on, I'm-here-to-tell-you complaint. That tendency to passive compliance, to a heedless endurance, is something to keep one's eyes on — in sharp focus.

I myself can occasionally summon the courage to complain,   9

but I cannot, as I have intimated, complain softly. My own instinct is so strong to let the thing ride, to forget about it — to expect that someone will take the matter up, when the grievance is
collective, in my behalf — that it is only when the provocation
is at a very special key, whose vibrations touch simultaneously a
complexus of nerves, allergies, and passions, that I catch fire and
find the reserves of courage and assertiveness to speak up. When
that happens, I get quite carried away. My blood gets hot, my
brow wet, I become unbearably and unconscionably sarcastic
and bellicose; I am girded for a total showdown.

Why should that be? Why could not I (or anyone else) on   10
that railroad coach have said simply to the conductor, "Sir" — I
take that back: that sounds sarcastic — "Conductor, would you
be good enough to turn down the heat? I am extremely hot. In
fact, I tend to get hot every time the temperature reaches 85
degr__" Strike that last sentence. Just end it with the simple
statement that you are extremely hot, and let the conductor infer the cause.

Every New Year's Eve I resolve to do something about the   11
Milquetoast in me and vow to speak up, calmly, for my rights,
and for the betterment of our society, on every appropriate occasion. Entering last New Year's Eve I was fortified in my resolve
because that morning at breakfast I had had to ask the waitress
three times for a glass of milk. She finally brought it — after I
had finished my eggs, which is when I don't want it any more. I
did not have the manliness to order her to take the milk back,
but settled instead for a cowardly sulk, and ostentatiously
refused to drink the milk — though I later paid for it — rather
than state plainly to the hostess, as I should have, why I had not
drunk it, and would not pay for it.

So by the time the New Year ushered out the Old, riding in   12
on my morning's indignation and stimulated by the gastric
juices of resolution that flow so faithfully on New Year's Eve, I
rendered my vow. Henceforward I would conquer my shyness,
my despicable disposition to supineness. I would speak out like a
man against the unnecessary annoyances of our time.

Forty-eight hours later, I was standing in line at the ski re- 13
pair store in Pico Peak, Vermont. All I needed, to get on with

my skiing, was the loan, for one minute, of a small screwdriver, to tighten a loose binding. Behind the counter in the workshop were two men. One was industriously engaged in servicing the complicated requirements of a young lady at the head of the line, and obviously he would be tied up for quite a while. The other — "Jiggs," his workmate called him — was a middle-aged man, who sat in a chair puffing a pipe, exchanging small talk with his working partner. My pulse began its telltale acceleration. The minutes ticked on. I stared at the idle shopkeeper, hoping to shame him into action, but he was impervious to my telepathic reproof and continued his small talk with his friend, brazenly insensitive to the nervous demands of six good men who were raring to ski.

Suddenly my New Year's Eve resolution struck me. It was   14
now or never. I broke from my place in line and marched to the counter. I was going to control myself. I dug my nails into my palms. My effort was only partially successful.

"If you are not too busy," I said icily, "would you mind   15
handing me a screwdriver?"

Work stopped and everyone turned his eyes on me, and I ex-   16
perienced that mortification I always feel when I am the center of centripetal shafts of curiosity, resentment, perplexity.

But the worst was yet to come. "I am sorry, sir," said Jiggs   17
deferentially, moving the pipe from his mouth. "I am not supposed to move. I have just had a heart attack." That was the signal for a great whirring noise that descended from heaven. We looked, stricken, out the window, and it appeared as though a cyclone had suddenly focused on the snowy courtyard between the shop and the ski lift. Suddenly a gigantic army helicopter materialized, and hovered down to a landing. Two men jumped out of the plane carrying a stretcher, tore into the ski shop, and lifted the shopkeeper onto the stretcher. Jiggs bade his companion goodby, was whisked out the door, into the plane, up to the heavens, down — we learned — to a near-by army hospital. I looked up manfully — into a score of man-eating eyes. I put the experience down as a reversal.

As I write this, on an airplane, I have run out of paper and   18
need to reach into my briefcase under my legs for more. I cannot

do this until my empty lunch tray is removed from my lap. I arrested the stewardess as she passed empty-handed down the aisle on the way to the kitchen to fetch the lunch trays for the passengers up forward who haven't been served yet. "Would you please take my tray?" "Just a *moment*, sir!" she said, and marched on sternly. Shall I tell her that since she is headed for the kitchen *anyway*, it could not delay the feeding of the other passengers by more than two seconds necessary to stash away my empty tray? Or remind her that not fifteen minutes ago she spoke unctuously into the loudspeaker the words undoubtedly devised by the airline's highly paid public relations counselor: "If there is anything I or Miss French can do for you to make your trip more enjoyable, *please* let us — " I have run out of paper.

I think the observable reluctance of the majority of Americans to assert themselves in minor matters is related to our increased sense of helplessness in an age of technology and centralized political and economic power. For generations, Americans who were too hot, or too cold, got up and did something about it. Now we call the plumber, or the electrician, or the furnace man. The habit of looking after our own needs obviously had something to do with the assertiveness that characterized the American family familiar to readers of American literature. With the technification of life goes our direct responsibility for our material environment, and we are conditioned to adopt a position of helplessness not only as regards the broken air conditioner, but as regards the overheated train. It takes an expert to fix the former, but not the latter; yet these distinctions, as we withdraw into helplessness, tend to fade away.   19

Our notorious political apathy is a related phenomenon. Every year, whether the Republican or the Democratic Party is in office, more and more power drains away from the individual to feed vast reservoirs in far-off places; and we have less and less say about the shape of events which shape our future. From this alienation of personal power comes the sense of resignation with which we accept the political dispensations of a powerful government whose hold upon us continues to increase.   20

An editor of a national weekly news magazine told me a few years ago that as few as a dozen letters of protest against an edi-   21

torial stance of his magazine was enough to convene a plenipotentiary meeting of the board of editors to review policy. "So
few people complain, or make their voices heard," he explained
to me, "that we assume a dozen letters represent the inarticulated views of thousands of readers." In the past ten years, he said,
the volume of mail has noticeably decreased, even though the
circulation of his magazine has risen.

When our voices are finally mute, when we have finally sup-   22
pressed the natural instinct to complain, whether the vexation is
trivial or grave, we shall have become automatons, incapable of
feeling. When Premier Khrushchev first came to this country
late in 1959 he was primed, we are informed, to experience the
bitter resentment of the American people against his tyranny,
against his persecutions, against the movement which is responsible for the great number of American deaths in Korea, for billions in taxes every year, and for life everlasting on the brink of
disaster; but Khrushchev was pleasantly surprised, and reported
back to the Russian people that he had been met with over-
whelming cordiality (read: apathy), except, to be sure, for "a few
fascists who followed me around with their wretched posters,
and should be horsewhipped."

I may be crazy, but I say there would have been lots more   23
posters in a society where train temperatures in the dead of winter are not allowed to climb to 85 degrees without complaint.

QUESTIONS ON MEANING AND PURPOSE

1. How does Buckley account for his failure to complain to the train
   conductor? What reasons does he give for not taking action when
   he notices that the movie he is watching is out of focus?
2. Where does Buckley finally place the blame for the average American's reluctance to try to "rectify irrational vexations"?
3. By what means does the author bring his argument around to the
   subject of political apathy?
4. What THESIS does Buckley attempt to support? How would you
   state it?

QUESTIONS ON WRITING STRATEGY

1. Buckley includes five stories in his essay, four of them taken from personal experience. Which support his thesis?
2. In taking to task not only his fellow Americans but also himself, does Buckley strengthen or weaken his charge that, as a people, Americans do not complain enough?
3. Judging from the vocabulary displayed in this essay, would you say that Buckley is writing for a highly specialized AUDIENCE, an educated but nonspecialized audience, or an uneducated general audience, such as most newspaper readers?
4. As a whole, is Buckley's essay an example of appeal to emotion or of reasoned argument? Give EVIDENCE for your answer.

QUESTIONS ON LANGUAGE

1. Define the following words: virile, doleful, sibilant (paragraph 2); supine (4); hectoring (5); unobtrusive, ambiguous (8); intimated, unconscionably, bellicose (9); ostentatiously (11); despicable (12); impervious (13); mortification, centripetal (16); deferentially (17); unctuously (18); notorious, dispensations (20); plenipotentiary, inarticulated (21); automatons (22).
2. What does Buckley's use of the capital A in *Authority* (paragraph 8) contribute to the sentence in which he uses it?
3. What is Buckley talking about when he alludes to "the Milquetoast in me" (paragraph 11)? (Notice how well the ALLUSION fits into the paragraph, with its emphasis on breakfast and a glass of milk.)

SUGGESTIONS FOR WRITING

1. Write about an occasion when you should have registered a complaint and did not; or, recount what happened when you did in fact protest against one of "the unnecessary annoyances of our time."
2. Write a paper in which you take issue with any one of Buckley's ideas. Argue that he is wrong and you are right.
3. Think of some disturbing incident you have witnessed, or some annoying treatment you have received in a store or other public place, and write a letter of complaint to whomever you believe responsible. Be specific in your evidence, be temperate in your language, and be sure to put your letter in the mail.

· H. L. Mencken ·

HENRY LOUIS MENCKEN (1880–1956) was a native of Baltimore, where for four decades he worked as newspaper reporter, editor, and columnist. In the 1920s, his boisterous, cynical observations on American life, appearing regularly in *The Smart Set* and later in *The American Mercury* (which he founded and edited), made him probably the most widely quoted writer in the country. Mencken leveled blasts at pomp, hypocrisy, and the middle classes (whom he labeled "the booboisie"). As editor and literary critic, he championed Sinclair Lewis, Theodore Dreiser, and other realistic writers. In 1933, when Mencken's attempts to laugh off the Depression began to ring hollow, his magazine died. He then devoted himself to revising and supplementing *The American Language* (fourth edition, 1948), a learned and highly entertaining survey of a nation's speech habits and vocabulary. Two dozen of Mencken's books are now in print, including *A Mencken Chrestomathy* (1949), a representative selection of his best writings of various kinds; and *A Choice of Days* (1980), a selection from his memoirs.

The Penalty of Death

Above all, Mencken is a humorist whose thought has a serious core. He argues by first making the reader's jaw drop, then inducing a laugh, and finally causing the reader to ponder, "Hmmmm — what if he's right?" The following still-controversial essay, from *Prejudices, Fifth Series* (1926), shows Mencken the persuader in top form. His work is enjoying a revival of attention nowadays — not so much for his ideas as for his style. No writer is better at swinging from ornate and abstract words to salty and concrete ones, at tossing a metaphor that makes you smile even as it kicks in your teeth.

Of the arguments against capital punishment that issue from uplifters, two are commonly heard most often, to wit:

1. That hanging a man (or frying him or gassing him) is a dreadful business, degrading to those who have to do it and revolting to those who have to witness it.
2. That it is useless, for it does not deter others from the same crime.

The first of these arguments, it seems to me, is plainly too   2
weak to need serious refutation. All it says, in brief, is that the work of the hangman is unpleasant. Granted. But suppose it is? It may be quite necessary to society for all that. There are, indeed, many other jobs that are unpleasant, and yet no one thinks of abolishing them — that of the plumber, that of the soldier, that of the garbage-man, that of the priest hearing confessions, that of the sand-hog, and so on. Moreover, what evidence is there that any actual hangman complains of his work? I have heard none. On the contrary, I have known many who delighted in their ancient art, and practiced it proudly.

In the second argument of the abolitionists there is rather   3
more force, but even here, I believe, the ground under them is shaky. Their fundamental error consists in assuming that the whole aim of punishing criminals is to deter other (potential) criminals — that we hang or electrocute A simply in order to so alarm B that he will not kill C. This, I believe, is an assumption which confuses a part with the whole. Deterrence, obviously, is *one* of the aims of punishment, but it is surely not the only one. On the contrary, there are at least a half dozen, and some are probably quite as important. At least one of them, practically considered, is *more* important. Commonly, it is described as revenge, but revenge is really not the word for it. I borrow a better term from the late Aristotle: *katharsis. Katharsis*, so used, means a salubrious discharge of emotions, a healthy letting off of steam. A school-boy, disliking his teacher, deposits a tack upon the pedagogical chair; the teacher jumps and the boy laughs. This is *katharsis*. What I contend is that one of the prime objects of all judicial punishments is to afford the same grateful relief (*a*) to the immediate victims of the criminal punished, and (*b*) to the general body of moral and timorous men.

These persons, and particularly the first group, are con-   4 cerned only indirectly with deterring other criminals. The thing they crave primarily is the satisfaction of seeing the criminal actually before them suffer as he made them suffer. What they want is the peace of mind that goes with the feeling that accounts are squared. Until they get that satisfaction they are in a state of emotional tension, and hence unhappy. The instant they get it they are comfortable. I do not argue that this yearning is noble; I simply argue that it is almost universal among human beings. In the face of injuries that are unimportant and can be borne without damage it may yield to higher impulses; that is to say, it may yield to what is called Christian charity. But when the injury is serious Christianity is adjourned, and even saints reach for their sidearms. It is plainly asking too much of human nature to expect it to conquer so natural an impulse. A keeps a store and has a bookkeeper, B. B steals $700, employs it in playing at dice or bingo, and is cleaned out. What is A to do? Let B go? If he does so he will be unable to sleep at night. The sense of injury, of injustice, of frustration will haunt him like pruritus. So he turns B over to the police, and they hustle B to prison. Thereafter A can sleep. More, he has pleasant dreams. He pictures B chained to the wall of a dungeon a hundred feet underground, devoured by rats and scorpions. It is so agreeable that it makes him forget his $700. He has got his *katharsis*.

The same thing precisely takes place on a larger scale when   5 there is a crime which destroys a whole community's sense of security. Every law-abiding citizen feels menaced and frustrated until the criminals have been struck down — until the communal capacity to get even with them, and more than even, has been dramatically demonstrated. Here, manifestly, the business of deterring others is no more than an afterthought. The main thing is to destroy the concrete scoundrels whose act has alarmed everyone, and thus made everyone unhappy. Until they are brought to book that unhappiness continues; when the law has been executed upon them there is a sigh of relief. In other words, there is *katharsis*.

I know of no public demand for the death penalty for ordi-   6 nary crimes, even for ordinary homicides. Its infliction would shock all men of normal decency of feeling. But for crimes involving the deliberate and inexcusable taking of human life, by men openly defiant of all civilized order — for such crimes it seems, to nine men out of ten, a just and proper punishment. Any lesser penalty leaves them feeling that the criminal has got the better of society — that he is free to add insult to injury by laughing. That feeling can be dissipated only by a recourse to *katharsis*, the invention of the aforesaid Aristotle. It is more effectively and economically achieved, as human nature now is, by wafting the criminal to realms of bliss.

The real objection to capital punishment doesn't lie against   7
the actual extermination of the condemned, but against our brutal American habit of putting it off so long. After all, every one of us must die soon or late, and a murderer, it must be assumed, is one who makes that sad fact the cornerstone of his metaphysic. But it is one thing to die, and quite another thing to lie for long months and even years under the shadow of death. No sane man would choose such a finish. All of us, despite the Prayer Book, long for a swift and unexpected end. Unhappily, a murderer, under the irrational American system, is tortured for what, to him, must seem a whole series of eternities. For months on end he sits in prison while his lawyers carry on their idiotic buffoonery with writs, injunctions, mandamuses, and appeals. In order to get his money (or that of his friends) they have to feed him with hope. Now and then, by the imbecility of a judge or some trick of juridic science, they actually justify it. But let us say that, his money all gone, they finally throw up their hands. Their client is now ready for the rope or the chair. But he must still wait for months before it fetches him.

That wait, I believe, is horribly cruel. I have seen more than   8
one man sitting in the death-house, and I don't want to see any more. Worse, it is wholly useless. Why should he wait at all? Why not hang him the day after the last court dissipates his last hope? Why torture him as not even cannibals would torture their victims? The common answer is that he must have time to make his peace with God. But how long does that take? It may be accomplished, I believe, in two hours quite as comfortably as

in two years. There are, indeed, no temporal limitations upon God. He could forgive a whole herd of murderers in a millionth of a second. More, it has been done.

QUESTIONS ON MEANING AND PURPOSE

1. Identify Mencken's main reason for his support of capital punishment. What is his THESIS?
2. In paragraph 3, Mencken asserts that there are at least half a dozen reasons for punishing offenders. In his essay, he mentions two, deterrence and revenge. What others can you supply?
3. For which class of offenders does Mencken advocate the death penalty?
4. What is Mencken's "real objection" to capital punishment?

QUESTIONS ON WRITING STRATEGY

1. How would you characterize Mencken's humor? Point to examples of it. In the light of his grim subject, do you find it funny?
2. In his first paragraph, Mencken pares his subject down to manageable size. What techniques does he employ for this purpose?
3. In paragraph 2, Mencken draws an analogy between the executioner's job and other jobs that are "unpleasant." How effective is this device? What flaw do you see in Mencken's argument by analogy? (For more on this fallacy, see page 447.)
4. At the start of paragraph 7, Mencken shifts his stance from concern for the victims of crime to concern for prisoners awaiting execution. Does the shift help or weaken the effectiveness of his earlier justification for capital punishment?
5. Do you think the author expects his AUDIENCE to agree with him? At what points does he seem to recognize the fact that some readers may see things differently?

QUESTIONS ON LANGUAGE

1. Mencken opens his argument by referring to those who reject capital punishment as "uplifters." What CONNOTATIONS does this

word have for you? Does the use of this "loaded" word strengthen or weaken Mencken's position? Explain.

2. Be sure you know the meanings of the following words: refutation, sand-hog (paragraph 2); salubrious, pedagogical, timorous (3); pruritus (4); wafting (6); mandamuses, juridic (7).

3. What emotional overtones can you detect in Mencken's reference to the hangman's job as an "ancient art" (paragraph 2)?

4. What does Mencken's argument gain from his substitution of the word *katharsis* for *revenge*?

SUGGESTIONS FOR WRITING

1. Write a paper in which you suggest one reform in current methods of apprehending, trying, and sentencing criminals. Supply EVIDENCE to persuade a reader that your idea would improve the system.

2. Write an essay in which you refute Mencken's case; or, take Mencken's side but use different arguments. Be sure to defend your stance, point by point.

· Flannery O'Connor ·

FLANNERY O'CONNOR was born in 1925 in Milledgeville, Georgia, attended college in her hometown, and later studied at the University of Iowa's School for Writers. Stricken with a fatal disease, lupus erythematosus, she returned home in 1951 to live out her short life in Milledgeville with her mother, to raise prize peacocks, and to write. O'Connor died in 1964. She is remembered for her short stories and for two novels, *Wise Blood* (1952) and *The Violent Bear It Away* (1960). *The Complete Stories of Flannery O'Connor* (1971) received a posthumous National Book Award. Famed for its Christian themes and its stark and at times humorous portrayals of country people who encounter the irrational, the grotesque, and the absurd, O'Connor's fiction has attracted steadily increasing notice from readers and critics alike. Her remarkable letters have been edited by Sally Fitzgerald in *The Habit of Being* (1979).

Total Effect and the Eighth Grade

This essay first appeared on March 21, 1963, in *The Bulletin*, a Catholic diocesan newspaper for which O'Connor wrote many articles and book reviews, though early on she once confided to a correspondent that she thought it "a wretched sheet" and apparently hoped to help improve it. *The Bulletin*'s editors changed the essay's title to "Fiction Is a Subject with a History; It Should Be Taught That Way." After the author's death, Sally and Robert Fitzgerald included "Total Effect and the Eighth Grade" in a selection of O'Connor's occasional prose called *Mystery and Manners* (1969).

In two recent instances in Georgia, parents have objected to their eighth- and ninth-grade children's reading assignments in modern fiction. This seems to happen with some regularity in cases throughout the country. The unwitting parent picks up his child's book, glances through it, comes upon passages of erotic detail or profanity, and takes off at once to complain to the school board. Sometimes, as in one of the Georgia cases, the teacher is dismissed and hackles rise in liberal circles everywhere.

The two cases in Georgia, which involved Steinbeck's *East* 2 *of Eden* and John Hersey's *A Bell for Adano*, provoked considerable newspaper comment. One columnist, in commending the enterprise of the teachers, announced that students do not like to read the fusty works of the nineteenth century, that their attention can best be held by novels dealing with the realities of our own time, and that the Bible, too, is full of racy stories.

Mr. Hersey himself addressed a letter to the State School 3 Superintendent in behalf of the teacher who had been dismissed. He pointed out that his book is not scandalous, that it attempts to convey an earnest message about the nature of democracy, and that it falls well within the limits of the principle of "total effect," that principle followed in legal cases by which a book is judged not for isolated parts but by the final effect of the whole book upon the general reader.

I do not want to comment on the merits of these particular 4 cases. What concerns me is what novels ought to be assigned in the eighth and ninth grades as a matter of course, for if these cases indicate anything, they indicate the haphazard way in which fiction is approached in our high schools. Presumably there is a state reading list which contains "safe" books for teachers to assign; after that it is up to the teacher.

English teachers come in Good, Bad, and Indifferent, but 5 too frequently in high schools anyone who can speak English is allowed to teach it. Since several novels can't easily be gathered into one textbook, the fiction that students are assigned depends upon their teacher's knowledge, ability, and taste: variable factors at best. More often than not, the teacher assigns what he thinks will hold the attention and interest of the students. Modern fiction will certainly hold it.

Ours is the first age in history which has asked the child 6 what he would tolerate learning, but that is a part of the problem with which I am not equipped to deal. The devil of Educationism that possesses us is the kind that can be "cast out only by prayer and fasting." No one has yet come along strong enough to do it. In other ages the attention of children was held by Homer and Virgil, among others, but, by the reverse evolutionary process, that is no longer possible; our children are too stupid now to enter the past imaginatively. No one asks the student if algebra pleases him or if he finds it satisfactory that some French verbs are irregular, but if he prefers Hersey to Hawthorne, his taste must prevail.

I would like to put forward the proposition, repugnant to most English teachers, that fiction, if it is going to be taught in the high schools, should be taught as a subject and as a subject with a history. The total effect of a novel depends not only on its innate impact, but upon the experience, literary and otherwise, with which it is approached. No child needs to be assigned Hersey or Steinbeck until he is familiar with a certain amount of the best work of Cooper, Hawthorne, Melville, the early James, and Crane, and he does not need to be assigned these until he has been introduced to some of the better English novelists of the eighteenth and nineteenth centuries.

The fact that these works do not present him with the realities of his own time is all to the good. He is surrounded by the realities of his own time, and he has no perspective whatever from which to view them. Like the college student who wrote in her paper on Lincoln that he went to the movies and got shot, many students go to college unaware that the world was not made yesterday; their studies began with the present and dipped backward occasionally when it seemed necessary or unavoidable.

There is much to be enjoyed in the great British novels of the nineteenth century, much that a good teacher can open up in them for the young student. There is no reason why these novels should be either too simple or too difficult for the eighth grade. For the simple, they offer simple pleasures; for the more precocious, they can be made to yield subtler ones if the teacher is up to it. Let the student discover, after reading the nineteenth-century British novel, that the nineteenth-century American novel is quite different as to its literary characteristics, and he will thereby learn something not only about these individual works but about the sea-change which a new historical

situation can effect in a literary form. Let him come to modern
fiction with this experience behind him, and he will be better
able to see and to deal with the more complicated demands of
the best twentieth-century fiction.

Modern fiction oftens looks simpler than the fiction that   10
preceded it, but in reality it is more complex. A natural evolution has taken place. The author has for the most part absented
himself from direct participation in the work and has left the
reader to make his own way amid experiences dramatically rendered and symbolically ordered. The modern novelist merges
the reader in the experience; he tends to raise the passions he
touches upon. If he is a good novelist, he raises them to effect by
their order and clarity a new experience — the total effect —
which is not in itself sensuous or simply of the moment. Unless
the child has had some literary experience before, he is not going to be able to resolve the immediate passions the book
arouses into any true, total picture.

It is here the moral problem will arise. It is one thing for a   11
child to read about adultery in the Bible or in *Anna Karenina,*
and quite another for him to read about it in most modern fiction. This is not only because in both the former instances adultery is considered a sin, and in the latter, at most, an inconvenience, but because modern writing involves the reader in the
action with a new degree of intensity, and literary mores now
permit him to be involved in any action a human being can perform.

In our fractured culture, we cannot agree on morals; we can-   12
not even agree that moral matters should come before literary
ones when there is a conflict between them. All this is another
reason why the high schools would do well to return to their
proper business of preparing foundations. Whether in the senior
year students should be assigned modern novelists should depend both on their parents' consent and on what they have already read and understood.

The high-school English teacher will be fulfilling his respon-   13
sibility if he furnishes the student a guided opportunity, through
the best writing of the past, to come, in time, to an understand-

ing of the best writing of the present. He will teach literature, not social studies or little lessons in democracy or the customs of many lands.

And if the student finds that this is not to his taste? Well,   14
that is regrettable. Most regrettable. His taste should not be consulted; it is being formed.

QUESTIONS ON MEANING AND PURPOSE

1. What faults in the usual methods of teaching fiction to high-school students does the author set forth? What remedies does she suggest?
2. List the targets of O'Connor's ire. Whose view is it that "our children are too stupid now to enter the past imaginatively" (paragraph 6)?
3. What objections does the author have to assigning contemporary novels in high school? Do you agree or disagree with her arguments? Why?
4. "Flannery O'Connor was just a prudish old maid who didn't want anyone reading about sex." How would you respond to that statement?
5. Where in her essay does the author express her views about the taste of students in eighth grade and high school?

QUESTIONS ON WRITING STRATEGY

1. How many of the arguments that O'Connor deals with in her essay are introduced in paragraphs 1–3?
2. Does the first sentence in paragraph 4 take you by surprise? If so, why? To what extent does it signal an abrupt change of direction?
3. What does O'Connor's TONE contribute to the impact of her words? In what passages is her attitude most clearly visible?
4. To what extent might a general AUDIENCE's reaction to O'Connor's essay differ from that of the audience for whom it was originally written?

QUESTIONS ON LANGUAGE

1. With the aid of your dictionary, if necessary, define the following words: unwitting, hackles (paragraph 1); fusty (2); repugnant, innate (7); precocious, sea-change (9).
2. What does O'Connor mean by "the devil of Educationism" and "the reverse evolutionary process" (paragraph 6)?
3. What are the CONNOTATIONS of the word *adultery* (paragraph 11)? Nowadays, where are you most likely to see the word used?

SUGGESTIONS FOR WRITING

1. In paragraph 5, O'Connor says, "English teachers come in Good, Bad, and Indifferent, but too frequently in high schools anyone who can speak English is allowed to teach it." In a brief essay, comment on that statement in the light of your own high-school experience. Keep in mind that using examples will lend vividness to your writing.
2. Write a paper in which you consider to what degree you think children and young adolescents should be protected from exposure to "any action a human being can perform." What forces in contemporary society militate against their being protected at all? Should such forces be resisted? If so, how?

· Martin Luther King, Jr. ·

MARTIN LUTHER KING, JR., (1929–1968) was born in Atlanta, the son of a Baptist minister, and was himself ordained in the same denomination. Stepping to the forefront of the civil rights movement in 1955, King led blacks in a boycott of segregated city buses in Montgomery, Alabama; became first president of the Southern Christian Leadership Conference; and staged sit-ins and mass marches that helped bring about the Civil Rights Act passed by Congress in 1964 and the Voting Rights Act of 1965. He received the Nobel Peace Prize in 1964. In view of the fact that King preached "nonviolent resistance," it is particularly ironic that he was himself the target of violence. He was stabbed in New York, pelted with stones in Chicago; his home in Montgomery was bombed; and at last in Memphis he was assassinated by a hidden sniper. On his tombstone near Atlanta's Ebenezer Baptist Church are these words from the spiritual he quotes at the conclusion of "I Have a Dream": "Free at last, free at last, thank God Almighty, I'm free at last." Martin Luther King's birthday, January 15, is now a national holiday.

I Have a Dream

In Washington, D.C., on August 28, 1963, King's campaign of nonviolent resistance reached its historic climax. On that date, commemorating the centennial of Lincoln's Emancipation Proclamation freeing the slaves, King led a march of 200,000 persons, black and white, from the Washington Monument to the Lincoln Memorial. Before this throng, and to millions who watched on television, he delivered this unforgettable speech.

Five score years ago, a great American, in whose symbolic shadow we stand, signed the Emancipation Proclamation. This momentous decree came as a great beacon light of hope to millions of Negro slaves who had been seared in the flames of with-

ering injustice. It came as a joyous daybreak to end the long
night of captivity.

But one hundred years later, we must face the tragic fact   2
that the Negro is still not free. One hundred years later, the life
of the Negro is still sadly crippled by the manacles of segregation
and the chains of discrimination. One hundred years later, the
Negro lives on a lonely island of poverty in the midst of a vast
ocean of material prosperity. One hundred years later, the Negro is still languishing in the corners of American society and
finds himself an exile in his own land. So we have come here today to dramatize an appalling condition.

In a sense we have come to our nation's capital to cash a   3
check. When the architects of our republic wrote the magnificent words of the Constitution and the Declaration of Independence, they were signing a promissory note to which every
American was to fall heir. This note was a promise that all men
would be guaranteed the unalienable rights of life, liberty, and
the pursuit of happiness.

It is obvious today that America has defaulted on this prom-   4
issory note insofar as her citizens of color are concerned. Instead
of honoring this sacred obligation, America has given the Negro
people a bad check; a check which has come back marked "insufficient funds." But we refuse to believe that the bank of justice is bankrupt. We refuse to believe that there are insufficient
funds in the great vaults of opportunity of this nation. So we
have come to cash this check — a check that will give us upon
demand the riches of freedom and the security of justice. We
have also come to this hallowed spot to remind America of the
fierce urgency of *now*. This is no time to engage in the luxury of
cooling off or to take the tranquilizing drugs of gradualism. *Now*
is the time to make real the promises of Democracy. *Now* is the
time to rise from the dark and desolate valley of segregation to
the sunlit path of racial justice. *Now* is the time to open the
doors of opportunity to all of God's children. *Now* is the time to
lift our nation from the quicksands of racial injustice to the solid
rock of brotherhood.

It would be fatal for the nation to overlook the urgency of   5
the moment and to underestimate the determination of the Negro. This sweltering summer of the Negro's legitimate discontent

will not pass until there is an invigorating autumn of freedom and equality. 1963 is not an end, but a beginning. Those who hope that the Negro needed to blow off steam and will now be content will have a rude awakening if the nation returns to business as usual. There will be neither rest nor tranquillity in America until the Negro is granted his citizenship rights. The whirlwinds of revolt will continue to shake the foundations of our nation until the bright day of justice emerges.

But there is something that I must say to my people who stand on the warm threshold which leads into the palace of justice. In the process of gaining our rightful place we must not be guilty of wrongful deeds. Let us not seek to satisfy our thirst for freedom by drinking from the cup of bitterness and hatred. We must forever conduct our struggle on the high plane of dignity and discipline. We must not allow our creative protest to degenerate into physical violence. Again and again we must rise to the majestic heights of meeting physical force with soul force. The marvelous new militancy which has engulfed the Negro community must not lead us to a distrust of all white people, for many of our white brothers, as evidenced by their presence here today, have come to realize that their destiny is tied up with our destiny and their freedom is inextricably bound to our freedom. We cannot walk alone.

And as we walk, we must make the pledge that we shall march ahead. We cannot turn back. There are those who are asking the devotees of civil rights, "When will you be satisfied?" We can never be satisfied as long as the Negro is the victim of the unspeakable horrors of police brutality. We can never be satisfied as long as our bodies, heavy with the fatigue of travel, cannot gain lodging in the motels of the highways and the hotels of the cities. We cannot be satisfied as long as the Negro's basic mobility is from a smaller ghetto to a larger one. We can never be satisfied as long as a Negro in Mississippi cannot vote and a Negro in New York believes he has nothing for which to vote. No, no, we are not satisfied, and we will not be satisfied until justice rolls down like waters and righteousness like a mighty stream.

I am not unmindful that some of you have come here out of great trials and tribulations. Some of you have come fresh from narrow jail cells. Some of you have come from areas where your quest for freedom left you battered by the storms of persecution and staggered by the winds of police brutality. You have been the veterans of creative suffering. Continue to work with the faith that unearned suffering is redemptive.

Go back to Mississippi, go back to Alabama, go back to   9 South Carolina, go back to Georgia, go back to Louisiana, go back to the slums and ghettos of our northern cities, knowing that somehow this situation can and will be changed. Let us not wallow in the valley of despair.

I say to you today, my friends, that in spite of the difficulties   10 and frustrations of the moment I still have a dream. It is a dream deeply rooted in the American dream.

I have a dream that one day this nation will rise up and live   11 out the true meaning of its creed: "We hold these truths to be self-evident; that all men are created equal."

I have a dream that one day on the red hills of Georgia the   12 sons of former slaves and the sons of former slaveowners will be able to sit down together at the table of brotherhood.

I have a dream that one day even the state of Mississippi, a   13 desert state sweltering with the heat of injustice and oppression, will be transformed into an oasis of freedom and justice.

I have a dream that my four little children will one day live   14 in a nation where they will not be judged by the color of their skin but by the content of their character.

I have a dream today.   15

I have a dream that one day the state of Alabama, whose   16 governor's lips are presently dripping with the words of interposition and nullification, will be transformed into a situation where little black boys and black girls will be able to join hands with little white boys and white girls and walk together as sisters and brothers.

I have a dream today.   17

I have a dream that one day every valley shall be exalted,   18 every hill and mountain shall be made low, the rough places will be made plain, and the crooked places will be made straight, and the glory of the Lord shall be revealed, and all flesh shall see it together.

This is our hope. This is the faith with which I return to the 19
South. With this faith we will be able to hew out of the mountain of despair a stone of hope. With this faith we will be able to transform the jangling discords of our nation into a beautiful symphony of brotherhood. With this faith we will be able to work together, to pray together, to struggle together, to go to jail together, to stand up for freedom together, knowing that we will be free one day.

This will be the day when all of God's children will be able 20
to sing with new meaning

> My country, 'tis of thee,
> Sweet land of liberty,
>   Of thee I sing:
> Land where my fathers died,
> Land of the pilgrims' pride,
> From every mountain-side
>   Let freedom ring.

And if America is to be a great nation this must become 21
true. So let freedom ring from the prodigious hilltops of New Hampshire. Let freedom ring from the mighty mountains of New York. Let freedom ring from the heightening Alleghenies of Pennsylvania!

Let freedom ring from the snowcapped Rockies of Colorado! 22
Let freedom ring from the curvaceous peaks of California! 23
But not only that; let freedom ring from Stone Mountain of 24
Georgia!

Let freedom ring from Lookout Mountain of Tennessee! 25
Let freedom ring from every hill and molehill of Mississippi. 26
From every mountainside, let freedom ring.

When we let freedom ring, when we let it ring from every 27
village and every hamlet, from every state and every city, we will be able to speed up that day when all of God's children, black men and white men, Jews and Gentiles, Protestants and Catholics, will be able to join hands and sing in the words of the old Negro spiritual, "Free at last! free at last! thank God almighty, we are free at last!"

QUESTIONS ON MEANING AND PURPOSE

1. What is the apparent PURPOSE of this speech?
2. What THESIS does King develop in his first four paragraphs?
3. What does King mean by the "marvelous new militancy which has engulfed the Negro community" (paragraph 6)? Does this contradict King's nonviolent philosophy?
4. In what passages of his speech does King notice events of history? Where does he acknowledge the historic occasion on which he is speaking?
5. To what extent does King's personal authority lend power to his words?

QUESTIONS ON WRITING STRATEGY

1. What examples of particular injustices does King offer in paragraph 7? In his speech as a whole, do his observations tend to be GENERAL or SPECIFIC?
2. Explain King's analogy of the bad check (paragraphs 3 and 4). What similarity do you find between it and any of the parables in the Bible, such as those of the lost sheep, the lost silver, and the prodigal son (Luke 15: 1–32)? (For analogy, see Chapter 7.)
3. What other analogy does King later develop?
4. What indicates that King's words were meant primarily for an AUDIENCE of listeners, and only secondarily for a reading audience? To hear these indications, try reading the speech aloud. What use of PARALLELISM do you notice?
5. Where in the speech does King acknowledge that not all of his listeners are black?
6. How much EMPHASIS does King place on the past? On the future?

QUESTIONS ON LANGUAGE

1. In general, is the language of King's speech ABSTRACT or CONCRETE? How is this level appropriate to the speaker's message and to the span of history with which he deals?
2. Point to memorable FIGURES OF SPEECH.
3. Define momentous (paragraph 1); manacles, languishing (2); promissory note (3); defaulted, hallowed, gradualism (4); inextricably

(6); mobility, ghetto (7); tribulations, redemptive (8); interposition, nullification (16); prodigious (21); curvaceous (23); hamlet (27).

SUGGESTIONS FOR WRITING

1. Has America (or your locality) today moved closer in any respects to the fulfillment of King's dream? Discuss this question in an essay, giving specific examples.
2. Argue in favor of some course of action in a situation that you consider an injustice. Racial injustice is one possible area, or unfairness to any minority, or to women, children, the old, ex-convicts, the handicapped, the poor. If possible, narrow your subject to a particular incident or a local situation on which you can write knowledgeably.

· Russell Baker ·

RUSSELL BAKER was born in Virginia in 1925 and earned his B.A. from Johns Hopkins University. A contributor to a number of magazines, including the *Ladies' Home Journal*, *McCall's*, *Sports Illustrated*, *Saturday Evening Post*, and the *New York Times Magazine*, he worked as a reporter for the Baltimore *Sun* from 1947 to 1954 and as a member of the Washington Bureau of the *New York Times* from 1954 to 1962, covering the White House. Since then he has written a widely syndicated column, "The Observer," in which humor and social criticism are blended. In 1979 he won the Pulitzer Prize for distinguished commentary. Among his most recent books are two collections of essays, *So This Is Depravity* (1980) and *The Rescue of Miss Yaskell and Other Pipe Dreams* (1983); and *Growing Up* (1982), the best-selling story of his own life, which won him the 1983 Pulitzer Prize for biography.

Universal Military Motion

Baker included a series called "Universal Military Motion" in *The Rescue of Miss Yaskell*, his 1983 collection of "Observer" columns. In this essay, with tongue firmly in cheek, he responds to a Pentagon proposal with a scheme of his own: one that will confuse the enemy and offer more protection to the MX missile system than its developers could have hoped for. See how well you think his plan would work.

The idea behind the MX missile system is sound enough. 1 Place bomb-bearing missiles on wheels and keep them moving constantly through thousands of miles of desert so enemy bombers will not have a fixed target. To confuse things further, move decoy missiles over the same routes so the enemy cannot distinguish between false missiles and the real thing.

As my strategic thinkers immediately pointed out, however, 2 the MX missile system makes very little sense unless matched by

an MX Pentagon system. What is the point, they asked, of in-
stalling a highly mobile missile system if its command center, the
Pentagon, remains anchored like a moose with four broken legs
on the bank of the Potomac River?

This is why we propose building 250 moveable structures so   3
precisely like the Pentagon that no one can tell our fake Pentagons from the real thing and to keep all of them, plus the real
Pentagon, in constant motion through the country.

Our first plan was to move only the real Pentagon, which   4
would be placed on a large flat-bottom truck bed and driven
about the countryside on the existing highway system. We immediately realized, however, that this would not provide sufficient protection against nuclear attack. The Pentagon is very big
and easily noticeable. When it is driven along at 55 miles per
hour, people can see it coming from miles away. It attracts attention. In short, it is a fat, easily detected target.

With 250 fake Pentagons constantly cruising the roads, the   5
problem is solved. Now, trying to distinguish the real Pentagon
from the fake Pentagons, enemy attackers will face the maddening problem of finding a needle in a haystack. With 251 Pentagons in circulation, the sight of a Pentagon on the highway will
attract no more attention than a politician's indictment. Thus
we foil the enemy's spies.

Still, to add another margin of security we will confuse mat-   6
ters further by building 1,500 Pentagon-shaped fast-food restau-
rants along the nation's highways.

Each will be an exact replica of the real Pentagon, at least as   7
seen from the outside. Inside, of course, they will be equipped to
provide all the necessities for producing acute indigestion, thus
providing the wherewithal of highway travel and, in the process,
earning the Government a little return on its investment.

Occasionally, when generals and admirals tire of touring   8
and yearn for a little stability, the real Pentagon will be parked
alongside the road to masquerade as a fast-food Pentagon. The
danger of highway travelers wandering in for a quick hot dog
and making trouble while the authentic Pentagon is in the
"parked" or "fast-food" mode has also been considered.

These interlopers will simply be told by receptionists that   9
hot dogs are in the back of the building and directed to walk the

long route around the Pentagon's outer ring. As they drop from exhaustion they will be removed by military police, carried to their cars, given free hot dogs and advised that next time they should enter their Pentagon fast-food dispensary through the rear door.

There are problems to be ironed out in the MX Pentagon, but we are too busy at the moment perfecting our MX Congress system to trifle with details. With 850 United States Capitols on the highway, we have an extremely touchy problem in deciding whether a Capitol or a Pentagon should have the right of way when they meet at an intersection.

10

QUESTIONS ON MEANING AND PURPOSE

1. Is Baker arguing *for* something, or *against* something? Explain.
2. Who are "my strategic thinkers" (paragraph 2)?
3. By what steps does the author's plan escalate?
4. What difficulties does Baker's plan blithely ignore?
5. Who and what are the targets of the author's SATIRE? Give EVIDENCE for your answer.

QUESTIONS ON WRITING STRATEGY

1. What role do exaggeration and oversimplification play in Baker's essay?
2. Where in his essay does the author make good use of UNDERSTATEMENT?
3. "Universal Military Motion" was originally written as a newspaper column. What constraints or limitations does such a form impose upon a writer? How well has Baker triumphed over them?
4. What segment of Baker's AUDIENCE would you expect to enjoy this essay most?

QUESTIONS ON LANGUAGE

1. Where in Baker's essay do FIGURES OF SPEECH add humor?
2. Do you believe the author to be serious when he uses the phrase *sound enough* in paragraph 1? Explain.

SUGGESTIONS FOR WRITING

1. Do a little research on the MX missile. In a paragraph sum up when it was conceived, what it can do, where and how it is meant to be used. Then, in a second paragraph, state your own argument for or against the necessity of deploying such a weapon.
2. Write a satire in which you attack some aspect of contemporary American life that seems to you absurd. Limit yourself to 500 or 600 words.

· Gloria Steinem ·

One of the foremost feminists of our day, GLORIA STEINEM was born in Toledo, Ohio, in 1934. After earning a B.A. degree from Smith College in 1956, she went to India on a Chester Bowles Asian fellowship. She is a contributing editor of *New York* magazine, which she helped to found in 1968. In 1971 she was also one of the founding editors of *Ms.,* for which she still writes regularly. She has been active in many political campaigns, civil rights organizations, peace movements, and women's groups. In 1972 *McCall's* magazine named her Woman of the Year, and in 1977 she held a Woodrow Wilson International Center for Scholars fellowship. She has written a number of magazine articles and three books, most recently *Outrageous Acts and Everyday Rebellions* (1983).

The Importance of Work

Steinem included "The Importance of Work" in *Outrageous Acts and Everyday Rebellions.* In her essay, she explores prevailing attitudes toward women in the workplace and suggests that having a paying job is as important to women as to men. Why, then, are women reluctant to say they work not only for money but for less tangible rewards as well?

Toward the end of the 1970s, *The Wall Street Journal* devoted an eight-part, front-page series to "the working woman" — that is, the influx of women into the paid-labor force — as the greatest change in American life since the Industrial Revolution.

Many women readers greeted both the news and the definition with cynicism. After all, women have always worked. If all the productive work of human maintenance that women do in the home were valued at its replacement cost, the gross national product of the United States would go up by 26 percent. It's just that we are now more likely than ever before to leave our poorly rewarded, low-security, high-risk job of homemaking (though we're still trying to explain that it's a perfectly good one and that the problem is male society's refusal both to do it and to give it an economic value) for more secure, independent, and better-paid jobs outside the home.

Obviously, the real work revolution won't come until all productive work is rewarded — including child rearing and other jobs done in the home — and men are integrated into so-called women's work as well as vice versa. But the radical change being touted by the *Journal* and other media is one part of that long integration process: the unprecedented flood of women into salaried jobs, that is, into the labor force as it has been male-defined and previously occupied by men. We are already more than 41 percent of it — the highest proportion in history. Given the fact that women also make up a whopping 69 percent of the "discouraged labor force" (that is, people who need jobs but don't get counted in the unemployment statistics because they've given up looking), plus an official female unemployment rate that is substantially higher than men's, it's clear that we could expand to become fully half of the national work force by 1990.

Faced with this determination of women to find a little independence and to be paid and honored for our work, experts have rushed to ask: "Why?" It's a question rarely directed at male workers. Their basic motivations of survival and personal satisfaction are taken for granted. Indeed, men are regarded as "odd" and therefore subjects for sociological study and journalistic reports only when they *don't* have work, even if they are rich and don't need jobs or are poor and can't find them. Nonetheless, pollsters and sociologists have gone to great expense to prove that women work outside the home because of dire financial need, or if we persist despite the presence of a wage-earning male, out of some desire to buy "little extras" for our families, or even out of good old-fashioned penis envy.

Job interviewers and even our own families may still ask salaried women the big "Why?" If we have small children at home or are in some job regarded as "men's work," the incidence of such questions increases. Condescending or accusatory versions of "What's a nice girl like you doing in a place like this?" have not disappeared from the workplace.

How do we answer these assumptions that we are "working"   6
out of some pressing or peculiar need? Do we feel okay about arguing that it's as natural for us to have salaried jobs as for our
husbands — whether or not we have young children at home?
Can we enjoy strong career ambitions without worrying about
being thought "unfeminine"? When we confront men's growing
resentment of women competing in the work force (often in the
form of such guilt-producing accusations as "You're taking
men's jobs away" or "You're damaging your children"), do we
simply state that a decent job is a basic human right for everybody?

I'm afraid the answer is often no. As individuals and as a   7
movement, we tend to retreat into some version of a tacti-
cally questionable defense: "Womenworkbecausewehaveto."
The phrase has become one word, one key on the typewriter —
an economic form of the socially "feminine" stance of passivity
and self-sacrifice. Under attack, we still tend to present ourselves
as creatures of economic necessity and familial devotion.
"Womenworkbecausewehaveto" has become the easiest thing to
say.

Like most truisms, this one is easy to prove with statistics.   8
Economic need *is* the most consistent work motive — for
women as well as men. In 1976, for instance, 43 percent of all
women in the paid-labor force were single, widowed, separated,
or divorced, and working to support themselves and their de-
pendents. An additional 21 percent were married to men who
had earned less than ten thousand dollars in the previous year,
the minimum then required to support a family of four. In fact,
if you take men's pensions, stocks, real estate, and various forms
of accumulated wealth into account, a good statistical case can
be made that there are more women who "have" to work (that
is, who have neither the accumulated wealth, nor husbands
whose work or wealth can support them for the rest of their
lives) than there are men with the same need. If we were going to
ask one group "Do you really need this job?" we should ask men.

But the first weakness of the whole "have to work" defense   9
is its deceptiveness. Anyone who has ever experienced dehu-
manized life on welfare or any other confidence-shaking depen-

dency knows that a paid job may be preferable to the dole, even when the handout is coming from a family member. Yet the will and self-confidence to work on one's own can diminish as dependency and fear increase. That may explain why — contrary to the "have to" rationale — wives of men who earn less than three thousand dollars a year are actually *less* likely to be employed than wives whose husbands make ten thousand dollars a year or more.

Furthermore, the greatest proportion of employed wives is 10 found among families with a total household income of twenty-five to fifty thousand dollars a year. This is the statistical underpinning used by some sociologists to prove that women's work is mainly important for boosting families into the middle or upper middle class. Thus, women's incomes are largely used for buying "luxuries" and "little extras": a neat double-whammy that renders us secondary within our families, and makes our jobs expendable in hard times. We may even go along with this interpretation (at least, up to the point of getting fired so a male can have our job). It preserves a husbandly ego-need to be seen as the primary breadwinner, and still allows us a safe "feminine" excuse for working.

But there are often rewards that we're not confessing. As 11 noted in *The Two-Career Couple*, by Francine and Douglas Hall: "Women who hold jobs by choice, even blue-collar routine jobs, are more satisfied with their lives than are the full-time housewives."

In addition to personal satisfaction, there is also society's 12 need for all its members' talents. Suppose that jobs were given out on only a "have to work" basis to both women and men — one job per household. It would be unthinkable to lose the unique abilities of, for instance, Eleanor Holmes Norton, the distinguished chair of the Equal Employment Opportunity Commission. But would we then be forced to question the important work of her husband, Edward Norton, who is also a distinguished lawyer? Since men earn more than twice as much as women on the average, the wife in most households would be more likely to give up her job. Does that mean the nation could do as well without millions of its nurses, teachers, and secre-

taries? Or that the rare man who earns less than his wife should
give up his job?

It was this kind of waste of human talents on a society-wide   13
scale that traumatized millions of unemployed or underem-
ployed Americans during the Depression. Then, a one-job-per-
household rule seemed somewhat justified, yet the concept was
used to displace women workers only, create intolerable depen-
dencies, and waste female talent that the country needed. That
Depression experience, plus the energy and example of women
who were finally allowed to work during the manpower shortage
created by World War II, led Congress to reinterpret the meaning of the country's full-employment goal in its Economic Act of
1946. Full employment was officially defined as "the employment of those who want to work, without regard to whether
their employment is, by some definition, necessary. This goal
applies equally to men and to women." Since bad economic
times are again creating a resentment of employed women — as
well as creating more need for women to be employed — we
need such a goal more than ever. Women are again being caught
in a tragic double bind: We are required to be strong and then
punished for our strength.

Clearly, anything less than government and popular com-   14
mitment to this 1946 definition of full employment will leave the
less powerful groups, whoever they may be, in danger. Almost
as important as the financial penalty paid by the powerless is the
suffering that comes from being shut out of paid and recognized
work. Without it, we lose much of our self-respect and our ability to prove that we are alive by making some difference in the
world. That's just as true for the suburban woman as it is for the
unemployed steel worker.

But it won't be easy to give up the passive defense of "we-   15
workbecausewehaveto."

When a woman who is struggling to support her children   16
and grandchildren on welfare sees her neighbor working as a
waitress, even though that neighbor's husband has a job, she
may feel resentful; and the waitress (of course, not the waitress's
husband) may feel guilty. Yet unless we establish the obligation
to provide a job for everyone who is willing and able to work,

that welfare woman may herself be penalized by policies that give out only one public-service job per household. She and her daughter will have to make a painful and divisive decision about which of them gets that precious job, and the whole household will have to survive on only one salary.

A job as a human right is a principle that applies to men as well as women. But women have more cause to fight for it. The phenomenon of the "working woman" has been held responsible for everything from an increase in male impotence (which turned out, incidentally, to be attributable to medication for high blood pressure) to the rising cost of steak (which was due to high energy costs and beef import restrictions, not women's refusal to prepare the cheaper, slower-cooking cuts). Unless we see a job as part of every citizen's right to autonomy and personal fulfillment, we will continue to be vulnerable to someone else's idea of what "need" is, and whose "need" counts the most. 17

In many ways, women who do not have to work for simple survival, but who choose to do so nonetheless, are on the frontier of asserting this right for all women. Those with well-to-do husbands are dangerously easy for us to resent and put down. It's easier still to resent women from families of inherited wealth, even though men generally control and benefit from that wealth. (There is no Rockefeller Sisters Fund, no J. P. Morgan & Daughters, and sons-in-law may be the ones who really sleep their way to power.) But to prevent a woman whose husband or father is wealthy from earning her own living, and from gaining the self-confidence that comes with that ability, is to keep her needful of that unearned power and less willing to disperse it. Moreover, it is to lose forever her unique talents. 18

Perhaps modern feminists have been guilty of a kind of reverse snobbism that keeps us from reaching out to the wives and daughters of wealthy men; yet it was exactly such women who refused the restrictions of class and financed the first wave of feminist revolution. 19

For most of us, however, "womenworkbecausewehaveto" is just true enough to be seductive as a personal defense. 20

If we use it without also staking out the larger human right to a job, however, we will never achieve that right. And we will 21 always be subject to the false argument that independence for women is a luxury affordable only in good economic times. Alternatives to layoffs will not be explored, acceptable unemployment will always be used to frighten those with jobs into accepting low wages, and we will never remedy the real cost, both to families and to the country, of dependent women and a massive loss of talent.

Worst of all, we may never learn to find productive, honored work as a natural part of ourselves and as one of life's basic pleasures.   22

QUESTIONS ON MEANING AND PURPOSE

1. What objection does Steinem raise to the *Wall Street Journal*'s definition of "the working woman"?
2. What is the author's response to accusations that women who work for pay are robbing men of their jobs and damaging their families? Or to the view that women of wealth ought not to work?
3. Sum up the author's objection to the justification most often given for women's holding down paid jobs: "Womenworkbecausewehaveto." According to Steinem, why do women resort to this defense?
4. According to the author, what benefits accrue to individuals and to society when full employment is the rule rather than the exception?
5. Does this essay appeal chiefly to reason or to emotion? Cite EVIDENCE for your answer.
6. For what, exactly, does Steinem argue? State her THESIS.

QUESTIONS ON WRITING STRATEGY

1. Where does Steinem's INTRODUCTION end and the body of her essay begin? What points in her introduction does the author choose not to pursue? What does her essay gain or lose from this decision?
2. What EFFECT does the author's use of statistics have on her argument?

3. What does Steinem achieve by casting the ideas in paragraph 6 into a series of RHETORICAL QUESTIONS — which she then answers herself in paragraph 7?
4. To what extent does the quotation in paragraph 11 strengthen Steinem's argument?
5. What is Steinem's point in paragraph 12? By what means does she make that point? What revelations in paragraph 13 buttress the material in paragraph 12?
6. What clues in Steinem's essay indicate that it was written for a general rather than a specialized AUDIENCE?

QUESTIONS ON LANGUAGE

1. Look up the following words if you need help defining them: touted (paragraph 3); truisms (8); rationale (9); autonomy, vulnerable (17); disperse (18).
2. What is a double-whammy (paragraph 10)? A double bind (13)?
3. How would you characterize Steinem's word choice: colorful, utilitarian, flowery, careless, or lyrical?

SUGGESTIONS FOR WRITING

1. In paragraph 6 of her essay, Steinem mentions two charges occasionally leveled at working women: "You're taking men's jobs away" and "You're damaging your children." Write an essay in which you reply to *one* of these accusations.
2. Write a brief argument attacking or agreeing with the old adage "A woman's place is in the home." A serious TONE is not required.

· Richard Rodriguez ·

The son of Spanish-speaking Mexican-Americans, RICHARD
RODRIGUEZ was born in 1944 in San Francisco. After graduation from Stanford, he continued his studies at Columbia, the
Warburg Institute in London, and the University of California, Berkeley. Now a writer and journalist, Rodriguez has
been living recently in Mexico City, preparing a book about
Mexico and California. His essays have appeared in *The
American Scholar, Change, Saturday Review* and other magazines; and he has published a widely discussed book of essays
in autobiography, *Hunger of Memory* (1982).

Aria: A Memoir of
a Bilingual Childhood

"Aria: A Memoir of a Bilingual Childhood" is taken from
Hunger of Memory. First published in *The American Scholar* in
1981, it contains both poignant memoir and persuasive argument. Setting forth his views of bilingual education, the author measures the gains and losses that resulted when English
gradually replaced the Spanish spoken in his childhood
home. To the child Rodriguez, Spanish was a private language, English a public one. Would the boy have learned
faster and better if his teachers had allowed him the use of his
native language in school?

I remember, to start with, that day in Sacramento, in a Cali-   1
fornia now nearly thirty years past, when I first entered a classroom — able to understand about fifty stray English words. The
third of four children, I had been preceded by my older brother
and sister to a neighborhood Roman Catholic school. But neither of them had revealed very much about their classroom experiences. They left each morning and returned each afternoon,
always together, speaking Spanish as they climbed the five steps

to the porch. And their mysterious books, wrapped in brown shopping-bag paper, remained on the table next to the door, closed firmly behind them.

An accident of geography sent me to a school where all my classmates were white and many were the children of doctors and lawyers and business executives. On that first day of school, my classmates must certainly have been uneasy to find themselves apart from their families, in the first institution of their lives. But I was astonished. I was fated to be the "problem student" in class.

The nun said, in a friendly but oddly impersonal voice: "Boys and girls, this is Richard Rodriguez." (I heard her sound it out: *Rich-heard Road-ree-guess.*) It was the first time I had heard anyone say my name in English. "Richard," the nun repeated more slowly, writing my name down in her book. Quickly I turned to see my mother's face dissolve in a watery blur behind the pebbled-glass door.

Now, many years later, I hear of something called "bilingual education" — a scheme proposed in the late 1960s by Hispanic-American social activists, later endorsed by a congressional vote. It is a program that seeks to permit non-English-speaking children (many from lower class homes) to use their "family language" as the language of school. Such, at least, is the aim its supporters announce. I hear them, and am forced to say no: It is not possible for a child, any child, ever to use his family's language in school. Not to understand this is to misunderstand the public uses of schooling and to trivialize the nature of intimate life.

Memory teaches me what I know of these matters. The boy reminds the adult. I was a bilingual child, but of a certain kind: "socially disadvantaged," the son of working-class parents, both Mexican immigrants.

In the early years of my boyhood, my parents coped very well in America. My father had steady work. My mother managed at home. They were nobody's victims. When we moved to a house many blocks from the Mexican-American section of town, they were not intimidated by those two or three neighbors who initially tried to make us unwelcome. ("Keep your brats away from my sidewalk!") But despite all they achieved, or perhaps because they had so much to achieve, they lacked any deep feeling of ease, of belonging in public. They regarded the people at work or in crowds as being very distant from us. Those were the others, *los gringos*. That term was interchangeable in their speech with another, even more telling: *los americanos*.

I grew up in a house where the only regular guests were my 7 relations. On a certain day, enormous families of relatives would visit us, and there would be so many people that the noise and the bodies would spill out to the backyard and onto the front porch. Then for weeks no one would come. (If the doorbell rang, it was usually a salesman.) Our house stood apart — gaudy yellow in a row of white bungalows. We were the people with the noisy dog, the people who raised chickens. We were the foreigners on the block. A few neighbors would smile and wave at us. We waved back. But until I was seven years old, I did not know the name of the old couple living next door or the names of the kids living across the street.

In public, my father and mother spoke a hesitant, accented, 8 and not always grammatical English. And then they would have to strain, their bodies tense, to catch the sense of what was rapidly said by *los gringos*. At home, they returned to Spanish. The language of their Mexican past sounded in counterpoint to the English spoken in public. The words would come quickly, with ease. Conveyed through those sounds was the pleasing, soothing, consoling reminder that one was at home.

During those years when I was first learning to speak, my 9 mother and father addressed me only in Spanish; in Spanish I learned to reply. By contrast, English (*inglés*) was the language I came to associate with gringos, rarely heard in the house. I learned my first words of English overhearing my parents speaking to strangers. At six years of age, I knew just enough words for my mother to trust me on errands to stores one block away — but no more.

I was then a listening child, careful to hear the very different 10 sounds of Spanish and English. Wide-eyed with hearing, I'd listen to sounds more than to words. First, there were English (gringo) sounds. So many words still were unknown to me that when the butcher or the lady at the drugstore said something, exotic polysyllabic sounds would bloom in the midst of their sentences. Often the speech of people in public seemed to me very loud, booming with confidence. The man behind the counter would literally ask, "What can I do for you?" But by being so firm and clear, the sound of his voice said that he was a gringo; he belonged in public society. There were also the high, nasal notes of middle-class American speech — which I rarely am conscious of hearing today because I hear them so often, but could not stop hearing when I was a boy. Crowds at Safeway or at bus stops were noisy with the birdlike sounds of *los gringos*. I'd move away from them all — all the chirping chatter above me.

My own sounds I was unable to hear, but I knew that I spoke English poorly. My words could not extend to form complete thoughts. And the words I did speak I didn't know well enough to make distinct sounds. (Listeners would usually lower their heads to hear better what I was trying to say.) But it was one thing for *me* to speak English with difficulty; it was more troubling to hear my parents speaking in public: their high-whining vowels and guttural consonants; their sentences that got stuck with "eh" and "ah" sounds; the confused syntax; the hesitant rhythm of sounds so different from the way gringos spoke. I'd notice, moreover, that my parents' voices were softer than those of gringos we would meet.

I am tempted to say now that none of this mattered. (In adulthood I am embarrassed by childhood fears.) And, in a way, it didn't matter very much that my parents could not speak English with ease. Their linguistic difficulties had no serious consequences. My mother and father made themselves understood at the county hospital clinic and at government offices. And yet, in another way, it mattered very much. It was unsettling to hear my parents struggle with English. Hearing them, I'd grow nervous, and my clutching trust in their protection and power would be weakened.

There were many times like the night at a brightly lit gasoline station (a blaring white memory) when I stood uneasily hearing my father talk to a teenage attendant. I do not recall what they were saying, but I cannot forget the sounds my father made as he spoke. At one point his words slid together to form one long word — sounds as confused as the threads of blue and green oil in the puddle next to my shoes. His voice rushed through what he had left to say. Toward the end, he reached falsetto notes, appealing to his listener's understanding. I looked away at the lights of passing automobiles. I tried not to hear any more. But I heard only too well the attendant's reply, his calm, easy tones. Shortly afterward, headed for home, I shivered when my father put his hand on my shoulder. The very first chance that I got, I evaded his grasp and ran on ahead into the dark, skipping with feigned boyish exuberance.

But then there was Spanish: *español*, the language rarely   14
heard away from the house; *español*, the language which seemed to me therefore a private language, my family's language. To hear its sounds was to feel myself specially recognized as one of the family, apart from *los otros*. A simple remark, an inconsequential comment could convey that assurance. My parents would say something to me and I would feel embraced by the sounds of their words. Those sounds said: *I am speaking with ease in Spanish. I am addressing you in words I never use with los gringos. I recognize you as someone special, close, like no one outside. You belong with us. In the family. Ricardo.*

At the age of six, well past the time when most middle-class   15
children no longer notice the difference between sounds uttered at home and words spoken in public, I had a different experience. I lived in a world compounded of sounds. I was a child longer than most. I lived in a magical world, surrounded by sounds both pleasing and fearful. I shared with my family a language enchantingly private — different from that used in the city around us.

Just opening or closing the screen door behind me was an   16
important experience. I'd rarely leave home all alone or without feeling reluctance. Walking down the sidewalk, under the canopy of tall trees, I'd warily notice the (suddenly) silent neighborhood kids who stood warily watching me. Nervously, I'd arrive at the grocery store to hear there the sounds of the gringo, reminding me that in this so-big world I was a foreigner. But if leaving home was never routine, neither was coming back.

Walking toward our house, climbing the steps from the sidewalk, in summer when the front door was open, I'd hear voices beyond the screen door talking in Spanish. For a second or two I'd stay, linger there listening. Smiling, I'd hear my mother call out, saying in Spanish, "Is that you, Richard?" Those were her words, but all the while her sounds would assure me: *You are home now. Come closer inside. With us.* "Sí," I'd reply.

Once more inside the house, I would resume my place in the   17
family. The sounds would grow harder to hear. Once more at home, I would grow less conscious of them. It required, however, no more than the blurt of the doorbell to alert me all over again to listen to sounds. The house would turn instantly quiet while my mother went to the door. I'd hear her hard English sounds. I'd wait to hear her voice turn to soft-sounding Spanish, which assured me, as surely as did the clicking tongue of the lock on the door, that the stranger was gone.

Plainly it is not healthy to hear such sounds so often. It is   18
not healthy to distinguish public from private sounds so easily. I remained cloistered by sounds, timid and shy in public, too dependent on the voices at home. And yet I was a very happy child when I was at home. I remember many nights when my father would come back from work, and I'd hear him call out to my mother in Spanish, sounding relieved. In Spanish, his voice would sound the light and free notes that he never could manage in English. Some nights I'd jump up just hearing his voice. My brother and I would come running into the room where he was with our mother. Our laughing (so deep was the pleasure!) became screaming. Like others who feel the pain of public alienation, we transformed the knowledge of our public separateness into a consoling reminder of our intimacy. Excited, our voices joined in a celebration of sounds. *We are speaking now the way we never speak out in public — we are together*, the sounds told me. Some nights no one seemed willing to loosen the hold that sounds had on us. At dinner we invented new words that sounded Spanish, but made sense only to us. We pieced together new words by taking, say, an English verb and giving it Spanish endings. My mother's instructions at bedtime would be lacquered with mock-urgent tones. Or a word like *sí*, sounded in

several notes, would convey added measures of feeling. Tongues lingered around the edges of words, especially fat vowels, and we happily sounded that military drum roll, the twirling roar of the Spanish *r*. Family language, my family's sounds: the voices of my parents and sisters and brother. Their voices insisting: *You belong here. We are family members. Related. Special to one another. Listen!* Voices singing and sighing, rising and straining, then surging, teeming with pleasure which burst syllables into fragments of laughter. At times it seemed there was steady quiet only when, from another room, the rustling whispers of my parents faded and I edged closer to sleep.

Supporters of bilingual education imply today that students   19
like me miss a great deal by not being taught in their family's language. What they seem not to recognize is that, as a socially disadvantaged child, I regarded Spanish as a private language. It was a ghetto language that deepened and strengthened my feeling of public separateness. What I needed to learn in school was that I had the right, and the obligation, to speak the public language. The odd truth is that my first-grade classmates could have become bilingual, in the conventional sense of the word, more easily than I. Had they been taught early (as upper middle-class children often are taught) a "second language" like Spanish or French, they could have regarded it simply as another public language. In my case, such bilingualism could not have been so quickly achieved. What I did not believe was that I could speak a single public language.

Without question, it would have pleased me to have heard   20
my teachers address me in Spanish when I entered the classroom. I would have felt much less afraid. I would have imagined that my instructors were somehow "related" to me; I would indeed have heard their Spanish as my family's language. I would have trusted them and responded with ease. But I would have delayed — postponed for how long? — having to learn the language of public society. I would have evaded — and for how long? — learning the great lesson of school: that I had a public identity.

Fortunately, my teachers were unsentimental about their re-   21
sponsibility. What they understood was that I needed to speak

public English. So their voices would search me out, asking me questions. Each time I heard them I'd look up in surprise to see a nun's face frowning at me. I'd mumble, not really meaning to answer. The nun would persist. "Richard, stand up. Don't look at the floor. Speak up. Speak to the entire class, not just to me!" But I couldn't believe English could be my language to use. (In part, I did not want to believe it.) I continued to mumble. I resisted the teacher's demands. (Did I somehow suspect that once I learned this public language my family life would be changed?) Silent, waiting for the bell to sound, I remained dazed, diffident, afraid.

Because I wrongly imagined that English was intrinsically a 22 public language and Spanish was intrinsically private, I easily noted the difference between classroom language and the language at home. At school, words were directed to a general audience of listeners. ("Boys and girls . . . ") Words were meaningfully ordered. And the point was not self-expression alone, but to make oneself understood by many others. The teacher quizzed: "Boys and girls, why do we use that word in this sentence? Could we think of a better word to use there? Would the sentence change its meaning if the words were differently arranged? Isn't there a better way of saying much the same thing?" (I couldn't say. I wouldn't try to say.)

Three months passed. Five. A half year. Unsmiling, ever 23 watchful, my teachers noted my silence. They began to connect my behavior with the slow progress my brother and sisters were making. Until, one Saturday morning, three nuns arrived at the house to talk to our parents. Stiffly they sat on the blue living-room sofa. From the doorway of another room, spying on the visitors, I noted the incongruity, the clash of two worlds, the faces and voices of school intruding upon the familiar setting of home. I overheard one voice gently wondering, "Do your children speak only Spanish at home, Mrs. Rodriguez?" While another voice added, "That Richard especially seems so timid and shy."

That Rich-heard! 24

With great tact, the visitors continued, "Is it possible for you 25 and your husband to encourage your children to practice their English when they are home?" Of course my parents complied.

What would they not do for their children's well-being? And how could they question the Church's authority which those women represented? In an instant they agreed to give up the language (the sounds) which had revealed and accentuated our family's closeness. The moment after the visitors left, the change was observed. "*Ahora*, speak to us only *en inglés*," my father and mother told us.

At first, it seemed a kind of game. After dinner each night,   26
the family gathered together to practice "our" English. It was still then *inglés*, a language foreign to us, so we felt drawn to it as strangers. Laughing, we would try to define words we could not pronounce. We played with strange English sounds, often over-anglicizing our pronunciations. And we filled the smiling gaps of our sentences with familiar Spanish sounds. But that was cheating, somebody shouted, and everyone laughed.

In school, meanwhile, like my brother and sisters, I was re-   27
quired to attend a daily tutoring session. I needed a full year of this special work. I also needed my teachers to keep my attention from straying in class by calling out, "*Rich-heard*" — their English voices slowly loosening the ties to my other name, with its three notes, *Ri-car-do*. Most of all, I needed to hear my mother and father speak to me in a moment of seriousness in "broken" — suddenly heartbreaking — English. This scene was inevitable. One Saturday morning I entered the kitchen where my parents were talking, but I did not realize that they were talking in Spanish until, the moment they saw me, their voices changed and they began speaking English. The gringo sounds they uttered startled me. Pushed me away. In that moment of trivial misunderstanding and profound insight, I felt my throat twisted by unsounded grief. I simply turned and left the room. But I had no place to escape to where I could grieve in Spanish. My brother and sisters were speaking English in another part of the house.

Again and again in the days following, as I grew increasingly   28
angry, I was obliged to hear my mother and father encouraging me: "Speak to us *en inglés*." Only then did I determine to learn classroom English. Thus, sometime afterward it happened: one day in school, I raised my hand to volunteer an answer to a question. I spoke out in a loud voice and I did not think it re-

markable when the entire class understood. That day I moved very far from being the disadvantaged child I had been only days earlier. Taken hold at last was the belief, the calming assurance, that I *belonged* in public.

Shortly after, I stopped hearing the high, troubling sounds of *los gringos*. A more and more confident speaker of English, I didn't listen to how strangers sounded when they talked to me. With so many English-speaking people around me, I no longer heard American accents. Conversations quickened. Listening to persons whose voices sounded eccentrically pitched, I might note their sounds for a few seconds, but then I'd concentrate on what they were saying. Now when I heard someone's tone of voice — angry or questioning or sarcastic or happy or sad — I didn't distinguish it from the words it expressed. Sound and word were thus tightly wedded. At the end of each day I was often bemused, and always relieved, to realize how "soundless," though crowded with words, my day in public had been. An eight-year-old boy, I finally came to accept what had been technically true since my birth: I was an American citizen. 29

But diminished by then was the special feeling of closeness at home. Gone was the desperate, urgent, intense feeling of being at home among those with whom I felt intimate. Our family remained a loving family, but one greatly changed. We were no longer so close, no longer bound tightly together by the knowledge of our separateness from *los gringos*. Neither my older brother nor my sisters rushed home after school any more. Nor did I. When I arrived home, often there would be neighborhood kids in the house. Or the house would be empty of sounds. 30

Following the dramatic Americanization of their children, even my parents grew more publicly confident — especially my mother. First she learned the names of all the people on the block. Then she decided we needed to have a telephone in our house. My father, for his part, continued to use the word gringo, but it was no longer charged with bitterness or distrust. Stripped of any emotional content, the word simply became a name for those Americans not of Hispanic descent. Hearing him, sometimes, I wasn't sure if he was pronouncing the Spanish word *gringo*, or saying gringo in English. 31

There was a new silence at home. As we children learned 32

more and more English, we shared fewer and fewer words with our parents. Sentences needed to be spoken slowly when one of us addressed our mother or father. Often the parent wouldn't understand. The child would need to repeat himself. Still the parent misunderstood. The young voice, frustrated, would end up saying, "Never mind" — the subject was closed. Dinners would be noisy with the clinking of knives and forks against dishes. My mother would smile softly between her remarks; my father, at the other end of the table, would chew and chew his food while he stared over the heads of his children.

My mother! My father! After English became my primary   33
language, I no longer knew what words to use in addressing my parents. The old Spanish words (those tender accents of sound) I had earlier used — *mamá* and *papá* — I couldn't use any more. They would have been all-too-painful reminders of how much had changed in my life. On the other hand, the words I heard neighborhood kids call their parents seemed equally unsatisfactory. "Mother" and "father," "ma," "papa," "pa," "dad," "pop" (how I hated the all-American sound of that last word) — all these I felt were unsuitable terms of address for *my* parents. As a result, I never used them at home. Whenever I'd speak to my parents, I would try to get their attention by looking at them. In public conversations, I'd refer to them as my "parents" or my "mother" and "father."

My mother and father, for their part, responded differently,   34
as their children spoke to them less. My mother grew restless, seemed troubled and anxious at the scarceness of words exchanged in the house. She would question me about my day when I came home from school. She smiled at my small talk. She pried at the edges of my sentences to get me to say something more. ("What . . . ?") She'd join conversations she overheard, but her intrusions often stopped her children's talking. By contrast, my father seemed to grow reconciled to the new quiet. Though his English somewhat improved, he tended more and more to retire into silence. At dinner he spoke very little. One night his children and even his wife helplessly giggled at his garbled English pronunciation of the Catholic "Grace Before Meals." Thereafter he made his wife recite the prayer at the start

of each meal, even on formal occasions when there were guests in the house.

Hers became the public voice of the family. On official busi- 35 ness it was she, not my father, who would usually talk to strangers on the phone or in stores. We children grew so accustomed to his silence that years later we would routinely refer to his "shyness." (My mother often tried to explain: both of his parents died when he was eight. He was raised by an uncle who treated him as little more than a menial servant. He was never encouraged to speak. He grew up alone — a man of few words.) But I realized my father was not shy whenever I'd watch him speaking Spanish with relatives. Using Spanish, he was quickly effusive. Especially when talking with other men, his voice would spark, flicker, flare alive with varied sounds. In Spanish he expressed ideas and feelings he rarely revealed when speaking English. With firm Spanish sounds he conveyed a confidence and authority that English would never allow him.

The silence at home, however, was not simply the result of 36 fewer words passing between parents and children. More profound for me was the silence created by my inattention to sounds. At about the time I no longer bothered to listen with care to the sounds of English in public, I grew careless about listening to the sounds made by the family when they spoke. Most of the time I would hear someone speaking at home and didn't distinguish his sounds from the words people uttered in public. I didn't even pay much attention to my parents' accented and ungrammatical speech — at least not at home. Only when I was with them in public would I become alert to their accents. But even then their sounds caused me less and less concern. For I was growing increasingly confident of my own public identity.

I would have been happier about my public success had I 37 not recalled, sometimes, what it had been like earlier, when my family conveyed its intimacy through a set of conveniently private sounds. Sometimes in public, hearing a stranger, I'd hark back to my lost past. A Mexican farm worker approached me one day downtown. He wanted directions to some place. "*Hijito,* . . . " he said. And his voice stirred old longings. Another time I was standing beside my mother in the visiting room of a Carmelite convent, before the dense screen which rendered the nuns shadowy figures. I heard several of them speaking Spanish in their busy, singsong, overlapping voices, assuring my mother that, yes, yes, we were remembered, all our family was remembered, in their prayers. Those voices echoed faraway family sounds. Another day a dark-faced old woman touched my shoulder lightly to steady herself as she boarded a bus. She murmured something to me I couldn't quite comprehend. Her Spanish voice came near, like the face of a never-before-seen relative in the instant before I was kissed. That voice, like so many of the Spanish voices I'd hear in public, recalled the golden age of my childhood.

Bilingual educators say today that children lose a degree of "individuality" by becoming assimilated into public society. (Bilingual schooling is a program popularized in the seventies, that decade when middle-class "ethnics" began to resist the process of assimilation — the "American melting pot.") But the bilingualists oversimplify when they scorn the value and necessity of assimilation. They do not seem to realize that a person is individualized in two ways. So they do not realize that, while one suffers a diminished sense of *private* individuality by being assimilated into public society, such assimilation makes possible the achievement of *public* individuality. 38

Simplistically again, the bilingualists insist that a student should be reminded of his difference from others in mass society, of his "heritage." But they equate mere separateness with individuality. The fact is that only in private — with intimates — is separateness from the crowd a prerequisite for individuality; an intimate "tells" me that I am unique, unlike all others, apart from the crowd. In public, by contrast, full individuality is achieved, paradoxically, by those who are able to consider themselves members of the crowd. Thus it happened for me. Only when I was able to think of myself as an American, no longer an alien in gringo society, could I seek the rights and opportunities necessary for full public individuality. The social and political advantages I enjoy as a man began on the day I came to believe that my name is indeed *Rich-heard Road-ree-guess.* It is true that my public society today is often impersonal; in fact, my 39 public society is usually mass society. But despite the anonymity of the crowd, and despite the fact that the individuality I achieve in public is often tenuous — because it depends on my being one in a crowd — I celebrate the day I acquired my new name. Those middle-class ethnics who scorn assimilation seem to me filled with decadent self-pity, obsessed by the burden of public life. Dangerously, they romanticize public separateness and trivialize the dilemma of those who are truly socially disadvantaged.

If I rehearse here the changes in my private life after my Americanization, it is finally to emphasize a public gain. The loss implies the gain. The house I returned to each afternoon was quiet. Intimate sounds no longer greeted me at the door. Inside there were other noises. The telephone rang. Neighborhood kids ran past the door of the bedroom where I was reading my schoolbooks — covered with brown shopping-bag paper. Once I learned the public language, it would never again be easy for me to hear intimate family voices. More and more of my day was spent hearing words, not sounds. But that may only be a way of saying that on the day I raised my hand in class and spoke loudly to an entire roomful of faces, my childhood started to end. 40

QUESTIONS ON MEANING AND PURPOSE

1. Rodriguez's essay is both memoir and argument. What is the thrust of the author's argument? Where in the essay does he set it forth?
2. How did the child Rodriguez react when, in his presence, his parents had to struggle to make themselves understood by "*los gringos*"?
3. What does the author mean when he says, "I was a child longer than most" (paragraph 15)?
4. According to the author, what impact did the Rodriguez children's use of English have on relationships within the family?
5. Contrast the child Rodriguez's view of the nuns who insisted he speak English with his adult view.

QUESTIONS ON WRITING STRATEGY

1. How effective an INTRODUCTION is Rodriguez's first paragraph?
2. Several times in his essay Rodriguez shifts from memoir to argument and back again. What is the EFFECT of these shifts? Do they strengthen or weaken the author's stance against bilingual education?
3. Twice in his essay (in paragraphs 1 and 40) the author mentions schoolbooks wrapped in shopping-bag paper. How does the use of this detail enhance his argument?
4. What AUDIENCE probably would not like this essay? Why would they not like it?

QUESTIONS ON LANGUAGE

1. Consult the dictionary if you need help defining these words: counterpoint (paragraph 8); polysyllabic (10); guttural, syntax (11); falsetto, exuberance (13); inconsequential (14); cloistered, lacquered (18); diffident (21); intrinsically (22); incongruity (23); bemused (29); effusive (35); assimilated (38); paradoxically, tenuous, decadent (39).
2. In Rodriguez's essay, how do the words *public* and *private* relate to the issue of bilingual education? What important distinction does the author make between *individuality* and *separateness* (paragraph 39)?
3. What exactly does the author mean when he says, "More and more of my day was spent hearing words, not sounds" (paragraph 40)?

SUGGESTIONS FOR WRITING

1. Write a brief personal history of your efforts to change your language habits.
2. Set forth a case in favor of the use of black English or of Spanish in public schools, contrary to Rodriguez's argument.
3. Try to define the distinctive quality of the language spoken in your home when you were a child. Explain any ways in which this language differed from what you heard in school. How has the difference mattered to you? (This language need not be a foreign language; it might include any words used in your family but not in the world at large: a dialect, slang, ALLUSIONS, sayings, FIGURES OF SPEECH, or a special vocabulary.)

—— POSTSCRIPT ON PROCESS ——

Richard Rodriguez

In this revealing comment on "Aria," Richard Rodriguez recalls the problem he faced as a student whenever a teacher would tell him, "Write about what you know." Somehow, his own life did not seem sufficient. Even when as a man he sought to explain his past, he felt a need to write with another purpose, to write "*about* something." Although here he tells of his personal experience as a writer, you will find that he also keeps you, the audience, clearly in mind.

"Aria" is a boy's story told in a man's voice. It is the story   1
about those years of my life when I sojourned between Spanish
and English, listening, keeping all that I knew to myself, behind
watchful eyes. I was a boy with too many words on my mind
and no one to trust.

From grammar school to college, my teachers offered peren-   2
nial encouragement: "Write about what you know." Every year
I would respond with the student's complaint: "I have nothing
to write about . . . I haven't done anything." (Writers, real writers, I thought, lived in New York or Paris; they smoked on the
back jackets of library books, their chores done.)

Stories die for not being told. Or they get told piecemeal too   3
late — too late the old lady remembers something (a path
through the blue forest; a communion veil) and none of her
grandchildren care to make sense of the mumbling. Or else —
and this may be true of the majority of stories untold — the
words are not there.

My story got told because I had received an education; my   4
teachers had given me the skill of stringing words together in a
coherent line. But it was not until I was a man that I felt any
need to write my story. A few years ago I left graduate school,
quit teaching for political reasons (to protest affirmative action).
But after leaving the classroom, as the months passed, I grew
desperate to talk to serious people about serious things. In the

great journals of the world, I noticed, there was conversation of a sort, glamorous company of a sort, and I determined to join it. I began writing to stay alive — not as a job, but to stay alive. I kept a sober house. I spent hours and hours alone — late at night, early in morning, inside on Sundays. A part-time writer, I called myself to myself, because I didn't want my life to pass. I didn't want my soul to wobble in my breast, to left, to right — a fat, trivial thing. Believe that if you want — it's true.

Even as you see my essay now, in cool printer's type, I look   5 at some pages and cannot remember having written them. Or else I can remember earlier versions — unused incident, character, description (rooms, faces) — crumbled and discarded. Flung from possibility. They hit the wastebasket, those pages, and yet, defying gravity with a scratchy, starchy resilience, tried to reopen themselves. Then they fell silent. I read certain other sentences now and they recall the very day they were composed — the afternoon of rain or the telephone call that was to come a few moments after, the house, the room where these sentences were composed, the pattern of the rug, the wastebasket. (In all there were about thirty or forty versions that preceded this final "Aria.") I tried to describe my experiences exactly, at once to discover myself and to reveal myself. Always I had to write against the fear I felt that no one would be able to understand what I was saying.

Throughout this essay you will notice that I pull back in   6 places, discuss bilingual education, the difference between private and public language, or theories of intimacy. I kept doing this when I wrote because I wanted to make sense of my experiences, hold them up to the light of common experience, as approximating some real light of day. I wanted "Aria" to be *about* something. Though now it does not seem to me crucial that our opinions — yours and mine — finally agree. As a writer, what I seek from you is an understanding.

Since "Aria" has been published, it has joined the debate   7 over bilingual education. There are inevitably readers who misunderstand, who think I am trying to present my life as a case study — the "Hispanic-American experience"; the "typical" immigrant child's experience. I intend no such thing. I have tried to describe only one life, one time, one street, the distance between my Spanish-speaking home and the corner Safeway.

As a reader, I have been struck by the way those novels and essays that are most particular, most particularly about one other life and time (Hannibal, Missouri; one summer; a slave; the loveliness of a muddy river) most fully achieve universality and call to be cherished. It is a paradox apparently: The more a writer unearths the detail that makes a life singular, the more a reader is led to feel a kind of sharing. Perhaps the reason we are able to respond to the life that is so different is because we all, each of us, think privately that we are different from one another. And the more closely we examine another life in its misery or wisdom or foolishness, the more it seems we take some version of ourselves. 8

It is, in any case, finally you that I end up having to trust not to laugh, not to snicker. Even as you regard me in these lines, I try to imagine your face as you read. You who read "Aria," especially those of you with your theme-divining yellow felt pen poised in your hand, you for whom this essay is yet another "assignment," please do not forget that it is my life I am handing you in these pages — memories that are as personal for me as family photographs in an old cigar box. 9

1. Write a persuasive essay in which you appeal primarily to either reason or emotion. In it, address a particular person or audience. For instance, you might direct your essay:

   To a friend unwilling to attend a ballet performance (or a wrestling match) with you on the grounds that such an event is for the birds

   To a teacher who asserts that more term papers, and longer ones, are necessary

   To a state trooper who intends to give you a ticket for speeding

   To a male employer skeptical of hiring women

   To a developer who plans to tear down a historic house

   To someone who sees no purpose in studying a foreign language

   To someone you are trying to persuade to sign a petition

   To a high-school class whose members don't want to go to college

   To an older generation skeptical of the value of "all that noise" (meaning current popular music)

   To an atheist who asserts that religion is a lot of pie-in-the-sky

   To the members of a library board who want to ban a certain book

2. Write a letter to your campus newspaper, or to a city newspaper, in which you argue for or against a certain cause or view. Perhaps you may wish to object to a particular feature, column, or editorial in the paper. Send your letter and see if it is published.

3. Write a short letter to your congressional or state representative, arguing in favor of (or against) the passage of some pending legislation. See a news magazine or a newspaper for a worthwhile bill to champion. Or else write in favor of some continuing cause: for instance, saving whales, reducing (or increasing) armaments, or providing more aid to the arts.

4. Write an essay in which you argue that something you feel strongly about be changed, removed, abolished, enforced, repeated, revised, reinstated, or reconsidered. Possible topics, listed to start you thinking, are:

   The drinking age
   Gun laws
   The draft

Low-income housing
Graduation requirements
The mandatory retirement age
ROTC programs in schools and colleges
The voting age
Movie ratings (G, PG, PG–13, R, X)
School prayer
Fraternities and sororities
Dress codes
TV advertising

FOR
FURTHER READING

· Jonathan Swift ·

JONATHAN SWIFT (1667–1745), the son of English parents who had settled in Ireland, divided his energies among literature, politics, and the Church of England. Dissatisfied with the quiet life of an Anglican parish priest, Swift spent much of his time in London hobnobbing with men of letters and writing pamphlets in support of the Tory Party. In 1713 Queen Anne rewarded his political services with an assignment the London-loving Swift didn't want: to supervise St. Patrick's Cathedral in Dublin. There, as Dean Swift, he ended his days — beloved by the Irish, whose interests he defended against the English government.

Although Swift's chief works include the remarkable satires *The Battle of the Books* and *A Tale of a Tub* (both 1704) and scores of fine poems, he is best remembered for *Gulliver's Travels* (1726), an account of four imaginary voyages. This classic is always abridged when it is given to children because of its frank descriptions of human filth and viciousness. In *Gulliver's Travels* Swift pays tribute to the reasoning portion of "that animal called man," and delivers a stinging rebuke to the rest of him.

A Modest Proposal

For Preventing the Children of Poor People in Ireland
from Being a Burden to Their Parents or Country,
and for Making Them Beneficial to the Public

Three consecutive years of drought and sparse crops had worked hardship upon the Irish when Swift wrote this ferocious essay in the summer of 1729. At the time, there were said to be 35,000 wandering beggars in the country: Whole families had quit their farms and had taken to the roads. Large landowners, of English ancestry, preferred to ignore their tenants' sufferings and lived abroad to dodge taxes and payment of church duties. Swift writes out of indignation and out of impatience with the many proposals to help the Irish offered in England without result.

Although printed as a pamphlet in Dublin, Swift's essay is clearly meant for English readers as well as Irish ones. When circulated, the pamphlet caused a sensation in both Ireland and England and had to be reprinted seven times in the same year. Swift is an expert with plain, vigorous English prose, and "A Modest Proposal" is a masterpiece of irony. (If you are uncertain what Swift argues for, see the discussion of *Irony* in Useful Terms.) The dean of St. Patrick's had no special fondness for the Irish, but he hated the inhumanity he witnessed.

It is a melancholy object to those who walk through this   1
great town[1] or travel in the country, when they see the streets, the roads, and cabin doors, crowded with beggars of the female sex, followed by three, four, or six children, all in rags and importuning every passenger for an alms. These mothers, instead of being able to work for their honest livelihood, are forced to employ all their time in strolling to beg sustenance for their helpless infants, who, as they grow up, either turn thieves for want of work, or leave their dear native country to fight for the Pretender in Spain, or sell themselves to the Barbados.[2]

I think it is agreed by all parties that this prodigious number   2
of children in the arms, or on the backs, or at the heels of their mothers, and frequently of their fathers, is in the present deplorable state of the kingdom a very great additional grievance; and therefore whoever could find out a fair, cheap, and easy method of making these children sound, useful members of the commonwealth would deserve so well of the public as to have his statue set up for a preserver of the nation.

But my intention is very far from being confined to provide   3
only for the children of professed beggars; it is of a much greater extent, and shall take in the whole number of infants at a cer-

[1]Dublin. — EDS.

[2]The Pretender was James Stuart, exiled in Spain; in 1718 many Irishmen had joined an army seeking to restore him to the English throne. Others wishing to emigrate had signed papers as indentured servants, agreeing to work for a number of years in the Barbados or other British colonies in exchange for their ocean passage. — EDS.

tain age who are born of parents in effect as little able to support them as those who demand our charity in the streets.

As to my own part, having turned my thoughts for many years upon this important subject, and maturely weighed the several schemes of other projectors,[3] I have always found them grossly mistaken in their computation. It is true, a child just dropped from its dam may be supported by her milk for a solar year, with little other nourishment; at most not above the value of two shillings, which the mother may certainly get, or the value in scraps, by her lawful occupation of begging; and it is exactly at one year that I propose to provide for them in such a manner as instead of being a charge upon their parents or the parish, or wanting food and raiment for the rest of their lives, they shall on the contrary contribute to the feeding, and partly to the clothing, of many thousands.

There is likewise another great advantage in my scheme, that it will prevent those voluntary abortions, and that horrid practice of women murdering their bastard children, alas, too frequent among us, sacrificing the poor innocent babes, I doubt, more to avoid the expense than the shame, which would move tears and pity in the most savage and inhuman breast.

The number of souls in this kingdom being usually reckoned one million and a half, of these I calculate there may be about two hundred thousand couples whose wives are breeders; from which number I subtract thirty thousand couples who are able to maintain their own children, although I apprehend there cannot be so many under the present distress of the kingdom; but this being granted, there will remain an hundred and seventy thousand breeders. I again subtract fifty thousand for those women who miscarry, or whose children die by accident or disease within the year. There only remain an hundred and twenty thousand children of poor parents annually born. The question therefore is, how this number shall be reared and provided for, which, as I have already said, under the present situation of affairs, is utterly impossible by all the methods hitherto proposed.

[3]Planners. — EDS.

For we can neither employ them in handicraft or agriculture; we neither build houses (I mean in the country) nor cultivate land. They can very seldom pick up a livelihood stealing till they arrive at six years old, except where they are of towardly parts;[4] although I confess they learn the rudiments much earlier, during which time they can however be looked upon only as probationers, as I have been informed by a principal gentleman in the country of Cavan, who protested to me that he never knew above one or two instances under the age of six, even in a part of the kingdom so renowned for the quickest proficiency in that art.

I am assured by our merchants that a boy or a girl before   7
twelve years old is no salable commodity; and even when they come to this age they will not yield above three pounds, or three pounds and half a crown at most on the Exchange; which cannot turn to account either to the parents or the kingdom, the charge of nutriment and rags having been at least four times that value.

I shall now therefore humbly propose my own thoughts,   8
which I hope will not be liable to the least objection.

I have been assured by a very knowing American of my ac-   9
quaintance in London, that a young healthy child well nursed is at a year old a most delicious, nourishing, and wholesome food, whether stewed, roasted, baked, or boiled; and I make no doubt that it will equally serve in a fricassee or a ragout.[5]

I do therefore humbly offer it to public consideration that of   10
the hundred and twenty thousand children, already computed, twenty thousand may be reserved for breed, whereof only one fourth part to be males, which is more than we allow to sheep, black cattle, or swine; and my reason is that these children are seldom the fruits of marriage, a circumstance not much regarded by our savages, therefore one male will be sufficient to serve four females. That the remaining hundred thousand may at a year old be offered in sale to the persons of quality and fortune through the kingdom, always advising the mother to let them

---

[4]Teachable wits, innate abilities. — EDS.
[5]Stew. — EDS.

suck plentifully in the last month, so as to render them plump and fat for a good table. A child will make two dishes at an entertainment for friends; and when the family dines alone, the fore or hind quarter will make a reasonable dish, and seasoned with a little pepper or salt will be very good boiled on the fourth day, especially in winter.

I have reckoned upon a medium that a child just born will weigh twelve pounds, and in a solar year if tolerably nursed increaseth to twenty-eight pounds. 11

I grant this food will be somewhat dear, and therefore very proper for landlords, who, as they have already devoured most of the parents, seem to have the best title to the children. 12

Infant's flesh will be in season throughout the year, but more plentiful in March, and a little before and after. For we are told by a grave author, an eminent French physician,[6] that fish being a prolific diet, there are more children born in Roman Catholic countries about nine months after Lent than at any other season; therefore, reckoning a year after Lent, the markets will be more glutted than usual, because the number of popish infants is at least three to one in this kingdom; and therefore it will have one other collateral advantage, by lessening the number of Papists among us. 13

I have already computed the charge of nursing a beggar's child (in which list I reckon all cottagers, laborers, and four-fifths of the farmers) to be about two shillings per annum, rags included; and I believe no gentleman would repine to give ten shillings for the carcass of a good fat child, which, as I have said, will make four dishes of excellent nutritive meat, when he hath only some particular friend or his own family to dine with him. Thus the squire will learn to be a good landlord, and grow popular among the tenants; the mother will have eight shillings net profit, and be fit for work till she produces another child. 14

Those who are more thrifty (as I must confess the times require) may flay the carcass; the skin of which artificially[7] dressed 15

---

[6]Swift's favorite French writer, François Rabelais, sixteenth-century author; not "grave" at all, but a broad humorist. — Eds.

[7]With art or craft. — Eds.

will make admirable gloves for ladies, and summer boots for fine gentlemen.

As to our city of Dublin, shambles[8] may be appointed for this purpose in the most convenient parts of it, and butchers we may be assured will not be wanting; although I rather recommend buying the children alive, and dressing them hot from the knife as we do roasting pigs.

A very worthy person, a true lover of his country, and whose virtues I highly esteem, was lately pleased in discoursing on this matter to offer a refinement upon my scheme. He said that many gentlemen of his kingdom, having of late destroyed their deer, he conceived that the want of venison might be well supplied by the bodies of young lads and maidens, not exceeding fourteen years of age nor under twelve, so great a number of both sexes in every county being now ready to starve for want of work and service; and these to be disposed of by their parents, if alive, or otherwise by their nearest relations. But with due deference to so excellent a friend and so deserving a patriot, I cannot be altogether in his sentiments; for as to the males, my American acquaintance assured me from frequent experience that their flesh was generally tough and lean, like that of our schoolboys, by continual exercise, and their taste disagreeable; and to fatten them would not answer the charge. Then as to the females, it would, I think with humble submission, be a loss to the public, because they soon would become breeders themselves; and besides, it is not improbable that some scrupulous people might be apt to censure such a practice (although indeed very unjustly) as a little bordering upon cruelty; which, I confess, hath always been with me the strongest objection against any project, how well soever intended.

But in order to justify my friend, he confessed that this expedient was put into his head by the famous Psalmanazar,[9] a native of the island Formosa, who came from thence to London above

16

17

18

---

[8]Butcher shops or slaughterhouses. — EDS.

[9]Georges Psalmanazar, a Frenchman who pretended to be Japanese, author of a completely imaginary *Description of the Isle Formosa* (1705), had become a well-known figure in gullible London society. — EDS.

twenty years ago, and in conversation told my friend that in his country when any young person happened to be put to death, the executioner sold the carcass to persons of quality as a prime dainty; and that in his time the body of a plump girl of fifteen, who was crucified for an attempt to poison the emperor, was sold to his Imperial Majesty's prime minister of state, and other great mandarins of the court, in joints from the gibbet, at four hundred crowns. Neither indeed can I deny that if the same use were made of several plump young girls in this town, who without one single groat to their fortunes cannot stir abroad without a chair, and appear at the playhouse and assemblies in foreign fineries which they never will pay for, the kingdom would not be the worse.

Some persons of a desponding spirit are in great concern   19
about that vast number of poor people who are aged, diseased, or maimed, and I have been desired to employ my thoughts what course may be taken to ease the nation of so grievous an encumbrance. But I am not in the least pain upon that matter, because it is very well known that they are every day dying and rotting by cold and famine, and filth and vermin, as fast as can be reasonably expected. And as to the younger laborers, they are now in almost as hopeful a condition. They cannot get work, and consequently pine away for want of nourishment to a degree that if any time they are accidentally hired to common labor, they have not strength to perform it; and thus the country and themselves are happily delivered from the evils to come.

I have too long digressed, and therefore shall return to my   20
subject. I think the advantages by the proposal which I have made are obvious and many, as well as of the highest importance.

For first, as I have already observed, it would greatly lessen   21
the number of Papists, with whom we are yearly overrun, being the principal breeders of the nation as well as our most dangerous enemies; and who stay at home on purpose to deliver the kingdom to the Pretender, hoping to take their advantage by the absence of so many good Protestants, who have chosen rather to leave their country than to stay at home and pay tithes against their conscience to an Episcopal curate.

Secondly, the poorer tenants will have something valuable   22
of their own, which by law may be made liable to distress,[10] and
help to pay their landlord's rent, their corn and cattle being already seized and money a thing unknown.

Thirdly, whereas the maintenance of an hundred thousand   23
children, from two years old and upwards, cannot be computed
at less than ten shillings a piece per annum, the nation's stock
will be thereby increased fifty thousand pounds per annum, besides the profit of a new dish introduced to the tables of all gentlemen of fortune in the kingdom who have any refinement in
taste. And the money will circulate among ourselves, the goods
being entirely of our own growth and manufacture.

Fourthly, the constant breeders, besides the gain of eight   24
shillings sterling per annum by the sale of their children, will be
rid of the charge of maintaining them after the first year.

Fifthly, this food would likewise bring great custom to tav-   25
erns, where the vintners will certainly be so prudent as to pro
cure the best receipts for dressing it to perfection, and consequently have their houses frequented by all the fine gentlemen,
who justly value themselves upon their knowledge in good eating; and a skillful cook, who understands how to oblige his
guests, will contrive to make it as expensive as they please.

Sixthly, this would be a great inducement to marriage,   26
which all wise nations have either encouraged by rewards or enforced by laws and penalties. It would increase the care and ten-
derness of mothers toward their children, when they were sure
of a settlement for life to the poor babes, provided in some sort
by the public, to their annual profit instead of expense. We
should see an honest emulation among the married women,
which of them could bring the fattest child to the market. Men
would become as fond of their wives during the time of their
pregnancy as they are now of their mares in foal, their cows in
calf, or sows when they are ready to farrow; nor offer to beat or
kick them (as is too frequent a practice) for fear of a miscarriage.

Many other advantages might be enumerated. For instance,   27
the addition of some thousand carcasses in our exportation of

[10]Subject to seizure by creditors. — Eds.

barreled beef, the propagation of swine's flesh, and improvements in the art of making good bacon, so much wanted among us by the great destruction of pigs, too frequent at our tables, which are no way comparable in taste or magnificence to a well-grown, fat, yearling child, which roasted whole will make a considerable figure at a lord mayor's feast or any other public entertainment. But this and many others I omit, being studious of brevity.

Supposing that one thousand families in this city would be constant customers for infants' flesh, besides others who might have it at merry meetings, particularly weddings and christenings, I compute that Dublin would take off annually about twenty thousand carcasses, and the rest of the kingdom (where probably they will be sold somewhat cheaper) the remaining eighty thousand.   28

I can think of no one objection that will possibly be raised against this proposal, unless it should be urged that the number of people will be thereby much lessened in the kingdom. This I freely own, and it was indeed one principal design in offering it to the world. I desire the reader will observe, that I calculate my remedy for this one individual kingdom of Ireland and for no other that ever was, is, or I think ever can be upon earth. Therefore let no man talk to me of other expedients: of taxing our absentees at five shillings a pound: of using neither clothes nor household furniture except what is of our own growth and manufacture: of utterly rejecting the materials and instruments that promote foreign luxury: of curing the expensiveness of pride, vanity, idleness, and gaming in our women: of introducing a vein of parsimony, prudence, and temperance: of learning to love our country, in the want of which we differ even from Laplanders and the inhabitants of Topinamboo:[11] of quitting our animosities and factions, nor acting any longer like the Jews, who were murdering one another at the very moment their city was taken:[12] of being a little cautious not to sell our country and   29

---

[11]District of Brazil inhabited by primitive tribes. — Eds.
[12]During the Roman siege of Jerusalem (A.D. 70), prominent Jews were executed on the charge of being in league with the enemy. — Eds.

conscience for nothing: of teaching landlords to have at least one degree of mercy toward their tenants: lastly, of putting a spirit of honesty, industry, and skill into our shopkeepers; who, if a resolution could now be taken to buy only our native goods, would immediately unite to cheat and exact upon us in the price, the measure, and the goodness, nor could ever yet be brought to make one fair proposal of just dealing, though often and earnestly invited to it.

Therefore I repeat, let no man talk to me of these and the like expedients, till he hath at least some glimpse of hope that there will ever be some hearty and sincere attempt to put them in practice.   30

But as to myself, having been wearied out for many years with offering vain, idle, visionary thoughts, and at length utterly despairing of success, I fortunately fell upon this proposal, which, as it is wholly new, so it hath something solid and real, of no expense and little trouble, full in our own power, and whereby we can incur no danger in disobliging England. For this kind of commodity will not bear exportation, the flesh being of too tender a consistence to admit a long continuance in salt, although perhaps I could name a country which would be glad to eat up our whole nation without it.   31

After all, I am not so violently bent upon my own opinion as to reject any offer proposed by wise men, which shall be found equally innocent, cheap, easy, and effectual. But before something of that kind shall be advanced in contradiction to my scheme, and offering a better, I desire the author or authors will be pleased maturely to consider two points. First, as things now stand, how they will be able to find food and raiment for an hundred thousand useless mouths and backs. And secondly, there being a round million of creatures in human figure throughout this kingdom, whose sole subsistence put into a common stock would leave them in debt two millions of pounds sterling, adding those who are beggars by profession to the bulk of farmers, cottagers, and laborers, with their wives and children who are beggars in effect; I desire those politicians who dislike my overture, and may perhaps be so bold to attempt an answer, that they will first ask the parents of these mortals whether they   32 would not at this day think it a great happiness to have been sold for food at a year old in this manner I prescribe, and thereby have avoided such a perpetual scene of misfortunes as they have since gone through by the oppression of landlords, the impossibility of paying rent without money or trade, the want of common sustenance, with neither house nor clothes to cover them from the inclemencies of the weather, and the most inevitable prospect of entailing the like or greater miseries upon their breed forever.

    I profess, in the sincerity of my heart, that I have not the least personal interest in endeavoring to promote this necessary work, having no other motive than the public good of my country, by advancing our trade, providing for infants, relieving the poor, and giving some pleasure to the rich. I have no children by which I can propose to get a single penny; the youngest being nine years old, and my wife past childbearing.   33

The most prominent British woman writer of our century, VIRGINIA WOOLF was born in London in 1882, the youngest daughter of Sir Leslie Stephen, a leading critic and editor. Frail in health as a child, she was educated mainly at home in her father's library. In 1904 she settled in the Bloomsbury district of London, joining an intellectual circle that came to include economist John Maynard Keynes and biographer Lytton Strachey. In 1917 she and her husband, Leonard Woolf, established the Hogarth Press, publisher of her own novels and of the first translated works of Sigmund Freud. In the 1920s her novels won wide attention. Woolf's techniques were then new and radical: in *Mrs. Dalloway* (1925) she explores characters' streams of consciousness; in *Orlando* (1928) her Elizabethan hero defies time and lives for centuries, changing into a woman in midlife. As an essayist and critic, Woolf is remembered especially for *The Common Reader* (in two series, 1925 and 1932), *The Death of the Moth* (1942), and *A Room of One's Own* (1929). In 1941, depressed by ill health and by World War II, she weighted her pockets with stones and stepped into a river.

What If Shakespeare Had Had a Sister?

A Room of One's Own was originally written as two long papers, delivered as lectures in 1928 before audiences largely consisting of women. In it Woolf considers the widespread discrimination suffered by women writers and artists down through English history. Recently the book's popularity has been renewed; many feminists and scholars in women's studies have paid it homage. From its third chapter, we reprint Woolf's famous speculation: Had Shakespeare had an equally gifted sister, what would have been her fate? We also include the book's valuable concluding paragraph, in which the author returns to the subject of Shakespeare's sister and imagines her reborn in the modern world.

It is a perennial puzzle why no woman wrote a word of that   1
extraordinary literature [of the time of Elizabeth I] when every
man, it seemed, was capable of song or sonnet. What were the
conditions in which women lived, I asked myself; for fiction,
imaginative work, that is, is not dropped like a pebble upon the
ground, as science may be; fiction is like a spider's web, attached
ever so lightly perhaps, but still attached to life at all four corners. Often the attachment is scarcely perceptible: Shakespeare's
plays, for instance, seem to hang there complete by themselves.
But when the web is pulled askew, hooked up at the edge, torn
in the middle, one remembers that these webs are not spun in
midair by incorporeal creatures, but are the work of suffering
human beings, and are attached to grossly material things, like
health and money and the houses we live in.

I went, therefore, to the shelf where the histories stand and   2
took down one of the latest, Professor Trevelyan's *History of England*. Once more I looked up Women, found "position of," and
turned to the pages indicated. "Wife-beating," I read, "was a rec-
ognised right of man, and was practised without shame by high
as well as low. . . . Similarly," the historian goes on, "the daughter who refused to marry the gentleman of her parents' choice
was liable to be locked up, beaten and flung about the room,
without any shock being inflicted on public opinion. Marriage
was not an affair of personal affection, but of family avarice, particularly in the 'chivalrous' upper classes. . . . Betrothal often
took place while one or both of the parties was in the cradle, and
marriage when they were scarcely out of the nurses' charge."
That was about 1470, soon after Chaucer's time. The next reference to the position of women is some two hundred years later,
in the time of the Stuarts. "It was still the exception for women
of the upper and middle class to choose their own husbands,
and when the husband had been assigned, he was lord and master, so far at least as law and custom could make him. Yet even
so," Professor Trevelyan concludes, "neither Shakespeare's
women nor those of authentic seventeenth-century memoirs,
like the Verneys and the Hutchinsons, seem wanting in personality and character." Certainly, if we consider it, Cleopatra must
have had a way with her; Lady Macbeth, one would suppose,

had a will of her own; Rosalind, one might conclude, was an attractive girl. Professor Trevelyan is speaking no more than the
truth when he remarks that Shakespeare's women do not seem
wanting in personality and character. Not being a historian, one
might go even further and say that women have burnt like bea-
cons in all the works of all the poets from the beginning of time
— Clytemnestra, Antigone, Cleopatra, Lady Macbeth, Phèdre,
Cressida, Rosalind, Desdemona, the Duchess of Malfi, among
the dramatists; then among the prose writers: Millamant,
Clarissa, Becky Sharp, Anna Karenina, Emma Bovary, Madame de Guermantes[1] — the names flock to mind, nor do they
recall women "lacking in personality and character." Indeed, if
woman had no existence save in the fiction written by men, one
would imagine her a person of the utmost importance; very various; heroic and mean; splendid and sordid; infinitely beautiful
and hideous in the extreme; as great as a man, some think even
greater. But this is woman in fiction. In fact, as Professor Trevelyan points out, she was locked up, beaten and flung about the
room.

A very queer, composite being thus emerges. Imaginatively   3
she is of the highest importance; practically she is completely in-
significant. She pervades poetry from cover to cover; she is all
but absent from history. She dominates the lives of kings and
conquerors in fiction; in fact she was the slave of any boy whose
parents forced a ring upon her finger. Some of the most inspired
words, some of the most profound thoughts in literature fall
from her lips; in real life she could hardly read, could scarcely
spell, and was the property of her husband.

It was certainly an odd monster that one made up by read-   4

[1]For this roster of great women characters of literature, Woolf draws
names first from drama: Greek tragedy (Clytemnestra, Antigone) and French
tragedy (Racine's *Phèdre*); the plays of Shakespeare (Cleopatra, Lady Macbeth,
Cressida, Rosalind, Desdemona) and John Webster (*The Duchess of Malfi*).
Then she names (in sequence) leading characters of William Congreve's com-
edy *The Way of the World*; of English novels (Samuel Richardson's *Clarissa
Harlowe*, W. M. Thackeray's *Vanity Fair*), a Russian novel (Leo Tolstoy's *Anna
Karenina*), and French novels (Gustave Flaubert's *Madame Bovary* and Marcel
Proust's series *Remembrance of Things Past*). — EDS.

ing the historians first and the poets afterwards — a worm winged like an eagle; the spirit of life and beauty in a kitchen chopping up suet. But these monsters, however amusing to the imagination, have no existence in fact. What one must do to bring her to life was to think poetically and prosaically at one and the same moment, thus keeping in touch with fact — that she is Mrs. Martin, aged thirty-six, dressed in blue, wearing a black hat and brown shoes; but not losing sight of fiction either — that she is a vessel in which all sorts of spirits and forces are coursing and flashing perpetually. The moment, however, that one tries this method with the Elizabethan woman, one branch of illumination fails; one is held up by the scarcity of facts. One knows nothing detailed, nothing perfectly true and substantial about her. History scarcely mentions her. . . .

Here am I asking why women did not write poetry in the   5 Elizabethan age, and I am not sure how they were educated; whether they were taught to write; whether they had sitting-rooms to themselves; how many women had children before they were twenty-one; what, in short, they did from eight in the morning till eight at night. They had no money evidently; according to Professor Trevelyan they were married whether they liked it or not before they were out of the nursery, at fifteen or sixteen very likely. It would have been extremely odd, even upon this showing, had one of them suddenly written the plays of Shakespeare, I concluded, and I thought of that old gentleman, who is dead now, but was a bishop, I think, who declared that it was impossible for any woman, past, present, or to come, to have the genius of Shakespeare. He wrote to the papers about it. He also told a lady who applied to him for information that cats do not as a matter of fact go to heaven, though they have, he added, souls of a sort. How much thinking those old gentlemen used to save one! How the borders of ignorance shrank back at their approach! Cats do not go to heaven. Women cannot write the plays of Shakespeare.

Be that as it may, I could not help thinking, as I looked at   6 the works of Shakespeare on the shelf, that the bishop was right at least in this; it would have been impossible, completely and

entirely, for any woman to have written the plays of Shakespeare in the age of Shakespeare. Let me imagine, since facts are
so hard to come by, what would have happened had Shakespeare had a wonderfully gifted sister, called Judith, let us say.
Shakespeare himself went, very probably — his mother was an
heiress — to the grammar school, where he may have learnt
Latin — Ovid, Virgil and Horace — and the elements of grammar and logic. He was, it is well known, a wild boy who poached
rabbits, perhaps shot a deer, and had, rather sooner than he
should have done, to marry a woman in the neighborhood,
who bore him a child rather quicker than was right. That esca-
pade sent him to seek his fortune in London. He had, it seemed,
a taste for the theatre; he began by holding horses at the stage
door. Very soon he got work in the theatre, became a successful
actor, and lived at the hub of the universe, meeting everybody,
knowing everybody, practising his art on the boards, exercising
his wits in the streets, and even getting access to the palace of
the queen. Meanwhile his extraordinarily gifted sister, let us
suppose, remained at home. She was as adventurous, as imaginative, as agog to see the world as he was. But she was not sent
to school. She had no chance of learning grammar and logic, let
alone of reading Horace and Virgil. She picked up a book now
and then, one of her brother's perhaps, and read a few pages.
But then her parents came in and told her to mend the stock-
ings or mind the stew and not moon about with books and papers. They would have spoken sharply but kindly, for they were
substantial people who knew the conditions of life for a woman
and loved their daughter — indeed, more likely than not she
was the apple of her father's eye. Perhaps she scribbled some
pages up in an apple loft on the sly, but was careful to hide them
or set fire to them. Soon, however, before she was out of her
teens, she was to be betrothed to the son of a neighboring
wool-stapler. She cried out that marriage was hateful to her, and
for that she was severely beaten by her father. Then he ceased to
scold her. He begged her instead not to hurt him, not to shame
him in this matter of her marriage. He would give her a chain of
beads or a fine petticoat, he said; and there were tears in his
eyes. How could she disobey him? How could she break his

heart? The force of her own gift alone drove her to it. She made up a small parcel of her belongings, let herself down by a rope one summer's night and took the road to London. She was not seventeen. The birds that sang in the hedge were not more musical than she was. She had the quickest fancy, a gift like her brother's, for the tune of words. Like him, she had a taste for the theatre. She stood at the stage door; she wanted to act, she said. Men laughed in her face. The manager — a fat, loose-lipped man — guffawed. He bellowed something about poodles dancing and women acting — no woman, he said, could possibly be an actress. He hinted — you can imagine what. She could get no training in her craft. Could she even seek her dinner in a tavern or roam the streets at midnight? Yet her genius was for fiction and lusted to feed abundantly upon the lives of men and women and the study of their ways. At last — for she was very young, oddly like Shakespeare the poet in her face, with the same grey eyes and rounded brows — at last Nick Greene the actor-manager took pity on her; she found herself with child by that gentleman and so — who shall measure the heat and violence of the poet's heart when caught and tangled in a woman's body? — killed herself one winter's night and lies buried at some crossroads where the omnibuses now stop outside the Elephant and Castle.[2]

That, more or less, is how the story would run, I think, if a   7
woman in Shakespeare's day had had Shakespeare's genius. But for my part, I agree with the deceased bishop, if such he was — it is unthinkable that any woman in Shakespeare's day should have had Shakespeare's genius. For genius like Shakespeare's is not born among laboring, uneducated, servile people. It was not born in England among the Saxons and the Britons. It is not born today among the working classes. How, then, could it have been born among women whose work began, according to Professor Trevelyan, almost before they were out of the nursery, who were forced to it by their parents and held to it by all the power of law and custom? Yet genius of a sort must have existed among women as it must have existed among the working

---

[2]In Southeast London, a district less colorful than its name. — EDS.

classes. Now and again an Emily Brontë or a Robert Burns blazes out and proves its presence. But certainly it never got itself on to paper. When, however, one reads of a witch being ducked, of a woman possessed by devils, of a wise woman selling herbs, or even of a very remarkable man who had a mother, then I think we are on the track of a lost novelist, a suppressed poet, of some mute and inglorious Jane Austen, some Emily Brontë who dashed her brains out on the moor or mopped and mowed about the highways crazed with the torture that her gift had put her to. Indeed, I would venture to guess that Anon, who wrote so many poems without signing them, was often a woman. It was a woman Edward Fitzgerald, I think, suggested who made the ballads and the folk-songs, crooning them to her children, beguiling her spinning with them, or the length of the winter's night.

This may be true or it may be false — who can say? — but what is true in it, so it seemed to me, reviewing the story of Shakespeare's sister as I had made it, is that any woman born with a great gift in the sixteenth century would certainly have gone crazed, shot herself, or ended her days in some lonely cottage outside the village, half witch, half wizard, feared and mocked at. For it needs little skill in psychology to be sure that a highly gifted girl who had tried to use her gift for poetry would have been so thwarted and hindered by other people, so tortured and pulled asunder by her own contrary instincts, that she must have lost her health and sanity to a certainty. No girl could have walked to London and stood at a stage door and forced her way into the presence of actor-managers without doing herself a violence and suffering an anguish which may have been irrational — for chastity may be a fetish invented by certain societies for unknown reasons — but were none the less inevitable. Chastity had then, it has even now, a religious importance in a woman's life, and has so wrapped itself round with nerves and instincts that to cut it free and bring it to the light of day demands courage of the rarest. To have lived a free life in London in the sixteenth century would have meant for a woman who was poet and playwright a nervous stress and dilemma which might well have killed her. Had she survived,

8

whatever she had written would have been twisted and deformed, issuing from a strained and morbid imagination. And undoubtedly, I thought, looking at the shelf where there are no plays by women, her work would have gone unsigned. That refuge she would have sought certainly. It was the relic of the sense of chastity that dictated anonymity to women even so late as the nineteenth century. Currer Bell, George Eliot, George Sand,[3] all the victims of inner strife as their writings prove, sought ineffectively to veil themselves by using the name of a man. Thus they did homage to the convention, which if not implanted by the other sex was liberally encouraged by them (the chief glory of a woman is not to be talked of, said Pericles, himself a much-talked-of man), that publicity in women is detestable. Anonymity runs in their blood. . . .

I told you in the course of this paper that Shakespeare had a   9
sister; but do not look for her in Sir Sidney Lee's life of the poet. She died young — alas, she never wrote a word. She lies buried where the omnibuses now stop, opposite the Elephant and Castle. Now my belief is that this poet who never wrote a word and was buried at the crossroads still lives. She lives in you and in me, and in many other women who are not here tonight, for they are washing up the dishes and putting the children to bed. But she lives; for great poets do not die; they are continuing presences; they need only the opportunity to walk among us in the flesh. This opportunity, as I think, it is now coming within your power to give her. For my belief is that if we live another century or so — I am talking of the common life which is the real life and not of the little separate lives which we live as individuals — and have five hundred a year each of us and rooms of our own; if we have the habit of freedom and the courage to write exactly what we think; if we escape a little from the common sitting-room and see human beings not always in their relation to each other but in relation to reality; and the sky, too, and the trees or whatever it may be in themselves; if we look

---

[3]Masculine pen names, respectively, of novelists Charlotte Brontë, Mary Ann Evans, and Aurore Dupin. — EDS.

past Milton's bogey,[4] for no human being should shut out the view; if we face the fact, for it is a fact, that there is no arm to cling to, but that we go alone and that our relation is to the world of reality and not only to the world of men and women, then the opportunity will come and the dead poet who was Shakespeare's sister will put on the body which she has so often laid down. Drawing her life from the lives of the unknown who were her forerunners, as her brother did before her, she will be born. As for her coming without that preparation, without that effort on our part, without that determination that when she is born again she shall find it possible to live and write her poetry, that we cannot expect, for that would be impossible. But I maintain that she would come if we worked for her, and that so to work, even in poverty and obscurity, is worth while.

[4]What bogey (or figure of dread) does Woolf think the invention of epic poet John Milton? Perhaps she means the terrifying Satan in *Paradise Lost*; perhaps, Milton's personification of the Father God. — EDS.

· George Orwell ·

GEORGE ORWELL was the pen name of Eric Blair (1903–1950).
For a full biographical note, see page 96.

Politics and
the English Language

In *1984*, a dictatorship tries to replace both spoken and written English with Newspeak, an official language that limits
thought by reducing the size of its users' vocabulary. (The
words *light* and *bad*, for instance, are suppressed in favor of
unlight and *unbad*.) This concern with language and with its
importance to society is constant in George Orwell's writings.
"Looking back through my work," he declares in an essay
("Why I Write"), "I see that it is invariably where I lacked a *political* purpose that I wrote lifeless books and was betrayed
into purple passages, sentences without meaning, decorative
adjectives, and humbug generally."

No English writer of the twentieth century wrote humbug more rarely than did Orwell. First published in 1946,
"Politics and the English Language" still stands as one of the
most devastating attacks on muddy writing and thinking ever
penned. To illustrate his argument Orwell carefully classifies
examples of clichés, vague and pretentious diction, and meaningless words. His six short rules for writing responsible prose
are well worth remembering.

Most people who bother with the matter at all would admit   1
that the English language is in a bad way, but it is generally assumed that we cannot by conscious action do anything about it.
Our civilization is decadent and our language — so the argument runs — must inevitably share in the general collapse. It follows that any struggle against the abuse of language is a sentimental archaism, like preferring candles to electric light or
hansom cabs to airplanes. Underneath this lies the half-con-
scious belief that language is a natural growth and not an instrument which we shape for our own purposes.

Now, it is clear that the decline of a language must ulti- 2
mately have political and economic causes: it is not due simply
to the bad influence of this or that individual writer. But an effect can become a cause, reinforcing the original cause and producing the same effect in an intensified form, and so on indefinitely. A man may take to drink because he feels himself to be a
failure, and then fail all the more completely because he drinks.
It is rather the same thing that is happening to the English language. It becomes ugly and inaccurate because our thoughts are
foolish, but the slovenliness of our language makes it easier for
us to have foolish thoughts. The point is that the process is reversible. Modern English, especially written English, is full of
bad habits which spread by imitation and which can be avoided
if one is willing to take the necessary trouble. If one gets rid of
these habits one can think more clearly, and to think clearly is a
necessary first step towards political regeneration: so that the
fight against bad English is not frivolous and is not the exclusive
concern of professional writers. I will come back to this presently, and I hope that by that time the meaning of what I have
said here will have become clearer. Meanwhile, here are
five specimens of the English language as it is now habitually
written.

These five passages have not been picked out because they 3
are especially bad — I could have quoted far worse if I had chosen — but because they illustrate various of the mental vices
from which we now suffer. They are a little below the average,
but are fairly representative samples. I number them so that I
can refer back to them when necessary:

> (1) I am not, indeed, sure whether it is not true to say that
> the Milton who once seemed not unlike a seventeenth-cen-
> tury Shelley had not become, out of an experience ever more
> bitter in each year, more alien [sic] to the founder of that Jes-
> uit sect which nothing could induce him to tolerate.
> Professor Harold Laski (Essay in *Freedom of Expression*).
> (2) Above all, we cannot play ducks and drakes with a na-
> tive battery of idioms which prescribes such egregious colloca-
> tions of vocables as the Basic *put up with* for *tolerate* or *put at a
> loss* for *bewilder.*   Professor Lancelot Hogben (*Interglossa*).

(3) On the one side we have the free personality: by definition it is not neurotic, for it has neither conflict nor dream. Its desires, such as they are, are transparent, for they are just what institutional approval keeps in the forefront of consciousness; another institutional pattern would alter their number and intensity; there is little in them that is natural, irreducible, or culturally dangerous. But *on the other side*, the social bond itself is nothing but the mutual reflection of these self-secure integrities. Recall the definition of love. Is not this the very picture of a small academic? Where is there a place in this hall of mirrors for either personality or fraternity?

Essay on psychology in *Politics* (New York).

(4) All the "best people" from the gentlemen's clubs, and all the frantic fascist captains, united in common hatred of Socialism and bestial horror of the rising tide of the mass revolutionary movement, have turned to acts of provocation, to foul incendiarism, to medieval legends of poisoned wells, to legalize their own destruction of proletarian organizations, and rouse the agitated petty-bourgeoisie to chauvinistic fervor on behalf of the fight against the revolutionary way out of the crisis.

Communist pamphlet.

(5) If a new spirit *is* to be infused into this old country, there is one thorny and contentious reform which must be tackled, and that is the humanization and galvanization of the B.B.C. Timidity here will bespeak cancer and atrophy of the soul. The heart of Britain may be sound and of strong beat, for instance, but the British lion's roar at present is like that of Bottom in Shakespeare's *Midsummer Night's Dream* — as gentle as any sucking dove. A virile new Britain cannot continue indefinitely to be traduced in the eyes or rather ears, of the world by the effete languors of Langham Place, brazenly masquerading as "standard English." When the Voice of Britain is heard at nine o'clock, better far and infinitely less ludicrous to hear aitches honestly dropped than the present priggish, inflated, inhibited, school-ma'amish arch braying of blameless bashful mewing maidens!

Letter in *Tribune*.

Each of these passages has faults of its own, but, quite apart 4
from avoidable ugliness, two qualities are common to all of

them. The first is staleness of imagery: the other is lack of precision. The writer either has a meaning and cannot express it, or
he inadvertently says something else, or he is almost indifferent
as to whether his words mean anything or not. The mixture of
vagueness and sheer incompetence is the most marked characteristic of modern English prose, and especially of any kind of
political writing. As soon as certain topics are raised, the concrete melts into the abstract and no one seems to think of turns
of speech that are not hackneyed: prose consists less and less of
words chosen for the sake of their meaning, and more and more
of *phrases* tacked together like the sections of a prefabricated
hen-house. I list below, with notes and examples, various of the
tricks by means of which the work of prose-construction is habitually dodged:

Dying Metaphors. A newly invented metaphor assists   5
thought by evoking a visual image, while on the other hand a
metaphor which is technically "dead" (e.g., *iron resolution*) has in
effect reverted to being an ordinary word and can generally be
used without loss of vividness. But in between these two classes
there is a huge dump of worn-out metaphors which have lost all
evocative power and are merely used because they save people
the trouble of inventing phrases for themselves. Examples are:
*Ring the changes on, take up the cudgels for, toe the line, ride rough-
shod over, stand shoulder to shoulder with, play into the hands of, no
axe to grind, grist to the mill, fishing in troubled waters, rift within
the lute, on the order of the day, Achilles' heel, swan song, hotbed.*
Many of these are used without knowledge of their meaning
(what is a "rift," for instance?), and incompatible metaphors are
frequently mixed, a sure sign that the writer is not interested in
what he is saying. Some metaphors now current have been
twisted out of their original meaning without those who use
them even being aware of the fact. For example, *toe the line* is
sometimes written *tow the line.* Another example is *the hammer
and the anvil,* now always used with the implication that the anvil gets the worst of it. In real life it is always the anvil that
breaks the hammer, never the other way about: a writer who

stopped to think what he was saying would be aware of this, and would avoid perverting the original phrase.

Operators or Verbal False Limbs. These save the trouble of picking out appropriate verbs and nouns, and at the same time pad each sentence with extra syllables which give it an appearance of symmetry. Characteristic phrases are: *render inoperative, militate against, make contact with, be subjected to, give rise to, give grounds for, have the effect of, play a leading part (role) in, make itself felt, take effect, exhibit a tendency to, serve the purpose of,* etc., etc. The keynote is the elimination of simple verbs. Instead of being a single word, such as *break, stop, spoil, mend, kill,* a verb becomes a *phrase,* made up of a noun or adjective tacked on to some general-purpose verb such as *prove, serve, form, play, render.* In addition, the passive voice is wherever possible used in preference to the active, and noun constructions are used instead of gerunds (*by examination of* instead of *by examining*). The range of verbs is further cut down by means of the *-ize* and *de-* formation, and the banal statements are given an appearance of profundity by means of the *not un-* formation. Simple conjunctions and prepositions are replaced by such phrases as *with respect to, having regard to, the fact that, by dint of, in view of, in the interests of, on the hypothesis that;* and the ends of sentences are saved from anticlimax by such resounding commonplaces as *greatly to be desired, cannot be left out of account, a development to be expected in the near future, deserving of serious consideration, brought to a satisfactory conclusion,* and so on and so forth.

Pretentious Diction. Words like *phenomenon, element, individual* (as noun), *objective, categorical, effective, virtual, basic, primary, promote, constitute, exhibit, exploit, utilize, eliminate, liquidate,* are used to dress up simple statements and give an air of scientific impartiality to biased judgments. Adjectives like *epochmaking, epic, historic, unforgettable, triumphant, age-old, inevitable, inexorable, veritable,* are used to dignify the sordid processes of international politics, while writing that aims at glorifying war usually takes on an archaic color, its characteristic words being:

realm, throne, chariot, mailed fist, trident, sword, shield, buckler, banner, jackboot, clarion. Foreign words and expressions such as *cul de sac, ancien régime, deus ex machina, mutatis mutandis, status quo, gleichschaltung, weltanschauung,* are used to give an air of culture and elegance. Except for the useful abbreviations *i.e., e.g.,* and *etc.,* there is no real need for any of the hundreds of foreign phrases now current in English. Bad writers, and especially scientific, political and sociological writers, are nearly always haunted by the notion that Latin or Greek words are grander than Saxon ones, and unnecessary words like *expedite, ameliorate, predict, extraneous, deracinated, clandestine, subaqueous* and hundreds of others constantly gain ground from their Anglo-Saxon opposite numbers.[1] The jargon peculiar to Marxist writing (*hyena, hangman, cannibal, petty bourgeois, these gentry, lackey, flunkey, mad dog, White Guard,* etc.) consists largely of words and phrases translated from Russian, German or French; but the normal way of coining a new word is to use a Latin or Greek root with the appropriate affix and, where necessary, the *-ize* formation. It is often easier to make up words of this kind (*deregionalize, impermissible, extramarital, nonfragmentatory* and so forth) than to think up the English words that will cover one's meaning. The result, in general, is an increase in slovenliness and vagueness.

Meaningless Words.   In certain kinds of writing, particularly   8
in art criticism and literary criticism, it is normal to come across
long passages which are almost completely lacking in meaning.[2]

---

[1]An interesting illustration of this is the way in which the English flower names which were in use till very recently are being ousted by Greek ones, *snapdragon* becoming *antirrhinum, forget-me-not* becoming *myosotis,* etc. It is hard to see any practical reason for this change of fashion: it is probably due to an instinctive turning-away from the more homely word and a vague feeling that the Greek word is scientific.

[2]Example: "Comfort's catholicity of perception and image, strangely Whitmanesque in range, almost the exact opposite in aesthetic compulsion, continues to evoke that trembling atmospheric accumulative hinting at a cruel, an inexorably serene timelessness. . . . Wrey Gardiner scores by aiming at simple bull's-eyes with precision. Only they are not so simple, and through this contented sadness runs more than the surface bitter-sweet of resignation." (*Poetry Quarterly.*)

Words like *romantic, plastic, values, human, dead, sentimental, natural, vitality,* as used in art criticism, are strictly meaningless in the sense that they not only do not point to any discoverable object, but are hardly ever expected to do so by the reader. When one critic writes, "The outstanding feature of Mr. X's work is its living quality," while another writes, "The immediately striking thing about Mr. X's work is its peculiar deadness," the reader accepts this as a simple difference of opinion. If words like *black* and *white* were involved, instead of the jargon words *dead* and *living,* he would see at once that language was being used in an improper way. Many political words are similarly abused. The word *Fascism* has now no meaning except in so far as it signifies "something not desirable." The words *democracy, socialism, freedom, patriotic, realistic, justice,* have each of them several different meanings which cannot be reconciled with one another. In the case of a word like *democracy,* not only is there no agreed definition, but the attempt to make one is resisted from all sides. It is almost universally felt that when we call a country democratic we are praising it: consequently the defenders of every kind of regime claim that it is a democracy, and fear that they might have to stop using the word if it were tied down to any one meaning. Words of this kind are often used in a consciously dishonest way. That is, the person who uses them has his own private definition, but allows his hearer to think he means something quite different. Statements like *Marshal Pétain was a true patriot, The Soviet Press is the freest in the world, The Catholic Church is opposed to persecution,* are almost always made with intent to deceive. Other words used in variable meanings, in most cases more or less dishonestly, are: *class, totalitarian, science, progressive, reactionary, bourgeois, equality.*

Now that I have made this catalogue of swindles and perversions, let me give another example of the kind of writing that they lead to. This time it must of its nature be an imaginary one. I am going to translate a passage of good English into modern English of the worst sort. Here is a well-known verse from *Ecclesiastes:* 9

> I returned and saw under the sun, that the race is not to the swift, nor the battle to the strong, neither yet bread to the

wise, nor yet riches to men of understanding, nor yet favor to men of skill; but time and chance happeneth to them all.

Here it is in modern English:

> Objective consideration of contemporary phenomena compels the conclusion that success or failure in competitive activities exhibits no tendency to be commensurate with innate capacity, but that a considerable element of the unpredictable must invariably be taken into account.

This is a parody, but not a very gross one. Exhibit (3), above, for instance, contains several patches of the same kind of English. It will be seen that I have not made a full translation. The beginning and ending of the sentence follow the original meaning fairly closely, but in the middle the concrete illustrations — race, battle, bread — dissolve into the vague phrase "success or failure in competitive activities." This had to be so, because no modern writer of the kind I am discussing — no one capable of using phrases like "objective consideration of contemporary phenomena" — would ever tabulate his thoughts in that precise and detailed way. The whole tendency of modern prose is away from concreteness. Now analyze these two sentences a little more closely. The first contains forty-nine words but only sixty syllables, and all its words are those of everyday life. The second contains thirty-eight words of ninety syllables: eighteen of its words are from Latin roots, and one from Greek. The first sentence contains six vivid images, and only one phrase ("time and chance") that could be called vague. The second contains not a single fresh, arresting phrase, and in spite of its ninety syllables it gives only a shortened version of the meaning contained in the first. Yet without a doubt it is the second kind of sentence that is gaining ground in modern English. I do not want to exaggerate. This kind of writing is not yet universal, and outcrops of simplicity will occur here and there in the worst-written page. Still, if you or I were told to write a few lines on the uncertainty of human fortunes, we should probably come much nearer to my imaginary sentence than to the one from *Ecclesiastes*.

As I have tried to show, modern writing at its worst does not consist in picking out words for the sake of their meaning and inventing images in order to make the meaning clearer. It consists in gumming together long strips of words which have already been set in order by someone else, and making the results presentable by sheer humbug. The attraction of this way of writing is that it is easy. It is easier — even quicker once you have the habit — to say *In my opinion it is a not unjustifiable assumption that* than to say *I think.* If you use ready-made phrases, you not only don't have to hunt about for words; you also don't have to bother with the rhythms of your sentences, since these phrases are generally so arranged as to be more or less euphonious. When you are composing in a hurry — when you are dictating to a stenographer, for instance, or making a public speech — it is natural to fall into a pretentious, Latinized style. Tags like *a consideration which we should do well to bear in mind* or *a conclusion to which all of us would readily assent* will save many a sentence from coming down with a bump. By using stale metaphors, similes and idioms, you save much mental effort, at the cost of leaving your meaning vague, not only for your reader but for yourself. This is the significance of mixed metaphors. The sole aim of a metaphor is to call up a visual image. When these images clash — as in *The Fascist octopus has sung its swan song, the jackboot is thrown into the melting pot* — it can be taken as certain that the writer is not seeing a mental image of the objects he is naming; in other words he is not really thinking. Look again at the examples I gave at the beginning of this essay. Professor Laski (1) uses five negatives in fifty-three words. One of these is superfluous, making nonsense of the whole passage, and in addition there is the slip *alien* for akin, making further nonsense, and several avoidable pieces of clumsiness which increase the general vagueness. Professor Hogben (2) plays ducks and drakes with a battery which is able to write prescriptions, and, while disapproving of the every-day phrase *put up with*, is unwilling to look *egregious* up in the dictionary and see what it means. (3), if one takes an uncharitable attitude towards it, is simply meaningless: probably one could work out its intended meaning by reading the whole of the article in which it occurs. In (4), the writer knows more or less what he wants to say, but an accumulation of stale phrases chokes him like tea leaves blocking a sink. In (5), words and meaning have almost parted company. People who write in this manner usually have a general emotional meaning — they dislike one thing and want to express solidarity with another — but they are not interested in the detail of what they are saying. A scrupulous writer, in every sentence that he writes, will ask himself at least four questions, thus: What am I trying to say? What words will express it? What image or idiom will make it clearer? Is this image fresh enough to have an effect? And he will probably ask himself two more: Could I put it more shortly? Have I said anything that is avoidably ugly? But you are not obliged to go to all this trouble. You can shirk it by simply throwing your mind open and letting the ready-made phrases come crowding in. They will construct your sentences for you — even think your thoughts for you, to a certain extent — and at need they will perform the important service of partially concealing your meaning even from yourself. It is at this point that the special connection between politics and the debasement of language becomes clear.

In our time it is broadly true that political writing is bad   12
writing. Where it is not true, it will generally be found that the writer is some kind of rebel, expressing his private opinions and not a "party line." Orthodoxy, of whatever color, seems to demand a lifeless, imitative style. The political dialects to be found in pamphlets, leading articles, manifestos, White Papers and the speeches of under-secretaries do, of course, vary from party to party, but they are all alike in that one almost never finds in them a fresh, vivid, home-made turn of speech. When one watches some tired hack on the platform mechanically repeating the familiar phrases — *bestial atrocities, iron heel, bloodstained tyranny, free peoples of the world, stand shoulder to shoulder* — one often has a curious feeling that one is not watching a live human being but some kind of dummy; a feeling which suddenly becomes stronger at moments when the light catches the speaker's spectacles and turns them into blank discs which seem to have no eyes behind them. And this is not altogether fanciful. A speaker who uses that kind of phraseology has gone some distance towards turning himself into a machine. The appropriate noises are coming out of his larynx, but his brain is not involved

as it would be if he were choosing his words for himself. If the speech he is making is one that he is accustomed to make over and over again, he may be almost unconscious of what he is saying, as one is when one utters the responses in church. And this reduced state of consciousness, if not indispensable, is at any rate favorable to political conformity.

In our time, political speech and writing are largely the defense of the indefensible. Things like the continuance of British rule in India, the Russian purges and deportations, the dropping of the atom bombs on Japan, can indeed be defended, but only by arguments which are too brutal for most people to face, and which do not square with the professed aims of political parties. Thus political language has to consist largely of euphemism, question-begging and sheer cloudy vagueness. Defenseless villages are bombarded from the air, the inhabitants driven out into the countryside, the cattle machine-gunned, the huts set on fire with incendiary bullets: this is called *pacification*. Millions of peasants are robbed of their farms and sent trudging along the roads with no more than they can carry: this is called *transfer of population* or *rectification of frontiers*. People are imprisoned for years without trial, or shot in the back of the neck or sent to die of scurvy in Arctic lumber camps: this is called *elimination of unreliable elements*. Such phraseology is needed if one wants to name things without calling up mental pictures of them. Consider for instance some comfortable English professor defending Russian totalitarianism. He cannot say outright, "I believe in killing off your opponents when you can get good results by doing so." Probably, therefore, he will say something like this: 13

"While freely conceding that the Soviet régime exhibits certain features which the humanitarian may be inclined to deplore, we must, I think, agree that a certain curtailment of the right to political opposition is an unavoidable concomitant of transitional periods, and that the rigors which the Russian people have been called upon to undergo have been amply justified in the sphere of concrete achievement." 14

The inflated style is itself a kind of euphemism. A mass of Latin words fall upon the facts like soft snow, blurring the outlines and covering up all the details. The great enemy of clear 15 language is insincerity. When there is a gap between one's real and one's declared aims, one turns as it were instinctively to long words and exhausted idioms, like a cuttlefish squirting out ink. In our age there is no such thing as "keeping out of politics." All issues are political issues, and politics itself is a mass of lies, evasions, folly, hatred and schizophrenia. When the general atmosphere is bad, language must suffer. I should expect to find — this is a guess which I have not sufficient knowledge to verify — that the German, Russian and Italian languages have all deteriorated in the last ten or fifteen years, as a result of dictatorship.

But if thought corrupts language, language can also corrupt   16
thought. A bad usage can spread by tradition and imitation, even among people who should and do know better. The debased language that I have been discussing is in some ways very convenient. Phrases like *a not unjustifiable assumption, leaves much to be desired, would serve no good purpose, a consideration which we should do well to bear in mind*, are a continuous temptation, a packet of aspirins always at one's elbow. Look back through this essay, and for certain you will find that I have again and again committed the very faults I am protesting against. By this morning's post I have received a pamphlet dealing with conditions in Germany. The author tells me that he "felt impelled" to write it. I open it at random, and here is almost the first sentence that I see: "(The Allies) have an opportunity not only of achieving a radical transformation of Germany's social and political structure in such a way as to avoid a nationalistic reaction in Germany itself, but at the same time of laying the foundations of a co-operative and unified Europe." You see, he "feels impelled" to write — feels, presumably, that he has something new to say — and yet his words, like cavalry horses answering the bugle, group themselves automatically into the familiar dreary pattern. This invasion of one's mind by ready-made phrases (*lay the foundations, achieve a radical transformation*) can only be prevented if one is constantly on guard against them, and every such phrase anesthetizes a portion of one's brain.

I said earlier that the decadence of our language is probably   17
curable. Those who deny this would argue, if they produced an argument at all, that language merely reflects existing social con-

ditions, and that we cannot influence its development by any direct tinkering with words and constructions. So far as the general tone or spirit of a language goes, this may be true, but it is not true in detail. Silly words and expressions have often disappeared, not through any evolutionary process but owing to the conscious action of a minority. Two recent examples were *explore every avenue* and *leave no stone unturned*, which were killed by the jeers of a few journalists. There is a long list of flyblown metaphors which could similarly be got rid of if enough people would interest themselves in the job; and it should also be possible to laugh the *not un-* formation out of existence,[3] to reduce the amount of Latin and Greek in the average sentence, to drive out foreign phrases and strayed scientific words, and, in general, to make pretentiousness unfashionable. But all these are minor points. The defense of the English language implies more than this, and perhaps it is best to start by saying what it does *not* imply.

To begin with it has nothing to do with archaism, with the salvaging of obsolete words and turns of speech, or with the setting up of a "standard English" which must never be departed from. On the contrary, it is especially concerned with the scrapping of every word or idiom which has outworn its usefulness. It has nothing to do with correct grammar and syntax, which are of no importance so long as one makes one's meaning clear, or with the avoidance of Americanisms, or with having what is called a "good prose style." On the other hand it is not concerned with fake simplicity and the attempt to make written English colloquial. Nor does it even imply in every case preferring the Saxon word to the Latin one, though it does imply using the fewest and shortest words that will cover one's meaning. What is above all needed is to let the meaning choose the word, and not the other way about. In prose, the worst thing one can do with words is to surrender to them. When you think of a concrete object, you think wordlessly, and then, if you want to describe the

18

---

[3]One can cure oneself of the *not un-* formation by memorizing this sentence: *A not unblack dog was chasing a not unsmall rabbit across a not ungreen field.*

thing you have been visualizing you probably hunt about till you find the exact words that seem to fit. When you think of something abstract you are more inclined to use words from the start, and unless you make a conscious effort to prevent it, the existing dialect will come rushing in and do the job for you, at the expense of blurring or even changing your meaning. Probably it is better to put off using words as long as possible and get one's meaning as clear as one can through pictures or sensations. Afterwards one can choose — not simply *accept* — the phrases that will best cover the meaning, and then switch round and decide what impression one's words are likely to make on another person. This last effort of the mind cuts out all stale or mixed images, all prefabricated phrases, needless repetitions, and humbug and vagueness generally. But one can often be in doubt about the effect of a word or phrase, and one needs rules that one can rely on when instinct fails. I think the following rules will cover most cases:

    (i) Never use a metaphor, simile or other figure of speech which you are used to seeing in print.
    (ii) Never use a long word where a short one will do.
    (iii) If it is possible to cut a word out, always cut it out.
    (iv) Never use the passive where you can use the active.
    (v) Never use a foreign phrase, a scientific word or a jargon word if you can think of an everyday English equivalent.
    (vi) Break any of these rules sooner than say anything outright barbarous.

These rules sound elementary, and so they are, but they demand a deep change in attitude in anyone who has grown used to writing in the style now fashionable. One could keep all of them and still write bad English, but one could not write the kind of stuff that I quoted in those five specimens at the beginning of this article.

I have not here been considering the literary use of language, but merely language as an instrument for expressing and not for concealing or preventing thought. Stuart Chase and others have come near to claiming that all abstract words are meaningless, and have used this as a pretext for advocating a kind of political quietism. Since you don't know what Fascism is, how can you struggle against Fascism? One need not swallow such absurdities as this, but one ought to recognize that the present political chaos is connected with the decay of language, and that one can probably bring about some improvement by starting at the verbal end. If you simplify your English, you are freed from the worst follies of orthodoxy. You cannot speak any of the necessary dialects, and when you make a stupid remark its stupidity will be obvious, even to yourself. Political language — and with variations this is true of all political parties, from Conservatives to Anarchists — is designed to make lies sound truthful and murder respectable, and to give an appearance of solidity to pure wind. One cannot change this all in a moment, but one can at least change one's own habits, and from time to time one can even, if one jeers loudly enough, send some worn-out and useless phrase — some *jackboot, Achilles' heel, hotbed, melting pot, acid test, veritable inferno* or other lump of verbal refuse — into the dustbin where it belongs.

A NOTE ON POLITICS
AND THE ENGLISH LANGUAGE

George Orwell's complaint that political language has to consist of "sheer cloudy vagueness" seems still to apply in our day. In February 1981, shortly after President Reagan's appointee as secretary of state appeared before Congress to be confirmed, *The Guardian*, an English newspaper, printed the following editorial, "Nuancing in the Dark." In the writer's opinion, Haig's diction and syntax deserve parody. By the pun *Clausewitz*, the editorial suggests that a holocaust like that of Auschwitz has been visited upon the English language.

> General Alexander Haig has contexted the Polish watchpot somewhat nuancely. How, though, if the situation decontrols, can he stoppage it mountingly conflagrating?
> Haig, in Congressional hearings before his confirmatory, paradoxed his auditioners by abnormalling his responds so that verbs were nouned, nouns verbed, and adjectives adverbized. He techniqued a new way to vocabulary his thoughts so as to informationally uncertain anybody listening about what he had actually implicationed.

At first it seemed that the general was impenetrabling what at basic was clear. This, it was suppositioned, was a new linguistic harbingered by NATO during the time he bell-wethered it. But close observers have alternatived that idea. What Haig is doing, they concept, is to decouple the Russians from everything they are moded to. An example was to obstacle Soviet Ambassador Dobrynin from personalizing the private elevator at Foggy Bottom. Now he has to communal like everybody else.

Experts in the Kremlin thought they could recognition the word-forms of American diplomacy. Now they have to afreshly language themselves up before suddenly told to knight their bishops and rook their pawns.

If that is how General Haig wants to nervous breakdown the Russian leadership he may be shrewding his way to the biggest diplomatic invent since Clausewitz. Unless, that is, he schizophrenes his allies first.

Evidently the parodist is recalling Haig's use of words and phrases such as "epistemologicallywise," "nuanced departures," "caveat my response," and "saddle myself with a statistical fence." For such dustbin language, the 1981 convention of the National Council of Teachers of English paid Haig the ironic tribute of their "Doublespeak Award" (an unwanted honor whose title recalls Orwell's Newspeak and Doublethink), citing him as "the most confusing, evasive, and contradictory public speaker of the year."

· Barbara W. Tuchman ·

BARBARA WERTHEIM TUCHMAN was born in 1912 in New York City. After her graduation from Radcliffe, she became an editorial assistant for *The Nation*, and in 1937 was assigned to Madrid as the magazine's observer of the Spanish Civil War. Later she worked as American correspondent for the *New Statesman and Nation* of London, and, during World War II, as an editor of Far East news for the Office of War Information.

It is as a historian that Tuchman has achieved her widest audience. Two of her eight studies in history have been Pulitzer Prize winners: *The Guns of August* (1962), an account of the outbreak of World War I, and *Stilwell and the American Experience in China* (1971). More recently she has published *A Distant Mirror: The Calamitous 14th Century* (1978); her selected essays, *Practicing History* (1981); and *The March of Folly* (1984). A writer who brings to history a journalist's willingness to do "legwork," Tuchman believes in visiting historic sites before describing them. Before she wrote *The Guns of August* she walked across battlefields in France and Belgium; and in doing research for *A Distant Mirror*, she retraced the steps of the fourteenth-century Crusaders. History, she maintains, has to be readable: "There should be a beginning, a middle, and an end, plus an element of suspense to keep a reader turning the pages."

An Inquiry into
the Persistence of Unwisdom
in Government

What did George III, Napoleon, Kaiser Wilhelm, Chiang Kai-shek, and countless other world leaders have in common? According to Barbara Tuchman, it was wooden-headedness: a refusal to face facts and to learn from experience. "An Inquiry into the Persistence of Unwisdom in Government," first published in *Esquire* (May 1980), contains an argument Tuchman was later to develop in a whole book, *The March of Folly*. In

this more concise survey, she ranges through history and
finds abundant evidence to support her stern opinion that,
from earliest times, wisdom has rarely prevailed among those
who govern — even those who in recent years have governed
the United States. Whether or not you agree with the author,
you will find this contemporary essay intelligent, frank, and
thought provoking.

A problem that strikes one in the study of history, regardless   1
of period, is why man makes a poorer performance of government than of almost any other human activity. In this sphere,
wisdom — meaning judgment acting on experience, common
sense, available knowledge, and a decent appreciation of probability — is less operative and more frustrated than it should be.
Why do men in high office so often act contrary to the way that
reason points and enlightened self-interest suggests? Why does
intelligent mental process so often seem to be paralyzed?

Why, to begin at the beginning, did the Trojan authorities   2
drag that suspicious-looking wooden horse inside their gates?
Why did successive ministries of George III — that "bundle of
imbecility," as Dr. Johnson called them collectively — insist on
coercing rather than conciliating the Colonies though strongly
advised otherwise by many counselors? Why did Napoleon and
Hitler invade Russia? Why did the kaiser's[1] government resume
unrestricted submarine warfare in 1917 although explicitly
warned that this would bring in the United States and that
American belligerency would mean Germany's defeat? Why did
Chiang Kai-shek[2] refuse to heed any voice of reform or alarm
until he woke up to find that his country had slid from under
him? Why did Lyndon Johnson, seconded by the best and the
brightest, progressively involve this nation in a war both ruin-
ous and halfhearted and from which nothing but bad for our

[1]Kaiser Wilhelm (1859–1941), grandson of Queen Victoria and emperor
of Germany, in part responsible for the outbreak of World War I. — EDS.
[2]Chinese general and statesman (1887–1975). President of China, 1948–
1949, and of Taiwan, 1950–1975. — EDS.

side resulted? Why does the present Administration continue to avoid introducing effective measures to reduce the wasteful consumption of oil while members of OPEC follow a price policy that must bankrupt their customers? How is it possible that the Central Intelligence Agency, whose function it is to provide, at taxpayers' expense, the information necessary to conduct a realistic foreign policy, could remain unaware that discontent in a country crucial to our interests was boiling up to the point of insurrection and overthrow of the ruler upon whom our policy rested? It has been reported that the CIA was ordered *not* to investigate the opposition to the shah of Iran in order to spare him any indication that we took it seriously, but since this sounds more like the theater of the absurd than like responsible government, I cannot bring myself to believe it.

There was a king of Spain once, Philip III, who is said to 3 have died of a fever he contracted from sitting too long near a hot brazier, helplessly overheating himself because the functionary whose duty it was to remove the brazier when summoned could not be found. In the late twentieth century, it begins to appear as if mankind may be approaching a similar stage of suicidal incompetence. The Italians have been sitting in Philip III's hot seat for some time. The British trade unions, in a lunatic spectacle, seem periodically bent on dragging their country toward paralysis, apparently under the impression that they are separate from the whole. Taiwan was thrown into a state of shock by the United States' recognition of the People's Republic of China because, according to one report, in the seven years since the Shanghai Communiqué, the Kuomintang rulers of Taiwan had "refused to accept the new trend as a reality."

Wooden-headedness is a factor that plays a remarkably large 4 role in government. Wooden-headedness consists of assessing a situation in terms of preconceived, fixed notions while ignoring or rejecting any contrary signs. It is acting according to wish while not allowing oneself to be confused by the facts.

A classic case was the French war plan of 1914, which con- 5 centrated everything on a French offensive to the Rhine, leaving the French left flank from Belgium to the Channel virtually unguarded. This strategy was based on the belief that the Germans would not use reserves in the front line and, without them, could not deploy enough manpower to extend their invasion through the French left. Reports by intelligence agents in 1913 to the effect that the Germans were indeed preparing their reserves for the front line in case of war were resolutely ignored because the governing spirits in France, dreaming only of their own offensive, did not want to believe in any signals that would require them to strengthen their left at the expense of their march to the Rhine. In the event, the Germans could and did extend themselves around the French left with results that determined a long war and its fearful consequences for our century.

Wooden-headedness is also the refusal to learn from experi-   6
ence, a form in which fourteenth-century rulers were supreme. No matter how often and obviously devaluation of the currency disrupted the economy and angered the people, French monarchs continued to resort to it whenever they were desperate for cash until they provoked insurrection among the bourgeoisie. No matter how often a campaign that depended on living off a hostile country ran into want and even starvation, campaigns for which this fate was inevitable were regularly undertaken.

Still another form is identification of self with the state, as   7
currently exhibited by the ayatollah Khomeini. No wooden-headedness is so impenetrable as that of a religious zealot. Because he is connected with a private wire to the Almighty, no idea coming in on a lesser channel can reach him, which leaves him ill equipped to guide his country in its own best interests.

Philosophers of government ever since Plato have devoted   8
their thinking to the major issues of ethics, sovereignty, the social contract, the rights of man, the corruption of power, the balance between freedom and order. Few — except Machiavelli,[3] who was concerned with government as it is, not as it should be — bothered with mere folly, although this has been a chronic and pervasive problem. "Know, my son," said a dying

---

[3]Italian statesman and political philosopher (1469–1527), author of *The Prince.* — Eps.

Swedish statesman in the seventeenth century, "with how little wisdom the world is governed." More recently, Woodrow Wilson warned, "In public affairs, stupidity is more dangerous than knavery."

Stupidity is not related to type of regime; monarchy, oligar- 9
chy, and democracy produce it equally. Nor is it peculiar to nation or class. The working class as represented by the Communist governments functions no more rationally or effectively in power than the aristocracy or the bourgeoisie, as has notably been demonstrated in recent history. Mao Tse-tung may be admired for many things, but the Great Leap Forward, with a steel plant in every backyard, and the Cultural Revolution were exercises in unwisdom that greatly damaged China's progress and stability, not to mention the chairman's reputation. The record of the Russian proletariat in power can hardly be called enlightened, although after sixty years of control it must be accorded a kind of brutal success. If the majority of Russians are better off now than before, the cost in cruelty and tyranny has been no less and probably greater than under the czars.

After the French Revolution, the new order was rescued 10
only by Bonaparte's military campaigns, which brought the spoils of foreign wars to fill the treasury, and subsequently by his competence as an executive. He chose officials not on the basis of origin or ideology but on the principle of "*la carrière ouverte aux talents*"[4] — the said talents being intelligence, energy, industry, and obedience. That worked until the day of his own fatal mistake.

I do not wish to give the impression that men in office are 11
incapable of governing wisely and well. Occasionally, the exception appears, rising in heroic size above the rest, a tower visible down the centuries. Greece had her Pericles, who ruled with authority, moderation, sound judgment, and a certain nobility that imposes natural dominion over others. Rome had Caesar, a man of remarkable governing talents, although it must be said that a ruler who arouses opponents to resort to assassination is probably not as smart as he ought to be. Later, under Mar-

---

[4]A French saying: "tools to those who can handle them". — EDS.

cus Aurelius and the other Antonines,[5] Roman citizens enjoyed good government, prosperity, and respect for about a century. Charlemagne was able to impose order upon a mass of contending elements, to foster the arts of civilization no less than those of war, and to earn a prestige supreme in the Middle Ages — probably not equaled in the eyes of contemporaries until the appearance of George Washington.

Possessor of an inner strength and perseverance that enabled him to prevail over a sea of obstacles, Washington was one of those critical figures but for whom history might well have taken a different course. He made possible the physical victory of American independence, while around him, in extraordinary fertility, political talent bloomed as if touched by some tropical sun. For all their flaws and quarrels, the Founding Fathers, who established our form of government, were, in the words of Arthur Schlesinger, Sr., "the most remarkable generation of public men in the history of the United States or perhaps of any other nation." It is worth noting the qualities Schlesinger ascribes to them: They were fearless, high-principled, deeply versed in ancient and modern political thought, astute and pragmatic, unafraid of experiment, and — this is significant — "convinced of man's power to improve his condition through the use of intelligence." That was the mark of the Age of Reason that formed them, and though the eighteenth century had a tendency to regard men as more rational than they in fact were, it evoked the best in government from these men.

For our purposes, it would be invaluable if we could know what produced this burst of talent from a base of only two million inhabitants. Schlesinger suggests some contributing factors: wide diffusion of education, challenging economic opportunities, social mobility, training in self-government — all these encouraged citizens to cultivate their political aptitudes to the utmost. Also, he adds, with the Church declining in prestige and with business, science, and art not yet offering competing fields of endeavor, statecraft remained almost the only outlet for men

12

13

[5]Name for several second-century Roman emperors, including Antoninus Pius, Marcus Aurelius, and Commodus. — Eds.

of energy and purpose. Perhaps the need of the moment — the opportunity to create a new political system — is what brought out the best.

Not before or since, I believe, has so much careful and rea-   14
sonable thinking been invested in the creation of a new political system. In the French, Russian, and Chinese revolutions, too much class hatred and bloodshed were involved to allow for fair results or permanent constitutions. The American experience was unique, and the system so far has always managed to right itself under pressure. In spite of accelerating incompetence, it still works better than most. We haven't had to discard the system and try another after every crisis, as have Italy and Germany, Spain and France. The founders of the United States are a phenomenon to keep in mind to encourage our estimate of human possibilities, but their example, as a political scientist has pointed out, is "too infrequent to be taken as a basis for normal expectations."

The English are considered to have enjoyed reasonably be-   15
nign government during the eighteenth and nineteenth centuries, except for their Irish subjects, debtors, child laborers, and other unfortunates in various pockets of oppression. The folly that lost the American colonies reappeared now and then, notably in the treatment of the Irish and the Boers,[6] but a social system can survive a good deal of folly when circumstances are historically favorable or when it is cushioned by large resources, as in the heyday of the British Empire, or absorbed by sheer size, as in this country during our period of expansion. Today there are no more cushions, which makes folly less affordable.

Elsewhere than in government, man has accomplished mar-   16
vels: invented the means in our time to leave the world and voyage to the moon; in the past, harnessed wind and electricity, raised earthbound stone into soaring cathedrals, woven silk brocades out of the spinnings of a worm, composed the music of Mozart and the dramas of Shakespeare, classified the forms of nature, penetrated the mysteries of genetics. Why is he so much

---

[6]South Africans of Dutch extraction. — EDS.

less accomplished in government? What frustrates, in that sphere, the operation of the intellect? Isaac Bashevis Singer,[7] discoursing as a Nobel laureate on mankind, offers the opinion that God had been frugal in bestowing intellect but lavish with passions and emotions. "He gave us," Singer says, "so many emotions and such strong ones that every human being, even if he is an idiot, is a millionaire in emotions."

I think Singer has made a point that applies to our inquiry.   17 What frustrates the workings of intellect is the passions and the emotions: ambition, greed, fear, face-saving, the instinct to dominate, the needs of the ego, the whole bundle of personal vanities and anxieties.

Reason is crushed by these forces. If the Athenians out of   18 pride and overconfidence had not set out to crush Sparta for good but had been content with moderate victory, their ultimate fall might have been averted. If fourteenth-century knights had not been obsessed by the idea of glory and personal prowess, they might have defeated the Turks at Nicopolis with incalculable consequence for all of Eastern Europe. If the English, 200 years ago, had heeded Chatham's[8] knocking on the door of what he called "this sleeping and confounded Ministry" and his urgent advice to repeal the Coercive Acts[9] and withdraw the troops before the "inexpiable drop of blood is shed in an impious war with a people contending in the great cause of publick liberty" or, given a last chance, if they had heeded Edmund Burke's[10] celebrated plea for conciliation and his warning that it would prove impossible to coerce a "fierce people" of their own pedigree, we might still be a united people bridging the Atlantic, with incalculable consequence for the history of the West. It did not happen that way, because king and Parliament felt it imperative to affirm sovereignty over arrogant colonials. The alterna-

[7]Author of novels and stories in Yiddish (b. 1904), now an American citizen and winner of the Nobel Prize for Literature in 1978. — EDS.

[8]William Pitt, earl of Chatham (1708–1788), British statesman who denounced his country's harsh measures against the American colonies. — EDS.

[9]A series of British laws, passed in 1774 in reaction to the Boston Tea Party, designed to close the port of Boston to commerce. — EDS.

[10]Burke (1729–1797) was a British statesman and orator. — EDS.

tive choice, as in Athens and medieval Europe, was close to psychologically impossible.

In the case we know best — the American engagement in   19
Vietnam — fixed notions, preconceptions, wooden-headed thinking, and emotions accumulated into a monumental mistake and classic humiliation. The original idea was that the lesson of the failure to halt fascist aggression during the appeasement era dictated the necessity of halting the so-called aggression by North Vietnam, conceived to be the spearhead of international communism. This was applying the wrong model to the wrong facts, which would have been obvious if our policy makers had taken into consideration the history of the people on the spot instead of charging forward wearing the blinkers of the cold war.

The reality of Vietnamese nationalism, of which Ho Chi   20
Minh had been the standard-bearer since long before the war, was certainly no secret. Indeed, Franklin Roosevelt had insisted that the French should not be allowed to return after the war, a policy that we instantly abandoned the moment the Japanese were out. Ignoring the Vietnamese demand for self-government, we first assisted the return of the French, and then, when, incredibly, they had been put to rout by the native forces, we took their place, as if Dien Bien Phu had no significance whatever. Policy founded upon error multiplies, never retreats. The pretense that North versus South Vietnam represented foreign aggression was intensified. If Asian specialists with knowledge of the situation suggested a reassessment, they were not persuasive. As a Communist aggressor, Hanoi was presumed to be a threat to the United States, yet the vital national interest at stake, which alone may have justified belligerency, was never clear enough to sustain a declaration of war.

A further, more fundamental error confounded our policy.   21
This was the nature of the client. In war, as any military treatise or any soldier who has seen active service will tell you, it is essential to know the nature — that is, the capabilities *and* intentions — of the enemy and no less so of an ally who is the primary belligerent. We fatally underestimated the one and foolishly overestimated the other. Placing reliance on, or hope in, South Viet-

nam was an advanced case of wooden-headedness. Improving on the Bourbons,[11] who forgot nothing and learned nothing, our policy makers forgot everything and learned nothing. The oldest lesson in history is the futility and, often, fatality of foreign interference to maintain in power a government unwanted or hated at home. As far back as 500 B.C., Confucius stated, "Without the confidence of the people, no government can stand," and political philosophers have echoed him down through the ages. What else was the lesson of our vain support of Chiang Kai-shek, within such recent experience? A corrupt or oppressive government may be maintained by despotic means but not for long, as the English occupiers of France learned in the fifteenth century. The human spirit protests and generates a Joan of Arc, for people will not passively endure a government that is in fact unendurable.

The deeper we became involved in Vietnam during the   22
Johnson era, the greater grew the self-deception, the lies, the false body counts, the cheating on Tonkin Gulf, the military mess, domestic dissent, and all those defensive emotions in which, as a result, our leaders became fixed. Their concern for personal ego, public image, and government status determined policy. Johnson was not going to be the first President to preside over defeat; generals could not admit failure nor civilian advisers risk their jobs by giving unpalatable advice.

Males, who so far in history have managed government, are   23
obsessed with potency, which is the reason, I suspect, why it is difficult for them to admit error. I have rarely known a man who, with a smile and a shrug, could easily acknowledge being wrong. Why not? I can, without any damage to self-respect. I can only suppose the difference is that deep in their psyches, men somehow equate being wrong with being impotent. For a Chief of State, it is almost out of the question, and especially so for Johnson and Nixon, who both seem to me to have had shaky self-images. Johnson's showed in his deliberate coarseness and compulsion to humiliate others in crude physical ways. No self-confident man would have needed to do that. Nixon was a

---

[11]Last house of the royal family of France. — EDS.

bundle of inferiorities and sense of persecution. I do not pretend to be a psychohistorian, but in pursuit of this inquiry, the psychological factors must be taken into account. Having no special knowledge of Johnson and Nixon, I will not pursue the question other than to say that it was our misfortune during the Vietnam period to have had two Presidents who lacked the self-confidence for a change of course, much less for a grand withdrawal. "Magnanimity in politics," said Edmund Burke, "is not seldom the truest wisdom, and a great Empire and little minds go ill together."

An essential component of that "truest wisdom" is the self- 24
confidence to reassess. Congressman Morris Udall made this point in the first few days after the nuclear accident at Three Mile Island. Cautioning against a hasty decision on the future of nuclear power, he said, "We have to go back and reassess. There is nothing wrong about being optimistic or making a mistake. The thing that is wrong, as in Vietnam, is *persisting* in a mistake when you see you are going down the wrong road and are caught in a bad situation."

The test comes in recognizing when persistence has become 25
a fatal error. A prince, says Machiavelli, ought always to be a great asker and a patient hearer of truth about those things of which he has inquired, and he should be angry if he finds that anyone has scruples about telling him the truth. Johnson and Nixon, as far as an outsider can tell, were not great askers; they did not want to hear the truth or to face it. Chiang Kai-shek knew virtually nothing of real conditions in his domain because he lived a headquarters life amid an entourage all of whom were afraid to be messengers of ill report. When, in World War I, a general of the headquarters staff visited for the first time the ghastly landscape of the Somme, he broke into tears, saying, "If I had known we sent men to fight in that, I could not have done it." Evidently he was no great asker either.

Neither, we now know, was the shah of Iran. Like Chiang 26
Kai-shek, he was isolated from actual conditions. He was educated abroad, took his vacations abroad, and toured his country, if at all, by helicopter.

Why is it that the major clients of the United States, a coun-   27
try founded on the principle that government derives its just
powers from the consent of the governed, tend to be unpopular
autocrats? A certain schizophrenia between our philosophy and
our practice afflicts American policy, and this split will always
make the policy based on it fall apart. On the day the shah left
Iran, an article summarizing his reign said that "except for the
generals, he has few friends or allies at home." How useful to us
is a ruler without friends or allies at home? He is a kind of luft-
mensch, no matter how rich or how golden a customer for
American business. To attach American foreign policy to a ruler
who does not have the acceptance of his countrymen is hardly
intelligent. By now, it seems to me, we might have learned that.
We must understand conditions — and by conditions, I mean
people and history — on the spot. Wise policy can only be made
on the basis of *informed*, not automatic, judgments.

When it has become evident to those associated with it that   28
a course of policy is pointed toward disaster, why does no one
resign in protest or at least for the peace of his own soul? They
never do. In 1917, the German chancellor Bethmann-Hollweg
pleaded desperately against the proposed resumption of unrestricted submarine warfare, since, by bringing in the United
States, it would revive the Allies' resources, their confidence in
victory, and their will to endure. When he was overruled by the
military, he told a friend who found him sunk in despair that
the decision meant "*finis Germaniae.*" When the friend said simply, "You should resign," Bethmann said he could not, for that
would sow dissension at home and let the world know he believed Germany would fail.

This is always the refuge. The officeholder tells himself he   29
can do more from within and that he must not reveal division at
the top to the public. In fact if there is to be any hope of change
in a democratic society, that is exactly what he must do. No one
of major influence in Johnson's circle resigned over our Vietnam
policy, although several, hoping to play it both ways, hinted
their disagreement. Humphrey, waiting for the nod, never challenged the President's policy, although he campaigned afterward
as an opponent of the war. Since then, I've always thought the
adulation given to him misplaced.

Basically, what keeps officeholders attached to a policy they   30
believe to be wrong is nothing more nor less, I believe, than the
lure of office, or Potomac fever. It is the same whether the locus
is the Thames or the Rhine or, no doubt, the Nile. When Herbert Lehman ran for a second term as senator from New York
after previously serving four terms as governor, his brother
asked him why on earth he wanted it. "Arthur," replied the senator, "after you have once ridden behind a motorcycle escort,
you are never the same again."

Here is a clue to the question of why our performance in   31
government is worse than in other activities: because government offers power, excites that lust for power, which is subject
to emotional drives — to narcissism, fantasies of omnipotence,
and other sources of folly. The lust for power, according to Taci-
tus,[12] "is the most flagrant of all the passions" and cannot really
be satisfied except by power over others. Business offers a kind
of power but only to the very successful at the very top, and
even they, in our day, have to play it down. Fords and Du
Ponts, Hearsts and Pulitzers nowadays are subdued, and the
Rockefeller who most conspicuously wanted power sought it in
government. Other activities — in sports, science, the professions, and the creative and performing arts — offer various satisfactions but not the opportunity for power. They may appeal to
status seeking and, in the form of celebrity, offer crowd worship
and limousines and recognition by headwaiters, but these are
the trappings of power, not the essence. Of course, mistakes and
stupidities occur in nongovernmental activities too, but since
these affect fewer people, they are less noticeable than they are
in public affairs. Government remains the paramount field of
unwisdom because it is there that men seek power over others —
and lose it over themselves.

There are, of course, other factors that lower competence in   32
public affairs, among them the pressure of overwork and over-
scheduling; bureaucracy, especially big bureaucracy; the contest
for votes that gives exaggerated influence to special interests and
an absurd tyranny to public opinion polls. Any hope of intelli-

---

[12]Roman historian (A.D. 55?–after 117). — EDS.

gent government would require that the persons entrusted with high office should formulate and execute policy according to their best judgment and the best knowledge available, not according to every breeze of public opinion. But reelection is on their minds, and that becomes the criterion. Moreover, given schedules broken down into fifteen-minute appointments and staffs numbering in the hundreds and briefing memos of never less than thirty pages, policy makers never have time to *think*. This leaves a rather important vacuum. Meanwhile, bureaucracy rolls on, impervious to any individual or cry for change, like some vast computer that when once penetrated by error goes on pumping it out forever.

Under the circumstances, what are the chances of improving the conduct of government? The idea of a class of professionals trained for the task has been around ever since Plato's *Republic*. Something of the sort animates, I imagine, the new Kennedy School of Government at Harvard. According to Plato, the ruling class in a just society should be men apprenticed to the art of ruling, drawn from the rational and the wise. Since he acknowledged that in natural distribution these are few, he believed they would have to be eugenically bred and nurtured. Government, he said, was a special art in which competence, as in any other profession, could be acquired only by study of the discipline and could not be acquired otherwise. 33

Without reference to Plato, the Mandarins of China were trained, if not bred, for the governing function. They had to pass through years of study and apprenticeship and weeding out by successive examinations, but they do not seem to have developed a form of government much superior to any other, and in the end, they petered out in decadence and incompetence. 34

In seventeenth-century Europe, after the devastation of the Thirty Years' War, the electors of Brandenburg, soon to be combined with Prussia, determined to create a strong state by means of a disciplined army and a trained civil service. Applicants for the civil positions, drawn from commoners in order to offset the nobles' control of the military, had to complete a course of study covering political theory, law and legal philosophy, economics, history, penology, and statutes. Only after passing through vari- 35 ous stages of examination and probationary terms of office did they receive definitive appointments and tenure and opportunity for advancement. The higher civil service was a separate branch, not open to promotion from the middle and lower levels.

The Prussian system proved so effective that the state was able to survive both military defeat by Napoleon in 1807 and the revolutionary surge of 1848. By then it had begun to congeal, losing many of its most progressive citizens in emigration to America; nevertheless, Prussian energies succeeded in 1871 in uniting the German states in an empire under Prussian hegemony. Its very success contained the seed of ruin, for it nourished the arrogance and power hunger that from 1914 through 1918 was to bring it down.   36

In England, instead of responding in reactionary panic to the thunders from the Continent in 1848, as might have been expected, the authorities, with commendable enterprise, ordered an investigation of their own government practices, which were then the virtually private preserve of the propertied class. The result was a report on the need for a permanent civil service to be based on training and specialized skills and designed to provide continuity and maintenance of the long view as against transient issues and political passions. Though heavily resisted, the system was adopted in 1870. It has produced distinguished civil servants but also Burgess, Maclean, Philby, and the fourth man.[13] The history of British government in the last 100 years suggests that factors other than the quality of its civil service determine a country's fate.   37

In the United States, civil service was established chiefly as a barrier to patronage and the pork barrel rather than in search of excellence. By 1937, a presidential commission, finding the system inadequate, urged the development of a "real career service . . . requiring personnel of the highest order, competent, highly trained, loyal, skilled in their duties by reason of long experience, and assured of continuity." After much effort and some   38

[13]British civil servants who in the 1970s were exposed as Russian spies. — EDS.

progress, that goal is still not reached, but even if it were, it would not take care of elected officials and high appointments — that is, of government at the top.

I do not know if the prognosis is hopeful or, given the un-   39
derlying emotional drives, whether professionalism is the cure. In the Age of Enlightenment, John Locke[14] thought the emotions should be controlled by intellectual judgment and that it was the distinction and glory of man to be able to control them. As witnesses of the twentieth century's record, comparable to the worst in history, we have less confidence in our species. Although professionalism can help, I tend to think that fitness of character is what government chiefly requires. How that can be discovered, encouraged, and brought into office is the problem that besets us.

No society has yet managed to implement Plato's design.   40
Now, with money and image-making manipulating our elective process, the chances are reduced. We are asked to choose by the packaging, yet the candidate seen in a studio-filmed spot, sincerely voicing lines from the TelePrompTer, is not the person who will have to meet the unrelenting problems and crucial decisions of the Oval Office. It might be a good idea if, without violating the First Amendment, we could ban all paid political commercials and require candidates (who accept federal subsidy for their campaigns) to be televised live only.

That is only a start. More profound change must come if we   41
are to bring into office the kind of person our form of government needs if it is to survive the challenges of this era. Perhaps rather than educating officials according to Plato's design, we should concentrate on educating the electorate — that is, ourselves — to look for, recognize, and reward character in our representatives and to reject the ersatz.

[14]English philosopher (1632–1704). — Eds.

USEFUL TERMS

Abstract and **Concrete** are names for two kinds of language. Abstract words refer to ideas, conditions, and qualities we cannot directly perceive: *truth, love, courage, evil, wealth, poverty, progressive, reactionary.* Concrete words indicate things we can know with our senses: *tree, chair, bird, pen, motorcycle, perfume, thunderclap, cheeseburger.* The use of concrete words lends vigor and clarity to writing, for such words help a reader to picture things. See *Image.*

Writers of expository essays tend to shift back and forth from one kind of language to the other. They often begin a paragraph with a general statement full of abstract words ("There is *hope* for the *future* of *motoring*"). Then they usually go on to give examples and present evidence in sentences full of concrete words ("Inventor *Jones* claims his *car* will go from *Fresno* to *Los Angeles* on a *gallon* of *peanut oil*"). Beginning writers often use too many abstract words and not enough concrete ones.

Allusion refers a reader to any person, place, or thing in fact, fiction, or legend that the writer believes is common knowledge. An allusion (a single reference) may point to a famous event, a familiar saying, a noted personality, a well-known story or song. Usually brief, an allusion is a space-saving way to convey much meaning. For example, the statement "The game was Coach Johnson's Waterloo" informs the reader that, like Napoleon meeting defeat in a celebrated battle, the coach led a confrontation resulting in his downfall and that of his team. If the writer is also showing Johnson's character, the allusion might further tell us that the coach is a man of Napoleonic ambition and pride. To observe "He is our town's J. R. Ewing" concisely says several things: that a leading citizen is unscrupulous, deceptive, merciless, rich, and eager to become richer — perhaps superficially charming and promiscuous as well. To make an effective allusion, you have to be aware of your audience. If your readers are not likely to recognize the allusion, it will only confuse. Not everyone, for example, would understand you if you alluded to a neighbor, to a seventeenth-century Russian harpsichordist, or to a little-known stock car driver.

Analogy is a form of exposition that uses an extended comparison based on the like features of two unlike things: one familiar or easily understood, the other unfamiliar, abstract, or complicated. See Chapter 7. For *Argument by Analogy* see the list of *Logical Fallacies* on page 447.

Argument is one of the four principal modes of writing, whose function is to convince readers. See Chapter 10.

Audience, for a writer, means readers. Having in mind a particular audience helps the writer in choosing strategies. Imagine, for instance, that you are writing two reviews of *Splash*, a movie about a mermaid: one for the students who read the campus newspaper, the other for amateur and professional filmmakers who read *Millimeter*. For the first audience, you might write about the actors, the plot, and especially dramatic scenes. You might judge the picture and urge your readers to see it — or to avoid it. Writing for *Millimeter*, you might discuss special effects, shooting techniques, problems in editing and in mixing picture and sound. In this review, you might use more specialized and technical terms. Obviously, an awareness of the interests and knowledge of your readers, in each case, would help you decide how to write. If you told readers of the campus paper too much about filming techniques, you would lose most of them. If you told *Millimeter*'s readers the plot of the film in detail and how you liked its humor, probably you would put them to sleep.

You can increase your awareness of your audience by asking yourself a few questions before you begin to write. Who are to be your readers? What is their age level? Background? Education? Where do they live? What are their beliefs and attitudes? What interests them? What, if anything, sets them apart from most people? How familiar are they with your subject? Knowing your audience can help you write so that your readers will not only understand you better, but more deeply care about what you say.

Cause and Effect is a form of exposition in which a writer analyzes reasons for an action, event, or decision, or analyzes its consequences. See Chapter 8.

Classification is a form of exposition in which a writer sorts out plural things (contact sports, college students, kinds of music) into categories. See Chapter 6.

Cliché (French) is a name for any worn-out, trite expression that a writer employs thoughtlessly. Although at one time the expression may have been colorful, from heavy use it has lost its luster. It is now "old as the hills." In conversation, most of us sometimes use clichés, but in writing they "stick out like sore thumbs." Alert writers, when they revise, replace a cliché with a fresh, concrete expression. Writers who have trouble recognizing clichés generally need to read more widely. Their problem is that, so many expressions being new to them, they do not know which ones are full of moths.

Coherence is the clear connection of the parts in a piece of effective writing. This quality exists when the reader can easily follow the flow of ideas between sentences, paragraphs, and larger divisions, and can see how they relate successively to one another.

In making your essay coherent, you may find certain devices useful. Transitions, for instance, can bridge ideas. Reminders of points you have stated earlier are helpful to a reader who may have forgotten them — as readers tend to do sometimes, particularly if your essay is long. However, a coherent essay is not one merely pasted together with transitions and reminders. It derives its coherence from the clear relationship between its thesis (or central idea) and all its parts.

Colloquial Expressions are those which occur primarily in speech and informal writing that seeks a relaxed, conversational tone. "My favorite chow is a burger and a shake" or "This math exam has me climbing the walls" may be acceptable in talking to a roommate, in corresponding with a friend, or in writing a humorous essay for general readers. Such choices of words, however, would be out of place in formal writing — in, say, a laboratory report or a letter to your senator. Contractions (*let's, don't, we'll*) and abbreviated words (*photo, sales rep, TV*) are the shorthand of spoken language. Good writers use such expressions with an awareness that they produce an effect of casualness.

Comparison and Contrast, two writing strategies, are usually found together. They are a form of exposition in which a writer examines the similarities and differences between two things in order to reveal their natures. See Chapter 4.

Conclusions are those sentences or paragraphs that bring an essay to a satisfying and logical end. They are purposefully crafted to give a sense of unity and completeness to the whole essay. The best conclusions evolve naturally out of what has gone before and convince the reader that the essay is indeed at an end, not that the writer has run out of steam.

Conclusions vary in type and length depending on the nature and scope of the essay. A long research paper may require several paragraphs of summary to review and emphasize the main points. A short essay, however, may benefit from a few brief closing sentences.

In concluding an essay, beware of diminishing the impact of your writing by finishing on a weak note. Don't apologize for what you have or have not written, or cram in a final detail that would have been better placed elsewhere.

Although there are no set formulas for closing, the following list presents several options:

1. Restate the thesis of your essay, and perhaps your main points.

2. Mention the broader implications or significance of your topic.

3. Give a final example that pulls all the parts of your discussion together.

4. Offer a prediction.

5. End with the most important point as the culmination of your essay's development.

6. Suggest how the reader can apply the information you have just imparted.

7. End with a bit of drama or flourish. Tell an anecdote, offer an appropriate quotation, ask a question, make a final insightful remark. Keep in mind, however, that an ending shouldn't sound false and gimmicky. It truly has to conclude.

Concrete: See *Abstract and Concrete.*

Connotation and **Denotation** are names for the two types of meanings most words have. Denotation is the explicit, literal, dictionary definition of a word. Connotation refers to the implied meaning, resonant with associations, of a word. The denotation of *blood* is "the fluid that circulates in the vascular system." The word's connotations range from *life force* to *gore* to *family bond*. A doctor might use the word *blood* for its denotation, and a mystery writer might rely on the rich connotations of the word to heighten a scene.

Because people have different experiences, they bring to the same word different associations. A conservative Republican's emotional response to the word *welfare* is not likely to be the same as a liberal Democrat's. And referring to your senator as a statesman evokes a different response, from him and from others, than if you were to call him a baby-kisser, or even a politician. The effective use of words involves knowing both what they mean literally and what they are likely to suggest.

Deduction is the method of reasoning from general to specific. See page 445.

Definition may refer to a statement of the literal and specific meaning or meanings of a word (*short definition*), or to a form of expository writing (*extended definition*). In the latter, the writer usually explains the nature of a word, a thing, a concept, or a phenomenon; in doing so the writer may employ narration, description, or any of the expository methods. See Chapter 9.

Denotation: See *Connotation and Denotation*.

Description is a mode of writing that conveys sensory evidence. See Chapter 2.

Diction is a choice of words. Every written or spoken statement contains diction of some kind. To describe certain aspects of diction, the following terms may be useful:

Standard English: words and grammatical forms that native speakers of the language use in formal writing.

Nonstandard English: words and grammatical forms such as *theirselves* and *ain't* that occur mainly in the speech of people of a particular social background.

Slang: certain words in highly informal speech or writing.

Colloquial expressions: words and phrases from conversation. See *Colloquial Expressions* for examples.

Regional terms: words heard in a certain locality, such as *spritzing* for raining in Pennsylvania Dutch country.

Dialect: a variety of English based on differences in geography, education, or social background. Dialect is usually spoken, but may be written. Maya Angelou's essay in Chapter 1 transcribes the words of dialect speakers: people waiting for the fight broadcast ("He gone whip him till that white boy call him Momma").

Technical terms: words and phrases that form the vocabulary of a particular discipline (*monocotyledon* from botany), occupation (*drawplate* from die-making), or avocation (*interval training* from running). See also *Jargon.*

Archaisms: old-fashioned expressions, once common but now used to suggest an earlier style, such as *ere*, *yon*, and *forsooth*. (Actually, *yon* is still current in the expression *hither and yon*; but if you say "Behold yon glass of beer!" it is an archaism.)

Obsolete diction: words that have passed out of use (such as the verb *werien*, "to protect or defend," and the noun *isetnesses*, "agreements"). *Obsolete* may also refer to certain meanings of words no longer current (*fond* for foolish, *clipping* for hugging or embracing).

Pretentious diction: use of words more numerous and elaborate than necessary, such as *institution of higher learning* for college, and *partake of solid nourishment* for eat.

To be sure, archaisms and pretentious diction have no place in good writing unless a writer deliberately uses them for ironic or humorous effect: H. L. Mencken has delighted in the hifalutin use of *tonsorial studio* instead of barber shop. Still, any diction may be the right diction for a certain occasion: The choice of words depends on a writer's purpose and audience.

Division is a form of expository writing in which the writer separates a single subject into its parts. See Chapter 6.

Effect, the result of an event or action, is usually considered together with *cause* as a form of exposition. See the discussion of cause and effect in Chapter 8. The term *effect* may also refer to the impression a word, sentence, paragraph, or entire work makes on its audience.

Emphasis is stress or special importance given to a certain point or element to make it stand out. A skillful writer draws attention to what is most important in a sentence, paragraph, or essay by controlling emphasis in any of the following ways:

Proportion: Important ideas are given greater coverage than minor points.

Position: The beginnings and ends of sentences, paragraphs, and larger divisions are the strongest positions. Placing key ideas in these spots helps draw attention to their importance. The end is the stronger position, for what stands last stands out. A sentence in which less important details precede the main point is called a *periodic sentence*: "Having disguised himself as a guard and walked through the courtyard to the side gate, the prisoner made his escape." A sentence in which the main point precedes less important details is a *loose sentence*: "Autumn is orange: gourds in baskets at roadside stands, the harvest moon hanging like a pumpkin, and oak and beech leaves flashing like goldfish."

Repetition: Careful repetition of key words or phrases can give them greater importance. (Careless repetition, however, can cause boredom.)

Mechanical devices: Italics (underlining), capital letters, and exclamation points can make words or sentences stand out. Writers sometimes fall back on these devices, however, after failing to show significance by other means. Italics and exclamation points can be useful in reporting speech, but excessive use sounds exaggerated or bombastic.

Essay refers to a short nonfiction composition on one central theme or subject in which the writer may offer personal views. Essays are sometimes classified as either formal or informal. In general, a *formal essay* is one whose diction is that of the written language (not colloquial speech), serious in tone, and usually focused on a subject the writer believes is important. (For example, see Barbara W. Tuchman's "An Inquiry into the Persistence of Unwisdom in Government.") An *informal essay*, in contrast, is more likely to admit colloquial expressions; the writer's tone tends to be lighter, perhaps humorous, and the subject is likely to be personal, sometimes even trivial. (See James Thurber's "University Days.") These distinctions, however, are rough ones: an essay such as Judy Syfers's "I Want a Wife" may use colloquial language and speak of personal experience, though it is serious in tone and has an undeniably important subject.

Evaluation is judging merits. In evaluating a work of writing, you suspend personal preference and judge its success in fulfilling the writer's apparent purpose. For instance, if an essay tells how to tune up a car and you have no interest in engines, you nevertheless decide how clearly and effectively the writer explains the process to you.

Evidence is the factual basis for an argument or an explanation. In a courtroom, an attorney's case is only as good as the evidence marshaled to support it. In an essay, a writer's opinions and generalizations also must rest upon evidence, usually given in the form of facts and examples.

Example, also called *exemplification*, is a form of exposition in which the writer illustrates a general idea. See Chapter 3. An example is a verbal illustration.

Exposition is the mode of prose writing that explains a subject. Its function is to inform, to instruct, or to set forth ideas. Exposition may call various methods to its service: example, comparison and contrast, process analysis, division, classification, analogy, cause and effect. Expository writing exposes information: the major trade routes in the Middle East, how to make a dulcimer, why the United States consumes more energy than it needs. Most college writing is exposition, and most of the essays in this book (those in Chapters 3 through 9) are expository.

Figures of Speech occur whenever a writer, for the sake of emphasis or vividness, departs from the literal meanings (or denotations) of words. To say "She's a jewel" doesn't mean that the subject of praise is literally a kind of shining stone; the statement makes sense because its connotations come to mind: rare, priceless, worth cherishing. Some figures of speech involve comparisons of two objects apparently unlike. A *simile* (from the Latin, "likeness") states the comparison directly, usually connecting the two things using "like," "as," or "than": "The moon is like a snowball," "He's lazy as a cat full of cream," "My feet are flatter than flyswatters." A *metaphor* (from the Greek, "transfer") declares one thing *to be* another: "A mighty fortress is our God," "The sheep were bolls of cotton on the hill." (A *dead metaphor* is a word or phrase that, originally a figure of speech, has come to be literal through common usage: "the *hands* of a clock.") *Personification* is a simile or metaphor that assigns human traits to inanimate objects or abstractions: "A stoop-shouldered refrigerator hummed quietly to itself," "All of a sudden the solution to the math problem sat there winking at me."

Other figures of speech consist of deliberate misrepresentations. *Hyperbole* (from the Greek, "throwing beyond") is a conscious exaggeration: "I'm so hungry I could eat a horse and saddle," "I'd wait for you a thousand years." Its opposite, *understatement*, creates an ironic or humorous effect: "I accepted the ride. At the moment, I didn't much feel like walking across the Mojave Desert." A *paradox* is a seemingly self-contradictory statement that, on reflection, makes sense: "Children are the poor man's wealth." (Wealth can be monetary, or it can be spiritual.)

Focus is the narrowing of a subject to make it manageable. Beginning with a general subject, you concentrate on a certain aspect of it. For instance, you may select crafts as a general subject, then decide your main interest lies in weaving. You could focus your essay still further by narrowing it to operating a hand loom. You can also focus your writing according to who will read it (*Audience*) or what you want it to achieve (*Purpose*).

General and **Specific** refer to words and describe their relative degrees of abstractness. General words name a group or class (*flowers*); specific words limit the class by naming its individual members (*rose, violet, dahlia, marigold*). Words may be arranged in a series from general to specific: *clothes, pants, jeans, Levis.* The word *cat* is more specific than *animal*, but less specific than *tiger cat*, or *Garfield.* See also *Abstract and Concrete.*

Generalization refers to a statement about a class based on an examination of some of its members: "Lions are fierce." The more members examined and the more representative they are of the class, the sturdier the generalization. Insufficient or nonrepresentative evidence often leads to a hasty generalization. The statement "Solar heat saves homeowners money" would be challenged by homeowners who have yet to recover their installation costs. "Solar heat can save homeowners money in the long run" would be a sounder generalization. Words such as *all, every, only,* and *always* have to be used with care. "Some artists are alcoholics" is more credible than "Artists are always alcoholics." Making a trustworthy generalization involves the use of *inductive reasoning* (discussed on pages 445–446).

Hyperbole: See *Figures of Speech*

Illustration is another name for the expository method of giving examples. See Chapter 3.

Image refers to a word or word sequence that evokes a sensory experience. Whether literal ("We picked two red apples") or figurative ("His cheeks looked like two red apples, buffed and shining"), an image appeals to the reader's memory of seeing, hearing, smelling, touching, or tasting. Images add concreteness to fiction — "The farm looked as tiny and still as a seashell, with the little knob of a house surrounded by its curved furrows of tomato plants" (Eudora Welty in a short story, "The Whistle") — and are an important element in poetry. But writers of essays, too, find images valuable in giving examples, in describing, in comparing and contrasting, and in drawing analogies.

Induction is the process of reasoning to a conclusion about an entire class by examining some of its members. See pages 445–446.

Introductions are the openings of written works. Often they state the writer's subject, narrow it, and communicate an attitude toward it (*Tone*). Introductions vary in length, depending on their purposes. A research paper may need several paragraphs to set forth its central idea and its plan of organization; on the other hand, a brief, informal essay may need only a sentence or two for an introduction. Whether long or short, good introductions tell us no more than we need to know when we begin reading. Here are a few possible ways to open an essay effectively:

1. State your central idea, perhaps showing why you care
about it.
2. Present startling facts about your subject.
3. Tell an illustrative anecdote.
4. Give background information that will help your reader understand your subject, or see why it is important.
5. Begin with an arresting quotation.
6. Ask a challenging question. (In your essay, you'll go on to
answer it.)

Irony is a manner of speaking or writing that does not directly state a
discrepancy, but implies one. *Verbal irony* is the intentional use of
words to suggest a meaning other than literal: "What a mansion!"
(said of a shack); "There's nothing like sunshine" (said on a foggy
morning). If irony is delivered contemptuously with intent to
hurt, we call it *sarcasm*: "Oh, you're a real friend!" (said to someone who refuses to lend the speaker a dime to make a phone call).
Certain situations also can be ironic, when we sense in them some
incongruity, some result contrary to expectation, or some twist of
fate: Juliet regains consciousness only to find that Romeo, believing her dead, has stabbed himself.

Jargon, strictly speaking, is the special vocabulary of a trade or profession; but the term has also come to mean inflated, vague, meaningless language of any kind. It is characterized by wordiness, abstractions galore, pretentious diction, and needlessly complicated
word order. Whenever you meet a sentence that obviously could
express its idea in fewer words and shorter ones, chances are that
it is jargon. For instance: "The motivating force compelling her to
opt continually for the most labor-intensive mode of operation in
performing her functions was consistently observed to be the single constant and regular factor in her behavior patterns." Translation: "She did everything the hard way." For more specimens of
jargon, see the examples George Orwell gives in "Politics and the
English Language" (For Further Reading).

Metaphor: See *Figures of Speech*.

Narration is the mode of writing that tells a story. See Chapter 1.

Nonstandard English: See *Diction*.

Objective and **Subjective** are names for kinds of writing that differ
in emphasis. In objective writing, the emphasis falls on the topic;
in subjective writing, it falls on the writer's view of the topic. Objective writing occurs in factual reporting, certain kinds of process
analysis (such as recipes, directions, and instructions), and logical
arguments in which the writer attempts to omit personal feelings
and opinions. Subjective writing sets forth the writer's feelings,
opinions, and interpretations. It occurs in friendly letters, jour-

nals, editorials, by-lined feature stories and columns in newspapers, personal essays, and arguments that appeal to emotion. Very few essays, however, contain one kind of writing exclusive of the other.

Paradox: See *Figures of Speech.*

Paragraph refers to a group of closely related sentences that develop a central idea. In an essay, a paragraph is the most important unit of thought because it is both self-contained and part of the larger whole. Paragraphs separate long and involved ideas into smaller parts that are more manageable for the writer and easier for the reader to take in. Good paragraphs, like good essays, possess unity and coherence. The central idea is usually stated in the topic sentence, often found at the beginning of the paragraph. All other sentences in the paragraph relate to this topic sentence, defining it, explaining it, illustrating it, providing it with evidence and support. Sometimes you will meet a unified and coherent paragraph that has no topic sentence. It usually contains a central idea that no sentence in it explicitly states, but that every sentence in it clearly implies.

Parallelism, or **Parallel Structure**, is a name for a habit of good writers: keeping ideas of equal importance in similar grammatical form. A writer may place nouns side by side ("*Time* and *tide* wait for no man") or in a series ("Give me *wind, sea,* and *stars*"). Phrases, too, may be arranged in parallel structure ("*Out of my bed, into my shoes, up to my classroom* — that's my life"); or clauses ("Ask not what your country can do for you; ask what you can do for your country").

Parallelism may be found not only in single sentences, but in larger units as well. A paragraph might read: "Rhythm is everywhere. It throbs in the rain forests of Brazil. It vibrates ballroom floors in Vienna. It snaps its fingers on street corners in Chicago." In a whole essay, parallelism may be the principle used to arrange ideas in a balanced or harmonious structure. See, for instance, James C. Rettie's essay " 'But a Watch in the Night,' " in which paragraphs 6 through 14 begin with transitions indicating when certain events took place. See the famous speech given by Martin Luther King, Jr. (Chapter 10), in which each paragraph in a series (paragraphs 11 through 18) begins with the words "I have a dream" and goes on to describe an imagined future. Not only does such a parallel structure organize ideas, but it also lends them force.

Paraphrase is putting another writer's thoughts into your own words. In writing a research paper or an essay containing evidence gathered from your reading, you will find it necessary to paraphrase — unless you are using another writer's very words with quotation marks around them. In paraphrasing, you rethink what the other writer has said, decide what is essential, and determine how you would say it otherwise. (Of course, you still acknowledge your source.) The purpose of paraphrasing is not merely to avoid copying word for word, but to adapt material to the needs of your own paper.

Although a paraphrase sometimes makes material briefer, it does not always do so; in principle, it rewrites and restates, sometimes in the same number of words, if not more. A condensation of longer material that renders it more concise is called a *summary*: for instance, a statement of the plot of a whole novel in a few sentences.

Person is a grammatical distinction made between the speaker, the one spoken to, and the one spoken about. In the first person (*I, we*), the subject is speaking; in the second person (*you*), the subject is being spoken to; in the third person (*he, she, it*), the subject is being spoken about. The *point of view* of an essay or work of fiction is often specified according to person: "This short story is told from a first person point of view." See *Point of View*.

Personification: See *Figures of Speech*.

Persuasion is a function of argument. See Chapter 10.

Point of View, in an essay, is the physical position or the mental angle from which a writer beholds a subject. Assuming the subject is starlings, the following three writers have different points of view. An ornithologist might write about the introduction of these birds into North America. A farmer might advise other farmers how to prevent the birds from eating seed. A bird-watcher might describe a first glad sighting of an unusual species. Furthermore, the *person* of each essay would probably differ. The scientist might present a scholarly paper in the third person; the farmer might offer advice in the second; the bird-watcher might recount the experience in the first. See *Person*.

Premise is a name for a proposition that supports a conclusion. In a *syllogism* we reason deductively from the major and minor premises to the conclusion that necessarily follows. See *Deduction*. In expository writing, premises are the assumptions on which an author bases an argument.

Prewriting generally refers to that stage or stages in the process of composition before words start to flow. It is the activity of the mind before setting pen or typewriter keys to paper, and may include evoking ideas, deciding on a topic, narrowing the topic, doing factual reading and research, defining your audience, planning and arranging material. An important stage of prewriting usually comes first: *invention*, the creation or discovery of ideas. Invention may follow from daydreaming or meditation, reading, keeping a journal, or perhaps carefully ransacking your memory.

As composition theorist D. Gordon Rohman has observed, prewriting may be defined as "the stage of discovery in the writing process when a person assimilates his subject to himself." In practice, the prewriting stage sometimes doesn't neatly end with the picking up of paper; reading, research, taking into account your audience, and further discovery may take place even while you write.

Process Analysis is a form of exposition that most often explains step by step how something is done or how to do something. See Chapter 5.

Purpose is a writer's reason for writing; it is whatever the writer of any work tries to achieve. To achieve unity and coherence, a writer identifies a purpose before beginning to write. The more clearly defined the purpose, the better the writer can concentrate on achieving it.

In trying to define the purpose of an essay you read, ask yourself, Why did the writer write this? or What was this writer trying to achieve? Even though you cannot know the writer's intentions with absolute certainty, an effective essay always makes some purpose clear.

Rhetoric is the study (and the art) of using language effectively. Often the modes of prose discourse (narration, description, exposition, and argument) and the various methods of exposition (exemplification, comparison and contrast, and the others) are called rhetorical forms.

Rhetorical Question indicates a question posed for effect, one that requires no answer. Instead, it often provokes thought, lends emphasis to a point, asserts or denies something without making a direct statement, launches further discussion, introduces an opinion, or leads the reader where the writer intends. Sometimes a writer throws one in to introduce variety in a paragraph full of declarative sentences. The following questions are rhetorical: "When will the United States learn that sending people to the moon does not feed them on earth?" — "Shall I compare thee to a summer's day?" — "What shall it profit a man to gain the whole world if he lose his immortal soul?" Both reader and writer know what the answers are supposed to be. (1. Someday, if the United States ever wises up; 2. Yes; 3. Nothing.) For examples of rhetorical questions used well, see Malcolm Cowley's essay "Vices and Pleasures: The View from 80."

Satire is a form of writing that employs wit to attack folly. Unlike most comedy, the purpose of satire is not merely to entertain, but to bring about enlightenment — even reform. Frequently, satire will employ irony — as in Jonathan Swift's "A Modest Proposal." For another illustration of this form see Russell Baker's "Universal Military Motion" (Chapter 10).

Sentimentality is a quality sometimes found in writing that fails to communicate. Such writing calls for an extreme emotional response on the part of an audience, although its writer fails to supply adequate reason for any such reaction. A sentimental writer delights in waxing teary over certain objects: great-grandmother's portrait, the first stick of chewing gum baby chewed (now a shapeless wad), an empty popcorn box saved from the World Series of 1952. Sentimental writing usually results when writers shut their eyes to the actual world, preferring to snuffle the sweet scents of remembrance.

Simile: See *Figures of Speech*.

Slang: See *Diction*.

Standard English: See *Diction*.

Strategy refers to whatever means a writer employs to write effectively. The methods set forth in each chapter of this book are strategies; but so are narrowing a subject, organizing ideas clearly, using transitions, writing with an awareness of your reader, and other effective writing practices.

Style is the distinctive manner in which a writer writes; it may be seen especially in the writer's choice of words and sentence structure. Two writers may write on the same subject, even express similar ideas, but it is style that gives each writer's work a personality.

Suspense is often an element in narration: the pleasurable expectation or anxiety we feel that keeps us reading a story. In an exciting mystery story, suspense is constant: how will it all turn out? — Will the detective get to the scene in time to prevent another murder? But there can be suspense in less melodramatic accounts as well. In reading Maxine Hong Kingston's "My Legal Father Enters America," we learn from the title how the story will turn out; the suspense lies in our desire to learn exactly how the father will succeed in defeating the U.S. Immigration Service.

Syllogism is a name for a three-step form of reasoning that employs deduction. See page 445 for an illustration.

Symbol is a name for a visible object or action that suggests some further meaning. The flag suggests country, the crown suggests royalty — these are conventional symbols familiar to us. Life abounds in such relatively clear-cut symbols. Football teams use dolphins and rams for easy identification; married couples symbolize their union with a ring.

In writing, symbols usually do not have such a one-to-one correspondence, but evoke a whole constellation of associations. In Herman Melville's *Moby Dick*, the whale suggests more than the large mammal it is. It hints at evil, obsession, and the untamable forces of nature. Such a symbol carries meanings too complex or elusive to be neatly defined.

More common in fiction and poetry than in expository writing, symbols can be used to good purpose in exposition because they often communicate an idea in a compact and concrete way.

Thesis is the central idea in a work of writing, to which everything else in the work refers. In some way, each sentence and each paragraph in an effective essay serve to support the thesis and to make it clear and explicit to an audience. Good writers, before they begin to write, often set down a *thesis sentence* or *thesis statement* to help them define their purpose. This thesis sentence, for instance, might have served Andrew Ward in writing his essay in Chapter 3: "The miserable old neighborhood gas station was preferable to the self-service station of today."

Tone refers to the way a writer regards subject, audience, or self. It is the writer's attitude, and sets the prevailing spirit of whatever he or she writes. Tone in writing varies as greatly as tone of voice varies in conversation. It can be serious, distant, flippant, angry, enthusiastic, sincere, or sympathetic. Whatever tone a writer chooses, usually it informs an entire essay and helps a reader decide how to respond.

Topic Sentence is a name for the statement of the central idea in a paragraph. Often it will appear at (or near) the beginning of the paragraph, announcing the idea and beginning its development. Because all other sentences in the paragraph explain and support this central idea, the topic sentence is a way to create unity.

Transitions are words, phrases, sentences, or even paragraphs that relate ideas. In moving from one topic to the next, a writer has to bring the reader along by showing how the ideas are developing, what bearing a new thought or detail has on an earlier discussion, or why a new topic is being introduced. A clear purpose, strong ideas, and logical development certainly aid coherence, but to ensure that the reader is following along, good writers provide signals, or transitions.

To bridge paragraphs and to point out relationships within them, you can use some of the following devices of transition:

1. Repeat words or phrases to produce an echo in the reader's mind.

2. Use parallel structures to produce a rhythm that moves the reader forward.

3. Use pronouns to refer back to nouns in earlier passages.

4. Use transitional words and phrases. These may indicate a relationship of time (*right away, later, soon, meanwhile, in a few minutes, that night*), proximity (*beside, close to, distant from, nearby, facing*), effect (*therefore, for this reason, as a result, consequently*), comparison (*similarly, in the same way, likewise*), or contrast (*yet, but, nevertheless, however, despite*). Some words and phrases of transition simply add on: *besides, too, also, moreover, in addition to, second, last, in the end.*

Understatement: See *Figures of Speech.*

Unity is the quality of good writing in which all parts relate to the thesis. (See *Thesis.*) In a unified essay, all words, sentences, and paragraphs support the single central idea. Your first step in achieving unity is to state your thesis; your next step is to organize your thoughts so that they make your thesis clear.

ESSAYS ARRANGED
BY SUBJECT

CHILDREN AND FAMILY

CONTEMPORARY ISSUES

COPING WITH LIFE

HISTORY

HUMOR AND SATIRE

LAW

MANNERS AND MORALS

PSYCHOLOGY AND BEHAVIOR

READING, WRITING, AND LANGUAGE

SCHOOL AND COLLEGE

SCIENCE AND TECHNOLOGY

SELF-DISCOVERY

SPORTS AND LEISURE

WARFARE AND WEAPONS

WOMEN

WORK AND BUSINESS

(Continued from page iv)

Peter Elbow, "Desperation Writing." From *Writing Without Teachers* by Peter Elbow. Copyright © 1973 by Oxford University Press, Inc. Reprinted by permission.

Joseph Epstein, "What Is Vulgar?" Reprinted from *The American Scholar*, Volume 51, Number 1, Winter, 1981/82. Copyright © 1981 by the author. Reprinted by permission of the publishers.

Paul Fussell, "Notes on Class." From *The Boy Scout Handbook and Other Observations* by Paul Fussell. Copyright © 1982 by Paul Fussell. Reprinted by permission of Oxford University Press, Inc.

Jeff Greenfield, "The Black and White Truth about Basketball." Reprinted by permission of The Sterling Lord Agency, Inc. Copyright © 1980, 1984 by Jeff Greenfield.

Dick Gregory, "If You Had to Kill Your Own Hog." From *The Shadow That Scares Me* by Dick Gregory. Copyright © 1968 by Dick Gregory. Reprinted by permission of Doubleday & Company, Inc.

Banesh Hoffmann, "My Friend, Albert Einstein." Reprinted with permission from the January 1968 *Reader's Digest*. Copyright © 1967 by The Reader's Digest Assn., Inc.

Martin Luther King, Jr., "I Have a Dream." Reprinted by permission of Joan Daves. Copyright © 1963 by Martin Luther King, Jr.

Maxine Hong Kingston, "My Legal Father Enters America." From *China Men*, by Maxine Hong Kingston. Copyright © 1977, 1978, 1979, 1980 by Maxine Hong Kingston. Reprinted by permission of Alfred A. Knopf, Inc.

Margaret Mead, "New Superstitions for Old — January, 1966." From *A Way of Seeing* by Margaret Mead and Rhoda Metraux. Copyright © 1966, 1970 by Margaret Mead and Rhoda Metraux. By permission of William Morrow & Co.

H. L. Mencken, "The Penalty of Death." From *A Mencken Chrestomathy*, by H. L. Mencken. Copyright 1926 by Alfred A. Knopf, Inc. and renewed 1954 by H. L. Mencken. Reprinted by permission, Alfred A. Knopf, Inc.

Arthur R. Miller, "Self-Defense: Can You Protect Yourself and Avoid the Slammer?" From *Miller's Court* by Arthur Miller. Copyright © 1982 by Arthur R. Miller. Reprinted by permission of Houghton Mifflin Co.

Jessica Mitford, "Behind the Formaldehyde Curtain." From *The American Way of Death* by Jessica Mitford. Copyright © 1963, 1978 by Jessica Mitford. Reprinted by permission of Simon & Schuster, Inc.

William Least Heat Moon, excerpt from *Blue Highways* by William Least Heat Moon. Copyright © 1982 by William Least Heat Moon. By permission of Little, Brown and Company in association with the Atlantic Monthly Press.

Flannery O'Connor, "Total Effect and the Eighth Grade." From *Mystery and Manners* by Flannery O'Connor. Copyright © 1957, 1961, 1963, 1964,

To the Student

We regularly revise the books we publish in order to make them better. To do this well we need to know what instructors and students think of the previous edition. At some point your instructor will be asked to comment on *The Bedford Reader*; now we would like to hear from you.

Please take a few minutes to complete this questionnaire and send it to Bedford Books of St. Martin's Press, 29 Commonwealth Avenue, Boston, Massachusetts 02116. We promise to listen to what you have to say. Thanks.

School _____

School location (city, state) _____

Course title _____

Instructor's name _____

Please rate the selections.

	Liked a lot	Okay	Didn't like	Didn't read
Thomas, *On Smell*	___	___	___	___
Thurber, *University Days*	___	___	___	___
Angelou, *Champion of the World*	___	___	___	___
Trillin, *It's Just Too Late*	___	___	___	___
Kingston, *My Legal Father Enters America*	___	___	___	___
Postscript on Process	___	___	___	___
Didion, *In Bed*	___	___	___	___
White, *Once More to the Lake*	___	___	___	___
Orwell, *The Moon under Water*	___	___	___	___

	Liked a lot	Okay	Didn't like	Didn't read
Dillard, *Lenses*	—	—	—	—
Postscript on Process	—	—	—	—
Miller, *Self-Defense*	—	—	—	—
Ward, *They Also Wait Who Stand and Serve Themselves*	—	—	—	—
Hoffmann, *My Friend, Albert Einstein*	—	—	—	—
Cowley, *Vices and Pleasures*	—	—	—	—
Rosenblatt, *Oops! How's That Again?*	—	—	—	—
Postscript on Process	—	—	—	—
Catton, *Grant and Lee*	—	—	—	—
Updike, *Venezuela for Visitors*	—	—	—	—
Rosenthal, *No News from Auschwitz*	—	—	—	—
Greenfield, *The Black and White Truth about Basketball*	—	—	—	—
Postscript on Process	—	—	—	—
Mitford, *Behind the Formaldehyde Curtain*	—	—	—	—
Petrunkevitch, *The Spider and the Wasp*	—	—	—	—
Elbow, *Desperation Writing*	—	—	—	—
Train, *For the Adventurous Few: How to Get Rich*	—	—	—	—
Postscript on Process	—	—	—	—
Syfers, *I Want a Wife*	—	—	—	—
Sheehy, *Predictable Crises of Adulthood*	—	—	—	—

	Liked a lot	Okay	Didn't like	Didn't read
Burke, *Classifying Proverbs*	——	——	——	——
Fussell, *Notes on Class*	——	——	——	——
Postscript on Process	——	——	——	——
Gregory, *If You Had to Kill Your Own Hog*	——	——	——	——
Rettie, *"But a Watch in the Night": A Scientific Fable*	——	——	——	——
Thoreau, *The Battle of the Ants*	——	——	——	——
Kennedy, *Writing with a DECmate II*	——	——	——	——
Postscript on Process	——	——	——	——
Vidal, *Drugs*	——	——	——	——
Sagan, *The Nuclear Winter*	——	——	——	——
Tobias, *Who's Afraid of Math, and Why?*	——	——	——	——
Winn, *The End of Play*	——	——	——	——
Postscript on Process	——	——	——	——
Wolfe, *Pornoviolence*	——	——	——	——
Mead, *New Superstitions for Old*	——	——	——	——
Twain, *Corn-Pone Opinions*	——	——	——	——
Epstein, *What Is Vulgar?*	——	——	——	——
Postscript on Process	——	——	——	——
Buckley, *Why Don't We Complain?*	——	——	——	——
Mencken, *The Penalty of Death*	——	——	——	——
O'Connor, *Total Effect and the Eighth Grade*	——	——	——	——

	Liked a lot	Okay	Didn't like	Didn't read
King, *I Have a Dream*	___	___	___	___
Baker, *Universal Military Motion*	___	___	___	___
Steinem, *The Importance of Work*	___	___	___	___
Rodriguez, *Aria*	___	___	___	___
Postscript on Process	___	___	___	___
Swift, *A Modest Proposal*	___	___	___	___
Woolf, *What If Shakespeare Had Had a Sister?*	___	___	___	___
Orwell, *Politics and the English Language*	___	___	___	___
Tuchman, *An Inquiry into the Persistence of Unwisdom in Government*	___	___	___	___

Are there any writers not included you would like to see added?

_____

_____

Any general comments or suggestions? _____

_____

_____

Name _____

Mailing address _____

Date _____